THE HUMAN PERSPECTIVE
Readings in World Civilization

❖ ❖ ❖

VOLUME I

❖ ❖ ❖

*The Ancient World
to the
Modern Era*

❖ ❖ ❖

THE HUMAN PERSPECTIVE
Readings in World Civilization
Second Edition

❖ ❖ ❖

VOLUME I

❖ ❖ ❖

The Ancient World to the Modern Era

❖ ❖ ❖

Lynn H. Nelson
University of Kansas

Steven K. Drummond
University of Kansas

Harcourt Brace College Publishers

Fort Worth   Philadelphia   San Diego   New York   Orlando   Austin   San Antonio
Toronto   Montreal   London   Sydney   Tokyo

Publisher	Christopher P. Klein
Acquisitions Editor	David Tatom
Developmental Editor	Susan Petty
Project Editor	Catherine Townsend
Production Manager	Cynthia Young
Art Director	Carol Kincaid

Harcourt Brace College Publishers may provide complimentary instructional aids and supplements or supplement packages to those adopters qualified under our adoption policy. Please contact your sales representative for more information. If as an adopter or potential user you receive supplements you do not need, please return them to your sales representative or send them to: Attn: Returns Department, Troy Warehouse, 465 South Lincoln Drive, Troy, MO 63379.

Address for Editorial Correspondence: Harcourt Brace College Publishers, 301 Commerce Street, Suite 3700, Fort Worth, TX 76102

Address for Orders: Harcourt Brace & Company, 6277 Sea Harbor Drive, Orlando, FL 32887 1-800-782-4479, or 1-800-433-0001 (in Florida)

ISBN: 0-15-501345-9

Library of Congress Catalog Number: 96-77709

Printed in the United States of America

6 7 8 9 0 1 2 3 4 5   016   10 9 8 7 6 5 4 3 2 1

In memory of Wilbert N. Drummond, Sr.

PREFACE TO THE SECOND EDITION

We have worked hard to have this second edition of *The Human Perspective* be more than a token revision. With the benefit of the accumulated experience of those who used the first edition in the classroom and who have been kind enough to offer us suggestions and advice, we believe that we have been able to present a more varied and usable collection of readings.

We have maintained two basic characteristics of the first edition—the use of substantial excerpts and the focus on social history. It has seemed proper, however, to include some works that have important social implications even if those implications are not immediately apparent. In such cases, we have provided more detailed, reflective introductory essays to assist the student in recognizing the significance of the work.

The first edition was organized around the themes of the individual, technological innovation, women and minorities, and recreation and education. Upon reflection, we have concluded that these emphases perhaps neglected to pay proper attention to human interaction and to the biological factors affecting human lives. As a consequence, we have added readings concerned with war, cultural and economic exchange, disease and medicine, and population. And we have increased the number of readings from forty-eight to seventy-five to accommodate this wider scope.

In the previous edition, we followed a fixed pattern in which each selection on a European subject was balanced and complemented by one on a similar non-European theme. This arrangement limited the selection of readings somewhat and has not been followed strictly in the present volumes. Non-European cultures are well represented, however, and the greater number of readings has allowed us to place more emphasis on areas such as Latin America and the Middle East.

Finally, we have increased the number of parts from three to four, in each volume, allowing us to provide useful introductory and transition material.

It is our hope that instructors and students will find the present selection and arrangement of materials both stimulating and illuminating. They will find that this edition, like its predecessor, is dedicated to the concept that history is properly the study of human beings and their achievements.

We would like to express our appreciation to the following individuals for their advice and suggestions in both the selection of materials and in the preparation of the accompanying apparatus: Professor Craig Lockard, University of Wisconsin at Green Bay; Professor Brendan Nagle, University of Southern California; and Professor Glee Wilson, Kent State University, Ohio. Judith Shaw of Pittsburgh State University and Michael Tate of the University of Nebraska at Omaha have been particularly helpful in providing suggestions derived from their classroom use of the first edition.

We have enjoyed the full support of the editorial staff of Harcourt Brace, and wish to extend our particular thanks to Carol Kincaid, Susan Petty, David Tatom, Catherine Townsend, and Cynthia Young for their assistance, encouragement, and forbearance.

Finally, we would like to make a special note of the personal encouragement offered over the years by Carolyn A. S. Nelson and Sherry S. Schirmer.

PREFACE TO THE FIRST EDITION

A steadily shrinking world has led history departments to increase their offerings of world history at the introductory level. But many of the instructors called on to teach these courses have had little formal training in non-Western areas. At the same time, most of their students have had little exposure to history other than that of the United States and could profit from materials of greater depth and interest than are found in traditional core texts. *The Human Perspective* grew out of a personal frustration at the unavailability of such materials. These two volumes seek to remedy this problem by providing an assortment of readings that both supplement the basic course materials and, through the attention given to non-Western subjects, compensate for the Western and European emphases of many texts.

The twenty-four essays in each volume are drawn largely from secondary accounts and fall into the general category of social history. They deal with the everyday lives of average men and women rather than the great deeds of leaders and heroes, with continuing patterns of activity rather than great events, and with the concrete rather than the abstract. Core texts in world history are generally good in establishing the traditional political, institutional, and economic framework of history. They are less satisfactory in fleshing out that framework and lending the study of history its proper human perspective. These volumes are intended to perform that function.

A special feature of *The Human Perspective* is a system of presentation that combines chronological, cultural, and topical criteria. In each volume, the readings appear in chronological order within three major historical divisions. In each historical division four of the readings concern Western and four non-Western cultures. All the readings relate to four topical categories: the life and times of individuals, technological innovations and their effect on societies, women and minorities, and education and recreation.

This first volume covers the period from 3000 B.C. to A.D. 1660, and its three historical divisions are the Ancient World, the Middle Ages, and the Premodern Era. Each of these parts opens with a chronological chart and a brief historical introduction that, together, outline the important movements of the age and place the readings in their historical context. Every reading has its own short introduction and is followed by a brief annotated bibliography. A set of discussion questions closes the part.

The parts all contain two readings on each topical theme, one Western and the other non-Western in emphasis. This organization allows the instructor a variety of approaches. To follow a chronological order within a given topic, for example, one might investigate technological innovation in the West by reading "The Birth of Writing," "The Stirrup and Its Impact on Medieval Society," and "Clocks: A Revolution in Time." Or one could take a comparative approach to the status of women in ancient times by reading "Women in Roman Society" and "The Position of Women in Han China."

The organization is not rigid, however, since many of the readings relate to more than one topic. To take just one of many examples, "The Life and Times of Margery Kempe" can be read as a portrait of an individual, the life of a medieval woman, or an account of the pilgrimage to Jerusalem (which could be regarded as a medieval recreational and educational pursuit). In other words, the readings do not stand alone in any category, but reinforce each other in various ways. The discussion questions are helpful in pointing out many such connections, as is the Topical Table of Contents, which lists each reading not only under the category that is its main focus but under other categories to which it is relevant.

This volume and its companion are meant to be useful at whatever level the instructor cares to employ them. One might assign individual selections simply as supplementary readings, or topical or chronological groups of readings as subjects for papers or discussions. One or more selections, along with their bibliographies, might serve as starting points for term papers. Finally, the discussion questions offer topics for student papers and reports, or might suggest themes around which to structure classroom presentations. In short, *The Human Perspective* is intended as a useful and rewarding tool in teaching and learning about the history of our world.

I acknowledge the valuable assistance and counsel I have received from Steve Drummond of Harcourt Brace Jovanovich in the conception and preparation of these volumes.

Those who helped in the initial stages of the project include John Dardess, University of Kansas; Bruce Garver, Richard Overfield, and Michael Tate, University of Nebraska at Omaha; Judith Shaw, Pittsburgh State University; Sister Georgia McGarry, Benedictine College; and James Falls and John Stack, University of Missouri at Kansas City. I am especially grateful to Stanley Chodorow, of the University of California at San Diego, who reviewed both volumes, and to James Summers for their advice and guidance, which helped significantly in shaping the text, and to Drake Bush and Catherine Fauver of Harcourt Brace Jovanovich for their encouragement and aid. Finally, my largest debt of gratitude is to my students, past and present, whose inquisitive minds provided the stimulus for this work.

LYNN H. NELSON

CONTENTS

PART III
EXPANDING HORIZONS: CHALLENGES
TO THE CLASSICAL HERITAGE, A.D. 500
TO 1350 175

PART IV
WORLDS OF CHANGE: THE CRISIS OF
THE CLASSICAL CULTURES, A.D. 1350

PART I

Origins

❖ ❖ ❖

40,000 TO 2500 B.C.

	40,000 B.C.	30,000 B.C.	20,000 B.C.
EUROPE	**ca. 40,000 B.C.** Homo Sapiens	**ca. 27,000 B.C.** World's oldest cave art, Provence **ca. 24,000 B.C.** Venus of Dolni Vestonice I World's oldest ceramic object	
SOUTHWEST ASIA AND AFRICA	**ca. 200,000 B.C.–40,000 B.C.** *The Roots of Language*		
SOUTH AND SOUTHEAST ASIA		**ca. 24,000 B.C.** Oldest raft, East Indies	
EAST ASIA	**ca. 50,000 B.C.** Beijing (Peking) man		**ca. 20,000 B.C.** Earliest sculpted Asian face
THE AMERICAS AND THE PACIFIC	**ca. 40,000 B.C.–30,000 B.C.** Pedra Furada, Brazil, possible human occupation **ca. 40,000 B.C.** First visitors to Australia **ca. 35,000 B.C.** Kow Swamp, Australia, modern human fossils found	**ca. 24,000 B.C.** "Los Angeles Man" human fossil	

10,000 B.C.	5000 B.C.	2500 B.C.
ca. 9000 B.C. Oldest remains of a bow and arrow, Germany **ca. 9000 B.C.** First domesticated dog, Germany	**ca. 6000–3000 B.C.** Greek Neolithic period	**ca. 3000–1000 B.C.** Greek Bronze Age **ca. 3800–2500 B.C.** Early Minoan **ca. 2800–1550 B.C.** Stonehenge
ca. 10,000 B.C. Ostrich eggshell drinking vessels, South Africa **ca. 8000 B.C.** Jericho walled village **ca. 8000 B.C.** *Bread or Beer*	**ca. 4000 B.C.** First cultivation of grapes for wine **ca. 3800 B.C.** First Nubian civilization	**ca. 3500 B.C.** City-states in Sumeria **ca. 3100 B.C.** Unification of Egypt **ca. 3000 B.C.** *The Origins of Agriculture in Africa* **ca. 2750 B.C.** *The First Heroic Age*
ca. 7000 B.C. Beginning of Neolithic period, Southeast Asia	**ca. 4000 B.C.** First Indian cities	**ca. 3000 B.C.** Earliest cloth known, Indus valley
ca. 10,500–300 B.C. Jōmon period, Japan **ca. 10,000 B.C.** Pottery vessels, Japan **ca. 5500 B.C.** Xinglongwa village in inner Mongolia	**ca. 5000–3000 B.C.** Yangshao culture, China **ca. 4000 B.C.** Agriculture in China	
ca. 10,000 B.C. Colonization of Alaska from across Bering Strait **ca. 10,000 B.C.** "Midland Woman"	**ca. 5000 B.C.** Peopling of the Caribbean **ca. 3700–1800 B.C.** Calusa people, Florida **ca. 3500 B.C.** First cultivated potatoes, Peru	**ca. 3000 B.C.** First pottery in the Americas, Ecuador

INTRODUCTION

Civilization emerged very late in the human experience. Behind its origin lies an extremely long developmental period. The most recent discoveries indicate that our ancestors have inhabited the earth for over four million years, and possibly even longer. Only the last 5,500 years represent the "historic" period in which humans have possessed the ability to record information. The account of human development during this earlier period is the province of archaeologists, prehistorians, and various other specialists, and our picture of this portion of the human story is changing rapidly.

One of the reasons for this advance is the development of new methods of inquiry other than physical anthropology that corroborate and elaborate on the fossil record. William Allman's "The Roots of Language" discusses two of these approaches, genetic analysis and paleolinguistics. Both confirm the conclusions of the archaeologists and physical anthropologists that all varieties of humans descend from a single primate species that emerged some millions of years ago, probably in Africa. Some 200,000 years ago, these early humans formed a small but well-defined community, and some 100,000 years ago they began to migrate out of Africa to populate the entire planet.

For some 90,000 years prior to the birth of civilization, these early humans roamed the Earth as nomadic hunters and food gatherers. This was the period known as the Paleolithic Era or Old Stone Age, and it was long believed that life during this time was, in a famous phrase, "nasty, brutish, and short." This attitude has changed with the realization that hunters and gatherers spend, on the average, four hours of light work daily to meet their basic needs and are able to use the remainder of the time in recreation, ritual, and socializing. This does much to explain the prevalence of so-called Garden of Eden stories in various cultures, all recalling a time in which the Earth yielded up its bounty gracefully and humans did not have to eat food that was wet with the sweat of their own labor. It would seem they may have recollections of a relatively carefree way of life that had been lost with the beginnings of civilization and history.

About ten thousand years ago, probably in the Middle East, humans succeeded in domesticating certain animals and plants, and the Neolithic Era, or New Stone Age, began. Humans were able to control their environment by means of these innovations, but at a considerable cost. The farmer-villagers and shepherds of this new age spent long and arduous hours of toil to fill their basic needs for subsistence, had to fight and die to protect their fields, and diverted an increasing amount of the fruits of their labor to support non-producing groups of warriors, rulers, and priests. There have been numerous suggestions as to why people gave up the relatively easy life of hunters and gatherers for the hard life of the peasant. Solomon Katz's article, "Beer or Bread: Which Came First?" deals with one such suggestion, that humans began the domestication of grain in order to secure a regular supply of beer.

Another yet unanswered question is whether there was a single Agricultural Revolution in the Near East that supplied the model and inspiration for the spread of agriculture and animal husbandry throughout the world, or whether various peoples at various times and places made the same advance independently. Robert July's "The Origins of Agriculture in Tropical Africa" presents the standard interpretation that agriculture was introduced rather late into Africa from Egypt. He suggests, however, that evidence may indicate that sub-Saharan African agriculture may have been an indigenous development occurring much earlier than is commonly supposed.

Whatever the cause, communities whose economies were based on the cultivation of grain and the utilization of domesticated animals proliferated throughout the Middle East. As time passed, the division of labor within these communities became more pronounced, and the chiefs of the communities' warrior groups seized political power at the expense of the mass of the population. Samuel Kramer, in "The First Heroic Age," portrays a period of Sumerian society in which this process was underway and in which the first stirrings of the Urban Revolution could be felt.

By about 3500 B.C., humans had effected the cultural achievements necessary to emerge from prehistoric society into a more complex social structure. A form of society emerged that was based on city life, written language and law, a division of labor, and advanced arts and sciences. With this development, the Historic Period had begun.

THE ROOTS OF LANGUAGE

HOW MODERN SPEECH EVOLVED FROM A SINGLE, ANCIENT SOURCE

William F. Allman

The diversity of languages and peoples of the Earth has long been a matter of interest, since language is a feature that both defines a group and differentiates it from other groups. The Hebrews explained this phenomenon by the tale of the Tower of Babel that can be found in the book of Genesis. There was a time, so the story went, when everyone spoke the same language. When settling in Sumeria, they decided to build a city with a great tower reaching to the heavens in order to set themselves apart from others by the magnitude of their accomplishment. God saw there was no limit to what such a united people could do, so he humbled them by making each speak a different language. They dispersed from their tower, carrying their separate languages across the earth.

This explanation was accepted throughout Europe until relatively recent times. Since the discovery by Sir William Jones, in 1786, that the ancient language of India was closely related to ancient Latin and Greek, scholars have tried to define the various families of language and to discover their origins. Since most of this study was conducted by Europeans, the greatest attention was paid to Indo-European, the great family that includes most of the languages of Europe, Iran, and northern India. Both legend and history suggested that the original Indo-Europeans had been a seminomadic people from the plains of southern Russia. Fighting from chariots, their chieftains led them in bloody invasions that carried them and their language from the western borders of China to the Atlantic Ocean. This view of their origin as a warlike and conquering people suited Westerners during a period in which the Europeans came to dominate the world.

This picture of Bronze Age society has changed remarkably during recent years, as further study and new techniques have altered our picture of the spread of the Indo-Europeans and have pushed back the history of language many thousands of years. The following selection discusses the research which has led many scholars to the conclusion that all languages and all human beings are descended from a common origin in Africa, and that the dispersion of humans throughout the world, and the differentiation of their languages as they migrated, probably began almost 100,000 years ago.

READING QUESTIONS

1. How do linguists trace the history of language?

2. How did the Indo-European languages spread?

3. Where did the Indo-European speakers originate?

4. How has our picture of the migrations of the North American Indians changed in recent years?

5. What is the evidence for an African origin of language and human beings?

I n 1786, Sir William Jones, an Englishman serving the Crown as a judge in India, turned a series of seeming coincidences into an extraordinary discovery about human nature. A scholar of the Orient by training, Jones had embarked on an effort to learn Sanskrit, the language in which many ancient Indian religious and literary texts are written. To his amazement, Jones found that Sanskrit's grammatical forms and vocabulary bore a striking resemblance to those of Greek and Latin, so much so that "no philologer could examine them all three without believing them to have sprung from some common source." As Charles Darwin was to assert almost a century later about the human body, Jones suggested that a fundamental part of the human psyche—language—had a hidden ancestry of its own.

Today, scientists are leading a new revolution in understanding the roots of language. While linguistic pioneer Noam Chomsky and his followers have focused on language as a psychological phenomenon, a small band of renegade scholars is revealing how languages are a product of cultural evolution. Sifting through modern tongues for linguistic "fossils" in the form of common words and grammatical structures, these "linguistic paleoanthropologists," many of whom have worked in obscurity in the Soviet Union, are reconstructing the pathways by which the world's roughly 5,000 languages arose from a handful of ancient "mother" tongues. A few radical linguists have gone even further, claiming they have reconstructed pieces of the mother of them all: The original language spoken at the dawn of the human species.

These linguistic findings are a windfall for archaeologists, anthropologists and other social scientists who are trying to piece together the

From William F. Allman, "The Mother Tongue," *U.S. News & World Report,* November 5, 1990, pp. 60–70.

story of the peopling of the earth. "We've come to realize," says Alexis Man-
aster Ramer, a researcher at Wayne State University in Detroit, "that a lot
of the answers to the big questions lie in something you might call anthro-
psycho-socio-linguistics." Language is an integral part of the cultural glue
that binds people together and signals their presence. Tracing the evolution
of language can reveal how ancient peoples migrated into new lands, for instance, just as reconstructing the vocabularies of lost languages can give researchers clues to what ancient people saw, ate and thought, or how one
culture coexisted—or collided—with another. The new linguistic findings
also neatly dovetail with conclusions drawn from a very different area of
evolutionary research. Comparisons of human genes worldwide have produced a "family tree" of the human race whose branches closely mirror the
branching of languages proposed by linguists, leading to the startling suggestion that all people—and perhaps all languages—are descended from a
tiny population that lived in Africa some 200,000 years ago.

ENGLISH PEDIGREE

The idea that languages are constantly evolving is obvious from looking at
English over time: Consider Shakespeare's Elizabethan "Shall I compare thee
to a summer's day?"; Chaucer's 14th-century, Middle English "Whan that

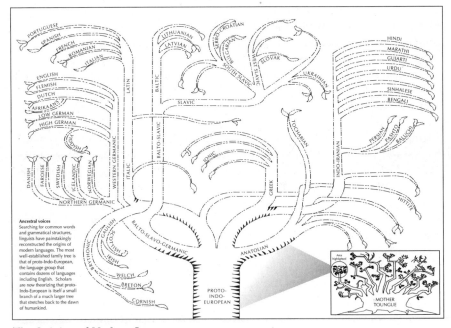

The Origins of Modern Languages

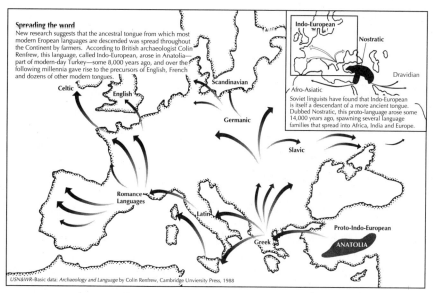

Spreading the word
New research suggests that the ancestral tongue from which most modern Eropean languages are descended was spread throughout the Continent by farmers. According to British archaeologist Colin Renfrew, this language, called Indo-European, arose in Anatolia—part of modern-day Turkey—some 8,000 years ago, and over the following millennia gave rise to the precursors of English, French and dozens of other modern tongues.

Celtic
English
Scandinavian
Germanic
Romance Languages
Latin
Slavic
Greek

Indo-European
Nostratic
Dravidian
Afro-Asiatic
Soviet linguists have found that Indo-European is itself a descendant of a more ancient tongue. Dubbed Nostratic, this proto-language arose some 14,000 years ago, spawning several language families that spread into Africa, India and Europe.

Proto-Indo-European
ANATOLIA

USN&WR–Basic data: *Archaeology and Language* by Colin Renfrew, Cambridge Unviersity Press, 1988

The Spread of Indo-European Languages

Aprille with his shourse sote," and the opening line from the eighth-century Old English epic *Beowulf:* "Hwaet! We Gar-Dena, in geardagum."

These dramatic sound changes within a single language are possible only because, with the exception of onomatopoeic words like sizzle, the sound of a word has no direct connection to its meaning, says Merritt Ruhlen, a scholar in Palo Alto, Calif., who is tracing the relationships among the world's languages. Like coins, words get their value from the community at large, which must agree on what they represent. The word *dog* may mean a furry creature with four legs and a wagging tail, for instance, but *hippopotamus* or *ziglot* would serve just as well, as long as both speaker and listener agreed on its meaning.

CREAM IN YOUR COFFEE

These arbitrary associations between sounds and meanings provide the key to reconstructing the linguistic past, says Ruhlen. Because any number of sounds could be associated with a particular meaning, the presence of similar-sounding words with similar meanings in two different languages suggests that both languages had a common ancestor. For instance, diners might order their coffee *au lait, con leche* or *latte,* depending on whether they are in a French, Spanish or Italian restaurant. Using these similar-sounding "daughter" words for milk and a knowledge of how the sounds of words change as languages evolve, linguists could come close to reconstructing the Latin form, *lacte,* even if this mother tongue of Romance languages were unknown.

Similar comparisons among words are what led Jones to suspect that Latin, along with Greek and Sanskrit, had descended from an even more ancient mother tongue. The word for the number three, for instance, is *tres* in Latin, *treis* in Greek and *tryas* in Sanskrit. Over the years, scholars following up on Jones's suggestion have demonstrated that dozens of languages, including English, Swedish, German, Russian, Polish, Hindi, Persian, Welsh and Lithuanian, are all descendants of this same ancient "proto-language." Called Indo-European by linguists, this mother tongue was spoken some 8,000 years ago, before the invention of writing, and is known only by the traces left behind in the vocabularies of its daughter languages.

From these remnants, however, linguists have reconstructed a vast lexicon of proto-Indo-European words, providing clues to the origins of the ancient people who spoke the language when they populated nearly all of Europe. According to recent work by two Soviet linguists, Thomas Gamkrelidze and Vyacheslav Ivanov, words for domesticated animals such as cows, sheep and dogs as well as plants such as barley, flax and wheat suggest that the people who spoke proto-Indo-European were farmers. Likewise, the prevalence of words evoking mountains and rapidly flowing rivers suggests the Indo-European people originally lived in a hilly terrain.

Using these and other linguistic clues, Soviet researchers have offered new evidence that Indo-European originated in an area known as Anatolia, which is now part of Turkey, and from there spread throughout Europe and the sub-Continent. Linguists had long thought that the Indo-European proto-language had originated in southern Russia and had been spread throughout Europe by hordes of conquering warriors. But Gamkrelidze, Ivanov and other Soviet scholars cite words in proto-Indo-European that appear to have been borrowed from the languages of Mesopotamia and the Near East, suggesting that the speakers of proto-Indo-European lived in close geographical proximity to these cultures. The proto-Indo-European word for wine, for instance, appears to have its ancient roots in the non-Indo-European Semitic word *wanju* and the Egyptian *wns.*

FARMING IN EUROPE

The Soviets' linguistic work has found unexpected support in new research by British archaeologist Colin Renfrew, who, unaware of the linguistic studies, independently determined that the Indo-European homeland was in Anatolia, based on a reassessment of the archaeological evidence. Renfrew suggests that it was farmers, not warriors, who were responsible for the spread of the Indo-European language into Europe. He notes that even if a farmer's offspring had moved only 10 miles from the family farm to set up farms of their own, the resulting wave of agriculture could have swept throughout Europe from Anatolia in about 1,500 years, carrying the Indo-European language with it. Because farming can support a larger number of people than hunting and gathering, the existing inhabitants of Europe were probably pushed out or adapted to farming on their own, says Renfrew.

While the existence of proto-Indo-European has been accepted among scholars for years, linguists have now begun to trace the lineage of languages back even further. Linguists studying languages from other areas of the world have identified ancestral mother tongues such as Altic, which gave rise to east Asian languages including Japanese and Korean, and Afro-Asiatic, the ancestor of Semitic. Working backward from reconstructions of Indo-European, Altic, Afro-Asiatic and several others, Soviet scholars have found that these ancestral tongues derived from an even more ancient language. Called "Nostratic," meaning "our language," this ancestral tongue was reconstructed independently by Soviet linguists Vladislav Illich-Svitych and Aharon Dolgopolsky during the 1960s, though their work was not translated into English until recently.

To re-create this ancient mother tongue, the Soviet scholars examined words considered by linguists to be the most stable parts of a vocabulary, such as names for body parts, personal pronouns and natural objects such as the sun and moon. Analyzing how the sounds for these words changed among Nostratic's various daughter languages, they were able to reconstruct hundreds of words. The Nostratic word for young man, for instance, is *majra,* which evolved into *merio* in Indo-European and thousands of years later became *mari* in French, meaning husband, and *marry* in English.

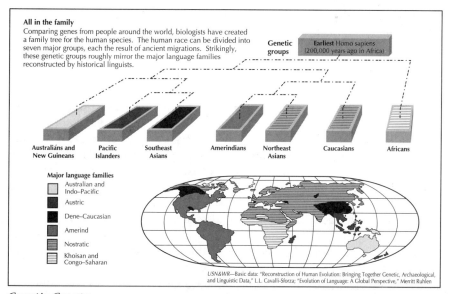

Genetic Groups

The reconstructed words of Nostratic vocabulary offer a glimpse of how the people who spoke the language lived, and they suggest a date when the language thrived. The absence of words for domesticated plants suggests the Nostratic speakers were probably hunter-gatherers, says Vitaly Sheveroskin, a former student of Dolgopolsky's who is now at the University of Michigan. Even more intriguing is the word *kuyna,* which can mean either dog or wolf: the "k" evolved into an "h" in Germanic languages, leading to *hound* in English. The ambiguity of meaning in the word suggests that wolves were in the process of becoming domesticated, says Sheveroskin, who notes that the oldest bones of dogs date to 14,000 years ago, giving a time frame when Nostratic was spoken. The speakers of Nostratic were well-traveled: Not only is the lexicon peppered with words that refer to "long journey" but over the next several thousand years, Nostratic split into several major language families as its speakers migrated from the Near East, their suspected homeland, into Europe, Persia and India.

The reconstruction of another such "macrofamily" of languages has given new clues to another mass migration, the original settling of the Americas. Joseph Greenberg, a linguist at Stanford University, recently proposed a controversial theory that all the languages spoken by Native Americans can be grouped into three families that correspond to three waves of migration from Asia into the New World thousands of years ago. The largest, oldest and most controversial group proposed by Greenberg is a macrofamily that he calls Amerind, which is made up of all the languages in South and Central America as well as many in North America. The other two language groups are Na-Dene, which includes tongues spoken by Native Americans in the Northwest as well as Navajo and Apache, and Eskimo-Aleut, which contains languages spoken mostly in the Arctic; this group was the last to arrive in the New World.

SCHOLARLY FUROR

Greenberg's theory has created a furor among linguists, even some of those who champion the deep reconstruction of languages. At a recent conference in Boulder, Colo., linguists attacked Greenberg's admittedly unconventional methodology, in which he compares common-sounding words across many languages rather than attempting to reconstruct the sound shifts that occurred when one tongue diverged from another. Yet Greenberg's defenders cite his track record: A classification of African languages he made 20 years ago created a similar furor among linguists and is now widely accepted.

Greenberg's theory is being given new weight by an upheaval in archaeological thinking about the peopling of the Americas. Archaeologists have long believed that the first migration to the New World occurred some 12,000 years ago—too short a time, some linguists argue, for the hundreds of Indian languages to arise from Greenberg's proposed Amerind mother tongue. But recently, several archaeological sites in the Americas have been shown to be far older than 12,000 years, suggesting that the first migration to the New World may have occurred much earlier—thus allowing more time for languages to diverge. One site, a rock shelter in Pennsylvania, has been dated at 16,000 years and another site in Chile may date back as far as 33,000 years. New studies that compare changes in the genes of Native Americans suggest that the date of the first migration might stretch back as far as 60,000 years.

Research on American languages is also throwing light on a longstanding linguistic mystery in Europe—as well as testifying to the remarkable wanderlust of ancient humans. Linguists have long wondered about the origins of Basque, a language spoken in the north of Spain that is one of the few non-Indo-European languages on the Continent. Soviet linguists have uncovered evidence that Basque is related to Na-Dene, and that both languages are part of yet another language macrofamily that includes tongues ranging from Chinese to the ancient Mediterranean tongue Etruscan. Called Dene-Caucasian, this ancient language was reconstructed in large part by Soviet linguist Sergei Starostin, another student of Dolgopolsky's. This wide-ranging tongue, spoken on both sides of the Bering Strait and at both ends of the Eurasian land mass, reflects the vast movements of ancient peoples who took their language with them and in some cases, such as Basque, kept it alive despite their being surrounded by other tongues.

The survival of an exotic linguistic island like Basque suggests that language, like genes, can sometimes serve as a marker for a distinct group of people. Historical linguistic studies are generating widespread interest among scientists involved in one of the most exciting new developments in science: Tracing the evolutionary history of human genes. "It's quite clear why you have a correlation between genes and language," says Stanford University geneticist Luigi Cavalli-Sforza, a pioneer in the new genetic techniques. "When the human expansion around the earth took place some 50,000 years ago, it caused a number of separations between groups that didn't communicate again, genetically or linguistically. As the genes become different, the languages become different, too."

Cavalli-Sforza and his colleagues recently examined genetic markers from 42 different indigenous peoples from around the world and used the divergence among the genes to construct a family tree for the entire human race. The tree shows the human diaspora over tens of thousands of years, as a single population split into several large groups and then into the smaller tribes that exist today.

AFRICAN SPLIT

More important, Cavalli-Sforza found that the groupings of the human family based on genetic evidence closely mirrored the language groupings laid out independently by historical linguists. The oldest split occurred between Africans and other world populations, reflecting the migration of Homo sapiens out of Africa. This split is reflected in languages as well: Africa's Khoisan languages, such as that of the !Kung San, which uses a clicking noise denoted by an exclamation point, is only distantly related to other languages in the world. A recent paleoanthropological discovery in the Near East of the oldest fossils of Homo sapiens gives a rough date for when this first split might have occurred: The fossils date back 92,000 years.

Another study that similarly traced the human genetic lineage suggests that all languages may have their roots in a small population that lived some 200,000 years ago. In their famed "Eve" hypothesis, Allan Wilson, Mark Stoneking and Rebecca Cann of the University of California at Berkeley traced genetic material from women around the world and concluded that all humans alive today are descendants of a tiny population of Homo sapiens that lived in Africa.

If the human race did arise from this small group of people, then it is likely they all spoke the same language, contends Sheveroskin. What's more, he says, the same techniques that gave rise to the reconstructions of ancient macro-families can also be used to dredge up bits of the original mother tongue of the human race. For example, the Nostratic word for leaf, *lapa,* is similar to *tlapa* in Dene-Caucasian and *dap* in Amerind. And the Amerind word for woman, *kuni,* closely resembles the Nostratic word for woman, *küni.* It is from this word that the English word *queen* is derived.

FLEAS AND IN-LAWS

Sheveroskin and other linguists have reconstructed dozens of words in this original mother tongue, which has been dubbed simply "proto-World." The word for I, for instance, is *ngai; nas* means nose. The linguists have also reconstructed proto-World words referring to body parts, fleas, in-laws and a category of words that referred to pairs of objects—reflecting, perhaps, a culture that before the invention of mathematics counted the world in ones, twos and many. *Niwha* and *hwina* refer simultaneously to life, breath and blood, but, strangely, notes Sheveroskin, there appear to be no words in proto-World that refer to human emotions.

In the end, discovering the roots of language is inexorably tied to the still unresolved task of defining what language is, and this is where the ultimate impact of the new linguistic research may lie. The deep connections between languages demonstrate that far from a mere communication device, language is the palette from which people color their lives and culture. Intimately connected to the human experience, language oils the gears of social interactions and solidifies the ephemera of the mind into literature, history and collective knowledge. It is the calling card of the human race;

announcing the presence not only of those alive today but, with its deep roots into the past, the ancient ancestors who came before us ❖

RECOMMENDED READINGS

Many linguists have been involved in recent years in the search for a common origin of human languages. The progress of their thought may be followed in Philip Lieberman, *On The Origins of Language; An Introduction to the Evolution of Human Speech* (New York: Macmillan, 1975); James H. Stam, *Inquiries into the Origin of Language: The Fate of a Question* (New York: Harper & Row, 1976); Derek Bickerton, *Roots of Language* (Ann Arbor, MI: Karoma, 1981); *The Genesis of Language: A Different Judgement of the Evidence,* ed. Marge E. Landsberg (Berlin and New York: Mouton de Gruyter, 1988); *Studies in Language Origins,* ed. Jan Wind et al. (Amsterdam and Philadelphia: J. Benjamins, 1989–); and *Sprung from Some Common Source: Investigations into the Prehistory of Languages,* ed. Sydney M. Lamb and E. Douglas Mitchell (Stanford, CA: Stanford University Press, 1991).

BREAD OR BEER

WHICH CAME FIRST?

Solomon H. Katz and Fritz Maytag

The Old Stone Age was an era in which small roving bands sustained themselves by hunting and gathering wild plants. Some time before 8000 B.C., however, some groups began the domestication of animals and the practice of agriculture, a process known variously as the Neolithic Revolution, the Agricultural Revolution, or the Biological Revolution. It was not a revolution in the sense of a sudden and drastic change, since the spread of these ideas throughout the world is not yet complete even now, and there are still groups of humans who survive by hunting and gathering. The Neolithic Revolution did represent a drastic change in the human condition, however.

Life was doubtless easier for the hunters and gatherers, who had to spend less time and labor securing their food than the Neolithic farmers spent in growing it. The relative ease of life before the introduction of agriculture is reflected in numerous accounts, such as that of the Garden of Eden, before humans were forced by progress "to earn their bread in the sweat of their brow." The Neolithic Revolution did demand that people settle down into a sedentary life and provide sufficient food for a great increase in population and the emergence of specialized, managerial classes.

But if the life of the hunters and gatherers had been easier and freer than that of the farmers, why was agriculture developed and why did people continue to pursue it? Increasing attention is being paid to the question of why groups of people developed agriculture and, despite its disadvantages for the individual, made it the basis of their social and economic organization. Many different suggestions have been advanced, but the question is still unanswered, and scholars still debate the matter hotly.

This selection discusses a stage of one of these debates. Almost half a century ago, it was suggested that grain was domesticated in order to make beer. Scholars rejected this theory on the grounds that the Neolithic farmers would not have wasted precious food in concocting an alcoholic luxury. This led to an attempt to brew beer in the most ancient manner known to determine how nutritious Neolithic beer might have been.

READING QUESTIONS

1. How did the debate between bread and beer arise?

2. Why did the brewers choose to use a Sumerian recipe?

3. What were their conclusions about the quality of ancient beer?

4. What contribution does this study make toward answering the question of why people developed agriculture?

I n the 1950s, Robert Braidwood of the University of Chicago published an article in *Scientific American* suggesting a cause-effect relationship between breadmaking and the domestication of cereal grains. He cited evidence from his excavations at Jarmo in the Taurus Mountains of modern Iraq. However, Jonathan D. Sauer, a well-known botanist from the University of Wisconsin, responded to Braidwood's article by asking if the earliest utilization of the domesticated cereals may have been for beer rather than bread. This query prompted Braidwood to organize a unique "symposium" for the journal *American Anthropologist* titled "Did man once live by beer alone?"

It was not an idle question. We now believe that barley was domesticated about 10,000 years ago in the highland region of the southern Levant. But it seems likely that wild grains were gathered long before then. What prompted the shift from hunting and gathering to agriculture? Many scholars have suggested that overexploitation of wild resources and climate change in the region are behind the transition. But barley can ferment naturally, as we shall explain, and the discovery of beer at an early date may well have been a significant motivating factor in hunter-gatherers settling down and farming the grain.

In his contribution to the symposium, Sauer, with simple elegance, explained that for hunter-gatherers the amount of work involved in cultivating grain would not have been worthwhile if the only reward was a little food. The desire for beer, he felt, might have been sufficient incentive for expending the effort to plant and raise the barley, which he believed to be the earliest crop.

Hans Helbaek, a botanist who had worked with Braidwood at Jarmo, argued that beer was *not* the cause for domestication, but a much later

From Solomon H. Katz and Fritz Maytag, "Brewing an Ancient Beer," *Archaeology* 44(4), July/August 1991, pp. 24–29.

development probably originating with the drying of grain for storage. The argument against Sauer's proposal was best articulated by botanist Paul Manglesdorf, who reasoned that, even though beer was a plausible incentive for the domestication of grain, it was not possible to "live on beer alone." "Did these Neolithic farmers," he asked, "forgo the extraordinary food values of the cereals in favor of alcohol, for which they had no physiological need? Are we to believe that the foundations of western civilization were laid by an ill-fed people living in a perpetual state of partial intoxication?" The majority of the respondents concluded that it was inconceivable that beer came before bread, and the issue was all but forgotten.

Last year the case was reopened. The Anchor Brewing Company of San Francisco, looking for a special event with which to celebrate the tenth anniversary of its new brewhouse, became aware of the Braidwood-Sauer debate after seeing an article on the subject in *Expedition* magazine published by The University Museum, University of Pennsylvania. The authors [Fritz Maytag is president of Anchor Brewing Company; Solomon Katz is a bioanthropologist at The University Museum] were intrigued by the beer-bread question, and conceived the idea of brewing a beer based on an ancient recipe. Such an effort would not only help answer the beer-bread question but might also shed new light on the ancient brewmaster's art.

We focused on the beer-making tradition of Mesopotamia because of its proximity to the region of the earliest cereal domestication. Ancient texts preserved on clay tablets indicate that the earliest beer was Sumerian. From all that we can determine, beer played an important role in Sumerian society, and was consumed by men and women from all social classes. In the Sumerian and Akkadian dictionaries being compiled by scholars today, the word for beer crops up in contexts relating to medicine, ritual, and myth. Beer parlors receive special mention in the laws codified by Hammurabi in the eighteenth century B.C. Apparently stiff penalties were dealt out to owners who overcharged customers (death by drowning) or who failed to notify authorities of the presence of criminals in their establishments (execution). High priestesses who were caught in such places were condemned to death by burning.

In combing the surviving Sumerian literature for a starting point, we examined the "Hymn to Ninkasi." This document, which dates to about 1800 B.C., sings the praises of the Sumerian goddess of brewing. The text, known from tablets found at Nippur, Sippar, and Larsa, had been translated by Miguel Civil of the Oriental Institute of the University of Chicago in 1964. Coded within the Hymn is an ancient recipe for beer. We would return to the Hymn time and again before attempting to brew the ancient recipe. On several occasions we met with Civil to discuss parts of the text that were vague or ambiguous. In responding to our questions, Civil was led to refine his translation of certain Sumerian words such as honey and wine. His revised translation of the hymn, presented here for the first time, allowed us to successfully re-create the Sumerian beer.

We then returned to Braidwood's question: Did beer come before bread? Although Sumerian beer was made several millennia after barley was first domesticated, the process used by the Sumerians is a "time platform" from which we can ask questions about earlier practices. When the "Hymn to Ninkasi" was written, beer was made using bread. But *bappir,* the Sumerian bread, could be kept for long periods of time without spoiling, and so it was a storable resource. We also know, from various annotations on bappir and beer in the Sumerian and Akkadian dictionaries, that bappir was eaten only during food shortages. In essence, making bread was a convenient way to store the raw materials for brewing beer.

The Hymn to Ninkasi

Borne of the flowing water (. . .),
Tenderly cared for by the Ninhursag,
Borne of the flowing water (. . .),
Tenderly cared for by the Ninhursag,

Having founded your town by the
    sacred lake,
She finished its great walls for you,
Ninkasi, having founded your town by
    the sacred lake,
She finished its great walls for you,

Your father is Enki, Lord Nidimmud,
Your mother is Ninti, the queen of the
    sacred lake.
Ninkasi, your father is Enki, Lord
    Nidimmud,
Your mother is Ninti, the queen of the
    sacred lake.

You are the one who handles the dough
    [and] with a big shovel,
Mixing in a pit, the bappir with sweet
    aromatics,
Ninkasi, you are the one who handles
    the dough [and] with a big shovel,
Mixing in a pit, the bappir with
    [date]-honey,

You are the one who bakes the bappir in
    the big oven,
Puts in order the piles of hulled grains,

Ninkasi, you are the one who bakes the
    bappir in the big oven,
Puts in order the piles of hulled grains,

You are the one who waters the malt set
    on the ground,
The noble dogs keep away even the
    potentates,
Ninkasi, you are the one who waters the
    malt set on the ground,
The noble dogs keep away even the
    potentates,

You are the one who soaks the malt in
    a jar,
The waves rise, the waves fall.
Ninkasi, you are the one who soaks the
    malt in a jar,
The waves rise, the waves fall.

You are the one who spreads the cooked
    mash on large reed mats,
Coolness overcomes,
Ninkasi, you are the one who spreads the
    cooked mash on large reed mats,
Coolness overcomes,

You are the one who holds with both
    hands the great sweet wort,
Brewing [it] with honey [and] wine
(You the sweet wort to the vessel)
Ninkasi, (. . .)
(You the sweet wort to the vessel)

The filtering vat, which makes
    a pleasant sound,
You place appropriately on [top of]
    a large collector vat.
Ninkasi, the filtering vat, which makes
    a pleasant sound,
You place appropriately on [top of]
    a large collector vat.

When you pour out the filtered beer of the
    collector vat,

It is [like] the onrush of Tigris and
   Euphrates.
Ninkasi, you are the one who pours out the
   filtered beer of the collector vat,
It is [like] the onrush of Tigris and
   Euphrates.

Which was more nutritious? Since Braidwood first raised the beer-bread question, we have learned that many traditional food preparation practices involve steps that lower the toxicity and improve the nutritional properties of plants, and become a regular part of traditional cuisine. For example, through fermentation of barley-derived sugars into beer, yeast decreases the levels of tannins, stomach-irritating chemicals, and increases the levels of B vitamins and essential amino acids. But for fermentation to occur, yeast cells need a higher concentration of sugar than is normally present in raw barley. Coincidentally, a unique property of sprouted barley seeds is their production of large amounts of enzymes that can convert starch into sugar. Barley thus has both starch and, in its sprouted form, enzymes that convert starch to sugar. The seeds can be sprouted any time of year, and the final product has excellent nutritional value and can have mildly intoxicating levels of alcohol. Collecting and processing wild barley seeds requires tremendous effort, and at the time of the transition to agriculture, barley was not the only exploitable food resource—in fact, many others were probably more accessible. It is hard to imagine that the effort spent collecting wild seeds would have been for producing loaves of bread. The alcohol content and higher nutritional levels of beer, however, might have been incentive enough.

Finally, it is worth noting that Nature herself may well have produced the first beer. After harvesting, wild barley seeds might have been placed in a container for storage. If the seeds were exposed to moisture they would sprout. Sprouted barley is sweeter and more tender than unsprouted seeds, and therefore more edible. Sprouted seeds might have been dried for later consumption. Exposed to airborne yeast and more moisture, the barley would have fermented, producing beer. We may never know when some brave soul actually drank the "spoiled" barley. But we do know that someone did. ❖

RECOMMENDED READINGS

The causes of the Neolithic Revolution are the subject of much speculation. Mark Nathan Cohen, *The Food Crisis in Prehistory: Overpopulation and the Origins of Agriculture* (New Haven: Yale University Press, 1977), finds the causes in overpopulation among the paleolithic hunter-gatherers; David Rindos, *The Origins of Agriculture: An Evolutionary Perspective* (Orlando: Academic Press, 1984), sees it as the result of social evolution.

The revolution itself is discussed in *Transitions to Agriculture in Prehistory,* ed. Anne Birgitte Gebauer and T. Douglas Price (Madison, WI: Prehistory Press, 1992), and in the somewhat old-fashioned, but nicely illustrated, work of Jonathan N. Leonard, *The First Farmers* (New York: Time-Life Books, 1973).

Somewhere in Central Africa, About 3000 B.C.

THE ORIGINS OF AGRICULTURE IN TROPICAL AFRICA

Robert W. July

Historians debate the question of whether human progress occurs primarily because of the diffusion of the knowledge of significant advances or because different groups of humans develop similar solutions to similar challenges. Progress is fostered in both ways, of course; observation is sufficient to establish that fact. Even though they were working half a world apart, Alfred Russell Wallace and Charles Darwin arrived almost simultaneously at the idea that natural selection was the driving force behind evolution. On the other hand, vast expanses of the American Middle West and Southwest remained grazing land until Russian immigrants at the end of the nineteenth century brought new strains of wheat and the techniques of dryland farming to America. An endless number of examples supporting either diffusion or independent development could be adduced, so it is unlikely that this particular problem is capable of being solved.

The same cannot be said for specific advances, and the nature of their spread among peoples is an important issue for the historian. The Romans, for instance, imported silk for centuries from China, where the means of its production were a closely guarded secret. The Romans did not relish the high prices that the merchants from the Silk Road demanded, but they had no choice, since they had no idea of how to manufacture the material themselves. Finally, in the time of Emperor Justinian (A.D. 527–565), Western ambassadors to the Chinese court managed to discover how silk was made and to smuggle some silkworm eggs past the Chinese border guards. When the Romans began producing their own silk, the prosperity and importance of the Silk Road began to decline. In this case, the knowledge that Western silk manufacture occurred through a form of diffusion is important to an understanding of the times.

Did the Agricultural Revolution spread through diffusion from its origin in or near Jericho in Palestine, or was it the result of independent developments in several centers? This is an important question for several reasons. The opinion is widely spread that human advances are made in response to challenges. The theory is that the increasing desiccation of North Africa and the Near East reduced the land available to paleolithic hunters and gatherers and forced them into closer and more continuous contact with the animals and plants on which they subsisted. Confined to an oasis, perhaps that of Jericho, they learned how food plants propagated and how animals could be controlled. This view of the process supports the image of "Man the Problem-Solver," a self-image that is a powerful force in shaping social values. It is no accident that industrialized societies value intelligence and measure it by tests that gauge the individual's ability to solve puzzles. Quickness and competitiveness, in addition to intelligence of a particular sort, are placed at a premium, and the value of other traits of character and personality are generally discredited. The "challenge and response" theory of human progress plays an important role in determining who is successful in our world.

There is another issue involved. Many scholars see the Urban Revolution as the logical and inevitable consequence of the Agricultural Revolution. Since the Urban Revolution occurred first in Mesopotamia, if we are to believe the archaeological evidence, it follows that the Agricultural Revolution must have begun somewhere nearby. This, too, has its ramifications. It assumes that the historical process evolves largely in response to economic factors and independently of human volition.

This appears to be the standard interpretation of the period between the end of the Old Stone Age and the beginning of the era of the Bronze Age empires, but it is not necessarily a settled issue. One could point to the wide variety of plants involved in the Agricultural Revolution in different parts of the world as suggesting the possibility of independent developments. One might also note that the Asian immigrants to the Americas came before the Agricultural Revolution reached them, but nevertheless developed their own agricultural systems based on corn and the potato.

What if the standard interpretation of this period of history is wrong? If the Agricultural Revolution occurred in several different places at different times and sometimes may have taken place without being forced by necessity, then what engine drives human progress? When one remembers that the Mayan did invent the wheel, but seem to have used it only for pull toys, one must consider the proposition that human curiosity and love of play may perhaps have a more important role than is generally believed.

The question is a significant one and is often hotly debated. The author of this selection adopts an evenhanded approach. While providing a relatively standard overview of the extension of agriculture and husbandry to sub-Saharan Africa, he also cites some intriguing evidence that the origins of the Agricultural Revolution in Africa may have been much earlier than is presently supposed, and that it may have occurred independently of outside influence.

READING QUESTIONS

1. What is the standard theory of how the Agricultural Revolution reached Africa?

2. What relevance does cotton have to the question of when and how agriculture arose in Africa?

3. What possible evidence exists for an early and independent development of agriculture in Africa?

T he change in human economy from food gathering to food production has rightly been regarded as a shift of monumental importance in human history, its implications as profound for man as the previous revolution of specialization and division of labor. First, it brought a vast increase in population, for it was now possible greatly to multiply and localize the supply of food. Even more significant was the shift from a nomadic to a settled form of social life. Hunting communities, obliged to move with the game and subject to seasonal water shortages, could never establish themselves long in one place and consequently could never produce and accumulate wealth above the bare necessities, which they were obliged to carry with them. As cultivation was introduced, however, man could look beyond immediate toward ultimate objectives. He could accumulate and preserve food for future consumption, utilizing the time freed for some other purpose than subsistence. He could continue the process of specialization, exempting certain individuals from the task of food production to follow other pursuits—war-making and statecraft, artistic endeavors, the practice of religion, the development of writing, the improvement of technology, and, in general, the acquisition of knowledge. Greater population density and a sedentary existence made possible for the first time an urban culture wherein exchange of goods and services and the communication of ideas became the natural order of things.

This food-producing revolution apparently did not begin in Africa but rather in the Middle East, where the cultivation of plants was practiced by villagers in ancient Judea as long ago as the tenth millennium before Christ. First at Jericho, and then at other sites, barley and wheat were domesticated by peoples who combined their new agricultural skills with a remarkable architectural virtuosity long celebrated in biblical annals. Similarly, when agriculture first appeared in Africa, it too was joined by a remarkable cultural flowering—the spectacular civilization of ancient Egypt.

The cultural changes that the introduction of agriculture brought to Egypt resulted from the unique fertility of the Nile floodplain, making

From Robert W. July, *A History of the African People,* 2nd ed. (New York: Charles Schribner's Sons, 1974), pp. 14, 18–21.

possible the application of political organization to economic productivity on a scale previously unknown. Elsewhere in Africa progress was much more modest. For one thing, there is considerable uncertainty as to when, where, and under what conditions the transformation from a food-gathering to a food-cultivating economy took place, but there clearly was no cultural revolution such as occurred in Egypt. The evidence, which is necessarily of a nonliterary nature, comes from archaeology, from historical botany, and from the analysis of African languages, sources that have been interpreted and collated with impressive ingenuity, yet that sometimes have brought forth conflicting hypotheses concerning the inception of agriculture in tropical Africa.

Those who have relied primarily on archaeological evidence have pieced together a picture of early civilizations in Africa that describes a relatively late shift from hunting societies to food producers. The special case of Egypt aside, several regions have been suggested as sources for cultivated crops developed from indigenous wild ancestors. The highlands of Ethiopia are thought to be the point of origin for the cereal called teff and the bananalike ensete plant; moreover, they may have been involved in the movement of wild cotton from the fringes of the Kalahari Desert to its cultivated form in the ancient Indus River valley. Some have identified East Africa as the breeding ground of certain indigenous millets, but more compelling is the claim for the West African savanna as a major cradle of early and independent agricultural activity.

Here, in the western Sudan, was domesticated a strain of millet known as fonio; here, too, were located a West African rice and the Guinea yam, both thought to have originated in the lake country of the upper Niger Valley. The rice came under cultivation there during the middle of the second millennium B.C., while the yam was domesticated as it was brought southward into the rain forest about four thousand years ago by peoples migrating before the growing desiccation of the Sahara region. As for fonio, it is found nowhere but in West Africa, a fact that has prompted the hypothesis that the western savanna must have served as one of the world centers for the independent discovery of plant cultivation, particularly of millets, which subsequently spread along the southern edge of the Sahara as far as Darfur in the Egyptian Sudan. An independent invention of agriculture in West Africa, the argument concludes, must have occurred as far back as the early sixth millennium B.C.; otherwise the savanna millets could not have diffused as far as the eastern Sudan before the arrival there of Egyptian wheat and barley coming up the Nile Valley.

Most authorities believe, however, that the agricultural movement was in fact from east to west, that knowledge of cultivation, originating in the Middle East, reached the Nile Delta, in the late sixth or early fifth millennium before Christ, then traveled southward along the Nile Valley, and finally westward across the southern edge of the Sahara into the central and western Sudan. Egyptian wheat and barley did not accompany the practice of cultivation, it is said, simply because local West African sorghum and millet were better suited to the savanna environment.

Much of this analysis is based on archaeological information—the finds in Palestine and numerous excavations in the Nile Valley, including evidence from the region of Khartoum estimated to be from the late fourth millennium B.C. In West Africa, however, such direct confirmation of agricultural activity does not extend beyond the early first-millennium sites of the Nigerian Nok culture, but further explorations may well expose earlier dating; witness the recent excavations deep in the forest area of western Nigeria establishing human habitation as long ago as eleven thousand years.

Despite the understandable reluctance of archaeologists to speculate on events unsupported by tangible evidence, other observers continue to urge a much more ancient beginning for agriculture in Africa and elsewhere. According to historical botanists the substantial variety and advanced evolution of many domesticated crops suggests a long period of anterior development, much longer than archaeological evidence alone appears able to sustain. Most major crops were already in use by 3000 B.C., some, like cotton, in highly evolved forms, and many geographically far removed from their points of origin as wild plants.

The example of cotton is instructive. It first appears in history about 3000 B.C. in the form of woven cloth at Mohenjo-Daro, centered in the ancient civilization of the Indus River valley. The cotton of Mohenjo-Daro came from a cultivated plant that had undergone much genetic and structural change but was nonetheless identifiable as the descendant of a wild ancestor still growing today along the edges of the Kalahari Desert in Southern Africa. Historical botanists have speculated at great length about the formidable questions of how, where, and by whom the cotton was domesticated, and what means were employed for transporting it thousands of miles by land and sea from its homeland to a far-off civilization apparently unconnected with Africa. Whatever may be the answers to these difficulties, it seems clear that a very long history of travel and cultivation must have preceded the fact of a flourishing cotton cloth industry in the Indus Valley fully five thousand years ago.

Indeed, some agricultural geographers have proposed that agriculture began far beyond the tenth-millennium Middle East cereals now generally regarded as the world's oldest examples of cultivated crops. If cotton had such an early start, would not food plants have been attempted much earlier still? If the Palestine grains are so ancient, why not a more remote cultivation based on wild roots and stems placed in the ground to sprout as they had been observed to do many times when tossed aside as refuse after a daily meal? Again, might not early hunters have gained control over their former quarry, offering the security and shelter of the camp in exchange for domestication? Such developments could have occurred in many places, although present speculation centers on the well-watered tropics of Southeast Asia where quasi-sedentary fishermen might have possessed the leisure time necessary for appropriate experimentation.

Africa, too, had its watercourses inhabited by fishing civilizations; more than that, historical linguists, through a technique known as glottochronology, have been able to follow language development in time, in the process producing interesting analyses concerning the early use of agricultural terms. Examining sub-Saharan African languages, they have traced words for domestic animals and agricultural implements that go back at least eight thousand years, evidence that teases the imagination with its possibilities for an ancient beginning of agricultural practice on the African continent. ❖

RECOMMENDED READINGS

The Old World: Early Man to the Development of Agriculture, gen. ed. Robert Stigler (New York: St. Martin's Press, 1974), provides an overview of human society prior to the Agricultural Revolution. The revolution itself is the subject of Donald O. Henry's *From Foraging to Agriculture: The Levant at the End of the Ice Age* (Philadelphia: University of Pennsylvania Press, 1989), which pays particular attention to the changing climate of the Near East and its effects on developments there.

James Mellaart, *The Neolithic of the Near East* (London: Thames & Hudson, 1975), offers a general account of the Neolithic period in the region; Peter J. Wilson, *The Domestication of the Human Species* (New Haven: Yale University Press, 1988), concentrates on the transformation of social organization and living patterns brought about by the new economy. The key archaeological site in establishing the growth of agriculture in the area as early as 8000 B.C. is the Palestinian town of Jericho, and Dame Kathleen Mary Kenyon, *Excavations at Jericho* (London: British School of Archaeology in Jerusalem, 1960–82), provides an excellent account of how these discoveries were made.

The selection refers to the use of cotton at Harappa and Mohenjo-Daro, the two major cities of the early Indus River civilization. Sir Robert Eric Mortimer Wheeler was one of the first to bring this culture to public notice. His *The Indus Civilization; Supplementary Volume to the Cambridge History of India,* 3rd ed. (Cambridge: University Press, 1968) was a definitive study for its day. Although it is now dated, it is still well worth reading as an introduction to the subject. Steven A. Weber, *Plants and Harappan Subsistence: An Example of Stability and Change from Rojdi* (New Delhi: Oxford & IBH, 1991), offers an up-to-date view of Indus agriculture and some consideration of the issue of the archaeological find of cotton cloth dating from a quite early period.

Sumeria, About 2750 B.C.

THE FIRST HEROIC AGE

Samuel Noah Kramer

The list of Sumerian innovations is impressive: schools, a calendar, astronomy, a sophisticated mathematical system, a complex theology and liturgy, a literature, a professional priesthood, city-states, public law-codes, and, above all, writing. The first great strides toward modern civilization occurred in Sumeria.

It is important to ask, however, what the social consequences of these developments were. Let us consider the Sumerian development of writing. How it occurred is relatively clear; needing to keep records of the quantities and varieties of things stored in their temples, Sumerian priests began the practice of scratching a simplified picture of the object or substance they wished to record, together with the number of scratches necessary to record its amount, on a lump of clay with the end of a stalk of reed.

In time, thousands of new signs were developed that bore little relationship to the object or idea they represented. Sumerian scribes now had a rich vocabulary and could record the hymns, laws, edicts, poems, and stories that have come down to us from that distant time. To master that vocabulary, however, required years of full-time and disciplined study. In this fashion, the first formal schools developed.

For the average men and women of the Sumerian city-states, however, this meant a loss of power and, with it, a loss of freedom. Information was controlled by the small number of individuals who were able to read and write; whoever monopolizes information invariably monopolizes power. A small and educated elite came to control what and how much was done, and when and where it was done.

As the Urban Revolution progressed, the mass of the Sumerian people were increasingly dominated by their professional priesthood and by the kings who eventually emerged from this priestly class. The relative freedom and equality of Old Stone Age society was replaced by bondage and hierarchy.

The following selection, although it is devoted to the first stirrings of epic poetry in Sumer, incidentally offers some indication of the early stages of this process. Kramer makes the point that the Sumerian epic poetry reflects an Heroic Age not unlike that of Achilles's Greece, Indra's

India, and Beowulf's Europe. Military power has come to be monopolized by a warrior chieftain and a band of professional fighters loyal to him personally. The chieftain and his followers, who were no doubt originally the young men of the community and their leader, have now become separate from the community and form a sort of aristocracy. The chieftain controls the council of elders and the assembly of the people that were once the organs of a more or less democratic society. "Wise men," distinguished by their memorization of stock praises and mythic genealogies, are also attached to the chieftain.

In time, of course, the descendants of the chieftains claim that they rule by the will of the gods, and their wise men, who have developed a system of writing, support them in this contention. The chieftains have become kings and their wise men have become priests. Most Heroic Ages are only a stage in the progressive bondage of the mass of the people.

READING QUESTIONS

1. What three Heroic Ages does Kramer note?

2. What are the form and content of the epic poems of an Heroic Age?

3. What are the characteristics of an Heroic Age?

4. When was the Sumerian Heroic Age?

istorians now generally realize (and this is largely to the credit of the English scholar H. Munro Chadwick) that the so-called Heroic Ages, which are come upon from time to time and from place to place in the history of civilization, represent not mere literary imagination but very real and significant social phenomena. Thus, to take only three of the better-known examples, there is the Greek Heroic Age, which flourished on the mainland of Greece toward the very end of the second millennium B.C.; the Heroic Age of India, which probably dates only a century or so later than that of Greece; and the Teutonic Heroic Age, which dominated much of northern Europe from the fourth to the sixth centuries A.D. All three of these Heroic Ages reveal a marked resemblance in social structure, governmental organization, religious concepts, and aesthetic expression. It is obvious that they owe their origin and being to similar social, political, and psychic factors.

From Samuel Noah Kramer, *History Begins at Sumer* (Garden City, NY: Doubleday, 1959), pp. 200-204.

The Sumerian heroic narrative poems constitute an epic literature which introduces a new Heroic Age to world history and literature—the Sumerian Heroic Age. Although it probably had its *floruit* toward the end of the first quarter of the third millennium B.C., and thus precedes by more than 1,500 years even the oldest of the three Indo-European Heroic Ages (that of the Greeks), its culture pattern is remarkably close to the culture pattern typical of the long-known Heroic Ages.

The Greek, Indian, and Teutonic Heroic Ages, as Chadwick concludes from relevant literary records, are essentially barbaric periods which show a number of salient characteristics in common. The political unit consists of a petty kingdom ruled by a king or prince who obtains and holds his rule through military prowess. His mainstay in power consists of the *comitatus,* a retinue of armed loyal followers who are prepared to do his bidding without question, no matter how foolhardy and dangerous the undertaking. There may be an assembly, but it is convened at the ruler's pleasure and serves only in an advisory and confirmatory capacity. The ruling kings and princes of the separate principalities carry on among themselves a lively, and at times friendly and even intimate, intercourse. They thus tend to develop into what may be termed an international aristocratic caste whose thoughts and acts have little in common with those of their subjects.

On the religious side, the three Indo-European Heroic Ages are characterized by a worship of anthropomorphic deities, which to a large extent seem to be recognized throughout the various states and principalities. These gods form organized communities in a chosen locality, though, in addition, each god has a special abode of his own. There are few traces of a chthonic or spirit cult. At death the soul travels to some distant locality that is regarded as a universal home and is not reserved for members of any particular community. Some of the heroes are conceived as springing from the gods, but there is no trace of heroic worship or hero cults. All these features common to the Heroic Ages of Greece, India, and Northern Europe are shared by the Heroic Age of Sumer.

But the parallelism extends even further. Indeed, it is particularly apparent on the aesthetic plane, especially in literature. One of the notable achievements of all four of these Heroic Ages was the creation of heroic narrative tales—in *poetic form*—that were to be spoken or sung. They reflect and illuminate the spirit of the age and its temper. Impelled by the thirst for fame and name so characteristic of the ruling caste during a Heroic Age, the bards and minstrels attached to the court were moved to improvise narrative poems or lays celebrating the adventures and achievements of kings and princes. These epic lays, with the primary object of providing entertainment at the frequent courtly banquets and feasts, were probably recited to the accompaniment of the harp or lyre.

None of these early heroic lays have come down to us in their original form, since they were composed when writing was either altogether unknown or, if known, of little concern to the illiterate minstrel. The written epics of the Greek, Indian, and Teutonic Heroic Ages date from much later

days, and consist of highly complex literary redactions in which only a selected number of the earlier lays are imbedded, and these in a highly modified and expanded form. In Sumer, there is good reason to believe, some of
the early heroic lays were first inscribed on clay five to six hundred years
following the close of the Heroic Age, and then only after they had undergone considerable transformation at the hands of priests and scribes. However, it should be carefully noted that the copies of the Sumerian epic texts
which we have at present date almost entirely from the first half of the second millennium B.C.

The written epics of the three Indo-European Heroic Ages show a number of striking similarities in form and content. In the first place, all the
poems are concerned primarily with individuals. It is the deeds and exploits
of the individual hero that are the prime concern of the poet, not the fate or
glory of the state or community. Moreover, while there is little doubt that
some of the adventures celebrated in the poems have a historical basis, the
poet does not hesitate to introduce unhistorical motifs and conventions,
such as exaggerated notions of the hero's powers, ominous dreams, and the
presence of divine beings. Stylistically, the epic poems abound in static epi-
thets, lengthy repetitions, and recurrent formulas, and in descriptions that
tend to be overleisurely and unusually detailed. Particularly noteworthy is
the fact that all the epics devote considerable space to speeches.

In all these respects, the pattern of Sumerian heroic poetry is similar to
the pattern of Greek, Indian, and Teutonic epic material. Since it is hardly
likely that a literary genre so individual in style and technique as narrative
poetry was created and developed independently, at different time intervals, in Sumer, Greece, India, and Northern Europe, and since the narrative
poetry of the Sumerians is by all odds the oldest of the four, it seems reasonable to conclude that in Sumer may be found the origin of epic poetry.

To be sure, there are a number of outstanding differences between the
Sumerian epic material and that of the Greeks, Indians, and Teutons. For example, the Sumerian epic poems consist of individual, disconnected tales of
varying length, each of which is restricted to a single episode. There is no
attempt to articulate and integrate these episodes into a larger unit. This was
first achieved by the Babylonian poets, who borrowed, modified, and
molded the relatively brief and episodic Sumerian tales—particularly in
their "Epic of Gilgamesh"—with the view of fashioning an epic of considerable length and complexity. There is relatively little characterization and
psychological penetration in the Sumerian material. The heroes tend to be
broad types, more or less undifferentiated, rather than highly personalized
individuals. Moreover, the incidents and plot motifs are related in a rather
static and conventionalized style; there is little of that plastic, expressive
movement which characterizes such poems as Homer's *Iliad* and *Odyssey*.
Another interesting difference: Mortal women play hardly any role in Sumerian epic literature, while they have a very prominent part in Indo-European
epic literature. Finally, in the matter of technique, the Sumerian poet gets
his rhythmic effects primarily from variations in the repetition patterns. He

makes no use whatever of the meters or uniform line so characteristic of Indo-European epics.

At present we can identify nine epic tales varying in length from one hundred to more than six hundred lines. Two of these revolve about the hero Enmerkar; two revolve about the hero Lugalbanda (in one of these Enmerkar, too, plays a considerable role); and five revolve about the most famous of the three heroes, Gilgamesh. All three are known from the Sumerian king list, a historical document which, like our epic material, has been found inscribed on tablets dating from the first half of the second millennium B.C. The list was probably composed in the last quarter of the third millennium B.C. In the king list, these three heroes are stated to be the second, third, and fifth rulers of the first dynasty of Erech, which, according to the Sumerian sages, followed the first dynasty of Kish, which in turn followed immediately upon the flood. ❖

RECOMMENDED READINGS

The discovery of Sumerian civilization has been the joint effort of archaeologists and historians. The foremost of the archaeologists was Sir Leonard Woolley, who presented an account of the initial excavations at the great Sumerian city of Ur in *Excavations at Ur: A Record of Twelve Years' Work* (New York: Crowell, 1954). His major work, *Ur of the Chaldees,* was first published in 1929 but has been revised by P.R.S. Moore and published as *Ur 'of the Chaldees': A Revised and Updated Edition of Sir Leonard Woolley's Excavations at Ur* (Ithaca, NY: Cornell University Press, 1982). More recent archaeological work in the region is discussed in *Fifty Years of Mesopotamian Discovery: The Work of the British School of Archaeology in Iraq, 1932-1982,* ed. John Curtis (London: British School of Archaeology in Iraq, 1982).

Samuel Noah Kramer has been a leader in translating Sumerian texts and presenting them to the English-reading public. *The Sumerians: Their History, Culture, and Character* (Chicago: University of Chicago Press, 1963) is an excellent general account. *Cradle of Civilization* (New York: Time-Life Books, 1969) by the same author is a handsomely illustrated presentation. The reader might find Kramer's *In the World of Sumer: An Autobiography* (Detroit: Wayne State University Press, 1986) an interesting account of a lifetime of scholarly work. A recent exposition of Sumerian civilization may be found in Harriet E. W. Crawford, *Sumer and the Sumerians* (Cambridge and New York: Cambridge University Press, 1991).

Other famous epics, all appearing in several editions each, are the *Ramayana* and *Mahabharata* of India; the *Iliad* and *Odyssey* of Greece; the *Aeniad* of Rome, *Beowulf, The Song of the Nibelungs, The Song of Roland,* and *The Song of the Cid,* of medieval Europe; and *Digenis Akritas* of the Byzantine Empire. *Hiawatha,* for the United States, and *Martin Fierro,* for Argentina, are two modern attempts at epic poetry. *The Song of the Cid* is distinguished by the fact that it has been made into a motion picture, *El Cid,* that manages to capture much of the epic spirit of the era.

DISCUSSION QUESTIONS

PART ONE: ORIGINS, 40,000 TO 2500 B.C.

1. The question of where, when, and how human beings first developed, appeared, or were made is one that has fascinated people since the beginning of recorded time, and it continues to be a matter of intense interest. Why are these questions so important, or are they? What difference does it make that we know something about the origins of humanity? Or does it make any difference at all?

2. The attempt to trace "human origins" depends largely on how one defines "human." What traits or characteristics can be described as unique to human beings? If you think that there are in fact such traits, how do you think they arose and what function do they serve? We often use the term "human nature." How would you define "human nature"?

3. Some scholars suggest that the difference between humans and other animals is only a matter of degree and that many supposedly human traits are in fact possessed by other animals. How valid do you think that position is? To what extent does the converse hold true? Do human beings display traits that are normally thought of as characteristic of animals? What about the territorial imperative, courtship displays and rituals, pecking orders, pack mentality, and so forth?

4. If the hunting and gathering way of life is so much easier, why did humans abandon it for agriculture and animal husbandry? Do you think the life of a nomadic hunter and food gatherer might have been better or happier than your own? Why or why not? Much of the free time of the hunters and gatherers is spent in religious and social ritual. What part do such rituals play in your life, and how important are they to you? Why?

5. Early writing was complex and very difficult to learn, and remained so for some 2,000 years, until the development of an alphabetic script. Why did it take so long to improve the art of writing? Was it in the interests of kings and scribes that there be a form of writing that could be mastered by all? Consider the function of writing in Egypt and Sumeria. How did writing serve to protect and enhance the power of a privileged minority?

6. Humans generally group themselves in societies in which a small group dominates and to some degree exploits the rest. Is that a true statement? If you think it is, why do people allow themselves to be treated in such

fashion for so long? Is it a reflection of some innate characteristic of "human nature" or is it a matter of social control? What are some of the means by which ruling classes control the mass of the population? Do you see any such control mechanisms influencing your own work, and, if so, in whose interests are they being applied?

PART II

The Ancient World

❖ ❖ ❖

2500 B.C. TO A.D. 500

	2500 B.C.	2000 B.C.	1500 B.C.	1000 B.C.
EUROPE		**ca. 1850–1600 B.C.** Immigration of Indo-European tribes **ca. 1628 B.C.** *The Eruption of Thera* **ca. 1600–1000 B.C.** Mycenaean period, Greece	**ca. 1400 B.C.** Fall of Minoan Crete **ca. 1180 B.C.** Trojan War **ca. 1150 B.C.** Destruction of Mycenaean citadels	**ca. 900 B.C.** Etruscan colonists come to Italy **776 B.C.** *The First Olympics* **ca. 750 B.C.** Period of Greek colonization; *The Greeks Reach Out* **ca. 700 B.C.** Hesiod
SOUTHWEST ASIA AND AFRICA	**ca. 1500–2000 B.C.** Egyptian Old Kingdom **ca. 2500 B.C.** Great Pyramid of Giza **ca. 2370 B.C.** Sargon of Akkad, Akkadian Empire **ca. 2100 B.C.** Oldest iron from Africa, central Nigeria	**ca. 1900–1450 B.C.** Kerma culture, Nubia **ca. 1792–1750 B.C.** Hammurabi **ca. 1650 B.C.** Hyksos invade Egypt **ca. 1500 B.C.** Amosis founds Egyptian New Kingdom	**ca. 1300–1200 B.C.** New Hittite Kingdom **ca. 1275 B.C.** *The Scribe Ramose* **ca. 1200 B.C.** Philistines settle on coast of Canaan **ca. 1150 B.C.** Moses leads Hebrews out of Egypt **ca. 1100 B.C.** *The Roots of Restriction*	**ca. 750 B.C.** Kushites conquer Upper Egypt **ca. 750–612 B.C.** Assyrian Empire **ca. 626–539 B.C.** Chaldean Empire **ca. 587 B.C.** Nebuchadnezzar destroys Solomon's Temple
SOUTH AND SOUTHEAST ASIA	**ca. 2300–1750 B.C.** Harappan civilization, Indus River valley	**ca. 2000 B.C.** Chicken and elephant domesticated, Indus valley	**ca. 1500–1000 B.C.** Aryans invade India; *Rig Veda*	**ca. 1,000–500 B.C.** Vedic period **ca. 563–483 B.C.** The Buddha **540–468 B.C.** Vardhamana
EAST ASIA	**ca. 2500 B.C.** Horse domesticated, central Asia **ca. 2500–2000 B.C.** Lung Shan culture, China	**ca. 2000 B.C.** First cultivated rice, southern China **ca. 1800 B.C.** Legendary Asia culture, China **ca. 1600–1027 B.C.** Chang Bronze Age culture		**ca. 1027–772 B.C.** Western Zhou Dynasty, China **ca. 770–256 B.C.** Eastern Zhou Dynasty, China
THE AMERICAS AND THE PACIFIC		**ca. 2000 B.C.** First metalworking in Peru **ca. 2000 B.C.** Immigrants from Indonesia settle Melanesia	**ca. 1500 B.C.** First oceangoing outrigger canoes, South Pacific **ca. 1300 B.C.** Fiji and western Polynesia settled	**1000 B.C.–A.D. 200** Olmec civilization, Mexico **ca. 1000–200 B.C.** Chavin civilization, Andes **ca. 1000 B.C.** First domesticated llama, Peru

500 B.C.	A.D. 1	A.D. 300	400	500
ca. **510 B.C.** Roman Republic founded ca. **500 B.C.** Beginning of Greek *polis* **499–479 B.C.** Persian Wars **451 B.C.** First Roman law code **431–404 B.C.** Peloponnesian War **336–323 B.C.** Alexander the Great; *The Greeks in Central Asia* **100 B.C.–A.D. 300** *The Roman Outlook*	**A.D. 14** Death of Augustus **A.D. 100** *Commerce on and Beyond the Frontier* **A.D. 161 180** Marcus Aurelius **A.D. 212** All freeman become Roman citizens	**303–311** Persecution of Christians **312** Conversion of Constantine **391** Christianity becomes Roman State Religion	**410** Visigoths sack Rome **476** *The Fall of Rome* ca. **480–543** Benedict of Nursia **481–511** Clovis, king of Franks **493–526** Theodoric the Ostrogoth	
ca. **549–333 B.C.** Persian Empire **500 B.C.–A.D. 200** Nok culture, West Africa **323 B.C.** Seleucid and Ptolemaic empires **270 B.C.–A.D. 350** Meroe culture, Nubia **247 B.C.** Parthian Kingdom established **63 B.C.** Palestine incorporated into Roman Empire	**A.D. 33** Crucifixion of Jesus **A.D. 70** Romans destroy Jerusalem **A.D. 250** Axum (Ethiopia) controls Red Sea trade	ca. **300** Ethiopia becomes Christian **330** Constantinople capital of Roman (Byzantine) Empire **354–430** St. Augustine	**400** Indonesians from Java and Sumatra settle in Madagascar. Introduce new type of banana	
ca. **500 B.C.–A.D. 500** *Student Life in Ancient India* **327–326 B.C.** Alexander the Great invades India **321–301 B.C.** Chandragupta, founder of Mauryan Empire, India **321–181 B.C.** Mauryan Empire **262–232 B.C.** Ashoka, Mauryan emperor	ca. **100 B.C.–A.D. 100** Bhagavad Gita ca. **A.D. 100–240** Kushan Empire, north India ca. **A.D. 100** Funan civilization, Vietnam	ca. **321–550** Gupta Empire, India	ca. **450** Buddhist monastery at Ajanta	
ca. **551–479 B.C.** Confucius *The Confucian Tradition* ca. **300 B.C.** Invention of wheelbarrow, China **221–206 B.C.** Qin dynasty, first Chinese Empire **202 B.C.–A.D. 220** Han dynasty, China ca. **202 B.C.–A.D. 220** *The Position of Women in Han China*	ca. **A.D. 100** *The Silk Roads* ca. **A.D. 100** *China's Invention of Paper* **A.D. 140–186** Emperor Wu, Han Dynasty, China ca. **A.D. 145–190** Sima Qian, Chinese historian	ca. **300–700** Ku Fun period, Japan **311** Sack of Luoyang, China **365–427** Tao Jian, Chinese poet	**420–588** Wei Dynasty, China ca. **450** Intro of Chinese writing to Japan	
ca. **300 B.C.** Earliest Eskimo tools, harpoon, and oil lamp	ca. **A.D. 100–800** Moche Kingdom, Peru ca. **A.D. 200–900** Classic Age of Maya	ca. **300** Rise of Hopewell Indian chiefdoms, North America ca. **300** Settlement of eastern Polynesia		

INTRODUCTION

The first civilizations emerged during the fourth millennium B.C. along the banks of mighty rivers. Such settlements arose first along the banks of the lower Tigris and Euphrates rivers and then in the valley of the Nile and the valleys of the Indus and Yellow rivers (India and China, respectively).

These civilizations developed, in large part, as a result of technological innovations that helped to revolutionize society. Improved irrigation techniques, new staple crops, the introduction of the wheel and of the plow all contributed to a more concentrated and complex lifestyle. The use of bronze for weaponry was another of the innovations of the period, and the Bronze Age empires were greatly influenced by their dependence on this alloy. The production of bronze required that tin, copper, fuel, and skilled metalworkers be brought together, a task that required the maintenance of complex trade routes and a high degree of central control. It was a worthwhile pursuit, however, because the few fighting men who could be armed and armored with this costly substance, and who could ride the swift war chariots that bronze fittings made possible, dominated the field of battle.

The rulers of the Bronze Age empires retained their power, and the loyalty of their warrior aristocracy, because they monopolized the supply of bronze. Chieftains of outlying states were eager to buy the bronze that would secure their own power, and so the Bronze Age empires were rich, powerful, and secure. These rulers and their aristocratic officials lived in walled cities from which they controlled and taxed the people of the surrounding countryside. Egypt was somewhat different in that geography protected the valley of the Nile from most foreign invaders and permitted the development of a highly centralized state and stable society. The selection entitled "The Scribe Ramose and the Valley of the Kings" portrays one individual's life during the high point in this civilization and illustrates the importance of government, culture, and ritual in this society.

This situation ended with the introduction of inexpensive iron. Even poor peoples could equip themselves with iron weapons, challenge those who had controlled bronze, and overthrow their walled cities. Carol Meyers, in "The Roots of Restriction: Women in Early Israel," portrays this age as that of the origin of the Hebrews, peasants who rose up and destroyed the Canaanite and Philistine cities of the plain. In the new Iron Age, the state that could put the greatest number of armed men in the field was usually victorious, the size of populations grew, and iron implements opened up new lands for settlement. Meyers notes how this drive for population increase influenced the early Hebrews in ways that have persisted down to the present day.

With the declining influence of the Bronze Age centers of culture, dynamic new Iron Age societies such as Korea, Southeast Asia, Palestine, and

Greece began to arise on their peripheries. Greek merchants and colonists, for instance, spread Greek culture and merchandise throughout the Mediterranean littoral. Lionel Casson, in "The First Olympics: Competing 'for the Greater Glory of Zeus,'" describes the exuberant combination of religion and sports in which the Greeks celebrated their common culture and marked its expansion. M. I. Finley, in "The Greeks Reach Out," strikes a more somber note, concluding that the driving force behind Greek expansion was the inability of their homeland to support any significant increase in population.

Another feature of the disintegration of the Bronze Age empires was the collapse of their elaborate systems of theology and ritual. Both Meyers and Casson illustrate the appearance of popular ethical religious systems, but the age was also one of conscious philosophic inquiry, the age of Hesiod, Joel, Buddha, Lao-tze, and K'ung-fu-tzu. Tu Wei-ming, in "The Confucian Tradition in Chinese History," examines K'ung-fu-tzu's reaction to the collapse of the Chou empire, and his development of a philosophic system that would continue to guide Chinese thought and action to the present day.

With the passage of time, Iron Age empires arose from the debris of their Bronze Age predecessors. These new states, although not existing in isolation from one another and often contributing to the growth of each other, each developed distinct cultures. It was from this belt of four Eurasian civilizations that satellite civilizations emerged, some evolving by 500 B.C. into the great empires of classical antiquity. Included in this group were the Persian Empire, the Alexandrian Empire and its successors; the Mauryan Empire in India; the Roman Empire; and the Ch'in and Han imperial dynasties in China.

Each empire possessed its own cultural characteristics and social structures. In "Student Life in Ancient India," Jeannine Auboyer indicates the combination of caste, initiation, and mysticism of Mauryan society that has remained a salient characteristic of Indian culture. "The Position of Women in Han China" illustrates how China's first woman scholar, Pan Chao, used her talents to instruct women in their proper role within the conservative society of the Han empire.

The amount of contact between cultures increased dramatically after 500 B.C. As a matter of fact, more contact occurred during this period than in the era from A.D. 500 to 1500. The Roman and Han empires traded extensively via both land and sea routes, and "The Silk Roads: A History" and "China's Invention of Paper" offer examples of both direct and indirect modes of exchange. On a smaller scale, "Commerce on and Beyond the Frontier" illustrates how Roman influences were carried first to the farthest reaches of their empire and then beyond, to the "barbarian" peoples beyond their borders.

These empires did not endure long after A.D. 500, but fell, at least for a time, under the control of invaders from beyond their frontiers. "The Fall of

Rome" offers an explanation of why this occurred in the western portion of the Roman Empire. The achievements of the Han, Mauryan, Sassanid Persian, and Roman empires were such, however, that they set a cultural standard for their respective regions that persists to the present day. It is for this reason that the period between 200 B.C. and A.D. 500 is sometimes called the Age of the Classical Empires.

THE ERUPTION OF THERA

Floyd W. McCoy and Grant Heiken

History students are always warned to beware of "monocausationalism,"
the ascribing of a single cause to a complex event or even a number of
events. Generally speaking, this is a very good precept and should not be
restricted to history students. One need only remember Adolf Hitler's insis-
tence that all of Germany's difficulties were caused by Jews, and the
"Final Solution" to which this belief led, to recognize that monocausation-
alism is not only poor history, but dangerous politics as well. One of Mur-
phy's laws is applicable: "For every complex problem there exists a simple,
clear, reasonable, and absolutely wrong solution."

People nevertheless appear to take a perverse pleasure in contemplat-
ing theories that present such simple, clear, and reasonable solutions. It is
almost traditional that every ten years a new reason for the fall of the
Roman Empire appears in the popular press. The most recent solution to
this old and complex question is that a change in the climate of the
Mediterranean made it impossible for the Romans to feed themselves, and
so they were too weak to withstand the Germanic invasions. Before that,
the reason was that the Romans used lead glaze on their pottery and lead
water pipes. They all got lead poisoning and went slightly crazy. Before
that, the Romans all had malaria; before that, they engaged in deficit
spending; before that, they spent too much money on the military, and so
forth.

Archaeological excavations on the Greek island of Thera, in the
Aegean Sea, began in the late 1960s. They revealed that the modern island
is only the remnant of a larger volcanic island that had blown apart over
3,500 years ago. Scientists were at that time beginning to have a much
better idea of how responsive the Earth's waters and air are to stimuli
such as decreased atmospheric ozone, small rises in the temperature of
parts of the oceans, and increased atmospheric dust, and the findings at
Thera aroused immediate interest.

There was still another consideration at work. It is not an easy matter
to acquire the funds for archaeological investigation and it is even harder
in Greece, where there are many potential sites and many applicants for
government funds. The suggestion that the eruption of Thera may have

been the basis for the legend of the lost continent of Atlantis came first from some of the supporters of the archaeologists working on Thera. The suggestion was sufficient to bring journalists to the island and to gain international publicity for the excavations at Thera.

By the time the first year's work was done, another theory had arisen that ash and tidal waves produced by the eruption had so devastated Crete that the Minoan civilization there collapsed. A theory that was advanced only as a suggestion to the scholarly community was enthusiastically accepted as proven by magazines and the popular press. It seemed clear that at least a portion of the public who were interested in such matters were ready for some hyperbole in the matter of Thera.

Popular writers and sensational journals turned attention to Thera and were soon crediting the eruption with turning the Nile River red with volcanic dust, of parting the Red Sea for the fleeing Israelites as a secondary effect of the tidal wave it caused; of stopping the sun at Joshua's command (although the author did not explain how the eruption managed to do this—particularly more than forty years after it had parted the Red Sea), of destroying Cretan civilization with falling ash and a tidal wave, of starting the Trojan War; and of causing or influencing a number of other well-known events.

There were few protests from archaeologists, although some scholars in Greece grumbled that the leader of the Thera excavations was so adept at generating interest that he was draining funds from other and more worthy projects. Thera's fame brought in tourists, government grants, and foundation endowments. These were sufficient to sponsor several years of what became the most thorough and modern archaeological investigation ever made of such a large Aegean site.

With the passage of time, however, the eruption at Thera has been shown to have had far less effect than even sober investigators had once supposed, although research into the matter is still not yet complete. What has been discovered, however, is enough data to provide a very full picture of the daily life of an outpost of Cretan civilization and a detailed record of the catastrophe that befell it.

This selection provides a balanced account of what actually occurred on Thera on that fateful day in 1628 B.C. It is far less dramatic than much of what has been written on the subject, but it is considerably more accurate. The excavators at Thera, together with those still working at Pompeii, have carried out the most thorough on-site investigations of volcanic eruptions on record, and they have contributed a great deal to knowledge of the exact sequence of events during such an occurrence.

McCoy's short treatment has been included not only for its intrinsic interest, but also because it offers some food for thought. It suggests that the Earth and its people may not be as fragile as is commonly supposed, and it illustrates that such matters as the excavation of a Bronze Age site on an obscure Aegean island holds the power to attract the attention normally reserved by the public for television stars and president's widows.

READING QUESTIONS

1. Why is the area of the Aegean the scene of so many volcanic eruptions?

2. What were the phases of the eruption of Thera?

3. What was the effect of the eruption?

Minoan Crete was the pride of the Aegean world at the opening of the Late Bronze Age (seventeenth through mid-fifteenth century B.C.). From key administrative centers like Knossos and Mallia on the north coast and Phaistos with the nearby harbor town of Kommos in the south, Minoan influence and trade extended in all directions—to Egypt, the Levant, and Cyprus to the south and east, but especially to the north and the Aegean islands. Excavations at Ayia Irini, on the island of Keos off the coast of Attica, and at Phylakopi on Melos have revealed settlements with close ties to Minoan culture. The emerging Mycenaean society on the Greek mainland was also strongly influenced by Crete. Kastri on the island of Kythera and Triandha on Rhodes may well have been Minoan colonies. Akrotiri on the volcanic island of Thera, or Santorini, in the southern Aegean was another flourishing Minoan town.

Akrotiri, however, was foredoomed. Like Pompeii some 1,700 years later, it would be destroyed by a massive volcanic eruption. The magnitude of that eruption, likened to the devastating explosion of Krakatoa off western Java in 1883, has been the subject of intense scrutiny by both archaeologists and geologists. Akrotiri, of course, was never reoccupied, and some scholars have speculated that its destruction spawned the legend of the lost continent of Atlantis. Romantic visionaries have even tried to link the eruption to ancient events such as the parting of the Red Sea during the Exodus and with the Ten Plagues in Egypt.

What was the effect of the eruption on Minoan civilization? Some have suggested that it created a major catastrophe for Minoan Crete—earthquakes and tidal waves destroying sites, ash burying and killing crops. Other scholars believe the blast had little effect outside Akrotiri, a view to which we now subscribe, particularly concerning the effects of the ash fall—research continues on the effects produced by earthquakes, tsunamis, and climate perturbations, all of which could have been significant. What we can now reconstruct with some certainty are the events of the final days of Thera, the

Floyd W. McCoy and Grant Heiken, "Anatomy of an Eruption," *Archaeology*, May/June 1990, pp. 42–49.

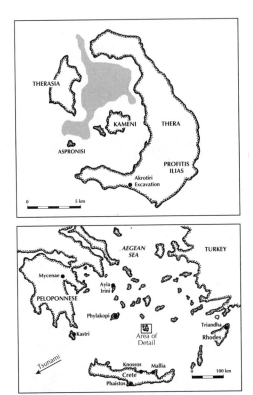

Located on a geologic hot spot, modern Thera and neighboring Aspronisi and Therasia, created during the Late Bronze Age eruption, surround the Kameni Islands, the product of more recent volcanic activity (at top, the Kameni Islands as seen from Thera). While the eruption reshaped Thera, its effects on Minoan civilization remain a matter of debate.
From "Anatomy of an Eruption," Archaeology, *May/June 1990, p. 44.*

island's geography in Minoan times, and the aftermath of that cataclysmic eruption.

In the fall of 1628 B.C., what might have been another bright day on Thera was darkened by falling ash. The rain of cold gritty particles followed months of unusual and unaccountable phenomena: low-intensity earthquakes, larger tremors, landslides, and variations in the flow of hot springs. Now the ash was ankle-deep on the south coast at Akrotiri. It was time to go; the island's inhabitants were leaving, taking with them anything of value they could carry.

One of the largest volcanic eruptions in recorded history had started. A mile or more beneath Thera, viscous magma was rising to the surface, following conduits of older eruptions. Although a new phenomenon to the Minoans, volcanic activity had been the dominant theme in the geologic history of the island for more than 100,000 years. At least seven major eruptions are known to have taken place, the last some 16,000 years before, each leaving distinctive deposits of ash and lava—the multicolored stratigraphy so spectacularly displayed in the island's seaside cliffs.

Hours after the departure of the Minoans, the earth's crust gave way beneath Thera. The consequent release of pressure freed dissolved gasses in the magma, much like uncorked champagne. The molten rock frothed, magma rose explosively. When the magma hit seawater, it became even more explosive. A major eruption was in progress, and the Minoan island was being reshaped just as it had been so often in the past.

Far beneath the Aegean, the geologic plates bearing the continents of Africa and Europe collide, creating volatile conditions on the surface. The northern edge of the African plate, overridden by the European plate, is forced downward until, at a depth of 50 to 75 miles, the rock melts. This molten rock then rises to collect in the shallow subsurface and later erupts at the surface; Thera sits on top of just such a geologic hot spot. How often and with what frequency these eruptions occur remains unknown. The events of the Late Bronze Age described above, however, are typical of the activity immediately preceding such an eruption.

Minoan artifacts beneath ash levels on the adjacent islet of Therasia, discovered during pumice quarrying for construction of the Suez canal in the mid-nineteenth century, first attracted the attention of a local physician. This discovery led to the first detailed examination of Thera's stratigraphy by a French geologist, Ferdinand André Fouqué, in 1879. Today, geologists have identified the ash from Thera throughout the Aegean and Mediterranean seas, on many of the surrounding islands, in lakes in Turkey, and as far away as the Nile Delta. Archaeologists have identified the ash at sites on Thera, Crete, and Rhodes. The regional extent of this ash is dramatic documentation of the enormous impact the volcanic event had on the Late Bronze Age world.

We have restudied Thera, and the adjacent islets of Therasia and Aspronisi, applying new knowledge from studies of large, caldera-forming eruptions elsewhere in the world. This has led to a better understanding of the Late Bronze Age event sequence and an interpretation of what the island looked like before the eruption.

In common with many other large explosive eruptions, the event on Thera progressed in four major stages, preceded by a minor precursor eruption. In the course of this precursor activity, ash was dispersed to the south over a small area of Thera leaving four distinct thin layers, each about a half inch thick. This suggests that four small eruptions of fine gray ash occurred, probably prompting the Minoans to leave. These steam-rich plumes of ash probably rose only a few hundred yards for a few hours each, a spectacular sight to any Minoans remaining in the vicinity.

An enormous plume charged with pumice and ash, rising perhaps 17 miles, well into the stratosphere, marked the first major phase of the eruption. It must have begun shortly after the precursor activity stopped, because there is no indication that wind or rain had time to erode the uppermost surface of the precursor ash layers. The gigantic plume deposited four-inch diameter chunks of pumice (frothy volcanic glass that can float on water) in layers up to six yards thick on Thera and Therasia. Variations in the intensity of this explosive activity produced faint layering in the deepening deposit.

Vast rafts of pumice produced during this stage of the eruption apparently drifted throughout the Aegean and eastern Mediterranean to accumulate on the beaches of Melos, Cyprus, Turkey, Israel, and Egypt. The finer-sized ash was dispersed to the south and east by stratospheric winds to blanket a wide area: about two inches fell on eastern Crete, as much as 12 inches were deposited on Kos, up to three feet accumulated on Rhodes, and it settled in the seawater leaving a submarine layer as much as a yard thick in the Aegean and inches thick in the eastern Mediterranean.

All in all, it was a gritty mess for Minoans living downwind of Thera, such as those on Crete. But is was a mess that was largely an inconvenience, not unlike the results of the Mount St. Helens eruption in 1981. At Akrotiri on Thera, it was a different matter. The buildings and walls of the town were buried under pumice and ash from the first phase. This was more an entombment than leveling, and structural damage was largely limited to collapsed roofs and walls.

Then a dramatic change in the character of the eruption took place, signaling the start of the second phase as seawater poured into the vent, reacting violently with the rising magma. The result was steam blasts that produced towering plumes so densely laden with volcanic debris that they periodically collapsed, sending repeated flows of ash, pumice, and steam surging away at high speed from the vent at ground level. While the pumice fell during the first phase in horizontal layers, like snow draped over the countryside, the second stage phreato-magmatic surges, as they are termed, left a different signature: sweeping dunelike and rippled beds. The transition between the first and second stages of the main eruption was abrupt, and this is reflected in the sharp boundary between the deposits with no indication of erosion.

These flows were particularly destructive, and their violent nature is particularly evident at Akrotiri. None of the town's structures is preserved in the surge deposits—portions of buildings and walls not buried in the pumice-fall deposits of the first phase were leveled by the violent surges of the second phase. More than just a frightening spectacle, anyone on the island or within several miles of the shore would have been killed instantly by these surges, which can flow over water for short distances.

Transition into the third eruptive phase was gradual. The border between the deposits from the second and third phases is often indistinct, noticeable only by the disappearance of dunelike beds. The deposits left by the third phase are the thickest of the succession, up to 56 yards deep, a heterogeneous mixture of ash, pumice, and large rock fragments.

How this massive third phase level was deposited is still a mystery. Layers beneath many of the large lithic blocks indicate that the material was thrown through the air, forming pits upon impact. But the types of rock represented by the blocks are the same as those found in lava flows that occur on present-day Therasia and in the northern part of Thera, and there is evidence for localized volcanic mud flows. Whatever the means of deposition, geophysical evidence indicates the material was deposited at much lower temperatures than during the first and second phases.

The fourth and last eruptive phase consisted of ground-hugging, hot, gaseous clouds containing ash and small lithic pieces that chilled and thickened at the shoreline—forming the present-day coastal plains along most of Thera, especially near the airport and Akrotiri, and along northern and western Therasia. The phase left thin deposits (about a yard thick) near the caldera, but considerably deeper (up to 40 yards) along coastal areas. Locally, eroded surfaces between the third and fourth phase deposits indicate brief rainstorms probably concurrent with eruptive activity.

This was the end of the eruption, a sequence of events that may have lasted for a few days or weeks. To Therans who attempted to return, the sight must have been astounding—the island's shape and topography were changed, steaming white-gray ash and pumice mantled the landscape, and the sea was covered with rafts of floating pumice.

Now that we have a thorough understanding of the eruption sequence, we can attempt to re-create the geography of the pre-eruption island. The bulls-eye pattern of pumice deposits from the first phase of the eruption pinpoints a vent just north of the modern-day Kameni Islands. Since pumice is produced when there is no water reacting with the erupting magma, we know that this vent was located on dry land.

Surges characteristic of the second phase, however, occur when there is explosive interaction with water at the vent, in quantities that implicate seawater. Because the surges flowed away from the source, we can trace that source by following the dunelike structures and rippled surfaces in the deposits. This study suggests that the center of the second phase of the eruption was south of the phase one position; we therefore assume the vent moved south to a new position that was within the sea.

The quantities of lithic fragments from lava flows in the northern portion of the island, and the thickness of the phase three deposit, suggest a large volume of erupted debris, expelled by the collapse that formed the modern-day caldera north of the Kameni Islands. Phase four was the final degassing of the magma, carrying with it whatever solid ash and lithic fragments were left in the vent.

Like today, Thera had a central bay surrounded by steep slopes and cliffs of spectacular beauty. During the Late Bronze Age, however, an extensive land mass existed in what is now the northern sector of the bay. We are not certain whether this was a broad low plain or a large island. Before the eruption, the central bay was open to the sea through the channel that exists today between Akrotiri peninsula and Aspronisi Island. The other two channels in today's topography (between Aspronisi and Therasia and between Therasia and Thera) were created by collapse during the volcanic activity, most likely in the third phase. The collapse of the channel between Aspronisi and Therasia islands produced the major tsunami (seismic sea-wave), which traveled out toward the southwest passing between Crete and the Greek mainland. For this we have deep-sea evidence of redeposited muds stirred by the passage of the tsunami, and suggests minimal tsunami effects toward the eastern Mediterranean region.

Thera never had a lofty, central, conical peak that collapsed to form the bay we see today. At least two overlapping calderas—an older one to the south, and the Late Bronze Age caldera to the north (they are topographically distinct below sea level)—form today's huge depression that is flooded by the sea. Small eruptions of lava from Roman times up until 1950 have formed the Kameni Islands, which lie along the common boundary of the two calderas.

Corroborating field evidence for our interpretation comes from numerous patches of Late Bronze Age volcanic debris mantling slopes that face inward toward the present-day depression—remnants of pre-Late Bronze Age eruption caldera walls that formed steep slopes during Minoan times.

What shaped this earlier caldera, which could have served the Minoans as a harbor? Exposed in the cliffs of Thera, well below the Late Bronze Age eruptive deposits, are two distinct white bands of ash and pumice produced by large explosive eruptions about 100,000 years ago, both as big as the Late Bronze Age eruption. Collapse associated with these older eruptions probably formed the southern caldera. Preservation of the caldera and its surrounding steep slopes for 100,000 years is not surprising, considering the slow rates of erosion and slope modification processes in the Mediterranean climate.

Much discussion has been concerned with the effects of the ash on Crete. By extrapolating from the deep-sea record, we feel that about two inches of ash were deposited on the central-eastern part of the island, certainly not enough to cause damage to crops or buildings, and quickly eroded or mixed into soils.

How often do these huge eruptions occur? This is a major subject of volcanological research and no answer can be given. On Thera the timing varies between perhaps only a few thousand years to 16,000 years, the span between the last pre-Late Bronze Age explosive event that produced a caldera and the Minoan eruption. When will the next occur? It's hard to say, but when it does it will be just as dramatic as the eruption witnessed by the Minoans. We leave for others the problem of what became of the Therans, forced to flee their island home and seek refuge on Crete, other Aegean islands, or the mainland.❖

RECOMMENDED READINGS

The archaeological excavations of Thera began in earnest in 1968-69, and the early findings of an enormous volcanic eruption quickly caught the public's attention, especially when it was suggested that the memory of a sudden disappearance of a large part of the island prompted Plato's discussion of the lost continent of Atlantis. Two books soon appeared, stressing that connection: Angelos Georgiou Galanopoulos, *Atlantis: The Truth Behind the Legend* (London: Nelson, 1969), and John Victor Luce, *The End of Atlantis: New Light on an Old Legend* (London: Thames & Hudson, 1969). The theory that the eruption of Thera destroyed the Cretan empire was put forward in Sir Denys Lionel Page, *The Santorini Volcano and the Desolation of Minoan Crete* (London: Society for the Promotion of Hellenic Studies, 1970).

Within a few years, however, attention turned to the results being obtained by continued archaeological work, an aspect of Thera that is presented in Christos Doumas, *Thera: Pompeii of the Ancient Aegean: Excavations at Akrotiri, 1967-79* (London: Thames & Hudson, 1983). The comparison with the eruption of Vesuvius and the sudden entombment of Pompeii and Herculaneum is inevitable. That disaster is minutely chronicled by Robert Etienne, *Pompeii: The Day a City Died* (New York: H.N. Abrams, 1992). Another comparable event is discussed in *Krakatau, 1883—The Volcanic Eruption and Its Effects,* ed. Tom Simkin and Richard S. Fiske (Washington, DC: Smithsonian Institution Press, 1983).

A recent work providing a most readable overview of the entire story of Thera and the men who brought its ancient culture to light is that of Charles R. Pellegrino, *Unearthing Atlantis: An Archaeological Odyssey* (New York: Random House, 1991).

Egypt, 1275 B.C.

THE SCRIBE RAMOSE AND THE VALLEY OF THE KINGS

John Romer

Ancient Egyptian civilization lasted for almost 3,000 years, from approximately 3200 to 332 B.C. It was marked by a remarkable continuity and permanence unparalleled in history. The Egyptians never forgot their archaic past, and it was their realization of the enduring nature of the state—a sense of changelessness—that most typified Egyptian civilization. Security and order, so essential to Egyptian society, were provided by a strong central government headed by a king (pharaoh) who was a god. Civilized life emanated from the divine king, and life everlasting for Egypt's pharaohs was the sustaining principle of Egyptian civilization. These dominating characteristics of Egyptian society all are present in the following selection by John Romer. He tells a vivid story of a 3,000-year-old village located in the fabled Valley of the Kings near Thebes. Housed within this village was a community of quarrymen, stonemasons, and artists. These artists and craftsmen were responsible for creating the tombs in which the pharaohs would reside for eternity.

The scribe Ramose was one of the many artists who worked and lived in the Valley of the Kings. For some forty years he checked and listed, measured and registered the work at the tomb, and maintained the records of the rations of food and supplies sent to the village. He belonged to that astute middle class of learned men who proved so necessary to the successful operation of the state machine. The art of writing was not easily mastered, and a prospective scribe spent years at school. The teaching was monotonous and the discipline hard, but those who graduated became highly respected and well-trained professionals.

The following selection manages to convey a sense of the daily lives of ordinary individuals residing in a small village—individuals living in a carefully ordered state dominated by the ceremony of life and death.

READING QUESTIONS

1. How did Ramose gain his elevated position in the world?

2. How did the villagers earn their livings?

3. What sort of religion did Ramose practice, and what did he hope to gain?

4. Why was so much attention, expense, and labor expended on tombs and burials?

I
n 1275 BC, in the fourth year of the reign of King Ramesses II, a young scribe named Ramose was working, so he tells us, in one of the royal temples, counting and listing the herds of cattle sent from estates up and down the Nile valley. Unusually for Thebes, where inheritance of profession was usual, Ramose had not followed his father Amenemheb in his profession as a messenger carrying instructions and reports between the state officials at Thebes, though it must have been Amenemheb's constant attendance upon the bureaucrats that had first brought his son to the notice of one of the scribes. These men were the counters and recorders of the state, and as the grinders of gods' wheels, the millers rather than the grist of their society, they formed an astute middle class. One of these men, then, took the messenger's boy into the scribal schools that many such officials ran and there taught him the skills of writing and accountancy. The young Ramose was shown the use of the equipment that made up a scribe's kit and which was also the honoured badge of that profession: the small slates on which the raw pigments for the inks were ground; the circular dishes in which the fine-ground pigments were mixed with their binders to make the inks; the smoothing stones with which the papyrus writing sheets were burnished to allow the brushes a smooth progress; the method of preparing the reeds that served as brushes by carefully chewing their ends to separate their stiff fibres enabling them to hold the ink; the rectangular wooden palettes, with places for small cakes of ink and a central slot to hold a dozen brushes; and the special knotting that was used to tie all these pieces together with a cord to make a single portable kit. Ramose was also taught the prayers that all scribes recited before they started work, along with the gentle ritual of sprinkling drops of water in honour of the spirits of the profession's patrons. He had to memorize the 700-odd hieroglyphic signs and their flamboyant cursive equivalents used in the records of the royal administration. And finally, by the hypnotic process of repetition, the boy was filled with elaborate repertoire of form and phrase that made up the literary language of the state.

These scribes' schools were hard, their morality, the backbone of the state, strict and straight. Later in his life, one scribe recalled that his training

From John Romer, *Ancient Lives: Daily Life in Egypt of the Pharaohs* (New York: Holt, Rinehart & Winston, 1984), pp. 6-7, 13-15, 19-22, 23-25, 26.

had consisted of having his back beaten to allow words to enter his ear. Certainly such training did little to cultivate originality. What it did produce, however, were generations of stolid men set for lifetimes in the state machine—pleasant lives engrossed in bureaucracy and the care of large households. If such training filled the scribes with arduous virtues, these were usually leavened in the individual by a fine wit and an awareness of the dignity of life appropriate to a nation of good farmers. There was a genuine social tenderness in Egypt which had, at its root, an instinctual piety. From the whores and drunks of the Theban beerhalls to the highest officials in the land, everybody lived in a world inhabited by mortals and gods alike. And just as Ramose and his friends understood the sanctity of the structure of this carefully ordered state, so they appreciated their role within it. They also understood that, like the gods and kings, as a part of this intricate coalition of men and gods, they too might live forever.

Yet with all their yearnings for immortality, few people ever consciously attempted to preserve the most precious of modern conceptions: personality. Scribe Ramose, for example, has memorialized himself, his wife, his concubines and his farmhands on dozens of monuments. In the course of a long life he built three chapels, supported a large household and died a well-to-do and respected leader of his community. Yet a careful sifting of the detritus of all this activity will reveal, with but a few moving exceptions, only the public face of the man. But this too is important, for this is the vision that a Theban scribe held of himself—one indeed which he has handed down to us with great care.

Ramose worked for some forty years in the Valley of the Kings, an arid intractable place where no plant would ever grow, yet the seeds that he helped to place there in the dry rock were very fruitful, for they were the dead kings of Egypt, a vital element in the bargain that the Egyptians had struck with their gods: a contract between ordered civilization and natural forces. Held amidst of the ceremonial of life and death, the kings of Egypt were the earthly representatives of the divine order, orchestrators of the marvellous balance struck between the fruitful rhythms of nature and the regular ordering of society. The death of a king was a potentially destructive event for the state, a random brutal happening that had to be methodically joined, carefully subsumed, into that same fruitful order of nature.

When Scribe Ramose first went to work in the Great Place the floor of its valley was much lower than it is today, a network of water-cut v-shaped channels partly choked with flints and stones which had rolled down from the slopes above. In the sides of these channels stood the doorways of the tombs of the new dynasty kings, surrounded by fresh piles of white stone chippings that stood like blobs of cream on the gold-crusty patina of the desert valley. In between the tombs, white paths passed in and out of the dry channels and up and down the hills and screes at the valley's head. Water jars were set up at intervals in the valley and they dripped as their porous clay allowed a gradual surface evaporation, cooling their contents. In the valley's centre stood a conglomeration of huts and store-houses that served the needs of the workmen. Apart from the visiting commissions of nobles, a vizier and even, occasionally, the King himself, the valley usually held about 100 men and, as they worked, lived and slept there, the noise and bustle of them all must have been much like that of any small village; but this was a community of quarrymen, stonemasons and artists, even occasionally a scholar priest sent to set out and correct the sacred texts of the royal underworld, and they worked with the calm authority of experts.

The tombmakers and their families lived in an isolated desert village on the west bank. To go home from the Great Place they had to climb the path running past the medjay's fortress with its three steps, out on to the horizon of Thebes with its sweeping view of the river valley, then turn southwards along a rim of cliffs, the western horizon of Thebes. Their village was set under these cliffs, isolated from the rest of Thebes, by a walk of some two miles along paths that swung round the sheltering desert hills, squeezed past the white walls of the royal temples, then went straight over the flat fields on a high silty causeway to the ferry-landing where they could cross to the city on the eastern bank.

Scribe Ramose had gone to live in this unique community when he began work in the royal tomb, and the change in his life was dramatic. Most Thebans, after all, lived a noisy communal life, largely out of doors. Now Ramose had left all that and moved to the quiet valley of the royal tombs and a remote yet tight-packed village filled with expert craftsmen: distinctive and unusual people, men of special knowledge and careful values, men who made the figures of the gods. Most Thebans lived in simple dusty houses with whitewashed walls and a few rough furnishings; a world of limited colour and texture. Of Ramose's possessions only his scribal kit, the emblem of his profession, would have been well made and of elegant proportions. The luxurious trappings of the court and the temples, elegant and ethereal objects, were magical symbols of status and rank, remote emblems of power. And every one of these strange things was unique, glowing with the touch of the craftsmen who made it, men whose lives were saturated in deep colours, absorbed in the careful values of their hybrid art. Ramose had joined a community of such people, a hot-house isolated from the bustling farmers and peasants who made up the bulk of Egyptian society.

He took a house in the oldest part of the village, close to and on the same side of the street as the gang foreman, Kaha. Just as the work at the tomb was divided by tradition between two gangs, each under its own foreman, so the village was split into two halves, east and west, by a street so narrow that you could stretch out your arms and touch the walls on either side. When Ramose came there were about seventy houses in the village, each similar in its design, with four ill-lit rooms running behind one another; two large family rooms of some five yards by four yards being followed by a smaller kitchen and storeroom. A stair gave access to the roof where the family would sleep in the hot summer nights. Though modest by modern standards, about the same size as a small terraced house of the last century, Ramose's village house probably held larger rooms than any he had lived in before. All the village houses were of a more regular, more compact, design than the usual dwellings in Thebes and many of them had ovens and cellars, cut from the desert rock. Dark, but with whitewashed walls reflecting the sunlight which fell from small slots in the roof, their public rooms held cushioned couches, neat wooden chairs and cabinets of rush and wood, all set on simple matting. On one of the walls there was a family shrine containing a little stela with a prayer carved on it and with busts, perhaps, of the ancestors standing close by. The largest room was probably reserved for gatherings of friends, for there was no square, no open ground, near the village where people could meet in the evenings. So we may imagine villagers seated in a parlour, bright beams of light holding in them the smoke from the ovens and dust hovering in the air. The white wooden door is open to the street, old friends make music together, play games or simply sit and talk, and children run in and out and all around.

When Ramose arrived at the village it was entirely contained inside long rectangular walls, with only one doorway, on its northern side, which opened into the central lane, the village high street. The village plan was like a fish skeleton, its spines the walls that partitioned the houses one from another, its backbone the narrow high street. The fish lay with its mouth, the gate, pointing up the valley to the north, and its tail some 140 yards away at the lowest point. As the high street was probably roofed over, from a distance the whole settlement would have had the appearance of a single low dusty-brown building with one small doorway, entirely filling the bottom of the desert valley.

Outside the village's north wall, on the high ground, was a group of temples, small versions of the huge stone temples of the state gods, some of which were already hundreds of years old in Ramose's time. Outside the south wall, the village rubbish was dumped so that it flowed further down the valley floor. The hillsides around the village were peppered with tomb shafts and covered with small mud-brick chapels and miniature pyramids, rows and rows of small white buildings with bright painted doorways. The main cemetery was on the western hillside, running down a slope from the little cliff at its top and almost touching the village wall. A network of paths and ramps, serving both as processional ways for funerals and to give access to the chapels containing the cults of the village ancestors, ran right through the cemetery, and on feast days the villagers would go to their family chapels to share their meals with their ancestors and make offerings to them at the family altars. Statues and pictures of the dead stood in the chapels and in the houses of the living. The spirits of the dead mingled freely with the living at the little village: Scribe Ramose started to make a tomb and chapel for himself in the cemetery even before he had found a wife.

Although the sturdy little curved wall that surrounded the oldest houses of the village had been built in the old dynasty, during the reign of King Tuthmosis I, tradition held that it has been this King's father, King

Amenhotep I, who had founded the community; some two and a half centuries later Vizier Paser's administration considered King Amenhotep, now a god, to be the owner of the village and its houses. With his wife, Queen Nefertari, the dead King was the revered patron of the village, with his shrine at the heart of the village temples. At times of festival the King's statue was taken from its shrine and carried through the village, and served as a popular oracle. In deference to their founder, the King's name, though common enough amongst ordinary Thebans, was seldom used in the families of the tombmakers.

In fact, even before King Amenhotep's time, there had been a group of houses in the valley. They had grown up on either side of the desert track which later became the village high street. The well-ordered village that King Tuthmosis had girded with his wall had been built above some of these more open-planned houses, and consisted of a dozen or so dwellings on each side of the path, all with the number and size of rooms and installations which became the standard pattern for the later houses in the village. In all probability, these houses had held tombmakers and craftsmen too, since they were situated in the heart of the Theban cemeteries; though these early villagers also seem to have worked upon temples and royal building projects and nobles' tombs in every capacity from stonemasons to artists and architects. At all events, their community had thrived sufficiently by the end of the dynasty to have seen another dozen houses added on to the outside of the western wall.

Then the troubles that accompanied the end of the old dynasty affected the village, and it seems that the tombmakers were taken away from Thebes to live in a new town in the middle of Egypt that the heretic King Akhenaten had founded as the centre of his new state. There they performed the same tasks as at Thebes, and in the process learnt many of the vivid artistic mannerisms of that eccentric period as well as its special skills of carving relief in stone and plaster. Their return to their old, now ruined, village came with the rise of the new dynasty under King Horemheb as a part of the restoration of the ancient state religion at Thebes. It was now that the Mayor of Thebes began the reform of the village and the work in the royal tomb that was to be so brilliantly concluded by Vizier Paser. Written news of the village at this time is almost non-existent; fortunately a litigant in a legal dispute of a much later date inadvertently recorded the beginning of the enlargement of the gangs and the further spread of the village in a deposition concerning the ownership of a tomb in the village cemetery:

> [In] year seven of King Horemheb [1313 BC], on the day of induction of my father Hay [i.e. on the day he joined the village], the Mayor of Thebes, Djutmose, apportioned the places that were in the village cemetery to the workmen—and he gave the tomb of Amenmose to Hay, my father—as my mother, Hel, was—[Amenmose's] daughter and he has no male child.

Vizier Paser's reorganization of the village was far more comprehensive than Mayor Djutmose's had been. When Ramose arrived the village houses had more than doubled in number, some twenty dwellings being added to each side of the high street and others built beyond the village entrance in the north wall. The southern end of the high street was extended across an open patch of ground, which had provided stabling for the village's cows and donkeys, by cutting through the old wall of Tuthmosis I. The new housing plots laid out on either side of it were generally larger than the older houses in the village and had been taken over by the longer-established village families, who later extended their domains southwards into other unoccupied plots as their succeeding generations needed houses of their own. At this time many of the village houses were given limestone doorposts engraved with the names of their occupants. As with villages everywhere, many of the houses would later be known by these names long after their original inhabitants had died. . . .

As well as making their own tombs, some of the villagers still made chapels and vaults in the Theban cemeteries. The villager Poy, on the other hand, a most experienced draughtsman who had worked in all the royal tombs of the new dynasty up to that of King Ramesses II, painted nobles' coffins with traditional scenes and patterns. Other villagers had special knowledge of the elaborate rituals which had to be performed upon such coffins to enable them to come alive and become living receptacles for the mummies which fitted so tightly inside them. Many of the tombmakers worked in this lucrative cottage-industry, supplying tomb furnishings to wealthy Thebans. Providing a wide variety of such esoteric talents, and with a ready market amongst the multitudes of priests and bureaucrats in the capital, the village flourished. Following Paser's reorganization, the village households, around eighty at their maximum, held some twenty-five interrelated families, and many of their members had, like Poy, served for generations in the royal tombs. All these people, the families of the scribes, the foremen and the men of the two gangs, were bound together by strong feelings of loyalty and pride.

Ramose was about thirty-five when he moved into this exclusive community. In his neat hand, he recorded the exact date on a flake of limestone: 'Made scribe in the Place of Truth in year five, third month of the season of inundation, day ten [13 September 1275 B.C.] of the King of Upper and Lower Egypt, Usermaatre Setepenre, Son of Re, Ramesses Beloved-of-Amun.' In a state where official appointments normally passed down through families it is an unusual record, for such an announcement would have been an inadvertent notice of a father's death and hardly a cause for celebration. Ramose's words, however, reflected a pride in his promotion, the most important event in his life. So proud, indeed, was Ramose of his new job that he also celebrated it high on the rocks of a nearby desert valley, the Place of Beauty where many queens and princes were buried. There, at the valley's head, the scribe scrambled up the cliffs high above the doorway of an unfinished tomb and, using the red ochre of his scribe's palette, he drew a picture of himself kneeling at prayer and, once again, wrote his name, his new title and the date of his appointment.

At his new job, Ramose checked and listed, measured and registered just as he had done in the storerooms of the temple of the King's Scribe Amenhotep; and not only with regard to the work at the tomb, as the scribes also kept records of the rations of food and supplies sent to their village. Lacking both soil and water, the village's needs were entirely supplied from outside: they were either sent from the warehouses of the royal temples or by the retainers working directly for the tombmakers and their families. Labourers tended a continuous line of donkeys that carried earthenware jars filled with water out across the desert to the bone-dry village and all the village's grains, vegetables, meats and fish arrived by the same route. Everything indeed, except the honey that the villagers collected from their own desert hives, was sent up to them from the fertile valley. And Ramose the scribe oversaw and checked these deliveries and reported upon them to the office of the vizier: 'The wages of the necropolis have been delivered, being absolutely complete, without any arrears.'

These provisions were delivered in bulk to the village and scribes divided them into rations which reflected the status of each house-holder in his work at the tomb. As a scribe, Ramose's grain ration—grain and emmer (a species of wheat) for bread; barley for beer; the two village staples—was on a par with that of the foremen, and about a third more than the amounts issued to the workmen's families. Ramose's grain ration was about four hundredweight a month, which would amply support a household of twelve or fourteen people. By village reckoning this was worth the equivalent of a little over one and a half pounds of copper—eight *deben,* the abstract measure used as a standard when bartering goods and services. The grain ration, sent directly from the warehouses of the royal temples, was the pith of the village economy.

Many of the other supplies to the village, such as fresh fish and vegetables, were provided by the village auxiliary servants. River fishermen brought their catch straight from the village's own Nile fishing-boats, gardeners brought bunches of vegetables from their fields, potters supplied the village households with domestic utensils, woodcutters brought fuel for cooking and heating. Sometimes when extra hands were needed at the royal tomb, these village servants would be called in to help. . . .

Apparently Ramose had arrived at the village a single man, for he married a village woman named Mutemwia, whom he called, in affectionate abbreviation, 'Wia'. Their household held many of Wia's relatives as well as several of the female servants allotted to each of the village households for chores such as grinding the grain ration into flour and making bread and beer. Usually such village servants were required to work in rotation in different village households, and it was possible for individual villagers to sell their household's share in this work ration. One of Ramose's close neighbours recorded exactly such a bargain. 'Third month of the summer season, day twenty-one, the day when the mistress—gave the day of her servant to the workman Any; being ten days each month, 120 days per year, [and for four years] 480 days. [Here is] the list of silver which Any gave her.' The list that follows makes it clear that these servants' labours were worth very little; another of Ramose's neighbours swapped his share of a woman's working time in his house for a wickerwork sieve and a small basket.

For the most part, it was the handful of scribes in the village who wrote these humble records of village life, for along with their official duties at the royal tomb and the village they also acted as the villagers' own scribes. Sometimes they composed petitions for them: prayers to the gods or pleas to the office of the vizier for the redress of earthly wrongs. 'I am the aged servant of my Lord since the seventh year of King Horemheb—I acted as medjay of the west of Thebes guarding the walls of the Great Place and I was appointed chief of the medjay, an excellent reward, because of my good behaviour—' begins a petition to the Vizier composed by one of Huy's scribes on behalf of Mininuiy who, at the time of the petition, had guarded the Great Place and its workers for more than fifty years.

By transforming the villagers' spoken words into formal written documents the scribes imbued their simple declarations with a gravity beyond speech, a metamorphosis that must have received tangible corroboration from the very bulk of the stone flakes and the sherds of pottery—both called ostraca—on which much of the village business was recorded. It is easy to imagine that such solid documents appeared to the villagers to be self-contained entities with a veracity of their own, powerful abstractions which gave a special gravity to the day-to-day affairs of their small community. As the creators of such marvellous things, Huy, Ramose and the other scribes of the village were especially important people. ❖

RECOMMENDED READINGS

For further reading on the daily lives of the Egyptians in the later dynasties, see Pierre Montet, *Everyday Life in the Days of Ramesses the Great* (Philadelphia: University of Pennsylvania Press, 1981). An interesting work on tomb building in Egypt is Morris Beirbrier, *The Tomb-builders of the Pharaohs* (New York: Charles Scribner's Sons, 1985). A good introduction to ancient Egypt is John A. Wilson, *The Culture of Ancient Egypt* (Chicago: University of Chicago Press, 1956).

Palestine, About 1200 B.C.

THE ROOTS OF RESTRICTION

WOMEN IN EARLY ISRAEL

Carol Meyers

The Bronze Age had been an aristocratic era in which power was concentrated in city-states that sometimes coalesced into great empires. The acquisition of the tin, copper, and fuel necessary to make bronze, and the maintenance of the skilled artisans needed to smelt and shape it, were complex processes that required substantial investments and some coordinating authority. Bronze technology thus promoted the concentration of wealth and power in the hands of the few. The wealthy found it necessary to protect themselves and their possessions, and the lands of the late Bronze Age were dominated by small towns surrounded by massive fortifications. Inside these walls, a complex bureaucracy evolved to support the rulers, increasingly elaborate religious rituals were devised to secure divine support for the ruling classes, and the powerful few enjoyed a relatively opulent lifestyle. All of this was maintained by an agricultural peasantry living outside the walls, a peasantry that had no choice, since their simple farming tools were no match for the bronze weaponry and body armor of the chariot-driving aristocracy.

All of this began to change with the emergence of iron making. Iron was, and is, relatively plentiful and can be heated and worked by even an untrained hand. Moreover, iron is stronger than bronze. With iron tools, the peasantry could open up lands that Bronze Age societies could not tame; with iron weapons, they could challenge the power of the Bronze Age aristocracy. This was the state of affairs in Palestine in about 1200 B.C. Central authority was weakening in the Egyptian Empire, and imperial authorities could no longer regulate affairs in Palestine. The seven major Philistine city-states of the plains were alone in facing a resurgent peasantry.

Carol Meyers examines the emergence and expansion of the Hebrew peasantry within this milieu, with particular attention to the problems posed by their need to increase their numbers to settle new lands and to occupy newly conquered lands. She finds that many biblical injunctions were designed to meet these particular problems and that the Covenant liberated both men and women but also defined their respective functions in meeting the challenges facing the Hebrews. That process was one in which women played a critical role.

READING QUESTIONS

1. What was the nature of early Hebrew society?

2. What challenges did the early Hebrews face?

3. What factors acted to limit their numbers?

4. How were the status and role of women defined by the Covenant?

5. How and why did that status change with the passage of time?

I f the emerging interest in reconstructing all dimensions of a crucial era in human history is to be expressed in thorough and balanced investigation, then it cannot do what so much of social history in the past has done, systematically omit or slight roughly half of humanity. In the natural and social history of any groupings of people, that slighted half—women—controls certain unique and critical functions within society. As the Harvard social historian David Herlihy puts it, women "carry the new generation to term, sustain children in early life, and usually introduce the young to the society and culture of which they will be a part. [In other words,] women begin the processes through which human cultures strive to achieve what their individual members cannot—indefinite life, immortality."

Moreover, an examination of women's social position, while eminently cogent and important for historical studies of any period of our past, becomes extraordinarily pertinent and imperative in consideration of biblical society, especially in its formative and idealistic period. That specific period is the one in which the biblical community was formed, a community bound in covenant with God through the leadership of Moses and developing its characteristics and radical new way of looking at the world and living in that world in the few centuries after Moses and before the Davidic monarchy. Archeologically, this formative period coincides with the closing decades of the Late Bronze Age and the beginning of centuries of the Iron Age in Palestine.

Concern for the evaluation of the social history of women during the early Israelite experience arises from the fact that this is precisely the period in which one of the major—if not *the* major—transitions occurred in

From Carol Meyers, "The Roots of Restriction: Women in Early Israel," *Biblical Archaeologist* *41*(1), March 1978, pp. 91-92, 94-101.

the history of the position and role of women in the world. Some three thousand years of male dominance in western civilization, and in particular in religious institutions, have clouded our vision of the prebiblical past and have led to the belief that the exclusion of females from regular leadership, at least in public and/or religious life, has been the norm in human history. Further, it is difficult, psychologically and emotionally, to deal with the fact that the liberating principles of Mosaic Israel and the egalitarian society which it set about to establish turned out to be the very force which caused a dramatic turnabout in the history of women. Yet, as more and more material from the ancient world becomes available to us, the realities of the status of women in ancient societies, including their role in religious life, are becoming invisible behind the double veils of time and misapprehension. It is being discovered that the position and role of women in society were very different in some crucial areas than what they became subsequent to the beginnings of Israel.

Early Israel, it has been shown, constituted a radical break with the city-state feudalism and nation-state imperialism of Late Bronze Age Palestine. The description of the motivation for that break (and the implementation through the Yahwistic covenant of a liberating replacement for city-state oppression) involves an understanding of the life of the peasantry. The natural resources of Palestine could no longer support an inflated urban bureaucracy and thus Late Bronze Age peasant society was at the subsistence level. The so-called Israelite "Conquest" represents a return of a full share of the products of the land to the people, a cessation of the continuous draining contributions to urban bureaucracies. The fact that nearly half of the Book of Joshua is concerned with tribal allotments points to the early Israelite recovery of land so that the people, according to their several tribes, would derive the benefit therefrom.

Claims to land ownership, once the domination of the city-based power structures had broken down, depended to a great extent on populating that land (cf. Exod 23:23–30). In addition to establishing local tribal control over certain territories formerly administered by oppressive city-states, the Israelite federation was about to embark upon the settlement of previously uninhabited territories, namely, the core of Palestine, the central hill country.

This territory was largely empty throughout the Bronze Age, except for occasional, usually minor sites near springs and in valleys. Generally poor soil and scarce water supplies precluded significant habitation, particularly if Bronze Age urban centers siphoned off a portion of the meager productivity. If anything, the Late Bronze Age had even fewer settlements in the hill country proper than the preceding Middle Bronze Age centuries.

The ensuing Iron Age, in sharp contrast, brought an extensive settlement of this region.

Technically, the storage of water in lined cisterns, the introduction of iron in the manufacture of farm tools, and the development of methods of agricultural terracing resolved the environmental difficulties and made this demographic shift possible. An enormous amount of human energy was required, however, to clear land that had never before been tilled, to build homes and villages where none had existed, and to cut back forests and undergrowth that had covered the landscape since time immemorial.

This understanding of early Israel as an agrarian peasantry is dispelling the romantic attachment to the notion of a biblical bias in favor of some sort of bedouin or seminomadic ideal. This understanding likewise affords an appreciation of a biblical undercurrent protesting—understandably so considering the ills and evils of Late Bronze Age Canaanite cities—against urban life. The first city, for example, is built according to biblical tradition by the first murderer (Gen 4:17). The concluding exhortation of the Holiness Code (Lev 26:25-26) links city life—"if you gather within your cities"—with famine, disease, and violence. The negative experience underlying such a bias is clear. The orientation of the period of the judges rejected the urban centers. In this process there arose social sanctions, ultimately translated into law, which strengthened and favored land-based village life.

Against this background, what was life like for roughly half the population? How were women to do their share in espousing and furthering the Yahwistic ideals of a free peasantry? Thus far, two major issues emerge in the attempt to answer these questions. Both of these had dramatic effects upon women and, while seemingly independent of each other, may prove ultimately to be interrelated.

The first issue concerns the biological need for productivity, the need to effect a population increase. Israel was obsessed both with having descendants to inherit its portion and with keeping its land-holdings within its kinship-based groups.

To begin with, the death rate was clearly highest among the preadult population. In one tomb group, 35% of the individuals died before the age of five, and nearly half of the individuals did not survive the age of eighteen. For those who did survive to adulthood, another clear pattern existed: the mortality rate of females in the child-bearing years greatly exceeded that of the males.

In a population in which the life expectancy for men would be 40, women would have a life expectancy closer to 30. Consequently, it should not be surprising that the elders of any ancient tribal system were males, since a greater proportion of males would have survived into the chronological seniority which was at the basis of political seniority and leadership. It is no wonder that ancient biologists, Aristotle among them, proclaimed that the males of all species live longer than the females. It is a relatively modern phenomenon that the converse is true for humans. Women in antiquity were a class of humanity in short supply.

Paleo-pathologists have established that the cause of half, if not more, of all deaths, whatever the age of the individual at the time of death, was the presence of endemic parasitic disease, that is, infections which occur in a community more or less all the time without much alteration in their effects from year to year or even century to century.

The biblical term "pestilence" (*deber*) seems to be used in reference to such endemic disease. Very young children and old people, being the most susceptible to such infections, were the most likely to succumb. This fact is archeologically evident in the high infant mortality rate as well as in the scarcity of people past forty. To put it bluntly, in normal times, families would have had to produce twice the number of children desired in order to achieve optimal family size.

The outbreak of epidemics, or the *abnormal* occurrence of acute infectious disease, reduced the usual low life expectancy even further. Epidemiological statistics, for historic periods in which records were kept, show the devastating effects of plague upon mortality rates. For example, in the plague-free early medieval years in Europe, life expectancy has been estimated as being between 35 and 40 years. For the generations during and immediately following the Black Death (1348-49), which introduced an epoch of recurring plagues, the average life expectancy was as low as 17 or 18 years. It took nearly 100 years or more thereafter for life spans to creep back up to around 30.

The Bible has a word that seems to describe such abnormal outbreaks of disease. This word, *maggephah,* normally translated "plague" (as opposed to "pestilence"), appears in several biblical accounts, chiefly in certain non-priestly narratives of Numbers, and also once in Exodus. Despite the layers of later explanations, these passages have preserved certain critical incidents of Israel's formative period and thus provide important information about public health and population density.

Epidemic disease was clearly rampant. This clustering of biblical texts dealing with the age of Moses and using the word "plague" or *maggephah* reflects a public health crisis. Furthermore, nearly every extrabiblical source from the Late Bronze Age indicates the devastation wrought by epidemic infections. Perhaps the most famous of these is the Plague Prayer of Mursilis, though disruption and devastation because of plague are recorded in other sources such as the Amarna letters. A similar situation did not occur again in Palestine until 200–250 years later in the period of the Philistine wars, for which there is another clustering of biblical texts reflecting a plague situation.

The biblical passages cited above as well as the extrabiblical sources mentioned can be associated with what has been identified archeologically as a massive disruption of the urbanized life of the petty kingdoms—or kinglets—in Palestine at the end of the Late Bronze Age. City after city suffered violent destruction. In many cases, if not all, the termination of Bronze Age culture in these cities is marked archeologically by a thick layer of ashes, indicating a conflagration of major proportions.

These burnings of cities, it seems, are an aftermath of military conquest or overthrow rather than a part of it. If anything, military conflicts or guerilla warfare took place outside the city walls, so well constructed were the fortifications of the Late Bronze cities. It is quite possible that the widespread burnings were not so much related to military actions as they were to a kind of primitive and desperate public health measure. The fiery destruction of plagues needed to be fought with fire. Immediately following the recollection of the destructive plague of Baal Peor in Num 31:21–23, the instructions to the Israelite warriors stipulate that "only the gold, the silver, the bronze, the iron, the tin, and the lead, everything that can stand the fire, you shall pass through the fire, and it shall be clean. Nevertheless, it shall also be purified with the water of impurity; and whatever cannot stand the fire you shall pass through the water." Thus, the unconscionable *ḥerem,* or utter destruction of cities as presented in the book of Joshua, perhaps can be seen as a kind of plague control. It is difficult in the western world today, with relatively little experience of such epidemics, to grasp the enormity of the plagues and the staggering death tolls which devastated the premodern world. Yet, the effort must be made to comprehend the drastic measures taken to stop epidemics in light of the ancient context.

Recognition of the existence of a period of widespread plague and death at the end of the Late Bronze Age is crucial, because that factor even more than famine and warfare (or at least in combination with those other two evils) created a life situation—or rather a death situation—of monumental proportions. The measures taken within the emergent Israelite community to deal with this situation are the ones that profoundly affected the lives of the female segment of the population.

Plague severely reduced the population of the peasantry at the time when sheer numbers counted most. The normal difficulties in maintaining rural population in Palestine were compounded dramatically during this period. The biological creativity of females, a matter of vital concern even in normal times because of high infant mortality rates and the often fatal complications of childbearing, was most sorely needed in the aftermath of plagues. The devastation of plague had caused a demographic crisis. The repeated biblical exhortation, "Be fruitful and multiply," is singularly appropriate to this situation.

The strength and solidarity of the family were the basis for the vitality of the restored peasantry in early Israel and its ability to occupy the hill country of Palestine. At the most basic level, Israelite society urgently required a replenishment and even a surge in population to combat the effect of the famine, war, and disease at the end of the Late Bronze Age and to provide the human factor necessary for normal agricultural efforts. Moreover, this need for population increase was intensified as settlement of virgin areas proceeded. In addition to their specifically biological contribution, the full participation of women in the chores of a land-based economy was essential. Further, since males were called away for occasional military duty in the absence of a standing army, the woman's role in managing all aspects of a household would increase.

From all perspectives, then, female creativity and labor were highly valued in early Israel. This female worth was not biological exploitation but rather part of the full cooperation of all elements in society in pursuing the goals of the Israelite people. Further, the early Iron Age experience of Israel was within the liberating matrix of the Covenant with Yahweh, which emphasized ethical concerns and sought to maintain all human dignity. The precepts of the Decalogue and the Covenant Code are dedicated passionately against the exploitation of any groups of human beings or even animals. The Fifth Commandment (Exod 20:12) bears this out. Both parents are to be honored, for on the two together depends the existence of Israel. The second part of this commandment is not a vague generality but rather an intrinsic complement of the familiar first half of that commandment ("Honor your father and your mother"). It expresses a hope for continued life and a restoration of public well-being: "that your days may be long in the land which the Lord your God gives you" (i.e., that life expectancies will stabilize above the low level characteristic of plague epochs).

The Bible generally reflects the fact that there were relatively fewer women of child-bearing age than men of the same age, a condition which Israel shared with the rest of the ancient world. Perhaps the existence of the *mohar,* translated variously as "bride price" or "marriage present," illustrates one way in which the community dealt with a shortage of marriageable women. The *mohar* may be a compensation to the bride's family, since a daughter contributed through her work to a parent's household. This bride-gift, a kind of reverse dowry, indicates that grooms had to compete for relatively few brides. Likewise, the financial burden of setting up a new household lay with the male, another indication of the socio-economic dimensions of the shortage of brides. The dowry was rarely if ever bestowed in biblical times. Fathers did not need to entice husbands. (Compare European history: it is perhaps not until the central Middle Ages that a combination of relative peace and a new urban economy brought about a relative increase in female population and led to the reversal of the terms of marriage. Girls became excess economic burdens and fathers gave dowries and paid for weddings to entice young men to take these girls off their hands.)

Beyond this, however, the intensified need for female participation in working out the Mosaic revolution in the early Israelite period can be seen in the Bible. Looking again at Numbers 31, an exception to the total purge of the Midianite population is to be noted. In addition to the metal objects which were exempt from utter destruction, so too were the "young girls who have not known man by lying with him" (Num 31:18). These captives, however, were not immediately brought into the Israelite camp. Instead, they and their captors were kept outside the camp for seven days in a kind of quarantine period. (Note that the usual incubation period for the kinds of infectious diseases which could conceivably have existed in this situation is two or three to six days.) Afterward, they thoroughly washed themselves and all their clothing before they entered the camp. This incident is hardly an expression of lascivious male behavior; rather, it reflects the desperate need for women of child-bearing age, a need so extreme that the utter destruction of the Midianite foes—and the prevention of death by plague—as required by the law of the *ḥerem* could be waived in the interest of sparing the young women. The Israelites weighed the life-death balance, and the need for females of child-bearing age took precedence.

Such a source of female population, however, was not to be regularized. Instead, the extraordinary needs for female reproductive power in the tribal period precipitated strong sanctions against the expending of sexual energy in ways that either detracted from the primary reproductive channels or interfered with the strengths of nuclear family life or the transmission of family-based land ownership. The whole array of sexual customs and rules which exist in the Bible and which had the ultimate effect of relegating women to a narrowed and eventually subordinate position in later biblical times are in many cases radical changes from what had existed previously in the ancient world. These changes, which limited human sexual contacts and options, must be reconsidered in light of the demographic crisis of early Israel. Sanctions that eventually became expressed in biblical laws dealing with incest, rape, adultery, virginity, bestiality, exogamy, homosexuality, and prostitution require reexamination and reevaluation within the dynamics of the socio-economic situation and human crisis of the earliest days of Israel. The dimension of purity and polemic in sexual sanctions is not to be ignored; but the role of the concern for repopulation and the need for human resources must also enter the picture.

This is a vast project and one which is beyond the scope of this paper. However, progress can tentatively begin by looking at one expression of sexuality and the way the societal pressures of ancient Israel transformed it. Harlotry is a good example, since it leads directly to considering the second major issue which effected the turnabout in the status of women in ancient society.

Until the period of the Judges, the existence of harlotry was an accepted, if not condoned, fact. Courtesans and prostitutes have existed at least since the dawn of recorded history without accompanying moral judgment or moral condemnation of harlotry *per se*. It was a legitimate though not necessarily desirable occupation for some women. In the Genesis story of Judah and Tamar, Tamar is not condemned for her temporary identification as a prostitute nor is Judah condemned for lying with her, except insofar as it signaled an evasion of his responsibilities toward his sons' widow (Genesis 38). Similarly, Rahab the harlot of Jericho is actually a heroine who helped the Israelite spies, in return for which they spared the destruction of her family (Joshua 2 and 6).

By the time that biblical legislation records attitudes toward harlotry, a considerable change had occurred. Lev 19:29 is explicit: "Do not profane your daughter by making her a harlot, lest the land fall into harlotry and the land fall into wickedness." A father was responsible in the patriarchal system for his daughters. He was to limit their choice of occupation. Prostitution was not a possibility. The priorities and values of early Israelite existence had made family-centered life the chief, if not the only, course of action for a young woman.

There was another reason for closing out the option of harlotry in early Israel beside the need to have all available women of child-bearing years integrated into self-sufficient families. Harlotry was closely associated with the special use of sexual energy involved in ritual or cultic prostitution in the nature religions of the ruling urban elites. The efforts to secure productivity in the Israelite village and rural settings were to be separated from the rituals of the fertility cults. The sexual fetishism of Late Bronze Age society was "integrated into the hierarchic social order."

Because Israel rejected that order and also rejected the magical and mythological associations between the human reproductive process and the ritual enactment of such process, it of necessity prohibited the involvement of cult functionaries, male or female (Deut 23:17), in such sexual activity.

In biblical law, the particular emphasis on the dissociation of the priests from harlotry can only be understood in this context. In Lev 21:7, 14-15, priests are commanded to marry virgins. They are forbidden to marry any of four categories of women (widows, divorcees, "defiled" women, and harlots) whose sexual energies may already have been somewhat dissipated and whose fitness for child-bearing may have been reduced. Harlots in this law are not singled out as detestable or illegal members of society at large. However, in the same passage, the daughters of priests are condemned to burning by fire should they play the harlot (v 9). This extraordinarily strong penalty for prostitution is aimed specifically at women who lived near or in the Israelite sanctuary area, the daughters of priests. It indicates the danger of pagan cultic expression that existed when men and women were together in cultic contexts, a danger that to some extent necessitated the removal of one of the two sexes from cultic services.

In the Bible, it is apparent which sex was barred from cultic leadership, but the reasons for such a limitation have not been properly explored. The priesthood of the Old Testament represents a radical break with the nature of priesthoods in the history of the ancient world; the priesthood of biblical religion is, from the outset, portrayed as a strictly and absolutely male profession.

The traditional answer to the query as to why the priesthood is male no doubt would have invoked the notion that the anthropomorphizing tendencies in the Bible made God out to be a male deity, some sort of macho warrior at one end or loving father at the other end. Male deities would naturally require a male priesthood. This response, however, does not account for the nonsexuality and nonhumanity of Yahweh's unity. Gender-oriented language for Yahweh is metaphoric. Furthermore, in addition to the all-too-familiar andromorphic images of Yahweh, there are a multitude of gynomorphic images, once one is open to reading them as such.

Still, the establishment of an exclusively male priesthood was in a sense a natural development at the end of the 2nd millennium. While a few millennia earlier a female priesthood in service of the Great Mother might have been the paradigm, the urban social systems of the Bronze Age were male dominated. Male deities outnumbered the goddesses. Thus, the kings, priest-kings, and priests were the dominant figures and provided the models for early Israel.

The priesthood before the monarchy was no doubt a decentralized and purposefully limited factor in Israelite life. The egalitarian economy of the reestablished peasantry of the period of the Judges rejected the bureaucratic concentration of wealth that an elaborate priesthood requires. Circumscribed as it may have been, a priesthood nevertheless was established and thus siphoned off some portion of manpower as well as some economic surplus. The possibility of female service within any sort of cultic context could be eliminated purely on the basis of the felt priorities of early Israel in its allocation of human energies. Female energies were desperately needed in the family setting.

Partially as a rejection of the mythological and cultic sexuality of pre-biblical religion and its integral connection with the urban power centers, and partly under pressures to concentrate female energies within the home and family, the Israelite priesthood emerged as a male occupation. In ancient Israel, thousands and thousands of years of female participation in this most crucial of all public institutions, an organized cultus, were terminated. One might speculate as to whether or not women might have entered priestly roles once the demographic crisis had been alleviated were it not for the continued attraction of the nature religions, particularly after the establishment of the monarchy and the return to urbanized life as the dominant mode in Israel. Thereafter, the social sanctions against such occupations as harlotry achieved the status of divine laws governing a priesthood distinct from that of pagan religion. From that situation, the moral judgment upon this kind of female sexual activity outside the family was only a step away.

Two major factors, then, appear to be primary causes of the profound change that occurred in the status and role of women during premonarchic Israel. The first was the drastic need to concentrate human energy, male and female, into family life and into intensive cultivation of the land, including considerable new territory. This meant a sex ethic, the primary societal function of which was to make childbirth and sexuality within the family crucial societal goals. Reversing the devastating depopulation of the Late Bronze Age was an enormous task. Likewise, setting about to reemphasize an agricultural economy and even to settle new lands was a highly ambitious goal which called for the labor of women alongside men. The second factor was the rejection of pagan deities in favor of a covenant with a unified Yahweh. In cultic terms, this translated into a male priesthood. Neither of these two factors *within their contemporary settings* was particularly exploitive of male or female. On the contrary, strong female involvement in an agricultural economy and in the birth of new generations of Israelites who would literally inherit the land meant that women and men worked together to achieve the covenant ideals.

It is indeed an irony of history, then, that this very tight channeling of female (and male) energies into domestic affairs, which was a liberating event in its own time, became, ultimately, the *raison d'etre* for continued and exclusive confinement of female energies to that sphere. A functional restriction to meet a demographic crisis of critical proportions became so deeply engrained that with the passing of the crisis the restrictions remained and ultimately became the basis for ideologies of female inferiority and subordination. Once the pattern of female nonparticipation in other spheres of life—the priesthood in particular—became established, society adhered to it in ways that became limiting and oppressive to women.

This was particularly true with the establishment of the monarchy and a gradual movement toward urbanization. Women became less important as participants in economic survival and therefore diminished in social importance. They were also the first to suffer when urban centers drained off the productivity of the land to support the monarchy and the military. Hard work under conditions of increased population and reduced nutrition meant even greater risks of death in childbirth. The introduction of slave wives under the phenomenal growth of the Davidic empire no doubt also contributed to the reduced importance of women. Thus, it was likely during the monarchy that the functional restriction of women in society became transformed gradually into an ideological restriction. ❖

RECOMMENDED READINGS

The historical context for the early history of the Hebrew people is provided by Donald B. Redford, *Egypt, Canaan, and Israel in Ancient Times* (Princeton, NJ: Princeton University Press, 1992) and *Early Israel: A New Horizon* (Minneapolis: Fortress Press, 1990). Archaeology and texts are used to portray early Israelite life and customs in David Meilsheim, *The World of Ancient Israel,* trans. Grace Jackman (New York: Tudor, 1973), and Niels Peter Lemche, *Early Israel: Anthropological and Historical Studies on the Israelite Society Before the Monarchy,* trans. Frederick H. Cryer (Leiden: E.J. Brill, 1985). The Canaanites and Philistines are studied in Niels Peter Lemche, *The Canaanites and Their Land: The Tradition of the Canaanites* (Sheffield, UK: JSOT Press, 1991), and the somewhat technical work of John F. Brug, *A Literary and Archaeological Study of the Philistines* (Oxford, UK: BAR, 1985). Trude Krakauer Dothan considers the evidence for identifying the Philistines with the sea peoples, including Greek pirates, mentioned by the Egyptians records in *People of the Sea: The Search for the Philistines* (New York: Macmillan, 1992).

Greece, 776 B.C.

THE FIRST OLYMPICS

COMPETING "FOR THE GREATER GLORY OF ZEUS"

Lionel Casson

The geographical nature of Greece, with its mountainous terrain and surrounding sea, discouraged political unification among the ancient Greeks. They dwelled in autonomous city-states located from the Black Sea to the coast of Spain. The Mediterranean's shores were widely populated with Greek colonies. Despite this wide dispersion, the Greeks possessed a feeling of commonality. They were extremely proud of their Greek heritage and considered anyone who did not share in it a barbarian.

The ancient Olympic Games, first held in 776 B.C. at Olympia in western Greece, typified the Panhellenic ("all Greek") spirit. For more than a thousand years—until at least A.D. 261—athletes from all parts of the Greek world met and competed with one another at Olympia. The Games, held every fourth summer without a break, despite wars and political upheaval, served as a binding force in Greek life.

The original Olympic Games were part of a religious festival dedicated to the god Zeus. Although the festival chiefly was devoted to the worship of the gods, to sacrifices, offerings, and prayers, the Greek passion for competitive games gained for athletics an important place in the festivities.

The following selection by Lionel Casson describes the earliest Olympic Games. While stressing the religious nature of the Games, he offers insights into the various athletic contests, the participants, and the audience. Casson pays special attention to the reasons for the Games' popularity and to the fundamental differences between the ancient and the modern Games.

READING QUESTIONS

1. How did the ancient Olympics come about?

2. What were the major events in the ancient Olympics?

3. How did one prepare to be a contestant?

4. Why did the ancient Olympics persist for so long?

ne midsummer day in the year we calculate to have been 776 B.C., a 200-meter dash was run in a rural backwater in southwestern Greece, and a young local named Coroebus won it. It was an obscure event in an obscure spot but it earned him immortality: he is the first Olympic victor on record.

It came about this way. Not far from his hometown, in the place called Olympia, was a primitive sanctuary to the Greeks' chief god, Zeus. Festivals for the deity had been going on there for centuries. For some reason the people in charge decided to embellish what was traditionally done: they would offer up, in addition to the customary sacrificial victims and prayers, the honor of an outstanding athletic performance. So they organized a race, the race Coroebus won.

The next embellished festival was scheduled for 772 B.C.—and from then on, every four years, it took place more or less without a break for more than a millennium, right up to A.D. 261. And what began as a simple neighborhood affair soon burgeoned into a celebrated spectacle, boasting a dozen or so different events that pulled in contestants and viewers from all over. They came from the whole ancient world, from as far away as what are now France and Syria. There were other religious festivals, some very important, whose programs included sports, too, but none ever attained the prestige of the Olympics. Then as now, a victory there was the be-all and end-all for all truly serious athletes.

Despite the growing renown of the Olympics, despite the fact that it attracted tens of thousands of people, the time and place were constant: everybody had to make the long and arduous pilgrimage to the out-of-the-way sanctuary. And when there, everybody, right up to champions of the highest repute and backers who sometimes were heads of state, had to submit to the arrangements, rules and regulations enforced by a local committee—about ten worthy citizens of Elis, the chief town of the area.

That was the way things were at the beginning and that is how the ancient games continued to be: for the greater glory of Zeus, not to improve the political image of any particular state or leader, as is sometimes the case today. And there was little fine talk of promoting international goodwill or anything like that. At the time the festival was launched and for four centuries afterward, the Greeks were organized into a multitude of little independent states, and one or more of these was always at war with another. When the date of the festival drew near, heralds were sent out to announce

From Lionel Casson, "The First Olympics," *Smithsonian,* June 1984, pp. 64-73 a sacred truce so that those who wanted to attend could make their way through the battle lines to get to Olympia. After a while, the truce was lengthened to three months or so because travel time increased as spectators and contestants flocked in from farther and farther away.

For some centuries there were no athletic facilities whatsoever at Olympia, just an open space in which a running track would be paced off, areas for the discus and javelin throw laid out, and so on. Finally, by about 500 B.C., a few amenities had come into existence: a stadium for the runners and a hippodrome for the horse and chariot races (but no stands with seats for the spectators, just a sloping embankment to sprawl on), a bathhouse for the athletes, a headquarters building for the Olympic committee, and, of course, a temple to Zeus. Progress was slow because funding depended upon contributions.

In ancient times, since the games were part of a religious ceremony, no admission could be charged. As it happens, Elis was not poor, but it was in no position all by itself to undertake a building program of the size needed. It was able to start work on Zeus' temple only when a successful war against a neighbor provided enough booty for the labor and materials. Many of the other improvements came, if at all, from generous wealthy states or individuals.

There was not even a gymnasium until sometime after 200 B.C.; the athletes worked out wherever they could. Though eventually there was the equivalent of a VIP hotel, there were never any facilities at all for ordinary spectators. They arrived hot and tired and stayed that way during the five days the festival lasted. The rich were not too badly off: they slept in tents that their retinue of slaves put up. Most, however, slept in the open and munched on bread, cheese and olives, and drank wine they had brought along or bought from itinerant vendors. Sanitation was rudimentary or non-existent and water, from springs and cisterns, was always in short supply. It was not until the second century A.D., after the games had been going on for about 900 years, that Herodes Atticus of Athens, at the time probably the richest Greek in the world, finally gave the place an aqueduct and a proper water system. In addition to all this, there was the heat and dust of a Greek summer and the flies—so bad that it is said the citizens of Elis used to offer up a special sacrifice to Zeus to keep them away from Olympia. The story goes that all a master had to do to make a sulky slave turn angelic was to threaten to take him along to the games.

"Aren't you all jammed in together?" asked the Greek philosopher Epictetus of the would-be spectators. "Isn't it hard to get a bath? Don't you get drenched when it rains? Don't you get fed up with the din and the shouting and the other annoyances?" The answer in every case was a resounding Yes!— but this did not stop people from coming in droves. After all, the Olympics gave them, as ours do us, the one chance in four years to see many of the world's very best athletes in action. And there were other rewards. They could attend the sacrifices and services—which, now that the festival had gained such fame, were impressive ceremonies. They could get a look at some of Greece's finest works of art: a gigantic statue of Zeus in his temple was one of the Seven Wonders of the Ancient World, and all over the sanctuary grounds were statues of other deities and of winning athletes. Imagine today's Olympics being held, say, in Rome during Easter Week and you get some idea of why so many made the long journey and put up with all the discomforts.

Like a number of key features of Greek life, the games were for males only. With the exception of a special priestess, married women were barred from entrance—and on pain of death, no less. Since the assemblage of spectators was joined by the kinds of people who lived off crowds—pickpockets, beggars, con men, pimps, prostitutes—it was no place for respectable unmarried women. (Other festivals eventually ran events for women athletes, but never the early Olympics.) On one occasion a matron from a great sporting family, who could not bear not seeing her son compete, sneaked in dressed as a trainer; when he was victorious, she enthusiastically vaulted the barrier that marked off the trainers' section and, in so doing, revealed her sex. Out of respect for the family's long line of winners she was spared execution, but a ruling was passed stating that trainers, like athletes, were to go around naked.

Shortly after 500 B.C. the program of sports reached its more or less final form—three days of major competition given over to about a dozen different events. It most likely started with the most spectacular, the chariot race. The number of entrants varied each year; at a comparable festival, the Pythian Games held in Delphi, there were as many as 41. The competitors lined up, each standing in a two-wheeled chariot that was light, like a modern trotter's gig, but pulled by a team of four horses that would be driven at the fastest gallop they could generate. They made 12 laps around the course—about nine kilometers—with 180-degree turns at each end. As at our Indianapolis 500, viewers enjoyed not only the excitement of a race but, the titillation that comes from the constant presence of danger: as the teams thundered around the turns, or one chariot tried to cut over from the outside to the inside, crashes and collisions were common and doubtless often fatal. In one celebrated race at the Pythian Games, competition was so lethal that only one competitor out of several dozen managed to finish!

Next came the horse race, and it, too, offered the spice of danger because jockeys rode bareback on earth just churned up by the chariots. Both of these events were strictly for the very rich; owning a racehorse in ancient times was like owning a Rolls-Royce today, and owning a chariot and team was like owning a fleet of four of them. In the very beginning the owners may have done their own driving and riding, but they soon turned these jobs over to professionals. The prize, however, went only to the owners. Once, for example, a famous mare named Αὔρα (Breeze) threw her rider at the very beginning of the race, but being well trained, covered the course in perfect style and came in first; the judges awarded her owner the prize. Women owners, who could not even get inside the grounds to watch, could yet win a prize this way, and there are the names of some in the lists of Olympic victors.

The chariot and horse races were the showiest events. But the crowd's favorites tended to be the body-contact sports—wrestling, boxing and the pancratium (a combination of the two)—which the arrangers of the program shrewdly scheduled for the fourth day, the latest possible. Wrestling was the mildest of the three. Unlike today's wrestling, the contestants were on their feet most of the time, since three falls ended a match and even touching the ground with the knees constituted a fall. Ancient wrestlers, like our TV mammoths, ran to size and beef. A certain Milo, who lived around 500 B.C., was so mighty a man that a whole series of fabulous stories grew up about him: that every day he packed away seven and a half kilos each of meat and bread, washing it down with seven and a half liters of wine; that he once carried a full-grown bull around the stadium, then cooked and ate it; that he could tie a band around his head and snap it by swelling his veins.

Fight crowds in any age like to see blood, and ancient boxing supplied plenty. The men fought with their hands wrapped in tough leather thongs, they fought continuously with no rounds and they fought till one was knocked out or gave up. It was a rare boxer who, after several years in the sport, still had uncaliflowered ears and all his teeth; boxers' battered physiognomies became a favorite butt of contemporary satirists, whose humor was crueler than ours.

The bloodiest and most popular event was the pancratium, or "all-powerful contest," a modified free-for-all. The contestants punched, slapped, kicked or wrestled, and the bout was over when one was knocked out, gave up or—as happened every now and then—died. No holds were barred, not even the stranglehold, and much of the time, as with today's wrestlers, the contestants were thrashing about on the ground, since a fall did not matter. One pancratiast actually developed a technique in which he would throw himself on his back with his opponent on top and work from there; he was never beaten. There was also biting and gouging, though these were theoretically illegal. The end usually came when one man got such a hold that the other quit to avert a broken bone or dislocated joint.

The first Olympic event to be recorded, Coroebus' race, was a straight run the length of the course, in effect a 200-meter dash. Soon a second race was introduced: down the course and back, a 400-meter dash. A long-distance run was added of nearly 4,800 meters, and then even a dash in which contestants ran in armor. These were the only track events; the marathon in today's games is a modern idea. The field events were three: broad jump, discus throw, javelin throw. They were never independent contests but always part of a curious mix called the "pentathlon," the "five-contest": the jump, discus and javelin followed by a 200-meter dash and a wrestling match. If a man took three of the five he was the winner.

It is hard to see how any one athlete could develop high skill in so many different sports. Yet the pentathlon was one of the earliest items in the

Olympic program. It was sandwiched in between the spectacular horse events of the second day and popular body-contact bouts of the fourth. The modern Olympics, begun in 1896, made things easier by deleting the wrestling. After 1924, the men's pentathlon was dropped entirely, although the Olympics had already instituted a quiet different competition, known as the "modern pentathlon," involving, among other things, horsemanship and pistol shooting. The 1984 games included, at least for women, a version that goes the ancient pentathlon two better: a heptathlon—a seven-part contest, all track and field.

The fifth and last day was devoted to prize giving. Winners formed a procession and marched to the Temple of Zeus. It was an ancient version of the ticker-tape parade, since bystanders along the route showered them with leaves and flowers. At the temple, each was handed what ancient athletes considered the most precious object in the world, the victor's olive wreath. Its intrinsic value may have been nil, but it was worth a fortune to the man who walked away with it. An Olympic victory, as it happens, was just as great an honor for a winner's fellow townspeople as for himself, and they sometimes showed their gratitude by voting him a cash bonus—sometimes even a pension for life—as well as other perquisites. Moreover, Olympic champions were welcomed as contestants at festivals where bountiful cash prizes were awarded.

All such benefits were for winners only. Vince Lombardi would have been right at home in the ancient Olympics. Winning was everything; there were no seconds or thirds, no Greek equivalents of silver or bronze medals. And modesty in victory was not required. It was expected that a winner would savor his triumph to the full, would publicly exult in it. The Greeks did not go in for our ceremonious "sportsmanship," the generous congratulations of the vanquished. Far from it: losers were jeered and, hiding their heads in shame, slunk away. Even their mothers treated them with scorn. "The wreath or death" was the motto.

Greek record keeping, too, was very different. Almost no records were kept of the actual distance a winner jumped, or threw the discus or javelin, or the exact time it took to win any of the races. In ancient Greek, there isn't even a way to say "set a record" or "break a record." What interested people were "firsts."

In the beginning, Olympic athletes tended to be aristocrats. Only they had enough free time to go in for the extended work needed to train a man up to championship standard, as well as the free time and the money to travel to the festival every four years. Besides, most aristocrats had a good head start since wrestling, running and other sports were the way Greece's gilded youth spent its leisure. As the years passed, though, lesser folk managed to enter the competition, and in increasing numbers. Perhaps this was what prompted a famous crack by Alexander the Great, a very fine runner, when he was urged to enter the dash: "Only if the contestants are kings." One reason that common folk came to compete more was that hometowns took as much pride in a victory as did the victor himself. When a promising lad turned up, they would subsidize him; they did for their athletes what American corporations today do for ours. And once the lad had racked up a win, between bonuses and prize money at other cash-paying festivals, he was set for life. One ancient Olympic victor was offered 30,000 drachmas—the 1984 equivalent of at least half a million dollars in purchasing power—just to take part in some local festival; our barnstorming tennis stars do not do much better. Then as now, the popularity of a man's sport made a difference. Where cash prizes were given, the reward for a win in the pancratium could be six times that for a win in the pentathlon.

There was a price to be paid for getting into the charmed circle of Olympic winners, the same price paid today: endless, grueling training under the iron rule of the best coaches to be found. These had their special techniques, some of which make sense, some of which do not. Runners, for example, were probably paced by men on horseback. Boxers shadowboxed and worked out with the punching bag. Wrestlers worked out with partners called "statues" in the Greek sports jargon. Pancratiasts worked out with a punching bag heavier than the boxer's type, and they not only practiced punching it but kicking it as well. They also let it bash them on the head, presumably to accustom that member to a bash from a fist.

Trainers had their hang-ups about food, then as now. When it came to fish, to eat or not to eat depended on the kind of seaweed the fish fed on. As for meat, pork from pigs pastured along the shore was taboo, since the chances were they had fed on the sea garlic that flourished there. One trainer refused to let his charges go to dinner parties on the grounds that intelligent conversation would cause headaches.

All entrants were eventually compelled by the rules to train continuously for the ten months prior to opening day. The last month of training was conducted at Elis under the gimlet eyes of the judges. This procedure immeasurably improved the competition since any who saw themselves clearly outclassed would quietly take off to avoid the shame of defeat.

The word "judges," when applied to the ancient Olympic committee, is a misnomer. Although the Greeks called them that, judging was only a small part of their duties. They checked the credentials of the competitors, supervised their training at Elis, served as referees and umpires, heard complaints of fouls and bribery. They were chosen by lot from a list of wealthy locals likely known as generous contributors.

If chosen, a man got the chance to be an absolute autocrat within the area of his competence and to display his importance by strutting about in a special purple robe and carrying a whip, followed by whip-carrying flunkeys. For the judges could punish athletes who had broken training—or committed fouls or accepted bribes—not only by fines or expulsion from the games but also by scourging, a most unusual procedure since Greek practice was never to lay a whip on a freeman (this was something reserved for slaves). Money from the fines went to erect statues of Zeus inscribed with appropriate sentiments, e.g.: "Show that you win at Olympia with the speed of your feet and the strength in your body, and not with money." The bribes seem not to have come from gamblers or betting combines but from fellow athletes who wanted a victory desperately enough to try buying it. Hometowns were so fervently behind their boys that even bribery did not faze them. When an Athenian pentathlete was fined for trying to bribe his way to a win, the Athenians sent out a top advocate to plead for him; when that failed, they paid the fine themselves.

The original Olympic Games endured for so long because they were part of a religious festival, an offering to the great god Zeus. Ironically, what kept them going was also what brought them to an end. As more and more of the ancient world turned to Christianity, Zeus was gradually forced to abdicate his throne. The Olympics were held, regularly as clockwork, down to A.D. 261, when a threatened invasion of barbarians, the Herulians, interrupted the long sequence. The Games were quickly resumed and continued—whether unbroken or not we do not know—until 393, the year in which the Roman Emperor Theodosius I, a fervent Christian, ordered the closing of all pagan centers. The site was abandoned. Over the centuries it was devastated by invaders, battered by earthquakes and gradually covered by silt from floodwaters of a nearby river. All this, together with endless years of neglect, left it buried until a British traveler found it in 1766. In 1875 the first of a number of German archaeological teams set about a systematic excavation.

Soon afterward, a French aristocrat, Baron Pierre de Coubertin, was passionately promoting the cause of athletics in general and a revival of the Olympic Games in particular. Resurrection of the site spurred him to even greater efforts, and in 1896 he finally achieved his dream: the first modern international Olympic Games. But they were held in urban Athens, not rural Olympia—the modern spectator took a dim view of sleeping alfresco, or even under a tent.❖

RECOMMENDED READINGS

For further readings on the Olympics and Greek athletics in general, see E. Norman Gardiner, *Athletics of the Ancient World* (Chicago: Ares Publications, 1978); H. A. Harris, *Greek Athletes and Athletics* (Bloomington: Indiana University Press, 1967); M. I. Finley and H. W. Pleket, *The Olympic Games: The First Thousand Years* (London: Chatto & Windus, 1976); Rachel Sargent Robinson, *Sources for the History of Greek Athletics* (Chicago: Ares Publications, 1980); Thomas Scanlon, *A Bibliography for Greek and Roman Athletics* (Chicago: Ares Publications, 1984).

Greece, 750 B.C.

THE GREEKS REACH OUT

M. I. Finley

Throughout much of the Eurasian continent, the city-states characteristic of the Bronze Age gave way to the kingdoms and empires of the Iron Age. The chariot-driving warrior aristocracy was driven from the field, and from power, by masses of inexpensively armed foot soldiers protected by iron-clad shields and wielding iron swords and iron-tipped spears. Wars were won by whoever could put the most men in the field, and small states were swallowed up by their larger neighbors.

This was not the case in Greece, however. Protected by the mountainous terrain of the peninsula, the small city-states of Greece survived the advent of the iron revolution and the disappearance of their warrior aristocracy. In 490 B.C. and again in 479, the Greeks successfully beat off the attacks of the great Persian Empire and even contrived to maintain a measure of independence under the empire of Alexander the Great and his successors in the 300s and 200s. Not until the arrival of the Romans in 146 B.C., did the Greek city-state succumb to the dominant political form of the age.

But the Greeks did more than merely survive. Beginning in about 750 B.C., the Greeks reached out, establishing colonies throughout the Mediterranean and Black seas, and spreading Greek influences throughout the region. Unlike the sea-borne empires of later centuries, however, Greek expansion did not create some ancient Mediterranean superpower; wherever they went, the Greek colonists and traders established small and independent city-states much like those that they had left. Scholars have long speculated on the reasons for this expansion and the conservative form it took.

In the following selection, M. I. Finley examines this matter. Although he finds the causes for the persistence of the city-state among the Greeks elusive, he concludes that the Greek colonists had been forced from their home cities by simple population pressure and the social unrest that it caused. Greek expansion had been essential to the survival of the city-states themselves.

READING QUESTIONS

1. What were the Greek city-states like, and how had they survived into the era of expansion?

2. What was the relationship of a Greek colony to its mother city?

3. Into what areas did the Greeks expand?

4. What was the relationship of trade to colonization?

T wo phenomena which mark the Archaic Age are the emergence and slow development of the characteristically Greek community-structure, the *polis* (conventionally and not very aptly translated 'city-state'), and the vast diffusion of Hellas in the course of about two hundred years, from the southeastern end of the Black Sea almost to the Atlantic Ocean.

It has already been noted that in the Dark Age the community had only a shadowy existence as a political organism. How the shadow acquired substance is a process we cannot trace, but at the heart lay the creation of institutions which subjected even the most powerful men to *formal* organs and rules of authority. This was no simple task; tension between the organs of the community and the power drives of ambitious individuals remained a disturbing factor in Greek society not only in the archaic period but also in the classical. One step was the elimination of kingship,[1] a step which was curiously unnoticed in Greek legends and traditions. The contrast in this respect with early Roman history could scarcely be greater. In time, the Romans developed a very full and detailed story of the reigns of their kings, each in turn, climaxed by the expulsion of the last of them, Tarquinius Superbus in 509.[2] The abolition of kingship was a story of a revolt from Etruscan overlordship, and that explains something of its attraction and its tenacity in Roman legends. The Greeks lacked such a stimulus. And their silence about this aspect of their past suggests that anyway,

---

[1] Sparta was the one survival. It should also be noted that the word *basileus,* "king," remained in use for such officials as the magistrates in charge of religious affairs in Athens, without any implication of royal status.

[2] See, for example, the first two books of Livy's history (available in the Penguin volume of Livy entitled *The Early History of Rome*).

From M. I. Finley, *Early Greece: The Bronze and Archaic Ages* (New York: W. W. Norton, 1970), pp. 90–99.

despite the Agamemnons and Ajaxes of the Homeric poems, their real Dark Age rulers were petty chieftains within a framework of 'many kings', whose disappearance from the scene was undramatic and unmemorable. Without them, the nobles were compelled to formalize the previously informal advisory bodies we see in action in the Homeric poems. So there arose councils and offices (which we call 'magistracies', borrowing the word from the Latin), with more or less defined prerogatives and responsibilities, and with a machinery for selection and rotation, all confined within the closed group of the landowning aristocracy.

These communities were small and independent (unless subjected by force). Following the normal Mediterranean residential pattern, they had an urban centre, even if it were no more than a village, where many of the people resided (especially the wealthy). The town square, an open space, was reserved: it was flanked by the main civic and religious buildings, but easy access was carefully maintained so that the people could all be assembled when required. That was the agora in its original sense, a 'gathering-place', long before shops and stalls began to encroach, so that the common 'marketplace' translation of the word *agora* is rarely quite right and sometimes just wrong. Usually there was also an acropolis, a high point to serve as a citadel for defence. Essentially town and country were conceived as a unit, not, as was common in medieval cities, as two antagonistic elements. This was built into the language, which equated the community with people and not with a place. An ancient Greek could express the idea of Athens as a community or as a political unit only by saying 'the Athenians'. The word 'Athens' was very rarely used in any sense other than geographical; one travelled to Athens but one made war with the Athenians. Of course, the tempo of development among these farflung autonomous communities was very uneven, and there were considerable variations in the end-product. The community of the eighth and seventh centuries had a long way to go before it became the classical *polis*. Nevertheless, the embryo was there in the early Archaic period.

The fragmentation which characterized Hellas is partly explained by geography. Much of the terrain in Greece proper is a chequer-board of mountains and small plains or valleys, tending to isolate each pocket of habitation from the other. In Asia Minor the coastal region had roughly the same structure and therefore encouraged a comparable settlement-pattern. The Aegean islands were also mountainous and they were mostly very small. But the geography is not a sufficient explanation, and especially not of later Greek developments. It cannot explain, for example, why the whole of Attica was politically united whereas neighbouring Boeotia, which is not much larger, contained twelve independent city-states who on the whole successfully resisted the efforts of the largest, Thebes, to dominate them; nor why a tiny island like Amorgos had three separate *poleis* right through the classical era; nor, above all, why the Greeks transplanted the small community to Sicily and southern Italy, where both the geography and self-preservation should have argued for embracing much larger territories within single political structures. Clearly there was something far greater at stake, a conviction that the *polis* was the only proper structure for civilized life, a conviction which Aristotle (*Politics* 1253a7 *ff.*) summed up, in the last days of Greek independence, when he defined man as a *zoön politikon,* a being destined by nature to live in a *polis.*

Land communication from one pocket to another was slow and cumbersome, sometimes actually impossible in the face of resistance. Inland waterways were almost wholly lacking, and therefore the sea became the normal Greek highway, even for relatively short distances wherever possible. In antiquity the Greeks became the people of the sea *par excellence,* and yet their attitude to it was notably ambiguous: it was the home of those pleasant nymphs, the Nereids, but it was ruled over by Poseidon, whom men feared and appeased but never loved. Nevertheless, when they were forced into a continuous movement of expansion, from the middle of the eighth century, they took to the sea, going west and northeast. By the end of the Archaic Age, Hellas covered an enormous area, from the northern, western and southern shores of the Black Sea, through western Asia Minor and Greece proper (with the Aegean islands) to much of Sicily and southern Italy, then continuing west along both shores of the Mediterranean to Cyrene in Libya and to Marseilles and some Spanish coastal sites. Wherever they went, they settled on the edge of the sea, not in the hinterland.

The sea was not the only common environmental feature of these farflung regions. Ecologically they shared (with few exceptions) what we popularly call a 'Mediterranean' climate and vegetation, permitting and even inducing an outdoor existence still familiar in our day. Summers are hot and sunny, winters are tolerable and usually free from snow on the shores and in the plains, olives and grapes grow freely, flowers abound, the plains produce cereals and vegetables, the sea is rich in fish, and there is adequate pasture on the hillsides (rich in places), at least for the smaller animals. Nothing is as a rule luxuriant, and therefore agriculture and pasturage need constant attention, but on the other hand the requirements of housing, and especially of warmth, can be met by fairly primitive means. Only metals and wood suitable for such purposes as shipbuilding cause serious difficulties from short supply: they are available only in restricted, and sometimes rather distant, localities. Fresh water may also be a problem, hence the stress in legend and reality on springs and fountains.

Schematically the Greek 'colonization' movement may be conceived as two long waves (not counting the earlier settlement of Asia Minor). The western one began about 750 B.C. and continued in full swing until the middle of the next century, with a secondary wave going on for about another century, when the process was essentially completed. Migration to the northeast began before 700 with settlements in the Thracian region, in nearby islands such as Thasos and in the Troad in Asia Minor, followed from about 650 with further movement into the Hellespont area and then along both shores of the Black Sea, not stopping until the end of the sixth century, at the mouth of the Don on the north coast and at Trapezus (now Trebizond) at the southeastern end. Ancient accounts of these movements are not very helpful. One reasonably sober example, the accepted story of the foundation of Syracuse in Sicily as repeated by the geographer Strabo (VI 2, 4), reads like this:

> Archias, sailing from Corinth, founded Syracuse about the same time that Naxos and Megara [also in Sicily] were established. They say that when Myscellus and Archias went to Delphi to consult the oracle, the god asked whether they preferred wealth or health. Archias chose wealth and Myscellus health, and the oracle then assigned Syracuse to the former to found, and Croton [in Southern Italy] to the latter. . . . On his way to Sicily, Archias left a part of the expedition to settle the island now called Corcyra [modern Corfu]. . . . The latter expelled the Liburni who occupied it and established a settlement. Archias, continuing on his journey, met some Dorians . . . who had separated from the settlers of Megara; he took them with him and together they founded Syracuse.

Such mythical overtones and the stress on a few individuals and their quarrels, rather than on the broader social aspects, are characteristic of most of the traditions. On the other hand, these accounts are more 'historical' than the still vaguer and more confused ones about the drift to Asia Minor early in the Dark Age. Whereas the earlier migrations were probably more in the nature of chancy, haphazard flights, what was now happening was an organized shift of population, though still in small numbers; group emigration systematically arranged by the 'mother-cities'.

The common Greek word for such a new settlement abroad, *apoikia,* connotes 'emigration' and lacks the implication of dependence inherent in our 'colony'. As a rule, each *apoikia* was from the outset, and by intention, an independent community, retaining sentimental, and often religious, ties with its 'mother-city', but not a subject either economically or politically. Indeed, their independence helped preserve friendly relations with their old homes on the whole, free as they were from the irritations and conflicts commonly aroused under colonial conditions. The designation 'mother-city', it should be added, was often a slightly arbitrary choice; many of the new foundations were established by settlers joining together from more than one place in the old Greek world.

According to the commonly accepted chronological scheme, based on archaeology and Greek antiquarian efforts, the earliest colony was Cumae near Naples shortly before 750 B.C. (more precisely, the island now known as Ischia, from which Cumae was then founded), settled from Chalcis and Eretria, the two leading cities of Euboea (active at the same time at Al Mina in the Levant). Chalcis was also the mother-city of Sicilian Zancle (later Messina), of Rhegium on the Italian side of the straits, and of Naxos, Leontini and Catania (Katane in Greek) in eastern Sicily, all traditionally founded by 730. They were joined in Zancle by other Euboeans, in Rhegium by Messenian exiles, and in Leontini by Megarians. Syracuse was founded at the same time by Corinthians and unspecified 'other Dorians'; Sybaris in southern Italy in about 720 by men from Achaea with a sprinkling from Troezen in the Peloponnese; Gela in southern Sicily in 688 by Cretans and Rhodians. Thereafter foundations were further complicated by 'inner' migrations, as some colonies became mother-cities in turn, while emigrants continued to come from the east. Thus, Himera was established about 650 from Zancle with a contingent of Syracusan exiles; Selinus between 650 and 630 from Megara Hyblaea in eastern Sicily; Cyrene about 630 from the Aegean island of Thera; Massalia (Marseilles) about 600 by Phocaeans from Asia Minor; and Akragas (modern Agrigento) in 580 from Gela together with migrants coming directly from the latter's own motherland, Rhodes.

This list is not complete and none of the traditional dates is secure. Enough has been said to indicate the chronology of the movement, which has been archaeologically substantiated in its general outline, to underscore the way the settlements clung to the sea, and to reveal the number, diversity and geographical spread of the Greek communities involved. There is no need to repeat with a catalogue of the north Aegean and Black Sea foundations, for which both the literary and the archaeological evidence is much poorer. Settlement on the Thracian coast of the Aegean Sea began late in the eighth century, and again the cities of Euboea were in the vanguard, as shown by the name of the promontory Chalcidice (from Chalcis). Soon other Aegean islands came into the picture, Paros, Rhodes, and above all Chios. And then, as the movement went beyond the Aegean coast to the shores of the Black Sea, Miletus became the dominant mother-city (followed by Megara). If all the references to Milesian activity were taken too literally, that city itself would have been totally depopulated, and that is further proof of the restricted role of a 'mother-city'.

The lands to which the Greeks migrated, both east and west, were all inhabited, by a variety of peoples at different levels of development, that is to say, by people with different interests in the newcomers and different capacities of resistance. The Etruscans of central Italy were strong enough to stop Greek expansion at a line drawn from the Bay of Naples, and sufficiently advanced to borrow from the Greeks their alphabet, much of their art, and elements of their religion. The Sicels, however, like the Thracians or the Scythians in the north Aegean and Black Sea areas, were less advanced technically and socially. Some were apparently reduced to a semi-servile labour force, though the evidence is thin and confused. Others were pushed inland, where they maintained an uneasy and complicated relationship with the Greeks in the following centuries.

A study of the list of mother-cities (and of those which seem to have taken no part in colonization) shows that there was little correlation between type of community and colonizing city. In particular, there is nothing in the list to justify the once widely held view that the colonizing activity was *chiefly inspired* by commercial interests. Emphasis on the words 'chiefly inspired' is important. The intention is not to deny the commercial aspect of colonization altogether, in particular the oft repeated need for metals. The island of Ischia, the first western settlement, had some iron, and anyway it was a gateway to the relatively rich ore-bearing regions of central Italy. Foundations on both sides of the Straits of Messina soon followed, evidently to control that narrow roadway to the western Italian coast. The first settlers seemed to know where they were headed, and the information could have come only from traders who had already been in the area. When this is said, however, it explains very little of the centuries-long movement of dispersion. Sicily, for example, had no metal and little else to attract Greek merchants, except in occasional ventures, and the same was true of the Black Sea hinterland. Archaeological evidence of Greek activity earlier than the first colonists is almost impossible to find. In the end, the central question is that of the motivation of the men who actually migrated, who left their homes in Greece, the islands of Asia Minor, to settle permanently in unfamiliar, and sometimes hostile, regions, essentially independent of their mother-cities from the start. They were not the same people as the traders, who did not abandon their home-bases, and so their interests were far from identical. Nor did merchants constitute a significant element in the migrants who followed, to join the original settlers, or in the secondary colonies, such as Himera and Akragas, which in time split off from the earlier ones.

The distinction is emphasized by the small number of genuine trading-posts which were eventually established, such as the places called Emporium (which in Greek means literally 'trading-station' or 'market-centre') in Spain (now Ampurias) and at the mouth of the River Don; or the very interesting settlement at Naucratis in the Nile Delta, where the Pharaohs concentrated the representatives of a number of Greek states, chiefly in Asia Minor, who conducted trade with Egypt. The small number of these posts is revealing, as well as their relatively late foundation—Spanish Emporium was set up by Massalia, which was itself not founded before 600; Naucratis can be dated somewhat earlier than Massalia, whereas Russian Emporium was substantially later. But the most decisive point is that these were not proper Greek *poleis,* but, like Al Mina before them, meeting-points between the Greek world and the non-Greek, whereas all the other new settlements—to be counted in the dozens and eventually in the hundreds—were, from the beginning, Greek communities in all respects. That meant, above all, that they were basically agrarian settlements, established by men who had come in search of land. They settled near the sea and they welcomed good anchorage, but that was a subordinate consideration. Hence, numerous as were the Greek communities in southern Italy, there was none at the best harbour on the east coast, the site of Roman Brundisium (modern Brindisi). Hence, too, the aristocracy of Syracuse, which became the greatest of the new communities in the west, were called *gamoroi,* which means literally 'those who divided the land'.

In the final analysis, the one feature which all the mother-cities had in common was a condition of crisis severe enough to induce the mobilization of the resources required for so difficult a venture as an overseas transplantation—ships, armour and weapons, presumably tools, seed and supplies—and to create the necessary psychology as well. Behind the traditional stories of personal feuds, quarrels and murders which the later Greeks associated with some of the individual foundations, there lies a deeper and

broader social conflict. One must not exaggerate the spirit of Viking adven-
turism in Archaic Greece.

A tantalizingly brief passage in Herodotus (IV 153) about the foundation
of Cyrene from Thera gives us a clue, with the help of an early fourth-
century inscription from Cyrene which purports to be the text of the pact
of the first settlers. What Herodotus says is this: 'The Therans decided to
send out one brother from among brothers, selected by lot, from each of the
seven districts of the island, and that Battos should be their leader and king.
On these terms they dispatched two fifty-oared ships.' The inscription adds
that the penalty for refusing to go was death and confiscation of property,
and that volunteers were also accepted. Numbers were therefore small—two
hundred at the most—and no women were included, which reminds us of
the suggestion already made about the first movement into Asia Minor, that
the earliest migrants took their wives from among the natives where they
settled. And there was compulsion, although families with only sons seem to
have been exempt. Why such pressure? We are not told. For Herodotus and
for the people who later inscribed the 'pact' in Cyrene itself, the story is all
tied up with orders from Apollo at Delphi and with a sanction for the Battiad
dynasty which had seized power in Cyrene. That takes us back to the mythical explanations characteristic of most of the foundation stories. But the factual core remains, and though we do not know the precise situation, we
cannot doubt the existence in Thera in the middle of the seventh century
B.C. of an excess of population, and hence of the potential, if not yet the reality, of social conflict. Nor that the same was the case wherever active colonizing was being fostered, and probably often compelled. ❖

RECOMMENDED READINGS

Anthony M. Snodgrass, *Archaic Greece: The Age of Experiment* (London: J.M. Dent,
1980), and Raphael Sealey, *A History of the Greek City States, ca. 700-338 B.C.* (Berkeley: University of California Press, 1976), offer a good background to the era of Greek
expansion; the process of colonization is studied in Irad Malkin, *Religion and Colonization in Ancient Greece* (Leiden: E.J. Brill, 1987).

Something of the wondering spirit of the era may be caught in the pages of Herodotus,
The Histories (many editions). Homer, *The Odyssey* (many editions), is in many ways a
romance of discovery and exploration as is the story of Jason and the search for the
Golden Fleece. Both have been made into motion pictures which, although they take
some liberties with their text, convey the sense of adventure and the thrill of the unknown that marked the original works. The culmination of Jason's voyage has been
cast in dramatic form by Euripides's somber *Medea*.

China, 479 B.C.

THE CONFUCIAN TRADITION IN CHINESE HISTORY

Tu Wei-ming

Iron metallurgy came late to China, but its social and political effects were devastating. The chariot-driving Bronze Age aristocracy was replaced by cavalry and peasant infantry, and the Chou dynasty (ca. 1100 B.C.–403 B.C.) disintegrated, leaving in its wake a number of petty contending principalities. This was the beginning of the Age of Warring States (403 B.C.–218 B.C.). In China as elsewhere, the collapse of the Bronze Age empires and the fall of their priestly castes left people to explain to themselves what had befallen them and to devise personal rules to guide them in the new and tumultuous times. The result was the rise of teachers such as Buddha in India, Joel in Israel, and Hesiod in Greece, and the spread of their doctrines.

K'ung-fu-tzu, Master K'ung, or Confucius, was the leading teacher in China. Ignoring the imperial pantheon of deities of early times, he concentrated on the ethics of human actions as the means of bringing order into an age of chaos. He taught that leaders should be motivated by service to others, righteousness, integrity, conscientiousness, and, above all, humanity. They should strive to combine these inner virtues with outer culture and—for want of a better term—manners. The logical extension of this doctrine was that power should be wielded in a humane manner by individuals who displayed both inner and outer merit. This vision proved so strong that Confucius's teachings formed the basis of education in China for the next 2,500 years.

Tu Wei-ming discusses the importance of the Confucian ethic to both China and the various cultures around it. No one can study Eastern civilization without quickly becoming aware of the deep and continuing influence that the teachings of Master K'ung continue to exert upon all aspects of life and thought.

READING QUESTIONS

1. What was the purpose of education for Confucius?

2. What is the *Analects* and what is its importance?

3. How did Confucius define the quality of humanity?

4. What is filial piety and why was it considered so important by Confucius?

C onfucianism, a generic Western term that has no counterpart in Chinese, is a worldview, a social ethic, a political ideology, a scholarly tradition, and a way of life.[1] Although Confucianism is often grouped together with Buddhism, Christianity, Hinduism, Islam, Judaism, and Taoism as a major historical religion, it is not an organized religion. Yet it has exerted profound influence on East Asian political culture as well as East Asian spiritual life. Both in theory and practice Confucianism has made an indelible mark on the governments, societies, educational practices, and family life of East Asia. It is an exaggeration to characterize traditional Chinese life and culture as "Confucian," but for well over two thousand years Confucian ethical values have served as a source of inspiration as well as the court of appeal for human interaction at all levels—individual, communal, and national—in the Sinic world.

Confucianism was not an organized missionary tradition, but by the first century B.C. it had spread to those East Asian countries that were under the influence of Chinese literate culture. In the centuries following the Confucian revival of Sung times (A.D. 960–1279), Confucianism was embraced in Chosŏn dynasty Korea beginning in the fifteenth century and in Tokugawa Japan beginning in the seventeenth century. Prior to the arrival of the Western powers in East Asia in the mid nineteenth century the Confucian persuasion was so predominant in the art of governance, the form and conduct of elite education, and the moral discourse of the populace that China, Korea, and Japan were all distinctively "Confucian" states. In Southeast Asia, Vietnam and Singapore were also influenced by Confucianism.

---

[1] The adjective "Confucian" derives from "Confucius," the Latinization of K'ung Fu-tzu, or Master K'ung. The term "Confucianism" was coined in Europe only in the eighteenth century. It is used, not entirely accurately, to translate the Chinese term *ju-chia,* which literally means "family of scholars," signifying a genealogy, a school, or a tradition of learning. Please note that my citations from the *Analects* are given by book and verse number and thus are the same for any edition.

From Tu Wei-ming, "The Confucian Tradition in Chinese History," in Paul S. Ropp, ed., *Heritage of China: Contemporary Perspectives on Chinese Civilization* (Berkeley: University of California Press, 1990), pp. 112–117.

THE LIFE OF CONFUCIUS

Considering Confucius's tremendous importance, his life seems starkly un-dramatic, or as a Chinese expression has it, "plain and real." The plainness and reality of Confucius's life, however, illustrate his humanity not as a re-vealed truth but as an expression of self-cultivation, the ability of human ef-fort to persevere in the endless but ennobling tasks of self-improvement and humanitarian service. The faith in the possibility that ordinary human be-ings can become awe-inspiring sages and worthies is deeply rooted in the Confucian heritage and the insistence that human beings are teachable, im-provable, and perfectible through personal and communal endeavor is typi-cally Confucian.

Confucius was born in 551 B.C. in Ch'ü-fu in the small feudal state of Lu (in modern Shantung province), which was noted for its preservation of the traditions of ritual and music of the Chou civilization. Confucius's ancestors were probably members of the aristocracy who had become virtual poverty-stricken commoners by the time of this birth. His father died when Confu-cius was only three years old. Instructed first by his mother, Confucius distinguished himself as an indefatigable learner in his teens. He recalled to-ward the end of his life that his heart was set on learning at fifteen (2.4, that is, book 2, chapter 4 of the *Analects*).

Confucius served in minor government posts managing stables and keeping books for granaries before he married a woman of similar back-ground when he was nineteen. He may already have acquired a reputation as a multitalented scholar at an early age. Confucius's mastery of the six arts—ritual, music, archery, charioteering, calligraphy, and arithmetic—and his familiarity with the classical traditions, notably poetry and history, enabled him to start a brilliant teaching career in his thirties.

Confucius is known as the first private teacher in China, for he was in-strumental in establishing the art of teaching as a vocation, indeed as a way of life. Before Confucius aristocratic families hired tutors to educate their sons and government officials instructed their subordinates in the necessary techniques, but he was the first person to devote his whole life to learning and teaching for the purpose of transforming and improving society.

For Confucius the primary function of education is to provide the proper way of training noblemen (*chün-tzu*), a process that involves constant self-improvement and continuous social interaction. Although he emphatically noted (14.25) that learning is "for the sake of the self" and that the end of learning is self-realization, he found public service a natural consequence of true education. Confucius confronted learned hermits who challenged the validity of his desire to serve the world; he resisted the temptation to "herd with birds and animals" (18.6), to live apart from the human community, and opted to try to transform the world from within. For decades Confucius was actively involved in the political arena wishing to put his humanist ideas into practice through governmental channels.

In his late forties and early fifties Confucius served first as a magistrate, then as an assistant minister of public works, and eventually as minister of justice in the state of Lu. But his political career was short-lived. At fifty-six, when he realized that his superiors were uninterested in his policies, he left the state of Lu in an attempt to find another feudal state in which to render his service. Despite his political frustration he was accompanied by a growing circle of students during this self-imposed exile of almost thirteen years. His reputation as a man of vision and mission spread. At the age of sixty-seven, he returned home to teach and to preserve his cherished classical traditions by writing and editing. He died in 479 B.C. at the age of seventy-three. According to the *Records of the Historian* seventy-two of his students mastered the "six arts," and three thousand people claimed to be his followers.

THE *ANALECTS* AS THE EMBODIMENT OF CONFUCIAN IDEAS

The *Analects* (*Lun-yü*), the most revered sacred text in the Confucian tradition, was probably compiled by the second generation of Confucius's disciples.[2] Based primarily on the master's sayings, which were preserved in both oral and written transmissions, the *Analects* captures the Confucian spirit in form and content in the same way that the Platonic dialogues underscore the Socratic pedagogy. The purpose in compiling this digest of Confucius's statements seems not to have been to present an argument or to record an event but to offer an invitation to its readers to take part in an ongoing conversation. Dialogue is used to show Confucius in thought and action, not as an isolated individual, but as a center of human relationships.

Confucius's life as a student and teacher exemplified the Confucian idea that education is a ceaseless process of self-realization. When one of his students reportedly had difficulty describing him, Confucius came to his aid: "Why did you not simply say something to this effect: he is the sort of man who forgets to eat when he engages himself in vigorous pursuit of learning, who is so full of joy that he forgets his worries, and who does not notice that old age is coming on?" (7.18).

The community that Confucius created through his inspiring personality was a scholarly fellowship of like-minded men of different ages and different backgrounds from different states. They were attracted to Confucius because they shared his vision and in varying degrees took part in his mission to bring moral order to an increasingly fragmented polity. This mission was difficult and even dangerous. The master himself suffered from joblessness,

---

[2] For a good translation of the *Analects* see D. C. Lau, trans. *The Analects* (Harmondsworth: Penguin, 1979).

homelessness, starvation, and, occasionally, life-threatening violence. Yet, his faith in the survivability of the culture that he cherished and the workability of the approach to teaching that he propounded was so steadfast that he convinced his followers as well as himself that Heaven was on their side. When Confucius's life was threatened in K'uang, he said: "Since the death of King Wen [founder of the Chou dynasty], does not the mission of culture (*wen*) rest here in me? If Heaven intends this culture to be destroyed, those who come after me will not be able to have any part of it. If Heaven does not intend this culture to be destroyed, then what can the men of K'uang do to me?" (9.5).

This expression of self-confidence may give the impression that there was presumptuousness in Confucius's self-image. However, Confucius made it explicit that he was far from attaining sagehood and that all he really excelled in was "love of learning" (5.28). In this sense Confucius was neither a prophet with privileged access to the divine nor a philosopher who has already seen the truth, but a teacher of humanity who is an advanced fellow traveler on the way to self-realization.

As a teacher of humanity, Confucius stated his ambition in terms of human care: "To bring comfort to the old, to have trust in friends, and to cherish the young" (5.26). Confucius's vision of the way to develop a moral community began with a holistic reflection on the human condition. Instead of dwelling on abstract ideas, such as the state of nature, Confucius sought to understand the actual situation of a given time and use this understanding as a point of departure. His aim was to restore trust in government and to transform society into a moral community by cultivating a sense of human caring in politics and society. To achieve this aim, the creation of a scholarly community, the fellowship of *chün-tzu* (noblemen), was essential. In the words of Confucius's disciple, Tseng Tzu, the true nobleman "must be broad-minded and resolute, for his burden is heavy and his road is long. He takes humanity as his burden. Is that not heavy? Only with death does his road come to an end. Is that not long?" (8.7). However, the fellowship of *chün-tzu,* as moral vanguards of society, did not seek to establish a radically different order. Its mission was to reformulate and revitalize those institutions that were believed to have maintained social solidarity and enabled people to live in harmony and prosperity for centuries.

An obvious example of such an institution is the family. The role and function of the family was related in the *Analects* when Confucius was asked why he did not take part in government. He responded (2.21) by citing a passage from an ancient classic, the *Book of Documents,* "Simply by being a good son and friendly to his brothers a man can exert an influence upon government!" This passage shows that what one does in the confines of one's private home is politically significant. This position is predicated on the Confucian conviction that the self-cultivation of each person is the root of social order and that social order is the basis for political stability and universal peace. The assertion that family ethics are politically efficacious must be seen in the context of the Confucian conception of politics as "rectification" (*cheng*). In this conception rulers are supposed to govern by moral leadership and exemplary teaching rather than by force. The government's responsibility is not only to provide food and security but also to educate the people. Law and punishment are the minimum requirements for order; but social harmony can only be attained by virtue, which is achieved through ritual performance. To perform ritual is to take part in a communal act to promote mutual understanding.

One of the fundamental Confucian values that ensures the integrity of ritual performance is filial piety. Confucius believed that filial piety was the first step toward moral excellence. He seemed to contend that the way to enhance personal dignity and identity is not to alienate ourselves from our family but to cultivate our genuine feelings for our parents. To learn to embody the family in our minds and hearts is to enable ourselves to move beyond self-centeredness or, to borrow from modern psychology, to transform the enclosed private ego into an open self. Indeed, the cardinal Confucian virtue, *jen* (humanity), is the result of self-cultivation. The first test for our self-cultivation is our ability to establish meaningful relationships with our family members. Filial piety does not demand unconditional submissiveness to parental authority; rather it demands recognition of and reverence for our source of life.

The purpose of filial piety, as the Greeks would have it, is "human flourishing" for both parent and child. Confucians see it as an essential way of learning to be human. They are fond of applying the family metaphor to the community, the country, and the universe. They prefer to address the emperor as the Son of Heaven, the king as ruler-father, and the magistrate as the "father-mother official" because they assume that implicit in the family-centered nomenclature is a political vision. When Confucius responded that taking care of family affairs is itself active participation in politics, he made it clear that family ethics are not merely a private, personal concern. Rather, family ethics make possible the realization of the public good.

In response to a question from his favorite disciple, Yen Hui, Confucius defined humanity as "conquer yourself and return to ritual" (12.1). This interplay between inner spiritual self-transformation (the master is said to have freed himself from four things: "opinionatedness, dogmatism, obstinacy, and egoism" [9.4]) and social participation enabled Confucius to be "loyal" (*chung*) to himself and "considerate" (*shu*) of others (4.15). Understandably, the Confucian golden rule is "Do not do unto others what you would not want other to do unto you" (15.23). Confucius's legacy, laden with profound ethical implications, is captured by his "plain and real" appreciation that learning to be human is a communal enterprise: "A man of humanity, wishing to establish himself, also establishes others, and wishing to enlarge himself, also enlarges others. The ability to take as analogy what is near at hand can be called the method of humanity" (6.28). ❖

RECOMMENDED READINGS

Fung Yu-lang, *A Short History of Chinese Philosophy,* ed. Derk Bodde (New York: Macmillan, 1948), provides an excellent general introduction to Chinese philosophy; Arthur F. Wright, *The Confucian Persuasion* (Palo Alto, CA: Stanford University Press, 1960), offers some stimulating insights into Confucianism in particular. Arthur F. Waley sets Confucianism in its wider cultural and social context in *Confucianism and Chinese Civilization* (Stanford: Stanford University Press, 1975). The standard English translation of the basic Confucian text is still Arthur F. Waley, *The Analects of Confucius* (New York: Allen & Unwin, 1938), although there are now several others available. Ch'u Chai and Winberg Ch'ai, eds. and trans., offer a representative sampling of later Confucian texts in *The Sacred Books of Confucius and Other Confucian Classics* (New York: Bantam, 1965). There are several biographies of Confucius, all of which are as much legend as fact. Raymond S. Dawson, *Confucius* (New York: Hill & Wang, 1982), provides one of the more recent of these. The reader who wishes to pursue Confucianism further would do well to turn to David L. Hall, *Thinking Through Confucius* (Albany: State University of New York Press, 1987).

Afghanistan, About 320 B.C.

THE GREEKS IN CENTRAL ASIA

A FRONTIER EXPERIENCE

Frank L. Holt

The eastern shores of the Mediterranean Sea have been an object of contention between Eastern and Western powers throughout the ages. Egypt, with its wealth and power, had generally been able to repel eastern invaders from a region that the Pharaohs considered their proper sphere of influence. In so doing, Egypt protected the infant civilizations of the Aegean Sea. The authority of the Pharaohs began to wane by the middle of the tenth century B.C., however, and Egypt was unable to resist the power of the Assyrian Empire. In 525 B.C., Egypt was occupied by a new and expanding Persian Empire, and for two centuries remained the westernmost province of a Middle Eastern empire that extended to the Indian Punjab.

There was no power to oppose the further westward expansion of the Persians except the collection of independent Greek city-states of the islands and shores of the Aegean Sea. Most of these states that lay on the shores of Asia Minor succumbed to the Persians by about the year 500 B.C., and the Persian emperor dispatched a force to test the resolve of the western states in 490. It was soundly defeated by the well-armored close-order infantry formation of Athens, and the effectiveness of the Greek hoplite warriors fighting in an unshakable phalanx became apparent to the Persians. From being easy prey, the Greeks had become a distinct threat and an inspiration to those considering rebellion against their Persian overlords.

From the Persian point of view, the Greeks had to be crushed as a lesson to others tempted to oppose Persian power. In 489, the Persian emperor Xerxes (zerk'-sees) led a massive expedition against the West. In The Persian Wars, *Herodotus chronicles the series of desperate battles in which the Persian land and sea forces were destroyed and Persian dreams of Western conquests were ended. Searching for the causes of the Greeks' victory against such odds, he concludes the Greeks triumphed because they were free, while their opponents were slaves of an absolute master.*

This same sense of freedom, however, doomed the alliance that had defeated the Persians and led to a state of civil war that left the city-states of Greece weakened and antagonistic. The kings of Macedon, to the north, moved into this vacuum and began to bring about some degree of unity through coercion and conquest. In 338 B.C., the Macedonians defeated their last effective opposition in the region and established their dominion. It was a precarious dominance, however, and Alexander, having just succeeded to the throne in 336 and facing a series of revolts, knew he had to do something to gain the loyalty of his new and quarrelsome subjects. He announced his intention of avenging the Persian invasions of 490 and 480, gathered an army, crossed over into Asia Minor, and attacked the empire.

Whatever his original intentions might have been, a series of victories led to his conquest of the entire Persian Empire and the birth of the idea of unifying East and West into a harmonious whole. He married a Persian princess and urged his followers to take native wives. He consolidated native leaders and armies with his own forces and established Greek cities, colonized by soldiers from his armies, wherever he went. What the result might have been had he lived to carry out this grand vision can only be guessed, since Alexander died in 323 B.C., only thirteen years after having crossed over into Persian territory.

His successors contrived to maintain control over the fragments of Alexander's empire, and the region between the Mediterranean Sea and the Indus River became imbued with Greek culture. Greek influences in art and literature passed from this area to influence India and even China, and Eastern influences were transmitted to the West. When the Romans replaced Alexander's successors in the course of the first and second centuries B.C., they inherited a heavily Westernized frontier zone that they were able to defend against a resurgent Persian Empire.

By and large, this frontier held until A.D. 632, almost a thousand years after Alexander had established it. By 650, however, the entire region was in the hands of Muslim Arab conquerors. The Persians may have been conquered militarily and converted in their faith, but they were victorious in cultural and intellectual matters. By 750, the leading Muslim scientists, scholars, poets, and artists were almost all Persian. The capital of the Islamic Empire was moved to Baghdad in Mesopotamia, where it remained for the next five hundred years.

Nevertheless, the Greek heritage of Alexander's empire survived in the region and played an important role in the intellectual achievements of the Muslims. When western Europe began to recover its Greek heritage in the course of the twelfth and thirteenth centuries, it was a Greek heritage that had been preserved by the Muslim inhabitants of the region that Alexander of Macedon had thought to transform into a multicultural empire. In the end, it was clear he had been successful.

The following selection discusses Bactria, the easternmost region of Alexander's empire, and illustrates how the Greek tradition endured, and even flourished, in places far from its home.

READING QUESTIONS

1. What was the geographical position of Bactria within Greek civilization?

2. What does his coinage tell us about King Agathocles and his kingdom?

3. Why did Alexander the Great invade Bactria?

4. What political factor allowed Alexander to gain a victory under such difficult circumstances?

ncient Bactria and the surrounding regions of Sogdiana, Margiana, Aria, Drangiana, Arachosia, and 'India' lay within the heartland of continental Eurasia in an area which now extends across the disputed borders of six modern nations. The entire region is part of the vast and varied geological system identified with Central Asia. Although best known for its open steppe, the principal feature of this system is the wide range of mountains descending in a diagonal line from Lake Baykal in the northeast to the Hindu Kush in the southwest.

Historically, this great divide has defined the cultural limits of three very important civilizations: the Chinese, Iranian, and Indian. But, like the Alps, this formidable 'barrier' is breached in numerous places and thus allows access along certain routes from one cultural center to the next, as the existence of the famous Silk Road attests. The central location of ancient Bactria within the larger system of Central Asia explains its special significance as a cultural and commercial crossroads.

Over two thousand years ago, when today's Afghanistan was the heartland of a kingdom called Bactria, it was ruled by an extraordinary line of some three dozen kings and queens. History has erased them all too well, so that only the deeds of a handful have survived. The rest we know only through numismatics, the study of coins still saved in the greedy fist of history's effacing hand.

Thus, for example, if not for the coins struck in his name somewhere in Central Asia sometime in the second quarter of the second century B.C., we would know nothing at all about King Agathocles 'The Just' of Bactria. None of his decrees has ever been found; no city or monument bearing his name

From Frank L. Holt, *Alexander the Great and Bactria* (Leiden and New York: E. J. Brill, 1988), pp. 1-3, 11, 44-49, 50-51.

has yet been brought to light. Whatever accounts were written of his reign by ancient authors have long since disappeared. And yet, this monarch and his money represent far more than a phantom image of a forgotten past; they are part of a remarkable episode of central importance to the histories of several civilizations.

This King Agathocles, after all, was a man of two worlds, a scion of east and west. His scattered coinage has been found on both sides of the Hindu Kush; yet, much of it seems to be as thoroughly Mediterranean as his name. He issued beautiful Greek silver coins on the Attic standard with his skillful carved portrait on one side, and a standing Zeus holding Hecate on the other. On smaller denominations struck in bronze or nickel, Agathocles chose Dionysos and the panther as his types. The inscriptions they bore are naturally Greek: BASILEOS AGATHOKLEOYS ["belonging to King Agathocles"], with the epithet DIKAIOS ["The Just"] added to his later issues. These coins suggest that Agathocles, though ruling a kingdom in Central Asia, was certainly a Greek who governed subjects of Hellenic culture.

But on the other hand, Agathocles issued the coins of a very different world. He struck bronze and silver coins of Oriental type that were square or rectangular in shape, and which portrayed the gods of India rather than Greece. These deities have been variously identified as Vishnu, Shiva, Vasudeva, Buddha, and Balarama. With Greek retained on some bilingual issues, these coins of Indian type were generally inscribed in either Brahmi or Kharoshthi (derived from Aramaic) script. This is the money of 'Rajane Agathuklayasa', a monarch whose subjects required a native currency in the local scripts of North-West India.

Agathocles/Agathuklayasa was indeed a man of two worlds, a Bactrian king of the borderlands between Greek and Indian culture. An additional Persian influence upon his realm is evident in the Aramaic origins of Kharoshthi lettering, while neighboring China and Scythia certainly contributed to the complex mix of civilizations in his ancient homeland. The kingdom of Agathocles is thus a subject of interest to scholars in many fields. Classicists, for example, may easily recognize Bactria's significance as the easternmost edge of Greek civilization, the historical horizon of the Hellenistic world. Land-locked in surroundings so unlike those of their Mediterranean heritage, the Bactrian Greeks demonstrated the full measure of their culture's adaptability to an alien environment. In fact, nothing so broadened the bounds of Greek history and culture beyond the proverbial 'frog-pond' of Plato as the Bactria of Agathocles.

Yet, from a vantage point among the mountains of Afghanistan rather than the monuments of the Acropolis, it is clear that Bactria was not simply the most remote of all Greek states; it was also an irrepressible center of Central Asian cultures never wholly subdued by the invasions of Iranians, Greeks, Indians, and others. Greek 'conquerors' and colonists were never alone nor omnipotent in Bactria, and the success of their stay required the accommodation of non-Greeks no less numerous or civilized than they. The coins of Agathocles/Agathuklayasa provide eloquent testimony to this hybrid nature of Bactria's history.

Bactria was brought into the historical spotlight by Alexander the Great's invasion of the Persian Empire. The swift passage of the Graeco-Macedonian army from Asia Minor to eastern Iran in four short years, during which Alexander journeyed to Siwah and won three major battles elsewhere, contrasts sharply with the next phase of the operation: the prolonged and costly three-year campaign in Bactria and Sogdiana. This circumstance gave to the Greeks a long, unfavorable look at the land and people of Central Asia. What they saw and what they wrote reflects, of course, a region thrown into confusion by the presence of a substantial military force. The Bactria that we are able to see in this period was anything but 'normal', and the invaders were anything but impartial in their judgements. Thus, if the native population was called savage because it dispersed to the protection of mountain strongholds instead of blissfully farming and conducting trade, the modern historian must not be inclined to believe Plutarch that the Bactrians were always barbarians in the worst possible sense until civilized by Alexander's army.

In this troubled age, the first Bactrians to face Alexander were apparently two thousand military colonists in Asia Minor who fought at the Granicus River in 334 B.C. In time, the Macedonians' steady advance required a much greater commitment to the cause of Persia's defense. After Darius III lost the major engagement at Issus in 333 B.C., the levies from the eastern satrapies were summoned to the west. At Gaugamela in 331 B.C. where the fate of the Persian Empire would be decided, the Bactrians and their neighbors played a major role in Darius' plan of defense. Indeed, this important arm of the Persian forces was commanded by Bessus, one of the most prominent men of the empire and destined to be Darius' self-appointed successor. Bessus was not only the satrap of Bactria, but also a member of Darius' own household.

In light of earlier events, the special status of this Bactrian satrap makes perfect sense and continues into the reign of Darius III the pattern set by Darius I. The sequel, too, comes as no great surprise. Defeated by Alexander for the final time at Gaugamela, Darius resolved to find safety in a predictable place: the redoubtable satrapy of Bactria. But Darius the king was not successful and he was murdered before Bactria could be reached. The assassin was Bessus himself, together with his Bactrian, Sogdian, and Scythian supporters.

Whatever else may have motivated the murder of Darius, it is clear that Bessus aimed not only to remove the king, but to replace him. With his power base in Bactria, Bessus acted no differently than all the known Bactrian satraps who preceded him. In fact, it was only a short time later that Bessus assumed the royal insignia as the Great King of Persia. A single problem remained for the man who would be king—Alexander claimed that right as well.

It was not as mere king of Macedonia, but also as ruler of Persia that Alexander crossed the Hindu Kush into Bactria during the spring of 329 B.C. Having reacted quickly to Bessus' challenge, Alexander presented himself quite openly as the 'legitimate' Persian king and treated Bessus as a rebel. Alexander created a Persian court, adopted important elements of Persian dress, experimented with Persian protocol, instituted Persian military units, and made certain that he himself performed the familial duties of his Persian predecessor. Alexander not only maintained much of Achaemenid administrative structure, but he also made every effort possible to keep prominent Persians in high positions. Thus, in the extreme east, Alexander took the risk of granting satrapal authority to such men as Satibarzanes, Amedines, Proexes, Tyriaspes, Artabazus, Oxyartes, Arsaces, and others. While most of these satraps were subsequently replaced, it is clear that Alexander was compelled to gamble on their loyalty during the most dangerous period of his easternmost campaigns in order to enhance his image as Great King. The element of risk was indeed very great, as Satibarzanes' revolt made plain from the start, but this only proves how important it was in this area to preserve the outward appearance of Achaemenid rule.

By every means possible, Alexander acted the part of a Persian king who must suppress a rebellious Bactrian satrap. In this there was no dawning of a new age in the east—it was merely Achaemenid business as usual in Bactria. It is important, therefore, to see in Alexander's invasion of Central Asia the perpetuation of a pre-Greek political pattern. Alexander clearly plotted his course *within* the long tradition of Persian rule in the East, not against it. As such, there was no sharp transfer of political authority from Achaemenid to Argead, nor from barbarian to Greek, during Alexander's 'conquest' of Bactria. In fact, so effective was Alexander's appeal to continuity and legitimacy that there was no immediate need for a military conquest at all. As long as Alexander acted out the traditional role of a relatively unobtrusive Persian king, his march through Bactria and Sogdiana was largely uncontested. The ease with which the king traversed this entire area is often overshadowed by the long and bitter war he subsequently waged there, but it must be remembered that Alexander never had to join battle against Bessus. This failure of Bessus to mount any real opposition against his rival can best be explained in political rather than military terms.

It is not difficult to understand how Bessus was beaten by Alexander's political propaganda. Bessus himself had murdered the Achaemenid king, not Alexander or his army. Bessus could only hope to show that his own leadership was superior to Darius', and that by kinship and deeds he was the man to preserve the eastern empire from Alexander. Bessus' reputation, exaggerated no doubt by the Battle of Gaugamela, spent itself quickly. Alexander cut off Bessus' eastern escape route by turning his flank via Arachosia and occupying the main passage of the Hindu Kush. The foundation of Alexandria *sub Caucaso* provided a safeguard there, while numerous villages supplied the advancing army. Then, against the formidable rigors of the Hindu Kush, Alexander and his army crossed into Bactria to test the deeds of Bessus.

When Bessus first established himself at Bactra as King Artaxerxes, his power appeared quite formidable. He called upon his various Scythian allies for support and had some eight thousand Bactrians under arms. Yet, Bessus' plan was a scorched-earth defense to slow if not stop Alexander's advance. Rather than hold the passes leading into Bactria, or fortify the principal cities of the region, Bessus chose instead to abandon the heartland of his 'kingdom'. It was a doomed decision, but he had no other—Alexander had already stolen a political victory.

Although Alexander's army was greatly weakened by the severities of Bactria's climate and terrain, there was no effort to stop its advance. Indeed, the principal cities of Bactria actually opened their gates to Alexander while Bessus' army of Bactrians deserted and disbanded to their native villages; 'Artaxerxes' was forced to withdraw into Sogdiana with those who had not yet changed their loyalty. With the aid of the local inhabitants, Alexander and his troops were reprovisioned by the time they marched unopposed into the very capital of the satrapy.

It is generally argued, of course, that the speed or direction of Alexander's march was not anticipated by Bessus, and the latter was thus forced to fall back in haste. This may be true, as far as it goes; but, the important question is how Alexander's destitute army moved so successfully through devastated territory. The one thing Alexander could not do was conduct sieges without supplies. Thus, the amazing thing is that Alexander did not have to take cities, not even the well-fortified Bactra. These fortresses would have hoarded foodstuffs in advance as the remainder was destroyed by Bessus' torches. If the latter's retreat were indeed part of a larger plan, the cities could greatly slow Alexander or close ranks behind him if he passed. Yet, Alexander was helped, not hindered, by the Bactrians. Bessus had lost support as satrap no less than as 'King Artaxerxes'.

All of this suggests that Bessus could not organize a 'nationalistic uprising' at all against a 'hated foreign invader'. Bessus' only strategy, a scorched-earth policy, proved ineffective because his Bactrian army deserted and his fortresses—even his capital—chose not to defend their walls. In an area renowned before and after for its guerrilla forces and the staunch resistance of its cities and towns, this quiet submission of Bactria is quite notable. Alexander himself was somewhat surprised and off-guard as a result of this easy success. Anxious to capture his forsaken rival, he left a Persian, Artabazus, as his own satrap in Bactra with a small garrison; then Alexander and his main force marched without supplies into the Turkestan desert. Without water and supplies, this march from Bactra to the Oxus was a terrible disaster. Again it was the weather which played havoc with Alexander's army, not a Persian enemy, and again the stricken Macedonians were not attacked while indisposed.

It was the arrival of Alexander at the Oxus, in fact, which prompted the complete betrayal of Bessus. Spitamenes and the other chief associates of Bessus arrested the "usurper" (tearing from him his royal insignia) and made arrangements to deliver him up to Alexander for punishment. Spitamenes himself joined Ptolemy, who had been sent ahead with a detachment of troops for the purpose, in escorting the chained 'criminal' to Alexander the 'rightful king'. Thus was Bessus, like other Bactrian satraps before him, the victim of his own ambition.

The interrogation, mutilation, and later execution of Bessus by Alexander and the Persian nobility were all calculated to underscore that Bessus' crime was not merely the murder of Darius, but also his onerous claim to the Persian throne in defiance of Alexander. By Persian practice and with Persian support, Alexander eliminated the 'false Artaxerxes' and assumed his unchallenged place as Darius' successor. This was a political victory based upon Persian precedent in the east, and it in no way signified the sudden end of the Achaemenid era or the beginning of Greek rule in Bactria. As long as Alexander's authority could be accepted by the native peoples of Bactria, there was no real hint of a Macedonian conquest. In this sense, the advance of Alexander into Central Asia was not yet a turning point in the history of Bactria-Sogdiana. The king was imitative, not innovative, and this was the key to his early success. It was only when Alexander aimed for something more than political recognition that he and his army were opposed, and that a Greek frontier was gradually forced upon the land and people of Bactria.❖

RECOMMENDED READINGS

There is an extensive literature on Alexander the Great, enough to justify book-length bibliographies. Nancy J. Burich, *Alexander the Great: A Bibliography* (Kent, OH: Kent State University Press, 1970) is dated, but provides a good introduction to various aspects of the subject. A. B. Bosworth, *Conquest and Empire: The Reign of Alexander the Great* (Cambridge, UK, and New York: Cambridge University Press, 1988), offers an overview of Alexander's life and times; Vincent Arthur Smith, *The Early History of India from 600 B.C. to the Muhammadan Conquest, Including the Invasion of Alexander the Great*, 4th ed., rev. (Oxford, UK: Clarendon Press, 1967), and Pierre Herman Leonard Eggermont, *Alexander's Campaigns in Sind and Baluchistan and the Siege of the Brahmin Town of Harmatelia* (Louvain: Louvain University Press, 1975), discuss his Eastern campaign. The routes of this expedition are retraced and described by the eminent Asian explorer Sir Aurel Stein, in *On Alexander's Track to the Indus; Personal Narrative of Explorations on the Northwest Frontier of India, Carried Out Under the Orders of H. M. Indian Government* (London: Macmillan, 1929). Alexander's commanders and successors are discussed by Waldemar Heckel, *The Marshals of Alexander's Empire* (London and New York: Routledge, 1992).

The most important single source for Alexander's campaigns is the work of Arrian, selections from which may be found in the Loeb Classical Library volume, *Arrian*, trans. E. Iliff Robson (London: W. Heinemann; New York, G.P. Putnam's Sons, 1929-33). Another Loeb Library volume is that of Quintus Curtius Rufus, *History of Alexander*, trans. John C. Rolfe (Cambridge: Harvard University Press; London: W. Heinemann, 1946), whose treatment is much later and more imbued with legend. An unknown author, called the Pseudo-Callistenes by scholars, wrote a fantastic account of Alexander's adventures and feats that became the basis for the widespread tradition of Alexander romance. Selections from the Western versions may be found in *The Romances of Alexander*, trans. Dennis M. Kratz (New York: Garland, 1991); and translations of an Armenian and Persian version may be found in *The Romance of Alexander the Great*, trans. Albert Mugrdich Wolohojian (New York: Columbia University Press, 1969); and *Iskandarnamah: A Persian Medieval Alexander-Romance*, trans. Minoo S. Southgate (New York: Columbia University Press, 1978).

India, 300 B.C.

STUDENT LIFE IN ANCIENT INDIA

Jeannine Auboyer

Ancient Indian society was dominated by an extremely rigid Hindu caste system. Individuals belonged to hereditary groups that were socially separated from other groups by strict regulations and restrictions. Every Indian was required to follow a hereditary occupation set down and perpetuated by the caste system. The social order that evolved in ancient India, although strict, did provide a sense of order to one of antiquity's most diverse civilizations. Originally the system was composed of four castes. At the top was the class of Brahmans, or priests. Next came the ksatriyas, *or warriors and nobles. Below them were the* vaisyas, *or merchants and farmers. Lowest of all were the* sudras, *or serfs. Each class possessed its own particular function in this social scheme.*

Every facet of life, including education, was affected by the social organization. The official pursuit of knowledge was available only to the three upper classes. Education in ancient India, although somewhat restricted by the caste system, was extremely effective. Despite an emphasis on philosophy, great strides were made in the sciences. Knowledge of chemistry, astronomy, and mathematics, in particular, was highly developed in the ancient period and, proportionally, exceeded the general state of knowledge prevailing in other ancient civilizations.

The following excerpt from Jeannine Auboyer's Daily Life in Ancient India *offers an interesting insight into India's educational structure. From her description of the daily activities of students and the instructional methods employed by teachers, a picture emerges of a very rigorous, disciplined, and productive educational system. The author, while stressing the ceremonial and moral aspects involved in a formal education, also reveals the human side of a student's life.*

READING QUESTIONS

1. What was the Brahmanic initiation and what did it signify?

2. What were the Brahmanic "schools" like?

3. What was taught in these schools?

4. What seems to have been the point of this education?

5. What other types of schools were there in ancient India?

hen a boy reached the age of four or five, he had to leave aside his childish games and start learning the alphabet. For the next few years he was taught reading and elementary arithmetic, either by a tutor who gave him lessons at home (which was the case in brāhmaṇ families and in the families of averagely well-off *kṣatriyas),* or else by going to the village school or the local school in his town.

The school for giving elementary instruction was usually attached to the neighbouring brāhmaṇic temple, and consisted of a house built as a quadrilateral around a central courtyard planted with a few banana- and mango-trees; the house served also as a home for the teacher. The classes were held in the open air. The teacher, rod in hand, sat on a low stool, surrounded by groups of pupils squatting on the ground. Each child held on his knees a small board, on which he traced, with the aid of a reed pen and a little pot of ink by his side, the figures and letters which the teacher demonstrated. A cage containing a parrot would stand in one corner of the courtyard, and the teacher's *vīṇā* hung on one of the walls. When the lesson was over, the boys had a recreation period during which they were taught wrestling and archery. This was followed by a rest period, when the children sat on stools and recited by heart whole passages from the texts that they had been taught earlier that day.

But these were only preliminary exercises. The child did not form part of the Āryan community prior to his brāhmaṇic initiation, and was not entitled to ritual instruction.

THE BRĀHMAṆIC INITIATION

This initiation was restricted to the first three castes. The age at which it was undergone depended on the caste, being eight in the case of a brāhmaṇ, eleven for a *kṣatriya* and twelve for a *vaiśya.* It was a most important sacrament, called *upanayana* or 'second birth', and opened the way to the ritual instruction which was indispensable for a child if he was to become a

From Jeannine Auboyer, *Daily Life in Ancient India* (New York: Macmillan, 1966), pp. 166–176.

grhastha eventually. This, then, was the beginning of an entirely new life and was considered a most solemn occasion.

It took place at various seasons, according to the caste: in spring for a brāhman, in summer for a *kṣatriya,* and in autumn for a *vaiśya.* In the same way, the ritual varied for the three castes, that involving the brāhmans being the most comprehensive.

Since the day of the ceremony must necessarily be a lucky date, it was carefully fixed after astrological calculations. Early in the morning, the postulant completed a careful toilet. The barber shaved his skull smooth all around the ritual topknot. Then he was given a meal. After this he decked himself out with his finest ceremonial clothes and accessories.

During this time, his future spiritual teacher (*guru*)— who was due to officiate at the ceremony and supervise its successive stages—had arrived, accompanied by his assistants, all fellow-brāhmans. He had already celebrated a morning service. Now, parents, servants and guests were grouped around the sacred fire to await the young boy's arrival. Near the hearth were arranged the objects necessary to his initiation: a stone (perhaps a millstone), a new garment, a black antelope skin, a sacred cord, a belt, and a cane made of *palāśa* wood (*Butea frondosa*) or *bilva* wood (*Aegle marmelos*). The guru had also ensured that there was a sufficient supply of logs for the sacred fire.

The postulant took his place next to his future teacher; they both stood side by side, their hands clasped, and the guru turned his face successively east and west. While murmuring appropriate formulas, he then invited the neophyte to mount the stone, stepping onto it with his right foot first, and pronounced the wish that the boy should remain as firm and stable as the stone beneath him. After this, the guru removed the garment that the boy was wearing and made him knot around his loins the new cloth that he had got ready beforehand, while using ritual phrases to wish him long life. Then he draped the sacred 'thread' (*yajñopavīta*) over the boy's left shoulder, and under his right arm. This cord consisted of three threads, each of nine twisted strands; the new initiate was bound to wear it throughout his life, and never to remove it or break it, under pain of a severe penance. The guru now presented the boy with his belt, and knotted it three times successively around his waist. Finally, he placed over his new pupil's shoulders the antelope skin which was to serve him as a cloak and endow him symbolically with strength and valour.

Master and pupil then engaged in a dialogue, during which their future relationship was defined. Cupping his hands, the guru had them filled with water by one of his assistants, while the child said to him: 'I have come here to become a student (*brahmacārin*). Initiate me. I wish to be a student, under the inspiration of the god Savitṛ.' By way of reply, the guru asked him: 'What is your name?' 'I am called _____ ' replied the pupil, pronouncing in public for the first time the secret name given him at birth. The guru continued: 'Do you descend from the *gotra* of the sage _____ ?', mentioning the name of the line's supposedly original ancestor. 'I do descend from the *gotra* of that sage.' 'Do you declare that you are a *brahmacārin?'* 'I declare that I am a *brahmacārin,'* Then the guru sprinkled the water that he had been holding in his cupped hands over the boy's joined hands, three times, while pronouncing his new name and saying: 'I initiate you.' Immediately after this, he grasped the child's right hand between his own and murmured a series of *mantras* designed to commend his new pupil to the gods, so that they might bless his progeny, and endow him with strength, wealth, good health and mastery of the Vedic science. Then he made the boy turn round in a complete circle while looking up at the sun, thus repeating the ritual which the father had carried out soon after his birth. Next, he touched the boy over the heart, expressing the hope that his new pupil should feel affection for him and that their two natures might prove well-matched. Then he asked him: 'Whose *brahmacārin* are you?' 'Yours,' replied the child respectfully. 'I am your guru,' confirmed the master. The latter now walked silently around the ritual fire, with his pupil on his right, touched him over the heart once again, and repeated the circling of the fire. Finally, placing his hand on the young initiate's shoulder, he recited to him briefly a list of the duties he would be required to perform during the ensuing months: keeping the sacred fire alight, drinking only water, helping domestically in the hermitage, forgoing any sleep during the daytime, and remaining silent until he had replenished the supply of fuel for the fire.

The second part of the ceremony took place either immediately following the first part or, alternatively, one year later. In this, the initiate was taught the sacred formula (*Gāyatrī*) which he would later have to pronounce during each daily rite when he had become a master of the house. Seated by the side of his guru, the new initiate said to him: 'Recite, if you please.' The master contented himself with pronouncing the supremely sacred syllable which comprehends all the others: '*Ōm.'* Following the pattern of the ritual, the pupil continued: 'Recite the *Savitr.'* And the guru chanted the formula of the daily service: 'Let us think on the lovely splendour of the god Savitr [the Sun], that he may inspire your minds.' To complete the ceremony, the master had his pupil swallow three mouthfuls of water, then handed his cane to him and walked alone round the fire while the pupil heaped logs on it.

The ceremony was over. While the guru was being presented with a cow (or its equivalent value), as well as the garment he had removed from his new pupil, the pupil himself had left the assembly, clad in the antelope skin and holding his cane high enough for its tip to be level with his nose. For the first time in his life, he was going to beg his food and that of his guru, a gesture which he would be repeating daily from then on. In actual fact, he went straight to his mother who was only too pleased to provide him with all the provisions he might require, but he still walked to the village afterwards in a symbolic quest for food. On returning, he reported to his guru what he had been able to collect in the way of offerings. Under the latter's supervision, he prepared their meal and, when given permission, ate. For the rest of the day he remained silent.

From now on, he belonged wholly to his guru. He had to follow him into his hermitage, serve him assiduously, and receive his teaching attentively. It amounted, in fact, to several years of austere existence consecrated to celibacy and a study of the sacred texts.

STUDENT LIFE AND TEACHING METHODS

The young boy who had just been initiated and had received the title of *brahmacārin* or 'brāhmaṇ student' had, as a result, left his family to go and live in a hermitage in company with his guru—his spiritual teacher—and, usually, several fellow-students.

Hermitages of this nature were usually situated at the verge of a forest, in some peaceful, isolated spot. They consisted of a few circular bamboo huts thatched with fronds, with a single door on a raised hearth, and lit sometimes by only a small square window. In a suitable place, an area had been carefully weeded and covered with a surface of sand, to be fit to receive in its centre the ritual fire and the small pavilion on columns which served to shelter it.

The students were subject, here, to a rigorous discipline, within the framework of which they received religious and scientific instruction. They slept on a litter of rushes, arose before dawn, and had as their first duty that of greeting their guru reverently by touching his feet. They were required to show total and prompt obedience towards him, standing upright with their hands pressed together whenever they addressed him. The guru was not a tyrant, and made every effort to teach his pupils the rules without ever misrepresenting the truth.

Outside the many hours devoted to study, the students' principal task was to cut the wood needed for the sacred fire, to chop the logs into equally proportioned faggots, to clean the emplacement with their hands, to water it, and to gather from the hearth the cinders which served to execute pious marks on the face and body. Twice a day, morning and evening, the wood-pile had to be replenished; and they, as well as their master, saluted the sun twice a day, as it rose and as it set. It fell to them, also, to go and beg their daily food, barefoot and clad in a dark-coloured tunic or an antelope skin. Their diet was simple and excluded both meat and honey; during periods of fast, they went without salt and spices, and slept on the bare ground. They ate only two meals a day, once in the morning and again in the afternoon. Their toilet was to be undertaken without complacency, and their hair was not shaved but allowed to grow, being rolled into a coil. Like many hermits, they often wore a skirt made from a sort of fibre (*valkala*) obtained by crushing the bark of certain trees between two stones. They were trained to become physically tough: they did not shelter when it rained, and had only their antelope skin to protect them from cold and damp; when they swam across a river, they did not wipe their bodies dry afterwards, even in winter. The equipment in use at the hermitage was so simple as to be rudimentary, consisting almost entirely of ewers for drinking water, protected by filters to keep out insects, water-jugs for washing and cooking purposes, spoons for use in the sacramental rites, and a few axes for chopping wood.

The greater part of the day was set aside for study. At the beginning of his stay, the *brahmacārin* learned to accomplish the rites of the *saṃdhyā* which were celebrated at sunrise, at midday and in the evening; in the course of his first instruction, he learned not only to recite the sacred formulas correctly but also to control his breathing, to breathe in and out through a single nostril, to drink water in ritual fashion, to sprinkle holy water in the prescribed fashion and to pour libations into the ritual fire. After this, the guru taught him the Veda, proceeding from the point of instruction that he had reached in the little school he had attended as a small child. Each day the guru gathered his pupils around him to teach them the Veda. There might be as many as fifteen pupils, and the lessons continued for several hours at a time, while they sat on the ground, attentive to his every word. The method he used consisted in making them repeat correctly after him, word by word, whole passages of sacred script. To ensure that their memory remained perfect, he used mnemonic techniques: each word was repeated independently then together with the word preceding it, then in the reverse order—and each verse was repeated once again before the following one was tackled. Thanks to these exercises, tradition was transmitted orally, and accurately, from one generation to another.

He taught them not only the Veda but also the contingent sciences necessary for a full understanding, that is to say, phonetics, etymology, grammar, prosody, literature, chemistry, astronomy and mathematics. These last three sciences were particularly highly developed in India during that epoch, and proportionately far in advance of the general state of knowledge prevailing in other ancient civilizations: by the sixth century AD, Indian scholars already knew how to extract square roots and cube roots in the classic manner still used today; algebra was in wide use, using sines, cosines and versines, as well as quadratic equations with unknown quantities. Many other knowledges might also be communicated to the young students, including such arts as snake-charming, demonology and divination. The *kṣatriya* at the hermitage were, in addition, taught swordsmanship and archery, as well as the plastic arts, painting, music and dancing, all of these being activities normally forbidden to brāhmaṇs.

At the same time, the guru did his best to instil into his young disciples the moral rules of their respective caste, exhorting them to conquer within themselves all sensuality, anger, jealousy and greed. He preached sobriety to them, and forbade them to indulge in idle gossip, calumny, lying, frivolity or insults towards 'living people'. To this end, he taught them the principles which had been set forth for the use of *brahmacārin* from time immemorial, and encouraged them to apply these precepts by grading his charges in order of their intelligence and amenability. To undertake successfully the weighty task of moulding the character of these young people, it was of course indispensable that the guru himself should be endowed with a solid

Vedic culture and a faultless moral sense. Being descended from a family where teaching was a hereditary occupation, and having been brought up in the same way as his own pupils, he usually possessed the necessary general qualities and took his role to heart. The means of discipline that he made use of were moral and persuasive rather than physical; he regarded corporal punishment as repugnant, and had recourse to it only as a last resort. Also, he refused to accept gifts of money or presents from his pupils, considering that it would be reprehensible for him to be beholden to those whose mentor he was. There did exist, nevertheless, bad masters who not only demanded cash fees but even showed favouritism towards those who paid them the largest amounts. On the other hand, a student was entitled to take legal proceedings against his guru, if he could prove that he had been maltreated. And, in any case, he was free to leave his master at any time.

It was, in fact, quite common for a *brahmacārin* not to stay with one guru for the whole of his student period, but to go from one to another, learning from each what he considered that particular guru was best qualified to teach. The duration of these studies varied considerably; theoretically, twelve years were allowed for each Veda—which would have meant that a comprehensive Vedic instruction would have lasted forty-eight years. Obviously, this period was, in practice, considerably less, although students in their thirties were by no means rare. In any case, these years were not continuous: the scholastic year lasted only five and a half months, or six months at the most, from July to January approximately, but even then the months of study were broken by numerous public holidays. And, in addition, any number of events provided sufficient reason for work to be suspended: thunder and lightning, eclipses, frost, sandstorms; or the birth of a child in the locality, a wrestling match, the death of the village chief; or any one of a series of seasonal festivals. If the most studious initiates regretted these interruptions, there was nothing to stop them pursuing their private studies during the vacation.

The hermitages were not the only centres of higher learning. There were, in addition, several well-known universities where young brāhmaṇs went to attend the lectures of India's most distinguished professors. The most celebrated universities were those of Taxila (in present-day Pakistan), Banāras, and Kāñchī in the south. These were real university cities, containing several clusters of colleges, most of which were subsidized by charitable foundations or royal donations. The number of students living in these university cities was very high: in Banāras, for instance, there were as many as five hundred in a single college. The form of teaching followed the same rules as those that applied in hermitages or with private tutors, and the students performed identical services for their particular professor.

Apart from these brāhmaṇic universities, there were others of equal importance, founded by Buddhists and Jains. The most famous was the university of Nālandā, in the state of Bihār, where novices desiring to enter the Buddhist order were trained, but which also taught the Veda, Hindu philosophy, logic, grammar and medicine. The most celebrated teachers of the time lectured there, and foreign scholars made long stays in the university, so adding to the ferment of intellectual activity. The monasteries and colleges covered a vast expanse of ground, each unit being enclosed within its own outer walls. And, for thirty or forty miles around, the countryside was dotted with hermitages in which several hundred students gathered each year, raising the total number of students in this whole great centre to some five thousand. Huge buildings and smaller pavilions served as residences, kitchens, refectories, store-rooms and cellars; there were also assembly halls and lecture rooms. Pools and artificial lakes had been constructed to provide for bathing and ritual ablutions. A whole population circulated in the streets of this great conglomeration: laics of all ages, women (for some students were married), and even children. The temples and sacred monuments which dominated the surrounding area with their splendour were also places of pilgrimage, where marriages were sometimes celebrated.

The termination of a young man's studies (*samāvartana*) was marked by a series of rites. There was no specific age at which his studies were considered completed; with the *kṣatriya* it was usually at the age of sixteen (but often later than that), since that was the age at which a young man supposedly started growing a beard. Repeating the ceremony of tonsure of his childhood, the student had his cheeks shaved for the first time in a ceremony with the evocative title of 'gift of a cow' (*godāna*) which was, equally, a sacrament. Having proved himself and having completed the normal number of terms, the student asked permission from his guru to leave him and become a *snātaka*, 'one who has bathed'. Having obtained his agreement, he had then to make certain preparations and acquire all the objects that would be needed for the ceremony, for his master as well as for himself. For each of them he obtained two sets of clothing, a turban, a pair of golden ear-rings, a necklace with a precious stone, a pair of wooden sandals, an umbrella, a cane, as well as a garland threaded with seeds for massaging the body, unguents with a sandalwood base, pomade for the eyes, and a piece of wood from a 'pure' tree for the sacrificial fire. Then he bought a cow and assorted foodstuffs to distribute to the brāhmaṇs.

When these preparations were completed, the young man took a ritual bath which enabled him to assume the state of *snātaka*, made a ritual offering of water, and performed an adoration of the sun. The guru then invited him to sit down on a bullock's skin and proceeded to cut his hair and beard, his body hair and finger and toe nails, making a mound of these clippings which he confided to a person considered well-intentioned towards the young man who buried them in a stable or other appropriate place, as his mother had done on the occasion of the ceremony of tonsure when he was three years old.

The young man then cleaned his teeth and performed nasal ablutions so that his mouth and nose should be ritually purified. After he had sprinkled himself with holy water and had sanctified the objects which he would be using from then on, he put on two pieces of clothing, and the necklace which was to ensure him long life and health. Then he anointed his eyes, and put on his ear-rings, as a sign of double protection. After rubbing his hands with ointment, he passed them over his head to ward off headaches, then over his limbs; finally he looked at himself in a mirror. The guru now gave him the turban, the umbrella which would thenceforward symbolize his status as a *snātaka* because it was the symbol of the sky above his head, and, signalling to him to rise, a pair of sandals designed to lead him safely forward and protect him 'from all sides'. Finally he proffered him the bamboo cane which had the same protective character, especially against the wickedness of mankind and the rapacity of thieves. Thus equipped, the student placed on the sacred fire the log he had specially chosen beforehand. He spent the rest of the day meditating in solitude.

The moment of departure was approaching, but his first departure was only a pretence: he climbed into a bullock-cart after touching the yoke and praying that his own limbs would have the same force and vigour, and allowed himself to be carried to the home of a brāhman friend who had prepared a reception for him. He was received with all the honour due a distinguished guest. After this, he returned to his professor's abode to take final leave of him. The guru required him to serve him a meal composed of his favourite dishes. The young man then offered him the presents he had got ready. Finally, he set off on the road leading to his own home and family, being careful to take his first step with the right foot.

As soon as he could see the roof of his home in the distance, he stopped and made obeisance. When passing through the door he paused to pronounce a formula of thanksgiving and to touch the two doorjambs. He saluted his parents with appropriate respect and greeted the other members of his family joyously. He was welcomed with honour and the village organized a splendid reception for him.

In the normal course of things, he would marry immediately on his return and, from being a *snātaka,* would become a *gṛhastha* (a 'master of the house'). ❖

RECOMMENDED READINGS

A more detailed study of ancient Indian education is provided in P. K. Mookerjī, *Ancient Indian Education, Brahmanical and Buddhist* (Livingston, NJ: Orient Book Distributors, 1974). Other texts dealing briefly with education along with other aspects of daily life are Padmini Sengupta, *Everyday Life in Ancient India* (New York: Oxford University Press, 1950), and Yagyendra Bakadur Singh, *Social Life in Ancient India* (New Delhi: Light and Life Publishers, 1981).

THE ROMAN OUTLOOK

OTHER PEOPLES

J.P.V.D. Balsdon

A king rules his people; an emperor rules his peoples. A kingdom, consequently, possesses a commonality of tradition and culture that usually provides a firm base for stability. An empire, by contrast, is a collection of peoples brought together for the most part unwillingly, and its administrators must be constantly concerned with the task of promoting tolerance and establishing institutions to promote and maintain unity. At the same time, however, it must attempt to prevent the ruling class from being absorbed into the subject population. The degree to which an empire can balance these conflicting requirements is often a key to understanding its policies.

One of the more common methods employed by imperial administrators is to pursue an official policy based on tolerance and, if not equality, at least on the assertion that individual merit will be recognized regardless of the individual's race, color, or creed. At the same time, however, the administration condones or even encourages feelings of intolerance and contempt among the rulers. Such feelings might be hidden behind such rationalizations as "White Man's Burden," but they remain no less potent.

The Romans were quite intolerant of other peoples; one might say they were bigoted in many respects. The Romans saw the inhabited world as an island of Roman virtue, bravery, and cultivation, surrounded by a sea of peoples who did not, for one reason or another, reach the standards required for acceptance by the Romans. The Africans were cowardly and mendacious, the Spaniards were brave but uncultured, the Greeks were cultured but effete, the Germans were brave but uncouth, the Jews were learned but arrogant, the Irish had no redeeming trait, and the Syrians were fit only to be incompetent slaves. In fact, the Romans appeared to have a genius for being disgusted by whatever peculiarities they found in other peoples.

How can one account for such different qualities among those whom the Roman stoic philosophers insisted were part of the Brotherhood of Man? The Romans believed that the differences among people were caused by the different environments in which they dwelled. Cold made people brave; heat made them clever. So Germans were brave and stupid, and

African Numidians were clever and cowardly. Abundance made people cultivated; sparseness made them moral. So the British were barbarous, and the Asians generally were effete and insincere. Too much of any influence was quite as pernicious as too little. The Romans, of course, believed that they lived in the best of climes, that happy medium that made people brave and clever, moral and urbane.

This selection stresses the degree to which assimilation of Roman speech and dress, attitudes and manner of living, was considered to be the essential requirement for alien peoples to be accepted by the Romans. And yet the natives of Rome found it difficult to accept the Spaniards Martial and Seneca, and the Asian Strabo. Despite a massive literature produced on the peoples of the empire, despite the frequent travels—official and private—by Romans to the farthest reaches of the empire and beyond, and despite the fact that many Romans had close commercial or social connections with the people of the provinces, the Romans seem never to have developed any clear understanding of their fellow subjects. Prejudice needs ignorance to survive.

READING QUESTIONS

1. What was the greatest failing of Easterners in the opinion of the Romans?

2. How did they regard the inhabitants of Gaul?

3. What was their experience with the Egyptians?

(1) NORTH AND SOUTH

If you were decently educated, you knew that the inhabited world was only in a sense 'flat', being part of a rounded, though not completely spherical, earth: it was an island, as it were, but not quite circular, measuring just under 9,000 miles from East to West and under 4,000 miles from South to North, and surrounded by Ocean, as peripheral voyages of discovery had in large part proved. Were it not for the isthmus connecting Egypt with Arabia, it would consist of two islands. There were various inland seas opening out into Ocean: the Persian Gulf, the Arabian Gulf, the great *mare internum*— the Mediterranean, Adriatic, Aegean and Euxine—and also, opening into the northern Ocean, the Caspian or Hyrcanian Sea.

From J. P. V. D. Balsdon, *Romans and Aliens* (Chapel Hill: University of North Carolina Press, 1979), pp. 59-71.

At one extreme was the frozen North, home of the Hyperboreans; Ireland, whose inhabitants were completely savage and led a miserable life because of the cold, being a fringe-country, due north of Britain. There was the Danube, in summer a river, in winter a frozen highway. There were the long summer days and short nights of the far North, Britons 'content with minimal darkness'. About the North you could believe what you liked; Cassius Dio thought there were people in Scotland, the unclad Caledonii and Maeatae, who, in flight from their enemies, lived for days on end in marshy bogs, only their heads protruding above the surface, kept alive by a diet of marsh weeds. At the other extreme was the torrid South, the country of the Ethiopians, the 'cinnamon country'.

The physique and character of the inhabitants of the southern and northern extremities of the world were profoundly different, the difference deriving from proximity to the sun or remoteness from it.

The southern people—the Ethiopians, the Numidians, the Mauretanians, whose name was thought by a false derivation to derive from the Greek word *mauros,* 'black'—were small (though Pliny oddly describes them as tall) and burnt black by the sun; they were shrill-voiced, strong-legged. The sun drew the blood to their heads; so they were quick-witted. On the other hand they suffered from blood-deficiency and were therefore afraid of losing the small amount of blood that they possessed. In consequence they were like haemophilics, terrified of being wounded; so they made bad fighters in hand-to-hand battle.

The South was the snake country, its menace graphically described by Lucan. It was where the spotted cats and so many of the wild beasts (and hunters) for the Games came from, their transport vividly illustrated in the mosaics at Piazza Armerina in Sicily.

Northerners, on the other hand, were deep-voiced palefaces, full-blooded and as fighters courageous to the point of foolhardiness, warlike but undisciplined. Their humours sank into their legs (so they were tall) and, in the absence of sun, not drawn up into their heads.

Romans were superior to northerners in intelligence, to southerners in physical strength.

(II) EAST AND WEST

There was a great rift between East and West, partially bridged by the Greeks who, though regarded by unsympathetic Romans as easterners, shared—indeed were themselves the origin of—many Roman prejudices.

Together with the prejudices of one half of the world against the other there went a very considerable ignorance. When told of Nero's Olympic victories, the simple Spaniards thought that he had fought and defeated people called Olympians. Greeks in general were as ignorant of the West as they were unanxious to visit it. Germans, of course, and for many the British, were beyond the pale. Galen stated, 'I am no more writing for Germans than for wolves and bears.' And there was disparagement even of a highly cultured city like Lugdunum in Gaul. The younger Pliny was surprised that there were bookshops in the town and Cassius Dio considered its citizens crude and unsophisticated even by Roman standards. Aulus Gellius describes the mocking of a Spanish-born Latin *rhetor* by a number of Greek smarties from Asia Minor, men who were the embodiment of Greek cultural conceit.

East and West had their marvels, often exaggerated in the telling.

In the far East India was a kind of never-never land which you could read about in books as fantastic as *Gulliver's Travels,* in particular in the work of the over-credulous Megasthenes who had actually travelled to Bengal at the time of Seleucus I and had spent a period at the Court of king Candragupta. No story about India was too fantastic to be true—there were people who slept in their ears, for instance—and the country literally flowed with milk and honey. It was the country of the great rivers, the Indus in particular and the Ganges, and of the great animals, elephants and tigers. It had its caste system, the most interesting being the wondermen, the Brahmans, vegetarians, wearing no wool or leather, indeed often no clothes at all, men of immense physical self-control, completely celibate for thirty-seven years (after which they married as many wives as they could, careful not to impart the secrets of their philosophy to them, and bred earnestly) and the Garmanes, medicine men who could determine the sex of unborn children. And there were the naked sophists who made prophecies until they had been proved wrong three times, after which they had to be quiet.

Nearer home was Egypt, whose history extended further into the remote past than that of any other country. Peculiar to Egypt were the pyramids and, greatest wonder perhaps of the whole world, partly because its origin was so uncertain, the Nile flood.

Chief wonder of the West (and North) were the great Atlantic tides; it has even been suggested that Posidonius' prime purpose in going to Cadiz was in order to study them. Many people believed that the migration of the Cimbri from the sea coast in the late second century BC had been caused by a specially large high tide from which they fled.

If westerners were crude and uncultured, they were tough and warlike; softness, effeminacy, lack of enterprise and courage marked the unwarlike oriental. If Roman soldiers on the western frontier of the Empire were tougher than those in the East, that was because the enemy whom they might at any time be called on to confront was so much more formidable. This was something that Tacitus stressed. For roughly 210 years, he wrote in AD 98, Rome had been in conflict with the Germans, and the history was one of recurrent Roman disasters. What comparable threat was offered by the Parthians?

Valerius Maximus, describing the decadent conduct of Metellus Pius and his suite in Spain in the seventies BC, wrote, 'And this not in Greece or Asia, by whose luxury severity itself might be corrupted, but in rough (*horrida*), warlike (*bellicosa*) Spain.'

Martial contrasted the tough Spaniard (himself) with the cissy Greek. Troops recruited in the East were shocked in AD 69 by the rough appearance and crude speech of delegates from the western legions. For themselves, conscious of the good things of life which they enjoyed, the eastern legions greeted with horror the thought of transfer to the West; they had only to think of the weather for a start.

The oriental's dress was unmanly, the burnouse, and so was his way of fighting with bow and arrow, a matter of tip and run, in contrast to cold steel, which was the essence of fighting in the West and the North, 'where men were men'.

The softness of the oriental was partly a matter of heredity, the result of subservience through long generations to the rule of kings—'Let Syria be slave, and Asia and the East, which is accustomed to kings'—and it was partly environmental, induced by the soft climate and by the luxury products of the East, the rich and extravagant things in life, the scents, the preservatives, exotic tastes, exotic smells, rich jewels. Silk came from the East, and fine linen, by contrast with the coarse but serviceable woollen garments, smelly cloaks in particular, which came from Spain and Gaul, greasy and so waterproof. Amber was unusual, an elegant extravagance which came from the North, not from the East.

Easterners displayed all the decadence of over-civilisation, as Tacitus might have written when he belittled the 'eastern peril' by contrast with the menace which was constituted by the free Germans.

Of that 'decadence', a stern Roman might have said, there were two outward and visible signs.

The first was the ecstatic character of all the eastern mystery religions, so different from the man-to-man relationship of a Roman with his traditional gods.

The second—not that a Roman would so have described it—was a surfeit of good manners, a tendency to agree, however insincerely, with what was said rather than commit the rudeness of disagreement, a readiness to give presents and to give them so charmingly that, if a Roman was half-asleep, he failed to recognise that what he was receiving was, by Roman standards, nothing less than a bribe. Sometimes, of course, the presents were in fact gross bribes and recognised as such by both parties to the transaction; but sometimes the Roman law against receiving bribes was almost unduly strained—in the case of Julius Bassus, for instance, 'that simple and incautious man', who as governor of Bithynia technically broke the law, but whose action had plenty of precedents. People in Bithynia sent him presents on his birthday and at the Saturnalia and he in return sent presents to them. What he called presents the prosecution in Rome described as 'theft and extortion'.

Flattery may be an exaggeration, it may be a corruption, of good manners, and flattery which had come easily to suggest to the Hellenistic monarchs that they were more than human and in fact divine, which had created the institution of ruler-cult, could not easily adopt a different attitude to Roman administrators, once Rome annexed the Hellenistic kingdoms into her empire. Good men, Flamininus in Greece, the admirable Mucius Scaevola in Asia, were so treated, Flamininus being made the object of religious cult, Scaevola giving his name to newly established games, the 'Mucia' in Asia. Even better men (perhaps) remembered that they were Romans and refused the proffered honours—Cicero, for instance, who in Cilicia refused to accept the dedication of statues and four-horse chariots in his honour. Bad men were just as likely to be honoured, in the hope that such flattery might effect an improvement in them. 'Verria' were established by the Greeks in Sicily.

The embarrassment which attended such honours in the Republic ended with the institution of the principate, after which there was at Rome, to eastern eyes, one super-Hellenistic king, the Emperor. His name was associated in cult with Rome (itself already a somewhat nebulous object of worship) and all was well. The new imperial cult was an acceptable form of loyalty, an effective bond of unity, which was allowed, with government encouragement, to spread even into Italy, and the western provinces.

Not, of course, that the emperor was a god in his lifetime; official policy was absolutely clear on that point. But in the East the exuberance of good manners (or flattery) could not so easily be checked. We possess the edict in which on his accession the emperor Claudius explained, in accepting certain honours and refusing others, from the city of Alexandria, that he was not a god or anything like it. The edict was published, introduced with a short preamble, by the Prefect of Egypt, 'that everybody might have the chance of reading the words of the god Caesar'. The governor obviously chose to forget for a moment that he was a Roman and instead to address the Alexandrians in their own language.

There were, of course, ways of honouring people short of cult. In the second century AD we know that the Rhodians greatly enjoyed erecting statues in honour of individuals from whom they had received benefits. As a result the island was littered with such statues, three thousand of them, and as new statues cost money, what could be better (or cheaper) than to take an old statue, the statue of some forgotten worthy of the past, erase the dedication and give it a new name and inscription?

No manners are so good as to be able to resist evil communications; and so, to western thinking, the influence of the East on the West was always a corrupting influence. This was shown by the degeneration of Macedonians in the Hellenistic world and by the disintegration of the migrant Gauls after they settled down in Asia Minor. And in the eyes of the Roman moralist this was the source of the degeneration of Roman morals from the time when Roman troops penetrated the Greek East in the early second century BC.

The intellectual and cultural tide flowed all the time from East to West. Astronomy and arithmetic were discoveries of the Phoenicians, geometry of the Egyptians; humane culture was derived by Rome from Greece. Then from the East came oriental religions, astrology and the false trickery of magic (*magicae vanitates*). All that the West exported to the East, the Roman legal system apart, was a taste for gladiators, a taste which, for all its cultural heritage, the East was anything but reluctant to acquire.

If a Roman looked round the world, he saw *humanitas* in Greece and—not every Greek would have agreed with him—in Rome (perhaps, also, in a vague way in distant India), and he found it elsewhere in those who had been properly romanised (in some cases, Tacitus would have said, over-romanised). These were the children of light; everywhere else was shrouded in the darkness of barbarism. Inside the Empire Cicero contrasted the barbarous Africans, Spaniards and Gauls on the one hand with the Greeks of Asia Minor on the other; the Sardinians, too, were *homines barbari*. Northern peoples were particularly barbaric in Strabo's opinion, having no civilised traditions, though in religion at least the Romans had eliminated some barbarisms from Gaul. Once you crossed the Rhine, there was no civilisation whatever: *immanitas barbariae*. Germans, by Velleius Paterculus' account—and he had fought against them—were able to talk (they were born liars) and were physically recognisable as human beings, but that was all. Thracians were particularly uncivilised, a people without comprehension of freedom in the view of Apollonius of Tyana, best left to tyrants, the only form of government they were fit for. In the East, Armenians were *barbari,* and so were Parthians.

(III) OTHER PEOPLES IN PARTICULAR

The nearest non-Romans were the inhabitants of Sicily, Sardinia and Corsica. Sicilians, who were largely Greek, were famed for their sharp intelligence and clever wit. At the other extreme, Sardinians, ferocious, unattractive brigands and congenital liars, this being a part of their Punic legacy, had no better name than had the climate of their island. There was an old saying in Rome, 'Sardinians for sale; if one is bad, the others are worse.' Yet, as inscriptions show, they were recruited in large numbers for the Roman navy; they evidently made good sailors.

Corsicans were less notorious, as their island was less productive and more thinly populated. They spoke a barbarous language. Diodorus said that they made good slaves, Strabo that they made very bad slaves indeed, since it was impossible to train them satisfactorily; you might buy one for a trifling sum, but you would always regret your purchase.

Spain and Gaul alike were divided into an early civilised and romanised South (Baetica, the earliest district outside Italy to receive Roman settlers, and Gallia Narbonensis which was 'more like Italy than a province') and a tougher North and West, the effort of whose conquest was not forgotten— Caesar's campaigns in Gaul and, in Spain, two centuries of horrible warfare before Augustus beat the Spaniards to their knees in 25 BC (and Agrippa had to beat them to their knees again six years after that). The fine military qualities of Spaniards were never depreciated by Roman writers. However, they settled down quickly, adopted the Latin language, provided Rome with soldiers, literary men and administrators and were, in general, the best possible advertisement for romanisation. They had only one colourful peculiarity, apart from the golden wool of their sheep and the infestation of their country by rabbits, *cuniculosa Celtiberia:* they cleaned their teeth in urine, and even bathed in it.

Gauls were the better—the more civilised, that is to say—the nearer they were to Rome. Nearest of all were the Gauls of the Po valley who after 90 BC were not Gauls any longer, but Latins and, after Julius Caesar, Romans. These were the Gauls whose highest ambition it was, according to the elder Cato, to be good soldiers and good talkers—Carcopino's Frenchmen who, under Julius Caesar, conquered France and did so much to build the Roman empire. They did indeed form the bulk of Caesar's legionaries, and they provided the first Gallic senators whose elevation so deeply shocked the fastidious, Cicero chief among them. And it was Cisalpine Gaul which supplied late Republican and early imperial Rome with the outstanding literary talent of a Catullus, a Virgil and a Livy.

Over the Alps, Narbonese Gaul, unique already in being a western outpost of Greek civilisation, soon caught the Roman infection. Massilia (Marseilles) had been Rome's oldest ally in the days of the city's freedom and, after Claudius, the province's Roman senators, like those from Sicily and, to the end of the second century, those of no other province, were allowed to return home on visits to their property without having to seek the emperor's permission. The reputation of Marseilles' highly respected university was established early, with prominent Romans among its students and from here culture was to spread northwards into the backwoods, where one day there would be important universities at Bordeaux and at Trier.

To the north of Narbonensis, the huge, long-haired, pale, often blue-eyed and trousered Gauls, addicted—unlike the Romans—to the wearing of gold and silver ornaments, necklaces and bracelets, had two weaknesses: they were impetuous and improvident and, therefore, terrifying as they might be, men and women alike, at first confrontation, they collapsed quickly if faced by resolute opposition; they lacked staying power. Moreover, they were not adaptable to climates and conditions apart from those in which they were nurtured and in particular were unable to support heat or thirst or to exercise moderation in the enjoyment of—for them, exotic—luxuries like hot baths, cooked food and wine.

Northern Gauls were not clever; they were highly credulous and they were braggarts (and yet, with all this, Diodorus thought them intelligent). They had their bards and their Druids whom, as the focus of Gallic nationalism and as perpetrators of human sacrifice, the Romans made it their policy to eliminate. Their young men, willing participants in homosexual practices, were liberal with their favours.

A sportsman would urge you not to forget that Gaul produced the finest breed of sporting dog in the world, appropriately enough since every kind of hunting flourished in Gaul, beagling, fox-hunting and stag-hunting. Fine hounds, and fine horses.

The British were hardly civilised and were inhospitable, only better than the Irish, who were without any redeeming virtues whatever. The one fact generally known about the British was that they painted their bodies with woad. A girl of British extraction who could pass at Rome as city-born—and there was one in Martial's time—was a prodigy. Still, Agricola saw virtue in some of the better-class young men in Britain who accepted the new educational opportunities which he offered; they might not acquire the same depth of culture as their counterparts in Gaul, but they were more quick-witted. We have an instance of the quick wit of one prominent Scotch woman, who in repartee was more than a match for the empress Julia Domna.

Thought of Britain provoked the question: had the place really been worth conquering at all? Would the empire not in fact have been the better without it? There was kudos in the fact that, by including it, the Roman empire extended beyond Ocean; but economically it brought no gain and was, in fact, a dead loss.

The inhabitants of the Balkan countries up to the Danube were generally considered to be rough, tough and uncouth. It was unusual, Polybius wrote, to find a Thracian who was sober or gentle. Velleius Paterculus, who served under Tiberius in the suppression of the Pannonian revolt of AD 6, had the poorest opinion of Pannonians, as indeed of other northern peoples; the Pannonians were not to be trusted; they had adopted Roman ways too quickly and, as a result, their culture was only skin-deep. We have Ovid's unflattering account of the people who lived on the western shores of the Black Sea.

Once you moved into the hinterland of Asia Minor, you were in the country that the slaves came from, the people so roundly abused by Cicero in his defence of Flaccus. What were the common sayings? 'A Phrygian is the better for a beating'; 'Try the poison on a Carian.' But Cappadocians were the commonest target of abuse. They spoke vile Greek, if they spoke Greek at all, and though they were often tall and made good litter-bearers (as did Bithynians and Syrians), they were as a general rule both stupid and dumb. Abusing Piso, in whose consulship he had been exiled, Cicero said, 'Insensitive, tasteless, tongue-tied, a dawdling apology for a man, a Cappadocian, you might think, who had just been picked out of a crowd of slaves under the auctioneer's hammer.' Paphlagonians, according to Lucian (who, as a Syrian, should have known what he was talking about) were 'rich and uneducated'.

The Syrian was the slave *par excellence.* 'Like Jews,' Cicero said, 'Syrians were born slaves'; some had been sold into slavery by their families. Indeed Syria and Asia Minor supplied the largest number of slaves whose country of origin can be identified.

Syria provided Rome with tall litter-bearers—also with bakers, cooks, hairdressers, singers and dancers. Syrians were sharp, quick to learn but not always impressively honest. Artful Dodgers, in fact.

But there was a very positive side to Syrian enterprise. The Phoenicians, after all, had been the greatest sailors in Mediterranean history, and in the early Empire Syrians (like Arabs in the East) were great traders. 'The Syrian slave came early to the West; the Syrian trader followed.'

From being provincial subjects, some acquired the Roman citizenship, the gallant ship-captain Seleucus of Rhosos from Octavian as triumvir. Finally, by the end of the second and start of the third centuries AD there was Syrian blood in the imperial family itself.

An origin by which a man might feel embarrassed? So Severus Alexander is said to have felt. Lucian, on the other hand, made no bones about it.

With the Syrians as natural slaves Cicero coupled the Jews. Jews were 'superstitiosi' and their 'superstition' involved a great number of distasteful peculiarities—the recurrent Sabbath, and excuse for idleness, circumcision, dietary tabus and there was Jewish proselytising activity, for the exposition of their scriptures in the synagogue had the attraction of a philosophy lecture and was something unparallelled in other cults. But what was worse was Jewish exclusiveness, their division of humanity into Jews and Gentiles, just as the Greeks divided humanity into Greeks and Barbarians. This exclusiveness, easily construed as misanthropy, was nowhere more evident than in their refusal to participate in the gaiety and rejoicing of imperial festival-days. Greeks had never liked Jews and, where there were large Jewish communities in a single city, Alexandria for instance or Antioch in Syria, they were like oil and water; there was no mixture. Nor was any love lost between Jews and their Arab neighbours. No pagan writer, Greek or Roman, had any great sympathy with the Jews.

Concerning the Arabs there was a nice fable that once upon a time the god Hermes' cart, loaded with mischief of all sorts, broke down in their country and was plundered by the natives. This explained why Arabs were 'liars and impostors, who did not know the meaning of truth'.

Egyptians generally were regarded by the Romans with hatred and contempt, and sometimes little distinction was made between Egyptians proper and Egyptian Greeks. 'An unwarlike and treacherous people', according to Florus; basely abject at one extreme, rashly foolhardy at the other, according to Achilles Tatius.

Romans of the senatorial class can have known little of Egypt itself except at second hand. In the Republic it was a foreign country and in the Empire senators were not allowed to visit the province without the express permission of the Emperor. It is significant that the younger Pliny, a prominent figure at the Roman Bar, did not know that Roman citizenship could not be given to an Egyptian unless he first possessed the citizenship of Alexandria. Augustus had barred the Roman Senate to Egyptians and it was not until the time of Caracalla that the rule was broken.

Yet clever Egyptians—'eruditi' is Apuleius' epithet for Egyptians (*Flor.* 6), and nobody doubted the existence of such men—climbed to positions of importance in Rome, favourites of the emperor to whom they owed their position, but of few others. There was the teacher Apion under Gaius, an Egyptian who had acquired Alexandrian citizenship, and, more important, Crispinus, a native of Memphis, who was perhaps Prefect of the Praetorian Guard under Domitian, a man to whom Martial toadied and whose memory Juvenal flogged, and there was the renegade Alexandrian Jew, Tiberius Alexander, also perhaps Prefect of the Guard at the end of his very distinguished career, a man whose statue, Juvenal suggested, was best used as a public lavatory.

Roman writers who visited Egypt, not being senators, were Seneca as a young man (his uncle was Roman governor) and Juvenal, who was exiled by Domitian, perhaps to Syene; his unqualified hatred for Egypt and Egyptians is expressed in his fifteenth satire.

In the eyes of most Romans Egypt consisted of Alexandria and a vast hinterland, the country inhabited by native Egyptians, while the population of Alexandria consisted predominantly of Greeks and Jews who were always at one another's throats. The Jews had the bad qualities of Jews everywhere; the Alexandrians, whether slave-children from the gutter or garrulous public representatives, were smart-alecs, boastful, ineffective, cheekily impertinent, particularly to those in authority whether in Egypt or in Rome, where their puerile abuse of Roman emperors who sat in judgment on them is recorded in the surviving *Acts of the Pagan Martyrs.* Particularly in the fact that until Septimius Severus they had no senate, they thought that they were discriminated against by Rome.

Concerts and horse-racing roused them to a pitch of frenzy.

A Roman who was in Egypt at the time of Julius Caesar was the author of the *Bellum Alexandrinum.* He wrote, 'If I was briefed to defend Alexandrians and to establish that they were neither treacherous nor irresponsible, I could make a long speech, but it would be a wasted effort.'

Yet the Alexandrians' very beautiful city was the largest in the empire after Rome, and the most cosmopolitan, a gateway to the deep South and to the far East.

Egypt was the home of the cult of Isis and of Serapis, which attracted converts in all parts of the Mediterranean. It was the home also, and the fact was notorious, of fantastic animal-worship of a widespread parochial kind; here one animal or bird was worshipped, there another: the cat, the ichneumon (which ate crocodile eggs), the dog, the hawk, the ibis, the wolf, the crocodile, the eagle and the goat. Besides which there were the great cults of the bull Apis at Memphis and, second in importance, of the bull Mneuis at Heliopolis.

'Who knows not what monsters demented Egypt worships?'

The devotion of Egyptians to animals was such as to inspire the admiration of the most sentimental of English spinsters. They denied themselves food for the animals' sake.

They did not display such considerate affection towards their fellow-men but instead behaved frequently as bloodthirsty fanatics. A Roman soldier was lynched in the late Republic because he accidentally killed a cat. The frenzied conflict of two villages described by Juvenal in his fifteenth satire ended in a cannibalistic orgy and blood was often shed as a result of religious animosity. When the Kynopolites (inhabitants of Dogstown and dog-worshippers) ate a snouted fish (*oxyrhynchus*), the Oxyrhynchites had their revenge by sacrificing and eating a dog. This in Plutarch's time, who records that peace was only restored after intervention by the Roman authorities. In the days of Egyptian independence the bestial savagery of civil conflict in Alexandria—where many of the offenders must have been Greeks—was recorded with horror by Polybius.

Africa, though it was in due course to produce lawyers, administrators, even emperors, and writers of genius and to possess in architecture the finest of Roman monuments, was a province whose inhabitants did not enjoy the highest cultural esteem. There were Numidians, Berbers and descendants of the Carthaginians, whose language was still widely spoken, fickle and untrustworthy, surviving examples of *Punica fides*. Africans, too, were thought of as over-sexed, like some of their wild animals whose mongrel offspring from male animals of other species produced the famous Greek observation which in Latin has become proverbial, 'Ex Africa semper aliquid novi'. Africa was the country of two women of fatal charm, Dido in legend and Sophonisba in romantic history, to whom the young Massinissa so badly lost his heart that Scipio had to lecture him on the virtue of self-control—Massinissa who survived a broken heart when young and was still fathering children in his late eighties. Such was Hannibal's self-control in refusing the enjoyment of captive women as bedfellows that, Justin states, nobody would believe that he had been born in Africa.

African women were very fertile, commonly producing twins, just as Egyptian women, thanks to the water of the Nile, produced triplets.

(IV) PATRONS AND CLIENTS

Popular generalisations apart, anthropological curiosity about different peoples on the part of educated Romans was satisfied by books like Strabo's or Pomponius Mela's on Geography, by wide-ranging histories like that of Posidonius or by encyclopedias like the *Natural Histories* of the elder Pliny. Much of the information available to such writers came from the first-hand records of Roman administrators; we have seen what Velleius Paterculus thought of the Germans and Pannonians and what the author of the *Bellum Alexandrinum* thought about the character of the Alexandrians. More importantly, there were the memoirs of important generals like Suetonius Paulinus and Domitius Corbulo in the Empire, who naturally took a vivid interest in the character of the peoples against whom they campaigned, just as Caesar, whether or not all that appears in the *Bellum Gallicum* was written by him, showed an anthropological interest in the Gauls, the Germans and the British. There were Romans, obviously, who had a great gift for understanding and getting on well with particular native peoples, the elder Africanus and Sertorius in Spain, Rutilius Rufus in Greek Asia Minor and Agricola in Britain.

Among the aristocracy in Rome there were individuals and families who enjoyed a particular relationship with particular provinces, a relationship derived from personal administration in a province (Cicero's close relationship with Sicily dated from the year when he was one of the two quaestors in the island) or inherited, perhaps as a consequence of the achievement of an ancestor in the province's conquest; in this way the Fabii and Domitii Ahenobarbi had a particular interest in southern Gaul and the Claudii Marcelli in Sicily. Or it might derive from a leading Roman's appearance on behalf of the provincials in the Roman law courts. In such cases the relationship was, in Roman language, the relationship of patron and clients. And though this relationship lost much of its reality in the Empire, when the Emperor emerged as a universal father-figure, leading advocates in the courts might still establish a close connexion with a particular province as a result of their advocacy of that province's interests, as was the case—*patrocinii foedus*—of the younger Pliny and Spanish Baetica.

Through administration in a province a Roman might have a bond of hospitality (*hospitium*) with particular provincial families, and provincial cities and even provinces themselves sometimes adopted a senator or Eques as 'patron', a relationship for which there is much inscriptional evidence, which descended from generation to generation in the patron's family.

Such relationship might give a boost to *dignitas* and be something to boast about in the courts, but there is no evidence that it resulted in any particularly close knowledge of the provincials themselves.❖

RECOMMENDED READINGS

Literature on the subject of Roman racial and ethnic attitudes is scattered, and much of it is untranslated. The work from which the selections was drawn is the fullest treatment in English on the subject. Those interested in the subject would do well to begin with a classic work on Roman life and customs: Jerome Carcopino, *Daily Life in Ancient Rome: The People and the City at the Height of the Empire,* trans. E. O. Lorimer; ed. Henry T. Rowell (New Haven: Yale University Press, 1968). The granting of Roman citizenship was a point at which the Roman attitudes toward their subject peoples became explicit. The standard treatment of the subject is that of A. N. Sherwin-White, *The Roman Citizenship,* 2nd ed. (Oxford, UK: Clarendon Press, 1973).

Many Roman authors discuss "aliens" in passing, but Tacitus, *The Germania of Tacitus,* ed. Rodney Potter Robinson (Hildesheim and New York: Georg Olms Verlag, 1991), provides an unusually full picture of the Germans living along the Rhine and Danube frontiers. In so doing, he exemplifies many of the attitudes of an educated Roman of the times. Steven Drummond and Lynn Nelson, *The Western Frontiers of Imperial Rome* (Armonk, NY: M.E. Sharpe, 1994), draw on Tacitus and others in their evaluation of Roman attitudes. Noting that the Romans seemed concerned with minor points such as height, hairstyle, beards, and whether one wore trousers or togas, the authors conclude that such preoccupations are the essential elements of prejudice.

THE POSITION OF WOMEN IN HAN CHINA

T'ung-tsu Ch'u

Women remained in the political, social, and economic background in most ancient societies, even though their functions were recognized as extremely important. In few cases, however, do we possess as detailed an account of the role and status of women as that provided in Lessons for Women *by Pan Chao, China's first woman scholar. Women in ancient China were greatly restricted by a complex web of law and tradition, and were taught almost from birth to be subservient to men. The ideal female was characterized by a humble, yielding, and respectful attitude toward males, and Pan Chao's work constituted a manual for cultivating such an attitude. It also provides an excellent source of information on the status of women in Han society, and T'ung-tsu Ch'u draws heavily on it in the following selection.*

The Han Empire (206 B.C.–A.D. 220) was an authoritarian state in which the original principles of Confucius were elaborated into a blueprint for a highly structured and compliant society based on the traditional Chinese extended family. We have seen how Tu Wei-ming's account of Confucian philosophy, in "The Confucian Tradition in Chinese History," emphasizes the virtue of filial piety and should not be surprised to learn that the author based this view on a treatise composed during the Han period and ascribed to Confucius. Nor should we be surprised to note that Pan Chao's guide for female deportment was written during the height of Han power.

In Han China, the subservient role of women was dictated by the tradition that the woman left her father's family to join that of her husband. Women born into a family lacked regard because they would eventually leave it, and those who had married into it were always considered almost as intruders whose presence was tolerated only because they were necessary to worship at the ancestral tomb and perpetuate the family line.

READING QUESTIONS

1. What was the woman's proper role in the family? Were there exceptions to this?

2. What was the economic role of women?

3. How were relationships different in those families allied by marriage
    with the imperial house?

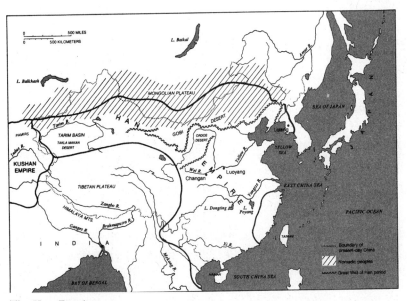

The Han Empire

WOMAN'S STATUS IN THE FAMILY

Humility and weakness were the patterns of behavior set for women in ancient Chinese society under the principle that women were inferior to men.
Pan Chao elaborated on this point in her famous *Lessons for Women:*

> In ancient times, people put a baby girl on the ground on the third day
> after her birth. . . . To lay the baby on the ground signifies that she is infe-
> rior and weak, and that she should humble herself before others. . . . To be
> modest, yielding, and respectful; to put others first, and herself last; not to
> mention it when she does a good deed; not to deny it when she commits a

From T'ung-tsu Ch'u, "The Position of Women in Han China," in Jack L. Dull, ed., *Han Social Structure* (Seattle and London: University of Washington Press, 1972), pp. 49–62.

wrong; to bear disgrace and humiliation; and always to have a feeling of fear—these may be said to be the ways in which she humbles herself before others. . . .

Yin and yang are not of the same nature; men and women behave differently. Rigidity is the virtue of the yang; yielding is the function of the yin. Strength is the glory of men; weakness is women's good quality. Thus in self-cultivation, nothing equals respect for others; in avoiding confrontation with strength, nothing equals compliance. Therefore it is said that the way of respect and compliance is woman's great li (proper rule of conduct).

Women were always taught to be submissive to the authority of men. The I-li and the Li-chi mention three stages of subordination for a woman: to her father when she is a girl, to her husband when married, and to her son after the death of her husband. Since every child was under the absolute control of the father, the first stage of subordination needs no special comment. The real subordination to a man began with marriage: the husband had full authority over his wife. By the time of the Han the recognition of such authority by society led to the development of the theory of san-kang, the three dominations. Under this theory the husband should dominate his wife in much the same way the ruler dominates his ministers and the father dominates his sons. Thus a wife was expected to serve her husband respectfully and obediently. Pan Chao instructed her daughters that a wife should never treat with contempt, quarrel with, or scold her husband. Such actions, as she saw it, would anger her husband and destroy the harmonious matrimonial relationship.

The model of an obedient wife is the wealthy woman who returned to her father's family all the luxurious garments and ornaments she had received as dowry, and who wore short clothes made of hempen cloth when she learned that her husband was displeased with her and had complained about her way of living. She said to him, "Since I am at your service, I only follow your orders." The case in which both the mother and the son came to apologize to the father and did not dare ascend to the main room until he accepted their apology illustrates the humble submission of the wife and the dignity and authority of the husband. It also suggests that both the wife and the children were under the authority of the family head. Teng Chih, whose son had received a gift from a corrupt official, shaved the head of his wife and his son to acknowledge this fault to Empress Dowager Teng, his younger sister. Since shaving the head, k'un, was a regular punishment in Han times, Teng's action implied that his wife was punished for her failure to fulfill the role of a mother.

But not all women acted passively and subordinately, for we also have records of women of strong personality and extraordinary ability. The daughter of Ma Jung, an outstanding scholar and official, was very eloquent and was able to overturn her husband's arguments when, on their wedding night, he attempted to ridicule her and her father. A woman with a strong personality was usually able to influence her husband directly or indirectly. There are two recorded instances in which a husband's intention to dwell in seclusion was influenced by his wife's encouragement. Occasionally a wife was responsible for changing her husband's whole way of thinking. A young man who found and picked up a piece of gold was ashamed of himself, threw away the gold, and went to study with a teacher when his wife told him it was improper to possess things belonging to others. When he returned home to visit her one year later, she told him that returning before his study was completed was like cutting the unfinished cloth on a loom. Convinced, as well as depressed, by her words, he went back to study and did not return for seven years. Apparently it is not an exaggeration to say that the man owed his education to his wife's efforts and that she greatly influenced his personality.

Usually a wife was allowed to be active only in domestic affairs; she was not supposed to be interested in social and political activities and was not allowed to interfere in such matters, which were considered exclusively men's affairs. However, a woman who had extraordinary determination might take an active part in men's business. An official's wife who was skilled in writing essays and calligraphy frequently wrote letters for her husband. A woman of strong personality might even dominate her husband in his official affairs. When Grand General Ho Kuang sent a representative to tell Imperial Chancellor Yang Ch'ang that they had decided to dethrone the emperor, Yang Ch'ang was so frightened he did not know what to say. Then his wife warned him: "This is an important affair of the empire. Now the Grand General has decided after deliberation and sent one of the Nine Ministers to report it to you. If you do not respond promptly, are not of the same mind as the Grand General, and hesitate without decision, you will be killed first." Then she and her husband talked together with the guest, and Yang Ch'ang promised to obey Ho Kuang's order. Obviously, it was she who made the decision and dominated her husband. However, women of such dominating character and broad insight in politics were rare.

A wife who could manage and dominate her husband was usually respected and looked up to by him. It was said that Liang Chi's beautiful wife was very jealous and was able to manage and control him. She made him remove the Liangs from government positions and replace them with members of her family. He did not dare to keep his concubine openly, and had to hide her child. Finally she seized the concubine, cut off her hair, and beat her. In this unusual situation it seems that the expected "wife-subordinate-to-husband" pattern was reversed.

The status of the mother in the family needs special attention. Theoretically, children were under the authority of their parents, and no distinction was made between father and mother. The children were supposed to be filial to both and obey both. However, the mother's status was conditioned by another basic principle: a wife was inferior to her husband. Thus the mother's status was also inferior to the father's. The point that there was only one supreme head in the family, and that the mother was not as superior as the father, was usually emphasized by ancient scholars. A child wore a full three years' mourning for his father, but he only wore one year's mourning for his mother when the father was still alive. It was explained that since three years' mourning was assigned for the father, the supreme head of the family, the mourning for the mother had to be reduced. Therefore, the mother was also under the control of the family head, the husband and father, and she was expected to obey him. There was no problem when father and mother agreed; but when disagreement and conflict arose, the father's authority took precedence. This point has already been discussed regarding the authority of the parents to arrange the marriages of their children. I have also indicated that both mother and children were under the authority of the same family head.

The problem of the mother's status was more complicated after the death of her husband. Theoretically, no one in the family was superior to a mother after the death of her husband; so she should have had the highest authority. But it was also held that a woman should obey her son after the death of her husband, which was in keeping with the belief that women were inferior to men. So the two theories were in conflict: If a son was to obey the will of his father and mother, how could a mother be expected to obey her son and be subordinate to him? Was there a change in the status of the mother and of the son after the father's death? Since a woman was unlikely to be a family head and it was usually the son who became the head if there were no other senior male members of the family, it seems that there was a change in the son's status when he became a family head. However, it does not follow that there was a change in the mother's status and that the mother was under the son's authority. On the contrary, there are indications that a son was still subject to his mother's authority after the death of his father. The mother's authority over a son is clearly illustrated in "The Peacock Flies to the Southeast." In this poem the mother becomes angry with her son, who wants to keep his wife in the family; finally, on the mother's orders, the wife is sent away. Sometimes a mother even had a voice in her son's public life. Yen Yen-nien, a grand administrator who resorted to severe punishments to maintain law and order, was merciless in killing powerful and evil persons. Once his mother came from her native town to Lo-yang to visit him. She disapproved of his harsh policy and refused to go to his official residence. She allowed him to see her only after he had removed his hat and kowtowed; she then rebuked him and told him to be benevolent to the people, and he again kowtowed and apologized.

In short, there is no evidence to support the theory that a mother was subordinate to her son after the death of the father. I am inclined to think that it would be misleading to treat the so-called mother's subordination and the other two kinds of subordination on the same basis.

WOMEN'S STATUS IN SOCIETY

Professional and Economic Status

Most women engaged in weaving and domestic work; even the wife of an imperial chancellor did some weaving in her home. But women in wealthy families were not usually expected to undertake productive tasks; only the women of poor families had to work. The family's profession generally conditioned the kind of work a woman was supposed to do; the women in farmers' families, for example, usually had to work on the farm. Weaving was the most common profession for women, either to provide clothing for the family or to supplement the family income. Usually women's work provided only a part of the family income, but occasionally a woman had the full responsibility of supporting her family when her husband was not engaged in productive work. For example, the wife of a gambler managed to support his mother. And I have already mentioned the husband who left home and engaged in study for seven years. During his absence his wife wove to support her mother-in-law and sometimes even managed to send supplies to him. It was not uncommon for a woman who had lost her husband to become the sole support of her family, often undergoing great hardship. One widow sold silk fabrics to support herself and her son. Another widow with a twelve-year-old son made a living by making straw sandals in the capital. He was able to study for more than ten years and finally became an official; without his mother's support he would have remained an office boy in the commandery government and would not have had a chance for an official career. Liu Pei was also supported by his widow-mother who made shoes and straw mats.

Some women of well-to-do families engaged in profitable businesses, and such trade sometimes provided opportunities for them to associate with customers of the upper class. A mother who sold pearls frequently went to the family of a princess; because of this connection her son became a paramour of the princess.

The most successful woman entrepreneur in ancient China was a widow whose husband's family owned cinnabar mines in Szechwan and who was able to keep and manage the business. Because of her great wealth she was well known all over the empire and was treated as his guest by the First Emperor of Ch'in, who built a terrace in her honor. But such great success for a woman was unparalleled in Chinese history. It would have been impossible for a woman to accumulate so much wealth if her family had not left the well-developed enterprise to her. However, her managerial ability in operating such a big enterprise should not be overlooked.

Only a few occupations were open to women. Since magic was very popular in Ch'in and Han times, and since there was a division of labor based upon sex, there was a considerable demand for sorceresses. But because sorcery was a humble profession, the status of a sorceress and her family must have been inferior.

The profession of a woman physician was a respected one. Sometimes opportunities for social mobility were given to her family members because of her professional connections with important families. A woman physician was an intimate friend of the wife of the grand general, and through his influence her husband was promoted to a higher post. The brother of one woman physician, who was the personal physician of the empress dowager, was appointed prefect and was later promoted to the post of grand administrator.

Perhaps singing and dancing were the most common professions for girls. Some cities were noted for providing singing and dancing girls, and there were specialists who brought up girls of poor families and trained them to dance and sing. Beautiful girls with such skills were usually sought by the families of nobles, officials, and wealthy commoners. They served as entertainers in the family as well as giving sexual satisfaction to their masters. Since the occupation of these girls was not respected by society, their status was very inferior. However, a singing girl who was able to win the favor of her master sometimes ascended to a superior status and at times even brought social mobility to her father's family. The mother of the First Emperor of Ch'in was originally a dancing girl owned by a wealthy merchant. Empress Wei was originally a singing girl of a princess. Her brother, Wei Ch'ing, became grand general, and her sister's son, Ho Ch'ü-ping, was appointed general (*chiang-chün*), a post next only to Wei Ch'ing's. Empress Chao was also a dancing girl in the family of a princess; because of her, her father was ennobled marquis. Wang Weng-hsü, who was the daughter of a poor family and who entered the family of the heir apparent as a singing girl, became the favorite of the son of the heir apparent. She gave birth to the future Emperor Hsüan. When he ascended the throne, Weng-hsü's mother, as well as her two brothers, were ennobled and became wealthy. Later, the son of the elder brother, Wang Chieh, was appointed general of chariots and cavalry (*chü-ch'i chiang-chün*), and the son of the younger one, Wang Shang, became the imperial chancellor. Overnight, the status of the family changed entirely because of the singing girl.

Chinese women of Ch'in and Han times were not usually given as much education as men. Yet there were some outstanding women scholars. Most of them were daughters of great scholars. When Fu Sheng, a Ch'in erudite (*po-shih*) and a specialist in the *Shang-shu*, was too old to give lectures, Ch'ao Ts'o was sent by the Han government to take lessons from Fu's daughter. It was Pan Chao, the daughter of Pan Piao, who completed the unfinished parts of the *Han-shu*, written by her brother, Pan Ku, and from whom Ma Jung learned the meaning of the text. Ts'ai Yung had a large collection of books and lost all of them during the war. After his death, his daughter, Ts'ai Yen, who could recite many of them, wrote them down at the request of Ts'ao Ts'ao. However, no woman was occupied as a teacher; probably there was no demand for women professional teachers.

Women were never appointed officials, although Pan Chao was summoned by Emperor Ho to continue the editing of the *Han-shu*, and she was frequently ordered to write essays when precious items of tribute were offered to the emperor. Furthermore, she was treated as a teacher by the empress and some of the concubines. When Empress Dowager Teng personally attended the court, Pan Chao also participated in government affairs. Although she was given no official title, her son was ennobled as marquis and appointed chancellor of the state of Ch'i, apparently as a reward for her role and merit in the court.

Political Status

Most women were not directly concerned with politics, nor were they given the chance to engage in government affairs. Women did not usually have a status in the political mechanism; however, some had influence in politics because of the political status of their husbands. The case of the wife of an imperial chancellor who urged her husband to accept the decision to dismiss the emperor, mentioned above, illustrates this point.

Because a woman usually had no independent status of her own, her status depended on her family's—on her father's or brother's when she was unmarried and on her husband's or son's when she was married. However, the daughter of an emperor or a king, who held the title of princess and had a political status similar to a king or marquis, usually conditioned the status of her husband and his family. Thus a man who married a princess not only shared the income of her fief but also had a superior status. Usually only a marquis could be the husband of a princess. In one instance even the paramour of a princess was able to make friends with the emperor and high officials. Another paramour of a princess almost succeeded in getting the title of marquis and a high post. Certain political and legal privileges were given to the son of a princess. Since the daughter of an emperor always had a status comparable to a marquis, and her fief was classified as a marquisate, her eldest son inherited her fief and became a marquis. The son of a princess had a special legal status: when he was accused of a crime, permission had to be obtained from the emperor before he could be tried and punished—a kind of legal privilege enjoyed by members of the imperial family, the heir of a marquis, and officials of certain ranks.

Because a princess was superior in status to her husband and his family members, there was a tendency to reverse the usual pattern of wife-subordinate-to-husband. Hsün Shuang complained about this, saying in a memorial that the domination of a princess over her husband was contrary to the universal principle of *yin-yang*. In one instance a princess summoned her husband to come to her chamber and ordered him to lie under the bed while she was with her paramour. Finally the husband was unable to overcome his anger and killed the princess; he and his siblings were executed on the order of the emperor.

A woman's status might also become independent of her father's or brother's status because of her connection with the imperial family; her new independent status would then condition the status of her father's family. Mobility and superior status were always given to the family of a woman who entered the inner palace by marriage. Usually a man was ennobled as a marquis when his daughter became empress. Also, the mother of an empress or empress dowager was sometimes ennobled. The women so ennobled held the title of baronet (*chün*) and had a status similar to that of a princess. Brothers and sometimes brothers' sons of an empress dowager were also ennobled as marquises. Furthermore, the father, brother, or some other member of a consort family often held such important official posts as imperial chancellor or grand general; this meant that great political power was concentrated in the hands of a member of the consort family. In short, the superior political and social status, as well as the political power, enjoyed by a consort family was made possible because of the woman's status. The change of family status was very striking; many families of poor and humble origin were immediately elevated into the highest social stratum when women of those families became empresses.

Since the social mobility and the power of a consort family were based entirely on one of its female members, she had a new status in the family, influence which she had not previously enjoyed and which was certainly not enjoyed by a woman under ordinary conditions. She was respected by all her family members, including her seniors, for her new status gave her the power to control the male members of her family. When Empress Dowager Tou was angry at her elder brother, Tou Hsien, he was confined in the palace. Fearing that he might be punished by death, he asked to lead an expeditionary force to fight against the Hsiung-nu in order to redeem his guilt. The action illustrated in this case is certainly contradictory to the accepted principle that a younger brother or sister was subordinate to his or her elder siblings.

Even the "daughter-subordinate-to-father" pattern might be reversed. A man divorced his wife, and years later one of his daughters became empress. The empress ordered her father to take back her divorced mother, who had remarried and was now a widow. Commanding a father was an action against the basic principle of the father's superior authority, and obviously it was her political status that gave her the power to do it. Her mother was divorced long before the daughter became empress. Apparently her disapproval of her father's action had been on her mind for a long time, but she would never have been able to change the marital life of her parents had she not become empress. Both Tou Wu, the father of Empress Dowager Tou, and Ho Chin, the elder brother of Empress Dowager Ho, were unable to carry out their plans to dismiss all the eunuchs because the two empress dowagers disagreed with their suggestions. Since the father or elder brother of an empress dowager was a minister of the state, he was obliged to treat her as his superior and accept her orders.

In the court the empress dowager enjoyed a superior status more or less comparable to the emperor's. It was often said that there existed only one ruler in the empire. For this reason even the father of Liu Pang had to give up his role of father and assume a humble role in the presence of his son who became the emperor; this action greatly pleased the latter. But it seems that an emperor's attitude toward his mother was different. The emperors showed affection and respect to their mothers, and often behaved humbly before them. When Empress Dowager Po learned that the heir apparent and the king of Liang had been accused by the prefect of official carriages (*kung-chü ling*) of not dismounting before the palace gate, Emperor Wen took off his hat and apologized to her for not having brought up his sons strictly. She then sent a messenger to pardon the heir apparent and the king of Liang so that they could enter the palace. Again, when the king of Liang died, Empress Dowager Tou wept and said that the emperor had killed his son. Emperor Ching was sad and tried to please her by ennobling all the children of the late king.

When a dispute between two members of different consort families, Tou Ying and T'ien Fen, led to a court debate, the empress dowager was greatly angered. Refusing to eat when the emperor came to dine with her, she complained: "Now I am still alive, and yet people oppress my younger [half-]brother. When I die they will all treat him as fish and meat. How can you, the emperor, act like a stone statue?" The emperor apologized and said: "Both [Tou and T'ien] are consort family members; therefore, a court debate was held. Otherwise this would be a case to be settled by a judicial official." Tou Ying was executed, evidently under the pressure of the empress dowager.

The empress dowager often exerted great influence upon the emperor. Empress Dowager Tou was fond of Huang-Lao doctrines, and as a result Emperor Ching and all members of the Tou family had to read Lao-tzu and honor his methods. Under the influence of Empress Dowager Wang, Emperor Wu, who was about to select an imperial chancellor and a grand commandant (*t'ai-wei*), gave the posts to Tou Ying and T'ien Fen respectively. Several examples show that an empress dowager could influence the decision of the emperor and thus interfere with his administration. An official who was considered loyal by Emperor Ching was put to death under the pressure of Empress Dowager Tou. She also caused the dismissal of three top officials during the reign of Emperor Wu. The emperor did not reappoint T'ien Fen, one of the three officials dismissed by the empress dowager, until after her death. Emperor Ai had to dismiss Fu Hsi because Empress Dowager Fu disliked him.

At times the emperor even allowed the empress dowager to play a formal role in the court. Top officials serving under Emperor Wu were required to present copies of memorials to Empress Dowager Tou as well as to the throne. The power of an empress dowager who attended the court in person was even greater. She was in a position to make important decisions and to issue orders, thus assuming the role of a ruler. In the Early Han two empress dowagers attended the court and practically controlled the government. In the Later Han nine emperors were under the domination of empress dowagers; there were altogether six empress dowagers who attended the court. Their success in manipulating power varied according to their ability and personality and also depended on the personality of the young emperor, the power of the consort family, the existence and the influence of rival forces, and so on; but there is one thing common to all cases—the empress dowagers all took advantage of the immaturity of the emperors. Thus Empress Dowager Wang attended court when the nine-year-old Emperor P'ing ascended the throne. All the emperors of the Later Han who were under the domination of an empress dowager were very young.

Ordinarily an empress dowager was expected to relinquish power to the emperor when he reached maturity. Empress Dowager Liang attended the court when Emperor Huan was fifteen, but announced her retirement three years later. However, Empress Dowager Teng, the most powerful woman ruler in Later Han, was able to remain in power even after the emperor was of age. At first she placed a hundred-day-old infant on the throne; after his death she put a ten-year-old boy on the throne. She ruled until her death, at which time Emperor An was twenty-seven years old; thus she held power continuously for about sixteen years. The *Hou-Han-shu* states that she exercised the power of an emperor, and that the emperor merely sat on the throne with folded hands.

Since the empress dowager could not run the government by herself, she had to rely upon her father or brother, to whom she entrusted the actual administration of government affairs. Thus a member of the consort family always held the key government position when the empress dowager attended the court personally. Through the cooperation of the empress dowager and the consort family members, both the inner palace and the outer court were under their control. ❖

RECOMMENDED READINGS

For further readings on women in ancient China, see Albert O'Hara, *The Position of Women in Early China* (Westport, CT: Hyperion Press, 1980), and Florence Ayscough, *Chinese Women: Yesterday and Today* (New York: Da Capo Press, 1975). A very informative study of Pan Chao, the author of *Lessons for Women,* is provided by Nancy Lee Swann in *Pan Chao: Foremost Woman Scholar of China* (New York: Russell & Russell, 1968). Women's sexuality is discussed in Robert Van Gulick, *Sexual Life in Ancient China* (Atlantic Highlands, NJ: Humanities Press International, 1974). An interesting view of women's life at court is available in C. P. Fitzgerald, *The Empress Wu* (London: Cresset Press, 1968).

The Old World, About A.D. 100

THE SILK ROADS

A HISTORY

Paul Lunde

Economists sometimes emphasize the distinction between "needs" and "wants," commodities that are necessary to people and goods that are only desired by them. Although such a distinction is useful in analyzing modern economic systems, historians often find that it is not an easy matter to distinguish between what the people of a given era actually need and what they merely desire. Much of the history of the world has turned upon the exchange of goods that appear to have little intrinsic value to the people trading them.

The story of the Silk Roads, which united China and the Mediterranean and flourished between A.D. 50 and A.D. 220, is an excellent case in point. After centuries of development, relatively secure and direct routes connected the Roman Empire with Han China to the mutual satisfaction of both. Roman gold flowed into Han China, but the Chinese did little significant with it. They used paper and silver for money, and their finest metallurgy was in bronze, not gold. They also obtained jade from stations along the way and carved it into astonishingly intricate and beautiful forms. Perhaps the object most illustrative of these imports of jade and gold, however, was that found by archaeologists in an imperial tomb. The body in the tomb was found to be completely encased in a suit constructed of hundreds of tiles of polished jade, each bound to the others with gold wire.

For their part, the Romans obtained silk, literally worth its weight in gold to them. Anyone who has handled pure silk knows there is something very special about it. Soft to the touch and as light as a feather, it seems to generate its own gentle warmth. It can accept the most brilliant dyes or the palest pastels and hold its colors for decades. Silk can be a delight to the eye and the touch, but it hardly seems to warrant the exertions and expense the Romans underwent to obtain it. Nevertheless they did so. The Silk Roads flourished for over two centuries and the Romans continued to attempt to reopen the routes long after they had collapsed.

Viewed only as routes of economic exchange, the Silk Roads might appear to have been only another example of infinite complexity of human fancy, but they were more than simply routes of economic exchange. Ideas flowed back and forth along with the caravans of silk, gold, and jade. One of the limitations of economic history is the fact that the tangible goods exchanged are well documented, but the intangibles are left largely unrecorded.

READING QUESTIONS

1. What role have the nomads of central Asia played in the history of the Old World?

2. Why did the Han Empire extend its power westward?

3. How did the opening of the Silk Roads affect the Roman Empire?

4. What brought the "Golden Age of the Silk Roads" to an end?

The Chinese, like the Greeks—but perhaps with more reason—divided the world into civilized and barbarian. They, like their counterparts in India, Mesopotamia and Egypt, had had to face the fierce mounted bowmen of the steppes, and to survive had had to adopt their enemies' methods of warfare.

The pattern established in the second millennium BC—the settled, agriculturally-based urban civilizations of China, India and the Middle East regularly exposed to attack by mounted horsemen from Central Asia—did not end with the settling of the Indo-European speaking nomads. As they were transformed, as a result of the success of their own conquests, into urban civilized peoples themselves—Greeks, Romans, Persians and Indians—they in their turn had to defend themselves against new attacks by mounted horsemen from the Eurasian steppes—Parthians, Huns, Turks and finally Mongols. The last great wave of invasion out of Central Asia occurred in the early 15th century of our era, when Tamerlane and his Turkic- and Mongolian-speaking hordes devastated the Middle East.

It is no wonder that Ibn Khaldun, the 14th-century Arab philosopher of history, saw the history of the Middle East in terms of urban peoples periodically assaulted by mounted nomads, who then adopted the civilized ways of the peoples they conquered, became thereby decadent and in their turn submitted to a new wave of nomadic invaders. Had Chinese historians been able to read Ibn Khaldun, they would have found his paradigm borne out by their own experience.

From Paul Lunde, "The Silk Roads: A History," *Aramco World* 39(4), July/August 1988, pp. 14, 17, 20, 24, 28, 32, 35, 39.

No fully satisfactory explanation has ever been offered for the periodic explosion of nomadic peoples from—or through—Central Asia, but the pattern is clear: The region has historically been a sort of dynamo generating population movements that have affected Europe, Asia and America since the beginning of human occupation of the Eurasian landmass.

The Chinese fear of the peoples to the west was therefore not without foundation. In the third century BC the short-lived but powerful Qin Dynasty linked up a series of earlier bulwarks and formed the Great Wall, effectively separating the settled and cultivated lands of China from the nomadic herdsmen without. The Great Wall stretches from Gansu to Manchuria, a distance of 2,400 kilometers (1,500 miles). It was an effective defence against nomads who lacked both siege machinery and the inclination for sustained warfare.

It was not, however, impermeable. By the time of the subsequent Han Dynasty in the second century BC, the Chinese were regularly trading silk and grain for horses and jade with the western barbarians—horses which they employed to withstand the attacks of those same barbarians. Some of this silk, passed from hand to hand, found its way into Greek and Indian hands for perhaps the first time. Northern nomads had been familiar with it for hundreds of years, but now it began to filter into the markets of the large urban centers of western Asia. Significantly, our word *China,* like the Persian and Greek names for the country, comes from Qin (pronounced *chin*), the name of the dynasty that first united China and built the Great Wall.

The energetic and commercially minded Greeks established trading colonies on the coast of Asia Minor very early, and the wealth accumulated in them has become proverbial—"rich as Croesus," we say, naming the king of Lydia, in present-day Turkey. These Greek colonies had been tolerated by the Persians, but during the fifth century BC the two expanding powers came into conflict. Darius, from his capital at Susa in southern Persia, had waged a successful war against the Medes and their Babylonian allies, and succeeded in taking the Medean capital of Ecbatana—Hamadan, in present-day Iran—and forming a great empire stretching from the Oxus to the Tigris. His ambitions extended to Anatolia, and he succeeded in taking Sardis, the Lydian capital, and subjugating the Greek colonies on the coast. He then attacked Macedonia and Greece itself, and was only stopped by the heroic Athenians at Marathon, in 490 BC. His son Xerxes won the battle of Thermopylae and razed Athens, only to be defeated in the famous naval battle at Salamis and driven out of Greece.

These events, which loom so large in Greek and European history, had two consequences that were to change the face of Asia. One was administrative: Darius established a system of roads linking major Persian cities with the Mediterranean coast, and this Royal Road, leading from Susa to Sardis, was to become the main trade route—and the preferred line of march—across the Anatolian Plateau to the wealthy cities of Mesopotamia and beyond. The road was garrisoned and supplied with caravanserais, with amenities for travelers, at regular intervals. The world was suddenly a smaller place, and the enormous extent of the Persian Empire—at its height it included all of the Middle East and Egypt—meant that markets and producers that had formerly been separated by hostile powers were now united under a single rule.

But the other consequence of the Persian attack on Greece was a bitter hatred of Greek for Persian, and this was what in the end destroyed the empire so carefully constructed by Cyrus, Xerxes and Darius. In 334 BC Alexander of Macedon, 23 years old, landed on the Anatolian coast, intent on avenging the Persian attack.

At the head an army of 10,000 men, Alexander defeated Darius II, Great King of the Persians, first at Issus, in 333 BC, and then, crushingly, at Gaugamela, "The Place of the Camels," two years later. In the interval between the two battles, Alexander captured Tyre, Sidon and Gaza, conquered Egypt and founded Alexandria, destined to become perhaps the greatest intellectual and commercial center of all time. After Gaugamela, Alexander marched on Babylon, Susa, Persepolis (which he burned to the ground) and Ecbatana. He extended his sway beyond the Oxus, founding a city on the Jaxartes River, and taking Bactria, in modern Afghanistan, and Sogdiana, in what is now the Uzbek Soviet Socialist Republic—two places that for centuries thereafter would play an important role in the trade with China.

Alexander's lightning attack on India, his return march through the desert to Susa and Babylon and his sudden death are the stuff of legend, and his conquest of the mighty Persian empire with so few men—perhaps no more than 80,000 at the most—left an indelible impression on the literature and art of the East.

The frontiers of Europe had been extended to the Ganges, and the effects are almost incalculable. The Greeks were exposed to very ancient and civilized societies, with their own customs, languages, literatures, dress and luxuries. By a happy coincidence, Alexander's conquests took place at a time when Greek art and thought were in fullest flower, and the peoples of Asia were quick to adopt—and adapt—the esthetics of Greece. The results were astonishing, and a single example speaks volumes: a carved stone head of Buddha whose style is Greek and whose features are recognizably those of the idealized Alexander of Greek sculpture.

On Alexander's death, the conquered territories were divided among his successors, Seleucus and Ptolemy. Seleucus took the lion's share, ruling over most of Anatolia, Syria, Mesopotamia, Persia and Afghanistan. Ptolemy took Egypt and the important dyeing industries. Seleucus created a new capital city, Antioch, which he founded in 300 BC on the banks of the Orontes River, where it flows from Syria into Turkey. This was to become one of the most important cities of its time in the east, rivaling even Alexandria.

He founded another city, on the Tigris not far from the modern city of Baghdad, and named it after himself, Seleucia. Antioch communicated with the Mediterranean and was linked—by the roads built by Darius—with the cities of Anatolia and Mesopotamia; Seleucia, in today's Iraq, lay close to the headwaters of the Arabian Gulf and on the caravan route to Palmyra. The two cities were thus ideally located across a number of intersecting trade routes. The old Medean capital of Ecbatana lay on the route that ultimately led to China, although at this date there is as yet no evidence of organized commercial exchange.

The stage, however, was set, and information about China—garbled, shrouded in legend—began to percolate into the Greek-speaking cities of the Seleucids. At the same time, Greek artisans, painters and musicians who had flocked to the frontier cities founded by Alexander in Persia and today's Afghanistan—each a classic Greek city, complete with baths, temples and public meeting places—began to spread their influence into Central Asia by means of trade and travel along the Silk Roads.

Under the Han Dynasty, the Chinese began moving tentatively westward. Almost certainly unaware of the dramatic changes that had taken place in the Greco-Persian political balance of western Asia, they were preoccupied with the perennial problem of the barbarians at the gates. They needed horses, and had heard that the best and strongest horses in the world—capable of carrying a heavily armored rider—were bred in the valleys of Ferghana, beyond the Tian Shan mountains.

This report reached the ears of the Han emperor Wu as a result of a mission he sent westward in 138 BC in order to form an alliance with a nomadic group that the Chinese historics call the Yue-zhi. His goal was to oppose a huge tribal confederation formed by the Xiong-nu, who may have been the people we know as Huns, and who were threatening China's borders. The mission was led by Zhang Qien, who followed the ancient route to Kashgar, where he was unfortunately captured and held prisoner by the Xiong-nu. Eventually he succeeded in escaping and making his way back to China, bringing valuable reports of affairs in Central Asia, and most interestingly, of Bactria, where he had actually been.

By this time, Bactria and Sogdiana were no longer part of the Seleucid Empire, the eastern portions of which had fragmented into independent satrapies or been conquered by the Parthians, another nomad people of uncertain origins. But Bactria—today's Balkh, in northern Afghanistan—preserved its character as a Greek city. Zhang Qien was surprised to see Chinese products—bamboo and cloth—there, and asked where they had been obtained. He was told that they had been bought in India.

Bactria was joined to India by a 4,200-kilometer (2,600-mile) road that passed across the Hindu Kush, through the Khyber Pass and drove diagonally across the subcontinent to the Bay of Bengal, following the course of the Ganges. It was built by Chandragupta, founder of the Maurya dynasty, who met and befriended Alexander in 325 BC, and who, two years later, drove the Greeks out of India. He ruled northern India from his capital of Pataliputra—on the site of modern Patna—where he maintained friendly intercourse with the Greeks of Bactria and beyond, despite the defeat he inflicted on Seleucus in 305 BC.

A Greek ambassador named Megasthenes spent a number of years at Chandragupta's capital and, in about 302 BC, wrote a long and fascinating description of it, which contains the earliest certain reference to trade with China. He says that in the bazaars of Pataliputra goods from Mesopotamia, the Greek cities of Asia Minor, and China were available; he specifically mentions silks, embroideries and brocades, all of Chinese origin, as well as medicinal plants, ivory, gold, jewels, and rugs—these last probably from western Asia and Mesopotamia.

The Chinese trade goods seen by Megasthenes in Pataliputra may well have reached India overland from China; if so, this is evidence that the Silk Roads were operating even before the Qin and Han Dynasties.

It is certain, however, that Indian trade goods, art objects and ideas were passing north along Chandragupta's road to Taxila, across the Hindu Kush to Bactria, and then spreading through Central Asia, reaching China along the Steppe Route and the Imperial Highway.

Zhang Qien's visit to Bactria was much later—some 47 years after the fall of the Mauryan Empire, which came to an end in 185 BC. But the bamboo and cloth he saw were not the only Chinese products to reach Bactria. The Bactrian kings struck beautiful cupro-nickel coins, the earliest of which were minted in 170 BC—long before Zhang Qien's visit. In view of the high melting point of nickel, which was beyond the reach of the technology of the time, the metal of which these coins are made must be a natural alloy. Since this particular alloy only occurs in the Chinese province of Yunnan, there must have been trade in ore or metal between Bactria and China.

Yet nowhere is such trade mentioned. Other archeological discoveries in the Bactrian area also show how little we actually know of the trans-Asian trade of the second century BC. Coins—probably passed from hand to hand by tribesmen—have been found near Lake Balkash, in the Kazak Soviet Socialist Republic, which were minted near the Bosporus in the fourth century BC; a charming glass vase made in Alexandria in the second century BC has been found on the banks of the Yellow River, in the heartland of China. A gold cup with a richly embossed floral design, made somewhere in the Hellenistic world, has been found in Siberia. All of these finds are probably a result of "relay trade"—or perhaps of booty taken by nomad bands—but they still show how far goods could travel from their points of origin.

Zhang Qien finally returned to Xian after an absence of 13 years, the original 100 members of his mission reduced to two. He brought news of many lands and peoples unheard of in China—Ferghana, Parthia, Bactria, Babylonia, Syria and India. The impact on the Chinese was comparable to the impact on the Greeks of the conquests of Alexander: New worlds—and new markets—were opened, and China's isolation ended.

Many Chinese embassies were dispatched to Central Asia in order to procure the fabled horses of Kokand, a city on the Jaxartes River in the region of Ferghana—horses which Zhang Qien had failed to bring back to his emperor.

Because the Chinese had finally crushed the Xiong-nu in 121 BC and settled garrisons in the Gansu Corridor, where the Imperial Highway passes beyond the protection of the Great Wall, these embassies were able to travel
unharmed across the Tarim Basin. And when the people of Kokand repeatedly refused to part with their fine breeding stock, the emperor Wu
launched a 60,000-man army against the city, capturing it in 102 BC after a
bitter siege. At a single stroke, China gained dominion over the entire Tarim
Basin, the vital key to the Silk Roads.

Four years earlier, the Chinese had sent an embassy to the Parthian ruler
Mithridates II, who had come to the throne in 124 BC and established
Parthian rule throughout Persia and Mesopotamia. The Chinese embassy had
been joyfully received in the Parthian capital of Hecatompylos—"City of a
Thousand Gates"—where they were particularly intrigued by the Syrian jugglers and acrobats they saw. The Parthians in turn sent their ambassador to
Xian, and the diplomatic relations thus established between China and the
Parthians of the Iranian plateau were to endure hundreds of years. The two
nations—and their successors—controlled the vital and most dangerous
stretches of the Silk Roads, and—as long as such intermediaries as the Sog-
dians co-operated—the precious silks of China and their superb steel
weapons could be exchanged for the furs, gold, jade, horses and carpets coveted by the Chinese.

The Romans learned of the Chinese from the Greeks, who usually called
them "Seres" and whose word for the Han capital was *Sera.* The Latin word
for silk, *serica,* is the origin of ours.

The Romans conquered the remaining Greek provinces of Asia Minor in
188 BC and in 113 BC the Roman province of Asia was created. It was thus not
long before the Romans came into conflict with the Parthians. What began
as a series of naval expeditions against pirates in the eastern Mediterranean
quickly led to the Roman conquest of Syria, which became a Roman province
in 62 BC. Only Palmyra, the great caravan city in the desert, retained its independence. It played an important role as a transit center until the third
century of our era, and some of the earliest surviving Chinese silks have
been found in its ruins.

It was during these years of expansion in the Middle East that Rome first
became acquainted with silk. Pliny the Elder, who composed his *Natural
History* between AD 60 and 79, knew that silk came from China, but thought
it grew on trees—a persistent misconception. The silk that was already
reaching Rome in Pliny's day was unwoven, and he specifically mentions
how Roman women first dressed the thread and then wove it themselves.
"Thus," says Pliny, "does work have to be increased, thus are the ends of the
earth traversed—all so Roman women may expose their charms through
transparent cloth."

It is possible that the Romans had not yet seen the marvellous dyed silks
woven and embroidered in China itself, for in 53 BC, when Marcus Crassus,

consul and triumvir of Rome and governor of the Roman province of Syria, sought to emulate Alexander and march to the east against the Parthians, his panicked legions—legions that had for hours bravely withstood the onslaught of the terrible Parthian cavalry—fled in confusion when the Parthians unfurled their glittering banners of Chinese silk.

That battle of Carrhae was one of the worst defeats ever suffered by Rome. Crassus and his son were killed, 20,000 legionnaires died and 10,000 were led in captivity to Margiana—the city later known to the Arabs as Marv.

When peace of a sort was finally established between the Romans and the Parthians, the Silk Roads entered their golden age—literally golden, for in the Romans the Chinese had found the ideal customer for their wares. Romans paid for unwoven Chinese silk in gold—weight for weight. And they could not seem to get enough.

Within 50 years of the battle of Carrhae, the Roman senate was already promulgating sumptuary laws, forbidding men to wear silk. No attention was paid, and demand for silk only increased. The peace established by Augustus throughout the empire, and Roman control of the Mediterranean and most of the Middle East, meant that all the ancient trade routes—the Silk Roads to China, the Incense Road to South Arabia, the Spice Road to India—all now converged on Rome. Roman control of the port cities of the eastern Mediterranean, with their ancient tradition of dyeing textiles red and purple with the murex shellfish, allowed the Romans to produce textiles to their own specifications. The undyed silk, packed in standard skeins, was dyed in Syria and sent on to Rome to be woven.

It has been estimated that silk accounted for some 90 percent of Rome's imports from China, but iron, lacquer and cinnamon also made the long, arduous journey. Rome in return sent mostly gold.

China has been called the graveyard of gold, for the Chinese tended to hoard the streams of precious metal that poured out of Rome. China clung to the use of silk as a currency, and the gold that found its way there never reappeared. Though it circulated to a certain extent within China, it was not used to purchase foreign luxuries. This meant that for centuries the Romans were constantly searching for new supplies of gold. By the early Middle Ages these supplies began to dry up, and Europe was cut off from eastern luxuries because it could not pay for them, at least on the former scale. Pliny the Elder estimated that Rome was losing 45 million sesterces a year to China.

Roman attempts to solve the problem of their deficit by trying to seize control of Parthia, thereby eliminating the middleman and reducing prices, had the opposite effect to that intended. The insecurity that resulted from the Roman attack only made Chinese silk more expensive.

Despite the vastly increased knowledge of the East that resulted from the Roman colonization of Syria and Egypt, and despite their constant trade with India and China, the Romans never solved the secret of silk manufacture.

Pausanius, the first-century author of a detailed guide book to Greece, is the classical author who came closest to the truth: He knew silk was produced by some kind of insect. But Pliny, Strabo and Virgil all believed silk to be vegetable in origin.

Nor did Roman knowledge of China itself advance much beyond the Greeks'. Because silk arrived in Rome both overland via Central Asia and by sea via India or the Arabian Gulf, Romans tended to think that there were *two* silk-producing countries far to the east.

Toward the end of the first century a Macedonian merchant named Maes Titianos sent agents to carry out a reconaissance of the Silk Roads. They estimated the distance from Hierapolis in Syria—not far from present-day Aleppo—to Sera, as they called Xian, at about 11,000 kilometers (6,800 miles). Titianos' agents then reported a list of stages on the northern route around the Tarim Basin, some of which have been identified with existing places—"Cassia" seems to be Aksu, for example. Marinos of Tyre, the Greek geographer who preserved the account of this first known exploration of the Silk Roads, bitterly laments the paucity of information brought back: "In the course of a seven-month journey they didn't bring back a single bit of information worth recording."

This was probably not the fault of Titianos' agents: The Parthians strictly controlled traffic through their territory, jealously guarding their monopoly. There is even evidence that they refused to let Han ambassadors pass to establish direct contact with the Romans. The agents were probably only able to obtain a hearsay account of the journey—or perhaps a written list of its stages, which we know was available.

The Parthians' power began to wane in the second century of our era. Their place as intermediaries was briefly filled by the Kushans, descendants of the Yue-zhi visited by Zhang Qien so many years before. But in AD 220 the Han dynasty fell and China disintegrated. Rome too, began to lose its hold on its eastern provinces. By the third century the great days of the Silk Roads were but a memory. ❖

RECOMMENDED READINGS

Robert J. Collins, *East to Cathay: The Silk Road* (New York: McGraw-Hill, 1968), offers a good general account of the route; Shih Min-hsiung, *The Silk Industry in Ching China,* trans. E-tu Zen Sun (Ann Arbor: Center for Chinese Studies, University of Michigan, 1976), offers a comprehensive account of Chinese silk production at the height of the Western trade. The magnificent scenery, coupled with the remoteness and difficulty of the route, continues to attract travelers and writers. A few of the more recent accounts of travels along the route are those of Jan Myrdal, *The Silk Road: A Journey from the High Pamirs and Ili Through Sinkiang and Kansu,* trans.

Ann Henning (New York: Pantheon Books, 1979); Peter Hopkirk, *Foreign Devils on the Silk Road: The Search For the Lost Cities and Treasures of Chinese Central Asia* (London: Murray, 1980); and Wei-chuan Wen's photographic essay, *Xinjiang, The Silk Road: Islam's Overland Route to China* (New York: Oxford University Press, 1986). There are also numerous earlier accounts, one of which is that of Sir Aurel Stein, who presents a good example of the Victorian explorer at his best in *Sand-Buried Ruins of Khotan: Personal Narrative of a Journey of Archaeological and Geographical Exploration in Chinese Turkestan* (London: Hurst and Blackett, 1904).

CHINA'S INVENTION OF PAPER

Thomas F. Carter

The Chinese, from approximately 500 B.C. to the beginning of the fifteenth century A.D., far surpassed the Western world in the area of scientific and technological discovery. Even a summary listing of such Chinese innovations as the mechanical clock, printing, the magnet, and gunpowder, of basic engineering devices such as the driving belt and the chain drive, of the wheelbarrow, and of nautical techniques like the stern-post rudder demonstrates China's dominating position in scientific and technological achievement during this period. China served as the source and the transmitter to the West of innumerable discoveries and inventions. Generally, the transmission of technology to the West occurred indirectly, with innovations passing through intermediaries until the West received them with no clear idea of the source.

Earlier selections demonstrate society's continual need for improved methods of information processing. The following excerpt from Thomas F. Carter's The Invention of Printing in China and Its Spread Westward *deals with a second technological innovation that also greatly enhanced the maintenance of large quantities of recorded information, the invention of paper by the ancient Chinese. Carter describes the gradual development process leading to the origin of paper and proceeds to discuss the transmission of the process to the West. The arrival in thirteenth-century Italy of this fully developed technological innovation was essential for still another information-processing revolution—books and the emergence of printing in the West.*

READING QUESTIONS

1. About when and by whom was paper invented?

2. What writing materials were used by the Chinese before the development of paper?

3. How have Chinese records concerning the inventions of paper been corroborated?

4. How and about when did paper manufacture reach the West?

Back of the invention of printing lies the use of paper, which is the most certain and the most complete of China's inventions. While other nations may dispute with China the honor of those discoveries where China found only the germ, to be developed and made useful to mankind in the West, the manufacture of paper was sent forth from the Chinese dominions as a fully developed art. Paper of rags, paper of hemp, paper of various plant fibers, paper of cellulose, paper sized and loaded to improve its quality for writing, paper of various colors, writing paper, wrapping paper, even paper napkins and toilet paper—all were in general use in China during the early centuries of our era. The paper, the secret of whose manufacture was taught by Chinese prisoners to their Arab captors at Samarkand in the eighth century, and which in turn was passed on by Moorish subjects to their Spanish conquerors in the twelfth and thirteenth centuries, is in all essential particulars the paper that we use today. And even in our own times China has continued to furnish new developments in paper manufacture, both the so-called "India paper" and papier-mâché having been introduced from China into the West during the nineteenth century.

Though the invention of paper is carefully dated in the dynastic records as belonging to the year A.D. 105,[1] the date is evidently chosen rather arbitrarily, and this invention, like most inventions, was a gradual process. Up to the end of the Chou dynasty (256 B.C.), through China's classical period, writing was done with a bamboo pen, with ink of soot, or lampblack,[2] upon slips of bamboo or wood. Wood was used largely for short messages, bamboo for longer writings and for books. The bamboo was cut into strips about nine inches long and wide enough for a single column of characters. The wood was sometimes in the same form, sometimes wider. The bamboo strips, being stronger, could be perforated at one end and strung together, either with silken cords or with leather thongs, to form books. Both the wooden strips and those of bamboo are carefully described in books on antiquities, written in the early centuries of the Christian era. The abundance of wooden and bamboo slips excavated in Turkestan conforms exactly to the early descriptions.

---

[1] Three years before A.D. 105, paper is mentioned in the biography of Empress Têng (A.D. 81–121).

[2] There is a tradition that grew up in the T'ang dynasty that during the Chou dynasty writing was done as a rule by cutting in the bamboo or wood with a knife.

From Thomas F. Carter, *The Invention of Printing in China and Its Spread Westward* (New York: Ronald Press, 1955), pp. 3–8.

The invention of the writing brush of hair,[3] attributed to the general Mêng T'ien in the third century B.C., worked a transformation in writing materials. This transformation is indicated by two changes in the language. The word for chapter used after this time means "roll"; the word for writing materials becomes "bamboo and silk" instead of "bamboo and wood." There is evidence that the silk used for writing during the early part of the Han dynasty consisted of actual silk fabric.[4] Letters on silk, dating possibly from Han times, have been found together with paper in a watchtower of a spur of the Great Wall.

But as the dynastic records of the time state, "silk was too expensive and bamboo too heavy." The philosopher Mo Ti, when he traveled from state to state, carried with him many books in the cart tail. The emperor Ch'in Shih Huang set himself the task of going over daily a hundred and twenty pounds of state documents. Clearly a new writing material was needed.

The first step was probably a sort of paper or near-paper made of raw silk. This is indicated by the character for paper, which has the silk radical showing material, and by the definition of that character in the *Shuo wên,* a dictionary that was finished about the year A.D. 100.

The year A.D. 105 is usually set as the date of the invention of paper, for in that year the invention was officially reported to the emperor by the eunuch Ts'ai Lun. Whether Ts'ai Lun was the real inventor or only the person in official position who became the patron of the invention (as Fêng Tao did later with printing) is uncertain. In any case his name is indelibly connected with the invention in the mind of the Chinese people. He has even been deified as the god of papermakers, and in the T'ang dynasty the mortar which Ts'ai Lun was supposed to have used for macerating his old rags and fish nets was brought with great ceremony from Hunan to the capital and placed in the imperial museum. The following is the account of the invention, as written by Fan Yeh in the fifth century in the official history of the Han dynasty, among the biographies of famous eunuchs:

> During the period Chien-ch'u (A.D. 76–84), Ts'ai Lun was a eunuch. The emperor Ho, on coming to the throne (A.D. 89), knowing that Ts'ai Lun was a man full of talent and zeal, appointed him a *chung ch'ang shih.* In this position he did not hesitate to bestow either praise or blame upon His Majesty.
>
> In the ninth year of the period Yung-yüan (A.D. 97) Ts'ai Lun became *shang fang ling.* Under his instruction workmen made, always with the

---

[3] It seems clear that the brush may already have had a long history before the time of Mêng T'ien. Archaeological proof is given by the evidence of brush writing on Yang-shao pottery (*ca.* 2000 B.C.), on jade, and on oracle bones of the late Shang period (*ca.* 1300–1028 B.C.).

[4] While in China the use of silk as material for writing quickly gave way to paper, silk remained the usual material for painting for several centuries and has never been entirely displaced.

best of materials, swords and arrows of various sorts, which were models to later generations.

In ancient times writing was generally on bamboo or on pieces of silk, which were then called *chih*. But silk being expensive and bamboo heavy, these two materials were not convenient. Then Ts'ai Lun thought of using tree bark, hemp, rags, and fish nets. In the first year of the Yüan-hsing period (A.D. 105) he made a report to the emperor on the process of paper-making, and received high praise for his ability. From this time paper has been in use everywhere and is called the "paper of Marquis Ts'ai."

The biographical note goes on to tell how Ts'ai Lun became involved in intrigues between the empress and the grandmother of the emperor, as a consequence of which, in order to avoid appearing before judges to answer for statements that he had made, "he went home, took a bath, combed his hair, put on his best robes, and drank poison."

Two statements in this quotation have received ample confirmation from discoveries along the Great Wall and in Turkestan. In March, 1931, while exploring a Han ruin on the Edsin-gol, not far from Kharakhoto, the Swedish archaeologist Folke Bergman discovered what is probably the oldest paper in the world. It was found along with a Chinese iron knife stuck in a leather sheath, a badly shriveled water sack of leather, a crossbow arrow with bronze head and reed shaft, many manuscripts on wood, silk rags (including a piece of polychrome silk), and an almost complete raincoat made of twisted grass strings. Lao Kan, who later made a report on this precious piece of paper, informs us that of the seventy-eight manuscripts on wood the great majority were dated between the fifth and seventh years of Yung-yüan (a reign period covering the years A.D. 89–105). On the latest was written: "5th day of the 1st moon of the 10th year of Yung-yüan," or February 24, A.D. 98. Mr. Lao agrees that, just because the last of the dated wooden slips bears a dated inscription, one cannot conclude that everything in the hoard was cached away in that year. Nevertheless, he surmises that about this time, possibly a few years later (whether before or after Ts'ai Lun's historic announcement will never be known), the paper was manufactured and dispatched to this lonely spot in modern Ninghsia province. Other pieces of paper of early times discovered in Turkestan date from about a century and a half after the announcement by Ts'ai Lun.

The statement concerning the materials used has also been thoroughly confirmed. Examination of paper from Turkestan, dating from the third to the eighth centuries of our era, shows that the materials used are the bark of the mulberry tree; hemp, both raw fibers and those which have been fabricated (fish nets, etc.); and various plant fibers, especially China grass (*Boehmeria nivea*), not in their raw form but taken from rags.

The discovery of rag paper in Turkestan, while confirming the statement in the Chinese records, came as a surprise to many Western scholars. From the time of Marco Polo until some seventy years ago, all oriental paper had been known as "cotton paper," and it had been supposed that rag paper was a German or Italian invention of the fifteenth century. Wiesner and Karabacek in 1885–87 showed, as a result of microscopic analysis, that the large quantity of Egyptian paper which had at that time recently been brought to Vienna, and which dated from about A.D. 800 to 1388, was almost all rag paper. A subsequent examination of the earliest European papers showed that they, too, were made in the main from rags. The theory was then advanced and generally believed that the Arabs of Samarkand were the inventors of rag paper, having been driven to it by their inability to find in Central Asia the materials that had been used by the Chinese. In 1904, this theory suffered a rude shock. Dr. Stein had submitted to Dr. Wiesner of Vienna some of the paper he had found during his first expedition to Turkestan, and Dr. Wiesner, while finding in it no pure rag paper, did find paper in which rags were used as a surrogate, the main material being the bark of the paper mulberry. The theory was changed to suit the facts. The Arabs of Samarkand were no longer the first to have used rags in the production of paper, but the first to have produced paper *solely* of rags. Finally, in 1911, after Dr. Stein's second expedition, paper of the first years of the fourth century was laid before Dr. Wiesner and was found to be a pure rag paper! Rag paper, supposed until 1885 to have been invented in Europe in the fifteenth century, supposed until 1911 to have been invented by the Arabs of Samarkand in the eighth century, was carried back to the Chinese of the early fourth century, and the Chinese record, stating that rag paper was invented in China at the beginning of the second century, was substantially confirmed.

The use of paper, so far superior to bamboo and silk as a writing material, made rapid headway. It was still, however, regarded as a cheap substitute. Extensive improvements in its manufacture were made by Tso Po, a young contemporary of Ts'ai Lun. The records of the next centuries contain abundant references to the use of paper and to certain special fancy and beautiful papers that appeared from time to time. In Turkestan, at each point where excavations have been undertaken, the time when wooden stationery gave way to paper can be fairly accurately dated. By the time of the invention of block printing all of Chinese Turkestan, so far as excavations show, was using paper. The use of paper in China proper had apparently become general much earlier.

The papers found in Turkestan show a certain amount of progress, especially in the art of loading and sizing to make writing more easy. The earliest papers are simply a net of rag fibers with no sizing. The first attempt to improve the paper so that it would absorb ink more readily consisted of giving the paper a coat of gypsum. Then followed the use of a glue or gelatine made from lichen. Next came the impregnation of the paper with raw dry starch flour. Finally this starch flour was mixed with a thin starch paste, or else the paste was used alone. Better methods of maceration also came into use that proved less destructive of the fibers and produced a stronger paper. All these improvements were perfected before the invention was passed on to the Arabs in the eighth century and before the first block printing in China began. So far as an invention can ever be said to be completed, it was a completed invention that was handed over to the Arabs at Samarkand. The papermaking taught by the Arabs to the Spaniards and Italians in the thirteenth century was almost exactly as they had learned it in the eighth. The paper used by the first printers of Europe differed very slightly from that used by the first Chinese block printers five centuries or more before.❖

RECOMMENDED READINGS

A more detailed account of the invention of paper is provided in Tsuen-Hsuin Tsien, *Written on Bamboo and Silk—the Beginnings of Chinese Books and Inscriptions* (Chicago: University of Chicago Press, 1962), and in *Ancient China's Technology and Science,* compiled by the Institute of the History of Natural Sciences, Chinese Academy of Sciences (Beijing: Foreign Language Press, 1983). For a fascinating study of China's technological contributions to the West, see Joseph Needham, *The Grand Titration: Science and Society in East and West* (London: Allen & Unwin, 1969). A truly outstanding presentation of Chinese technology and science is found in Joseph Needham's very scholarly multivolumed *Science and Civilization in China* (Cambridge and New York: Cambridge University Press, 1954).

On the Roman Frontier, About A.D. *100*

COMMERCE ON AND BEYOND THE FRONTIER

Steven K. Drummond and Lynn H. Nelson

When dealing with great states and empires, historians tend to concentrate their attention on the heartland and to note what is occurring on the frontiers only insofar as it reflects or affects the affairs of the metropolis. Americans are less prone to the preoccupation, since so much of their own national heritage is the product of the frontier experience; in fact, their nation itself was at one time only one of a number of the frontiers of the British Empire.

Unlike the British frontiers, the Roman frontier was not intended to support economic development but to provide the heartland of the empire with an effective and inexpensive defense against the warlike Germanic peoples to the north and east. The following selection discusses how the inhabitants of the frontier developed a dynamic economic system that eventually eclipsed that of the interior of the empire. Merchants from these frontier regions went out among the Germans to trade, and the Germans reciprocated by settling near the frontier and delivering goods to sell to the Romans. By A.D. *100, Germans and frontier Romans were united in a single commercial system, and Roman silver coins were the money of exchange on both sides of the border.*

The "Fall of the Roman Empire" in the West did not alter this situation much. The "barbarian" invaders were in fact the Romans' old trading partners, people who had absorbed many Roman ways through their long association with the Romans. The frontier fortresses that the Romans had built to defend their frontiers continued as trading centers between German and Latin Europe; Cologne, Mainz, Vienna, Budapest, Belgrade, Sofia, and others have continued as great cities to the present day. In attempting to seal off their part of Europe, the Romans succeeded in laying the foundations of a civilization that would embrace the entire continent.

READING QUESTIONS

1. What was the importance of amber as an object of trade?

2. What were the major routes of Roman trade beyond the frontier?

3. How did the Roman authorities use the trade with the Germans as a political tool?

4. How did geography and transportation contribute to the economic development of the frontier districts?

FRONTIER TRADERS

During the reign of the emperor Nero (A.D. 54–68), a young Roman, serving as the agent of the merchant Julianus, undertook a trading expedition to the Baltic. Leaving from the great legionary fortress and trading town of Carnuntum on the Danube, he and his men traveled some six hundred miles north along one of the most well-known of the trade routes into free Germany. This route led northwards up the valley of the March, through the Moravian Gates, and into the German plain. From the upper Oder, the trail proceeded towards Kalisz in upper Poland, where it reached the lower Vistula and the famous "Amber Coast" of the Baltic. The trip from Carnuntum along the amber route to the Baltic took about two months, although a merchant passing this way could spend considerably longer if he stopped to bargain at the numerous trading posts that lay along the route and offered travellers accommodations and the opportunity to purchase local wares.[1] Needless to say, this was not a new trail, but one that had existed from prehistoric times, joining Baltic and Mediterranean lands. The young Roman trailblazer's adventures were well-publicized, however, and the large amount of amber he brought back helped to focus Roman attention on this and other products of the North.

Amber quickly became an object of fascination for the Romans, and gladiatorial, circus, and theater performances sometimes featured displays of crude amber, amber jewelry, and amber-colored accessories. The fossilized resin of the prehistoric firs of the Baltic valley, amber possessed a number of unusual qualities. Soft to the touch, it grew warm when held in the hand. Hair and bits of lint were attracted as if by magic to a cloth that had been stroked by a piece of amber. If one were to rub a piece of amber against a pin or needle and then float the needle on some water, one would find that the needle pointed always toward the north, as if pointing the way to the lands from which the amber had come. The Roman populace, who

From Steven K. Drummond and Lynn H. Nelson, *The Western Frontiers of Imperial Rome* (Armonk, NY: M. E. Sharpe, 1994), pp. 101–126.

were a superstitious lot at best, seized upon amber as a sovereign defense against the dangers of the evil eye. There were few Roman parents who felt that they could not afford at least a small piece of amber for a bracelet or necklace to protect their children from the envious and malevolent witches who seemed to abound in the early Empire. For this and many other reasons, there continued to be a steady and significant demand within the Empire for northern amber. The amber route became a well-travelled path, in which a wide variety of Roman and northern goods passed back and forth between the numerous middlemen who took up residence along the road.

These Roman traders did more than pass goods from hand to hand. They went out from the amber route to trade their wares with nearby tribesmen for local products such as honey, beeswax, furs, rosins, and even the luxuriant hair of German women to make wigs for the noble ladies of Rome. It was not a secure life; when a tribe began to feel that life, the gods, or their neighbors were treating them unfairly, their first reaction was often to kill the Roman merchants who dwelled or passed among them, usually in the most unpleasant manner they could think of. Other Roman traders soon came to take their place, however. For many Romans, the frontier was not a barrier, but rather a point of departure from which to seize the opportunities that German trade presented. Many lost their lives in the pursuit of profit far beyond the frontier of the Empire, but the hope of riches and the assurance of adventure lured others to replace them.

The basic geography of the frontier virtually ensured that Roman trade and commerce would be carried far beyond the lines established by the Roman army and that such commerce would eventually stimulate the manufacturing potential of the frontier districts themselves. The Romans had sought defensible military positions and had found them in the Rhine and Danube rivers, but these rivers were also the hearts of great watersheds, and the tributary waters of the frontier led north, into free Germany, as well as south into the border provinces of the Empire. These water routes northward made trade not only possible, but almost inevitable. Indeed, trade beyond the frontier was well-developed even before the frontier itself was firmly fixed; Roman merchants had established themselves far beyond the Rhine by the mid-first century A.D.

Tacitus reports that there was a concentration of Roman traders by this time among the Marcomanni, who inhabited the region of Bohemia. They had been encouraged to settle in the Marcomanni capital by the leader of the tribe, and had stayed on because of the profit possible in supplying the Marcomanni with Roman export goods. By the end of the century, they appear to have lost their Roman identity and adapted to German ways.[2] The abundance of Roman goods found in archaeological sites in this region indicates that this early merchant colony was quite active,[3] and the entire account suggests the complex nature of commerce beyond the frontier. It was not a simple matter of Germans and Romans; the trading network often developed its own peculiar population, a half-German, half-Roman merchant folk who acted as intermediaries between the two cultures. There is no history of these people, but incidental references by Roman historians make it quite clear that they existed and that they played an important role in carrying Roman goods and influences deep into German lands. One wonders if the German killings and mistreatment of Roman merchants may not sometimes have been the result of these Germanized traders' attempts to eliminate unwanted competition.

The trade routes were often as complex and varied as the people who travelled them. In the west, for instance, Roman trade goods were apparently carried from the frontier to the lands of the Elbe, but some of these goods were apparently transshipped down this and other rivers of northern Germany to markets established at the rivers' mouths.[4] The merchants from the German interior, carrying a mixed cargo of Roman export and German goods, were met here by other traders, most probably Frisians, who were carrying Roman goods by sea for trade all along the German and Norwegian coast.[5] Still other merchants attending these northern markets bought Roman wares from both Frisians and the traders from the interior and carried them into the Baltic. Archaeologists have traced such wares across the base of Jutland and discovered several concentrations in the Danish islands. It would appear that Danish merchants traded their Roman wares along the Baltic coast, often in competition with similar goods carried from the region of the Elbe across to the Vistula and then northward to the coast.[6] Such complex systems indicate that Roman imports were important goods in a large and far-flung German trading economy.

This fact was of major significance to the Roman government. Roman traders supplied frontier tribes the wares with which those tribes carried on commerce with their neighbors, and this gave the Romans a certain degree of control over their German neighbors. They could reward a friendly tribe by increasing its access to Roman export goods and thus allow it to expand its commerce with its neighbors and increase its wealth. Conversely, pressure could be placed upon a tribe by limiting the Roman wares it could acquire, and thus place it at an economic disadvantage in obtaining the materials it needed from other tribes. Finally, on those rare occasions when a tribe attacked the frontier, trade with the Romans was automatically ended, and the whole tribe soon began to feel the effects of the lack of exchangeable commodities. Although plunder could remedy that deficiency for a time, the disruption of normal commerce could not help but soon alienate the hostile tribe's neighbors, who were, after all, gaining no profit from the situation.

The inhabitants of the frontier districts were probably less concerned with the value of the German trade as a device for controlling the frontier tribes than they were with the profits to be gained from its pursuit. For the frontier districts, there were three distinct aspects to this commerce: the trade by which Roman goods were carried beyond the frontier for exchange among the Germans; the trade by which the Germans, usually border tribesmen, brought their goods to frontier stations for exchange with local merchants; and the local production of export wares to supply both types of commerce.

Generally speaking, trade beyond the frontiers of Britain appears to have been negligible, although a certain amount of Irish goods probably found their way to British markets, particularly in the western part of the island.[7] There was little that the Picts and Scots of the North could offer in the way of exchange, and there is little evidence of any attempt on the part of the Romans to stimulate a desire for Roman wares among them. The result was that Roman influences were very slight among the northern tribes, and, since the Romans could not influence them through the control of commerce, the natives of the North of the island remained particularly unpredictable and hostile. Elsewhere along the frontier, however, traders were active in carrying their wares to markets beyond the frontier. From the Rhine districts, Roman merchants generally moved up the Rhine's eastern tributaries. The Lippe, with the fortress of Vetera (Xanten) at its base, the Ruhr from Asciburgium and probably the Sieg from Bonn all facilitated trade with the Germans, but the Lahn and the Main rivers, the latter overlooked by the fortress at Mainz, were probably the most important routes for long-range trade. These streams provided easy access to the broad lowlands near the Elbe and, eventually, to the Baltic. Trade in the Danubian region appears to have been just as extensive as along the Rhine and perhaps even more important to the Empire. Roman traders ranged along the amber route to the Baltic, as well as its western branch that led to Bohemia and the region of the Elbe. Some from the lower reaches of the Danube may have used the Black Sea route to reach southern Russia and even penetrate up the great rivers of the region, although there is less solid evidence for this than for the other routes mentioned.

TRADE AS A MEANS OF CONTROL

Although trade with the border tribes occurred all along the Rhine-Danube frontier, and many frontier fortresses had special facilities to accommodate this activity, it was of greatest significance along the Danube. The border tribes of the region, the Marcomanni, Quadi, and Dacians, were numerous, well-organized, and relatively sophisticated. They were also dangerous adversaries, and the most desperate struggles in the history of the Roman army of the frontier were waged against these peoples. It was because of their presence that the bulk of the army of the frontier was garrisoned along the Danube. Nevertheless, it was important to the Roman government that commerce be maintained with these peoples. Not only did the Roman frontier districts depend heavily upon German imports of leather, horses, cattle, and the like, but it was essential that the government have control of commerce as a possible implement of foreign policy. Several treaties made with the Germans testify to the Roman government's concern with this commerce. Trading immediately along the frontier posed a clear danger to military security, but its continuation was necessary.

The imperial government maintained a policy of encouraging frontier trade generally, but strictly controlling its conduct. Tacitus remarked that the Hermundiri, a frontier tribe dwelling north of the upper Danube and allies of the Romans, were

> . . . the only Germans who trade with us, not only on the riverbank, but deep inside our lines, in the brilliant colony that is the capital of Raetia (Augsburg). They come over where they will, and without a guard. To other nations we only show our arms and our camps; to them we expose our palaces and our country-mansions and they do not covet them.[8]

This policy of controlling trade was continued until the disintegration of the western frontier. As late as 369, an agreement between the Eastern Emperor Valens and the Goths restricted German traders to two locales on the Danube.[9] By and large, the policy was effective. Although the frontier tribes along the Danube were dangerous and restive, and serious wars had to be waged against them, the fact that war interrupted commerce and ended their ability to acquire Roman export goods tended to act as a brake upon their hostile tendencies. After the battle of Adrianople in 378, for instance, the victorious Visigoths found all their opportunities for trade with the Romans had been cut off. Without their accustomed Roman imports, they soon found themselves in such straits that they sued for peace.[10]

TRANSPORT

Imperial restrictions on frontier trade and its extending or withdrawing trade as a means of controlling the border tribes must have had an unsettling effect upon the merchants of the frontier districts.[11] A number of factors no doubt made the German trade unpredictable enough without adding imperial manipulation of the merchants' activities. The complex of trade routes and the existence of various independent groups of shippers might mean, for instance, that a merchant carrying a load of glassware, at a great investment of time, expense, and personal danger, to a market at the mouth of the Elbe, might find the market glutted by similar shipments brought in by Frisians to sell to Danes who had already bought such wares from Danubian merchants at the mouth of the Oder. Or he might find that the entire trade route system had been closed by a war breaking out between two far-off tribes, fighting to the death for some typically incomprehensible German reason. Despite such uncertainties, however, the German trade continued along the frontier, and eventually encouraged the growth of a considerable manufacturing potential in these districts along the edge of the Empire. The German trade, and the manufacture of export goods to supply it, became a virtual monopoly of the frontier.[12]

The basic reason for this development lay in the fact that there was no effective all-water route from the heartland of the Empire to its European frontier districts. Overland transport was both expensive and slow in the ancient world and was avoided when possible. Transport and packaging technology was, as a consequence, poorly developed. The Romans generally employed pack animals when possible, but when the weight of the load demanded, they would use carts. Such carts were drawn by oxen, which served as the primary draft animal prior to the adoption of the horse collar in the early medieval period. Since the Romans had not developed such basic wagon technology as tandem harnessing, eveners, wheel bearings, or pivoted front axles, their carts were limited to light loads and were both clumsy and easily worn out. They were poorly-suited for rough roads or cross-country hauling, and their maximum traction was two animals. Pack mules could cover about fifty miles per day on a relatively regular basis, but their loads were necessarily light and they required grain while travelling. Ox-drawn carts could carry more freight, but could manage only about twenty miles in the same time.[13]

Given the small maximum loads and the great time required to cover any appreciable distance, the costs of land-transport were exorbitant. Long-distance hauling and the shipment of bulk commodities was simply not cost effective, nor could any enterprising merchant afford the excessive turn-around times required by overland freighting. The result was that whenever possible, the Romans relied on water transport. Roman traders could never view the Rhine and Danube as limits or barriers when their tributaries offered clear water access to the interior of Germany. Throughout the history of the Roman frontier districts, they served as jumping-off places for traders ranging deep into the interior. While the imperial administration may have viewed the frontier districts as the boundaries of the Empire, their inhabitants saw them also as the fringe of the vast lands of free Germany. The contrast between the government's view of the frontier as a static line and its inhabitants' perception of the frontier as a dynamic region contributed to the existence of a sentiment for continued imperial conquest, as opposed to the government's official anti-expansionist policies.

The limitations of overland transport had other profound effects on the frontier districts and their inhabitants. The basins of the Rhine and Danube were separated from that of the Mediterranean by short, but costly and time-consuming, overland routes. As a consequence, trade and commerce between the heartland of the Empire and its continental frontier, although extensive, was not unlimited, and the two tended to form separate economic regions. At the same time, the importance of the North Sea, Rhine and Danube as a water-route uniting the frontier districts was accentuated. Divorced by overland barriers from their heartland and connected closely to each other by their water-routes, it was easy for the frontier districts to develop and maintain a sense of separate identity. The relative high cost of goods imported from the imperial heartland provided an opportunity for small-scale local manufacturers and producers to compete successfully for the regional military market as well as in the production of export goods for the German trade. Some luxury goods, such as fine wines, were of such great value per unit of weight, that their export from the imperial heartland continued to be a profitable pursuit.[14] By and large, however, as time passed, an ever-greater portion of production for both local consumption and export came to be concentrated in the frontier districts.

The significance of the fact that the frontier districts were separated from the Empire by an overland barrier was not lost on the Romans. In A.D. 58, Lucius Antistius Verus, an energetic governor of Upper Germany, developed a plan to link the Saône and Moselle by a canal, using army engineers to provide the planning and frontier troops to furnish the labor. In reporting this event, Tacitus enthusiastically noted that this would have allowed goods from the Mediterranean to be shipped up the Rhone and Saône, via the canal to the Moselle, and thence to the Rhine and North Sea, thus eliminating the need of overland transport.[15] Strikingly enough, Aelius Gracilis, the governor of Gallia Belgica (modern northern France and Belgium), where the canal would be built, refused to allow the frontier troops to enter his province. Tacitus attributed his action to jealousy and quoted his argument that the project would please the inhabitants of Gaul and cause the emperor concern. Tacitus implies that this is merely an excuse, but it is more likely that Aelius Gracilis realized that an all-water route from the Mediterranean would benefit the producers and manufacturers of southern Gaul to the detriment of the inhabitants of his own province. It is not improbable that other such schemes were frustrated by the same type of resistance. The inhabitants of the frontier regions must have realized that their isolation from the large-scale production centers of the South worked to their advantage and that it was in their interests to keep it that way.❖

NOTES

1. Pliny, *Naturalis Historia,* ed. H. Rackham (Cambridge University Press, 1938), 37: 45. Olwen Brogan, "Trade Between the Roman Empire and the Free Germans," *JRS* 26 (1936): 196.

2. Tacitus, *Annales,* 2: 62. M. P. Charlesworth, *Trade-Routes and Commerce of the Roman Empire* (New York: Square Publishers Inc., 1970), pp. 187–188, 208, 215, 217, states that even before Caesar, merchants had penetrated into the Rhine valley. As early as Caesar's time, merchants were engaged in trade with Britain, and during the reign of Augustus, trade relations were kept up with this region. Among the items exported from Britain were gold, silver, iron, hides, cattle, sheep, wool, dogs, cloth, and slaves.

3. R. M. Wheeler, *Rome Beyond the Imperial Frontiers* (London: G. Bell & Sons Ltd., 1955), p. 7.

4. Pliny, 37: 45.

5. Brogan, p. 196.

6. For German traders in the region of the Elbe, see Brogan, p. 196, who also suggests that some of the sailors of the lower Rhine, mostly Germanic, may have traded along the north German coast.

7. Some few Roman coins have been found in Ireland, particularly in the Boyne valley of Meath, which might indicate trade with Britain. The coins may, however, have reached Ireland indirectly, through Welsh traders.

8. Tacitus, *Germania,* ed. D. R. Stuart (New York: Macmillan Co., 1916), 41.

9. Ammianus Marcellinus, *Rerum Gestarum Libri Qui Supersunt,* ed. Wolfgang Seyfarth, 2 vols. (Leipzig: Teubner, 1978), 17; 9, 10.

10. Wheeler, *Rome Beyond the Imperial Frontiers,* p. 15.

11. Although evidence is, naturally enough, lacking, it would appear more than likely that such government restrictions would have led to extensive smuggling. It would have been difficult for the government to control such an activity along the entire length of the frontier, particularly when a sizeable portion of the local population would have supported it. It was generally forbidden to trade armor or weapons to the Germans, but the numerous finds of such items in German burials and other archaeological sites indicate that this government regulation sat rather lightly on the shoulders of the frontier traders.

12. C. R. Whittaker, "Trade and Frontiers in the Roman Empire," *Trade and Famine in Classical Antiquity,* ed. P. Garnsey and C. R. Whittaker (Supplement Volume 8; Cambridge UK: Cambridge Philological Society, 1983), considers the general phenomenon, while Olwen Brogan, "Trade between the Roman Empire and the Free Germans." *Journal of Roman Studies* 26 (1936): 196-223, is dated but still worth reading as an introduction to the German trade. Otto Schlippschuh, *Die Händler im römischen Kaiserreich in Gallien, Germanien und den Donauprovinzen Ration, Noricum und Pannonien* (Amsterdam: Hakkert, 1974), provides a general view of the activities of traders, while Jurgen Kunow, *Der romische Import in der Germania libera bis zu den Markomannenkriegen: Studien zu Bronze- und Glasgefassen* (Neumunster: K. Wachholtz, 1983), confines himself to two important wares. V. Sakar, "Roman Imports in Bohemia," *Fontes Archaeologici Pragenses* 14 (1970), considers the extent and variety of Roman trading to a single region.

13. See Christoph Wilhelm Roring, *Untersuchungen zu römischen Reisewagen* (Koblenz: Numismatischer Verlag G. M. Forneck, 1983), for a discussion of Roman wagon technology. J. Mertens, "The Military Origins of Some Roman Settlements in Belgium," *Rome and Her Northern Provinces,* ed. Brian Hartley and John Wacher (Gloucester: Alan Sutton Publishing Ltd., 1983), p. 39, suggests that the failure of the Romans to develop more efficient harnessing indicates that their transport technology was sufficient for their needs. In northern Europe, the terrain would have impeded freight wagons in any event, so one

may conclude that water transport and pack animals made the development of more efficient means of hauling unnecessary.

14. Wheeler, pp. 47–48.

15. Tacitus, *Annales,* 13: 53.

RECOMMENDED READINGS

The literature on Roman trade beyond its frontiers is scattered and much of it is in languages other than English. The classic study of the subject is R. M. Wheeler, *Rome Beyond the Imperial Frontiers* (London: G. Bell & Sons, 1935), and the subject of frontier trading in particular is considered in C. R. Whittaker, "Trade and Frontiers in the Roman Empire," ed. P. Garnsey and C. R. Whittaker, *Trade and Famine in Classical Antiquity* (Cambridge Philological Society, Supplement Vol. 8 (1983): 118) and Anthony Birley, "The Economic Effects of Roman Frontier Policy," *The Roman West in the Third Century,* ed. A. King and M. Henig (Oxford, UK: British Archaeological Reports S-109, 1981), 39–54.

Specific trading systems are analyzed by Olwen Brogan, "Trade Between the Roman Empire and the Free Germans," *Journal of Roman Studies* 26 (1936): 196–223; Ioan Glodariu, *Dacian Trade with the Hellenistic and Roman World* (British Archaeological Reports supplementary series, 8. Oxford: British Archaeological Reports, 1976); and L. Macinnes, "Baubles, Bangles and Beads: Trade and Exchange in Roman Scotland," *Barbarians and Romans in North-West Europe,* ed. J. C. Barrett, A. P. Fitzpatrick, and L. Macinnes (Oxford, UK: British Archaeological Reports S-471, 1989), pp. 108–116.

Archaeological evidence of the extent and nature of Roman trade with their German neighbors may be found in Hans Norling-Christensen, "Danish Imports of Roman and Roman Provincial Objects in Bronze and Glass," *Congress of Roman Frontier Studies, 1949,* ed. Eric Birley (Durham: University of North Carolina Press, 1952), p. 76, and V. Sakar, "Roman Imports in Bohemia," *Fontes Archaeologici Pragenses* 14 (1970).

THE FALL OF ROME

Arther Ferrill

The screen darkens and the ominous beat of a single kettledrum is heard. The screen then brightens, with a map of the Roman Empire in white surrounded by Barbarian Lands in black. As the black spreads into the pristine whiteness of the Roman Empire, clangs, shouts, and screams are heard in the background while a solemn voice intones, "In the fifth century, barbarian hordes from the North swarmed over the Roman Empire, burning the temples, and sacking the cities. The lamp of civilization burned low through a thousand years until [the sound of a trumpet peals] the Rebirth of the Human Spirit called the REHN-AY-SAHNS" and the word REN'AISSANCE appears at the bottom of the screen.

This is a typical view of the fall of the Roman Empire, and most of us have probably watched a similar episode in some educational film or another. It is a false view, however; there were not hordes, and they were—for the most part—not barbarians. There were no temples; they had years before been converted into Christian churches. Most of all, however, this dramatic sequence jumps right over the important question of how "The Grandeur That Was Rome" could have fallen before these handfuls of wandering cattlemen.

New theories are advanced periodically. The Romans went crazy from drinking water from lead pipes and cooking food in clay pots with lead glaze. They all got malaria. The educated classes stopped having children, so the Romans became stupid. The Emperor Honorius was an idiot whose hobby was feeding chickens. The Romans became Christians and were too concerned with the next world to do anything about the present one.

Arther Ferrill attempts to cut through all of these bright ideas to reach a single, rational cause. He finds it in the decay of discipline and skill in the Roman army of the West. The Romans had hired Germans to do their fighting for them but expected them to fight in the same manner as the Roman legions of old. The morale and training of these troops were inadequate for the task of fighting in close-ordered ranks. The Western Empire fell because it allowed the effectiveness of its armed forces to decay beyond the point of repair.

READING QUESTIONS

1. What reasons have been advanced for the weakness of late Western Roman armies?

2. When did the weakness of the Western army become apparent?

3. What role did Stilicho play in this weakening?

4. What was the importance of Roman military training?

W hen the adherents of the 'Late Antique' school use the word 'transformation' in describing the fall of Rome, they mean it as an explanation as well as a description. The transformation they see from Rome to the Middle Ages developed over centuries, not years. Yet the fall of Rome in the West was more than a process—it was also an event, one that occurred rather suddenly, in the same sense at least in which the fall of the British Empire after World War II required about a generation but can nevertheless be said to have been sudden.

If one takes 476 as the date of the fall, and looks back merely a hundred years to 376, one can see an empire still strong, still as large as the Empire of Augustus, still respected by its foes across the imperial frontiers. Furthermore, it was defended by an army that continued to fight effectively despite the catastrophe in Persia under Julian, a strategic blow that cannot be laid at the feet of the legions.

On the other hand, 376 was itself an important year in Roman history. It was then that the Visigoths, driven by the pressure of the Huns and the Ostrogoths, crossed the Danube with the emperor's permission to settle permanently in Roman territory. Thus began a series of invasions (for the crossing of the Danube soon turned into an invasion) that led in a hundred years to the fall of the Western Roman Empire. It is easy with hindsight to regard that fall as inevitable, to emphasize the vulnerability and fragility of the Roman Empire.

One cannot argue, as in the case of modern Britain, that the loss of empire 'cushioned' Rome's fall in the world. The Empire had been so inextricably identified with Rome itself that the fall of the Empire *was* the fall of Rome.

From Arther Ferrill, *The Fall of the Roman Empire* (New York: Thames & Hudson, 1986), pp. 161–169.

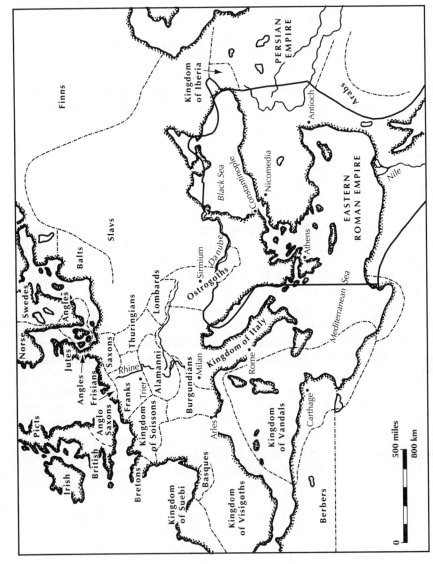

Europe in AD 476. The Western Roman Empire no longer existed. The Byzantine Empire survived until the fifteenth century.

To see Roman history from Marcus Aurelius on, as the story of a troubled giant, as so many historians do, a decaying empire, the victim of 'cultural and world-political Angst', is to miss the point. Some historians, recognizing the common fallacy, turn the problem around and ask why the Empire survived so long. Both tendencies, however, have the same effect—to direct attention away from a consideration of the factors that led to the disappearance of the Western Roman Empire in the last half of the fifth century; one by seeking the causes in the much too distant past and the other by accepting the fact as inevitable.

The Roman Empire on the eve of Adrianople was not obviously on a downhill course. Nor had Roman citizens lost faith in their destiny to rule the world. The Empire was strong, despite a recent defeat in Persia, and it continued to show remarkable strength in the devastating thirty or so years between the defeat at Adrianople and the sack of Rome by Alaric. Since the days of the Punic Wars the strategic strength of Rome had consisted to a certain extent in the ability of the Empire to suffer tactical defeats in the field and yet mobilize new forces to continue the fighting.

Even after AD 410 some of that resilience remained, but there was one difference, particularly in the West. Rome had almost stopped producing its own soldiers, and those it did draw into military service were no longer trained in the ancient tactics of close-order formation though they tried to fight that way. Many historians have argued, either directly or more often by emphasizing other causes, that the fall of Rome was not primarily a military phenomenon. In fact, it was exactly that. After 410 the emperor in the West could no longer project military power to the ancient frontiers. That weakness led immediately to the loss of Britain and within a generation to the loss of Africa. One need not produce a string of decisive battles in order to demonstrate a military collapse. The shrinkage of the imperial frontiers from 410 to 440 was directly the result of military conquests by barbarian forces. To be sure, the loss of strategic resources in money, material and manpower compounded the mere loss of territory and made military defence of the remainder of the Empire even more difficult. It is simply perverse, however, to argue that Rome's strategic problems in the 440s, 50s and 60s were primarily the result of financial and political difficulties or of long-term trends such as gradual depopulation.

The modern historian must keep in mind the fact that Rome in the East did not fall, and any explanation of the fall of Rome must also account for its survival in Byzantium. Why was the East to marshal its military resources, to survive the barbarian invasions and to emerge under Justinian in the sixth century with a burst of military power, sufficient to reconquer, at least temporarily, parts of the West? Some specifically military explanations can be set aside. Recruitment in the Late Empire was difficult, but too much has been made of imperial legislation on that score. Even in the great days of the Roman Empire, for example in the last years of Augustus, recruitment could be a problem during military crises. In the fourth and fifth centuries it was no greater a problem in the West than in the East, at least not until western difficulties were highly exacerbated by military and territorial losses. The strategic strength of the East behind the impenetrable walls of Constantinople is often emphasized as a factor in the survival of the Byzantine Empire, but one must look also at the elements of weakness in the West.

In fact, of course, the sack of Rome, the loss of Britain and of Africa, and parts of Gaul and Spain, dealt heavy blows to the military capacity of the Western emperor. If one begins the story of Rome's fall with the year 440, the collapse of the West and not of the East is easy enough to explain. By 440 western forces were much weaker than those of the East. That was not true, however, on the last day of the year 406, the day Vandals, Suebi and Alamanni crossed the frozen Rhine and moved into Gaul. In 406, on paper, western power was as great as eastern. Stilicho had driven Alaric and Radagaisus out of Italy. Indeed on behalf of the West he had dealt more effectively with Alaric than eastern generals had done. Yet in the short period, 407–10, the West received an ultimately fatal blow. After 410 it was never again militarily as strong as the East. Barbarians were permanently established in Gaul and Spain, and Britain had been lost.

One could argue, as I am inclined to do, that even after 410 the emperor of the West had not lost all military options, that he might yet have restored Roman military power, if not in Britain, at least in the rest of the Western Empire. But military losses in 407–10 were sufficient to make a major difference between the strategic, projective military power of the Eastern and Western emperors. Those few years constitute a turning point after which it is no longer necessary to explain why the West fell and the East survived.

Why, then, did the West do so badly in 407–10? To a certain extent, as we have seen, the strategic strength of the East contributed to the fall of the West. Constantinople was heavily defended. No barbarian tribe could possibly hope to storm those walls. Furthermore, the emperor in the East was better able to afford the heavy subsidies barbarian leaders demanded in the years after Adrianople, though in fact the West also paid a heavy monetary price for peace.

Perhaps the most popular approach to the explanation of Rome's fall, if we can set aside the examination of those long-term causes such as depopulation, race mixture, political and economic deterioration, lead poisoning and other fashionable theories, has been to find a scapegoat, to see in an error or errors of human judgment the fatal mistake that caused the tragedy. Although this approach has often been ridiculed in recent times, it is not without merit. Leaders do matter. Strategic decisions produce successful or unsuccessful results. The weight of history, in the form of long-term trends, may impose limitations on the military mind, but a good general or political leader will bear the burden and solve his strategic problems one way or another.

The Emperor Honorius has been asked by ancient and modern historians alike to take far too much of the blame for Rome's fall. Partly that is because

Rome suffered its great humiliation in 407–10 under his rule, and since he did not prevent it, he must undoubtedly be held responsible for it. As citizens we apply this kind of standard to our present leaders, and it is perhaps not unreasonable to do the same for leaders of the past. On the other hand, if it is possible to be right and still lose, Honorius may have done just that. He does not deserve the criticism he uniformly gets for doing nothing, since doing nothing was almost certainly, for him, an 'active' or conscious strategy, not simply negligence, a strategy that might in fact have worked if someone had not opened a gate to Rome for Alaric's Visigoths in August 410.

Stilicho's role in the fall of the West is harder to assess, and he has had vigorous attackers and defenders. That he was much too interested in affairs in Constantinople rather than in Italy is certain. Whether he can also be accused of having let Alaric escape on several occasions when the barbarian leader might have been crushed is impossible to determine on the basis of the inadequate surviving evidence. To those who see the fall of Rome as a matter of trends, Stilicho's efforts are of no concern. Presumably if he had not left Alaric free to sack Rome, someone else would have sacked it. How can even Rome fight trends? But in fact the fate of the Western Roman Empire might have been very different had events in 407–10 taken another course. Insofar as human agency might have prevented them, the failure of Stilicho is significant. His inability to shape a better future for the Western Roman Empire was much more the result of actual mistaken judgment (leading to his execution in 408) than was the failure of Honorius. Stilicho was wrong; Honorius was unlucky.

It is also true, however, that the army itself underwent significant deterioration between 378 and 410, more so in the West than in the East. In the fourth century the western army had been the better one. It was the eastern army that had been defeated in Persia and at Adrianople, but at the Frigid River in 394 Theodosius had beaten the western army with the help of twenty thousand Visigoths, who attacked Arbogast and Eugenius in line of column suffering extraordinarily heavy losses (50 per cent). The loss at the Frigidus undoubtedly demoralized the western army to a certain extent, but it must have been much more humiliated by its treatment at the hands of Stilicho, who commanded it from 395 to 408.

At that time there was a reaction in the East against the use of Germans in the Roman army, but in the West Stilicho imposed the Theodosian policy of barbarization. First, with the western army in the Balkans he failed to crush Alaric on at least two occasions, and then, during the successful campaigns in Italy from 401 to 405 against Alaric (who got away again, twice) and Radagaisus, Stilicho relied heavily on barbarian troops. His use of barbarians became a matter of controversy and contributed to his downfall in 408. For that reason 'barbarization' in this period is often treated as a political problem (which it was), and little consideration has been given to the probable effect the policy had on the proud army of the West.

There is no way of knowing, unfortunately, to what extent the central, mobile army in Italy, by 408, was a traditional Roman army and to what extent it had become overwhelmed by barbarian influences. Possibly, if the resources of Britain and Gaul had been united with the army of Italy in the crisis of 408-10, it might have been possible to have defeated Alaric again, but the revolt of Constantine prevented that kind of cooperation, and Honorius decided to pursue a strategy of exhaustion rather than to bring Alaric to battle. Such a policy was extremely humiliating for the army. General Sir John Hackett has said: 'An army's good qualities are best shown when it is losing.' To fight on in the face of certain defeat requires much more than courage. But the army of the West in the crisis of 408-10 was not allowed to fight at all, and after what it had suffered earlier at the hands of Stilicho, this was the crushing blow. Never again was the emperor of the West the military equal of his eastern counterpart.

In the aftermath of 410 Constantius and Aëtius had done the best they could to maintain Rome's reduced position in the West. Constantius was the better strategist of the two, and his skilful use of naval power did give the regime, now in Ravenna, a new lease of life. Aëtius was unfortunately too interested in Gaul at the expense of Italy, Spain and particularly Africa. The loss of Carthage was a double blow to Rome since the emperor in the West had relied heavily on African grain and because the resources of the African city now strengthened the Vandal kingdom. Declining revenues and territory made recruitment difficult, and the true Roman contingent of the army that fought Attila at Châlons was the object of ridicule. In the last twenty years of the Western Empire, after the death of Valentinian III, the central government in Italy relied exclusively on barbarians until the latter finally, in 476, put one of their own officers in as king and abolished the emperorship in the West.

It is clear that after 410 the Roman army no longer had any special advantage, tactically, over barbarian armies—simply because the Roman army had been barbarized. Hans Delbrück has argued that Roman strength had always been strategic rather than tactical, that man for man Roman armies were no better than Germanic ones:

> Vis-a-vis civilized peoples, barbarians have the advantage of having at their disposal the warlike power of unbridled animal instincts, of basic toughness. Civilization refines the human being, makes him more sensitive, and in doing so it decreases his military worth, not only his bodily strength but also his physical courage.

Delbrück goes on to say that Roman tactical organization and training merely 'equalized the situation'.

This is stuff and nonsense. Rome's army had always been small, relative to the population of the Empire, because Roman training and discipline gave it an unparalleled advantage in tactically effective, close-order formation. By 451, to judge from the speech Attila gave to the Huns at the battle of

Châlons, the feeble remnant of the once-proud legions still fought in the ancient formation, but apparently without the training and discipline. Without them, close order was worse than no order at all. Romans could be expected to huddle behind their screen of shields; Visigoths and Alans would do the fighting. As the western army became barbarized, it lost its tactical superiority, and Rome fell to the onrush of barbarism. ❖

RECOMMENDED READINGS

The bibliography on the fall of the Roman Empire is quite extensive, and Alden M. Rollins, *The Fall of Rome: A Reference Guide* (Jefferson, NC: McFarland, 1983), offers a thorough listing of these works, particularly those in English, up to 1982. The most famous treatment of the subject is that of Edward Gibbon's *The Decline and Fall of the Roman Empire*. This is available in many editions, but among the most common is the three-volume set first published by Modern Library in 1932. Lionel Gossman, *The Empire Unpossess'd: An Essay on Gibbon's Decline and Fall* (New York: Cambridge University Press, 1981), offers one of several excellent analyses of Gibbon's approach to the matter.

The question undergoes regular reevaluations, of which Michael Grant, *The Fall of the Roman Empire: A Reappraisal* (Radnor, PA: Annenberg School Press, 1976), is a good example. The Heath series on Problems in European Civilization includes a good appraisal of the nature of the "fall" in Donald Kagan, *The End of the Roman Empire: Decline or Transformation?* (Lexington, MA: Heath, 1978). Different authors have considered the question from different points of view. Jaroslav J. Pelikan, *The Excellent Empire: The Fall of Rome and the Triumph of the Church* (San Francisco: Harper & Row, 1987), for instance, traces the rise of the Church to fill the vacuum left with the collapse of Roman civil authority.

Walter Goffart, in *Barbarians and Romans, A.D. 418–584: The Techniques of Accommodation* (Princeton, NJ: Princeton University Press, 1980) and *Rome's Fall and After* (London: Hambledon Press, 1989), discusses the amalgamation of the Romans and their conquerors after the collapse of the independent Western Empire.

DISCUSSION QUESTIONS

PART TWO: THE ANCIENT WORLD, 2500 B.C. TO A.D. 500

1. The original Olympic Games were a costly affair and were justified as being religious festivals in honor of the god Zeus. Do you think this was the real reason that people participated in, supported, and attended the Games, or was it simply an excuse? Who benefited from the Games, and what rewards did they earn? What connection do you see between sports and religion? Freud said that athletic competition could serve as a substitute for war. Do you think the Olympic Games may have partly fulfilled this function?

2. You will have observed that most of the education discussed in "Student Life in Ancient India" consisted of the student's learning the prayers and rituals necessary to establish himself as a member of a privileged caste. Was this a legitimate function for an educational system, and to what extent do you think it harmed or benefited Indian society? Does modern education to some extent perform the same function? Is a "Liberal Education" a legitimate educational goal, or is it primarily a means of setting members of the college-educated class apart from their less advantaged peers?

3. It has been suggested that the treatment of women as inferiors is the most fundamental and pervasive form of discrimination and exploitation. Based on your reading of "The Roots of Restriction: Women in Early Israel" and "The Position of Women in Han China," to what extent would you agree with that proposition? Why should gender discrimination be so extensive and enduring? Who really profits from such customs? Would all of a society not benefit from utilizing the abilities of women to their full extent? If so, why have societies generally failed to do so?

4. Some technological innovations are less important in themselves than in the way they facilitate other technological developments. What were the immediate advantages of papermaking, and what other advances did it make possible? Why did the art of papermaking take so long to reach western Europe?

5. Some historians suggest that the course of events is directed not so much by human decisions as by the effect of certain basic factors, such as the size and structure of a society's population. Based on "The Roots of Restriction" and "The Greeks Reach Out," to what extent do you consider that position to be valid? Why do societies have such difficulty in

controlling their own numbers, and what devices do they use to do so? What sort of effects does the structure of our population have on our own society, and how far reaching are these effects?

6. We generally consider commerce to be a purely economic matter, the exchange of goods in the pursuit of profit. Do you think there may be more to it than that? Why were the Silk Roads so important, since they served primarily to carry expensive and unnecessary luxury goods from one end of Eurasia to the other? What factors encouraged German-Roman frontier trade? What value does trade have apart from the exchange of goods?

7. Many books and articles have been written attempting to explain the fall of the Western Roman Empire. Do you consider this a significant question or not? If it is not a significant question, why do you think it has aroused such interest over such a long period?

8. You have seen that some technological developments tend to concentrate power in the hands of a few, and others tend to disperse it among many. What major "aristocratizing" inventions of the past can you think of, and what significant "democratizing" ones? How have these technological developments affected the states and societies in which they were introduced? What do you consider the dominant technology of the modern world? Do you think it is aristocratizing or democratizing?

9. You have seen that the status and freedom of women were greatly restricted in early Israel and Han China. What were the various tools used to keep women in an inferior position? Are similar devices still in use in society today? What exceptions did the Hebrews and Chinese make in these restrictions, and why?

10. We have noted that the Roman, Sassanian, Mauryan, and Han empires each established the "Classical" tradition for their regions. Why was this so? Why have these cultural traditions continued to endure, and why have people constantly returned to them as models? What elements of Roman heritage do you see in the world about you?

PART III

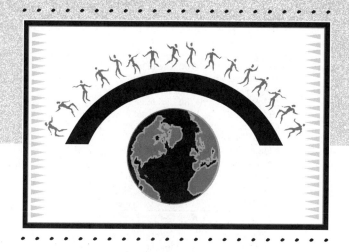

Expanding Horizons:
Challenges to the
Classical Heritage

❖ ❖ ❖

A.D. 500 TO 1350

Region	500	600	700	800	900
AND AFRICA	**536–552** Gothic Wars in Italy **568** Lombards invade Italy **586** Conversion of Recared I, Spain **590–604** Pope Gregory I	**679–714** Pepin II, The rise of the Carolingians	**ca. 700** *The Stirrup and Its Impact on Medieval Society* **732** Charles Martel defeats the Arabs **768–814** Charles the Great; crowned emperor, 800	**ca. 800** *Bodo: A Peasant in Charlemagne's Time* **849** Birth of Alfred the Great **864–865** Conversion of the Bulgars	**910** Monastery of Cluny founded **955** Otto I defeats Magyars
	527–565 Byzantine Emperor Justinian **534** *Corpus Juris Civilis* **572** Sassanian dynasty restores Persian frontier	**ca. 662** *Jewish-Muslim Relations: The Formative Years* **662** *Hegira* of Muhammad **627** Heraclius defeats Persians **661** Umayyad dynasty founded, Damascus	**700** Rise of trading state of Ghana, western Sudan **730** Byzantine Iconoclastic movement **750** Abbasid caliphate founded, Baghdad **786–809** Caliph Harun-al-Rashid		**900–1200** Kalomo culture, southern Zambia **969** Fatimids conquer Egypt **976–1025** Basil the Bulgar Slayer **998–1030** Mahmud of Ghazna
ASIA	**ca. 500** *The Travels of Sānudāsa the Merchant* **ca. 500** Khmers conquer Funan	**ca. 650** Rock-cut architecture, Tamil, southern India	**700–799** Borobudur stupa, Java **ca. 711** Early Arab incursions into north Africa **ca. 788–820** Shankara, Indian philosopher		
	552–710 Asuka period, Japan **552** Buddhism in Japan **581–617** Sui Dynasty, China	**607** "Constitution" of Prince Shotoku, Japan **618–907** Tang Dynasty, China	**701–763** Li Bo, Chinese poet **710–784** Nara period, Japan **751** Battle of Talas, near Samarkand **774–835** Kukai, Shingon Buddhism **794–1185** Heian period, Japan	**ca. 844** Buddhist persecutions **ca. 850** *Gunpowder and Firearms in Medieval China*	**960–1127** Northern Song Dynasty, China **995–1027** Fujiwara Michinaga, ruler of Japan
THE PACIFIC	**ca. 500–1000** Ulúa culture, Honduras **ca. 500** Caribbean eating habits shift from land to sea animals	**ca. 600–1000** Huari Empire, Andes	**ca. 700–1500** Cahokia Mississipan culture **ca. 770** Toltecs build Tula	**800** First settlement of New Zealand from Polynesia	**900–1325** Toltec Empire

1000	1100	1200	1250	1300 1350
1054 Schism between Latin and Greek churches **1066** Norman conquest **1075–1122** Investiture controversy **1080** Christians take Toledo	**ca. 1100** *The Life of the Nobility* **1150** First gothic church, St. Denis **ca. 1150** *Natural History of Medieval Women* **ca. 1155** Peasant Alpaix born **ca. 1182–1226** Francis of Assisi **1185–1200** Epidemic and famine	**1215** *Magna Carta* **1216** Dominian order established **ca. 1225–1274** Thomas Aquinas	**1276–1337** Giotto **ca. 1280** Transmission of gunpowder to the West **ca. 1280** *Clocks: A Revolution in Time*	**ca. 1300** *The Medieval Tournament* **1302** Unam Sanctam **1305–1377** Avignon papacy **1315–1317** Great famine **1347–1354** Black death
1035 Muslim Almoravid movement, Senegal **1071** Battle of ~~Manzikert; Seljuk~~ Turks take Jerusalem **1096–1100** First crusade	**ca. 1100** Kanem Empire, Lake Chad **ca. 1100** *The Impact of the Crusades* ~~**1185** Timbuktu~~ center of learning **1174–1193** Saladin, Sultan, Ayyubid Dynasty	**ca. 1200–1546** Mali Empire, west Africa **1204–1261** Latin Empire of ~~Constantinople~~ **1220** Mongol invasion of southwest Asia **1242** Mongol armies reach Adriatic	**1260** Mongols defeated by Mamluks **1291** Acre conquered ~~by Mamluks~~	**ca. 1300** Rise of Yoruba states, west Africa **1332–1406** Ibn-Khaldun, Arabian traveler **1350** Kongo Dynasty established
1044–1278 Pagan Empire, Burma **1070** Van Mieu Temple of Literature, Vietnam	**1100–1150** Angkor Wat, Kampuchea **1170** Height of Srivijaya kingdom, Java	**ca. 1200-1300** *The Thirteenth Century World System* **1206–1526** Delhi sultanate	**1293** Mongol expedition to Java **1296–1316** Aladain Khalji	
ca. 1000 *Heian Japan: The Good People* **1010** Tale of Genji **1069–1076** Wang Anshi, Chinese reformer **1090** Clock tower of Su Sung, China	**1127–1279** Southern Song Dynasty, China **1162–1227** Genghis Khan (Tèmujin) **1185–1333** Kamakura shogunate, Japan	**1215–1223** Mongols conquer central Asia, Russia, north China	**1260–1290** Kublai Khan, Mongol Dynasty, China **1271–1295** Marco Polo in China **1279–1368** Yüan Dynasty, China	**1300** Zen Buddhism **1336–1408** Ashikaga shogunate, Japan
1000 Vikings settle Greenland, discover North America **1000** Mesa Verde cliff dwellings, southwest United States **1000–1150** Mimbres people, New Mexico				**1325** Rise of Aztec Empire

INTRODUCTION

The period from the fourth to the twelfth century is often characterized in European history textbooks as the "Dark Ages," an era of poverty and stagnation commencing with the fall of the Roman Empire and ending only with the advent of the Italian Renaissance. Although this view is exaggerated, it has a certain validity when one contrasts conditions in western Europe at the time with those prevailing elsewhere in the Old World empires. The nomadic attacks of the fourth century had caused considerable disruption in all of these civilizations, and the fifth century saw the establishment of barbarian states on territories previously controlled by imperial forces. The sixth century, however, was a period of recovery. The Ephthalite invaders of India lost all cohesiveness and unity by 549; the Sassanian dynasty succeeded in restoring Persia's previous frontiers in 572; and China was reunited under the Sui dynasty in 589. Imperial recovery was limited only in the Mediterranean lands. Here, Justinian's effort at reunification ceased with his death in 565, and western Europe was abandoned to its Germanic conquerors.

Left to its own devices, western Europe lacked the population and resources to maintain, much less to restore, the civilization and culture the Romans had established there. After yet another wave of barbarian attacks in the ninth century, the Europeans were hard-pressed even to secure their own survival. This survival was secured by locally based mounted warriors who undertook both the government and defense of the West. "Bodo: The Life of a Peasant in Charlemagne's Time" depicts how completely the life of the mass of the population was subordinated to the needs and desires of this military aristocracy. Although all of the empires used heavy cavalry and local initiative against the nomadic horsemen along their frontiers, nowhere except in Europe did this military arrangement come to dominate government and society completely. In "The Stirrup and Its Impact on Medieval Society," Lynn White suggests that the reason for this was that nowhere else was heavy cavalry so fully developed as in Europe, but it would seem that the Europeans simply lacked the resources to maintain both a civil and military authority. The Europeans' meager wealth and manpower, organized in a compartmentalized and overwhelmingly agricultural society, were almost entirely directed to the task of maintaining the warhorses and warriors on which the region depended for its defense. The European selections in this part all reflect, in one way or another, the comparative poverty of the region during this period and the subordination of its resources to the military needs of feudalism.

The picture elsewhere in the lands of the Old World empires was one of dynamism and expansion. If Europe was agricultural and isolated, the other civilizations were commercial and cosmopolitan. The era of the Guptan Empire (320-535) was a golden age for India. Buddhist missionaries carried their faith northward and eastward to China, Korea, and even Japan. Meanwhile, traders carried India's material culture, as well as its religion, to Burma, Thailand, Ceylon, and Indonesia. This age of exploration and expansion gave rise to a vigorous culture, of which "The Travels of Sānudāsa the Merchant" is a charming example. This great maritime movement was terminated only by the Muslim seizure of Indian Ocean commerce during the seventh century.

The expansion of Muslim power carried the Arabic language and culture far beyond the borders of the Arabian Peninsula. Islam was established as a faith by 622 and as a political force ten years later. "Jewish-Muslim Relations: The Formative Years" provides an account of the events of those ten years, focusing on the struggle between Muhammad and his followers and the Jewish tribes of the oasis town of Medina. By 750, the Muslims had subjugated the Persian Empire to the north, had expanded as far as France to the west, and, to the east, had reached beyond the Indus River and to the frontier of the Chinese Empire. Arab ships dominated both the Mediterranean Sea and the Indian Ocean, and Arab merchants were trading throughout the entire belt of civilization and beyond.

Nor did the Chinese lag behind in this era of expansion. Armed forces of the T'ang dynasty (618–907) followed the great Silk Road that led across the Eurasian continent to the markets of the Mediterranean, a route detailed in Part II in "The Silk Roads: A History." In an early example of the flag following trade, Chinese imperial control was eventually extended as far as Kashgar and Khotan in central Asia. For the most part, however, Chinese dynamism was an internal affair, reflected in great increases in population and economic wealth, and the growing perfection of the Chinese social and political order. Something of the stability and creativity of China is demonstrated in Joseph Needham's "The Development of Gunpowder and Firearms in Medieval China." Although the Chinese had developed gunpowder and used it in warfare as early as the tenth century, it had had little real effect on Chinese affairs. The introduction of gunpowder and cannon helped to destroy the feudal society of western Europe, but Chinese society was not so fragile.

China had regained its position as the center of Eastern culture, and Chinese influences spread far beyond the borders of the empire. In the Japanese islands, these influences, coupled with the pacification of the aboriginal inhabitants, gave rise to an aristocracy of rarified manners and delicate culture. "Heian Japan: 'The Good People' and Their Lives" describes this accomplished but short-lived court society.

Western Europe began to develop economic strength and a degree of political stability with a sudden turn in its fortunes around the year 1000. Its enemies either embraced Christianity or fell into disunity, an unaccustomed degree of peace settled over the land, and population, production, and wealth began to increase. Society also began to change; "The Natural History of Medieval Women" illustrates how women lost economic value in the new commercial and manufacturing economy, and lost status and rights as a result.

Europe did not accept its good fortune gracefully, partly because it had been geared for war too long. In "The Life of the Nobility," Marc Bloch describes how the fighting aristocracy slowly transformed itself into a hereditary nobility, a process that reached an absurd culmination in the elaborate spectacles described in "The Medieval Tournament."

The Europeans also turned their military might outward and, for a brief period, succeeded in seizing control of Palestine from the Muslims. In "The Impact of the Crusades on Muslim Lands," Philip Hitti discusses how the Christian attacks in fact reinvigorated the disunited and squabbling western world of Islam. Although they were paltry when compared to the creative capacities of the Chinese, technological advances the Europeans began to make were small but important. The development of the mechanical clock in about 1280, discussed in "Clocks: A Revolution in Time," had profound effects on a developing and changing Europe.

By 1350, the Mongols had established an Asian empire that reopened the routes that had once united the Old World. A new political and economic balance had been struck, and a complex system of economic exchange had been established. Janet Abu-Lughod describes this pattern in "The Thirteenth-Century World System." Goods and ideas were once again flowing throughout the Eurasian continent, as were germs and viruses. The revival of long-distance commerce and trade condemned millions of people to death. Long isolated, Europe perhaps suffered the most severely and developed attitudes and institutions consonant with an age of recurrent plagues, wars, and famines.

It was in this troubled fashion that the Old World entered the early modern era.

The reading selections in this part therefore constitute a study in contrasts: poverty, parsimony, and a niggardly husbanding of scant resources in western Europe, contrasted with the wealth, expansion, sophistication, and exuberance of Islam, India, and China.

India, About A.D. *500*

THE TRAVELS OF SĀNUDĀSA
THE MERCHANT

J. A. B. Van Buitenen

This selection from the tale of Sānudāsa the Merchant is a small part of a great collection of Sanskrit romances dating perhaps to the eighth century. The action is set earlier still, in the period of the great Guptan Empire of India, from the fourth through the seventh centuries, a time when Indian civilization was being spread by trade into Southeast Asia, Indonesia, and elsewhere on the littoral of the Indian Ocean. Sānudāsa was not a historical figure but an ideal type. In Western literature, the hero of a quest is usually a warrior or thief, such as Jason, Ulysses, or Aeneas. In the East, it is more often a merchant, such as Sinbad or Sānudāsa. Sānudāsa fulfills his destiny by striving for profit, but, as this selection demonstrates, the Indian concept of profit encompasses more than simple considerations of economic gain.

Despite its sprightliness and almost comic resolution, the story of Sānudāsa is in fact a highly moral tale. We have seen in Jeannine Auboyer's account of the schools of ancient India that the caste system was fundamental to an understanding of Indian culture and society. In a cycle of births and rebirths, the individual climbed closer and closer to the ultimate goal of Nirvana by performing his proper obligations, and sank lower and lower to the same degree that he failed to meet them. Sānudāsa was a Vaisya, a merchant, and he was neglecting the obligations of his status. Both the magnificent hymn of the Bhagavad Gita *and the tale of Sānudāsa the merchant illuminate the same principle, that neglect of one's proper functions is the greatest of faults.*

This selection begins somewhat abruptly, and requires some background. Sānudāsa was the rich and pampered only son of a famous merchant of the city of Campa. By the time he had reached manhood and his father had died, his fastidiousness and self-righteousness made him a burden to his friends and useless to himself. His friends tricked him into getting drunk and making love to a prostitute of the city. Sānudāsa was so captivated by these pleasures that he stayed with the prostitute and quickly spent his entire fortune on her. She then threw him out of her house. Returning to his own home, he was told it had been sold and that

his destitute mother, wife, and child had been forced to move to the Pau-
pers' Quarter on the outskirts of the city.

READING QUESTIONS

1. Why does Sānudāsa embark on his journey?

2. What parallels does Sānudāsa see between the *Bhagavad Gita* and his own expedition for gold?

3. What role did the hermit play in Sānudāsa's education?

4. How had Sānudāsa been tricked by his mother and his friends?

S lowly I trod along the road to the village of the poor, and I looked at the dispossessed, wasted by consumption, more dead than alive. Then, under a common nīm tree, I saw my little son Dattaka. He was surrounded by a band of children. He was the king and the others his ministers and subjects, and he was sharing with them the little balls of half-ripe barley which he had brought. One of the boys who played the chamberlain snatched the ball that was reserved for the king and swallowed it hungrily. Dattaka, robbed of his single piece, began to scream for his mother. He ran to a little cabin, the front yard of which was littered with rubbish. A fence of straw mats ran around the place, but it was rotten and loose, and the roof let sun and moon in through an infinite number of holes.

I followed Dattaka to the front yard. A servant girl recognized me and went in to tell Mitrāvatī. My mother came out in great confusion and embraced me, even in the state I was in. She held me tight and did not move or even breathe, as though at last she had found rest in a deep sleep. The poor woman who had lost her husband and only today had found her son washed me with her tears which were neither hot nor cold. Then I saw my wife. She was hiding in a corner of the hut and—But why enlarge on the misery of it all? She was the image of poverty itself.

By rubbing my skin carefully with kodrava grains still in the husk, my mother removed the stuff which that malicious wench at the brothel had smeared on me. A water pitcher had to be borrowed next door to give me a

From *Tales of Ancient India*, trans. J. A. B. Van Buitenen (Chicago: University of Chicago Press, 1959), pp. 227–229, 243–253.

hot bath; it was full of holes patched with lac, the brim was chipped, the neck cracked. The servant who was giving me my bath broke this miserable pitcher in a moment of carelessness, and the woman who owned it beat her breast and screamed wildly. "Ayi, my little pitcher, my princess of a pitcher, now you are gone and the world is empty and my mother dead. Mother got you as a present from her family when she married, and I cry over you as my second mother. . . ."

My heart grew weak with compassion for the woman who was weeping so pitifully; and I cut my cloak in two and gave her one half. Like elephants who drink the water in which they have bathed I ate a soup of kodrava seasoned with rice gruel; but it took effort. Enough! You have heard too much already about life of the poor, and hearing more can only upset a man of your sensibilities.

Somehow I got through a night that lasted a hundred thousand years. An inescapable gloom came over me, and when morning broke, I said to my mother: "I shall return to your house with four times more than I have wasted—or I shall never return. You, mother, you must pass your days as if you had never had a son or as if your son had died, with whatever distraction your misery and your labor can provide."

"Don't go, my child," she begged. "I shall do the meanest kind of work to keep you alive and happy with your wife and son."

"Praised be the life of the talented man who lives on the wretched labor of his old mother! Stop worrying about me, mother. Are you not the wife of a man whose mind was as lofty as the Meru?"

My insistence won out, and I bowed to my mother and departed from that terrible colony of the poor as from the inferno itself. My mother followed me a long way, giving me all kinds of good advice. "Go to Tāmraliptī, son. My brother Gangadatta lives there, and when a man is in need, his mother's people are his only refuge. An intelligent man leaves his father's relations alone, for they are his born enemies!"

She gave me a bowl full of rice cakes, and with a last word of advice she turned back. I went on and took the road that goes east. On the road I saw a company of travelers from foreign parts. Their umbrellas and sandals were worn, and they carried old leather haversacks and cooking pots slung over the shoulder. They looked exactly as I did; but when they saw me, they said to one another in pitying voices, "Aho, look at the cruel workings of fate! Who would have thought to see the upright Sānudāsa in this state? But why should we pity him? He has not lost his fortune yet: for so long as a man of character has not lost his talents, he has lost nothing!"

Sānudāsa then underwent a series of adventures—shipwreck, robberies, persecution—always seeking to make his fortune and always failing. Despite offers of help and pleas to return home, he continued his quest. Profit had become more than simply a means of freeing his family from the horrors of poverty; it had become the only means by which Sānudāsa felt he could justify his own existence.

One day I met a merchant by the name of Acera who was going to the Gold Countries with a large company of traders. I embarked with him on his ship, and when we had completed part of our journey on sea, we landed, beached our ship, and continued on land down the coast.

When the sun reddened at dusk, we halted in wooded country at the foot of a majestic mountain whose peak pierced the clouds. That night, after we had finished eating and were sitting on our beds of leaves, the caravan leader gave us instructions.

"Merchants, when we are climbing the mountain, tie your rucksacks with provisions tightly to your backs with three windings of rope and hang your leather oil-flasks around your necks. While climbing, use a flexible and sturdy cane stick, not too dry or brittle, and hold it firmly with both your hands. Any fool who uses any other kind of stick is bound to get killed on the mountain. They call this the Cane Trail. It is like the great Lord of Obstacles, and it seeks to frustrate all the efforts of those who are driven by the prospects of gold."

He sounded discouraging; but, devoured by our cupidity, we did as he told us. When one of our party had already climbed a good part of the way, the end of his cane broke; and, like a warrior whose bowstring is cut by a blade, he tumbled and fell to the valley. All the others in our party made it to the summit. We mourned our companion's death and made him a water oblation. We passed the night on the peak.

The next morning we traveled a long way until we found a river full of large rocks that were shaped like cows, horses, goats, and sheep. Acera, at the head of our column, stopped us from going any farther.

"Don't touch the water, don't! Hey, there, stop at once, stop! Any fool who touches this water is changed into stone. Can't you see for yourselves, friends? Now look at the bamboo trees across the river. There is a sharp wind blowing this way which bends the trees all the way across to this bank. Get a firm grip on one of these bamboos with both your hands, but it should not be too brittle, soft, rotten, or dry. When the wind dies down, the bamboos will straighten themselves and swing you, if you are careful enough, to the other bank. But if anybody holds onto the wrong kind of bamboo, he'll fall in the river and be turned into stone. This is the Bamboo Trail, and it is terrifying like the Last Trail itself. But with some agility and luck any one with courage can jump it."

Like the fool who entered the demon's cave at the sorcerer's bidding, we did what he wanted. One of us had got hold of a thin bamboo; it broke and he fell; and, abandoning his petrified body, he went to God's heaven. We climbed down our bamboos and left the river far behind. We made an oblation of water for his soul at another river where we camped.

The next morning when we had covered about five leagues, I saw in front of me an extremely narrow ledge which snaked along the side of a horrifying abyss. The bottom receded from sight in an intense darkness which even the sun was afraid to penetrate. Acera instructed the travelers.

"We must make a smoking fire with damp wood, leaves, and straw. The highlanders will come out when they see the smoke, to sell us their mountain goats which are covered with tiger skins. You have got to buy them, giving saffron, indigo, or śakala-dyed clothes or even sugar, rice, vermilion, salt, or oils in exchange. Mount the goats and carry bamboo poles with you, then ride on to the circuitous ledge, death's crooked eyebrow. . . .

"Now it is possible that on the ledge there will be another party of travelers returning with gold from the gold mines, and we may come face to face with each other halfway. And that means we die in the ravine with our gold or our hopes. The ledge is too narrow for a goat train to pass or to turn. Therefore we need a powerful man who is used to handling a spear and has a butcher's experience to ride at the head of our train. One man like that can kill off an entire row of enemies as long as he is not himself slain by the enemies. This terrible road is known as the Goat Trail. Those who don't mind the fall are sure to meet Bhṛgu!"

Acera was interrupted by the arrival of a band of tribesmen, armed with tall bows, who drove a troop of goats ahead of them. When the buying and selling was done, they departed. The travelers bathed and prayed in loud voices to Śiva and Kṛṣṇa. Thereupon the long train of goats carrying the travelers started along, moving fast enough, yet precisely balanced like a becalmed ship on the high seas. I was the seventh from the rear, and Acera, immediately behind me, the sixth. As we were riding on, we heard in the distance ahead of us the loud clatter of bamboos striking against one another—zing zing!—and the cries of men and beasts—meh meh! and aah aah!—as they fell into the abyss of darkness and mud, terrifying even to a brave man's heart.

A moment later the ranks of the enemy were annihilated save for one man, and in our own ranks the seventh from the rear had suddenly become the first. Our leader prodded me: "Come on, what are you waiting for? There is only one enemy left. Send him to heaven!"

The man opposite me threw his bamboo stick away, folded his hands at his forehead, and, now that his entire caravan had been destroyed and he was left unprotected, sought my protection. "My family is perishing," he cried, "and I am the only one left to continue it. Don't destroy it completely by cutting down the last branch! My parents are blind, and I, their only son, their only love, am the stick to guide them. Brother, don't kill me!"

I thought, "Damn the life that is smeared with the filth of sin, thrice damn the gold that must be won by killing the living. Let the wretch kill me. He clings to life, and his life means sight to the dead eyes of his parents."

Red with rage and pale with despair Acera sneered at me between clenched teeth in a harsh and hissing voice. "Ayi! stupid ass, have you no sense of time? This is not the time to use pity, but to use a sword. Bah, you and your theories: we know all about your pity in practice! Are you going to sacrifice sixteen for the sake of one scoundrel? Kill him and his goat, and at least fourteen lives are saved. If you don't, he and you and the goats and all of us will perish. A man's life is sacred and should not be sacrificed to save one scoundrel! 'One must always protect one's self, with one's wife as well as one's wealth,' " and so on and so forth. He read me a sermon as long as the Bhagavadgītā, prompting me to an act of cruelty as Viṣṇu prompted Arjuna. Deeply ashamed, blaming myself for the cruelty of my deed, I struck my enemy's goat very lightly on the legs. And as the animal sank like a ship in the ocean of darkness, the traveler who sailed it drowned with his cupidity. We came away from the perilous road like the survivors from the Bhārata wars: our thin ranks annihilated, seven saved their souls but lost their hearts.[1]

We continued our journey through the country until we reached a Ganges. There we offered a handful of water, mixed with our tears, to our dead. Soon our grief, bitter though it was, gave way to our appetite; for man knows no pain like the pain of hunger. We prepared our meal and lay down on a bed of leaves.

When the leader woke us up, our eyes were still heavy from too little sleep. "These goats," he said, "have to be killed. We shall eat the meat; the skins we turn inside out and sew up to form sacks. Then we wrap ourselves in these sacks—no room for squeamishness here, it will only delay us!—in such a way that the bloody inside is turned outside. There are birds here as large as the winged mountains of legend, with beaks wide as caverns. They come here from the Gold Country. They will mistake us for lumps of meat and carry us in their beaks through the sky all the way to the Gold Country. That is what we must do."

I said, "It is true what people say, 'Throw this gold away that cuts your ears!' How could I be so cruel as to kill my goat, this good spirit that has saved me from peril as virtue saves a man from hell? I am done with money and done with living if I have to kill my best friend to save the life he gave me."

Acera said to the travelers, "Everyone kill his own goat. And take Sānudāsa's goat out of the way." One of the traders took my goat somewhere and came back with a goatskin hanging from his stick.

"I swapped Sānudāsa's goat for another," he said. "Look, I have its skin here." But I recognized it: it was the skin of my own goat. "You did not take it out of the way," I cried, "you *put* it out of the way!"

Thereupon, taking our leader's word for it, we prepared ourselves for a voyage through the sky, which is more terrible than a voyage by sea because there is no way of escape. Soon all the heavens were filled with huge gray birds thundering ominously like autumn clouds. Under the wind of their wings the heavy tree trunks on the mountain were crushed to the ground as though they were the mountains' wings being cut by the blades of Indra's arrows. Seven birds swooped down and carried the seven of us, each with his heart in his throat, to the sky. One bird was left without its share, and,

---

[1] The conflict described in the *Mahābhārata*, of which the *Bhagavadgītā* is a part.

cheated out of its expectations, it started to tear me violently away from the bird that had got me. This started a gruesome fight between the two vultures, each greedy for its own share, which, like the battle of Jaṭāyus and Rāvaṇa, terrified all the inhabitants of heaven. I was torn between the two birds, passing from beak to beak and sometimes rolling over the ground. I prayed to Śiva. Their pointed beaks and claws, hard as diamond points, ripped the skin until it was worn like a sieve. I was dragged from the torn skin bag and tumbled into a pond of astonishing beauty.

I rubbed my bloodsmeared body with lotuses and bathed. Next I made a thanksgiving offering to the gods and the fathers, and only then tasted the nectar of the pond. I sank down on the shore and lay until I was rested. My eyes wandered over the woods that had been the scene of prodigious adventures and forgot the anxieties of the battle between the giant birds, forgot them like a man who has escaped from the Hell of the Swordblades to stroll in Paradise. There was not a tree with a withered or faded leaf; not one was burned by lightning and brushfire or empty of bloom and fruit. The blossoms of cadamba, malatī and kunda jasmine, and spring creepers were thickly dotted by armies of bees. The ground was covered with a carpet of grass four fingers high, blue-green like Śiva's throat, and as soft as rabbit fur. Lions, tigers, peacocks, snakes, and all kinds of game lived peaceably like hermits on nothing but leaves, flowers, water, and wind. My eyes did not tire of looking as I roamed in the woods.

Then I discovered a faint track, a path made by some man's footsteps. Slowly I followed the track, which led me far into the woods to a river with low banks and shallow bed; both bottom and banks were covered with precious stones and gold-dust. I crossed the stream, bathed, and paid homage to the gods and my elders.

Near the riverbank I saw a hermitage surrounded by banana trees where monkeys were crouching quietly. And within the hermitage I saw a great hermit with a matted tuft of hair, golden like a flash of lightning, who was sitting on a sheaf of dwarf kuśa grass like the image of the sacrificial fire resting in the womb of a pit, its base and kindling sprinkled with butter oblations.

When I approached to greet him, he was like a rising moon of graciousness, like a winter sun without summer glare. His cheeks were moist with tears of joy as he spoke to me: "A blessing to merchant Sānudāsa!"

I thought, "Then it is true that hermits have second sight, for he sees what is hidden to the eyes of the flesh. My name, which could have been anything, and the vocation that governs my action—he has named them before he was told."

While I was thinking, he directed me to a grass cushion, and I sat down slowly for I was embarrassed. But the recluse smiled and said, "It is as you think, my boy. But the mere mention of a name is none too miraculous a feat of austerity. I know everything about you: how Dhruvaka and his friends inveigled you into drinking spirits, how you met the harlot Gaṅgā in the park, and from there on until your escape from the battle of the birds, the very mouth of death, and your arrival here.

"Yes, you have seen ships wrecked and you have explored inaccessible mountains, forests, and rivers. Why have you toiled so tirelessly? Ah, your mother Mitrāvatī will tell you that. You expended all that effort just to find gold. It is within your reach now; don't despair any longer, for where can the gold go? It is easy to find for people with energy and intelligence, for a man of character like you who listens to the counsel of one like me. Stay in my hermitage for a few days; you will sleep in a hut of leaves and eat the fruits of trees."

So I ate forest fare, nutritious, invigorating, and purifying; and it tasted so good that I lost all taste for grown vegetables. And as I slept on the bed of leaves I had made in a hut of foliage, I learned to hate Gangadatta's house with its high-legged couches. Yet, although these simple joys which are outside a common man's experience made me oblivious of my sorrows, I never forgot that my mother was living in a slum. The misfortunes I had suffered so far till my abortive journey through the sky I now regarded as blessings; for misfortune that leads to the discovery of gold is fortune indeed!

One day I saw a celestial chariot arrive from heaven, splendid like Mount Meru; it had come for the sage, the incarnation of his merit. Heavenly maidens alighted, illuminating the forest with their radiance, as flashes of lightning alight from a beloved rainbow-hued cloud. They bowed before the prince of hermits, made a circumambulation to honor him, and returned to heaven like the rays of the moon.

One girl had remained behind. The hermit raised her to his breast, and with his eyes streaming and his voice stammering for joy, he said, "Gandharvadattā my daughter, you must forget me and devote yourself to your father Sānudāsa!"

I thought that her meticulous attentiveness was merely mockery, and I felt like a humble attendant of Śiva's whom the great White Goddess is amused to greet respectfully. One day I asked her, "Who is he? And who are you?"

"Listen," she said and told their history. "The sage, who is the sitting stone of all hermits, is of the clan of Bharadvāja. He is Bharadvāja of the Aerial Spirits whose science he has sought to acquire. So powerful were his mortifications that Indra himself was perturbed and worried lest he be thrown off his mountain throne. Even as he lay in the arms of his wife, Indra could not help thinking that there was a hermit somewhere. When Nārada, the messenger of the gods, reported that this hermit was Bharadvāja, Viṣṇu summoned Suprabhā, the daughter of the king of Gandharvas, the celestial musicians.

" 'It is common knowledge in all the worlds,' Viṣṇu said, 'that you surpass even Urvaśī, however vain she may be of her youth, her beauty, and her charms. Therefore, my lovely girl, go to Bharadvāja and attend to him so that your beauty and charm be suitably rewarded.'

"Suprabhā tried her best to seduce the saint with all the stratagems of love, with words, glances, and meaningful gestures, but the saint's mind remained fixed on truth. When she failed, even though she spent years, she was so discouraged that she became his handmaiden. She did all the chores so well, plucking flowers, fetching water, sweeping the cell, that the sage was pleased and asked her to choose a boon.

" 'Sir,' she said, 'your imperturbability has made a mockery of charms for which the wives of all thirty-three gods envy me. Beauty, ornaments, garlands, and ointments are valueless to women unless their value can be measured by their power to arouse the passions of their men. Therefore I pray you, if you are pleased to grant me a boon, then may you, the greatest man in the world, be a man to me! If a young girl's heart is smitten with love, what greater boon is there than a husband who charms her eyes and heart? Please, although you hate passion, submit to your mercy and love me so that you may restore my charm to me!"

"He was agreeable and gave her one daughter; for even a contrary man will be won in the end by devotion. Suprabhā took the girl to the house of her father Viśvavasu, and she reared her there and educated her in the arts and sciences. Then the king of the Gandharvas took his granddaughter to Bharadvāja and asked him to give her a name. The name the sage gave her was full of meaning. 'Let her be Gandharvadattā,' he said, 'the Gift of the Gandharva, for you have given her to me.'

"So a girl was born to Bharadvāja and Suprabhā and given the name Gandharvadattā. And I am this girl," she concluded.

One dark night I happened to notice that the trees on a rocky hillock were aglow with a golden light. I thought, "This hill must be pure gold ore. That is a piece of luck to find gold here! It will bring me luck." What sense I had was caught in the noose of greed, and I completely filled one large hut with rocks. When Gandharvadattā the next morning saw the rocks, she asked me what they were, and I told her. She told her father, and he called me.

"This is not gold ore, my boy," he said, "just rock. That golden glow you saw in the darkness comes from the herbs. Sunlight obscures it, but at night it spreads freely. You see nothing but gold, even in rocks: thus a man with a jaundiced eye sees the whole world yellow. At the right time I myself shall arrange for your gold and your return to Campā. It will be soon now. Now free yourself of your confusions!"

It took me a whole day of increasing misery to throw out the rocks which had taken an hour of increasing contentment to bring in.

Then one day the hermit handed me a lute made of tortoise shell and said, "Hear what I am going to say and do as I tell you. The story which Gandharvadattā has told you about me is true; she is indeed my daughter. She is the future bride of the future emperor of Aerial Spirits: the goddess that rose from the ocean could never be any but Viṣṇu's bride. You must take Gandharvadattā to Campā and give her to the emperor. I shall tell you how you can recognize him, and you must plant the signs firmly in your memory. Every six months you will assemble all the Gandharvas, and when they are assembled, Gandharvadattā will chant for them the 'Hymn to Nārāyana.' If one of the Gandharvas is able to accompany her song on the lute and to chant it himself, you must give him my daughter."

("Sire, he predicted exactly what you yourself would do at the meeting of the Gandharvas, everything, including your chanting the hymn and accompanying her on your lute!")

The sage continued. "Children, you have been bored for a long time now. To relieve your boredom, start for Campā."

I threw myself at his feet; and my happiness made me so nervous that the whole long night had passed before I fell asleep.

When I woke up, I heard the divine music of two wooden vīnās and a flute, enchanting to ear and heart, and, interrupted by the crowing of cocks, the loud benedictions and greetings of heralds which at once dispelled my sleep. Wide awake now, I found myself in a palaquin framed in gold and aglitter with precious stones. It stood on a shining clean stone floor in the center of a pavilion that was thatched with colorful silks which were supported by polished golden tentpoles. Gandharvadattā was sitting in the lap of a blue crystal bench under an awning to bar the sun, and she was playing her vīnā with great concentration. My pavilion was surrounded by a host of smaller tents in flamboyant colors, and their beautifully dressed proprietors happily moved between the sacks of gold that filled their tents. Merchants were busily buying and selling such costly wares as gold and jewelry, and all around the encampment crowded herds of camels and bullocks. But how could a dumb man describe the spectacle? Impossible! No man has ever seen such wealth in all his dreams.

I asked Gandharvadattā, "What is this miracle? Is it fantasy, is it magic, is it a dream?"

"These are the fruits of Bharadvāja's austerities," she said, "which have become a very Tree of Wishes. For if rightly observed the mortifications of the just have a power that is beyond the imagination. You can spend as you wish, for your wealth has no limit. Spend it on anybody, worthy or worthless, but don't bury it in the ground. Don't worry how to gain; worry how to spend! You can draw forever on Bharadvāja's mountain of gold. And don't worry any more about when you will see your mother. Campā is only ten miles from this caravan camp." She was like wisdom whose soul is Certainty, and as she spoke, all my doubts about magic or dream dissolved instantly.

Then I saw Dhruvaka, the scoundrel. He did not dare to look me in the face, and he hung his head; and so did his friends around him. Getting up from my bed, I hugged him affectionately and gave him my own chair; his embarrassment vanished at once. Grandly he favored his friends with a gracious word or two, an embrace, and a seat, strictly according to seniority.

Soon after, all Campā's people came out dancing behind their dancers and surrounded the caravan. They were uproariously happy, so happy indeed that several of them lost their breath—one found it back in the end, but another died. I showered presents on the crowd: delicacies of food and drink, jewels, robes, garlands, perfumes, and liberal quantities of gold. And especially did I rescue from the hell of poverty those who had had to clean their streets with cowdung when I passed by on my way back from the brothel.

At last I said to Dhruvaka, "Friend, get my mother out of that ghastly slum and bring her to her own house. Give the owner a hundred times as much as he paid when he bought it from my mother. Perish the life of a man who can see his wealthy mother in a poor man's quarters and live!"

Dhruvaka smiled. "Madame poor? Who has seen the Ganges run dry? The house is her own and her wealth as solid as ever. But now that you have returned, she will bloom like a lotus pond in the moonlight."

Day and night passed like an instant, and early the next morning I rode into Campā, as Kubera into Alakā.[2] Preceded by a parade of all the different guilds, I went along the highways and avenues to call upon our glorious king. I prostrated myself before him at a respectful distance, but the king addressed me joyfully and embraced me without dissimulation. When he had honored me with costly gems and robes without end, he said, "Son, now go and see your mother." I filled the insatiable hellhole of royal cupidity with a mass of gold and precious stones that was worth Mount Meru and, surrounded by the king's boon companions and chanting brahmins, returned to my old house. It is a wonder I was not trampled by the townspeople who with the energy that only rapture can arouse danced wildly in the streets to the soft beat of drums. But when they saw my mother from a distance, carrying in her hand the little bowl with the water of hospitality, the crowd shrank away in confusion. For the masses of commoners are unnerved by the sight of a lady and disperse as darkness disperses before the full moon.

> *His mother then revealed to Sānudāsa that he had been tricked. She had not been destitute and his family had not been forced to live in a slum. It had all been a deception concocted by her, the king of Campā, and all his friends and relations. They had sought to force him to become a man and to seek his fulfillment as a merchant in search of profit. This he had done, and his fame would live forever.* ❖

RECOMMENDED READINGS

Long a classic survey, Vincent A. Smith, *The Oxford History of India,* 3rd ed., ed. Mortimer Wheeler et al. (Oxford: UK: Clarendon Press, 1958), presents a detailed account, concentrating on political history. Romila Thapar, *A History of India,* Vol. I (New

---

[2] The residence of the god of wealth.

York: Penguin Books, n.d.), provides an easily available history of India from the Aryan invasions to the coming of the Mughals in 1576. Hugh Tinker, *South Asia: A Short History* (New York: Frederick A. Praeger, 1966), provides a brief survey that includes not only India, but also Pakistan, Sri Lanka, Burma, and Nepal. Francis Watson, *A Concise History of India* (New York: Charles Scribner's Sons, 1975), is briefer still, but contains some excellent illustrations. A. L. Bashan, *The Wonder That Was India,* 3rd ed. (New York: Taplinger, 1968), is a general account of Indian civilization to the coming of the Mughals. Organized topically, its chapters include State, Society, Everyday Life, Art, Religion, and Language and Literature, as well as a series of appendixes on special aspects of the Indian heritage such as the calendar, mathematics, and astronomy. Perhaps the classic account of early Indian society, however, is that of Jeannine Auboyer, *Daily Life in Ancient India from 200 B.C. to 700 A.D.,* trans. Simon W. Taylor (New York: Macmillan, 1965). Topically organized, it covers a wide range of ancient Indian life. The best available economic history is that of Rajaram N. Saletore, *Early Indian Economic History* (Bombay: N. M. Tripathi, 1973). Lucille Schulberg, *Historic India* (New York: Time-Life Books, 1968), provides a richly illustrated work with a readable historical text.

The revival of Sanskrit during the Guptan age forms part of the general survey of A. B. Keith's standard work, *A History of Sanskrit Literature* (Oxford, UK: Oxford University Press, 1928). Guptan literature available in translation includes Kalidasa, *The Cloud Messenger,* trans. Franklin and Eleanor Edgerton (Ann Arbor: University of Michigan Press, 1964); *The Kama Sutra of Vasyayana,* trans. Richard F. Burton (New York: Dutton Paperback, 1964); and the *Panchitantra,* trans. Arthur W. Ryder (Chicago: University of Chicago Press, 1956). Fa-hsien's account of his travels in Guptan India may be read in *The Travels of Fa-hsien,* trans. K. A. Giles (Cambridge, UK: Cambridge University Press, 1923).

Arabia, A.D. 622

JEWISH-MUSLIM RELATIONS

THE FORMATIVE YEARS

Norman A. Stillman

Muslims consider their religion to have been established in A.D. 622 and date their calendar from that year. It was in 622 that Muhammad fled his enemies in Mecca and, with a band of his followers, took up residence in Medina, an oasis city some 200 miles to the north. Islam in fact already existed as a religion, and Muhammad had gained a number of converts to the faith. It was during the next ten years at Medina, however, that the movement became institutionalized and developed its characteristic political, economic, and social doctrines. Many of these appear to have been responses to specific problems Muhammad and his followers faced during those formative years.

One of the pressing issues was to define the proper relationship between Muslims and nonbelievers. How should Muslims react to people who rejected Muhammad's teaching, especially since such rejection was tantamount to denying the truth of the Prophet's message? How could Muslims tolerate communities of such people within Islamic lands? This was not an abstract question: There existed at Medina a long established Jewish community that had become an integral element within the social and economic structure of the oasis.

The following article traces the relationship between Muslims and Jews during those formative years. Muhammad and his followers had to move slowly, since it was they who were in the minority and the Jews in the majority. Relatively few in number, without much in the way of material wealth and lacking powerful allies, the Muslims would have been at the mercy of the Jewish inhabitants had the Jews recognized the danger the Muslims presented and united against them. That did not happen, however. By the time the Jewish communities did awake, it was too late. The Muslims had established their dominance in the region, and the great expansion of Islam had begun.

READING QUESTIONS

1. To what religious influences was the young Muhammad exposed?

2. Why was Muhammad invited to come to Yathrib?

3. How did the Jewish community at Yathrib regard Muhammad?

4. How did Muhammad eliminate the opposition of the Jewish tribes?

5. What was the effect of Muhammad's conquest of the Jewish oasis of Khaybar?

Jews had been living in the Arabian Peninsula centuries before the birth of the Prophet of Islam. The dates and circumstances surrounding their arrival are shrouded in legend, and even the most valiant attempts at reconstructing the history of this very early period are sheer speculation. The Jewish communities in the advanced urban civilizations of ancient South Arabia most likely date back to biblical times. The legendary encounter between Solomon and the Queen of Sheba (Arabian Saba') attests to the antiquity of Israelite-Arabian contacts. This was the Arabia Felix of classical geographers, a land of incense and spices and a way station on the routes to eastern Africa, on the one hand, and India and the Orient, on the other.

Jewish settlers had already established themselves in the oasis communities of northern Arabia by the latter part of the Second Temple period. Although this area was not as culturally felicitous as the southern region, it was not by any means totally an Arabia Deserta. Jews could find a livelihood in date-growing, caravan commerce, and in the crafts. Their ranks must have been swelled by refugees who fled Judea after the rebellions against Rome collapsed in a sea of blood in 70 and 135 C.E. By the time Muhammad was born, sometime around the year 571, Jews were not only to be found in considerable numbers in Arabia but were well integrated into the life and culture of the peninsula. Like their pagan neighbors, the Jews spoke Arabic, were organized into clans and tribes, and had assimilated many of the values of desert society. They formed alliances and participated in intertribal feuds. The odes of the pre-Islamic Jewish poet al-Samaw'al b. ʿAdiyā' reflect the same rugged ethos of *muruwwa,* or manly virtues, as expressed in countless poems by non-Jewish Arabs. Jewish influence in Arabia was significant enough that for a short time Judaism was adopted by the royal house of the Yemenite kingdom of Ḥimyar under Yūsuf Asʿar Dhū Nuwās (ruled ca. 517–25), who was killed while trying to repel an overwhelming Ethiopian

From Norman A. Stillman, *The Jews of Arab Lands: A History and Source Book* (Philadelphia: The Jewish Publication Society of America, 1979), pp. 3–21.

invasion. Although the spiritual influence of the Jews was strong in pagan Yemen, they themselves probably constituted a relatively small proportion of the population.

Despite their high degree of assimilation into Arabian society, Jews were still viewed as a separate group with their own peculiar customs and characteristics. Arab poets of the pre-Islamic period (assuming that a substantial part of the poetry attributed to them is genuine) occasionally refer to Jewish religious practices, and the Koran frequently mentions such typical Jewish institutions as the Sabbath, *kashrut,* and the Torah. The daily language spoken by Jews among themselves with its admixture of Aramaic and Hebrew words seemed to the Arabs a dialect all its own. Some of these Aramaic terms and concepts, however, passed unnoticed into the speech of Arabs at large. So too, religious ideas, ethical notions, and homiletic lore were disseminated among the pagan Arabs who came into close contact with Jews. The same could be said with regard to the Christians of Arabia who, like the Jews, formed a distinct religious community while at the same time being highly assimilated.

The young man Muḥammad had probably met many Jews and Christians. His hometown of Mecca was a great mercantile éntrepôt situated along the caravan route linking Yemen in the south with Byzantine Egypt and Syria-Palestine to the northwest and the Sasanian Empire to the northeast. According to Muslim tradition, Muḥammad had on more than one occasion accompanied caravans into Syria and had seen the piety of the Syriac monks, which made a deep and lasting impression upon him. He also encountered Christians and Jews in Arabia. The trade route to Syria passed through the Wādi 'l-Qurā (Valley of Villages), which had a large Jewish population. Farther north, on the fringes of the Byzantine territory, were Christian Arab tribes. So too, in northeastern Arabia on the border of Iraq, which was the administrative center of the Sasanian Empire, were large numbers of Christian Arabs. Those Jews and Christians with whom Muḥammad came into closest contact were merchants, either in Mecca itself, or at one of the annual fairs, such as the one held in nearby ʿUkāẓ.

Some of the merchants whom Muḥammad encountered probably acted as amateur missionaries, who in addition to their commercial activities spread the message of the one God. These self-appointed missionaries most certainly did not preach fine points of dogma or theology, but rather emphasized the moral and ethical essentials of monotheism to their pagan Arab listeners. Despite some obvious external differences between Christians and Jews, the message they preached seemed surprisingly the same. To wit, there is but one God, the Creator of heaven, earth, and all that is therein, Who has in His mercy and loving-kindness revealed to man what is required of him, and Who on the Last Day will call all souls before His great judgment seat, rewarding the righteous with eternal bliss and damning the sinner to everlasting torment. The code of conduct enjoined by these preachers was also striking in its sameness—"thou shalt not murder," "thou shalt not steal," "thou shalt not commit adultery," "oppress not the widow, the orphan, the stranger, or the indigent." As merchants, they also emphasized the obligation to maintain fair weights and measures and to be honest in business dealings.

The time was ripe in Arabia for this kind of proselytizing. There was a spiritual malaise in the peninsula not unlike that of the Mediterranean world in late antiquity. The traditional Arab paganism and polydemonism had become sterile and unsatisfying to many. The townspeople were becoming culturally and morally more sophisticated. Many freelance seekers of God, called *ḥanīfs* in Arabic tradition, set off on a pilgrim's progress toward monotheism without accepting either Judaism or Christianity. Some of these more sensitive souls were inspired with the belief that they had been chosen like the prophets of old to bring the Divine message to their own people.

One such soul was Muḥammad b. ʿAbd Allāh b. ʿAbd al-Muṭallib of the Hashemite clan of the tribe of Quraysh in Mecca. What differentiated him from other *ḥanīfs,* would-be prophets, and warners was the fact that he was a great religious genius. Muḥammad seems to have been particularly impressed by the preachers' frequent references to a book or scroll as divine authority. These missionaries would hold their scripture in hand, citing verses in the original language and then translating them into broken Arabic. The moral lessons cited were often driven home by picturesque homiletic tales. Muḥammad eventually came to the profound religious conclusion that just as God was one, so was His message, which He had revealed to different peoples at different times in their own language. He began to wonder why God in His infinite mercy had not yet bestowed His saving word upon the Arab people who until now had been astray in night and were, therefore, condemned to perdition. How long were his people to remain in ignorance? Who would bring them God's heavenly scripture in their own language?

Muḥammad was, we are told, given to meditations and night vigils, inspired perhaps by the ascetic examples of anchorite monks who could be found here and there throughout the Syrian and Arabian deserts, or perhaps by the pious *ḥanīfs,* or even by Judeo-Christian sects such as the Ebionites. During one such vigil on a lonely mountainside not far from Mecca the answer to his question came: "Recite in the name of your Lord Who created . . ." It was he who had been chosen. He was about forty years of age at the time. Like most good prophets, Muḥammad was not entirely prepared for his theophany. He doubted his sanity. But soon he became convinced that God—Allah—had spoken to him through the angel Gabriel and was revealing to him a message in "clear Arabic." His sincerity convinced others. His first converts were members of his immediate household—his wife Khadīja, his adopted son Zayd b. Ḥāritha, and his cousin ʿAlī, who lived with them. Soon he began to meet with some success amongst his fellow Meccans. Even those, and they were the majority, who were not swayed by his preaching looked upon him as a man with spiritual powers. After all, he spoke in rhymed prose and swore strange oaths by natural phenomena, just like the *kāhins* (soothsayers) and *shāʿirs* (poets) who received their inspiration from the *jinn* (spirits). However, when Muḥammad's message of imminent Judgment before Allah came to its ultimate conclusion in a total rejection of traditional Arab paganism, then Muḥammad began to meet with stiff, hardcore opposition. Mecca was the leading religious center of pagan Arabia, and its shrine, the Kaʿba, was the object of an important annual pilgrimage. The religious and economic interests that he threatened were too great. His opponents accused him of being mad. They claimed that he was merely spouting words taught to him by others:

> Those who do not believe have said, "This is nothing but a lie which he has invented. Other people have helped him with it." They have come forth with injustice and falsehood. They have also said, "Fables of the ancients which he has copied. They are dictated to him morning and evening."
> We know that they say, "It is only a mortal who teaches him." But the speech of him to whom they refer is foreign, while this is clear Arabic language.

A period of ostracism and some persecution against the Prophet and his followers ensued. Finally, Muḥammad decided that the climate in Mecca was too inhospitable for continuing his mission there. In September 622, after having looked into the possibility of going to other towns, Muḥammad emigrated to the oasis community of Yathrib, also known as Medina, which lay about 250 miles to the north. For later Muslims, the year of the *Hijra* (Emigration) marks the beginning of the Islamic Era. And here, an entirely new phase of history begins.

For all intents and purposes, the story of Muslim-Jewish relations begins with Muḥammad's arrival in Medina. Prior to the *Hijra,* he had met individual Christians and Jews who had come to Mecca on business, as well as during his own travels. It has long been debated whether Muḥammad's principal monotheist informants were Jews or Christians. Abraham Geiger in the nineteenth century was the first to argue cogently for Jewish teachers. This view predominated until the 1920s when Tor Andrae and Richard Bell made strong cases for Christian mentors. More recently, S. D. Goitein has advanced very convincing arguments in favor of sectarian Jewish influences. Unfortunately, our sources, which are exclusively Muslim and from a much later period, are silent on this point, and all of the arguments have of necessity been based on the contents of the suras revealed to Muḥammad in Mecca. Be that as it may, it is indisputably clear that in Medina, Muḥammad came into daily face to face contact with a large, organized Jewish community. The encounter did not prove to be an auspicious one.

The fertile oasis of Yathrib had been settled by Jewish agriculturalists centuries before Muḥammad's arrival. The arabicized Aramaic by-name of the place, al-Madīna (the district), probably was given to it by the Jews themselves. They formed the majority of the population and were organized in tribes. The three most important were the Banū 'l-Naḍīr, the Banū Qurayẓa, and the Banū Qaynuqāʿ. The first two were priestly tribes known as

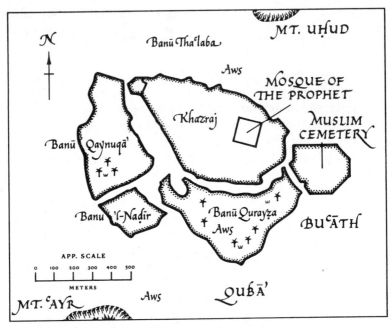

The tribes in Medina at the time of Muḥammad.

al-kāhinān (the two Kōhanīm) and Banū Hārūn (sons of Aaron). Medina was also inhabited by two large confederations of pagan Arabs—the Banū Aws and the Banū Khazraj. They had settled there sometime during the fifth century, having emigrated from southern Arabia after the catastrophic bursting of Ma'rib Dam. A long struggle for dominance ensued in which the Naḍīr and Qurayẓa sided with the Aws, while Qaynuqāᶜ allied itself with the Khazraj. Both sides were exhausted by the conflict, and it is in light of this that we must understand the invitation extended to Muḥammad by the Medinese.

Muḥammad's reputation had already begun to spread through western Arabia. Several Medinese had been converted to his new faith while visiting Mecca for the pilgrimage and enthusiastically proselytized among their own people upon their return. At the very time that Muḥammad was seeking a new home, members of both the Aws and Khazraj decided to invite him to come to Medina as its chief magistrate, who would provide much needed leadership in the strife-torn community by virtue of his spiritual gifts. His function was to be similar to that of the *ḥakam,* the wise neutral arbiter of intertribal disputes. The negotiations were delicate and involved two meetings near Mecca, at a pass called al-ᶜAqaba. At the second meeting, in June 622, seventy-five Medinese accepted Islam and swore allegiance to the Prophet, pledging to defend him as one of their own. Even the traditional

Muslim sources have noted that the readiness of the Medinese to accept Islamic monotheism was conditioned by their longtime association and familiarity with Jews.

The Jews had no part in inviting Muḥammad to Medina, and no Jews were present at the ʿAqaba negotiations. Yet the potential awkwardness of their presence in Medina under the new order was obvious to all. Fealty to the Prophet and his cause meant the dissolution of other bonds and alliances, and according to the laws of the desert, those not protected by alliances have no rights. Thus, it was clear to all concerned that eventually the Jews would have to go.

Most modern historians in the West have argued that Muḥammad came to Medina expecting to be accepted by the Jews there, and when he was rejected by them, he turned against them in pique, driving out two tribes and exterminating the third. The distinguished British scholar W. Montgomery Watt even goes so far as to speculate that "had the Jews come to terms with Muḥammad instead of opposing him . . . they might have become partners in the Arab empire and Islam a sect of Jewry." These notions do not give Muḥammad much credit either as a student of religion or as a politician. He would have been incredibly naïve to believe that the Jews would accept his new faith. He must have been aware that Jews did not recognize Christians, nor did Christians recognize Jews, nor did members of the different Christian sects recognize each other. Why then would they recognize him? On the other hand, he may have expected that the Jews of Medina would concede the validity of his mission to the Arab people. The God-fearing Gentiles had been granted a certain degree of acceptance by Jews in the hellenistic world, and those on the road to monotheism were probably still encouraged. There is internal evidence in the Koran for the view that Muḥammad was encouraged in his mission to the pagans of Mecca by his monotheist mentors. If Goitein is correct in surmising that these mentors in Mecca were sectarian Jews, then the fierce antagonism shown to the Prophet by the Medinese Jews is all the more understandable because it stems from the bitter conflict within Jewry at that time between the forces of orthodoxy and sectarianism. The Jewish opposition to Muḥammad was certainly in part political, although this does not seem to have been the predominant factor as some have suggested. For had the Jewish tribes of Medina been motivated by "the idea of exerting a considerable political influence over the oasis as a whole," they would have put up a united front against the political threat.

When Muḥammad arrived in Medina in September 622, his position was, naturally, rather precarious. Neither he nor his fellow emigrants from Mecca were in the best of financial circumstances. Not all of the people of Medina were wholehearted supporters of Muḥammad by any means. (These nonenthusiasts, some of whom may even have been opponents, have been dubbed with the uncomplimentary epithet of the Hypocrites by Muslim tradition.) He, therefore, had to proceed with some discretion until he could consolidate his position.

One of Muḥammad's first acts was the promulgation of a document that outlined the relationships between the various groups in Medina. This document looks like a covenant for the governance of the community and, thus, has been dubbed by many scholars the Constitution of Medina. To a certain extent it was a constitution, but in reality was only an interim step and was soon abandoned by Muḥammad when he had no further need of it. The document . . . is a masterpiece of *clair-obscur*. It is an eloquent testimony to Muḥammad's political foresight and diplomatic skill. The document confirmed the Jews as members of the Medinese community with certain rights and responsibilities. This status, however, was granted only as long as the Jews did not act wrongfully. The vagueness of this qualification was to provide Muḥammad with a legal avenue for changing their status at a later date.

The Jewish scholars of Medina must have been particularly irksome to Muḥammad. It was bad enough that they rejected his prophethood, but this, as already indicated, was understandable in a sense even to Muḥammad. That they openly contradicted what he had to say was worse. And that they ridiculed what seemed to them his glaring errors in relating biblical and midrashic narratives was unforgivable. The learned Jews attacked him on the level at which he was most vulnerable and at the time in which he could do least about it. His experimentation with certain Jewish pietist practices such as the fast of Yom Kippur (called in Arabic ʿAshūrāʾ) and prayer toward Jerusalem made no impression upon these rancorous opponents. There was little Muḥammad could do to them at this time except to continue with his own preparations for the war against Mecca and await the changes in circumstances when he would be able to punish those who had wronged him. He also became increasingly convinced during this period that the Jews' rejection of him was because of pride and contumacy. As he knew with an unshakable religious certainty that his revelations were true, he came to the logical conclusion that whatever the Jews were citing to contradict him must be false. He may already have heard sometime in the past the common Christian accusation that the Jews had corrupted the text of their Scriptures. In this, he may have been abetted by the Jewish renegade ʿAbd Allāh b. Salām. Like so many Jewish converts to Islam and Christianity in the Middle Ages, ʿAbd Allāh proved his zeal for his new faith by exposing the falseness of his former coreligionists who in their stubbornness denied or suppressed those signs in their sacred texts that foretold the coming of Muḥammad or Jesus, as the case may be.

The Muslims' first significant victory over the Meccans at Badr in 624 was just the sort of turning point Muḥammad had been waiting for. He now had the power and the prestige to begin moving against his enemies in Medina. Two pagan poets, one an old man, the other a woman with an infant at her breast, were assassinated for having written satirical verses about him. Shortly thereafter, he turned upon the weakest of the three Jewish tribes, the Banū Qaynuqāʿ, whose members were mainly craftsmen and artisans. After a short siege the Qaynuqāʿ surrendered unconditionally.

Muḥammad's position was still not so firmly established that he could act with complete impugnity, and when the Khazrajī chieftain ʿAbd Allāh b. Ubayy demanded that mercy be shown his former clients, the Prophet had to acquiesce. ʿAbd Allāh b. Ubayy thus earned himself a place in Islamic tradition as the arch-hypocrite, and the Jews of Qaynuqāʿ were able to leave Medina with some of their possessions. They eventually made their way to Adhriʿāt in Syria.

No historian has failed to notice the fact that the other two Jewish tribes did not come to the aid of their brethren. Clearly, the Jews did not grasp the nature of the conflict. It probably seemed to them to be a tribal and political affair of the traditional Arabian kind with which they were familiar, rather than a religious one. Besides, the Qaynuqāʿ had been on the opposing side of the Naḍīr, and Qurayẓa during the old Aws Khazraj struggles. Even the assassination of Kaʿb b. al-Ashraf, who was a chieftain of the Banu 'l-Naḍīr, did not fully change the Jews' perception of things. After all, Kaʿb had written verses satirizing Islam and insulting Muslim womanhood. Retaliation for such a slight to a group's honor was perfectly consistent with the heroic norms of Arab society in that period. Kaʿb was an Arab, through his father, as well as a Jew, through his mother. The new dimensions of the conflict were still not clear, but the Jews began to feel uneasy.

The defeat of the Muslim army at Mount Uḥud on March 23, 625, weakened Muḥammad's position somewhat. He needed a victory now to regain the lost prestige. Already some of his missionaries had been murdered by Bedouin tribesmen. He decided, therefore, to attack the Naḍīr. Like the Qurayẓa and the smaller Jewish clans, they had not come to the Prophet's aid at Uḥud because the battle took place on the Sabbath. They could barely conceal their satisfaction with the Muslim's defeat. Furthermore, they were wealthy and occupied some of the best land in Medina, while the Muslims were in difficult financial straits at the time. Muḥammad had already had unpleasant experiences trying to collect contributions or obtain loans from the Jews. On one such occasion Abū Bakr, a close companion of the Prophet, had been given the mocking retort: "We are not in need of Allah, whereas He seems to be in need of us. . . . We are rich compared to Him."

Muḥammad had no difficulty in finding a *casus belli*. On the basis of a divine revelation, he accused the Naḍīr of plotting against his life and ordered them to leave Medina. Expecting support from the Qurayẓa and from ʿAbd Allāh b. Ubayy and his partisans, they decided to resist the eviction decree. When the aid they had counted upon failed to materialize, they surrendered on the condition that they be allowed to leave with all their movable goods, except their arms.

Humility was never a virtue in old Arabian society, and the Naḍīr decided to go into exile with their heads held high. They departed for the Jewish oasis of Khaybar in an impressive caravan of 600 camels, which paraded through the heart of Medina to the music of pipes and timbrels. Their women unveiled their faces to flaunt their renowned beauty and sported all their finery. It is clear from all of the poetry composed upon the occasion that the Arabs were duly impressed—perhaps overly so. Two years later, the men of Naḍīr lost their lives, their wealth, and their women when the Muslims took Khaybar.

The lands of the Banu 'l-Naḍīr were divided among the Emigrants, who till then had no patrimony of their own in their adopted home and who were for the most part beholden to the Medinese Helpers for their livelihood. The Prophet's own share of land made him financially independent. The booty formed the basis for the new Muslim state treasury.

There remained only one important Jewish tribe in Medina—the Banū Qurayẓa. They must have been in a state of serious alarm by this time but were incapable of taking any action on their own. According to Muslim tradition, Kaʿb b. Asad, the Qurazī chieftain, had made a treaty with Muḥammad. This seems doubtful, however, and is probably the invention of later Muslim writers who wished to justify the harsh punishment that was meted out to the Qurayẓa. When the Meccans and their Bedouin allies moved toward Medina in 627, the Qurayẓa contributed to the defense effort by supplying spades, picks, and baskets for the excavation of the defensive trench along the exposed northern side of the oasis. During the brief siege of Medina, the Qurayẓa remained in their forts in a state of armed neutrality. Although they never committed any aggressive acts, their loyalty was questionable, for they allowed themselves to be approached by the enemy, who sought to win them over. The emissary from the besiegers was Ḥuyayy b. Akhṭab, a chieftain of the exiled Naḍīr who, according to some Muslim traditions, was the mastermind of the entire operation. This sort of parleying was quite common in Arabian warfare. Muḥammad himself attempted to buy off the Ghaṭāfān and Fazāra, the Bedouin allies of the Meccans.

The Qurayẓa were supposedly won over to the enemy, but they never could agree upon a course of action because they did not trust the Meccans entirely. In the end they did nothing. That they did nothing was of no account, for from the Muslim point of view, they had "sinned in their hearts."

The very day the besieging army turned away from Medina, Muḥammad attacked the Banū Qurayẓa. The Jewish tribe held out for twenty-five days. When all hope was gone they sought to surrender on the same terms as had the Naḍīr. This time the Prophet intended to make an example of them. He still could not act with complete disregard of public opinion. The degree of the Qurayẓa's treason was by no means clear. Muḥammad had previously spared the Banū Qaynuqāʿ at the request of their former allies the Khazraj. Many Awsites were now pleading that their former confederates be shown mercy. Always the master politician, Muḥammad stepped aside and appointed Saʿd b. Muʿādh to pass judgment upon them. Saʿd was a devout Muslim and a chieftain of the Aws, who was dying of wounds received during the siege against the Qurayẓa. Saʿd took the hint and condemned the adult males to death and the hapless women and children to slavery. Muḥammad then declared that this was none other than Allah's decision. Actually, it is clear from the Muslim sources that the Qurayẓa's fate had been decided even before their surrender. One of Muḥammad's emissaries, Abū Lubāba, who had advised the Qurayẓa to give up, had to perform penance for hinting to the Jews what their real fate would be.

The men of Qurayẓa were beheaded in the central marketplace of Medina, and their bodies thrown into large open trenches. Only two or three saved their lives through conversion. Between 600 and 900 men were slain. The slaughter of so many men was an extremely impressive act that enhanced Muḥammad's prestige throughout Arabia. Here was a man to be reckoned with. He was now absolute master in Medina. Some historians, such as Tor Andrae, H. Z. Hirschberg, and Salo Baron, have censured Muḥammad's savage treatment of the Jews of Qurayẓa. W. Montgomery Watt, on the other hand, has offered as strong an apologetic defense of Muḥammad's conduct on this occasion as might be expected from any devout Muslim. Neither blame nor vindication are in order here. We cannot judge the treatment of the Qurayẓa by present-day moral standards. Their fate was a bitter one, but not unusual according to the harsh rules of war during that period. As Rudi Paret has observed, Muḥammad had to be more concerned with adverse public opinion when he had some date palms cut down during the siege of the Naḍīr than when on a given day he had some 600 or more Jews put to the sword.

At that time Medina was not altogether devoid of Jews. There still remained a few individual Jews and some small, marginal clans that had not belonged to any of those principal Jewish tribes. These few individuals posed no threat whatsoever to Muḥammad and so were left unmolested for a while. Eventually, however, they were forced to sell their properties and leave the area.

Muḥammad had not forgotten the enmity the Jews had shown him. Neither had he forgotten that many members of the Naḍīr were now comfortably resettled in Khaybar. The Jews of this rich oasis must have clearly understood the danger they were in. Ḥuyayy b. Akhṭab had gone from Khaybar with his son to join the Meccan and Bedouin forces besieging Medina at the time of the Battle of the Trench. He had been killed after having fought alongside the Banū Qurayẓa. Another chieftain, Abu 'l-Rāfiʿ b. Abi 'l-Ḥuqayq, was assassinated in bed by some of Muḥammad's henchmen, who had stolen into Khaybar at night, aided by a Muslim who spoke the Jewish dialect of Arabic.

The Jews were anxious to ward off any calamity and were willing to enter into negotiations with the strongman of Medina. Muḥammad sent emissaries to Khaybar inviting the war chief of the Naḍīr, a man by the name of Usayr (Yusayr) b. Zārim, to come to Medina to parley. Usayr set off with thirty companions and a Muslim escort. Suspecting no foul play, the Jews went unarmed. On the way, the Muslims turned upon the defenseless delegation, killing all but one who managed to escape. "War is deception," according to an oft-quoted saying of the Prophet.

There was consequently no doubt in Khaybar that all-out war was inevitable. The Jews of Khaybar joined in a defense alliance with their coreligionists in the Fadak oasis and with several Bedouin tribes. For a while Muḥammad made no move, and the Jews of Khaybar felt the immediate danger of a Muslim attack was averted. The respite was only temporary.

Muḥammad advanced in force against Khaybar in May 628. The timing could not have been better. The Jews were not expecting the attack and were unprepared for an extended siege. The Muslims had been disappointed by the Prophet's recent abortive attempt to make a pilgrimage to Mecca and by his signing a truce with the Quraysh at al-Ḥudaybiyya. They needed a victory to raise their spirits. Furthermore, it was clear from the circumstances surrounding the incident at al-Ḥudaybiyya that most of the Bedouin were still not closely tied to the Umma (the Muslim community). Muḥammad needed to show them that it was worth their while to be allied to his cause.

The Jews of Khaybar put up a fierce resistance to the Muslims. The lesson to be learned from the fate of their Medinese coreligionists had not been lost upon them. Muḥammad was forced to fight it out with them, fortress by fortress. In the meantime, he was able to buy off the Khaybarīs' Bedouin allies and prevent any reinforcements from coming to the assistance of the besieged. The Jews of Khaybar were finally forced to surrender, but were able to do so on terms—except, that is, for the Naḍīr, who were given no quarter. In return for their personal safety and the right to retain their homes and property, the Khaybarī s agreed to pay the Umma one-half of their annual date harvest. The terms were burdensome, but not unusually harsh. Oasis dwellers customarily paid (and in many places still pay) "protection money" in the form of a share of their produce to neighboring Bedouin. As Salo Baron has noted, "this practice, far from being considered at that time a sign of political weakness, was freely indulged in also by the great Byzantine and Persian empires to secure peace from many unruly neighboring tribes."

The settlement made with the Jews of Khaybar was repeated with those of Fadak and the oases of the Wādi 'l-Qurā. These agreements became significant as legal precedents for the treatment of Jews and Christians in the later Islamic state. Once subdued and made tribute bearers, they were to be shown tolerance. Muslim sources differ on the details of the Khaybar treaty. One important clause that is common to most of the versions states that the Jews might remain in their homes only as long as the Muslims permitted, but could be expelled whenever the Umma saw fit to do so. Such a stipulation seems highly unlikely and is certainly a later interpolation inserted to justify the expulsion of Jews from the Hijaz under the Caliph ʿUmar (634–44). It is clear that the Jews had been kept on because of their valuable skills in agriculture. During the caliphate of ʿUmar, when the great conquests of the Middle East were taking place, vast numbers of prisoners of war were brought into Arabia as slaves. Many of these were peasant villagers. The Jewish labor force was no longer necessary; neither were the Jews at that time strong enough to force any concessions from the Umma. The Khaybarī Jews spread throughout the Middle East after their expulsion, many of them settling in Palestine. They were able to maintain their own distinct identity until at least the twelfth century. In later times they became popular figures in Arabic folklore.

The submission of Khaybar and the Jewish oases of the northern Hijaz produced the effect Muḥammad desired. His power, prestige, and influence waxed ever greater. Bedouin tribes, who until this time had sat upon the sidelines, flocked to his banner. Eighteen months after the conquest of Khaybar, Mecca surrendered peacefully, and its citizens accepted Islam. The surrender of Ṭā'if, Mecca's rival city, soon followed. Muḥammad had become the undisputed master of the Hijaz. Soon delegations from all over Arabia were coming to Medina to sign treaties acknowledging the supremacy of Allah's apostle. Many tribes requested missionaries to teach them and their brethren the new faith.

The Jews and Christians of Yemen in the south, and of Yamama, Nejd, and Bahrayn in the east, began to pay tribute to the new overlord. This tribute, called *jizya,* a word that probably indicated "compensation," was not originally the poll tax it was to become in later Islamic times, although it also had this meaning in Muḥammad's lifetime. The early treaties made between Muḥammad and the Jews of Maqnaᶜ on the Gulf of Aqaba or the Christians of Najran in Yemen clearly show that the initial *jizya* was in the form of an annual percentage of produce and a fixed quantity of goods. The payment of the *jizya* tribute by Jews and Christians received divine sanction in the autumn of 630, when the koranic verse was revealed that enjoined the Muslims to fight against the peoples of the Book "until they pay the *jizya* out of hand, and have been humbled" (Sura 9:29). The injunction was clear and unequivocal, even if the precise nuances of the Arabic phraseology were somewhat hazy. The non-Muslim was to be subjugated. He was to be made a tribute bearer, and he was to be humbled. Just how he was to be humbled was to be more explicitly defined as time went on. But the basis for his position in Muslim Arab society was permanently established by the eternal word of Allah.

In 632, Muḥammad set the precedent of making the *jizya* a poll tax. In his instructions to his representative in Yemen, he wrote:

> Any Jew or Christian who embraces Islam, sincerely and of his own accord, and practices the Islamic religion, is to be considered one of the Believers. He is to have the same rights and the same duties as they. However, no one who belongs to either Christianity or Judaism is to be dissuaded from it. Every adult, male or female, freeman or slave, must pay a dinar of full weight or its equivalent in garments. Whoever fulfills that has the protection of Allah and His Apostle. Whoever withholds that is the enemy of Allah, His Apostle, and the Believers altogether.

W. Montgomery Watt has questioned the authenticity of these instructions, suspecting that they had been altered by Muslim historians to "reflect the practice of a period later than Muḥammad's lifetime." However, since this universal poll tax of one dinar on all adults of both sexes was not the practice in later Islamic times, it seems highly unlikely that such a document, which differs considerably from eventual Islamic law, would be attributed to none other than the Prophet himself. It has been preserved in the *Sīra* and other early sources precisely because of its authenticity. Although later Muslim rulers were to depart from the specifics of this document, they faithfully maintained its spirit. The general guidelines for the treatment of the People of the Book were firmly established. When the Arabs went on to conquer their vast empire, they had clear proof through koranic text and had the administrative procedures of the Prophet himself to fall back upon.

In the same year that he established the poll tax, Muḥammad died after a brief illness. A period of instability followed. Some Arabs broke their ties to the Umma. Religious reformers and would-be prophets in other parts of the peninsula who had been overshadowed during Muḥammad's lifetime now tried to duplicate his success. Some Jews and Christians hoped to throw off the yoke of subjection. It took nearly one year to reestablish Muslim hegemony throughout Arabia. These local conflicts, known in Islamic tradition as the Wars of Ridda (Apostasy), formed the backdrop for the great conquests that were to follow immediately, almost as a coincidental outcome. Soon the entire Middle East with its enormous Christian, Jewish, and Zoroastrian populations would be under Muslim Arab rule. A new phase in the history of the Jews of soon-to-be-expanded Arab lands was about to commence. ❖

RECOMMENDED READINGS

The classic short survey of the history of the Muslims is Bernard Lewis, *The Arabs in history,* rev. ed. (New York: Harper & Row, 1966). H. A. R. Gibb, *Mohammedanism: An Historical Survey* (London: Oxford University Press, 1975), provides a thoughtful introduction to the basic tenets and development of the Islamic faith. Most students will find N. J. Dawood's translation of *The Koran* (New York: Penguin Books, 1974) both readable and handy. The broad sweep of Jewish history to the modern era may be followed in H. H. Ben-Sasson, *Trial and Achievement: Currents in Jewish History from 313* (Jerusalem: Keter Publishing House, 1974).

France, About A.D. 750

THE STIRRUP AND ITS IMPACT ON MEDIEVAL SOCIETY

Lynn White

Feudalism was not peculiar to western Europe; each of the great empires of Eurasia had adopted the armored warrior on horseback as the weapon to defeat the nomadic horsemen of central Asia. It must be admitted, however, that the mounted warriors of feudal Europe differed from their counterparts elsewhere. They used a heavy lance and the shock of mass charges to gain victory, whereas the "knights" elsewhere commonly used a bow and arrow or a javelin. In addition, the mounted warriors of western Europe dominated the field of battle until the close of the fourteenth century, far longer than elsewhere. Finally, Europe never did recover from the decentralization of its feudal age, but remained a collection of independent national entities in an era when the rest of the world was moving toward greater and more centralized empires. Historians have long asked why Europe appeared to have been so different.

Lynn White's contribution—to this discussion in particular and to historiography in general—lay in his realization of the close interrelationship between technology and society and his observation that apparently small technological developments can have major and far-reaching social and economic consequences. In this famous essay, he argues that the evolution of western European feudal society may have depended on something seemingly so obvious and simple as the stirrup.

"The Stirrup and Its Impact on Medieval Society" was one of the more important historical essays of recent times. It awakened an entire generation of historians to the importance of technology and, by so doing, permanently altered the nature of historical analysis and interpretation.

READING QUESTIONS

1. What was the effect of the necessity of maintaining heavy cavalry?

2. What were the necessary qualities of a feudal warrior?

3. How did European feudal military technology influence other cultures?

4. How did their particular kind of warfare affect the feudal warrior class?

The history of the use of the horse in battle is divided into three periods: first, that of the charioteer; second, that of the mounted warrior who clings to his steed by pressure of the knees; and third, that of the rider equipped with stirrups. The horse has always given its master an advantage over the footman in battle, and each improvement in its military use has been related to far-reaching social and cultural changes.

Before the introduction of the stirrup, the seat of the rider was precarious.[1] Bit[2] and spur[3] might help him to control his mount; the simple saddle[4] might confirm his seat; nevertheless, he was still much restricted in his methods of fighting. He was primarily a rapidly mobile bowman and hurler of javelins. Swordplay was limited because 'without stirrups your slashing horseman, taking a good broadhanded swipe at his foe, had only to miss to find himself on the ground'.[5] As for the spear, before the invention of the stirrup it was wielded at the end of the arm and the blow was delivered with the strength of shoulder and biceps.[6] The stirrup made possible—although it did not demand—a vastly more effective mode of attack: now the rider could lay his lance at rest, held between the upper arm and the body, and make at his foe, delivering the blow not with his muscles but with the combined weight of himself and his charging stallion.

---

[1] Cf. H. Müller-Hickler, 'Sitz und Sattel im Laufe der Jahrhunderte', *Zeitschrift für historische Waffen- und Kostümkunde*, x (1923), 9.

[2] R. Zschille and R. Forrer, *Die Pferdetrense in ihrer Formentwicklung* (Berlin, 1893); H. A. Potratz, 'Die Pferdegebisse des zwischenstromländischen Raumes', *Archiv für Orientforschung*, xiv (1941), 1-39; A. Mozsolics, 'Mors en bois de cerf sur le territoire du bassin des Carpathes', *Acta archaeologica* (Budapest), iii (1953), 69-109; M. Schiller, 'Trense und Kandare', *Wissenschaftliche Zeitschrift der Humboldt-Universität zu Berlin, Math.-naturwiss. Reihe*, vii (1957-8), 465-95.

[3] C. de L. Lacy, *History of the Spur* (London, 1911); J. Martin, *Der Reitersporn: seine Entstehung und früheste Entwicklung* (Leipzig, 1921); K. Friis-Johansen, 'Et bidrag til ryttarsporen aeldste historie', *Corrolla archaeologica in honorem C. A. Nordman* (Helsinki, 1952), 41-57.

[4] A. Schlieben, 'Reit- und Packsättel der Alten', *Annalen des Vereins für Nassauische Altertumskunde*, xxi (1889), 14-27; R. Norberg, 'Om förhistoriska sadlar i Sverige', *Rig*, xii (1929), 97-113; J. Werner, 'Beiträge zur Archäologie des Attila-Reiches', *Bayerische Akademie der Wissenschaften, Phil.-hist. Klasse, Abhandlungen*, Heft 38A (1956), 50-53; infra, p. 7, n. 1.

[5] D. H. Gordon, 'Swords, rapiers and horseriders', *Antiquity*, xxvii (1953), 75.

[6] As noted first, among scholars, by H. Delbrück, *Geschichte der Kriegskunst* (Berlin, 1900), i. 141.

From Lynn White, *Medieval Technology and Social Change* (Oxford, UK: Oxford University Press, 1976), pp. 1-2, 28-38.

The stirrup, by giving lateral support in addition to the front and back support offered by pommel and cantle, effectively welded horse and rider into a single fighting unit capable of a violence without precedent. The fighter's hand no longer delivered the blow: it merely guided it.[7] The stirrup thus replaced human energy with animal power, and immensely increased the warrior's ability to damage his enemy. Immediately, without preparatory steps, it made possible mounted shock combat, a revolutionary new way of doing battle.

What was the effect of the introduction of the stirrup in Europe?

The historical record is replete with inventions which have remained dormant in a society[8] until at last—usually for reasons which remain mysterious—they 'awaken' and become active elements in the shaping of a culture to which they are not entirely novel. It is conceivable that Charles Martel, or his military advisers, may have realized the potential of the stirrup after it had been known to the Franks for some decades. However, the present state of our information indicates that it was in fact a new arrival when he used it as the technological basis of his military reforms.

As our understanding of the history of technology increases, it becomes clear that a new device merely opens a door; it does not compel one to enter. The acceptance or rejection of an invention, or the extent to which its implications are realized if it is accepted, depends quite as much upon the condition of a society, and upon the imagination of its leaders, as upon the nature of the technological item itself. As we shall see, the Anglo-Saxons used the stirrup, but did not comprehend it; and for this they paid a fearful price. While semi-feudal relationships and institutions had long been scattered thickly over the civilized world, it was the Franks alone—presumably led by Charles Martel's genius—who fully grasped the possibilities inherent in the stirrup and created in terms of it a new type of warfare supported by a novel structure of society which we call feudalism.

The feudal class of the European Middle Ages existed to be armed horsemen, cavaliers fighting in a particular manner which was made possible by the stirrup. This *élite* created a secular culture closely related to its style of fighting and vigorously paralleling the ecclesiastical culture of the Church.[9]

---

[7] In the twelfth century Usāmah clearly defined the greater efficiency of shock combat and the new relation between man and horse: 'He who is on the point of striking with his lance should hold his lance as tightly as possible with his hand and under his arm, close to his side, and should let his horse run and effect the required thrust; for if he should move his hand while holding the lance or stretch out his arm within the lance, then his thrust would have no effect whatever, and would result in no harm' (*An Arab-Syrian Gentleman and Warrior in the Period of the Crusades: Memoirs of Usāmah ibm Munqidh*, ed. and tr. P. K. Hitti [New York, 1929], 69-70; cf. also 173 and 175 for relation of stirrup to the lance at rest).

[8] E.g. the mechanical crank; cf. *infra*, pp. 110-15.

[9] In its relationships with the ecclesiastical culture, chivalric culture seems to have been highly selective; e.g. E. R. Labande, 'Le "Credo" épique: à propos des prières dans les chansons de

Feudal institutions, the knightly class, and chivalric culture altered, waxed and waned; but for a thousand years they bore the marks of their birth from the new military technology of the eighth century.

While money had by no means gone out of circulation in the Frankish realm, the West of the eighth century was closer to a barter economy than was either contemporary Byzantium or Islam. Moreover, the bureaucracy of the Carolingian kingdom was so slender that the collection of taxes by the central government was difficult. Land was the fundamental form of riches. When they decided that it was essential to secure cavalry to fight in the new and very expensive manner, Charles Martel and his heirs took the only possible action in seizing Church lands and distributing them to vassals on condition of knight's service in the Frankish host.[10]

Fighting in the new manner involved large expenditures. Horses were costly, and armour was growing heavier to meet the new violence of mounted shock combat. In 761 a certain Isanhard sold his ancestral lands and a slave for a horse and a sword.[11] In general, military equipment for one man seems to have cost about twenty oxen,[12] or the plough-teams of at least ten peasant families. But horses get killed: a knight needed remounts to be effective; and his squire should be adequately mounted. And horses eat large quantities of grain, an important matter in an age of more slender agricultural production than ours.

Although in the Frankish realm the right and duty to bear arms rested on all free men regardless of economic condition, naturally the great majority could afford to come to muster only on foot, equipped with relatively inexpensive weapons and armour. As has been mentioned, even from this group Charlemagne tried to raise horsemen[13] by commanding that the less prosperous freemen should band together, according to the size of their lands, to equip one of their number and send him to the wars.[14] Such an arrangement

---

geste', *Mémoires et documents publiés par la Société de l'École des Chartes,* xii. ii (1955), 62-80, shows that these knightly prayers contain chiefly Biblical materials, and far less apocryphal and legendary matter than is to be found in the iconography of contemporary churches.

[10] Prejudice against confiscation of Church lands was so strong that by 755 the Carolingians began to require the holders of such *precariae verbo regis* to pay to their former clerical owners one-fifth of the produce annually. Clarifying much earlier confusion, G. Constable, 'Nona et decima: an aspect of Carolingian economy', *Speculum,* xxxv (1960), 224-50, shows that these payments were quite distinct from the regular tithe which was due from all lands.

[11] H. Wartmann, *Urkundenbuch S. Gallen* (Zürich, 1863), i. 34, no. 31.

[12] *Lex ribuaria,* xxvi. 11, *MGH, Leges,* v. 231; cf. Delbrück, op. cit. iii. 4; Kaufmann, op. cit. i. 339, n. 1.

[13] Fehr, op. cit. 118-19, shows that the effort of A. Dopsch, *Wirtschaftsentwicklung der Karolingerzeit* (Weimar, 1913), ii. 18-19, to prove that this plan of sharing military burdens is older than Charlemagne rests upon a misinterpretation of a capitulary of 825 (*MGH, Cap.* i. 325, c. 3).

[14] *MGH, Cap.* i. 134, c. 2; cf. Brunner, *Deutsche Rechtsgeschichte,* 2nd edn. (Munich, 1928), ii. 273-5.

would be hard to administer, and it did not survive the confusion of the later ninth century.[15] But inherent in this device was the recognition that if the new technology of warfare were to be developed consistently, military service must become a matter of class. Those economically unable to fight on horseback suffered from a social infirmity which shortly became a legal inferiority. In 808 the infelicitous wording of a capitulary *De exercitu promovendo* distinguishes 'liberi' from 'pauperes':[16] the expression is legally inexact, but it points to the time when freedom was to become largely a matter of poverty. Two capitularies of 825 show how rapidly concepts were moving. One separates 'liberi' from 'mediocres quippe liberi qui non possunt per se hostem facere'; while the other refers to those latter as 'liberi secundi ordinis'.[17] With the collapse of the Frankish empire, the feudality which the Carolingians had deliberately created, in terms of the new military method of mounted shock combat, to be the backbone of their army became the governing as well as the fighting *élite*. The old levy of freemen (although not all infantry) vanished, and a gulf appeared between a warrior aristocracy and the mass of peasants. By about the year 1000, *miles* had ceased to mean 'soldier' and had become 'knight'.[18]

The feudal aristocrat might, indeed, be a ruler, but this was incidental to his being a warrior. A student of medieval poetry has remarked that the 'essential note of true knighthood is to put down wrong-doers—not a magistracy but a substitute or supplement for magistracy'.[19] The image of the cavalier reflected in his literature shows that his self-respect was based primarily on two ideal virtues: loyalty to his liege (after the troubadours had done their work, to his lady as well), and prowess in combat. Both *loiautee* and *proesce* were integral to feudal origins.

The members of the feudal class held their lands and enjoyed their status by reason of loyalty in regard to their obligation of knight's service. Gradually the concept was broadened to include other 'aids', notably assisting at the court of one's liege lord. But the original and basic knight's service was mounted shock combat. When the central royal authority evaporated during the later ninth century, subinfeudation assured that the concept of feudal loyalty remained vigorous. Feudal tenures quickly became hereditary, but

---

[15] It last appears in 864; cf. *MGH, Cap.* ii. 310.

[16] *MGH, Cap.* i. 137, c. 2.

[17] Ibid. 329, c. 1; 325, c. 3; cf. K. Bosl, 'Freiheit und Unfreiheit: zur Entwicklung der Unterschichten in Deutschland und Frankreich während des Mittelalters', *Vierteljahrschrift für Sozial- und Wirtschaftsgeschichte*, xliv (1957), 206-7.

[18] G. Duby, *La Société aux XIᵉ et XIIᵉ siècles dans la region mâconnaise* (Paris, 1953), 231; F. L. Ganshof, 'Les Relations féodo-vassaliques aux temps post-carolingiens', *Settimane di studio del Centro Italiano di Studi sull'Alto Medioevo*, ii (1955), 83-85; K. J. Hollyman, *Le Développement du vocabulaire féodal en France pendant le haut moyen âge* (Paris, 1957), 129-34.

[19] G. Mathew, 'Ideals of knighthood in late fourteenth-century England', *Studies in Medieval History presented to F. M. Powicke* (Oxford, 1948), 360.

they could be inherited only by one able to fulfill the duty of knight's service. Elaborate rules for the wardship of minors, and regulations requiring widows and heiresses to marry, guarded this essential requirement for enfiefment.

The chivalric class never repudiated the original condition of its existence; that it was endowed to fight, and that anyone who could not or would not meet his military obligations forfeited his endowment. The duty of knight's service is the key to feudal institutions. It is 'the touchstone of feudalism, for through it all else was drawn into focus; and its acceptance as the determining principle of land-tenure involved a social revolution'.[20]

The feudal sense that the enjoyment of wealth is inseparable from public responsibility chiefly distinguishes medieval ideas of ownership from both classical and modern. The vassal class created by the military mutation of the eighth century became for generations the ruling element of European society, but through all subsequent chaos, and despite abuses, it never lost completely its sense of *noblesse oblige,* even when a new and rival class of burghers revived the Roman notion of the unconditional and socially irresponsible possession of property.

The second element in a knight's pride, prowess, was inherent in the adequate performance of his service. Quite apart from the cost of arms and horses, the new mode of fighting necessarily destroyed the old Germanic idea that every freeman was a soldier. Mounted shock combat was not a business for part-time warriors: one had to be a skilled professional, the product of a long technical training, and in excellent physical condition. Towards the middle of the ninth century Hrabanus Maurus quotes a Frankish proverb that to learn to fight like a knight one must start at puberty. Even more significant is Hrabanus's indication that in his time the households of great lords had already become schools in which boys were trained in the chivalric arts, probably including practice in the tilt-yard.

Stenton has remarked that 'the apprenticeship which preceded knighthood is the most significant fact in the organization of feudal society'.[21] It welded together a self-conscious, cosmopolitan military caste, aware of its solidarity and proud of its traditions, an essential part of which was great rivalry among knights in feats of arms. When a youth was at last admitted to the guild of knights, he was professionally committed to slaying dragons. The new mode of combat, with its high mobility and fearful impact, opened fresh fields for deeds of individual prowess. The old days were gone of standing in formation in the shieldwall and thrusting and hacking. While in the feudal age major battles were often planned carefully, and executed with

---

[20] H. A. Cronne, 'The origins of feudalism', *History*, xxiv (1939), 253.

[21] F. M. Stenton, *First Century of English Feudalism, 1066-1166* (Oxford, 1932), 131.

admirable discipline by squadrons of knights,[22] the emotional life of the chivalric warrior was highly individualized. Long passages of the *chansons de geste* are devoted to blow-by-blow accounts of mighty encounters which can be appreciated only if one pictures the technical interests of the feudal audience. And at last, in Froissart's *Chronicle,* the chivalric world produced a philosophy of history which announced the recording of great feats of arms for the edification of posterity to be the chief duty of Clio.[23]

Keeping physically fit and dexterous in the use of arms in shock combat were the presuppositions of ability to display both loyalty to the liege and prowess in battle. To that end the chivalric stratum developed and elaborated a deadly and completely realistic game of war—the tournament. In 842 there was a formidable passage at arms near Strassburg in the presence of Charles the Bald and Louis the German, and evidently at that time such events were not exceptional.[24] However, concrete evidence about such knightly free-for-alls is scanty until the twelfth century. Thereafter they 'formed the pastime of the higher class up to the Thirty Years War'.[25]

As the violence of shock combat increased, the armourer's skill tried to meet it by building heavier and heavier defences for the knight. Increasingly he became unrecognizable beneath his carapace, and means of identification had to be developed.[26] In the Bayeux Tapestry of the late eleventh century the pennons are more individualized than the shields. By the early

---

[22] P. Pieri, 'Alcuni quistioni sopra la fanteria in Italia nel periodo comunale', *Rivista storica italiana,* l (1933), 567–8; J. F. Verbruggen, 'La Tactique militaire des armées de chevaliers', *Revue du nord* xxix (1947), 161–80, and his *De krijgskunst in West-Europa in de middeleeuwen, IXe tot begin XIVe eeuw* (Brussels, 1954), esp. 52–58, 148–54, destroy the conventional view that medieval battles were disorderly slaughter. On the contrary, knights habitually fought, both in the field and at tournaments, in *conrois* of from twelve to forty horsemen operating as a shock-combat group and placing great stress upon maintaining a line formation at the charge.

[23] *Chroniques de J. Froissart,* ed. S. Luce (Paris, 1869), i. 1: 'Afin que les grans merveilles et li biau fait d'armes, qui sont avenu par les grans guerres de France et d'Engleterre et des royaumes voisins, dont li roy et leurs consaulz sont cause, soient notablement registré et ou temps present et a venir veu et cogneu, je me voel ensonnüer de l'ordonner et mettre en prose.'

[24] Nithard, iii. 6, *MGH, Scriptores,* ii. 667: 'Ludos etiam hoc ordine *saepe* causa exercitii frequentabant.' Cf. F. Niederer, *Das deutsche Turnier im XII. und XIII. Jahrhundert* (Berlin, 1881), 7.

[25] R. C. Clephan, *Defensive Armour* (London, 1900), 77. K. G. T. Webster, 'The twelfth-century tourney', in *Anniversary Papers by Colleagues of G. L. Kittredge* (Boston, 1913), 227–34, and N. Denholm-Young, 'The tournament in the thirteenth century', in *Studies in Medieval History presented to F. M. Powicke* (Oxford, 1948), 240–68, emphasize the brutal realism of the tourney as practice for war.

[26] That identification, not merely ornamentation, was the functional reason for the emergence of heraldry is indicated by the fact that the earliest term for arms is *cunuissances* or *conoissances; cf.* R. Chabanne, *Le Régime juridique des armoiries* (Lyons, 1954), 3–4. Since all warriors, until our age of camouflage, have decorated their arms, we should beware of discovering heraldry in the early tenth century when Abbo, *De bellis Parisiaci urbis,* i. l. 256–7, in *MGH, Scriptores,* ii. 783, says that from the walls of besieged Paris 'nihil sub se nisi picta scuta videt'.

twelfth century, however, not only armorial devices but hereditary arms were coming into use in France, England, and Germany.[27] It is not playing tricks with semantics to insist that the feudal knight himself, and his society, knew who he was in terms of his arms. The exigencies of mounted shock combat, as invented by the Franks of the eighth century, had formed both his personality and his world.

Wherever the Carolingian realm extended its vast borders, it took its mode of fighting, its feudal institutions, and the seeds of chivalry. In Italy, for example, although anticipations of feudal relationships can be discovered in the Lombard kingdom, the feudal combination of vassalage and benefice was introduced by Charlemagne's conquest of the late eighth century.[28] But even where Frankish institutions and attitudes did not penetrate, their mode of fighting could not be disregarded.

In Byzantium the new military technology of the Franks was making itself felt by the time of Nicephoras II Phocas (963-9) who, because of the great increase in the cost of arms, felt compelled to raise the value of the inalienable minimum of a military holding from four to twelve pounds of gold.[29] Here, as in the West, military change on such a scale involved profound social change. As Ostrogorsky remarks, it 'must certainly have meant that the Byzantine army would henceforth be composed of a different social class. The heavily armed soldiers of Nicephoras . . . could no longer be the old peasant militia'.[30] Like their Germanic neighbours, the Greeks increased their emphasis on cavalry to the point where, in the tenth century, the garrison of Constantinople consisted of four regiments of horse as compared with one of infantry.[31]

Even the forms and uses of Byzantine arms came to be copied from the West. The earliest Frankish pictures of the lance held at rest come from the end of the ninth century; the first Byzantine representations are of the tenth

---

[27] P. Gras, 'Aux origines de l'héraldique: La décoration des boucliers au début du XIIᵉ siècle, d'après la Bible de Citeaux', *Bibliothèque de l'École des Chartes,* cix (1951), 198-208; A. R. Wagner, *Heralds and Heraldry in the Middle Ages* (Oxford, 1956), 13-17; C. U. Ulmenstein, *Über Ursprung und Entstehung des Wappenwesens* (Weimar, 1935), 15, 56-60.

[28] P. S. Leicht, 'Gasindi e vassali', *Rendiconti della Reale Accademia Nazionale dei Lincei, Classe di scienze morali, etc.,* ser. 6, iii (1927), 291-307, and 'Il feudo in Italia mell'età carolingia', *Settimane di studio del Centro Italiano di Studi sull'Alto Medioevo,* i (1954), 71-107.

[29] F. Dölger, *Regesten der Kaiserurkunden des oströmischen Reichs* (Munich, 1924), i. 93, no. 721: J. and P. Zepos, *Jus graecoromanorum* (Athens, 1931), i. 255-6. P. Lemerle, 'Esquisse pour une histoire agraire de Byzance: les sources et les problèmes', *Revue historique,* ccxx (1958), 53, rightly deplores the lack of special studies of Byzantine armament which would permit us to judge exactly the basis of Nicephoras Phocas's drastic action.

[30] In *Cambridge Economic History of Europe,* i (Cambridge, 1941), 208; cf. E. H. Kantorowicz, '"Feudalism" in the Byzantine Empire', *Feudalism in History,* ed. R. Coulborn (Princeton, 1956), 161-2. Lemerle, loc. cit., n. 4, challenges Ostrogorski on this point; but whatever Nicephoras Phocas's intentions, would not the result of his decree be to raise the endowed soldier to a higher social class?

[31] C. Diehl and G. Marcais, *Le Monde oriental de 395 à 1081* (Paris, 1936), 464.

to eleventh centuries.[32] By about the year 1000 the demands of mounted shock combat had led the Franks to modify the older circular or oval shield by lengthening it to a pointed kite shape which gave greater protection to the knight's left leg.[33] A century later this is found in Constantinople.[34] Moreover, the cross-bow, which the West had invented, or revived, or borrowed from China in the later tenth century as an 'anti-tank gun' to penetrate the massive new armour, was a complete novelty to Anna Comnena in Byzantium at the time of the First Crusade.[35]

Nor was Islam exempt, even before the First Crusade, from the contagion of Frankish military ideas. In 1087, when Armenian architects built the Bāb an-Naṣr, one of the three great gates of Cairo, it was decorated with a frieze of shields, some round, but some rounded above and pointed below such as we see the Normans carrying in the Bayeux Tapestry.[36] The Arabic word for such pointed shields, *tārīqa,* is derived from the French *targe.*[37] By Saladin's day, the Muslims were using several kinds of cross-bows;[38] they employed the new method of shock combat, and their word for the heavy lance, *qunṭariya,* was either of Greek or Romanic derivation.[39] They much admired the brilliance of the Christian painted shields,[40] and there can be little doubt that the basic concept of Saracenic heraldry is a reflection of the Frankish. By the later thirteenth century the tournament on the Western pattern was practised by the Muslim chivalry of Syria and Egypt.[41] Perhaps most significant is the admiration with which al-Herewī (d. A.D. 1211) describes the

---

[32] A. Goldschmidt and K. Weitzmann, *Die byzantinische Elfenbeinskulpturen des X.-XIII. Jahrhunderts* (Berlin, 1930), i, nos. 12, 20; also no. 98*e,* of the twelfth century, in which the authentic portion of a modern forgery shows two Byzantine riders charging each other with lances at rest. D. Koco, 'L'Ornamentation d'un vase à mesurer du Musée Cluny et les "Stecci" bosniaques', *Artibus Asiae,* xv (1952), 198, fig. 2, shows a Bosnian tombstone of the later Middle Ages with two knights wearing helmets of oriental design but equipped with Western shields, and jousting with the lance at rest.

[33] For a West German ivory of *c.* 1000, cf. H. Schnitzler, *Der Dom zu Aachen* (Düsseldorf, 1950), pl. 59; for the Catalan Farfa Bible, fols. 94ᵛ, 161ʳ, 342ʳ, 352ʳ, 366ᵛ, see *infra,* p. 150; for the Codex aureus Epternachensis, fol. 78, datable *c.* 1035–40, cf. A. Grabar and C. Nordenfalk, *Early Medieval Painting* (New York, 1957), 212.

[34] *Octateuch* of the Library of the Seraglio, MS. 8, fols. 134ʳ, 136ᵛ, 139ʳ, 368ʳ; photographs in Princeton Index. For date, cf. K. Weitzmann, *The Joshua Roll* (Princeton, 1948), 6.

[35] *Alexiad,* tr. E. A. S. Dawes (London, 1928), 255.

[36] K. A. C. Cresswell, 'Fortification in Islam before A.D. 1250', *Proceedings of the British Academy,* xxxviii (1952), 114.

[37] C. Cahen, 'Un traité d'armurerie composé pour Saladin', *Bulletin d'études orientales de l'Institut français de Damas,* xii (1948), 137, 155, n. 2, 160.

[38] Ibid. 127-9, 150-1.

[39] Ibid. 134-6, 154-5.

[40] Ibid. 137, 155, n. 2; L. A. Mayer, *Saracenic Heraldry, a Survey* (Oxford, 1933), does not offer evidence of East–West influences.

[41] H. Ritter, 'La Parure des cavaliers [of ibn Huḍail] und die Literatur über die ritterlichen Kunste,' *Der Islam,* xviii (1929), 122, 127. W. B. Ghali, *La Tradition chevalresque des arabes* (Paris, 1919), 28, 32-33, concludes that the idea of an 'order' of knighthood was likewise adopted from the West in the twelfth century.

carefully co-ordinated battle tactics of the Franks, and the way cavalry and infantry gave mutual support.[42]

If such was the situation in the Levant, we should expect even greater Frankish influence upon Spanish Islam. We have already noted that the Moors developed their emphasis on cavalry a generation after Charles Martel's reform, and were possibly inspired by it. In any case by the thirteenth century the knights of the Reconquista were setting the styles for their Saracenic adversaries. Ibn Sa'īd tells us that 'Very often the Andalusian princes and warriors take the neighbouring Christians as models for their equipment. Their arms are identical, likewise their surcoats of scarlet or other stuff, their pennons, their saddles. Similar also is their mode of fighting with bucklers and long lances for the charge. They use neither the mace nor the bow of the Arabs, but they employ Frankish crossbows for sieges and arm infantry with them for their encounters with the enemy.[43]' Since the Berbers across the Strait of Gibraltar were not so often in contact with Christian arms, Ibn Sa'īd notes that they could use light equipment, whereas the Christian peril compelled the Spanish Muslim warriors to be 'weighed down by the burden of buckler, long thick lance and coat of mail, and they cannot move easily. Consequently their one aim is to stick solidly to the saddle and to form with the horse a veritable iron-clad whole.'

The most spectacular extension, however, of the Frankish military technology, together with all its social and cultural concomitants, was the Norman conquest of England. The Anglo-Saxons were acquainted with the stirrup,[44] but did not sufficiently modify their methods of warfare in terms of it. In Anglo-Saxon England there were seigniorial elements, as there had been in Merovingian Gaul; but there was little tendency towards feudalism or the development of an *élite* of mounted warriors.[45] Harold, his thegns and housecarls, rode stirrupped horses: at the battle of Stamford Bridge King Harold Hardrada of Norway said of him 'That was a little man, but he sat firmly in his stirrups'.[46] However, when they reached Hastings they dismounted to do battle on foot, in the old Germanic shieldwall[47] with which Charles Martel had defeated the Saracens at Poitiers.

---

[42] Ritter, op. cit. 147.

[43] Quoted by E. Lévi-Provençal, *L'Espagne musulmane au Xème siècle* (Paris, 1932), 146.

[44] For the Anglo-Saxon word, see *infra*, pp. 142–3. A stirrup of the Viking age has been found in the Thames; cf. *London Museum Catalogues, No. 1: London and the Vikings* (London, 1927), 39, fig. 17. On the use of cavalry by the invading Norsemen, see J. H. Clephan, 'The horsing of the Danes', *English Historical Review*, xxv (1910), 287–93, rather than F. Pratt, 'The cavalry of the Vikings', *Cavalry Journal*, xlii (1933), 19–21.

[45] Stenton, op. cit. 125, 130–1.

[46] *Heimskringla*, iv. 44, tr. S. Laing (London, 1930), 230. R. Glover, 'English warfare in 1066', *English Historical Review,* lxvii (1952), 5–9, defends the use of this late source for an understanding of the battle of Stamford Bridge.

[47] W. G. Collingwood, *Northumbrian Crosses of the Pre-Norman Age* (London, 1927), 172, fig. 211, shows an Anglo-Saxon relief of *c.* 1000 from Gosforth in Cumberland depicting an army with heavy swords and round shields overlapping to form a shieldwall.

At Hastings[48] the Anglo-Saxons had the advantage of position on the hill of Senlac; they probably outnumbered the Normans, they had the psychological strength of fighting to repel invaders of their homeland. Yet the outcome was certain: this was a conflict between the military methods of the seventh century and those of the eleventh century. Harold fought without cavalry and had few archers. Even the English shields were obsolete: the Bayeux Tapestry shows us that while the royal bodyguard fought with kite-shaped shields—probably a result of Edward the Confessor's continental education—most of the Anglo-Saxons were equipped with round or oval shields.[49] From the beginning William held the initiative with his bowmen and cavalry, and the English could do nothing but stand and resist a mobile striking power which at last proved irresistible.

When William had won his victory and the crown of England, he rapidly modernized, i.e. feudalized, his new kingdom. Naturally he preserved and incorporated into the Anglo-Norman order whatever institutions of the Anglo-Saxon régime suited his purpose; but innovation was more evident than continuity. Just as the Carolingians 300 years earlier had deliberately systematized and disciplined the long-established tendencies towards seigniority in Frankish society in order to strengthen their position, so William the Conqueror used the fully developed feudal organizations of the eleventh century to establish the most powerful European state of his generation.

Indeed, the England of the later eleventh century furnishes the classic example in European history of the disruption of a social order by the sudden introduction of an alien military technology. The Norman Conquest is likewise the Norman Revolution. But it was merely the spread across the Channel of a revolution which had been accomplished by stages on the Continent during the preceding ten generations.

Few inventions have been so simple as the stirrup, but few have had so catalytic an influence on history. The requirements of the new mode of warfare which it made possible found expression in a new form of western European society dominated by an aristocracy of warriors endowed with land so that they might fight in a new and highly specialized way. Inevitably this nobility developed cultural forms and patterns of thought and emotion in harmony with its style of mounted shock combat and its social posture; as Denholm-Young has said: 'it is impossible to be chivalrous without a horse.' The Man on Horseback, as we have known him during the past millennium,

---

[48] Cf. W. Spatz, *Die Schlacht von Hastings* (Berlin, 1896); A. H. Burne, *The Battlefields of England* (London, 1950), 19-45. In his brilliant reappraisal not only of Hastings but of the entire campaign of which it was the culmination, R. Glover, op. cit., 1-18, shows that Anglo-Saxons could fight effectively as cavalry, and explains some of the special circumstances which led to their reversion to infantry at Senlac. However (14, n. 3) he underestimates the iconographic conservatism of the Bayeux Tapestry in representing Norman methods of combat (cf. *infra*, p. 147), and his findings, as is remarked by G. W. S. Barrow, *Feudal Britain* (London, 1956), 34, do not alter the essential fact 'that Hastings was a decisive defeat of infantry by cavalry-with-archers'.

[49] K. Pfannkuche, *Der Schild bei den Angelsachsen* (Halle a. S., 1908), 52-53.

was made possible by the stirrup, which joined man and steed into a fighting organism. Antiquity imagined the Centaur; the early Middle Ages made him the master of Europe.❖

RECOMMENDED READINGS

The best general discussion of feudal society, and one that considers far more than simply its military character, is Marc Bloch, *Feudal Society* (Chicago: University of Chicago Press, 1961). Ronald W. Clark, *Works of Man* (New York: Viking Press, 1985), provides a general history of technology, stressing the close connection between technological development and social change. The technological accomplishments of medieval society are covered in Jean Gimpel, *The Medieval Machine: The Industrial Revolution of the Middle Ages* (New York: Penguin Books, 1977). Lynn White's approach and findings have been subjected to numerous critiques; one of the more extensive is that of R. H. Hilton and P. H. Sawyer, "Technical Determinism: The Stirrup and the Plow," *Past and Present* 24 (1963): 90–100.

BODO

THE LIFE OF A PEASANT IN CHARLEMAGNE'S TIME

Eileen Power

Although medieval western European society was overwhelmingly agricultural and its population mainly peasant, historians for many years were concerned almost exclusively with political developments and "great" men. Eileen Power was one of the first to devote herself to the task of attempting to reconstruct the daily life of the so-called common man and woman. Her essay on the peasant Bodo has remained a model of this type of history. Taking as her base the remarkable body of information provided by the estate book of the Abbey of St. Germain des Prés, she deftly creates a picture of rural life as it may have been lived near Paris at the opening of the ninth century.

READING QUESTIONS

1. How were the lands of the Abbey of St. Germain organized?

2. What were the obligations of the peasants?

3. What role did women play in the estate's economy?

4. What were the entertainments and pastimes of the peasants?

This book is chiefly concerned with the kitchens of History, and the first which we shall visit is a country estate at the beginning of the ninth century. It so happens that we know a surprising amount about such an estate, partly because Charlemagne himself issued a set of orders instructing the Royal stewards how to manage his own lands, telling them everything it was necessary for them to

From Eileen Power, *Medieval People* (Garden City, NY: Doubleday, n.d.), pp. 13–36.

know, down to the vegetables which they were to plant in the garden. But our chief source of knowledge is a wonderful estate book which Irminon, the Abbot of St. Germain des Prés near Paris, drew up so that the abbey might know exactly what lands belonged to it and who lived on those lands, very much as William I drew up an estate book of his whole kingdom and called it "Domesday Book." In this estate book is set down the name of every little estate (or *fisc* as it was called) belonging to the abbey, with a description of the land which was worked under its steward to its own profit, and the land which was held by tenants, and the names of those tenants and of their wives and of their children, and the exact services and rents, down to a plank and an egg, which they had to do for their land. We know to-day the name of almost every man, woman, and child who was living on those little *fiscs* in the time of Charlemagne, and a great deal about their daily lives.

Consider for a moment how the estate upon which they lived was organized. The lands of the Abbey of St. Germain were divided into a number of estates, called *fiscs,* each of a convenient size to be administered by a steward. On each of these *fiscs* the land was divided into seigniorial and tributary lands; the first administered by the monks through a steward or some other officer, and the second possessed by various tenants, who received and held them from the abbey. These tributary lands were divided into numbers of little farms, called manses, each occupied by one or more families. If you had paid a visit to the chief or seigniorial manse, which the monks kept in their own hands, you would have found a little house, with three or four rooms, probably built of stone, facing an inner court, and on one side of it you would have seen a special group of houses hedged round, where the women serfs belonging to the house lived and did their work; all round you would also have seen little wooden houses, where the household serfs lived, workrooms, a kitchen, a bakehouse, barns, stables, and other farm buildings, and round the whole a hedge carefully planted with trees, so as to make a kind of enclosure or court. Attached to this central manse was a considerable amount of land—ploughland, meadows, vineyards, orchards and almost all the woods or forests on the estate. Clearly a great deal of labour would be needed to cultivate all these lands. Some of that labour was provided by servile workers, who were attached to the chief manse and lived in the court. But these household serfs were not nearly enough to do all the work upon the monks' land, and far the greater part of it had to be done by services paid by the other landowners on the estate.

Beside the seigniorial manse, there were a number of little dependent manses. These belonged to men and women who were in various stages of freedom, except for the fact that all had to do work on the land of the chief manse. There is no need to trouble with the different classes, for in practice there was very little difference between them, and in a couple of centuries they were all merged into one common class of medieval villeins. The most important people were those called *coloni,* who were personally free (that is to say, counted as free men by the law), but bound to the soil, so that they could never leave their farms and were sold with the estate, if it were sold. Each of the dependent manses was held either by one family or by two or three families which clubbed together to do the work; it consisted of a house or houses, and farm buildings, like those of the chief manse, only poorer and made of wood, with ploughland and a meadow and perhaps a little piece of vineyard attached to it. In return for these holdings the owner or joint owners of every manse had to do work on the land of the chief manse for about three days in the week. The steward's chief business was to see that they did their work properly, and from every one he had the right to demand two kinds of labour. The first was *field work:* every year each man was bound to do a fixed amount of ploughing on the domain land (as it was called later on), and also to give what was called a *corvée,* that is to say, an unfixed amount of ploughing, which the steward could demand every week when it was needed; the distinction corresponds to the distinction between *week work* and *boon work* in the later Middle Ages. The second kind of labour which every owner of a farm had to do on the monks' land was called hand-work, that is to say, he had to help repair buildings, or cut down trees, or gather fruit, or make ale, or carry loads—anything, in fact, which wanted doing and which the steward told him to do. It was by these services that the monks got their seigniorial farm cultivated. On all the other days of the week these hard-worked tenants were free to cultivate their own little farms, and we may be sure that they put twice as much elbow grease into the business.

But their obligation did not end here, for not only had they to pay services, they also had to pay certain rents to the big house. There were no State taxes in those days, but every man had to pay an army due, which Charlemagne exacted from the abbey, and which the abbey exacted from its tenants; this took the form of an ox and a certain number of sheep, or the equivalent in money: "He pays to the host two shillings of silver" comes first on every freeman's list of obligations. The farmers also had to pay in return for any special privileges granted to them by the monks; they had to carry a load of wood to the big house, in return for being allowed to gather firewood in the woods, which were jealously preserved for the use of the abbey; they had to pay some hogsheads of wine for the right to pasture their pigs in the same precious woods; every third year they had to give up one of their sheep for the right to graze upon the fields of the chief manse, they had to pay a sort of poll-tax of 4d. a head. In addition to these special rents every farmer had also to pay other rents in produce; every year he owed the big house three chickens and fifteen eggs and a large number of planks, to repair its buildings; often he had to give it a couple of pigs; sometimes corn, wine, honey, wax, soap, or oil. If the farmer were also an artisan and made things, he had to pay the produce of his craft; a smith would have to make lances for the abbey's contigent to the army, a carpenter had to make barrels and hoops and vine props, a wheelwright had to make a cart. Even the wives of the farmers were kept busy, if they happened to be serfs; for the servile women were obliged to spin cloth or to make a garment for the big house every year.

All these things were exacted and collected by the steward, whom they called *Villicus,* or *Major* (Mayor). He was a very hard-worked man, and when one reads the seventy separate and particular injunctions which Charlemagne addressed to his stewards one cannot help feeling sorry for him. He had to get all the right services out of the tenants, and tell them what to do each week and see that they did it; he had to be careful that they brought the right number of eggs and pigs up to the house, and did not foist off warped or badly planed planks upon him. He had to look after the household serfs too, and set them to work. He had to see about storing, or selling, or sending off to the monastery the produce of the estate and of the tenants' rents; and every year he had to present a full and detailed account of his stewardship to the abbot. He had a manse of his own, with services and rents due from it, and Charlemagne exhorted his stewards to be prompt in their payments, so as to set a good example. Probably his official duties left him very little time to work on his own farm, and he would have to put in a man to work it for him, as Charlemagne bade his stewards do. Often, however, he had subordinate officials called *deans* under him, and sometimes the work of receiving and looking after the stores in the big house was done by a special cellarer.

That, in a few words, is the way in which the monks of St. Germain and the other Frankish landowners of the time of Charlemagne managed their estates. Let us try, now, to look at those estates from a more human point of view and see what life was like to a farmer who lived upon them. The abbey possessed a little estate called Villaris, near Paris, in the place now occupied by the park of Saint Cloud. When we turn up the pages in the estate book dealing with Villaris, we find that there was a man called Bodo living there. He had a wife called Ermentrude and three children called Wido and Gerbert and Hildegard; and he owned a little farm of arable and meadow land, with a few vines. And we know very nearly as much about Bodo's work as we know about that of a small-holder in France to-day. Let us try and imagine a day in his life. On a fine spring morning towards the end of Charlemagne's reign Bodo gets up early, because it is his day to go and work on the monks' farm, and he does not dare to be late, for fear of the steward. To be sure, he has probably given the steward a present of eggs and vegetables the week before, to keep him in a good temper; but the monks will not allow their stewards to take big bribes (as is sometimes done on other estates), and Bodo knows that he will not be allowed to go late to work. It is his day to plough, so he takes his big ox with him and little Wido to run by its side with a goad, and he joins his friends from some of the farms near by, who are going to work at the big house too. They all assemble, some with horses and oxen, some with mattocks and hoes and spades and axes and scythes, and go off in gangs to work upon the fields and meadows and woods of the seigniorial manse, according as the steward orders them. The manse next door to Bodo is held by a group of families: Frambert and Ermoin and Ragenold, with their wives and children. Bodo bids them good morning as he passes. Frambert is going to make a fence round the wood, to prevent the rabbits from coming out and eating the young crops; Ermoin has been told off to cart a great load of firewood up to the house; and Ragenold is mending a hole in the roof of a barn. Bodo goes whistling off in the cold with his oxen and his little boy; and it is no use to follow him farther, because he ploughs all day and eats his meal under a tree with the other ploughmen, and it is very monotonous.

Let us go back and see what Bodo's wife, Ermentrude, is doing. She is busy too; it is the day on which the chicken-rent is due—a fat pullet and five eggs in all. She leaves her second son, aged nine, to look after the baby Hildegard and calls on one of her neighbours, who has to go up to the big house too. The neighbour is a serf and she has to take the steward a piece of woollen cloth, which will be sent away to St. Germain to make a habit for a monk. Her husband is working all day in the lord's vineyards, for on this estate the serfs generally tend the vines, while the freemen do most of the ploughing. Ermentrude and the serf's wife go together up to the house. There all is busy. In the men's workshop are several clever workmen—a shoemaker, a carpenter, a blacksmith, and two silversmiths; there are not more, because the best artisans on the estates of St. Germain live by the walls of the abbey, so that they can work for the monks on the spot and save the labour of carriage. But there were always some craftsmen on every estate, either attached as serfs to the big house, or living on manses of their own, and good landowners tried to have as many clever craftsmen as possible. Charlemagne ordered his stewards each to have in his district "good workmen, namely, blacksmiths, goldsmiths, silversmiths, shoemakers, turners, carpenters, swordmakers, fishermen, foilers, soapmakers, men who know how to make beer, cider, perry and all other kinds of beverages, bakers to make pasty for our table, netmakers who know how to make nets for hunting, fishing and fowling, and others too many to be named." And some of these workmen are to be found working for the monks in the estate of Villaris.

But Ermentrude does not stop at the men's workshop. She finds the steward, bobs her curtsy to him, and gives up her fowl and eggs, and then she hurries off to the women's part of the house, to gossip with the serfs there. The Franks used at this time to keep the women of their household in a separate quarter, where they did the work which was considered suitable for women, very much as the Greeks of antiquity used to do. If a Frankish noble had lived at the big house, his wife would have looked after their work, but as no one lived in the stone house at Villaris, the steward had to oversee the women. Their quarter consisted of a little group of houses, with a workroom, the whole surrounded by a thick hedge with a strong bolted gate, like a harem, so that no one could come in without leave. Their workrooms were comfortable places, warmed by stoves, and there Ermentrude (who, being a woman, was allowed to go in) found about a dozen servile women spinning and dyeing cloth and sewing garments. Every week the harassed steward brought them the raw materials for their work and took away what they made. Charlemagne gives his stewards several instructions about the women attached to his manses, and we may be sure that the monks of St. Germain did the same on their model estates. "For our women's work," says Charlemagne, "they are to give at the proper time the materials, that is linen, wool, woad, vermilion, madder, wool combs, teasels, soap, grease, vessels, and other objects which are necessary. And let our women's quarters be well looked after, furnished with houses and rooms with stoves and cellars, and let them be surrounded by good hedge, and let the doors be strong, so that the women can do our work properly." Ermentrude, however, has to hurry away after her gossip, and so must we. She goes back to her own farm and sets to work in the little vineyard; then after an hour or two goes back to get the children's meal and to spend the rest of the day in weaving warm woollen clothes for them. All her friends are either working in the fields on their husband's farms or else looking after the poultry, or the vegetables, or sewing at home; for the women have to work just as hard as the men on a country farm. In Charlemagne's time (for instance) they did nearly all the sheep shearing. Then at last Bodo comes back for his supper, and as soon as the sun goes down they go to bed; for their hand-made candle gives only a flicker of light, and they both have to be up early in the morning. De Quincey once pointed out, in his inimitable manner, how the ancients everywhere went to bed, "like good boys, from seven to nine o'clock." "Man went to bed early in those ages simply because his worthy mother earth could not afford him candles. She, good old lady . . . would certainly have shuddered to hear of any of her nations asking for candles. 'Candles, indeed!' she would have said; 'who ever heard of such a thing? and with so much excellent daylight running to waste, as I have provided *gratis!* What will the wretches want next?' " Something of the same situation prevailed even in Bodo's time.

This, then, is how Bodo and Ermentrude usually passed their working day. But, it may be complained, this is all very well. We know about the estates on which these peasants lived and about the rents which they had to pay, and the services which they had to do. But how did they feel and think and amuse themselves when they were not working? Rents and services are only outside things; an estate book only describes routine. It would be idle to try to picture the life of a university from a study of its lecture list, and it is equally idle to try and describe the life of Bodo from the estate book of his masters. It is no good taking your meals in the kitchen if you never talk to the servants. This is true, and to arrive at Bodo's thoughts and feelings and holiday amusements we must bid good-bye to Abbot Irminon's estate book, and peer into some very dark corners indeed; for though by the aid of Chaucer and Langland and a few Court Rolls it is possible to know a great deal about the feelings of a peasant six centuries later, material is scarce in the ninth century, and it is all the more necessary to remember the secret of the invisible ink.

Bodo certainly *had* plenty of feelings, and very strong ones. When he got up in the frost on a cold morning to drive the plough over the abbot's acres, when his own were calling out for work, he often shivered and shook the rime from his beard, and wished that the big house and all its land were at the bottom of the sea (which, as a matter of fact, he had never seen and could not imagine). Or else he wished he were the abbot's huntsman, hunting in the forest; or a monk of St. Germain, singing sweetly in the abbey church; or a merchant, taking bales of cloaks and girdles along the high road to Paris; anything, in fact, but a poor ploughman ploughing other people's land. An Anglo-Saxon writer has imagined a dialogue with him:

> "Well, ploughman, how do you do your work?" "Oh, sir, I work very hard. I go out in the dawning, driving the oxen to the field and I yoke them to the plough. Be the winter never so stark, I dare not stay at home for fear of my lord; but every day I must plough a full acre or more, after having yoked the oxen and fastened the share and coulter to the plough!" "Have you any mate?" "I have a boy, who drives the oxen with a goad, who is now hoarse from cold and shouting." (Poor little Wido!) "Well, well, it is very hard work?" "Yes, indeed it is very hard work."

Nevertheless, hard as the work was, Bodo sang lustily to cheer himself and Wido; for is it not related that once, when a clerk was singing the "Allelulia" in the emperor's presence, Charles turned to one of the bishops, saying, "My clerk is singing very well," whereat the rude bishop replied, "Any clown in our countryside drones as well as that to his oxen at their ploughing"? It is certain too that Bodo agreed with the names which the great Charles gave to the months of the year in his own Frankish tongue; for he called January "Winter-month," February "Mud-month," March "Spring-month," April "Easter-month," May "Joy-month," June "Plough-month," July "Hay-month," August "Harvest-month," September "Wind-month," "October "Vintage-month," November "Autumn-month," and December "Holy-month."

And Bodo was a superstitious creature. The Franks had been Christian now for many years, but Christian though they were, the peasant clung to old beliefs and superstitions. On the estates of the holy monks of St. Germain you would have found the country people saying charms which were hoary with age, parts of the lay sung by the Frankish ploughman over his bewitched land long before he marched southwards into the Roman Empire, or parts of the spell which the bee master performed when he swarmed his bees on the shores of the Baltic Sea. Christianity has coloured these charms, but it has not effaced their heathen origin; and because the tilling of the soil is the oldest and most unchanging of human occupations, old beliefs and superstitions cling to it and the old gods stalk up and down the brown furrows, when they have long vanished from houses and roads. So on Abbot Irminon's estates the peasant-farmers muttered charms over their sick cattle (and over their sick children too) and said incantations over the fields to make them fertile. If you had followed behind Bodo when he broke his first furrow you would have probably seen him take out of his jerkin a little cake, baked for him by Ermentrude out of different kinds of meal, and you would have seen him stoop and lay it under the furrow and sing:

Earth, Earth, Earth! O Earth, our mother!
May the All-Wielder, Ever-Lord grant thee
Acres a-waxing, upwards a-growing,
Pregnant with corn and plenteous in strength;
Hosts of grain shafts and of glittering plants!
Of broad barley the blossoms,
And of white wheat ears waxing,
Of the whole land the harvest. . . .

Acre, full-fed, bring forth fodder for men!
Blossoming brightly, blessed become!
And the God who wrought with earth grant us gift of growing
That each of all the corns may come unto our need.

Then he would drive his plough through the acre.

The Church wisely did not interfere with these old rites. It taught Bodo to pray to the Ever-Lord instead of to Father Heaven, and to the Virgin Mary instead of to Mother Earth, and with these changes let the old spell he had learned from his ancestors serve him still. It taught him, for instance, to call on Christ and Mary in his charm for bees. When Ermentrude heard her bees swarming, she stood outside her cottage and said this little charm over them:

Christ, there is a swarm of bees outside,
Fly hither, my little cattle,
In blest peace, in God's protection,
Come home safe and sound.
Sit down, sit down, bee,
St. Mary commanded thee.
Thou shalt not have leave,
Thou shalt not fly to the wood.
Thou shalt not escape me,
Nor go away from me.
Sit very still,
Wait God's will!

And if Bodo on his way home saw one of his bees caught in a brier bush, he immediately stood still and wished—as some people wish to-day when they go under a ladder. It was the Church, too, which taught Bodo to add "So be it, Lord," to the end of his charm against pain. Now, his ancestors for generations behind him had believed that if you had a stitch in your side, or a bad pain anywhere, it came from a worm in the marrow of your bones, which was eating you up, and that the only way to get rid of that worm was to put a knife, or an arrow-head, or some other piece of metal to the sore place, and then wheedle the worm out on to the blade by saying a charm. And this was the charm which Bodo's heathen ancestors had always said and which Bodo went on saying when little Wido had a pain: "Come out, worm, with nine little worms, out from the marrow into the bone, from the bone into the flesh, from the flesh into the skin, from the skin into this arrow." And then (in obedience to the Church) he added "So be it, Lord." But sometimes it was not possible to read a Christian meaning into Bodo's doings. Sometimes he paid visits to some man who was thought to have a wizard's powers, or superstitiously reverenced some twisted tree, about which were hung old stories never quite forgotten. Then the Church was stern. When he went to confession the priest would ask him: "Have you consulted magicians and enchanters, have you made vows to trees and fountains, have you drunk any magic philtre?" And he would have to confess what he did last time his cow was sick. But the Church was kind as well as stern. "When serfs come to you," we find one bishop telling his priests, "you must not give them as many fasts to perform as rich men. Put upon them only half the penance." The Church knew well enough that Bodo could not drive his plough all day upon an empty stomach. The hunting, drinking, feasting Frankish nobles could afford to lose a meal.

It was from this stern and yet kind Church that Bodo got his holidays. For the Church made the pious emperor decree that on Sundays and saints' days no servile or other works should be done. Charlemagne's son repeated his decree in 827. It runs thus:

> We ordain according to the law of God and to the command of our father of blessed memory in his edicts, that no servile works shall be done on Sundays, neither shall men perform their rustic labours, tending vines, ploughing fields, reaping corn and mowing hay, setting up hedges or fencing woods, cutting trees, or working in quarries or building houses; nor shall they work in the garden, nor come to the law courts, nor follow the chase. But three carrying-services it is lawful to do on Sunday, to wit carrying for the army, carrying food, or carrying (if need be) the body of a lord to its grave. Item, women shall not do their textile works, nor cut out clothes, nor stitch them together with the needle, nor card wool, nor beat hemp, nor wash clothes in public, nor shear sheep: so that there may be rest on the Lord's day. But let them come together from all sides to Mass in the Church and praise God for all the good things He did for us on that day!

Unfortunately, however, Bodo and Ermentrude and their friends were not content to go quietly to church on saints' days and quietly home again. They used to spend their holidays in dancing and singing and buffoonery, as country folk have always done until our own gloomier, more self-conscious age. They were very merry and not at all refined, and the place they always chose for their dances was the churchyard; and unluckily the songs they sang as they danced in a ring were old pagan songs of their forefathers, left over from old May-day festivities, which they could not forget, or ribald

love-songs which the Church disliked. Over and over again we find the
Church councils complaining that the peasants (and sometimes the priests
too) were singing "wicked songs with a chorus of dancing women," or holding "ballads and dancings and evil and wanton songs and such-like lures of
the devil"; over and over again the bishops forbade these songs and dances;
but in vain. In every country in Europe, right through the Middle Ages to the
time of the Reformation, and after it, country folk continued to sing and
dance in the churchyard. Two hundred years after Charlemagne's death
there grew up the legend of the dancers of Kölbigk, who danced on Christmas Eve in the churchyard, in spite of the warning of the priest, and all got
rooted to the spot for a year, till the Archbishop of Cologne released them.
Some men say that they were not rooted standing to the spot, but that they
had to go on dancing for the whole year; and that before they were released
they had danced themselves waist-deep into the ground. People used to repeat the little Latin verse which they were singing:

Equitabat Bovo per silvam frondosam
Ducebat sibi Merswindem formosam.
    Quid stamus? Cur non imus?

Through the leafy forest, Bovo went a-riding
And his pretty Merswind trotted on beside him—
    Why are we standing still? Why can't we go away?

Another later story still is told about a priest in Worchestershire, who was
kept awake all night by the people dancing in his churchyard and singing a
song with the refrain "Sweetheart have pity," so that he could not get it out
of his head, and the next morning at Mass, instead of saying "Dominus vo-
biscum," he said "Sweetheart have pity," and there was a dreadful scandal
which got into a chronicle.

    Sometimes our Bodo did not dance himself, but listened to the songs of
wandering minstrels. The priests did not at all approve of these minstrels,
who (they said) would certainly go to hell for singing profane secular songs,
all about the great deeds of heathen heroes of the Frankish race, instead
of Christian hymns. But Bodo loved them, and so did Bodo's betters; the
Church councils had sometimes even to rebuke abbots and abbesses for listening to their songs. And the worst of it was that the great emperor himself,
the good Charlemagne, loved them too. He would always listen to a minstrel,
and his biographer, Einhard, tells us that "He wrote out the barbarous and
ancient songs, in which the acts of the kings and their wars were sung,
and committed them to memory"; and one at least of those old sagas, which
he liked men to write down, has been preserved on the cover of a Latin manuscript, where a monk scribbled it in his spare time. His son, Louis the
Pious, was very different; he rejected the national poems, which he had
learnt in his youth, and would not have them read or recited or taught; he

would not allow minstrels to have justice in the law courts, and he forbade idle dances and songs and tales in public places on Sundays; but then he also dragged down his father's kingdom into disgrace and ruin. The minstrels repaid Charlemagne for his kindness to them. They gave him everlasting fame; for all through the Middle Ages the legend of Charlemagne grew, and he shares with our King Arthur the honour of being the hero of one of the greatest romance-cycles of the Middle Ages. Every different century clad him anew in its own dress and sang new lays about him. What the monkish chroniclers in their cells could never do for Charlemagne, these despised and accursed minstrels did for him: they gave him what is perhaps more desirable and more lasting than a place in history—they gave him a place in legend. It is not every emperor who rules in those realms of gold of which Keats spoke, as well as in the kingdoms of the world; and in the realms of gold Charlemagne reigns with King Arthur, and his peers joust with the Knights of the Round Table. Bodo, at any rate, benefited by Charles's love of minstrels, and it is probable that he heard in the lifetime of the emperor himself the first beginnings of those legends which afterwards clung to the name of Charlemagne. One can imagine him round-eyed in the churchyard, listening to fabulous stories of Charles's Iron March to Pavia, such as a gossiping old monk of St. Gall afterwards wrote down in his chronicle.

It is likely enough that such legends were the nearest Bodo ever came to seeing the emperor, of whom even the poor serfs who never followed him to court or camp were proud. But Charles was a great traveller: like all the monarchs of the early Middle Ages he spent the time, when he was not warring, in trekking round his kingdom, staying at one of his estates, until he and his household had literally eaten their way through it, and then passing on to another. And sometimes he varied the procedure by paying a visit to the estates of his bishops or nobles, who entertained him royally. It may be that one day he came on a visit to Bodo's masters and stopped at the big house on his way to Paris, and then Bodo saw him plain; for Charlemagne would come riding along the road in his jerkin of otter skin, and his plain blue cloak (Einhard tells us that he hated grand clothes and on ordinary days dressed like the common people); and after him would come his three sons and his bodyguard, and then his five daughters. Einhard has also told us that

> He had such care of the upbringing of his sons and daughters that he never dined without them when he was at home and never travelled without them. His sons rode along with him and his daughters followed in the rear. Some of his guards, chosen for this very purpose, watched the end of the line of march where his daughters travelled. They were very beautiful and much beloved by their father, and, therefore, it is strange that he would give them in marriage to no one, either among his own people or of a foreign state. But up to his death he kept them all at home saying he could not forgo their society.

Then, with luck, Bodo, quaking at the knees, might even behold a portent new to his experience, the emperor's elephant. Haroun El Raschid, the

great Sultan of the "Arabian Nights," had sent it to Charles, and it accompanied him on all his progresses. Its name was "Abu-Lubabah," which is an Arabic word and means "the father of intelligence,"* and it died a hero's death
on an expedition against the Danes in 810. It is certain that ever afterwards
Ermentrude quelled little Gerbert, when he was naughty, with the threat,
"Abu-Lubabah will come with his long nose and carry you off." But Wido,
being aged eight and a bread-winner, professed to have felt no fear on being
confronted with the elephant; but admitted when pressed, that he greatly
preferred Haroun El Raschid's other present to the emperor, the friendly
dog, who answered to the name of "Becerillo."

It would be a busy time for Bodo when all these great folk came, for
everything would have to be cleaned before their arrival, the pastry cooks
and sausage-makers summoned and a great feast prepared; and though the
household serfs did most of the work, it is probable that he had to help. The
gossipy old monk of St. Gall has given us some amusing pictures of the excitement when Charles suddenly paid a visit to his subjects:

> There was a certain bishopric which lay full in Charles's path when he
> journeyed, and which indeed he could hardly avoid: and the bishop of this
> place, always anxious to give satisfaction, put everything that he had at
> Charles's disposal. But once the Emperor came quite unexpectedly and the
> bishop in great anxiety had to fly hither and thither like a swallow, and
> had not only the palaces and houses but also the courts and squares swept
> and cleaned: and then, tired and irritated, came to meet him. The most
> pious Charles noticed this, and after examining all the various details, he
> said to the bishop: "My kind host, you always have everything splendidly
> cleaned for my arrival." Then the bishop, as if divinely inspired, bowed his
> head and grasped the king's never-conquered right hand, and hiding his ir-
> ritation, kissed it and said: "It is but right, my lord, that, wherever you
> come, all things should be thoroughly cleansed." Then Charles, of all kings
> the wisest, understanding the state of affairs said to him: "If I empty I can
> also fill." And he added: "You may have that estate which lies close to your
> bishopric, and all your successors may have it until the end of time." In the
> same journey, too, he came to a bishop who lived in a place through which
> he must needs pass. Now on that day, being the sixth day of the week, he
> was not willing to eat the flesh of beast or bird; and the bishop, being by
> reason of the nature of the place unable to procure fish upon the sudden,
> ordered some excellent cheese, rich and creamy, to be placed before him.
> And the most self-restrained Charles, with the readiness which he showed
> everywhere and on all occasions, spared the blushes of the bishop and re-
> quired no better fare; but taking up his knife cut off the skin, which he
> thought unsavoury and fell to on the white of the cheese. Thereupon the
> bishop, who was standing near like a servant, drew closer and said: "Why
> do you do that, lord emperor? You are throwing away the very best part."
> Then Charles, who deceived no one, and did not believe that anyone would

* *Abu-Lubabah.*—It is remarkable that the name should have suffered no corruption in the
chronicles.

deceive him, on the persuasion of the bishop put a piece of the skin in his mouth, and slowly ate it and swallowed it like butter. Then approving of the advice of the bishop, he said: "Very true, my good host," and he added: "Be sure to send me every year to Aix two cartloads of just such cheeses." And the bishop was alarmed at the impossibility of the task and, fearful of losing both his rank and his office, he rejoined: "My lord, I can procure the cheeses, but I cannot tell which are of this quality and which of another. Much I fear lest I fall under your censure." Then Charles, from whose penetration and skill nothing could escape, however new or strange it might be, spoke thus to the bishop, who from childhood had known such cheeses and yet could not test them: "Cut them in two," he said, "Then fasten together with a skewer those that you find to be of the right quality and keep them in your cellar for a time and then send them to me. The rest you may keep for yourself and your clergy and your family." This was done for two years, and the king ordered the present of cheeses to be taken in without remark: then in the third year the bishop brought in person his laboriously collected cheeses. But the most just Charles pitied his labour and anxiety and added to the bishopric an excellent estate whence he and his successors might provide themselves with corn and wine.

We may feel sorry for the poor flustered bishop collecting his two cartloads of cheeses; but it is possible that our real sympathy ought to go to Bodo, who probably had to pay an extra rent in cheeses to satisfy the emperor's taste, and got no excellent estate to recompense him.

A visit from the emperor, however, would be a rare event in his life, to be talked about for years and told to his grandchildren. But there was one other event, which happened annually, and which was certainly looked for with excitement by Bodo and his friends. For once a year the king's itinerant justices, the *Missi Dominici,* came round to hold their court and to see if the local counts had been doing justice. Two of them would come, a bishop and a count, and they would perhaps stay a night at the big house as guests of the abbot, and the next day they would go on to Paris, and there they would sit and do justice in the open square before the church, and from all the district round great men and small, nobles and freemen and *coloni,* would bring their grievances and demand redress. Bodo would go too, if anyone had injured or robbed him, and would make his complaint to the judges. But if he were canny he would not go to them empty-handed, trusting to justice alone. Charlemagne was very strict, but unless the *missi* were exceptionally honest and pious they would not be averse to taking bribes. Theodulf, Bishop of Orleans, who was one of the Emperor's *missi,* has left us a most entertaining Latin poem, in which he describes the attempts of the clergy and laymen, who flocked to his court, to buy justice. Every one according to his means brought a present; the rich offered money, precious stones, fine materials, and Eastern carpets, arms, horses, antique vases of gold or silver chiselled with representations of the labours of Hercules. The poor brought skins of Cordova leather, tanned and untanned, excellent pieces of cloth and linen (poor Ermentrude must have worked hard for the month before the justices came!), boxes, and wax. "With this battering-ram," cries the shocked Bishop Theodulf, "they hope to break down the wall of my soul. But they would not have thought that they could shake *me,* if they had not so shaken other judges before." And indeed, if his picture be true, the royal justices must have been followed about by a regular caravan of carts and horses to carry their presents. Even Theodulf has to admit that, in order not to hurt people's feelings, he was obliged to accept certain unconsidered trifles in the shape of eggs and bread and wine and chickens and little birds, "whose bodies" (he says, smacking his lips) "are small, but very good to eat." One seems to detect the anxious face of Bodo behind those eggs and little birds.

Another treat Bodo had which happened once a year; for regularly on the ninth of October there began the great fair of St. Denys, which went on for a whole month, outside the gate of Paris. Then for a week before the fair little booths and sheds sprang up, with open fronts in which the merchants could display their wares, and the Abbey of St. Denys, which had the right to take a toll of all the merchants who came there to sell, saw to it that the fair was well enclosed with fences, and that all came in by the gates and paid their money, for wily merchants were sometimes known to burrow under fences or climb over them so as to avoid the toll. Then the streets of Paris were crowded with merchants bringing their goods, packed in carts and upon horses and oxen; and on the opening day all regular trade in Paris stopped for a month, and every Parisian shopkeeper was in a booth somewhere in the fair, exchanging the corn and wine and honey of the district for rarer goods from foreign parts. Bodo's abbey probably had a stall in the fair and sold some of those pieces of cloth woven by the serfs in the women's' quarter, or cheeses and salted meat prepared on the estates, or wine paid in rent by Bodo and his fellow-farmers. Bodo would certainly take a holiday and go to the fair. In fact, the steward would probably have great difficulty in keeping his men at work during the month; Charlemagne had to give a special order to his stewards that they should "be careful that our men do properly the work which it is lawful to exact from them, and that they do not waste their time in running about to markets and fairs." Bodo and Ermentrude and the three children, all attired in their best, did not consider it waste of time to go to the fair even twice or three times. They pretended that they wanted to buy salt to salt down their winter meat, or some vermilion dye to colour a frock for the baby. What they really wanted was to wander along the little rows of booths and look at all the strange things assembled there; for merchants came to St. Denys to sell their rich goods from the distant East to Bodo's betters, and wealthy Frankish nobles bargained there for purple and silken robes with orange borders, stamped leather jerkins, peacock's feathers, and the scarlet plumage of flamingos (which they called "phoenix skins"), scents and pearls and spices, almonds and raisins, and monkeys for their wives to play with. Sometimes these merchants were Venetians, but more often they were Syrians or crafty Jews, and Bodo and his fellows laughed loudly over the story of how a Jewish merchant had tricked a certain bishop, who craved for all the latest novelties, by stuffing a mouse with spices and offering it for sale to him, saying that "he had brought this most precious never-before-seen animal from Judea," and refusing to take less than a whole measure of silver for it. In exchange for their luxuries these merchants took away with them Frisian cloth, which was greatly esteemed, and corn and hunting dogs, and sometimes a piece of fine goldsmith's work, made in a monastic workshop. And Bodo would hear a hundred dialects and tongues, for men of Saxony and Frisia, Spain and Provence, Rouen and Lombardy, and perhaps an Englishman or two, jostled each other in the little streets; and from time to time there came also an Irish scholar with a manuscript to sell, and the strange, sweet songs of Ireland on his lips:

> A hedge of trees surrounds me,
> A blackbird's lay sings to me;
> Above my lined booklet
> The trilling birds chant to me.
>
> In a grey mantle from the top of bushes
> The cuckoo sings:
> Verily—may the Lord shield me!—
> Well do I write under the greenwood.

Then there were always jugglers and tumblers, and men with performing bears, and minstrels to wheedle Bodo's few pence out of his pocket. And it would be a very tired and happy family that trundled home in the cart to bed. For it is not, after all, so dull in the kitchen, and when we have quite finished with the emperor, 'Charlemagne and all his peerage,' it is really worth while to spend a few moments with Bodo in his little manse. History is largely made up of Bodos. ❖

RECOMMENDED READINGS

The classic survey of the medieval agrarian economy is that of Georges Duby, *Rural Economy and Country Life in the Medieval West,* trans. Cynthia Postan (Columbia: University of South Carolina Press, 1976). Descriptions of peasant life in periods later than Bodo's may be found in H. S. Bennett, *Life on a Medieval Manor: A Study of Peasant Conditions, 1150-1400* (Cambridge: Cambridge University Press, 1937), and George C. Homans, *English Villagers of the Thirteenth Century* (New York: W. W. Norton, 1941). Using a remarkable source of information provided by Inquisitorial records, Emmanuel Le Roy Ladourie has been able to reconstruct the lives, thoughts, and attitudes of the inhabitants of a French village during the period 1294 to 1324; his extraordinary work has been translated into English by Barbara Bray under the title *Montaillou: The Promised Land of Error* (New York: Vintage Books, 1979).

China, About A.D. 900

THE DEVELOPMENT OF GUNPOWDER AND FIREARMS IN MEDIEVAL CHINA

Joseph Needham

Joseph Needham is the world's leading authority on Chinese science, the editor of the definitive multivolume Science and Civilization in China. *The following selection, one in a series of four lectures he delivered in Hong Kong, addresses the early development of gunpowder and its employment in firearms in China. The introduction of these elements into western European warfare in the fourteenth century had far-reaching social and political consequences. It contributed significantly to the disappearance of feudal society and, after 1500, provided the Europeans with a powerful weapon for overseas conquest. Historians have long found it difficult to believe the Chinese could have developed gunpowder as early as the ninth century and experienced so little disruption of their own traditional social and political structure. The common conclusion has been that the Chinese viewed their discovery as a curiosity and a plaything and failed to appreciate its military potential as the Europeans were to do.*

Needham skillfully refutes this view by tracing the development of Chinese firearms. It is clear that the Chinese were using a gunpowder-fueled flamethrower in the 900s and grenades and bamboo-barreled guns soon after. It would seem that the Chinese were using cannon sometime before Europeans did and that the latter may have borrowed this device from the East. It is clear that the Chinese appreciated the military possibilities of gunpowder and exploited them extensively. Needham suggests that the reason gunpowder caused so much more disruption in European society than in China was the greater vulnerability of Western society of this type of weapon. That is a view worthy of considerable thought.

READING QUESTIONS

1. What are the sources attesting to the early development of gunpowder by the Chinese?

2. What was the "fire lance"?

3. Why did the use of gunpowder for military purposes not affect China as profoundly as it did western Europe?

T he development of gunpowder and gunpowder weapons was certainly one of the greatest achievements of the mediaeval Chinese world. One finds the beginning of it toward the end of the T'ang, in the +9th century, when the first reference to the mixing of charcoal, saltpetre (potassium nitrate), and sulphur is found. This occurs in a Taoist book which strongly recommends alchemists not to mix these substances, especially with the addition of arsenic, because some of those who have done so have had the mixture deflagrate, singe their beards, and burn down the building in which they were working.

Let us go back to some of the earliest experiments of which we have records which led to the invention of the gunpowder formula. In the first place, the ancient Chinese were very adept at the making of smoke, the burning of incense, and fumigation as such. This procedure was carried on for hygienic and insecticidal reasons, and it is found even in the *Shih Ching*, where the annual purification of dwellings, a New Fire ceremony, and so on are mentioned. The *Kuan Tzŭ* Book, not many centuries later, refers to the medicinal fumigation of houses, closing all the apertures, and we know that insecticidal plants like *Illicium* and *Pyrethrum* were used in those operations. Then we know also how from Ch'in and Han times onward Chinese scholars fumigated their libraries to keep down the depredations of bookworms.

The Chinese were really great smoke-producers. Toxic smokes and smoke-screens generated by pumps and furnaces in siege warfare are referred to in the military sections of the *Mo Tzŭ* book, dating from the −4th century. There may be sources earlier than that but we do not know them. The *Mo Tzŭ* book is certainly full of such toxic devices, and they prefigure the toxic smoke-bombs in the *Huo Lung Ching* of the +15th century, which come also in the *Wu Ching Tsung Yao* of +1044, which I shall quote below. This was a wonderful book, a "Compendium of the Most Important Military Techniques" compiled by Tsêng Kung-Liang[1] during the Northern Sung period. The sea-battles of the +12th century between the Sung and the Chin Tartars, as well as the civil wars and rebellions of the time, show many other examples of the use of toxic smokes containing lime and arsenic. Indeed, the earth-shaking invention, literally earth-shaking, of gunpowder itself sometime in the +9th century, as I've said, was closely related, because it derived

---

[1] Tsêng Kung-Liang, +998–1078, military encyclopaedist, whose book of 1044, *Wu Ching Tsung Yao,* gave the first gunpowder formulae in any civilisation.

From Joseph Needham, *Science in Traditional China: A Comparative Perspective* (Cambridge: Harvard University Press, 1981), pp. 27–31, 37–44, 55–56.

from incendiary preparation and its earliest formulae sometimes contained arsenic.

As always, of course, good things developed as well as bad things. For example, in +980 the monk Tsan-Ning[2] wrote in his *Ko Wu Ts'u T'an* (Simple Discourses on the Investigation of Things) that "when there is an epidemic of febrile disease, let the clothes of the sick persons be collected as soon as possible after the onset of the malady, and thoroughly steamed. In this way the rest of the family will escape infection." Now, that would have intrigued Louis Pasteur[3] and Joseph Lister.[4] The evil and beneficent effects of knowledge have always gone hand in hand, for such is man's nature.

Another important point, of course, was the early recognition of saltpetre, potassium nitrate. Until that was thoroughly understood, and the salt could be separated and crystallised, it was no good expecting the appearance of gunpowder. There is an interesting book, the *Chu Chia Shên P'in Tan Fa,* in the *Tao Tsang,* which gives much information about these things. Another story in a related book, the *Chin Shih Pu Wu Chiu Shu Chüeh* (Explanation of the Inventory of Metals and Minerals according to the Numbers Five and Nine), mentions the appearance of Sogdian Buddhist monks who knew about saltpetre in the +6th century and noticed its presence as an incrustation on the soil. There is an interesting quotation from the Lin-Te period of the T'ang (+664), when a certain Sogdian[5] monk called Chih Fa-Lin[6] came to China bringing with him some sutras in the Sanskrit language for translation.

> When he reached the Ling-Shih district in Fên-chou, he said, "This place must be full of saltpetre, why isn't it collected and put to use?" At that time he was in the company of twelve persons, and together they collected some of the substance and tested it but found it unsuitable for use, and not comparable with that produced in Wu-Ch'ang. Later they came to Tsê-chou and the monk said again that saltpetre must also occur in this region: "I wonder if it will be as useless as what we came across before?" Whereupon they collected the substance, and on burning it emitted copious purple flames. The Sogdian monk said, "This is a marvellous substance which can produce changes in the five metals, and when the various minerals are brought into contact with it they are completely transmuted into liquid form." And in fact its properties were indeed the same as the material from Wu-Ch'ang which they knew about already.

---

[2] (Lu) Tsan-Ning, +919-1001, Buddhist monk, scientist, chemist, and microbiologist.

[3] Louis Pasteur, 1822-1895, scientist, chemist, and microbiologist, founder of the science of bacteriology.

[4] Joseph Lister, 1827-1912, English surgeon, introducer of antisepsis.

[5] Sogdian. Sogdiana is the ancient region corresponding to more recent Bokhara. It is bounded by the Oxus River to the south, and by the Jaxartes to the north.

[6] Chih Fa-Lin, monk from Central Asia. Floruit ca. +664.

So here you have a mention of the potassium flame, the use of saltpetre as a flux in smelting, and its ability to liberate nitric acid, which would help the solution of inorganic substances hard to dissolve.

In the *Chu Chia Shên P'in Tan Fa* that I mentioned just now, there is an interesting account of experiments which may have been made by the great alchemist and physician Sun Szŭ-Mo[7] in about +600. One of the formulae says:

> Take sulphur and saltpetre two ounces each, grind them together, and then put them in a silver-melting crucible or refractory pot. Dig a pit in the ground and put the vessel inside it so that its top is level with the surface and cover it all round with earth. Take three perfect pods of the soap-bean tree, uneaten by insects, char them so that they keep their shape, and then put them in the pot with the sulphur and the saltpetre. After the flames have subsided, close the mouth and place three catties of glowing charcoal on the lid, and when this has been consumed, remove it all. The substance need not be cool before it is taken out; it has been subdued by fire.

Someone seems to have been engaged here, perhaps round about +650, in an operation designed, as it were, to produce potassium sulphate, and not therefore very exciting; but on the way he stumbled upon the first preparation of a deflagrating, and later explosive, mixture in the history of all civilisation. Exciting must have been the word for that. But of course he may not have realised quite what he was doing and what had really happened. . . .

Finally, among these early references, I would like to mention that interesting book, the *Chên Yüan Miao Tao Yao Lüeh* (Classified Essentials of the Mysterious Tao of the True Origin of Things). We do not know its exact date but it was probably about the middle of the 9th century. This is the book referred to above because it mentions no less than thirty-five different elixir formulae which the writer points out to be wrong or dangerous, though popular in his time. It tells of cases where people died after consuming elixirs prepared from mercury, lead, and silver; and of other cases where people suffered from boils or sores on the back after ingesting cinnabar; and of serious illness when people drank "black lead juice," possibly a hot suspension of graphite. Among the erroneous methods are boiling the ash obtained from burning mulberry wood and regarding it as *ch'iu chih* (autumn mineral), or mixing common salt, ammonium chloride, and urine, evaporating to dryness and calling the sublimate from that *ch'ien hung* (literally, lead and mercury). These look like falsifications intended to deceive. Finally, among all these methods which the writer warned were misleading and wrong, it says quite clearly that some of the alchemists had heated sulphur together with realgar (arsenic sulphide), saltpetre, and honey, with the result that their hands and faces had been scorched when the mixture deflagrated, and even their houses burned down. These things only bring Taoism

---

[7] Sun Szŭ-Mo, +581–672, eminent Sui and T'ang alchemist, wrote the *Tan Ching Yao Chüeh*.

into discredit, he claims, and alchemists should not do them. This passage is of outstanding importance because it is one of the first references in any civilisation to a deflagrative or explosive mixture, protogunpowder, combining sulphur with nitrate and a source of carbon.

After that, things started to happen quite rapidly. *Huo yao* was the common term for gunpowder in Chinese culture, the "fire chemical," and as we hardly ever meet with the term in any other context, its use is a sure indication that gunpowder is being talked about. There is one exception to that, namely its use in *nei tan,* inner alchemy, or what we call physiological alchemy, where it can have another significance; but generally speaking, it always refers to a gunpowder mixture of one kind or another. We meet with the first use of *huo yao* as a slow match for a flame-thrower in +919, and by the time we reach the year +1000 the practice of using gunpowder in simple bombs and grenades was coming into use, especially thrown or lobbed over from trebuchets, which got the name of *huo p'ao.*

The flame-thrower which used gunpowder as a slow match was indeed a fascinating piece of machinery. It is described and illustrated in the *Wu Ching Tsung Yao* of +1044, and it was a naphtha projector like the "syphon" of the Byzantine Greeks. Actually, it was a very interesting force-pump because it had two pistons on one piston rod, and it drew up from the tank below the naphtha or low-boiling-point petroleum fractions, then ignited the liquid and shot it forth for many yards. It must have been quite frightening for anyone trying to climb over a city wall.

The first formula for the composition also appeared in the *Wu Ching Tsung Yao* compiled by Tsêng Kung-Liang in +1044—a great deal earlier than the first appearances or references to any gunpowder composition in Europe. For those you have to go forward to +1327, contemporary with Mongol times, at best 1285. That is an important date to keep in mind because it was the first occurrence of any reference to the gunpowder formula in Occidental civilisation.

Of course, the bombs and grenades of the first part of the 11th century did not contain a brisant explosive like that which became known in the following two centuries when the proportion of nitrate was raised. At first the proportion of nitrate, which is the substance that provides the oxygen in the mixture, was low, but later on it was raised. These early forms of protogunpowder were more like rocket compositions, going off with a "whoosh." That could be quite frightening, but it was not a destructive explosion. By the middle of the 13th century, when the Mongols and the Sung Chinese were locked in combat, the proportion of nitrate was at last raised to the point where really destructive explosions could take place, walls could be blown up, and city gates broken in.

These followed the very important transition to the barrel gun. It occurred, we now think, in the middle of the +10th century, in other words in the Wu Tai (Five Dynasties) period, when the fire lance first came into existence—that's the *huo ch'iang,* the fire lance or fire spear. A most remarkable banner from Tunhuang has been discovered recently in the Musée

Guimet in Paris. It shows the Buddha meditating, and the hosts of Mara the Tempter all round the side, looking very fierce and throwing things at him. Many of them are dressed in military uniforms, and in one place there is a figure with three snakes in its headdress—a devil, in fact—holding in its hands a cylinder from which are issuing flames. The fact that flames are not going upward but are being shot forth horizontally is a clear indication that the object can be nothing but a fire lance. It must contain rocket composition, which is bursting forth like a miniature three-minute flame-thrower, producing the effect desired.

It is easy to see from this great importance of the availability of a natural form of tubing, the stem of the bamboo; and we would like to maintain that this was in fact the ancestor, the original ancestor, of all barrel guns and cannon of every kind. The fire lance played a very prominent part in the wars between the Sung and the Jurchen Chin Tartars from about +1100 onward. There exists, for example, a book by Ch'ên Kuei called the *Shou Ch'êng Lu,* a record of the defence of a city north of Hankow about +1120, in which is described the use of many of these *huo ch'iang* tubes filled with rocket composition and held upon the end of a spear. In my opinion, an adequate supply of these three-minute flame-throwers, passed on from hand to hand, must have effectively discouraged enemy troops from storming one's city wall.

By about +1230 we begin to have descriptions of really destructive explosions, as I said before, in the later campaigns between the Sung and the Yüan Mongols; and then, about 1280, comes the appearance of the true metal-barrel gun or cannon somewhere in the Old World. There has been a great deal of controversy and doubt as to where it first appeared, whether among the Arabs with their *madfaa,* as they were called, or possibly among the Westerners. Between +1280 and +1320 is the key period, the crucial period, for the appearance of metal-barrel cannon, but we have no doubt whatever that its real ancestry was the substantial bamboo tube of the Chinese fire lance.

We have to follow this a bit further through several developments of great significance before we can talk about other important inventions connected with gunpowder. I would like first of all to point out how easy and logical was the development of the fire lance from the flame-thrower, the "fierce fire oil machine," the *mêng huo yu chi,* using "Greek fire" (that is, naphtha) or distilled light petroleum fractions of low boiling point. First it turned out that the petrol-projector pump could be made into a portable hand-weapon flame-thrower. Second, gunpowder, even though very low in nitrate, had already been used in that force-pump as a slow magic igniter, so the transition was very easy. It is interesting to note that Greek fire itself goes back to a chemist named Collinicus in 7th-century Byzantium, and that naphtha was used freely in the wars of the Arabs, while by the 10th century the rulers of the Wu Tai period in China were often giving presents of it to each other. So much was being passed around in those days that the Chinese must have been distilling it themselves.

The fire lance lasted in use until quite recent times. There still exists a photograph taken on a pirate ship in the South China Seas about sixty or seventy years ago, which shows the fire lance in action. It was well calculated to set the rigging or the woodwork of another ship on fire, and it was employed right down to the beginning of the present century. . . .

We have seen that the fire lance, the *huo ch'iang,* was certainly in existence by +950 and very prominent by +1110. Of course, as I have said, the gunpowder which it contained was not a brisant explosive, but more like a rocket composition, deflagrating violently and shooting forth powerful flames, but not going off suddenly with a mighty bang. At first, fire lances were held manually by the fire-weapon soldiers, but by the time of the Southern Sung they were made of bamboo much larger in diameter, perhaps up to a foot across, and mounted on a framework of legs, sometimes even provided with wheels so as to make them moderately mobile. This gave rise to a weapon for which we have found it necessary to coin a word; and we call it an "eruptor," because nothing or almost nothing like it existed in the Western world. (There are one or two exceptions; for example, something of the same kind was trundled out by the defenders of Malta in the siege against the Turks in +1563, but they had no convenient name, and in our opinion they betrayed, together with many other things, their direct indebtedness to Chinese origins.)

Even more remarkable, these eruptors were so constructed as to shoot out projectiles along with the flames. Once again we need a new word for this, and we have decided to call these objects "co-viative" projectiles. They could be just bits of old iron, or even broken pottery or glass, but this system was quite different from the chain shot of later Napoleonic Europe, because there the function of the gunpowder was explosively propellant, and the chain shot took the place of the normal solid cannonball. The co-viative projectiles of the eruptors of the Sung and Yüan were more like case shot, which Mainwaring[8] in +1644 defined as "any kind of old iron, stones, musket-bullets or the like which we put into cases to shoot forth out of our great ordnance." But the difference was that in the older Chinese system the pieces of hard, sharp-edged rubbish were actually mixed with the rocket composition, the gunpowder. Other names for the case shot in later times were cannister shot and langrel, but none of these things were co-viative, since that belonged to a much earlier stage of the story. Generally the eruptors consisted of bamboo barrels mounted on carriages, but it was precisely in connection with these that the first metal barrels appeared, cast in bronze or iron, a most important event. It is most notable that metal-barrel eruptors preceded metal-barrel bombards and cannon.

One extraordinary fact is that before the end of the eruptor period, actual explosive shells were fired forth as co-viative projectiles, and that must

---

[8] Charles Mainwaring, +17th-century English gunner.

have been the time of their first invention. But eruptors with co-viative projectiles could be made small enough to be held manually, and by the late +13th and early +14th century, when all this was in its prime, co-viative arrow-launchers were also used. The arrows probably did not fly very far, since the gunpowder was not exerting its full propellant force, but for close combat on city walls their effects may have been impressive enough, especially against personnel armoured lightly or not at all. Pictures in late books show co-viative projectiles in hand-held eruptors or fire lances in their later form.

Lastly, there appeared the metal-barrel firearm characterised by two other basic features: first the use of high-nitrate gunpowder, and second the total occlusion of the muzzle (or front orifice) by a projectile (such as a bullet or cannonball) in such a way that the gunpowder exerted its full propellant effect. This type of firearm may be described as the true gun or cannon, and if it appeared in early Yüan times about 1280, as we suspect it did, its development had taken just about three and a half centuries since the invention of the first of the firearms, flame-throwers.

The bombard (as it may now be called) made its first appearance in Europe in +1327, as we know from the famous manuscript in the Bodleian Library at Oxford. We must not imagine that at this early time there was a long, smooth bore with parallel walls to guide the projectile to its destination. The first bombards of Europe were distinctively vase-shaped with a rounded belly and a muzzle that splayed outward like the mouth of a blunderbuss. The shooting, therefore, must have been very hit-or-miss, but presumably the charge of gunpowder was rammed down into the bombard and the ball packed into the narrowest part, and then, even if the gunners (bombardiers) could not aim accurately at anything, their bombards would have been quite useful against castle walls or city gates or the massed troops of men in close order that probably moved about in those days.

Now, the interesting thing is that we find Chinese drawings of just such bombards. Pictures exist of a whole set of them, mounted on a carriage, exactly similar in shape to the first European 14th-century ones. So the probability is that they originated in China and were copied exactly in the West, where the beginnings of the knowledge of gunpowder itself go back only to 1285 or so. If this probability is correct, it would mean that the purely propellant phase of gunpowder and shot, the culminating stage of all the gunpowder uses, was attained in China with these bottle-shaped bombards before any knowledge of gunpowder itself reached Europe at all. Or perhaps it was about the same time. In any case, the whole development, beginning with the first experiments of Sun Szǔ-Mo and his friends, would have taken just on seven centuries—which was not bad going for the Middle Ages. . . .

Second, and really last, in the gunpowder epic, we have the case of a socially devastating discovery which China could somehow take in her stride, but which had revolutionary effects in Europe. For decades, indeed for centuries, from Shakespeare's time onward, European historians have recognised in the first salvoes of the 14th century bombards the death-knell of the castle, and hence of Western military aristocratic feudalism. It would be tedious to enlarge upon this now. In one single year, 1449, the artillery train of the king of France, making a tour of the castles still held by the English in Normandy, battered them down one after another at the rate of five a month. Nor were the effects of gunpowder confined to the land. They had a profound influence also at sea, for in due time they gave the death-blow to the multi-oared, slave-manned galley of the Mediterranean, which was unable to provide gun platforms sufficiently stable for naval cannonades and broadsides. . . .

Socially, the contrast with China is particularly noteworthy. While gunpowder blew up Western military aristocratic feudalism, the basic structure of Chinese bureaucratic feudalism after five centuries or so of gunpowder weapons remained just about the same as it had been before the invention had taken place. The birth of chemical warfare had occurred, we may say, in the T'ang, but it did not find wide military use before the Wu Tai and the Sung, and its real proving grounds were the wars between the Sung Empire, the Chin Tartars and the Mongols in the 12th and 13th centuries. There are plenty of examples of its use by the forces of agrarian rebellions and it was employed at sea as well as on land, in siege warfare no less than in the field; but as there was no heavily armoured knightly cavalry in China, nor any aristocratic or manorial feudal castles, the new weapon simply supplemented those which had been in use before, and produced no perceptible effect upon the age-old civil and military bureaucratic apparatus, which each new foreign conqueror had to take over and use in his turn. ❖

RECOMMENDED READINGS

The standard work on Chinese science and technology is the multivolume *Science and Civilization in China,* ed. Joseph Needham (Cambridge: Cambridge University Press, 1959-). The Institute of the History of Natural Sciences of the Academy of Science of the People's Republic of China has compiled a volume containing a series of essays on important traditional Chinese technologies such as tea, porcelain, papermaking, and silk manufacture, *Ancient China's Technology and Science* (Beijing: Foreign Language Press, 1983). The importance of gunpowder to European overseas expansion is one of the themes of Carlo M. Cipolla, *Guns, Sails, and Empires: Technological Innovations and the Early Phases of European Expansion, 1400-1700* (New York: Pantheon, 1966).

HEIAN JAPAN

"THE GOOD PEOPLE" AND THEIR LIVES

Ivan Morris

The Heian period (794–1185 A.D.*) was a golden age of Japanese culture. Protected by the sea and having at last achieved domination over the Ainu aboriginals, the nobility of Japan entered a period of relative peace. At the same time, the influences of the great culture of T'ang China began to penetrate the islands along with a new spiritual inspiration in the form of Buddhism.*

In their capital of Heian, on the site of modern Kyoto, the nobles of the Japanese court cultivated Chinese literature, rarified manners, exquisite sensibilities, and elaborate rituals. Interestingly enough, however, it was the women of the Heian court whose views and insights have survived.

While the men wrote relatively uninspired Chinese verse, the noblewomen wrote detailed diaries and romances based on the court life that formed their world. The greatest of these were indisputably the Pillow Book *of Lady Sei Shonagon and Lady Murasaki's massive* The Tale of Genji. *Ivan Morris drew heavily on the latter in his work* The World of the Shining Prince. Court Life in Ancient Japan, *from which the following selection is drawn.*

The refined world of the Heian nobility of Japan contrasts sharply with the rough-and-ready—and often brutal—world of the feudal nobility of western Europe. It should be noted, however, that Heian nobles were eventually confronted by war bands of armed Buddhist monks. Having lost the ability even to defend themselves, they called in warrior clans to protect them. The warriors soon displaced the gentlefolk, and the world of the Shining Prince had come to an end.

READING QUESTIONS

1. How accurate were the portrayals of court life by Lady Sei Shonagun and Lady Murasaki?

2. What were the characteristics of an ideal Heian nobleman?

3. What was the Heian diet like?

I f the informed Westerner was asked to enumerate the outstanding features of traditional Japan, his list might well consist of the following: in *culture* Nō and Kabuki drama, Haiku poems, Ukiyoe colour prints, samisen music, and various activities like the tea ceremony, flower arrangement, and the preparation of miniature landscapes that are related to Zen influence; in *society* the two-sworded samurai and the geisha; in *ideas* the Zen approach to human experience with its stress on an intuitive understanding of the truth and sudden enlightenment, the samurai ethic sometimes known as *Bushidō,* a great concern with the conflicting demands of duty and human affection, and an extremely permissive attitude to suicide, especially love suicides; in *domestic architecture* fitted straw matting *(tatami),* large communal baths, *tokonoma* alcoves for hanging *kakemono;* in *food* raw fish and soy sauce *(tempura* and *sukiyaki* being judiciously excluded as Western importations). The list would of course be entirely correct. Yet not a single one of these items existed in Murasaki's[1] world, and many of them would have seemed as alien to her as they do to the modern Westerner.

The immense changes that occurred in Japan, especially during the Muromachi and Tokugawa periods, make it hard to reconstruct life in Heian Kyō; and the tidal waves of later Westernization impose a further barrier between us and the world inhabited by Murasaki. We do, however, have a compensating advantage. Vernacular literature, in particular *The Tale of Genji* and the *Pillow Book,*[2] gives us a remarkably detailed picture of daily life in Japanese patrician society during the tenth and eleventh centuries. When it comes to this sort of information, we are probably better served about Japan than about any other country at the time; and in Japan itself it is not until we reach the seventeenth century that we find a body of realistic writing with a similar amount of detail.

Of course, it is a one-sided picture, concentrated almost exclusively on the social and cultural aspects of life. From reading works like *The Tale of Genji, Gossamer Diary,* and the *Pillow Book* we should hardly guess that the men described were often leading figures in the government of the day and that they spent at least as much of their time in political intrigues as in those

---

[1] Murasaki Shikibu, a lady-in-waiting to the empress and the author of *The Tale of Genji. Genji* was the world's first novel and provides an excellent description of the Heian court during the tenth century.

[2] *The Pillow Book of Sei Shonagon* also reflects aristocratic life in Heian Japan.

From Ivan Morris, *The World of the Shining Prince: Court Life in Ancient Japan* (New York: Knopf, 1964), pp. 141–143, 144–149.

of an erotic nature. Still less should we imagine that many of them, especially members of the northern branch of the Fujiwara family, were hard-working officials, seriously devoted to their public duties. The old Minister of the Left in *The Tale of Genji* is one of the few characters in the romantic literature of the time who belong to the category described by Sir George Sansom when he writes of 'grave and industrious officials, men who were diligent in performing their ceremonial duties, scribbling their memoranda, issuing their orders and despatches, men steeped in official routine'.[3]

One reason is that many of the writers of the vernacular works were women who could have little detailed knowledge of matters like politics from which most of them were excluded. In his study of Sei Shōnagon Arthur Waley refers to the 'extraordinary vagueness of women concerning purely male activities'.[4]

Yet this is only part of the explanation. Writers like Murasaki would, it is true, tend to underplay the 'public' lives of their male characters. Yet from other sources we know that many of the men who attained positions of importance in the Heian administrative hierarchy were in fact singularly uninterested in their official responsibilities and preferred to pass their time in composing elegant poems in Chinese or supervising the punctilios of elaborate ceremonies rather than in carrying out the prosaic duties of public office. Still less were most of them prepared to administer their scattered manors in the provinces, which would mean spending precious days away from the capital, and worse still, dealing with dreary, boorish yokels. When Murasaki's gentlemen do venture into the countryside it is not to inspect their estates, or even to enjoy a day of hunting (the common male pastime in most aristocratic societies), but to compose poems on the autumn foliage or to keep a tryst at some mountain temple. Professor Oka emphasizes the debilitating effect on the Heian upper class of being almost totally divorced from the productive life of the country; and the separation of Heian Kyō from the rest of Japan undoubtedly helped to discourage the development of a vigorous, self-reliant approach among the metropolitan aristocrats.

The picture of the average Heian aristocrat that appears in literature and painting is likely to strike many Western readers as effeminate. The contemporary ideal of male beauty was a plump white face with a minute mouth, the narrowest slits for eyes and a little tuft of beard on the point of the chin. This—apart from the beard—was the same as the ideal of feminine beauty, and often in Murasaki's novel we are told that a handsome gentleman like

---

[3] Some Heian women (especially Dowager Empresses like Higashi Sanjō no In and Jōtōmon In) wielded great political power, but they were exceptions. Most women of the time, including all the writers with whose work we are familiar, were uninvolved in politics, though many of them took a keen interest in palace intrigues, state marriages, and promotions.

[4] For all her curiosity, Sei shows extremely little interest in what took place in the government offices, and none at all in the manors, from which her society derived its sustenance.

Kaoru is as beautiful as a woman. We know that Fujiwara no Korechika, the great Adonis of the day, had a perfectly round white face; here, as in many other respects, he was probably the model for the hero of *The Tale of Genji*. Having read the scenes in which ladies almost swoon at the thought of Prince Genji's physical charms, most Westerners (and many modern Japanese) are bound to be surprised by his rather epicene appearance in the scrolls, where he is depicted with a pasty complexion, almost imperceptible eyes, and an exiguous tuft of beard. Yet there is every reason to believe that the scrolls are faithful to Murasaki's ideal of male beauty.

We also have a good picture of what a Heian gentleman should *not* look like. The dark, hirsute Prince Higekuro (who is significantly named after his 'black beard') is physically the antithesis of Genji and Kaoru, and when Tamakazura, later to become his wife, looks with aversion at his dark, hairy face, we can judge what Murasaki Shikibu thought about the more masculine-appearing type of man.

The Heian gentleman powdered his face (the faces of badly-powdered men remind Sei of dark earth over which the snow has melted in patches) and used a generous amount of scent on his hair and clothes. The technique of mixing perfumes was highly developed. In an age when bathing was perfunctory and clothing elaborate and hard to clean, scent served a very useful purpose. It was, of course, no ready-made commodity, but the product of a complex and sophisticated art. Genji himself was much admired for the skill with which he prepared his own incense, whose distinctive aroma always announced his approach and lingered after his departure. In the case of Prince Niou, who on the whole is pictured as one of the more masculine of the male characters, the preparation of scents was something of an obsession. Both he and his friend Kaoru owe their names to this art; and nothing more symbolizes the ideals of this period, and contrasts it with the subsequent age of military heroes, than the fact that two of Murasaki's most respected male characters should be named 'Lord Fragrance' and 'Prince Scent'.

This somewhat feminine impression of the Heian gentleman is confirmed by what we read of his behaviour. During his visits to the nearby village of Uji, Prince Niou, who is certainly not intended to appear more pusillanimous than average, is terrified of being attacked by highway robbers or by men from Kaoru's manor. Few Western readers will fail to be impressed by the unabashed way in which Murasaki's heroes display their softer emotions. Genji and his companions lived in an age when the virtues of male impassivity had not yet come to be valued. Tears, far from being a sign of weakness, showed that a man was sensitive to the beauty and pathos of life. It is true that lachrymose heroes often figure in the history of the military period too; but it is a different sort of situation that reduces these robust men to tears. The warrior will weep at the death of his lord and thus display the sincerity of his grief; but the Heian gentleman is reduced to tears at the prospect of parting from his mistress, at the sight of a magnificent sunrise, or at the thought of someone else's loneliness. In her diary Murasaki describes the great Fujiwara no Michinaga weeping with joy when he sees the emperor arriving at the Gosechi festival; and in her novel the spectators are moved to tears by the beauty of Genji's dance. Love affairs are invariably attended by tears and the man is certainly not behindhand in this respect. After Prince Niou has spent his first night with Ukifune, he weeps at the thought of how hard it will be to arrange future meetings. Here Murasaki is not, as the modern reader might suspect, implying some weakness in the young man's character, but simply reminding us of his exquisite sensibility.

In drawing a picture of the Heian gentleman from a book like *The Tale of Genji* we must of course make full allowance for the fact that it is a work of fiction in which many of the characters, especially the more important ones, are idealized. In her descriptions of Genji, Niou, and Kaoru the author was presenting the ideal man, rather than the flesh and blood creatures whom she met at court, those all too human men who drank to excess, spoke in loud voices, and knocked on her door at night.

For some women the solid, sturdy, impassive male, to whom the grunt or the laconic remark comes easier than the flood of tears, provides a more attractive image; but Murasaki clearly preferred the sensitive and emotional type who might nowadays be described as unmanly. Here, as in her ideas about male physical beauty, she appears to have shared the standards of her time—standards that are reflected not only in women's diaries but in male works of fiction like *The Tale of the Hollow Tree.*

We can be sure that there were many gentlemen in Heian Kyō who worked hard and efficiently in their offices (how else could the Fujiwara Councils have functioned as well as they did?), who were perfunctory in their use of scent and powder, who, like Tachibana no Norimitsu in the *Pillow Book,* did not give a fig for poetry or literary quotations, and who conducted their love affairs expeditiously, with a minimum of tears and elegances. And even among the aristocracy nature no doubt created far more men with Higekuro's attributes than with the smooth features of a Kaoru.

Yet, so long as we are aware of its limitations, Murasaki's picture of the Heian male is valid and historically significant. For it was a man like Prince Genji, with his gentle nature, his sensitivity and his wide range of artistic skills, who represented the ideal of the age and who set the tone for the social and cultural life of the good people.

Not much is said about food in the vernacular literature of the time and virtually nothing in the Chinese-style writings. It was regarded as a vulgar subject and, while we hear a good deal about drinking parties, meals are hardly ever described. Sei Shōnagon disliked men who ate heavily; a gentleman, she tells us, should pick daintily at his dishes. One of the most distressing things about the lower orders is the way in which they wolf down their food.

As in China, rice was the staple diet, the polished variety being reserved mainly for the aristocracy. There were several rice dishes, some of which (like *mochi* rice cakes) are still current. Among the food that commonly accompanied the rice was seaweed and radishes. Fruits and nuts were eaten a great deal and also made into cakes; sugar, however, was not used. Ice was stored in special chambers, and in the hot months rich people enjoyed a sort of sherbet made of shaved ice and liana syrup. Fish was boiled, baked, or pickled, but, in the capital at least, it was not as a rule eaten raw until a later period; shell-fish like sea-ear *(awabi)* were especially popular. Meat was normally excluded because of Buddhist influence. Somewhat illogically, pheasant, quail, and other types of game were allowed; but, since there was little hunting, this was not an important part of the menu except in the very richest households. Among the common vegetables were sweet potatoes, egg-plants, carrots, onions, and garlic (the last having been introduced from Korea). In the reign of Emperor Ichijō a type of butter *(so)* was made of cow's milk, but it did not become popular and soon disappeared from the Japanese diet—so completely, indeed, that when the first Westerners arrived in the country their outstanding characteristic, apart from having red hair and bulging blue eyes, was that they were 'butter-stinking' *(bata-kusai)*.

Heian cuisine was remarkably little influenced by China's. Then as now great stress was placed on presentation, the food always being served with an eye to visual effect. But the dishes themselves lacked the variety and sophistication that, possibly under the influence of Taoism, had already made Chinese cooking among the finest in the world. The joys of the table did not rank high in Heian Kyō, and on the whole the food was poor in both culinary and nutritive value.

Non-alcoholic drink was limited almost entirely to water. Milk had been drunk during the Nara period, but had now lapsed from use and was held in almost the same aversion as in China. Tea was introduced in the ninth century by the founder of the Tendai sect, and was planted on Mount Hiei. The first Japanese sovereign to taste it was Emperor Saga, who was offered a cup by a Buddhist priest in 815. This mark of royal approval did not, however, win success for the new beverage. In Murasaki's time laymen used it almost exclusively for medical purposes, and it did not become popular for more than two hundred years.

In the tenth (as in the twentieth) century the great Japanese drink was rice wine. Already seven hundred years earlier Chinese travellers commented that the Japanese 'are much given to strong drink'. Heian literature provides ample evidence that the gentlemen of the time enjoyed wine and its effects. Drinking parties were extremely popular. Wine was poured for each guest in turn according to his rank; often people were expected to recite a poem or sing a song before raising the cup to their lips. There were several drinking games, in which the losers were obliged to drink the 'cup of defeat' *(basshu)*, and these frequently turned into drunken carousals.

Most of the numerous types of *sake* drunk in Murasaki's time were weaker than the present-day varieties; yet (owing, among other things, to the absence of fats from the traditional Japanese diet) they were all highly intoxicating. In her diary Murasaki complains about Michinaga's drunkenness, from which she suffered on more than one occasion. His elder brother, Michitaka, shared his taste for drink, as we can tell from the following passage in the *Pillow Book:*

> 'The gallery [of the Palace] was full of courtiers. His Excellency [Fujiwara no Michitaka] summoned servants from the Empress' Household and made them bring fruit and other dishes to be eaten with the wine. "Now let everyone get drunk!" he said. And in fact everyone did get drunk. The ladies-in-waiting began to exchange remarks with the gentlemen and they all found each other extremely amusing.'

A common form of entertainment among the officials was a drinking party at which those who had recently been promoted were made to take as much *sake* as they could hold—and sometimes rather more. So bibulous did these affairs become that the custom was repeatedly prohibited. Like most interdictions of this type, however, it had little effect, and the 'promotion parties' went on unabated. The traditional Japanese tolerance towards drunkenness was already well established in the Heian period. Women were not excluded from the pleasures of the cup. Sei Shōnagon expresses her disapproval of women drinkers, but she herself had the reputation of being a tippler. ❖

RECOMMENDED READINGS

An enormous number of commentaries and scholarly studies have been written on *The Tale of Genji*. Notable among these is Ivan Morris, *The World of the Shining Prince* (New York: Knopf, 1964), which provides an informative and delightful look at the life of the Heian aristocracy. For Heian institutional history, see *Medieval Japan: Essays in Institutional History,* ed. John W. Hall and Jeffrey P. Maas (New Haven: Yale University Press, 1974), about half of which deals with the Heian period. J. Puette, *Guide to the Tale of Genji* (Rutland, VT, and Tokyo: Charles E. Tuttle, 1983), is a helpful commentary that includes a brief analysis of each chapter of the *Tale.* Sir George Samson, *A History of Japan to 1334* (Stanford, CA: Stanford University Press, 1958), provides the standard general history of the period. Earl Miner, *An Introduction to Japanese Court Poetry* (Stanford, CA: Stanford University Press, 1968), is a classic study of poetry in medieval Japan.

Important translations of Heian literature include *The Pillow Book of Sei Shonagon,* 2 vols., trans. Ivan Morris (New York: Columbia University Press, 1967); *The Tales of Ise,* trans. H. Jay Harris (Rutland, VT, and Tokyo: Charles E. Tuttle, 1972); and *Okagami— The Great Mirror: Fujiwara Michinaga (966–1027),* trans. Helen Craig McCullough (Princeton, NJ: Princeton University Press, 1980). *Diaries of Court Ladies of Old Japan,* trans. Annie Shepley Omori and Kochi Dei (Boston: Houghton Mifflin, 1920), includes translations of the diaries of three women of the Heian period, including that of Murasaki Shikibu.

France, About A.D. *1100*

THE LIFE OF THE NOBILITY

Marc Bloch

Because the figure of the feudal knight is such an important element of Western culture, it is important to recognize the reality that lay behind the idealized picture of "the knight in shining armor." Marc Bloch, one of the most influential medieval historians of the twentieth century, realized that the society of feudal Europe was highly integrated; every institution influenced, and was in turn influenced by, other institutions. For this reason, Bloch reasoned, one could not properly discuss the feudal aristocracy of medieval Europe apart from the society in which they lived, and so he undertook to describe that society as a whole.

This selection from Feudal Society *portrays the feudal aristocracy on the eve of its transformation into a hereditary nobility. When the feudal aristocracy first emerged in the course of the ninth century, its members were selected by their ability to fight against the Saracens, Magyars, and Vikings who were attacking western Europe, and its function of providing protection and maintaining a modicum of law and order was clearly recognized. By the beginning of the eleventh century, however, the situation had changed greatly. There was now much less justification for the wealth and status enjoyed by the feudal aristocracy.*

In response to this challenge to their position, the nobles began cultivating elaborate codes of behavior such as courtesy and chivalry, ostentatious displays of wealth such as tournaments and largess, and elaborate patterns of speech such as the troubadour songs in order to set themselves off from the other classes of their society. By so doing, they closed their class to newcomers and became a hereditary caste, a nobility of blood that successfully defended its right to wealth and status as a birthright. The common view of the medieval knight is derived from this mystique, rather than the reality of the times. Marc Bloch describes not only that reality, but elements of the process by which the feudal aristocracy was transformed into something quite different from what it once had been.

READING QUESTIONS

1. Why was war so popular among the members of the feudal aristocracy?

2. What qualities made an ideal knight?

3. What was chivalry like in practice rather than in theory?

4. How would you characterize the relationship between men and women of the feudal aristocracy?

5. How did the troubadour tradition alter that relationship?

6. How did the aristocracy seek to set itself apart from other elements of medieval society?

I love the gay Eastertide, which brings forth leaves and flowers; and I love the joyous songs of the birds, re-echoing through the copse. But also I love to see, amidst the meadows, tents and pavilions spread; and it gives me great joy to see, drawn up on the field, knights and horses in battle array; and it delights me when the scouts scatter people and herds in their path; and I love to see them followed by a great body of men-at-arms; and my heart is filled with gladness when I see strong castles besieged, and the stockades broken and overwhelmed, and the warriors on the bank, girt about by fosses, with a line of strong stakes, interlaced. . . . Maces, swords, helms of different hues, shields that will be riven and shattered as soon as the fight begins; and many vassals struck down together; and the horses of the dead and the wounded roving at random. And when battle is joined, let all men of good lineage think of naught but the breaking of heads and arms; for it is better to die than to be vanquished and live. I tell you, I find no such savour in food, or in wine, or in sleep, as in hearing the shout "On! On!" from both sides, and the neighing of steeds that have lost their riders, and the cries of "Help! Help!"; in seeing men great and small go down on the grass beyond the fosses; in seeing at last the dead, with the pennoned stumps of lances still in their sides.'

Thus sang, in the second half of the twelfth century, a troubadour who is probably to be identified with the petty nobleman from Périgord, Bertrand de Born. The accurate observation and the fine verve, in contrast with the insipidity of what is usually a more conventional type of poetry, are the marks of an uncommon talent. The sentiment, on the other hand, is in no way extraordinary; as is shown in many another piece from the same social world, in which it is expressed, no doubt with less gusto, but with equal spontaneity. In war—'fresh and joyful war', as it has been called in our own

From Marc Bloch, *Feudal Society,* trans. L. A. Manyon (Chicago: University of Chicago Press, 1968), pp. 293-301, 307-311.

day by someone who was not destined to see it at such close quarters—the noble loved first and foremost the display of physical strength, the strength of a splendid animal, deliberately maintained by constant exercises, begun in childhood. 'He who has stayed at school till the age of twelve,' says a German poet, repeating the old Carolingian proverb, 'and never ridden a horse, is only fit to be a priest.' The interminable accounts of single combats which fill the epics are eloquent psychological documents. The reader of today, bored by their monotony, finds it difficult to believe that they could have afforded so much pleasure—as clearly they did—to those who listened to them in days of old; theirs was the attitude of the sedentary enthusiast to reports of sporting events. In works of imagination as well as in the chronicles, the portrait of the good knight emphasizes above all his athletic build: he is 'big-boned', 'large of limb', the body 'well-proportioned' and pitted with honourable scars; the shoulders are broad, and so is the 'fork'—as becomes a horseman. And since this strength must be sustained, the valiant knight is known for his mighty appetite. In the old *Chanson de Guillaume*, so barbarous in its tone, listen to Dame Guibourc who, after having served at the great table of the castle the young Girart, her husband's nephew, remarks to her spouse:

> *Par Deu, bel sire, cist est de de vostre lin,*
> *Et si mangue un grant braun porcin,*
> *Et a dous traitz beit un cester de vin.*
> *Ben dure guere deit il rendre a sun veisin.*

> By God! fair sire! he's of your line indeed,
> Who thus devours a mighty haunch of boar
> And drinks of wine a gallon at two gulps;
> Pity the man on whom he wages war!

A supple and muscular body, however, it is almost superfluous to say, was not enough to make the ideal knight. To these qualities he must add courage as well. And it was also because it gave scope for the exercise of this virtue that war created such joy in the hearts of men for whom daring and the contempt for death were, in a sense, professional assets. It is true that this valour did not always prevent mad panics (we have seen examples of them in face of the Vikings), nor was it above resorting to crude stratagems. Nevertheless the knightly class knew how to fight—on this point, history agrees with legend. Its unquestionable heroism was nurtured by many elements: the simple physical reaction of a healthy human being; the rage of despair—it is when he feels himself 'wounded unto death' that the 'cautious' Oliver strikes such terrible blows, in order 'to avenge himself all he could'; the devotion to a chief or, in the case of the holy war, to a cause; the passionate desire for glory, personal or collective; the fatalistic acquiescence in face of ineluctable destiny, of which literature offers no more poignant examples than some of the last cantos of the *Nibelungenlied;* finally, the hope of reward in another world, promised not only to him who died for his God, but also to him who died for his master.

Accustomed to danger, the knight found in war yet another attraction: it offered a remedy for boredom. For these men whose culture long remained rudimentary and who—apart from a few great barons and their counsellors—were seldom occupied by very heavy administrative cares, everyday life easily slipped into a grey monotony. Thus was born an appetite for diversions which, when one's native soil failed to afford the means to gratify it, sought satisfaction in distant lands. William the Conqueror, bent on exacting due service from his vassals, said of one of them, whose fiefs he had just confiscated as a punishment for his having dared to depart for the crusade in Spain without permission: 'I do not believe it would be possible to find a better knight in arms; but he is unstable and extravagant, and he spends his time gadding about from place to place.' Of how many others could the same have been said! The roving disposition was especially widespread among the French. The fact was that their own country did not offer them, as did half-Moslem Spain, or, to a less degree, Germany with its Slav frontier, an arena for conquests or swift forays; nor, like Germany again, the hardships and the pleasures of the great imperial expeditions. It is also probable that the knightly class was more numerous there than elsewhere, and therefore cramped for room. In France itself it has often been observed that Normandy was of all the provinces the richest in bold adventurers. Already the German Otto of Freising spoke of the 'very restless race of the Normans'. Could it have been the legacy of Viking blood? Possibly. But it was above all the effect of the state of relative peace which, in that remarkably centralized principality, the dukes established at an early date; so that those who craved the opportunity for fighting had to seek it abroad. Flanders, where political conditions were not very different, furnished an almost equally large contingent of roving warriors.

These knights-errant—the term is a contemporary one—helped the native Christians in Spain to reconquer the northern part of the peninsula from Islam; they set up the Norman states in southern Italy; even before the First Crusade they enlisted as mercenaries in the service of Byzantium and fought against its eastern foes; finally, they found in the conquest and defence of the Tomb of Christ their chosen field of action. Whether in Spain or in Syria, the holy war offered the dual attraction of an adventure and a work of piety. 'No need is there now to endure the monk's hard life in the strictest of the orders . . .' sang one of the troubadours; 'to accomplish honourable deeds and thereby at the same time to save oneself from hell—what more could one wish?' These migrations helped to maintain relations between societies separated from each other by great distances and sharp contrasts; they disseminated Western and especially French culture beyond its own frontiers. A case to strike the imagination is that of one Hervé 'the Francopol' who was taken prisoner by an emir in 1057 when in command on the shores of Lake Van. At the same time the bloodletting thus practised abroad by the most turbulent groups in the West saved its civilization from being extinguished by guerilla warfare. The chroniclers were well aware that at the start of a crusade the people at home in the old countries always breathed more freely, because now they could once more enjoy a little peace.

Fighting, which was sometimes a legal obligation and frequently a plea-sure, might also be required of the knight as a matter of honour: in the twelfth century, Périgord ran with blood because a certain lord thought that one of his noble neighbours looked like a blacksmith and had the bad taste to say so. But fighting was also, and perhaps above all, a source of profit—in fact, the nobleman's chief industry.

The lyrical effusions of Bertrand de Born have been mentioned above. He himself made no secret of the less creditable reasons which above all dis-posed him 'to find no pleasure in peace'. 'Why', he asks, 'do I want rich men to hate each other?' 'Because a rich man is much more noble, generous and affable in war than in peace.' And more crudely: 'We are going to have some fun. For the barons will make much of us . . . and if they want us to re-main with them, they will give us *barbarins*' (i.e. coin of Limoges). And again: 'Trumpet, drums, flags and pennons, standards and horses white and black—that is what we shall shortly see. And it will be a happy day; for we shall seize the usurers' goods, and no more shall beasts of burden pass along the highways by day in complete safety; nor shall the burgess journey with-out fear, nor the merchant on his way to France; but the man who is full of courage shall be rich.' The poet belonged to that class of petty holders of fiefs, the 'vavasours'—he so described himself—for whom life in the ances-tral manor-house lacked both gaiety and comforts. War made up for these de-ficiencies by stimulating the liberality of the great and providing prizes worth having.

The baron, of course, out of regard for his prestige as well as his inter-est, could not afford to be niggardly in the matter of presents, even towards vassals summoned to his side by the strictest conventions of feudal duty. If it was desired to retain them beyond the stipulated time, to take them farther or call on them more often than an increasingly rigorous custom appeared to permit, it was necessary to give them more. Finally, in face of the growing inadequacy of the vassal contingents, there was soon no army which could dispense with the assistance of that wandering body of warriors to whom adventure made so strong an appeal, provided that there was a prospect of gain as well as of mighty combats. Thus cynically, our Bertrand offered his services to the count of Poitiers: 'I can help you. I have already a shield at my neck and a helm on my head. . . . Nevertheless, how can I put myself in the field without money?'

But it was undoubtedly considered that the finest gift the chief could be-stow was the right to a share of the plunder. This was also the principal profit which the knight who fought on his own account in little local wars expected from his efforts. It was a double prize, moreover: men and things. It is true that the Christian code no longer allowed captives to be reduced to slavery and at most permitted a few peasants or artisans to be forcibly removed from one place to another. But the ransoming of prisoners was a general practice. A ruler as firm and prudent as William the Conqueror might indeed never release alive the enemies who fell into his hands; but most warriors were not so far-sighted. The ransoming of prisoners occasionally had more dreadful consequences than the ancient practice of enslavement. The author of the *chanson* of Girart de Roussillon, who certainly wrote from personal observation, tells us that in the evening after a battle Girart and his followers put to the sword all the humble prisoners and wounded, sparing only the 'owners of castles', who alone were in a position to buy their freedom with hard cash. As to plunder, it was traditionally so regular a source of profit that in the ages accustomed to written documents the legal texts treat it as a matter of course—on this point, the barbarian codes, at the beginning of the Middle Ages, and the thirteenth-century contracts of enlistment at the end, speak with the same voice. Heavy wagons followed the armies, for the purpose of collecting the spoils of war. Most serious of all, by a series of transitions almost unnoticed by the rather simple minds of the time, forms of violent action which were sometimes legitimate—requisitions indispensable to armies without commissariat, reprisals exacted against the enemy or his subjects—degenerated into pure brigandage, brutal and mean. Merchants were robbed on the highway; sheep, cheeses, chickens were stolen from pens and farmsteads—as was done, typically, by a small Catalan landowner of the early thirteenth century bent on annoying his neighbours of the abbey of Canigou. The best of men contracted strange habits. William Marshal was certainly a valiant knight. Nevertheless when, as a young and landless man travelling through France from tourney to tourney, he encountered on the road a monk who was running away with a girl of noble family and who candidly avowed his intention of putting out to usury the money he was carrying, William did not scruple to rob the poor devil of his cash, under the pretext of punishing him for his evil designs. One of his companions even reproached him for not having seized the horse as well.

Such practices reveal a signal indifference to human life and suffering. War in the feudal age was in no sense war in kid gloves. It was accompanied by actions which seem to us today anything but chivalrous; as for instance— a frequent occurrence, sometimes even in disregard of a solemn oath—the massacre or mutilation of garrisons which had held out 'too long'. It involved, as a natural concomitant, the devastation of the enemy's estates. Here and there a poet, like the author of *Huon of Bordeaux*, and later a pious king like St. Louis protested in vain against this 'wasting' of the countryside which brought such appalling miseries upon the innocent. The epics, the German as well as the French, are faithful interpreters of real life, and they show us a whole succession of 'smoking' villages. 'There can be no real war without fire and blood,' said the plain-spoken Bertrand de Born.

In two passages exhibiting striking parallels, the poet of *Girart de Roussillon* and the anonymous biographer of the Emperor Henry IV show us what the return of peace meant for the 'poor knights': the disdainful indifference of the great, who would have no more need of them; the importunities of money-lenders; the heavy plough-horse instead of the mettlesome charger; iron spurs instead of gold—in short an economic crisis as well as a disastrous loss of prestige. For the merchant and the peasant, on the contrary, peace meant that it was possible once again to work, to gain a livelihood—in short, to live. Let us appeal once more to the evidence of the observant *trouvère* of *Girart de Roussillon*. Outlawed and repentant, Girart with his wife wanders through the countryside. They meet some merchants, and the duchess thinks it prudent to make them believe that the exile whose features they think they recognize is no more. 'Girart is dead; I saw him buried.' 'God be praised,' the merchants reply, 'for he was always making war and through him we have suffered many ills.' At these words, Girart's brow darkened; if he had had his sword 'he would have smitten one of them'. It is a story based on actual experience and illustrates the fundamental hostility which separated the classes. It cuts both ways. For the knight, proud of his courage and skill, despised the unwarlike *(imbellis)* people—the villeins who in face of the armies scampered away 'like deer', and later on the townsmen, whose economic power seemed to him so much the more hateful in that it was obtained by means which were at once mysterious and directly opposed to his own activities. If the propensity to bloody deeds was prevalent everywhere—more than one abbot indeed met his death as the victim of a cloister feud—it was the conception of the necessity of war, as a source of honour and as a means of livelihood, that set apart the little group of 'noble' folk from the rest of society.

THE NOBLE AT HOME

Favourite sport though it was, war had its dead seasons; but at these times the knightly class was distinguished from its neighbours by a manner of life which was essentially that of a nobility.

We should not think of this mode of existence as having invariably a rural setting. Italy, Provence and Languedoc still bore the age-old imprint of the Mediterranean civilizations whose structure had been systematized by Rome. In those regions, each small community was traditionally grouped round a town or large village which was at one and the same time an administrative centre, a market, and a place of refuge; and consequently the normal place of residence of the powerful. These people continued as much as ever to inhabit the old urban centres; and they took part in all their revolutions. In the thirteenth century, this civic character was regarded as one of the distinctive traits of the southern nobility. In contrast with Italy, said the Franciscan Salimbene, a native of Parma, who visited the kingdom of St. Louis, the towns of

France are inhabited only by burgesses; the nobility live on their estates. But, though true in general of the period in which the good friar was writing, the contrast would not have been equally true of the first feudal age. Undoubtedly in the purely merchant cities which, especially in the Low Countries and trans-Rhenish Germany, came into being almost entirely from the tenth or the eleventh century onwards—Ghent, Bruges, Soest, Lübeck and so many others—the dominant caste was almost invariably composed of men grown rich through trade; though where there was a governor of princely rank a small body of vassals was sometimes maintained, consisting of unenfeoffed knights or those who came regularly to perform their turn of duty. In the old Roman cities such as Rheims or Tournai, on the other hand, groups of knights seem to have resided over a long period, many of them no doubt attached to the courts of bishops or abbots. It was only gradually and in consequence of a more pronounced differentiation of classes that knightly society, outside Italy and southern France, became almost entirely divorced from the urban populations properly so called. Although the noble certainly did not cease altogether to visit the town, he henceforth went there only occasionally, in pursuit of pleasure or for the exercise of certain functions.

Everything tended to induce him to live in the country. First, there was the habit, which was becoming more and more widespread, of remunerating vassals by means of fiefs, consisting in the vast majority of cases of rural manors; then there was the weakening of feudal obligations, which favoured the tendency among the retainers who had now been provided with fiefs to live each in his own home, far from the kings, the great barons, and the bishops, who controlled the towns; finally, a taste for the open air, natural to these sportsmen, played its part. There is a moving story, told by a German monk, of a count's son who had been dedicated by his family to the monastic life; on the day when he was first subjected to the harsh rule of claustration, he climbed up to the highest tower of the monastery, in order 'at least to feast his vagrant soul on the spectacle of the hills and fields where he might no longer roam'. The pressure of the burghers, who had very little desire to admit into their communities elements indifferent to their activities and their interests, accelerated the movement.

Thus whatever modifications it may be necessary to introduce into the picture of a nobility exclusively rural from the outset, it remains true that, ever since knights existed, a growing majority of them in the North and many even in the coastal regions of the Mediterranean ordinarily resided in a country mansion.

The manor-house usually stood in the midst of a cluster of dwellings, or nearby; sometimes there were several in the same village. The manor-house was sharply distinguished from the surrounding cottages, just as it was in the towns from the habitations of the poor—not only because it was better built, but above all because it was almost invariably designed for defence. The desire of the rich to protect their dwellings from attack was naturally as old as the social disorders themselves; witness those fortified *villae* whose appearance about the fourth century bears witness to the decline of the Roman peace. The tradition may have continued here and there in the Frankish period, but most of the 'courts' inhabited by rich proprietors and even royal palaces themselves long remained almost without permanent means of defence. It was the invasions of the Northmen or the Hungarians which, from the Adriatic to the plains of northern England, led not only to the repair or rebuilding of town ramparts, but also to the erection on every hand of the rural strongholds *(fertés)* which were destined to cast a perpetual shadow over the fields of Europe. Internal wars soon added to their number. The rôle of the great potentates, kings or princes, in this prolific building of castles, and their efforts to control it, will be dealt with later; for the present they need not detain us. For the fortified houses of the petty lords, scattered over hill and dale, had almost always been constructed without any authorization from above. They answered elementary needs, spontaneously felt and satisfied. A hagiographer has given a very exact account of them, although in an unsympathetic spirit: 'their purpose was to enable these men, constantly occupied with quarrels and massacres, to protect themselves from their enemies, to triumph over their equals, to oppress their inferiors'; in short, to defend themselves and dominate others.

As we have seen, the nobility had never been completely illiterate; still less had it been impervious to the influence of literature, though this was listened to rather than read. But a great step forward was taken when knights themselves became literary men. It is significant that the *genre* to which they devoted themselves almost exclusively up the thirteenth century was lyric poetry. The earliest of the troubadours known to us—it should be added that he was certainly not the first—ranked among the most powerful princes in France. This was William IX of Aquitaine (d. 1127). In the list of Provençal singers who followed him, as also a little later among their rivals, the lyric poets of the North, all ranks of the knighthood were abundantly represented—leaving aside, of course, the professional minstrels kept by the great. These short pieces, which were generally characterized by an intricate technique—sometimes amounting to deliberate hermeticism, the famous 'close' style *(trobar clus)*—were admirably suited for recital in aristocratic gatherings. The fact that the nobility was thus able to savour and to find genuine enjoyment in pleasures too refined to be appreciated by villeins naturally reinforced its sense of superiority. As the poems were usually set off by singing and instrumental accompaniment the charm of music was wedded to the charm of words, and exercised an equally potent influence. William Marshal, who had been so tough a fighter, on his deathbed, longing, but not daring, to sing himself, would not say farewell to his daughters till they had allowed him to hear for the last time the 'sweet sound' of some *rotrouenges.*[1] And it was while listening to Volker's fiddle in the calm

---

[1] [A *rotrouenge* was a type of song with a refrain, composed by the *trouvères.*]

night, that the Burgundian heroes of the *Nibelungenlied* fell into what was to be their last sleep.

Towards the pleasures of the flesh the attitude of the knightly class appears to have been frankly realistic. It was the attitude of the age as a whole. The Church imposed ascetic standards on its members and required laymen to restrict sexual intercourse to marriage and the purpose of procreation. But it did not practise its own precepts very effectively, and this was especially true of the secular clergy, among whom even the Gregorian reform purified the lives of few but the episcopate. Significantly, we are told with admiration of pious persons, parish priests, nay even abbots, of whom 'it is said' that they died virgins. The example of the clergy proves how repugnant continence was to the majority of men: it was certainly not calculated to inspire it in the faithful. As a matter of fact—if we exclude such intentionally comic episodes as Oliver's boasting about his virility in the *Pèlerinage de Charlemagne*—the tone of the epics is fairly chaste. This was because their authors did not attach great importance to describing goings-on which had in fact no epic quality. Even in the less reticent narratives of the age of 'courtesy', libertinism is commonly represented as something for which the womenfolk rather than the heroes are responsible. Here and there nevertheless a characteristic touch gives a hint of the truth—as in the old poem of *Girart de Roussillon* where we find a vassal, who is required to give hospitality to a messenger, providing him with a beautiful girl for the night. And doubtless those 'delightsome' encounters were not wholly fictitious which, according to the romances, the castles so happily facilitated.

The evidence of history is clearer still. The noble's marriage, as we know, was often an ordinary business transaction, and the houses of the nobility swarmed with bastards. At first sight, the advent of 'courtesy' does not seem to have effected any great change in these morals. Certain of the songs of William of Aquitaine sing the praises of sensual pleasure in barrack-room style and this attitude was to find more than one imitator among the poets who succeeded him. Nevertheless, with William, who was apparently the heir of a tradition whose origins elude us, another conception of love was already emerging—that 'courtly' love, which was certainly one of the most curious products of the moral code of chivalry. Can we conceive of Don Quixote without Dulcinea?

The characteristic features of courtly love can be summarized fairly simply. It had nothing to do with marriage, or rather it was directly opposed to the legal state of marriage, since the beloved was as a rule a married woman and the lover was never her husband. This love was often bestowed upon a lady of higher rank, but in any case it always involved a strong emphasis on the man's adoration of the woman. It professed to be an all-engrossing passion, constantly frustrated, easily jealous, and nourished by its own difficulties; but its stereotyped development early acquired something of a ritual character. It was not averse to casuistry. Finally, as the troubadour Geoffrey Rudel said, in a poem which, wrongly interpreted, gave rise to the famous legend of Princess Far-away, it was, ideally, a 'distant' love. It did not indeed reject carnal intercourse on principle, nor according to Andrew the Chaplain, who discoursed on the subject, did it despise minor physical grati-fications if obliged to renounce 'the ultimate solace'. But absence or obsta-cles, instead of destroying it, only enriched it with a poetic melancholy. If possession, always to be desired, was seen to be quite out of the question, the sentiment none the less endured as an exciting emotion and a poignant joy.

Such is the picture drawn for us by the poets. For courtly love is only known to us through literature and for that reason it is very difficult to de-termine to what extent it was merely a fashionable fiction. It is certain that, though tending in some measure to dissociate sentiment from sensuality, it by no means prevented the flesh from seeking satisfaction in a more direct way; for we know that with the majority of men emotional sincerity exists on several planes. In any case we may be sure that such an idea of amorous relationships, in which today we recognize many elements with which we have now become familiar, was at first a strikingly original conception. It owed little to the ancient arts of love, or even—although they were perhaps nearer to it—to the always rather equivocal treatises which Graeco-Roman civilization devoted to the analysis of masculine friendship. In particular the humble attitude of the lover was a new thing. We have seen that it was apt to express itself in terms borrowed from the vocabulary of vassal homage; and this was not merely a matter of words. The identification of the loved one and the lord corresponded to an aspect of social morality entirely character-istic of feudal society.

Still less, in spite of what has sometimes been said, was this code de-pendent on religious ideas. If we leave out of account a few superficial analogies, which are at the most only the result of environment, we must in fact recognize that it was directly opposed to them, although its adherents had no clear consciousness of this antithesis. It made the love of man and woman almost one of the cardinal virtues, and certainly the supreme form of pleasure. Above all, even when it renounced physical satisfaction, it subli-mated—to the point of making it the be-all and end-all of existence—an emotional impulse derived essentially from those carnal appetites whose legitimacy Christianity only admits in order to curb them by marriage (pro-foundly despised by courtly love), in order to justify them by the propaga-tion of the species (to which courtly love gave but little thought), and in order, finally, to confine them to a secondary plane of moral experience. It is not in the knightly lyrics that we can hope to find the authentic echo of the attitude of contemporary Christianity towards sexual relations. This is expressed, quite uncompromisingly, in that passage of the pious and clerical *Queste du Saint-Graal* where Adam and Eve, before they lie together under the Tree to beget 'Abel the Just', beg the Lord to bring down upon them a great darkness to 'comfort' their shame.

The contrast between the two moralities in their treatment of this sub-ject perhaps provides us with the key to the problem of social geography presented by these new preoccupations with romantic love. Like the lyrical poetry which has preserved them for us, they arose as early as the end of the eleventh century in the courtly circles of southern France. It was only a reflection of them which appeared a little later in the North—still in the lyrical form or through the medium of the romances—and which subsequently passed into the German *Minnesang.*

Now, it would be absurd to attempt to explain this fact by attributing some indefinable superiority to the civilization of Languedoc. Whether relating to the artistic, the intellectual or the economic sphere, the claim would be equally untenable. It would mean ignoring the French epic, Gothic art, the first efforts of philosophy in the schools between Loire and Meuse, the fairs of Champagne, and the teeming cities of Flanders. It is beyond dispute, on the other hand, that in the South the Church, especially during the first feudal age, was less rich, less cultivated, less active than in the northern provinces. No great works of clerical literature, no great movements of monastic reform emanated from that region. This relative weakness of the religious centres alone can explain the extraordinary successes achieved, from Provence to the region of Toulouse, by heresies fundamentally international; and it was also no doubt the reason why the higher ranks of the laity, being less subject to clerical influence, were relatively free to develop their own secular morality. Moreover, the fact that these precepts of courtly love were subsequently so easily propagated shows how well they served the new requirements of a class. They helped it to become aware of itself. To love in a different way from the generality of men must inevitably make one feel different from them.

That a knight should carefully calculate his booty or his ransoms and, on returning home, impose a heavy 'tallage' on his peasants provoked little or no criticism. Gain was legitimate; but on one condition—that it should be promptly and liberally expended. 'I can assure you,' said a troubadour when he was reproached for his brigandage, 'if I robbed, it was to give, not to hoard.' No doubt we are entitled to regard as a little suspect the insistence with which the minstrels, those professional parasites, extolled above all other duties that of generosity, *largesse,* 'lady and queen in whose light all virtues shine'. No doubt also, among the nobles of middle or lesser rank and still more perhaps among the great barons, there were always miserly or merely prudent individuals, more inclined to amass scarce coin or jewels in their coffers than to distribute them. It is none the less true that, in squandering a fortune that was easily gained and easily lost, the noble thought to affirm his superiority over classes less confident in the future or more careful in providing for it. This praiseworthy prodigality might not always stop at generosity or even luxury. A chronicler has preserved for us the record of the remarkable competition in wasteful expenditure witnessed one day at a great 'court' held in Limousin. One knight had a plot of ground ploughed up and sown with small pieces of silver; another burned wax candles for his cooking; a third, 'through boastfulness', ordered thirty of his horses to be burnt alive. What must a merchant have thought of this struggle for prestige through extravagance—which reminds us of the practices of certain primitive races? Here again different notions of honour marked the line of separation between the social groups.

Thus set apart by its power, by the nature of its wealth and its mode of life, by its very morals, the social class of nobles was toward the middle of the twelfth century quite ready to solidify into a legal and hereditary class. The ever more frequent use which from that time onwards seems to have been made of the word *gentilhomme*—man of good *gent* or lineage—to describe the members of this class is an indication of the growing importance attributed to qualities of birth. With the wide adoption of the ceremony of 'dubbing' or formal arming of the knight the legal class of nobility took definite shape.❖

RECOMMENDED READINGS

J. S. Critchley, *Feudalism* (London and Boston: Allen & Unwin, 1978), provides a general overview of the feudal system, but the reader might well begin with Marc Bloch, *French Rural History: An Essay on Its Basic Characteristics,* trans. Janet Sondheimer (Berkeley: University of California Press, 1966), who sets the bases for the feudal organization of Europe in its systems of landholding and tilling. Georges Duby, one of the most imaginative and original of a fine generation of French medievalists, has attempted to recreate feudal society in *The Three Orders: Feudal Society Imagined,* trans. Arthur Goldhammer (Chicago: University of Chicago Press, 1980).

Jean-Pierre Poly, *The Feudal Transformation: 900-1200,* trans. Caroline Higgitt (New York: Holmes & Meier, 1991), traces the growth of the feudal aristocracy to its transformation into a chivalric nobility; David Herlihy, *The History of Feudalism* (New York: Walker, 1971), illustrates the process with an excellent selection of readings from the period.

Feudalism was not monolithic, of course, and there are a series of studies of the operation of the system in various locales. Outstanding among these are Barbara English, *The Lords of Holderness, 1086-1260: A Study in Feudal Society* (Oxford, UK, and New York: Published for the University of Hull by Oxford University Press, 1979); Archibald Ross Lewis, *The Development of Southern French and Catalan Society, 718-1050* (Austin: University of Texas Press, 1965); and Theodore Evergates, *Feudal Society in the Bailliage of Troyes Under the Counts of Champagne, 1152-1284* (Baltimore: Johns Hopkins University Press, 1975).

Palestine, A.D. 1100

THE IMPACT OF THE CRUSADES ON MOSLEM LANDS

Philip K. Hitti

*For five hundred years after the fall of the Western Roman Empire, west-
ern Europe was overshadowed politically, economically, and culturally
in the Mediterranean world, first by the Byzantine Empire and then by
both the Byzantine Empire and Islam. By the year 900, the Muslims of
North Africa controlled the western Mediterranean, and a Muslim
fortress on the upper Rhine River collected tolls from the river traffic
passing beneath its walls. This had all changed by the year 1000. The
Muslim caliphate of Cordoba in Spain had disintegrated, the merchants
of the North Italian cities had wrested control of the sea, and the Muslim
leaders of the eastern Mediterranean had begun to fall into petty political
and doctrinal squabbles. In 1096, the Westerners seized the moment and
launched a holy war to reclaim the Bible lands for Christianity. The venture was a resounding success; by 1100, the western Christians were in
control of the Holy Land.*

*Western historians have generally regarded the Crusade as the mark
of European resurgence, and have concentrated on its effects on the
West. Philip Hitti focused his attention on subsequent developments in
the East, and found that their initial defeat in the First Crusade had
been, in many ways, the salvation of the Muslims. The Christian victory
had been possible only because of the Muslims' loss of a sense of unity
and the general incompetence of their leaders. The situation after the
victory of the Westerners called forth a new leadership, epitomized in the
figure of Saladin, and awoke in the Muslims a new sense of fellowship
and purpose. The presence of a common enemy did much to revivify
Muslim spirits and transform a decaying society into a militant and dynamic one.*

READING QUESTIONS

1. Why were the Christians victorious and how long did their dominance in
   the region of Palestine endure?

2. What was the effect of the Crusades on the Muslim political institutions
   of the region?

3. How did the Crusades affect the trade of the region?

4. How well did Christian missionary activity among the Arabs succeed?

Rich in picturesque episodes and dramatic events, the crusades were poor in the contribution they made to the edification or enlightenment of the area of their operation. The chain reaction of counter-crusades and of the anti-Christian and anti-western feeling they generated has not ceased. The festering sore they left refuses to heal, and scars on the face of the lands and on the souls of their inhabitants are still in evidence. As late as the twentieth century the anti-crusading ghost was invoked in connection with the mandates imposed on Syria and Iraq and the Anglo-French attack on Egypt in 1956.

At the launching of the crusading movement the religious unity of Islam had already been shattered, and its political state was fragmented. The caliphate, which personified the double unity, was then itself triple. The Umaiyad caliphate of Cordova was a traditional enemy of its counterpart in Baghdad, and both were considered illegitimate by the Shī'ite imamate of Cairo. The Baghdad caliphate had been subordinated since 1055 to newly Islamized Selchükid (Seljuk) Turks, whose loosely united—if not utterly disjointed—states and statelets had mushroomed all over the area, extending into Byzantine Anatolia. Almost every sizable city in Syria had its own Selchükid or Arab ruler, often at odds one with the other. Hostility between Ridvan (1095–1113) in Aleppo, who had Ismā'īlite leanings, and his orthodox brother Dukak (1095–1104) in Damascus formed, together with battles against crusaders, the central theme of their reigns. Shaizar on the Orontes near Hamah was defended by the Sunnite Arab Banū-Munqidh. Tripoli was under the Shī'ite Arab Banū-'Ammār. The Byzantines were seizing and losing towns along the coast and on Syria's northern frontier. Jerusalem, the ultimate crusading goal, was being tossed from one hand to another: in 1070 the Selchükid general Atsîz had wrested it from the Fātimids; in 1096 it had reverted to their control.

At the advent of the crusaders, therefore, not only was the unity of Islam fundamentally impaired but the possibility of its repair under Turkish or Arab aegis looked equally hopeless.[1] In fact, throughout its history, except

---

[1] For a different view see Steven Runciman, *A History of the Crusades* (3 vols., Cambridge, Eng., 1951–1954), III, 472–474.

From Philip Hitti, "The Impact of the Crusades on Moslem Lands," in Norman P. Zacour and Harry W. Hazard, eds., *The Impact of the Crusades on the Near East*, Vol. 5 in Kenneth W. Setton, gen. ed., *A History of the Crusades* (Madison: University of Wisconsin Press, 1985), pp. 33–36, 38–40, 41, 44–45, 49–50, 57–58.

This chapter was edited by Harry W. Hazard, after the author's death.

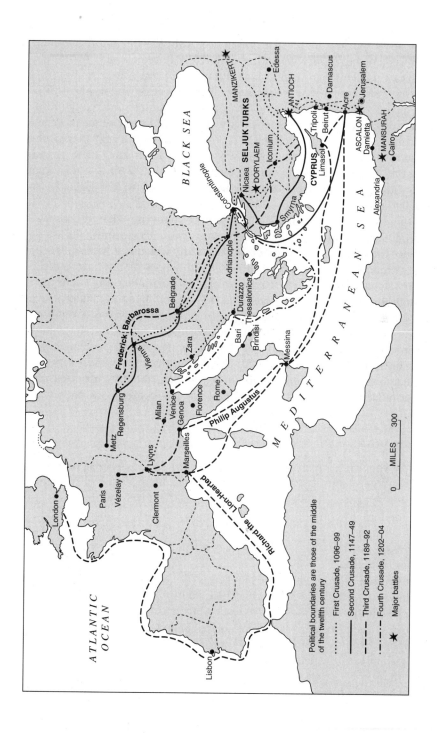

ATLANTIC OCEAN

London

Paris
Vézelay
Clermont

Lisbon

Richard the Lion-Hearted

Metz
Regensburg
Lyons
Milan
Venice
Genoa
Florence
Marseilles
Rome

Frederick Barbarossa
Vienna

Belgrade
Zara
Bari
Durazzo
Thessalonica
Brindisi
Messina

Adrianople

Philip Augustus

MEDITERRANEAN SEA

BLACK SEA

Constantinople

MANZIKERT
SELJUK TURKS
Nicaea DORYLAEM
Iconium
Smyrna

Edessa

ANTIOCH
Damascus
Beirut
Tripoli
Acre
Jerusalem
CYPRUS
Limasol
ASCALON
Damietta
MANSURAH
Cairo
Alexandria

Political boundaries are those of the middle
of the twelfth century

.... First Crusade, 1096–99
————— Second Crusade, 1147–49
– – – – Third Crusade, 1189–92
–·–·–·– Fourth Crusade, 1202–04
★ Major battles

MILES
0   300

for a short period under the Orthodox caliphs and another under the Umaiyads, Moslem unity was more nominal than real.

Into this semichaotic politico-military situation the crusading element was injected, and to it was owed the initial success, which constituted the bulk of the total success. One after another the states in the way of the crusaders were wiped off the map. First to fall (1097) was the most substantial and consolidated, that of Selchükid "Rūm," based on Nicaea. This victory restored to emperor Alexius I Comnenus (1081–1118) his lost province and delayed the Turkish—in the event, Ottoman—invasion of Europe for two and a half centuries. Next came Edessa (ar-Ruhā', Urfa), whose large Armenian population prompted a special detour. Unhesitatingly, Armenian Christians cast their lot with crusading Catholics. With them they shared common feelings of hostility to Turks and antipathy toward Byzantines. Edessa's ruler Țoros of the Roupenid dynasty enthusiastically welcomed Baldwin (February 6, 1098) and formally declared him son and heir. A month later the adopted son replaced the father (d. 1098). Antioch's surrender three months later, through the treachery of an Armenian officer commanding one of its towers, ended a long and arduous siege. Tripoli's Arab governor Ibn-'Ammār bought off the invaders, and contacts were established between the Franks and the Maronites, who furnished guides and forces. No serious resistance was offered until Jerusalem was reached. The fall of the third-holiest city in Islam evoked no more than an expression of regret from al-Mustazhir, the caliph-defender of Islam at Baghdad. But in the words of a contemporary poet:

> Tears are the least effective of weapons,
>   when swords illumine the fires of war.[2]

On Christmas day of 1100, count Baldwin of Edessa was crowned at Bethlehem as ruler of the Latin kingdom of Jerusalem. A few years thereafter Tripoli was captured by Raymond of Toulouse (d. 1105). With the creation of the kingdom, to which the county of Tripoli, the principality of Antioch (including Cilicia), and the county of Edessa were loosely held by feudal bonds, the mission of the cross-wearers was fulfilled, all within the compass of a few short years.

As refugees from Palestine flocked into Baghdad, a group of Sūfīs, merchants, and *faqībs* (canon lawyers) headed by a noble Hāshimite, forced the preacher in the grand mosque to descend from the pulpit, which they tore to pieces. At last the Arab caliph al-Mustazhir and the Selchükid sultan Berkyaruk bestirred themselves; they sent a token contingent.

Response to the challenge came from an unexpected quarter. It started with the son of a Turkish slave, Zengi, who from Mosul spread his domain through northern Syria and in 1144 took Edessa. The first to be lost, Edessa was the first to be regained. Its restoration marked the beginning of the end of the

---

[2] Ibn-al-Athīr, *Al-kāmil fī-t-ta'rīkh*, ed. Carl J. Tornberg (14 vols., Leyden and Uppsala, 1851–1876), I, 194.

Latin states. With it the spirit of the holy war *(jihād)* shifted to the Moslem camp. It sparked a dormant pan-Islamic spirit which materialized in counter-crusades that continued until the last crusader was thrown out of the land.

Zengi ushered in a series of counter-crusader heroes which included his son Nūr-ad-Dīn and culminated in the Kurdish Ṣalāḥ-ad-Dīn (Saladin) and the Mamluk Baybars. Nūr-ad-Dīn's capture of Damascus in 1154 removed the last barrier between his expanding kingdom and that of the Latins in Jerusalem. Saladin managed to inherit the Nūrid territory and built on the foundation of a united Syrian monarchy laid by his two predecessors. By the conquest of Jerusalem in 1187, following the dramatic victory of Hattin, the watershed in the military history of the crusades was reached and the unification of all Syria was potentially assured. Saladin's destruction of the Shī'ite Fāṭimid imamate of Cairo in 1171 was more than the ending of a dynasty; it was the destruction of the possibility of the future development there of a dissident Moslem power. Saladin's sultanate now extended from Diyār-Bakr to Nubia and included Hejaz. Thus did the crusades unwittingly contribute to reversing the centrifugal forces in political Islam and to halting sectarian expansion in religious Islam. A devout Sunnite, Saladin suppressed heterodoxy, championed orthodoxy, and more than any other Moslem hero personified the counter-crusading pan-Islamic spirit. With him the disunity, incompetent leadership, and low morale which had characterized Islam at the end of the eleventh century completed the shift to the enemy's side.[3]

This achievement, which began with Zengi and culminated in Saladin, may be considered the first both in chronology and in significance of the positive effects of the crusades on Moslem lands. The liquidation of the Selchükid and petty Arab states was the first of the negative effects.

Baybars resumed with telling effect the devastating blows of his great predecessor, specializing in taking Templars' and Hospitallers' castles, the main strongholds of the crusaders. His seizure of Antioch in 1268 ended the career of the second-oldest, and at this time the strongest, of the Frankish states. Not much more was left than mopping up.

The military ventures which technically began with pope Urban II's speech in 1095 and ended with the fall of Acre to Mamluk armies in 1291 had antecedents which may be traced back through Byzantine, Roman, and Alexandrian periods to earlier wars with Persians in the fifth century before Christ. Their counter-crusading sequels extended for centuries.[4]

Next to the political, the economic transformation was the most pronounced and important effect on Moslem lands. The crusader impact had its negative economic effects in the form of destruction of life and property, but, it should be remembered, the periods of peace were of longer duration

---

[3] For more details on early Moslem reaction to the crusades consult Emmanuel Sivan, *L'Islam et la croisade* (Paris, 1968), pp. 28–35.

[4] Aziz S. Atiya, *Crusade, Commerce and Culture* (Bloomington, Ind., 1962), pp. 146 ff., considers even the Ottoman Turkish invasion of Europe a counter-crusade.

than those of war. Trade—at least in the case of Genoese, Venetians, and Pisans, the shrewdest money-makers of the age—was a primary motivation in the venture.

Hitherto trade had flowed mostly from east to west, but now there was a strong reverse current, while the east-west stream was both enhanced and accelerated. The textile industry, as old as Phoenicia, the trade in spices, which went back to Sabaean-Roman days, the export of pottery and glass-ware from Sidon and Tyre, of drugs and perfume from Damascus, wines from Gaza, and sugar from the maritime plain—all these activities received fresh impetus as a result of opening new markets and widening old ones. Gold-work, ironwork, the manufacture of swords, silk, and soap, and the weaving of rugs flourished as never before. The incoming Europeans introduced no new techniques in industry, but crusaders, pilgrims, businessmen, and sailors returned to their homelands with newly acquired or developed desires and tastes for semitropical oriental products. Fabrics such as muslin (from Mosul), baldachin (from Baghdad), damask (from Damascus), sarcenet (from Saracen), and atlas *(aṭlas)* were increasingly in demand. New tastes, acquired for attar *('iṭr)*, sugar *(sukkar)*, ginger *(zanjabīl)*, and other aromatics, spices, and products of India and Arabia, had to be satisfied on behalf of returning crusaders through commercial channels. The Syrian merchant enlarged his traditional function as the middleman between east and west, between Europe on the one hand, and Arabia, India, and the Far East on the other, for the route around the Cape of Good Hope was not yet known. After Tyre, Acre, "the rendezvous of Moslem and Christian merchants from the four quarters of the world,"[5] became a flourishing center of maritime trade. From their Beirut warehouse (Ar. *funduq,* from Gr.) Venetians lost in value in one day 10,000 dinars' worth of pepper, a figure which gives an idea of the enormous riches accumulated in the agencies or factories of the Levant.[6]

Woolen fabrics from England, Flanders, France, and Italy went first to Venice or some other Italian port and thence on galleys to Syrian and Egyptian ports.[7] Venetians in Syria exchanged western for eastern glassware; Genoese and Florentines carried on the same kind of trade. Besides wool, linen was a desired commodity. Linen from Rheims normally passed through Marseilles on its route eastward. Pisa, Genoa, and Venice had with their fleets assisted in the conquest of the land and in return enjoyed commercial and political privileges, including the occupation of special quarters in certain cities. There their merchant colonies grew. From Syrian ports, trade found its way into the interior, into Mesopotamia, Persia, and even Central Asia.

---

[5] Ibn-Jubair, *Riḥlah,* ed. William Wright (E. J. W. Gibb Memorial Series, 5; London, 1852); revised by Martin J. de Goeje (Leyden, 1907), p. 303.

[6] See Ṣāliḥ ibn-Yaḥyâ, *Ta'rīkh Bairūt,* ed. Louis Cheikho (Beirut, 1902), p. 62.

[7] Wilhelm Heyd, *Histoire du commerce du levant au moyen-âge,* tr. Furcy Raynaud, II (Leipzig, 1886; repr. Leipzig, 1936, Amsterdam, 1967), 706.

Brisk trading and manufacturing enabled Moslem merchants, especially in the interior cities, to amass huge fortunes. Ibn-Jubair, who visited Syria in the 1180's, cites the case of two such Damascene merchants. He was impressed with the uninterrupted and unimpeded march of caravans between Egypt and Damascus through the "land of the Franks." His and later evidence leaves no doubt that Aiyūbid Syria enjoyed a period of unusual prosperity. By that time the shock of the invasion had abated and the two sides had evidently adjusted themselves to the strange new life. One scholar goes so far as to say that the occupation of Syria revolutionized the entire economy of commerce in the Mediterranean, helped to raise the country to the international level, and bestowed on it a prosperity previously enjoyed only under the Romans.[8] Another, however, representing the German school, dwells on the miseries of the natives—which they no doubt suffered in the early stages—and claims that Moslem citizens were expelled or exterminated systematically, native Christians were put to flight, and Palestine assumed a desolate aspect.[9]

To meet the financial needs of the new situation a larger supply and a more rapid circulation of money became necessary. The *byzantinus saracenatus,* probably the earliest gold coin struck by Latins, was minted in the Holy Land and bore an Arabic inscription. The Templars began to issue letters of credit and perform other banking functions. In fact, all three military orders—Templars, Hospitallers, and Teutonic Knights—which had started as charitable religious organizations and evolved into military institutions, gradually became to a certain extent commercial companies.

For the lower strata of Moslem society the conquest probably meant little by way of direct economic change. To them it was an exchange of one set of rulers, the Selchükids, strange in race and language, or native emirs unconcerned with their subjects' welfare, for another set of rulers, Europeans, equally strange and unconcerned. Local sultans and emirs, whether Turks or Arabs, had previously accorded territorial concessions *(iqtā'āt)* to their lieutenants for services rendered by troops under them. The mass of people lived as serfs on those feudal lands. Their daily life now went on unaffected. In country places a clearcut differentiation in treatment between Frankish-held and native-held domains hardly existed; only cities were delimited and subjected to customs duty. The crusaders belonged mostly to urban, not farming, populations, and when they lost a city to Moslems, it was usually stipulated that they evacuate it.

In the minor as in the fine arts, the easterners possessed an older, richer, and more highly developed tradition, placing the westerners almost entirely on the receiving end. Likewise in science, letters, and other purely

---

[8] Henri Lammens, *La Syrie: Précis historique* (2 vols., Beirut, 1921), I, 235.

[9] Hans Prutz, *Kulturgeschichte der Kreuzzüge* (Berlin, 1883; repr. Hildesheim, 1964), pp. 93, 95, 145.

intellectual achievements the Arabs had more to give than to receive, especially since soldiers and merchants formed the bulk of the colonists. When two differing cultures stand in confrontation, the normal flow is from the higher to the lower, and this case was no exception.

In his delightfully entertaining memoirs Usāmah (d. 1188) presents the most elaborate details about contemporary social intercourse between Moslems and Franks. A warrior, hunter, gentleman, poet, and man of letters, he defended his picturesque castle, Shaizar on the Orontes, in times of war and fraternized with the Franks in times of peace. In and around Hamah (Epiphania), in Ascalon ('Asqalān) and other Palestinian towns, in Sinai and Egypt, in Mosul and other places of Mesopotamia, he witnessed or took part in battles against Franks and Arabs, Christians and Moslems. The information he offers is often first-hand, candid, and unique. His appraisal of Frankish character no doubt reflects the then-prevailing Moslem public opinion. To him "the Franks are void of all zeal and jealousy" in sex affairs;[10] their methods of ordeal by water and duel are far inferior to the Moslem judicial procedure;[11] their system of medication appears odd and primitive when compared with the more highly developed system of the Arabs.[12] Usāmah credits them with possessing "the virtues of courage and fighting, but nothing else."[13] Again and again Usāmah draws the distinction between the outlandish, rude "recent comers" and the "acclimatized" Franks in Moslem lands.[14] One knight was on such intimate terms of friendship with Usāmah that he began to address him as "my brother."[15]

Many crusaders must have realized that baggy clothes and heavy headgear were preferable in a warm climate, and they consequently adopted native dress.[16] Their preference for native dishes is also attested. A Frank in Antioch who shunned European dishes employed an Egyptian cook, and never had pork in his kitchen,[17] but we know of no cases of Arabs adopting European clothes or preferring western food. For one thing, Islamic dietary laws involving pork and the manner of slaughter would stand in the way. Nor do we know by name any Moslem attracted by a visit to Europe. When the knight who called Usāmah "brother" asked Usāmah to permit his fourteen-year-old son to accompany the knight to Europe, Usāmah felt as if there fell upon his ears words which would never come out of the mouth of a sensible

---

[10] Usāmah Ibn-Muniqidh, *Kitāb al-i'tibār*, ed. Philip K. Hitti (Princeton, 1930), p. 135; tr. Hitti, *An Arab-Syrian Gentleman and Warrior in the Period of the Crusades* (*CURC*, 10; New York, 1929; repr. Beirut, 1964), p. 164.

[11] *I'tibār*, pp. 138–139; *Arab-Syrian Gentleman*, pp. 167–168.

[12] *I'tibār*, pp. 132 ff.; *Arab-Syrian Gentleman*, pp. 162 ff.

[13] *I'tibār*, p. 132; *Arab-Syrian Gentleman*, p. 161.

[14] *I'tibār*, pp. 134–135, 140–141; *Arab-Syrian Gentleman*, pp. 163–164, 169–170.

[15] *I'tibār*, p. 132; *Arab-Syrian Gentleman*, p. 161.

[16] Emmanuel G. Rey, *Les Colonies franques de Syrie* (Paris, 1883), pp. 11 ff.; Gustave Schlumberger, *Numismatique de l'Orient latin* (Paris, 1878; repr. Graz, 1954), p. 45.

[17] Usāmah, *I'tibār*, pp. 140–141; *Arab-Syrian Gentleman*, pp. 169–170.

man.[18] Nevertheless, he apologetically told his friend that the only reason for rejecting the request was the unusual attachment of the grandmother to her grandson.

The Christian military venture left Islam more militant, less tolerant, and more self-centered. In its formative stage Islamic culture enthusiastically entered upon the Greek heritage through the intermediacy of Syrian (Syriac-speaking) Christians. But the lowering of the crusading curtain shut it off entirely from that source. The venture created another barrier between Moslems and their Christian countrymen. The alienation between the two societies has lingered to the present.

But whereas Islam can show some items on the credit side of the balance sheet, eastern Christianity has hardly any to show. Its followers, upholders of a tradition more venerable than that of Rome or Byzantium, entrepreneurs of classical science and philosophies, liaison officers between east and west, were by the end of the crusading period weakened to the point of impotence. The enterprise which had its inception in the urge to defend Christendom came near to destroying Christendom's eastern wing.

We have thus far treated the area as a Moslem land with a Christian minority. But in Syria-Lebanon-Palestine the Christian minorities in total must have amounted to a majority at the dawn of the crusades, though not a united one.[19] In the aftermath of the crusades they dwindled into an insignificant minority. Especially strong were the Armenian and Greek Orthodox elements in Antioch, Edessa, and the rest of northern Syria, extending through Cilicia. In Palestine the Greek Orthodox alone probably formed half the total population. The western branch of the Syrian (Suryānī) church, commonly called Jacobite and once based in Edessa, was spread all over the area. Maronites controlled northern Lebanon. Copts were not numerous but did figure in the Egyptian population and manned high administrative and government positions. True, all these Christians were second-class citizens in the Moslem state, but their rights and obligations were clearly defined by the Koran and Islamic law and the adherents were generally reconciled to their status. The crusaders' advent introduced a most disturbing factor. It gave Moslems occasion to suspect their Christian neighbors of sympathy with their western coreligionists, and offered native Christians the temptation to turn collaborationists.

The Latins considered eastern Christians as schismatics, and Rome considered it its duty to "reunite" them with the mother church. Through pressure or persuasion and for political reasons certain groups yielded to the new disruptive force, were then cut off from their respective denominations, and became separate "Uniate" sects. But Moslems, rulers and ruled, were not fully cognizant of that fact and of its implications. To them

---

[18] *I'tibār*, p. 132; *Arab-Syrian Gentleman*, p. 161.

[19] Consult Claude Cahen, *La Syrie du nord à l'époque des croisades et la principauté franque d'Antioche* (IFD, BO, I; Paris, 1940), pp. 190–191.

Gregorian Armenians, Syrian Jacobites and Nestorians, Lebanese Maronites, Egyptian Copts, and Latin Franks were all simply Christians. They had to pay a heavy price after the restoration of Moslem control. Certain communities were decimated, others converted. With the exception of Lebanon, the area began to assume the Moslem aspect it still maintains.

One interesting and enduring byproduct of the crusades was the initiation of missionary work among Moslems. With the failure of Christians to subdue the "infidel" by force, the theory prevailed that his soul might be subdued by persuasion. The possibility of substituting peaceful, spiritual conquest for a military one took root as a reaction from the crusading methods and as a result of the newly generated interest in the east. Launched in the early thirteenth century, the missionary activity, with its many ramifications, has persisted down to the present time.

The two earliest missionary organizations were the Franciscan and the Dominican, both originating in Syria. Francis of Assisi himself started the mission named after him when in 1219 he arrived in Acre and sent eleven disciples across the land. This city became the headquarters of the Franciscan effort. He also presented himself before the Aiyūbid al-Kāmil, nephew of Saladin, in Egypt and discussed religion with him. About the same time the Dominican mission was launched; it established a convent in Damascus and another in Tripoli. The Carmelite order, monastic and contemplative rather than missionary, also had a Syrian origin; it was organized earlier by a veteran crusader and took its name from a Palestinian mountain.

The results of this early missionary effort among Moslems were disappointing. The protagonists thereupon sought new channels directed toward native Christian communities. The creation of the Uniate churches, Syrian and Greek, in the seventeenth and eighteenth centuries was the crowning achievement of Catholic missionary activity.

As the idea of converting Moslems was germinating in Christian minds, Mongol hordes were pouring into western Asia, thus providing the missionaries with a wider field for their activity. The victorious march of the Mongols landed them in Syria, where they and the crusaders found themselves facing a common enemy—the Moslems. Negotiations were carried on for concerted action. Embassies were exchanged with popes and kings. For a time these heathens from Central Asia flirted with Christianity. Hulagu, whose wife, Toqūz Khātūn (d. 1265), was a member of the east Syrian church, sympathized with this faith. His general Kitbogha, who had led the army triumphantly into Palestine, professed the same form of Christianity. But the routing of the Mongol army in 1260 at 'Ain Jālūt, the first major check the Mongols experienced, and the subsequent expulsion of the Franks from the land must have convinced these heathens that Islam was the more powerful religion.[20] In

[20] Laurence E. Browne, *The Eclipse of Christianity in Asia* . . . (Cambridge, Eng., 1933), p. 154.

1295 their seventh īl-khān, Ghazan, adopted the Arabic name Maḥmūd and de-clared Islam to be the Mongol state religion

In Europe the champion of the policy of peaceful penetration was a Catalan, Raymond Lull, who persuaded the king of Majorca to found a school of Arabic studies to train missionaries whose only weapons would be "love, prayers, and the outpouring of tears." Acting on Lull's plea the Council of Vienne in 1312 ordered the teaching of Arabic in the universities of Rome, Paris, Oxford, Bologna, and Salamanca. The study of Arabic led to the study of other oriental languages. In the course of the thirteenth and fourteenth centuries, Catholic bishoprics were established not only in Syria, Armenia, and Persia but also across Central Asia to eastern China.

In the wake of the missionary went the trader. Travelers and merchants, especially from Italy, penetrated by land from Acre to Peking. Others circumnavigated southern Asia from Basra to Canton. Both of these land and sea routes had been known to Moslems and frequented by them for centuries; but to Europeans the experience amounted to a discovery of anterior Asia and the Far East, resulting in an expansion of geographical knowledge that ranks in importance second only to that entailed by the discovery of the New World two centuries later. ❖

RECOMMENDED READINGS

Aziz Suryal Atiya has published a useful, although now somewhat dated, work, *The Crusade: Historiography and Bibliography* (Bloomington: Indiana University Press, 1962).

Steven Runciman, *A History of the Crusades* (New York: Harper & Row, 1964), is a readable general account; the collective work *A History of the Crusades,* 2nd ed., ed. Kenneth M. Setton, is perhaps the most thorough single treatment of the subject: Vol. 1. *The First Hundred Years,* ed. M. W. Baldwin (1955); Vol. 2. *The Later Crusades,* ed. R. L. Wolff (1962); Vol. 3. *The Fourteenth and Fifteenth Centuries,* ed. H. W. Hazard (1975); Vol. 4. *The Art and Architecture of the Crusader States,* ed. H. W. Hazard (1977) (Madison: University of Wisconsin Press, 1969–1989).

There are several accounts of the Crusades from the Muslim point of view, prominent among them Francesco Gabrieli, *Arab Historians of the Crusades; Selected and Translated from the Arabic Sources,* trans. E. J. Costello (London: Routledge & K. Paul, 1969); Amin Maalouf, *The Crusades Through Arab Eyes,* trans. Jon Rothschild (London: Al Saqi Books: Distributed by Zed Books, 1984); and Usamah ibn Munqidh, *Memoirs of an Arab-Syrian Gentleman; or, An Arab Knight in the Crusades: Memoirs of Usamah ibn-Munqidh (Kitab al-itibar),* trans. Philip K. Hitti (Beirut: Khayats, 1964).

THE NATURAL HISTORY OF MEDIEVAL WOMEN

David Herlihy

Medieval Europe was in many ways a marginal society, in which the individual's status and even survival depended at least in some measure on his or her ability to contribute to the group. The following selection shows how Europe's economic development affected the lives and status of women. Women were obviously necessary if society was to perpetuate itself, but their status depended on other factors. In the earlier Middle Ages, the economy was overwhelmingly agricultural, and women contributed their labor to the work in the fields and in raising the gardens that provided critical vegetable and fruit supplements to the overwhelmingly cereal diet of the day. The importance of these contributions can scarcely be overestimated. It should be remembered, however, that the eleventh-century boom in the European economy was characterized by the widespread construction of water mills. The function of these mills was to grind grain into flour, a task that had absorbed much female labor up to that time. The woman-hours saved in this manner were turned to agricultural work that generally raised the standard of living and made possible a significant growth of population.

Although their more arduous agricultural work increased the value of women and, therefore, their status, it also shortened their lives. Being in relatively short supply, women were the more highly valued and possessed protection and privileges. As time passed, the manufacturing sector—an area in which female labor was less needed—grew. As a consequence, the women of the later Middle Ages enjoyed the advantages of working less and living longer. The accompanying disadvantage, however, was that their economic value had declined and they consequently enjoyed a less elevated status. As David Herlihy points out in the following selection, the women of modern Western society still enjoy some of these advantages; they also continue to pay a heavy cost.

READING QUESTIONS

1. How did ancient and medieval scholars view the relative life expectancy of men and women, and to what did they attribute the differences?

2. When did the life expectancy of medieval women increase, and for what reasons?

3. What do Herlihy's biographical sketches of medieval women indicate about the status of females in medieval society?

V ersed in reconstructing all dimensions of past human experience, many modern social historians have become especially interested in women. Partly inspired by the contemporary feminist movement (whose advocates have correctly pointed out that the history of roughly half of humanity has been systematically slighted), these historians also recognize that in the natural and social history of any society, women have unique and critical functions. They carry the new generation to term, sustain children in early life, and usually introduce the young to the society and culture of which they will be a part. Women begin the processes through which human cultures strive to achieve what their individual members cannot—indefinite life, immortality.

Few historians are willing to accept the claims of sociobiologists, who find culture already programmed in genes and who subordinate cultural history to natural history. But most would agree that human societies and civilizations cannot be properly evaluated or appreciated without considering the basic biological experiences of their members. These crucial events—including the duration of life itself under various social and historical conditions, as well as the timing of nursing and weaning, sexual maturity, marriage and mating, reproduction, menopause, and aging—are often by no means parallel experiences for both men and women and can have radically different consequences for each sex.

The biological experiences of women throughout the Middle Ages are interesting because of the length of this particular period: we can observe a thousand years of women's careers and the contours of their lives. Data concerning the Middle Ages are notoriously intractable—difficult to find, difficult to interpret. But medieval scholars advanced some general comments on the biology of women, and a few of these ideas have come down to us; even some precious statistical information that illuminates how women fared in the real world. Finally, some biographies, chiefly of saints and queens, support our rudimentary knowledge of women's situations. All

From David Herlihy, "The Natural History of Medieval Women," *Natural History,* March 1978, pp. 56–67.

these sources have manifest gaps, but taken together, they present coherent pictures of medieval women. Although medievalists are often obliged to be jugglers and prestidigitators, they are not without pins or beans with which to play.

In the Middle Ages, life expectancies apparently varied sharply, in accordance with epidemiological conditions. For unclear reasons, western Europe was practically free of epidemics from the sixth to the fourteenth century, when the infamous Black Death of 1348–1349 introduced an epoch of recurrent and devastating plagues. From the thirteenth century on, we know the birth and death dates of many medieval nobles and townspeople, predominantly male, and can venture some estimates. In the plague-free years of the thirteenth century, people could expect to live between 35 and 40 years. In the stricken generations including and immediately following the Black Death, life expectancies fell to only 17 or 18 years. It thereafter slowly lengthened and averaged about 30 years during the fifteenth century.

Life expectancies for women shifted up or down in phase with this general movement. But simultaneously, a small, significant change was taking place. Women were beginning to survive better than men; they were acquiring an advantage in longevity that, in the Western world, they have not since relinquished.

Medieval natural philosophers concluded that women's chances for life were improving. The biologists of the ancient world—of whom the foremost was Aristotle—had affirmed that, saving unusual circumstances, males of all species live longer than females (hard work or excessive sexual indulgence might frustrate nature's intent and artificially shorten the male life span). Males represented the perfection of the human species; females were an imperfection of nature, albeit a happy one, in view of their essential contribution to propagation. The defective females passed through all stages of life quicker than the male. They reached sexual maturity sooner, aged earlier, and were the first to die. The ancient biologists thought that specific humors determined a person's temperament and believed that women's temperaments, dominated by cold and dry humors, hurried them toward the cold and dry state of death.

In the twelfth century, when a renaissance of learning began in western Europe, scholars reexamined the biological writings of Aristotle and other classics. Initially, medieval natural scientists repeated without elaboration the ancients' opinion that men, as perfect representations of the species, live longer than women. Then, in the thirteenth century, the foremost biologist of the age, Saint Albertus Magnus (Albert the Great), who died in 1280, treated the question of the relative longevity of the sexes in a novel fashion. In Albertus's view, the Philosopher, Aristotle, was indeed correct. Men live longer than women *naturaliter,* "according to the natural order." But women live longer than men *per accidens,* "by accident," by which Albertus apparently meant under the distinctive conditions of his period. He gives three reasons for women's longer life expectancy: sexual intercourse is less demanding on women than on men; menstruation flushes impurities from women's bodies; and women "work less, and for that reason are not so much consumed." We can question what Albertus meant by the judgment that the demands of sexual intercourse or the purgative functions of menstruation were accidental, but his observation that the burdens of labor lowered men's natural life expectancies is worth remembering.

Subsequently, other medieval authors also concluded that women live longer than men. Some even occasionally pointed out that women must be the superior sex because they live longer and thus fulfill nature's intent better than males. Learned opinion shifted and the ancient belief in the greater life expectancy of males was slowly abandoned.

This change in scholarly attitudes corresponded with an actual improvement in life expectancies for women. From the opening centuries of the Christian Era, we have tens of thousands of funeral inscriptions, from visible standing monuments and from tombstones uncovered by archeologists' excavations. These epigraphs give age at death and allow a rough calculation of the duration of life according to sex. The evidence seems to confirm Aristotle's opinion that at their death, men in these populations of the late ancient era were four to seven years older than women. However, there may be a bias in the data; presumably, the young wife who died prematurely was more likely to earn a memorial than the aged and forgotten widow. But we are certain that women were in short supply in ancient society, either through systematic infanticide of girls or through shorter life expectancies. The biological experience of the women—or baby girls—of classical antiquity was not especially happy.

Unfortunately, we have no comparable epigraphic evidence from medieval populations. The earliest surviving relevant data are sporadic surveys made by the great European monasteries, which wanted clear records of the rents they could expect from their lands. We have between fifteen and twenty of these studies, dating from the ninth century on and enumerating populations settled on particular estates or manors. The largest census was taken by the monastery of Saint Germain-des-Prés in Paris and covers lands that are now mainly Parisian suburbs. Monasterial surveys of the early medieval world characteristically show more men than women, with ratios as high as 130 men per 100 women. Women continued to be in short supply.

Of course, the monasteries may have counted males more carefully. Still, much indirect evidence suggests that women were both few and highly valued in early medieval society. The barbarian legal codes, passed down orally and finally redacted between the fifth and ninth centuries as Christianity spread and introduced literacy, characteristically imposed a fine, usually called a *Wergeld*, on anyone who caused a person's injury or death. The fines protecting women were usually as high as, and sometimes higher than, those protecting men, and women of childbearing age sometimes enjoyed special value. Moreover, in marriage arrangements, the groom brought the dowry to the bride. The male or his family assumed the principal costs of setting up the new household. This reverse dowry suggests that grooms had to compete for relatively few brides.

About 965, an Arab geographer, Ibrahim ibn-Iakub, described Slavic marriage customs, which, in many respects, were typical of all barbarian Europe. Ibrahim reported that the "marital price" required of grooms was so high that "if a man has two or three daughters, they are as riches to him; if, however, boys are born to him, this becomes for him a cause of poverty." Nearly the same complaint would be widely heard again in Europe during the late Middle Ages (1350-1500), but the sexual references would be exactly reversed.

From the eleventh or twelfth century, the relative number of women in medieval society, and presumably their life expectancies, rose. A rough estimate of life expectancies for the urban and rural population of Pistoia in Italy in 1427 is 29.8 years for women; 28.4 years for men. The shift is most apparent among the high nobility and in the towns. In Bologna in 1395, there were only 95.6 men for every 100 women; in fifteenth-century Nuremberg, there were 83.8 men per 100 women. Even in cities where the sex ratio favored men—as in Florence in 1427—women grew more numerous in the progression up the scale of ages and held an absolute majority among the elderly. Although many older women may have migrated to the city, women probably also survived better under conditions of urban life.

There are several reasons for women's improving chances of survival during the central Middle Ages (1000-1350). The establishment of strong governments and a stable political order lowered the level and reduced the incidence of violence. New ideals of chivalry restricted—although they by no means completely ended—women's active participation in warfare as fighters or as victims. Women fare better under peaceful conditions, when they do not run the constant risk of attack, rape, or abduction. But the most decisive changes were economic. Primitive agricultural economies, with their low production levels, used predominantly the labor of women, children, and the aged. In a famous description written in A.D. 98, the Roman historian Tacitus observed that among the barbarian Germans, women and children maintained the household economy, while adult males gave themselves over to war and indolence. This pattern probably was preserved well into the Middle Ages. But intensive cultivation requires heavy field work, which women cannot readily perform; peasant women in the late Middle Ages worked hard on their farms, but they were no longer alone.

Finally, the new urban economy offered little employment for women. They spun at home, prayed in convents, and labored as household servants, but they did not constitute a significant part of the urban labor force. Families considered their daughters burdens, unable to earn their keep. Girls were also burdens to prospective husbands, and so the terms of marriage turned against women. The reverse dowry all but disappeared, and the girl or her family had to meet the principal costs of marriage. Throughout the late Middle Ages, the social position of women visibly deteriorated, but so also did the social demands and pressures laid upon them. For women, less participation in economic life and diminishing social importance meant better chances of biological survival.

The other principal biological events in women's lives, menarche and menopause, are difficult to examine historically. Medieval medical writers, who abounded from the eleventh century on, commonly placed menarche at between twelve and fifteen years of age and menopause at fifty. But we have no way of knowing whether they were recording their own observations or merely echoing the ancient authorities. Both Roman law and canon law of the medieval Church set the age of puberty and of binding marriage at twelve years for girls and fourteen years for boys. Saint Augustine, who lived from 354 to 430, contracted to marry a girl "two years below the marriageable age"; presumably, she was ten. "I liked her," he reports in his *Confessions,* "and was prepared to wait." He was then thirty years old. Had his conversion to celibacy not intervened, the girl would have been married at age twelve or soon after, to a groom twenty years older. The pattern seems typical of Roman marriages within the privileged orders.

The medieval canonical requirement that girls be at least twelve years old at the consummation of their marriage was a lower bound. There are many indications that girls at menarche were closer to age fifteen than to age twelve. In the law of the seventh-century Visigoths, a girl was not considered capable of bearing children until age fifteen. In a manorial survey of the early ninth century, from the church of Saint Victor of Marseilles, girls are called "marriageable" only from age fifteen. The customs of Anjou in 1246 similarly give age fifteen as the date of presumed maturity for women.

Still, the traditional estimate of age twelve for menarche was not entirely unrealistic. To judge from marriage patterns, which we can discern from the fourteenth and fifteenth centuries on, rich urban girls tended to be very young at first marriage—younger than those of lower social station and younger even than peasant women. Chaucer's wife of Bath, a middle-class, urban woman, was first married at age twelve, and many urban women were already mothers by age fifteen. Social factors were important here: the rich were apparently eager to settle the future of their daughters as early as possible. But the evidence also hints that menarche came sooner among rich women, and amenorrhea (abnormal absence or suppression of the menses) was presumably less common among them. In consequence, rich women in marriage tended to be consistently more prolific than the poor.

Some dietitians argue that girls must achieve a certain critical amount of body fat to trigger menarche and also to sustain menstruation. The better diet and ease of living that rich Roman girls and their medieval counterparts enjoyed gave them low ages of menarche, close to the thirteenth year anticipated in Roman and canon law. Girls in the countryside and among the poor classes were probably at menarche closer to age fifteen—the year most commonly encountered in the barbarian codes, manorial surveys, and customary laws. Perhaps these same groups also experienced relatively early menopause. The laws of the Visigoths assume that a woman would no longer be fertile after age forty. Apart from what we have gleaned from legal sources, we can say little with certainty about these principal events in the female life cycle.

To add flesh and features to our portrait of women, we can rapidly review the lives of three real people—a peasant, a queen, and a bourgeoise. Our peasant is a woman named Alpaix. She was eventually canonized in the late nineteenth century, and even during the Middle Ages, her sanctity was so well recognized that, unlike most peasant women, she attracted a biographer.

Alpaix was born about 1155 in a village near Sens in northern France. Her biographer says that her father, a poor man, "earned his bread by the sweat of his face," by laboriously tilling the soil. Alpaix was the eldest child with several younger brothers. From an early age, she had to assist her father in the heavy work of cultivating the fields. As he drove his two oxen at the head of the plow, she marched alongside, goading the animals to more strenuous effort. When so ordered, she carried manure and sheep dung on her slight shoulders to the fields and gardens. Her young frame could not easily bear the weight, and her father, who seems to have felt no particular sympathy for her, lashed the burdens to her back. Besides her other chores, she had to lead the cattle and sheep to pasture and guard them as they grazed.

All this she did willingly, even on Sundays and festivals, when other peasant girls gave themselves over to dancing and "frivolous things." But then, at the age of twelve, she could no longer sustain the charges laid upon her. According to her biographer, "the tender maiden could no longer bear such heavy labors. Rather, her entire insides were broken and torn from the magnitude of unrelieved work. Drawing deep sighs from the depths of her heart, with the color of her lovely face all marred, she finally gave external, visible signs of her internal suffering. What more can be said? Gripped by unyielding weakness, she remained for an entire year recumbent on her hard and bitter bed, made of straw, without mattress and sheets. . . ." Ugly lesions appeared on her skin, and her body exuded such a repulsive odor that her family isolated her in a hut. For her sustenance, they delivered black bread daily to her door. But because she could no longer contribute to the household, her brothers demanded that no food be wasted upon her. Their heartless proposal implies that the favorable social position of the peasant woman was indeed linked to her labors.

After a year of excruciating pain, Alpaix was visited in a vision by the Virgin Mary, who cured her of her sores and smell. But Alpaix never recovered the use of her limbs and remained bedridden the rest of her life. She took no food apart from Communion, and died in 1211. Before the eyes of this ignorant, invalid peasant girl, spectacular visions paraded; she was allowed to contemplate the splendid court of heaven and terrifying scenes of hell. Her powerful visions gave her a reputation for sanctity, and pilgrims began to find their way to her bedside. Eventually a biographer arrived and preserved for modern historians an account of a girl's hard childhood in the medieval countryside.

Our medieval queen was also acquainted with holiness; she is Blanche of Castile, mother of Louis IX, or Saint Louis, king of France. She was born on March 4, 1188, in Valencia, Spain, the third daughter of King Alphonso VII and the granddaughter, through her mother, of Eleanor of Aquitaine, who had been, in succession, queen of France and of England. Blanche was taken to France, where on May 23, 1200, not long after her twelfth birthday, she married the French heir apparent, who would later reign as Louis VIII (1223–1226). The marriage was not consummated until 1205, when Blanche was sixteen years old. The delay probably indicates, not her own retarded menarche, but the youth of her husband, only a few months older than she.

According to differing sources, Blanche's marriage, which ended when Louis died in 1226, gave her either eleven or twelve children. Blanche's deliveries included one set of twins, born dead in 1213. The spacing of her children suggests that Blanche initially tried to nurse her babies, although the king's disposition and his absences on royal business may also have affected the rhythms of her births. Thus, three and a half years elapsed between the birth of her second baby, Philip (born September 9, 1209), and her next delivery on January 26, 1213, when the dead twins were born. No period of nursing followed here, and her next child, the future Louis IX, was born only fifteen months later. Another lengthy interval of two and a half years followed until the next child, presumably because Louis was being nursed by his mother. Thereafter, births in rapid succession (five or six of them in the eight years from 1219 to 1227) suggest that Blanche—now maturing and occupied with children, household, and the affairs of state—no longer suckled her babies but instead relied on wet nurses. Several tracts on nursing have survived from the thirteenth century, and the assumption in all of them is that the nurse was not likely to be the child's mother.

Blanche's career illustrates the powerful position that women could still attain among Europe's high nobility in the thirteenth century. Of course, given the shortage of males, many noble girls did not marry. Most of those who remained single were forced into the religious life and all but excluded from lay society. A woman lucky enough to marry often did so very young, produced babies in rapid succession, did not nurse her own children, and was likely to be relieved of the risks and burdens of childbearing by her husband's early death. Women frequently figured prominently as administrators and regents for their often absent, or short-lived, husbands and sons. At this elevated social level, a widow with children was not likely to remarry; rather, she would dedicate herself to defending and advancing her children's interest.

Blanche herself was effectively regent of France during the minority of her son Louis (1226–1234), and regent again during his absence on the ill-fated Egyptian crusade (1252). She dominated her son and tyrannized her

daughter-in-law; she even tried to prevent the royal couple from chatting together before retiring for the night. Surviving her husband by twenty-eight
years, Blanche died at the age of sixty-four in November 1254.

The woman who for us perhaps best represents the medieval bourgeoise
is Alessandra, daughter of Bardo dei Bardi. She was born in Florence in 1414.
We know a good deal about her because a Florentine book dealer named
Vespasiano da Bisticci wrote the story of her life. His work, probably the oldest surviving biography of a European woman who was neither a princess
nor a saint, tells us, for example, that Alessandra grew to be the tallest young
woman in Florence, delighted ambassadors by her grace in promenading
and in dancing, learned to read, and could do excellent needlework. She was
engaged to be married at age fourteen, but for unknown reasons, the marriage was delayed until 1432, when she was eighteen years old. She was
close to the average age of first marriage (17.8 years) for Florentine women
in 1427. We can make refined estimates because in that year, a large census
was taken of the city. Alessandra's husband, Lorenzo, was the son of
Palla di Nofri dei Strozzi, who in 1427 was Florence's richest citizen. Then
twenty-seven years old, Lorenzo was young by Florentine standards. The average age of first marriage for males in 1427 was 29.9 years. As Lorenzo was
the first-born son in Palla's family, he was probably permitted to marry
somewhat earlier. His new wife quickly produced three children in four
years—an indication that she was not nursing her own babies.

Disasters then struck Alessandra's family. In 1434, her father, an opponent of the Medici family, was exiled. He was sixty-six years old at the time;
Alessandra was twenty. This long generational distance of forty-six years between father and child seems typical of Florentine households. Alessandra's
unmarried sisters, left without dowries, were desperate. "What will become
of us?" they protested to their departing father. "In whose care will you
leave us?" Amid the continuing tumult of Florentine politics, Alessandra's
husband, Lorenzo, was similarly exiled in 1438, freeing her, at the age of
twenty-four, of the risk of further pregnancies. In 1427, the average age
of mothers at the birth of their middle children was twenty-six, the fathers'
average age was forty.

Lorenzo eked out a living as a tutor in the town of Gubbio, but in 1451
he was assassinated by a disgruntled student. He was forty-six at the time.
Alessandra, now widowed, had to raise her children alone. Her biographer
presents her as a model of dedication and sober deportment for young widows, of whom there were many in Florentine society. He mentions one
other, Caterina degli Alberti, who was married at fifteen, bore two children
over the next twenty-three months, lost her husband, and remained a widow
for the following sixty years. Alessandra herself remained a widow for seventeen years, and died in 1468, at the age of fifty-four.

The bourgeois woman, like the lady of the landed nobility, was very
young at first marriage, and her groom was even older than among the nobles. She, too, bore her babies in rapid succession, did not herself nurse

them, and through the death of her older husband, was more likely than the noblewoman to be free of the dangers of continual pregnancies. As a child bride married to a mature man, she probably had little influence on her husband and his generation. But as a young mother destined to have intimate and usually extended contact with her children, she could be a respected and influential figure for the young. Married women occupied a strategic position. As intermediaries between the distant generations of fathers and their children, they could readily shape the tastes and values of the young and thus profoundly influence the culture of the city. And widowhood seems to have suited women well. In Florence in 1427, more than half the adult population of women were widows.

Both the biological and social experiences of women changed substantially during the long medieval centuries. In the overwhelmingly rural world of the early Middle Ages, women enjoyed a high social value and entered marriage under favorable terms. But the bases of their preferment seem to have been the taxing physical labor they performed and the substantial contribution they made to the peasant household. With the growth and transformation of the medieval economy—and in particular the rise of towns from the twelfth century on—women's participation in the domestic economy grew restricted. Daughters no longer made a father rich and the terms under which they entered marriage turned against them. But this partial exemption of women from hard labor conferred some benefits: "they work less," observed Albertus Magnus, "and for that reason are not so much consumed." Women in modern Western history still enjoy some of the advantages and bear some of the penalties bequeathed to them by medieval society. We have yet to see what will happen to these advantages and penalties, in our own, rapidly changing times.❖

RECOMMENDED READINGS

The broader picture of the development of medieval family life and structure is discussed in David Herlihy, *Medieval Households* (Cambridge: Harvard University Press, 1985). Vern Bullogh and Cameron Campbell present another suggestion as to why the life expectancy of women appears to have increased during the later Middle Ages in "Female Longevity and Diet in the Middle Ages," *Speculum* 55 (1980): 317–325. A woman's view of the world of the late Middle Ages is provided by the remarkable book of decorum by Christine de Pisan, *The Treasure of the City of Ladies; or, The Book of Three Virtues* (New York: Penguin Books, 1985).

CLOCKS

A REVOLUTION IN TIME

David Landes

The ability to measure time is an essential need of an organized society. Throughout history, various methods of meeting this need have been devised. Initially, sundials were employed as instruments of measurement; later, water clocks and fire clocks were developed. However, each of these solutions to the problem of accurately measuring time had distinct flaws. Finally, a revolutionary development took place in thirteenth-century Europe—the invention of the mechanical clock. After some early refinements, Western society was able, due to this discovery, to measure time precisely. Few discoveries have been as significant for European technology, culture, and society as the invention of the mechanical clock.

David Landes's article examines the profound social and economic effects of the mechanical clock on Western civilization. Landes gives particular attention to the effect of the mechanical clock on the emerging urban social order of the thirteenth and fourteenth centuries, whose need for well-defined working time was essential for profitable enterprise. He describes the measurement of time as primarily an urban concern and contrasts the nature and needs of lay time with those of church time.

An important feature of Landes's examination of the invention of the mechanical clock is his comparison of early European and Chinese time-keeping methods. Prior to the thirteenth century, the two civilizations possessed similar timekeeping capacities. The author offers an interesting and plausible explanation of the reasons for Europe's success in effecting the transition to a superior timekeeping technology while China's timekeeping methods regressed to simpler devices.

READING QUESTIONS

1. In what respects were the early mechanical clocks superior to water clocks?

2. What were the uses of the early Chinese clocks?

3. Why was the Christian Church interested in the accurate measurement of time?

4. What function did the mechanical clock perform in medieval towns?

5. What effect has the miniaturization of the mechanical clock had on private life?

hen in the late sixteenth century Portuguese traders and Christian missionaries sought entry into China, they were thwarted by a kind of permanent quarantine. Chinese officials correctly perceived these foreigners as potential subversives, bringing with them the threat of political interference, material seduction, and spiritual corruption. The ban was not lifted for decades, and then only because Matteo Ricci and his Jesuit mission brought with them knowledge and instruments that the Celestial Court coveted. In particular, they brought chiming clocks, which the Chinese received as a wondrous device. By the time Ricci, after numerous advances and retreats, finally secured permission from the court eunuchs and other officials to proceed to Peking and present himself to the throne, the emperor could hardly wait. 'Where', he called, 'are the self-ringing bells?' And later, when the dowager empress showed an interest in her son's favourite clock, the emperor had the bell disconnected so that she would be disappointed. He could not have refused to give it to her, had she asked for it; but neither would he give it up, so he found this devious way to reconcile filial piety with personal gratification.

The use of these clocks as a ticket of entry is evidence of the great advance European timekeeping had made over Chinese horology. It had not always been thus. The Chinese had always been much concerned to track the stars for astrological and horoscopic purposes. For the emperor, the conjunctions of the heavenly bodies were an indispensable guide to action, public and private—to making war and peace, to sowing and reaping, to conceiving an heir with the empress or coupling with a concubine. To facilitate the calculations required, court mechanicians of the Sung dynasty (tenth and eleventh centuries) built a series of remarkable clock-driven astraria, designed to track and display the apparent movements of the stars. The clock mechanism that drove the display was hydraulic—a water clock (clepsydra) linked to a bucket wheel. As each bucket filled, it activated a release mechanism that allowed the big drive wheel to turn and bring the next bucket into position. The water clock in itself was no more accurate than such devices can be; but in combination with the wheel, it could be adjusted

From David Landes, "Clocks: A Revolution in Time," *History Today,* January 1984, pp. 19–26.

to keep time within a minute or two a day. By way of comparison, the ordinary drip or flow water clocks then in use in Europe probably varied by a half-hour or more.

These astronomical clocks marked a culmination. The greatest of them, that built by Su Sung at the end of the eleventh century, was also the last of the series. When invasion and war forced the court to flee, the clock was lost and its secret as well. From this high point of achievement, Chinese timekeeping retrogressed to simpler, less accurate instruments, so that when the Jesuits arrived some five hundred years later with their mechanical clocks, they found only objects that confirmed their comfortable sense of technological, and by implication moral, superiority.

Meanwhile European timekeeping made a quantum leap by moving from hydraulic to mechanical devices. The new clocks, which took the form of weight-driven automated bells, made their appearance around 1280. We don't know where—England possibly, or Italy—and we don't know who invented them. What we do know is that the gain was immense and that the new clocks very rapidly swept the older clepsydras aside. Since these first mechanical clocks were notoriously inaccurate, varying an hour or more a day, and unreliable, breaking down frequently and needing major overhauls every few years, one can only infer that water clocks left even more to be desired. The great advantage of the mechanical clock lay in its relative immunity to temperature change, whereas the drip or flow of the water clock varied with the seasons while frost would halt it altogether (the temperature did not have to go down to freezing to increase viscosity and slow the rate). In the poorly heated buildings of northern Europe, especially at night, this was a near-fatal impairment. Dirt was another enemy. No water is pure, and deposits would gradually choke the narrow opening. The instructions for use of a thirteenth-century water clock installed in the Abbey of Villers (near Brussels) make it clear that no one expected much of these devices: the sacristan was to adjust it daily by the sun, as it fell on the abbey windows; and if the day was cloudy, why then it was automatically ten o'clock at the end of morning mass.

Why Europe should have succeeded in effecting this transition to a superior technology and China not is an important historical question. Anyone who looked at the horological world of the eleventh or twelfth century would have surely predicted the opposite result. (He would have also expected Islam to surpass Europe in this domain.) The Chinese failure—if failure is the right word—cannot be sought in material circumstances. The Chinese were as troubled and inconvenienced by the limitations of the water clock as were the Europeans; it can get very cold in Peking. (The Chinese tried substituting mercury or sand for water, but mercury kills and neither behaves very well over time.) Instead the explanation must be sought in the character and purposes of Chinese timekeeping. It was, in its higher forms, a monopoly of the imperial court, as much an attribute of sovereignty as the right to coin money. In this instance, dominion over time and calendar was a major aspect of power, for it laid the cognitive foundation for imperial decisions in every area of political and economic life. So much was this the case that each emperor began by proclaiming his own calendar, often different from that of his predecessor; by so doing, he affirmed his legitimacy and identity.

Timekeeping instruments were therefore reserved to the court and certain of its officials; there was no civilian clock trade. Such great astronomical clocks as were built for the throne were undertaken as special projects, the work of a team assembled for the occasion. Each of these machines was a *tour de force,* and each built on earlier models, researched in the archives by way of preparation. There was, then, no continuous process of construction and emendation; no multiplicity of private initiatives; no dynamic of continuing improvement. Instead we have these occasional peak moments of achievement, highly fragile, vulnerable to political hostility and adventitious violence, easily buried and forgotten once the team of builders had dissolved or died.

Outside these rarefied circles, the Chinese people had little interest in time measurement for its own sake. Most of them were peasants, and peasants have no need of clocks. They wake with the animals in the morning, watch the shadows shorten and lengthen as the sun crosses the sky, and go to bed once night falls—because they are tired, illumination is costly and they must get up very early. They are not unaware of the passage of time, but they do not have to measure it. Time measurement is an urban concern, and in medieval China the authorities provided time signals (drums, trumpets) in the cities to mark the passage of the hours and warn the residents of such things as the closing of the gates to the separate quarters or neighbourhoods. But such noises could not easily be used to order the daily round of activities, for the Chinese did not number the hours sequentially; rather they named them, so that auditory signals transmitted limited information. Such as they were, they sufficed, for the organisation of work created no need for closer or continuous timing. The typical work unit was the household shop, comprising master, assistants, and apprentices. The day started at dawn, when the youngest or newest apprentice woke to make the fire and wake the rest; and work continued until night imposed its interruption. This mode of production set no artificial *clocktime* limited to labour; nature fixed the bounds.

In contrast, medieval Europe did have a constituency concerned to track and use time. This was the Christian church, especially those monastic orders that followed the rule of Benedict. This rule, which was defined in the sixth century, became over time the standard of monachal discipline in western Europe. The aim of the rule was to ensure that the entire day be ordered and devoted to the service of God—to pray above all, but also to work, which was defined as another kind of prayer. The daily prayer offices numbered seven (later eight), six (later seven) in the daytime and one at night. The institution of a nocturnal office was peculiar to Christianity and sharply differentiated it from the other monotheistic religions. It went back to the prayer vigils conducted by the earliest Christians in imminent expectation of the *parousia,* or second coming. It was these vigils that were later merged with the morning prayer to constitute the canonical hour known as matins.

The obligation to rise to prayer in the dark imposed a special condition on Christian worship. Whereas Jews (and later Muslims) set their times of prayer by natural events (morning, afternoon, and evening) that do not require the use of an artificial timekeeper, Christians needed some kind of alarm to wake to matins. In the cities of the Roman empire, the night watch could give the signal. In medieval Europe such municipal services had long disappeared, and most abbeys were located in rural areas. Each house, then, had to find its own way to satisfy the requirement, usually by means of an alarm device linked to a water clock. This would rouse the waker, usually the sacristan, who would then ring the bells that called the others to prayer. Most house rules—for although the principle was general, there was little uniformity in the details of practice—enjoined the sacristan to be scrupulous in his performance of this duty, for his neglect imperilled the salvation of his brethren (and the larger church) as well as his own. 'Nothing, therefore, shall be put before the Divine Office', says the Rule.

To the ordinary monk, getting up in the dark of the night was perhaps the hardest aspect of monastic discipline. Indeed the practical meaning of 'reforming' a house meant first and foremost the imposition (reimposition) of this duty. The sleepyheads were prodded out of bed and urged to the offices; they were also prodded during service lest they fail in their obligations. Where the flesh was weak, temptation lurked. Raoul Glaber (early eleventh century) tells the tale of a demon who successfully seduced a monk by holding the lure of sweet sleep:

> As for you, I wonder why you so scrupulously jump out of bed as soon as you hear the bell, when you could stay resting even unto the third bell . . . but know that every year Christ empties hell of sinners and brings them to heaven, so without worry you can give yourself to all the voluptuousness of the flesh . . .

The same Glaber confesses to two occasions when he himself woke late and saw a demon, 'come to do business with the laggards'. And Peter the Venerable, Abbot of Cluny in the twelfth century, tells the story of Brother Alger, who woke thinking he had heard the bell ring for nocturns. Looking around, he thought he saw the other beds empty, so he drew on his sandals, threw on his cloak, and hastened to the chapel. There he was puzzled not to hear the sound of voices lifted in prayer. Now he hurried back to the dormitory, where he found all the other monks fast asleep. And then he understood: this was all a temptation of the devil, who had awakened him at the wrong time, so that when the bell for nocturns really rang, he would sleep through it.

These, I suggest, are what we now know as anxiety dreams. They clearly reflect the degree to which time-consciousness and discipline had become internalised. Missing matins was a serious matter, so serious that it has been immortalised for us by perhaps the best known of children's songs:

> Frère Jacques, Frère Jacques,
> Dormez-vous? dormez-vous?
> Sonnez les matines, sonnez les matines,
> Ding, dang, dong; ding, dang, dong.

We know far less than we should like about monastic horology in the Middle Ages, and such information as we have is confused by the use of the general term *(h)orologium* for any and all kinds of timekeeper. It seems clear, however, that the century or two preceding the appearance of the mechanical clock saw important improvements in technique and a growing emphasis on the details of the monastic time service. The enhanced temporal consciousness may be related to the revival of monastic life after the millennium and in particular to the needs of the Cistercian order—that economic empire with its agricultural, mining, and industrial enterprises, its ever-turning water wheels, its large labour force of lay brethren, its place in the forefront of European technology.

One of the innovations of this period seems to have been the combination clepsydra/mechanical alarm. This worked as follows: when the water in the recipient vessel reached an appropriate height, it tripped a weight-driven escape wheel, so called because it meshed with pallets that alternately blocked and released it (allowed it to escape). This stop-go motion in turn imparted a to-and-fro oscillation to the rod or *verge* holding the pallets; hence the name *verge escapement.* Attach a small hammer to the end of the verge, and it could ring a bell. Put an oscillating cross bar on the end, and you had a controller for a clock.

The first clocks were probably alarms converted in this manner. The very name *clock* meant bell, and these were essentially machines to sound the passing hours. Their use entailed a drastic change in the character of European timekeeping. Because the mechanical clock beat at a more or less uniform rate, it sounded equal-length hours—what later came to be known as mean (average) time. But the standard of medieval Europe was the sun, and the hours were natural, equal fractions of the day and night. Thus as days got longer, daylight hours lengthened and night hours shrank; and vice versa. These seasonally variable hours (often called temporal hours) were easily measured by the water clock; all one had to do was change the scale with the seasons. But an automated bell was another story: changing the times of ringing to take account of changing hours would have been a difficult and time-consuming task. So Europeans learned a new time standard in which the sun rose and set at different hours as the days passed. This seems natural enough to us, but it must have come as a shock at first. (Some places chose to start their day at sunrise, which took care of one end of the problem, though not the other.)

In effect the new clock offered a rival time standard in competition with the older church time. It was not only the hours that differed; it was the signals also. The old water clocks did not sound public, tower bells. They told the time for the bell ringer, who usually rang, not the unequal, temporal hours, but the hours of prayer, the so-called canonical hours. These were not equally spaced and did not lend themselves to the kind of calculation we take for granted: how long since? how long until? It was equal hours that made this possible and thereby contributed significantly to the growing numeracy of the urban population. Insofar as the medieval church resisted the new time standard, it gave over an important symbol of authority to the secular power. Where once people punctuated their day by such marks as sext, none, and vespers, now they thought in terms of hours and, very soon, minutes.

The transition from church time to lay time was at once sign and consequence of the rise of a new, urban social order. The new machines appealed from the start to the rich and powerful, who made them the preferred object of conspicuous consumption. No court, no prince could be without one. But far more important in the long run was the rapid acceptance of the new instrument in cities and towns, which had long learned to regulate many aspects of civil life by bells—bells to signal the opening and closing of markets, waking bells and work bells, drinking and curfew bells, bells for opening and closing of gates, assembly and alarms. In this regard, the medieval city was a secular version of the cloister, prepared by habit and need to use the clock as a superior instrument of time discipline and management.

The pressure for time signals was especially strong in those cities that were engaged in textile manufacture—the first and greatest of medieval industries. There the definition of working time was crucial to the profitability of enterprise and the prosperity of the commune. The textile industry was the first to go over to large-scale production for export, hence the first to overflow the traditional workshop and engage a dispersed work force. Some of these workers—the *ciompi* in Florence, the 'blue nails' (stained by dye) in Flanders—were true proletarians, owning none of the instruments of production, selling only their labour power. They streamed early every morning into the dye shops and fulling mills, where the high consumption of energy for heating the vats and driving the hammers encouraged concentration in large units. Other branches of the manufacture could be conducted in the rooms and cottages of the workers: employers liked this so-called putting-out because it shifted much of the burden of overhead costs to the employee, who was paid by the piece rather than by time; and the workers preferred it to the time discipline and supervision of the large shops. They could in principle start and stop work at will, for who was to tell them what to do in their own home?

The bells would tell them. Where there was textile manufacture, there were work bells, which inevitably gave rise to conflict. Part of the problem was implicit in the effort to impose time discipline on home workers. In principle, payment by the piece should have taken care of the matter, with workers responding to wage incentives. In fact, the home workers were content to earn what they felt they needed, and in time of keen demand, employers found it impossible to get them to do more, for higher pay only reduced the amount of work required to satisfy these needs. The effort to bring the constraints of the manufactory into the rooms and cottages of spinners and weavers made the very use of bells a focus of resentment.

Meanwhile in the fulling mills and dyeshops the bells posed a different kind of problem, especially when they were controlled by the employer. Consider the nature of the wage contract: the worker was paid by the day, and the day was bounded by these time signals. The employer had an interest in getting a full day's work for the wages he paid; and the worker in giving no more time than he was paid for. The question inevitably arose how the worker could know whether bell time was honest time. How could he trust even the municipal bells when the town council was dominated by representatives of the employers?

Under the circumstances, workers in some places sought to silence the *werkclocke:* at Therouanne in 1367 the dean and chapter promised 'workers, fullers, and other mechanics' to silence 'forever the workers' bell in order that no scandal or conflict be born in the city and church as a result of the ringing of a bell of this type'. Such efforts to eliminate time signals never achieved success: as soon suppress the system of wage labour. Besides, once the work day was defined in temporal rather than natural terms, workers as well as employers had an interest in defining and somehow signalling the boundaries. Time measurement here was a two-edged sword: it gave the employer bounds to fill, and to the worker bounds to work. The alternative was the open-ended working day, as Chrétien de Troyes observed of the silk weavers of Lyons in the twelfth century:

> . . . nous sommes en grand'misère,
> Mais s'enrichit de nos salaires
> Celui pour qui nous travaillons.
> Des nuits grand partie nous veillons
> Et tout le jour pour y gagner

> . . . we are in great misery,
> The man who gets rich on our wages
> Is the man we work for.
> We're up a good part of the night
> And work all day to make our way . . .

It was not the work bells as such, then, that were resented and mis-trusted, but the people who controlled them; and it is here that the chiming tower clock made its greatest contribution. It kept equal hours and provided regular signals, at first on the hour, later on at the halves or quarters, and these necessarily limited the opportunities for abuse. With the appearance of the dial (from the word for day), of course, it was possible for all inter-ested parties to verify the time on a continuous basis.

The early turret clocks were very expensive, even when simple. Wrought iron and brass needed repeated hammering, hence much labour and much fuel. The casting of the bells was a precarious operation. The placement of the mechanism usually entailed major structural alterations. The construction and installation of a tower clock might take months if not years. Teams of craftsmen and labourers had to be assembled on the site and there lodged and boarded. Subsequent maintenance required the attendance of a resident technician, repeated visits by specialised artists, and an endless flow of replacement parts.

These costs increased substantially as soon as one went beyond simple timekeepers to astronomical clocks and/or automata. The medieval accounts show this process clearly: the sums paid to painters and wood-carvers bear witness to the growing importance of the clock as spectacle as well as time signal. The hourly parade of saints and patriarchs; the ponderous strokes of the hammer-wielding *jaquemarts;* the angel turning with the sun; the rooster crowing at sunrise; the lunar disc waxing and waning with the moon—and all these movements and sounds offered lessons in theology and astronomy to the up-gazing multitude that gathered to watch and wonder at what man had wrought. The hourly pageant was an imitation of divine cre-ation; the mechanism, a miniaturisation of heaven and earth. As a result, the show clock was to the new secular, urbanising world of the later Middle Ages what the cathedrals had been to the still worshipful world of the high Middle Ages: a combination of a sacrifice and affirmation, the embodiment of the highest skills and artistry, a symbol of prowess and source of pride. It was also a source of income—the lay analogue to the religious relics that were so potent an attraction to medieval travellers. When Philip the Bold of Burgundy defeated the Flemish burghers at Rosebecke in 1382 and wanted to punish those proud and troublesome clothiers, he could do no worse (or better) than seize the belfry clock at Courtrai and take it off to his capital at Dijon.

These public clocks, moreover, were only the top of the market. They are the ones that history knows best, but we know only a fraction of what was made. In this regard, the records are misleading: they have preserved the memory of a spotty, biased selection and largely omitted the smaller do-mestic clocks made to private order. As a result, it was long thought that the first mechanical clocks were turret clocks, and that the smaller domestic models were the much later product of advances in miniaturisation. Yet there was no technical impediment to making chamber clocks once the verge escapement had been invented. Indeed, since the mechanical clock is a development of the timer alarm, itself made to chamber size, small may well have preceded big.

Whichever came first, the one logically implied the other, so that we may fairly assume that both types of clock were known and made from the start. In the event, the first literary allusion to a mechanical clock refers to domestic timepieces. This goes back to the late thirteenth century, in Jean de Meung's additional verse to *Le roman de la rose*. Jean, a romantic poet of curiously worldly interest, attributes to his Pygmalion a fair array of chamber clocks:

> Et puis faire sonner ses orloges
> Par ses salles et par ses loges
> A roues trop subtillement
> De pardurable mouvement.

> And then through halls and chambers
> Made his clock chime
> By wheels of such cunning
> Ever turning through time.

By the end of the fourteenth century, hundreds of clocks were turning in western Europe. A new profession of horologers had emerged, competing for custom and seeking severally to improve their product. There could be no surer guarantee of cumulative technical advance. Few inventions in history have ever made their way with such ease. Everyone seems to have welcomed the clock, even those workers who toiled to its rules, for they much preferred it to arbitrary bells. *Summe necessarium pro omni statu hominum* was the way Galvano Fiamma, chronicler of Milan, put it when he proudly marked the erection in 1333 (?) of a clock that not only struck the hours but signalled each one by the number of peals. And this in turn recalls an earlier inscription on a clock installed in 1314 on the bridge at Caen:

> Je ferai les heures ouir
> Pour le commun peuple rejouir.

> I shall give the hours voice
> To make the common folk rejoice.

Even the poets liked the new clocks. That is the most astonishing aspect of these early years of mechanical horology, for no group is by instinct and sensibility so suspicious of technical innovation. Here, moreover, was an invention that carried with it the seeds of control, order, self-restraint—all virtues (or vices) inimical to the free, spontaneous imagination and contemplation so prized by creative artists. Yet it would be anachronistic to impute these ideals to the thirteenth and fourteenth centuries; they came much later. The medieval ideal was one of sobriety and control, along with due respect for worthy models. Besides, it was surely too soon to understand the potential of the new device for forming the persona as well as dictating the terms of life and work. Instead, the availability of this new knowledge gave all a sense of power, of enhanced efficiency and potential, of owner-ship of a new and valuable asset, whereas we, living by the clock, see igno-rance of or indifference to time as a release from constraint and a gain in freedom. Everything depends, I suppose, on where one is coming from. In any event, the early celebrators of the clock were no mere poetasters: thus Dante Alighieri, who sang in his *Paradise* (Canto X) the praises of the 'glori-ous wheel' moving and returning 'voice to voice in timbre and sweetness'— *tin tin sonando con si dolce nota* (almost surely a reference to a chamber clock, unless Dante had a tin ear), therein echoing the pleasure that Jean De Meung's Pygmalion took in his chiming clocks a generation earlier. And a half-century later we have Jean Froissart, poet but more famous as his-torian, composer of 'love ditties', among them *L'horloge amoureuse* (1369):

. . . The clock is, when you think about it,
A very beautiful and remarkable instrument,
And it's also pleasant and useful,
Because night and day it tells us the hours
By the subtlety of its mechanism
Even when there is no sun.
Hence all the more reason to prize one's machine,
Because other instruments can't do this
However artfully and precisely they may be made
Hence do we hold him for valiant and wise
Who first invented this device
And with his knowledge undertook and made
A thing so noble and of such great pride.

The invention and diffusion of the mechanical clock had momentous consequences for European technology, culture, and society—comparable in their significance to the effects of the later invention of movable type and printing. For one thing, the clock could be miniaturised and, once small enough, moved about. For this, a new power source was needed, which took the form of a coiled spring, releasing energy as it unwound. This came in during the fifteenth century and gave rise to a new generation of small do-mestic clocks and, by the early sixteenth, to the watch, that is, a clock small enough to be worn on the person. Domestic clocks and, even more, the watch were the basis of the private, internalised time discipline that charac-terises modern personality and civilisation—for better or worse. Without this discipline, we could not operate the numerous and complex activities required to make our society go. (We could, no doubt, have recourse to public signals, as in the army. But that would mean a very different kind of collectivity).

For another thing, the mechanical clock was susceptible of great improvement in accuracy, even in its smaller form. This potential lay in its revolutionary principle of time measurement. Whereas earlier instruments had relied on some continuous movement—of shadow (the sundial) or fluid (the clepsydra)—to track the passage of time, the mechanical clock marked time by means of an oscillating controller. This took the form of a bar or wheel swinging to and fro. The swings (pulses or beats) could then be counted and converted to time units—hours, minutes, and eventually subminutes. To the ancients who invented the sundial and water clock, a continuous controller on what we would now call the analogue principle seemed only logical, for it was an imitation of time itself, always passing. But in the long run, its possibilities for improvement were limited not only by the inherent flaws of sunlight (no use at night or in cloudy weather) and flowing liquids, but by the difficulty of sustaining an even, continuously moving display. Time measurement by beats or pulses, on the other hand—the digital principle—had no bounds of accuracy. All that was needed was an even, countable frequency. The oscillating controller of the first medieval clocks usually beat double-seconds. Frequency was decidedly uneven, hence the large variation in rate. It took almost four hundred years to invent a vastly superior controller in the form of the pendulum, which in its seconds-beating form could keep time within less than a minute a day. Today, of course, new controllers have been invented in the form of vibrating quartz crystals (hundreds of thousands or even millions of beats per second), which vary less than a minute a year; and atomic resonators (billions of vibrations per second), which take thousands of years to gain or lose a second. These gains in precision have been an important impetus to scientific inquiry; indeed, almost all of them came about because scientists needed better timekeeping instruments. How else to study process and rates of changes?

Finally, the clock with its regularity came to stand as the model for all other machines—the machine of machines, the essence of man's best work in the image of God; and clockmaking became the school for all other mechanical arts. No one has said it better than Lewis Mumford in *Technics and Civilization:*

> The clock, not the steam engine, is the key-machine of the modern industrial age . . . In its relationship to determinable quantities of energy, to standardization, to automatic action, and finally to its own special product, accurate timing, the clock has been the foremost machine in modern technics; and at each period it has remained in the lead: it marks a perfection toward which other machines aspire.

All of this was there in germ in the oscillating controllers of the first mechanical clocks. The builders of those clocks did not know what they had wrought. That the clock was invented in Europe and remained a European monopoly for some five hundred years, and that Europe then built a civilisation organised around the measurement of time;—these were critical factors in the differentiation of West from Rest and the definition of modernity.❖

RECOMMENDED READINGS

For further information on the history of clocks, see David S. Landes, *Revolution in Time: Clocks and the Making of the Modern World* (Cambridge: Harvard University Press, 1984); Ernest von Bassermann-Jordan, *The Book of Old Clocks and Watches,* 4th ed., rev. Hans von Bertele (New York: Crown, 1964); Eric Bruton, *The History of Clocks and Watches* (New York: Rizzoli, 1979); Carlo Cipolla, *Clocks and Culture, 1300-1700* (New York: Walker, 1967); Jacques Le Goff, *Time, Work, and Culture in the Middle Ages* (Chicago: University of Chicago Press, 1980); Lewis Mumford, *Technics and Civilization* (New York: Harcourt Brace Jovanovich, 1934); Joseph Needham, Wang Ling, and Derek J. de Solla Price, *Heavenly Clockwork: The Great Astronomical Clocks of Medieval China* (New York: Cambridge University Press, 1960).

Western Europe, About A.D. 1300

THE MEDIEVAL TOURNAMENT

Richard Barber

As time passed, the feudal nobles of western Europe began to lose their political and military functions to mercenaries, archers, and royal bureaucrats. Life became steadily more structured, with less and less scope for the skills of the heavily armored mounted warrior. As these people lost their primary functions in society, they began to seek other justifications for their position and privileges. In time, the feudal aristocracy evolved into the chivalric nobility.

The beginnings of this change are discussed in the selection entitled "The Life of the Nobility" by Marc Bloch, who directs his attention primarily to the growth of the troubadour tradition. In the following selection, Richard Barber traces the same evolution through the medium of the tournament, one of the most romanticized aspects of medieval life. The transformation of the feudal aristocracy into a hereditary nobility was reflected in the elaboration of the tournament from the rough-and-ready brawls of the twelfth century into the ritualized and structured pageants of the fifteenth and sixteenth centuries.

Barber provides the details of that development and demonstrates how the constant elaboration of the equipment, tactics, and format of the tournament finally destroyed it as a sport. It is interesting to note that the popular concept of the medieval knight—his manners, armor, weapons, horse, and traditions—is based on the artificial figure of the tournament competitor rather than on the actual warriors of the period.

READING QUESTIONS

1. When and in what form did the tournament originate?

2. How and why were tournament rules developed?

3. How did the objectives of the participants in tournaments change over time?

For all his involvement with higher ideals, the knight remained first and foremost a warrior; and he acquired his skill in arms in two ways: in real warfare, and in practice in arms off the battlefield. Training for war has existed since time immemorial; but when the conduct of war plays so important a part in society as in Europe in the tenth century, such training comes to occupy a quite exceptional place. In the absence of a central organisation with the means to supervise such training, it developed a formal outline of its own: the tournament. Although this brought together the most enjoyable elements of war, its pomp, its camaraderie, its delight in the display of physical skill, all tournaments retained a strong element of practice in arms until the status of the knight in war proper began to decline, and they lacked sufficient impetus of their own to survive as anything more than a pageant once their relevance to real war had disappeared. Yet tournaments must be firmly classified as sport, despite their military and political overtones, in that they very quickly became an end in themselves: although spectators of all classes were present at tournaments, they were primarily for the enjoyment of the participants. The ancient world had known nothing like them; for although tournaments resemble circuses in their exploitation of physical skill and courage for entertainment, and in their military overtones, the social stigma attached to appearance in the arena, whatever the circumstances, was very strong.

Perhaps the greatest difference between the tournament and the circus was that the former stemmed from a primitive element in social life, and not from the theatrical inventions of civilisation. Indeed, the very nature of the tournament's origins meant that its decline could not be avoided once it became the place for peacock vanities rather than strong arms and stout hearts. It harks back to the military games which Tacitus describes among the German tribes, but the exact development of these into mock warfare remains uncharted. We can catch a glimpse of Frankish games on horseback, a kind of competition in horsemanship which reappears later as the *buhurt*, a sport associated with and sometimes confused with the tournament, in which similar manœuvres, and occasionally very light armour and weapons, were used. But even the historians of the later Middle Ages, though much closer in time to the beginnings of the tournament, knew very little about it indeed. They could only produce, for the edification of their noble readers, descriptions of fictitious tournaments in the style of their own times, and the most arduous sifting of their fictions

From Richard Barber, *The Knight and Chivalry* (New York: Harper & Row, 1974), pp. 153–157, 162–170.

leaves nothing tangible whatsoever, save a clear *terminus ante quem:* the tournament did not come into being before the middle of the tenth century. Even the ambitious Georg Ruexner only takes us back to the year 938 for his first tournament, though his *Tournament Book; which is to say a true real and brief description of the beginnings, causes, origins, and derivations of the Tournament in the Holy Roman Empire . . .* provides us with a circumstantial list of those who took part in nine elaborate festivals in German towns before the year 1100, giving their shields and their varying fortunes in the lists. Yet if Ruexner, writing in the sixteenth century to curry favour with the Emperor Maximilian, is an extreme example, the myths had nonetheless begun to be woven in the thirteenth century, when the vogue first began, with the insertion of bald and apparently factual entries into older chronicles, which appear to record jousts under the Frankish kings Clovis and Pepin. Even the junketings attributed to Charlemagne's sons are part of these fancies.

After which it may be rather hard to accept the entry of a sober monkish chronicler of St Martin at Tours, under the year 1062, to the effect that one Godfrey of Preuilly was killed in a tournament in that year, a sport of which he had framed the rules. But at this point that myth conceals a certain degree of probability. It cannot have been much later than this period that these military games were formalised into a specific framework. That this took place in France is supported by the early name of such events: *conflictus Gallicus.* There is no means of saying whether Godfrey of Preuilly was responsible for this development. His name is merely the head of an ever-increasing roll of tourneyers who come to our notice after this date. By the beginning of the twelfth century there can have been few knights who did not know what a tournament implied. A charter of Henry I's reign provides that a vassal shall carry his lord's 'coloured lances' to London both for war 'and when I want to go overseas for tournaments'. As the opportunities for, and plunder from, private baronial warfare diminished, so the tournament grew in popularity.

The first great tournament of which we have reliable record is that held at Würzburg in 1127, described briefly by Otto of Freising and even this seems to have been more a military review than what we would now call a tournament. Although prohibitions on the tournament were supposedly issued by William and Henry I, it was not until the troubled times of Stephen's reign that the tournament first reached England; the king himself was reputed to be an enthusiastic participant. By 1130, there was sufficient following for this unchristian sport for Innocent II to be moved to prohibit it at the Council of Clermont, preaching that crusades were a better means of employing knightly exuberance than these wantonly fatal affairs. The theme was to be repeated many times: at the second and third Lateran Councils in 1139 and 1179, and by Eugenius III in 1148 at the Synod of Rheims; but the 'repugnant markets and festivals at which knights are wont to assemble by agreement and to fight together to prove their rashness and strength, which often leads to death and corruption of the soul', continued unabated. Knights who died in a tournament were permitted the last sacrament and extreme unction, but not church burial. In 1163, even the Archbishop of Rheims, with Thomas Becket's support, was unable to beg an exemption from this edict. Very often an automatic excommunication was in force for all the combatants as well. Despite these measures, the tournament was practised by the crusaders themselves, the first example being at Antioch in 1156, and at about the same time it appeared in Italy.

The new sport was thus well established by the third decade of the twelfth century; and with good reason. It provided an outlet for the exercise of knightly prowess which could no longer be expended in the old way in a society that was becoming more orderly and subject to restraints. The knight still occupied the position and maintained the attitudes that the previous centuries had given him; his very nature was conservative. But the last Viking raids were long past; the crusades were an alternative for the very dedicated, the very rich or the very pious; and large-scale warfare was rare. Since the whole outlook of the conservative knightly class was warlike, alternatives to full-scale war were vital as an outlet for their energies. Private war was certainly not uncommon, but with the increasing weight of central authority, both royal and papal, against it, only a very determined or very powerful baron could hope to wage it with success. Hence the arrival of the tournament was opportune, although neither pope nor king welcomed the armed gatherings; it seemed only to be the familiar devil of civil war in another guise, and their ideal remained a peace uninterrupted by either baronial revolts or baronial tournaments. But the knights' enthusiasm was already too great, and the powers that be had to extend a grudging toleration to the new sport. This is not to say that kings themselves disliked tournaments; the reverse was more often the case, because they were in many senses the first knights of their realms. When royal policy was concerned, the king as statesman was obliged to frown on tournaments as a possible source of disturbances; the king as knight more often than not took part, and enthusiasm easily overcame statesmanship.

The rise of the tournaments coincided with a number of other developments in the mediaeval world; most notably and closely with the emergence of a new literary culture. The first great works in everyday language are more or less contemporary with the establishment of the tournament as an international sport, and the trouvères or troubadours were essential to its greatness and to the fame which participants so eagerly sought. No monastic scholar writing in Latin was going to record such vain events, except as examples of devilish temptation to be shunned by God-fearing men who abhorred loose living (which filled an otherwise uneventful year in their records very nicely): or, more usually, as incidents in a political conflict, for when the knights of two hostile lords met in the lists, the tournament could—and often did—become a war in miniature.

Because the new literature only began to flourish about 1150, we glean little about the tournaments before that date, except for the vague indications of their growth in popularity already mentioned. Other traces come from later writers; unless mere monkish ignorance of worldly affairs explains Matthew Paris' description in the 1220s of a tournament as being fought in 'linen armour' (meaning perhaps a kind of padded overgarment), he may be thinking either of an earlier form of the sport or some kind of practice jousts.

The tournament was essentially two teams of knights, fighting under certain conditions, including a prescribed time limit (of part of one day) and prescribed weapons (either of war or with blunted points). From the very first, rules to prevent foul or dangerous blows were enforced, for the object was at least in theory friendly, even in the miniature war of the tournaments *à outrance.* Such rules must at first have been relatively simple, covering only the points of aim and means of holding a lance. But judges do not appear in early accounts; and if someone struck a foul blow, it is hard to see how redress was to be obtained. Only the rudimentary formal elements in a tournament distinguished it from a mere brawl; and the tone in which the Church thundered against them in the early days implies that mere brawls were often the result. There were no individual jousts; the contest was a *mêlée,* in which all the combatants took part; as a result, it was not uncommon for four or five knights to attack one, and the fighting was much rougher and cruder. Finally, the term 'lists' in the early tournaments did not imply an enclosure; until well into the next century it meant the barriers erected round the refuges, where a knight could retreat to rest or to repair his armour. The fighting might range over a wide area as a result and no set boundaries seem to have been arranged. If there were limits to the area of the contest, they were either very wide indeed—several square miles—or frequently ignored.

Until well into the thirteenth century, the tournament remained in practice, if not in theory, a miniature war. With no boundaries and no referees or judges, all sorts of outrages might occur, since the only tribunal was the general consensus of the participants; only later did the heralds responsible for announcing the tournament and organising the time and place have any effective say in the control of the actual fighting. Prizes were awarded by consensus of either the knights or spectators; but otherwise only those arrangements which had an obvious mutual benefit were generally adhered to, such as the refuges and the rules about foul blows and weapons. The latter were limited to sword and lance; but other weapons were sometimes introduced, as the Monk of Montaudon tells us at the end of the twelfth century, when in the list of the things he hates to see in the world he includes 'darts and quarrels [crossbow bolts] in tournaments'. Specific matters about which prior rulings had been made could also be enforced, such as the amount payable for ransoms. However, the word of honour did count for something, and agreements over surrender, although made in the heat of battle, were generally honoured, even if the defeated knight was usually handed over to the keeping of a reliable and sturdy squire.

The first signs of control appear in 1194, when Richard I licensed tournaments in England. Most of his restrictions were political, but in the stipulation that the earls of Salisbury, Clare and Warenne—three names which recur throughout the roll-calls of English tournaments—should act as general controllers and licencers of tournaments, the germ of a more formal attitude to the sport is present. Furthermore, each separate tournament was to be attended by two knights and two clerks, who were to administer an oath to keep the peace and not to pursue feuds in the lists, and also to collect the royal taxes imposed on those who took part.

About the same time there came about a decline in the system of patronage and retinues which figures so prominently in the tournaments of William Marshal's day. The retinues remained, but in much diminished form; even allowing for the usual exaggeration on the chronicler's part, the essence of William Marshal's tournaments was the large number of participants. By the middle of the thirteenth century the numbers indicated are in the region of 100 a side, and as the years pass so this number decreases. At the same time, jousts are first recorded. These may have started as a reaction against the chance and brute force which decided the fortunes of the *mêlée*. Fighting man to man, skill was all that counted, and the joust had the added advantage of being the only way of settling an argument as to which of two knights was the better.

As a result, by 1225 the lists had become much more civilised. Skill becomes much more important than mere endurance. Instead of William Marshal and his friends trampling over the vineyards and indulging in a cheerful but crude free-for-all, we have the faintly fantastical figure of Ulrich von Lichtenstein. The tournament for Ulrich was essentially part of the apparatus of courtly love, another reason for seeking individual glory. A great lord with a well-organised retinue was the real victor and hero of the old-style tournament, even if individuals had their share of the plaudits. But in fighting for one's lady's honour, the individual combat was essential.

Ulrich's great series of jousts in Italy, Austria and Bohemia in 1227 marks the first emergence of this form into prominence. At the same time it is the first transformation of the tournament by alien ideals, in that the show of gallantry is as important as the display of skill. Ulrich's narrative of his adventures is circumstantial, though he does stray into romance at intervals. It is often difficult to distinguish truth and fiction in his story; for instance, when he says that he went dressed as Frau Venus in honour of his lady, this might well be a figure of speech; but he goes on to describe the issue of a challenge to the knights of northern Italy and Austria, specifically mentioning this costume, and his stay incognito in Venice during the previous winter while he had the costume prepared. The terms of the challenge were that each comer who broke three spears with him was to receive a gold ring; if defeated, the challenger was to bow to the four corners of the earth in honour of Ulrich's lady, while if Ulrich was beaten, the victor was to take all his horses. The itinerary was carefully specified so that knights could find him easily, and ended in a great tournament at Klosterneuberg. If we are to believe Ulrich's own account, he broke, in one month's jousting, between 25 April and 23 May 1227, a total of 307 spears, a quite respectable number (though Gahmuret in Wolfram's *Parzival* is supposed to break 100 in a single day!). Indeed, the success of the enterprise was such that, thirteen years later, Ulrich undertook a journey dressed as King Arthur in honour of a new lady, when she in whose honour the 'Venus journey' had been made proved too cruel. But the idea did not bear repetition, and it ended suddenly after a local ban on tournaments.

The system of fighting depicted in Ulrich's poems introduces a number of entirely new elements. Skill, for the moment at least, becomes much more important, since instead of seeing who can withstand the opponents' blows the longest, the contest is limited in scope and form. Furthermore, scoring is introduced, which implies the presence of officials to record and supervise the actual events of the lists rather than the general conduct of the whole event. Most important of all, the tournament is becoming divorced from the practical side of war. For the object in these contests was to break one's own lance squarely on the opponent's shield, while deflecting his blow. Unhorsing might result (and meant complete victory, whether the spear was broken or not), but any form of unnecessary damage was to be avoided. In a real battle, lances were of less importance; they were useless after the first impact, and skill in swordplay—or other weapons, such as maces and pikes—was equally essential to the good warrior. Even in later years, when swordplay became increasingly important in jousts, the lance was never entirely abandoned. Hence a skilful jouster was not necessarily a skilful warrior.

However, the joust was not a rival to the tournament proper, but remained a supplementary exercise. Among the knights themselves, it was more highly esteemed because of the opportunities for personal glory; but the onlookers continued to prefer the spectacle of the *mêlée*. Indeed, it was not until the early fourteenth century that the joust was firmly established through Europe as part of the sport. The speed with which it spread is very hard to gauge, since the chroniclers fail to distinguish between the two: and our only mirror of the times is therefore in literary works. These would tend to confirm that the joust originated in Ulrich von Lichtenstein's homelands in Styria, and moved slowly north and west. The word itself is Germanic—*tijoste*—and the German romances have more scenes involving jousts than their French counterparts, which at first prefer to describe the enchantments and marvels encountered by knights-errant rather than an honest tournament. From the poets of both countries comes our reconstruction of the formal theory of the lists of this period, the basis for all later tournaments.

Any tournament was fought under certain preconditions. There were clear rules as to who was qualified to take part. Knights who had disgraced the order of knighthood were excluded at an early date, although at first only those actually guilty of criminal offences suffered under this proviso. With the rise of the courtly philosophy, those who had been guilty of unchivalrous behaviour suffered likewise; even if their most heinous sin was only to have repeated gossip about a lady, the offended party could denounce them and have them debarred from the lists. A knight could also be thrown out of the tournament (and beaten by the squires into the bargain) for such diverse offenses as buying goods to sell at a profit, deserting his lord in battle, destroying vineyards and cornfields, and, more essential, failing to prove his pedigree back to four great-grandfathers. He must not only be noble, but also be prepared to live up to his status. Such was the theory. In practice only a knight who was obviously ill-equipped or unskilled was likely to be turned away. Tournaments were usually open to anyone with the means and inclination to join in, but as the sport developed, certain practical distinctions arose. Competitors were matched against each other according to their skill, and events were graded accordingly. The most skilled were those reserved for the very expert knights. The weapons used could be either the *armes courtois,* a blunted sword and a lance without a point or with a coronal, a small knob with spokes shaped like a crown, on the end, or *armes à outrance* could be specified, in which case neither lance nor sword were blunted. The latter occasions were reserved for genuinely hostile combats, perhaps duels over points of honour, or for knights who were skilled enough to use such weapons with a minimum of injury to each other, though the weapons could be changed from *armes courtois* to *armes à outrance* half-way through a tournament.

The events within the tournament itself were similarly regulated, particularly the taking of prisoners and the interference of squires and servants. In the best tournaments of the thirteenth century jousting only was employed, not the sword fight, and the prime object was to unseat one's opponent, who then became a prisoner, but was at liberty to escape from the custody of the victor's squires if he did not give his word, although his horse and armour fell to the victor. More common were combats in which prisoners, once taken, agreed not to escape. The loser was therefore more reluctant to surrender, and the question was usually settled by a sword fight once a knight was unhorsed. Under both sets of rules squires and servants could only bring in new horses and weapons; but a third type allowed what was really a general free-for-all. This probably arose in small affairs where there were difficulties in finding enough heralds and other officers to run the tournament properly, and to prevent the attendants from joining in on behalf of their masters was difficult. They were therefore allowed to take prisoners for the latter, and the result was a mere brawl. Finally, there were the squires' tournaments, known as *buhurts,* descendants of the exercises on horseback of the twelfth century. These gave the most trouble of all. In 1234 they had to be banned in England because so much ill will was aroused. In 1288, at the 'Fair of Boston', two gangs of squires, pretending to hold a *buhurt,* dressed as friars and canons, burnt down half the town, and provided an excuse for renewed measures against tournaments proper.

The varying terms corresponded with a variety of motives. The free-for-alls were usually run for profit, the object being to make as much as possible out of ransoms and perquisites such as the armour and horse of the loser; but these were not suitable occasions for the wearing of ladies' favours and for fighting in their honour. Such contests, with ladies presiding, had as their goal the winning of individual renown; the knight exerted himself to gain approval in the eyes of the fair sex, and a mob of servants taking prisoners for him would win him no *doux baisers* and little honour. Tournaments for honour alone, where prizes were offered for the knight who acquitted himself best in the lists were the most highly regarded form, for those held in honour of ladies tended to degenerate into shows of elaborate gallantry; but where an individual prize was offered, skill was for once paramount.

Technique within the lists was fast becoming a complex independent art. By Wolfram von Eschenbach's time—early in the thirteenth century—five distinct 'runs' in tournament and joust were recognised. Two of these, *z'entmuoten* and *diu volge,* we cannot reconstruct with certainty. Two refer to multiple combats or *mêlées. Zem puneiz* was the usual form of charge, in which the massive warhorses were put into a canter, and thundered head-on towards each other, the target being the knight to the left. The lefthand aim was based on the simple reason that it was easiest to hold the spear steady by having it in the right hand and bracing it across the body at an angle of about fifteen degrees. The usual point of aim in this case would be the shield fastening of the opposing knight, which he would have in his left hand; four nailheads on the outside of the shield showed where it might be struck with the greatest chance of unseating him and least likelihood of danger or injury.

This manœuvre, simple in theory, must have called for good horsemanship and aim as well as a firm seat and not inconsiderable strength: the lances were about twelve feet in length and averaged three inches in diameter, being thicker towards the butt end, and tapering towards the point. As the years passed, more and more aids to keep the knight in the saddle were allowed until, with bootlike stirrups and a high pommelled saddle, man and horse were almost inseparable, and only the breaking of the lance was possible.

A more violent tactic was to try to ride down one's opponent by charging horse to horse as well as attempting to unseat him with the lance. This led to the heavy horse armour of the later Middle Ages, when the beast became a primitive form of tank: the gay trappings portrayed in the miniatures concealed more practical coverings beneath. Another possible manœuvre imposed a much more severe test on the knights' horsemanship. If it was agreed to use *zem treviers* beforehand, the knights would at a given signal, swing forty-five degrees to the right as they charged, and strike their opponents on the open side, thus avoiding their lances. The manœuvre must be to the right: if performed with a leftward swing the opponent can move his lance to meet the blow and still keep it across his body, while if he does this to counter a righthand swing he loses the leverage and must support it with his extended arm alone. To do this successfully good timing was essential or chaos would ensue, especially as the order had to be given at the last possible moment to prevent the enemy from doing a counter-manœuvre and defeating the purpose.

Ze rehter tjost was the simple joust, ridden between two knights only, with the same points of aim as in the *mêlée,* the four nails of the shield and the gorge or throat-armour. If the second aim was correctly taken, it might lift off his helm, even if it failed to sweep him clean out of the saddle. But if the armour was faulty or the lance point splintered, it could be very dangerous.

In all this the lance is the chief weapon. Until the middle of the thirteenth century, the sword was regarded as incidental, and the swordfight on horseback was unknown. It was only when the knights wished to prolong the issue beyond the breaking of three lances that the sword came into play. When one of the two was unhorsed, the other would dismount; otherwise both would dismount when the lances had been broken. The weapons were rebated, that is, blunted on both edges and with a rounded end instead of a point. If one knight failed to use the correct type of sword—and this could happen not only by guile but also by picking up the wrong weapon, and there were always sharp weapons to hand—the result could be fatal. An incident of this type at an English tournament at Walden in 1252 aroused considerable anger and unfavourable comment.

As the joust developed, it came more and more to resemble a rather crude form of fencing match or duel. A knight had to be able to break the three spears correctly at the outset; but the real business was done on foot. Due to the nature of swordplay and the armour, it became increasingly a trial of strength. Only a series of heavy buffets could bring a knight down without injury; and although injury was frequent enough, the skilled knight would fight until the sheer weight of his armour or the effort of heaving himself to his feet when knocked down had completely exhausted him. Hence the only alternative was to make the contest dependent on technical rulings. Elaborate means of scoring were therefore developed to give due weight to the accomplished rather than the purely strong knight. In John Tiptoft's set of rules for English tournaments, a late example drawn up in 1466, the system is carefully graded according to the degree of competence involved in each achievement. Unhorsing remained the most impressive feat; a knight who had unhorsed another would take precedence for the prize over all others. After unhorsing came striking 'coronal to coronal', that is, spear's tip to spear's tip; any knight who did this twice was a candidate for the prize. This was followed by striking the crest (on the helm) three . times, by breaking the most spears, and finally by any knight who was generally held to have stayed in the field longest and to have fought the best.

This system was the standard one for the last century and a half of jousting, and Tudor 'jousting cheques' which record the scores on this basis still survive.

If these definitions seem artificial at first, they would certainly encourage a good eye and a firm seat in the saddle. A strong practical streak remains in the rules: anyone striking the barrier of his opponent's saddle is to have one spear deducted from his total; anyone who strikes a horse is to be immediately expelled from the lists with dishonour; and anyone using a gauntlet which locks on to the spear (to give a steady and rigid grip) is to be disqualified.

As the object of the tourneyer changed, so did the organisation of the jousts. The feats of Ulrich von Lichtenstein and other knights who fought for their ladies' sakes were of no avail if there were no spectators to witness their triumph. So the few attendants of the early tournaments became a throng. Even in William Marshal's day we hear of ladies dancing with the knights before a tournament; but this was only a diversion to fill a few idle moments. The first step towards the establishment of the tournament as a formal social event is probably the curious institution of the mid-thirteenth century known as the 'round table'. It first appears in Flanders in 1235, and is certainly derived from the institution of the same name in the legends of King Arthur, just as Ulrich had chosen a legendary guise for both his 'journeys'. Tournaments were dangerous, and only too liable to arouse ill-feeling; and the round table may have started as a group of knights who met together before proceedings opened to swear mutual friendship and to agree on certain preconditions aimed at greater safety. Naturally, feasting would be called for beforehand and afterwards, and the affair might take three days instead of one. Such arrangements soon became standard for all tournaments.

The most marked development in the history of the tournament is its gradual restriction to a smaller and smaller group of knights. The decline in retinues, abolition of the squires' right to intervene and capture knights, and political restrictions all contributed to this trend. The costs, too, grew to huge proportions, partly as the cost of armour increased and partly as the pageantry involved grew more elaborate. Each knight was expected to retain heralds and minstrels, and the distribution of largesse was claimed by an ever-increasing circle of attendants. Hence from being a sport in which almost any knight could participate, it became an expensive hobby for the select few by the fourteenth century. Even before that, the knight who had ruined himself in tournaments was a familiar figure in the diatribes of the moralists attacking tournaments.

At the same time, the ethos of the tournament became more sophisticated. The virtues of the early tourneyers were chiefly a strong arm and a hard head; if they were also congenial company and liberal spenders, their success was assured. Towards the end of the twelfth century, the ideas of courtly love were adapted to the circumstances of the tournament, and the romantic ideals of the poets began to be reflected in real life. Honour and the lady's love were now the spur, and on the outcome of the lists depended the knight's success with his mistress. The old tournaments were more likely to end in a drinking bout than in elaborate social festivities and dances. Eventually the tournament itself was overshadowed by these, and became a mere adjunct of occasions such as weddings, knightings or coronations, a means of giving them added pageantry and colour.❖

RECOMMENDED READINGS

A general view of medieval warfare, arms, and armor is provided by A. V. B. Norman, *The Medieval Soldier* (New York: Thomas Y. Crowell, 1971). Sidney Painter, *French Chivalry: Chivalric Practices and Ideas in Medieval France* (Baltimore: Johns Hopkins University Press, 1940), is the classic study of chivalry. Painter also provides us with an excellent biography of an outstanding figure of English chivalry and the most famous tournament figure of his day in *William Marshall: Knight Errant, Baron and Regent of England* (Baltimore: Johns Hopkins University Press, 1933). Peter Vansittart, *The Tournament* (New York: Collier Books, 1962), a compelling impressionistic novel centering on a late medieval tournament, does much to convey the tenor of the times.

The World, About A.D. 1300

THE THIRTEENTH-CENTURY WORLD SYSTEM

Janet L. Abu-Lughod

An increasingly important interdisciplinary approach to the past called "world system analysis" combines features of economics, geography, and political science with history. The world system analysts avoid viewing states and societies as separate entities and attempt to characterize them in terms of their interaction with the other states and societies of their era. In this sense, world systems analysis goes beyond comparative history, since comparisons are used only to define the variations in the overall system. The objection may be made that the approach leads one too far from the actions and lives of human beings and presents history as the evolution of massive forces beyond human control, and there is certainly some justice in that view. On the other hand, world system analysts view affairs at a level of generality that removes them from the distortions introduced by national pride, religious bias, and a sense of cultural superiority.

Janet Abu-Lughod's analysis of the world system of the thirteenth century provides an excellent case in point. It is generally agreed that the European global domination that began about 1500 is one of the critical movements of modern history, and historians have advanced many possible causes for European success in this period. Abu-Lughod rejects each in turn, and suggests that the Europeans did not develop a new system of trade routes and economic relations, but simply took over those that Eastern societies had created during the period 1300 to 1500. She sees the cause of European success in this and partly in the economic decline of the East, but primarily because the Europeans possessed a new set of economic values. While the rest of the old world system benefited from multiple trading partners and had no great urge to dominate the entire system, the Europeans looked for great short-term gains at the expense of their partners. They brought to the economic world system a new sense of unbridled competition; European trade was not unlike European war.

READING QUESTIONS

1. What are the common reasons advanced for European dominance, and how does Abu-Lughod deal with them?

2. How might one characterize the world system of the period 1300 to 1500?

3. What causes economic advances and declines within a world system?

4. What single cause does Abu-Lughod believe led the western European states to force their way into the Eastern trading lanes?

From the end of the twelfth and well into the fourteenth century, a world trade system emerged that involved a vast region stretching between northwest Europe and China. Although it was not a global system, since it did not include the still-isolated continental masses of the Americas and Australia, it represented a substantially larger system than the world had previously known. It had newly integrated an impressive set of interlinked subsystems in Europe, the Middle East (including the northern portion of Africa), and Asia (coastal and steppe zones).

Although, naturally, this system was extremely *uneven,* integrating into the network only an archipelago of "world cities" elevated above a sea of relatively isolated rural areas and open stretches, such spottiness was not unique to the thirteenth century. Unevenness in itself does not invalidate the existence of an overarching system. Indeed, it is debatable whether the discrepancy between world city and hinterland in the thirteenth century was nearly as great as the gap that separates Tokyo or New York from rural Togo in today's world system.

Even though, when compared to the contemporary epoch, the thirteenth-century system of international trade and the production associated with it could not be described as either large scale or technologically advanced, it was substantially more complex in organization, greater in volume, and more sophisticated in execution, than anything the world had previously known. Nor was it basically inferior to what it would be in the sixteenth century.

Sophistication was evident in the technology of shipping and navigation, the social organization of production and marketing, and the institutional arrangements for conducting business, such as partnerships, mechanisms for pooling capital, and techniques for monetization and exchange. Thus, it is im-

From Janet L. Abu-Lughod, *Before European Hegemony: The World System A.D. 1250–1350* (New York and Oxford, UK: Oxford University Press, 1989), pp. 352–363.

portant to recognize that no simple, deterministic explanation can account for Europe's later hegemony. Explanations that concentrate on the special technological, cultural, psychological, or even economic characteristics of European society are not sufficient, since they tend to ignore the contextual changes in the preexistent system.

First, no enormous advances occurred in the sixteenth century in the all-important area of sea transport. Although European vessels were considerably better than they had been, they were still not superior to the Chinese ships Admiral Cheng Ho had paraded through the Indian Ocean in the early fifteenth century. Indeed, the threshold of true integration by sea was not attained until much later. Not until the development of the steamship in the nineteenth century did the shape of the world system dramatically alter.

Nor was there any quantum leap in the area of social invention (the organization of production, the financing of capital investment, the instruments of money and credit) in the sixteenth century. There, too, the rule is one of continuities and gradual advances through diffusion and elaboration, rather than decisive breakthroughs. To consider Arab commerce deficient because in the thirteenth century it did not have modern banks, or Chinese paper legal tender deficient because it lacked a gold standard, is illicit and anachronistic, since such institutions gradually grew in Europe as development continued. It is just as credible to propose that the primitive institutions of money and credit that existed in the nonwestern world in the thirteenth century would undoubtedly have continued to evolve, had that part of the world remained important to world trade. Failure to develop more sophisticated business techniques was a symptom of the demotion of the nonwestern world's power, not a cause of it.

Finally, given this earlier incipient world system in which no unity prevailed in culture, religion, or economic institutional arrangement, it is difficult to accept a purely "cultural" explanation for dominance. No particular culture seems to have had a monopoly over either technological or social inventiveness. Neither a unique syndrome of psychology, a special economic form of organizing production and exchange, nor any particular set of religious beliefs or values was needed to succeed in the thirteenth century. The fact that the "West won" in the sixteenth century, whereas the earlier system aborted, cannot be used to argue convincingly that *only* the institutions and culture of the West *could have succeeded.*[1]

Indeed, what is noteworthy in the world system of the thirteenth century is that a wide variety of cultural systems coexisted and cooperated, and that societies organized very differently from those in the west dominated the system. Christianity, Buddhism, Confucianism, Islam, Zoroastrianism,

---

[1] Eurocentric historians and social scientists have been tempted to attribute sixteenth-century European success to the unique success of alternatively, European "culture" or "capitalism" in its pure form.

and numerous other smaller sects often dismissed as "pagan" all seem to have permitted and indeed facilitated lively commerce, production, exchange, risk taking, and the like. And among these, Christianity played a relatively insignificant role.

Similarly, a variety of economic systems coexisted in the thirteenth century—from "near" private capitalism, albeit supported by state power, to "near" state production, albeit assisted by private merchants. Furthermore, these variations were not particularly congruent with either geographic region or religious domain. The organization of textile production in Kanchipuram was not unlike that in Flanders, whereas in China and Egypt larger scale coordination was more typical. The state built boats for trade in both Venice and China, whereas elsewhere (and even at different times in Genoa, China, and Egypt) private vessels were comandeered when the state needed them.

Nor were the underlying bases for economic activities uniform. Participating in the world system of the thirteenth century were (1) large agrarian societies such as India and China that covered subcontinents in expanse, in which industrial production was oriented mainly but not exclusively to the processing of agricultural raw materials; (2) small city-state ports such as Venice, Aden, Palembang, and Malacca, whose functions are best described as compradorial; (3) places as diverse as south India, Champagne, Samarkand, the Levant, and ports along the Persian Gulf, whose importance was enhanced by their strategic location at points where pathways between flanking trading partners met; and (4) places that contained valued raw materials unavailable elsewhere (fine-quality wool in England, camphor in Sumatra, frankincense and myrrh on the Arabian Peninsula, spices in the Indian archipelago, jewels in Ceylon, ivory and ostrich feathers in Africa, and even military slaves in eastern Europe). These resources did not *account* for the world system; they were *products* of it.

The economic vitality of these areas was the result, at least in part, of the system in which they participated. All these units were not only trading with one another and handling the transit trade of others, but had begun to reorganize parts of their internal economies to meet the exigencies of a world market. Production of certain fiber crops fed a growing demand for textiles abroad; increased acreage to graze sheep similarly supplied wool to spinners and weavers producing for export; an enlarged metallurgical sector satisfied burgeoning outside demands for weapons; and specialization in prospecting for camphor and precious metals or in growing pepper or other spices followed from export demands. These developments were all the result of the world system that, by the end of the thirteenth century, had made prosperity pandemic. The results of that effusive period of economic growth are reflected in the increased size of cities participating in it.

Yet, some fifty years later, the system began to unravel and, by the late fifteenth century, only small parts of it retained their former vigor. The cycle was coming to an end. Why? To say that economic expansions and contractions tend to be cyclical is no answer. It seems mystical to talk of Kondratieff (45–55 years) or other regularly recurring economic cycles as if they were forces in their own right, rather than more or less useful observational or measurement artifacts. It is true that a period of some hundred years of "rise" and fifty years of "fall" has been selected for study, but to some extent that was only for convenience. The cycle fits Europe best—and not by any accident. In fact, the limiting years were originally selected because of their congruence with a known fluctuation in European history. As seen, however, even in western Europe the beginning point varies from place to place, and the upturn, depending on the focus, could well have been placed earlier or later. The downturn point is less arbitrary, since it coincides with the demographically disastrous Black Death that most European historians agree set in motion deep structural changes on the continent.

The Middle Eastern cycle, however, would exhibit far different temporal "borders," if that region were being studied alone rather than in relationship to a world system that included northern Europe. The beginning of growing strength in the Middle East region comes as early as the eighth century, although the terminal phase varies from one subarea to another. After the eighth- to tenth-century "peak," which favored both Baghdad and Cairo, the histories of these two imperial centers diverge. Indeed, the high points of Egyptian medieval history are almost inverse images of Iraq's stagnation. Nor, in spite of the demographic decimations caused by the Black Death, did Egypt experience the marked decline that so many other portions of the world system did in the latter fourteenth century. The trade monopoly Venice and Cairo achieved through their uneasy and ambivalent alliance insulated both from the retrenchments engulfing their rivals. Cairo's final decline did not come until *after* the Portuguese circumnavigated Africa a century and a half later. The Ottoman conquest of Egypt in 1516 did not cause but merely confirmed this loss of position.

Farther east, the cycles were also not neatly synchronized. On the west coast of India, whose fate was linked so closely to the Middle East, the longer upswing phase of the· cycle paralleled the cycle in Egypt to which it was causally linked. In contrast, the increasing passivity, if not decline, on the east coast of India began before the fourteenth century and closely corresponded to the declining importance of the Srivijayan city-states, in turn linked to Chinese aggressiveness; the Chinese actively bypassed both the straits traders and the ports on the Coromandel coast, going directly to Quilon.

Across the northern steppelands, the cycle of integration and fragmentation was tied to changes in the empire established by the tribal confederation referred to as "the Mongols." The expanding phase came early in the thirteenth century, with maximum consolidation achieved by the early fourteenth century. In contrast, fragmentation and territorial losses (including China) characterized the second half of the fourteenth century. As earlier

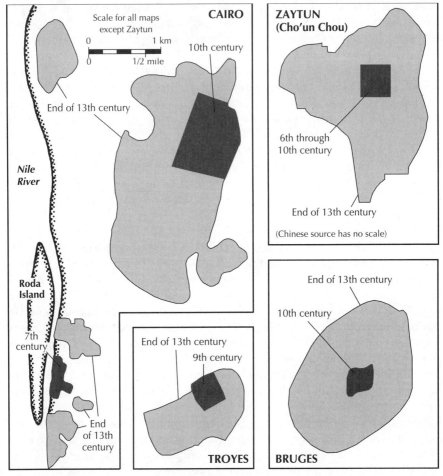

The growth of selected cities between the ninth/tenth and the end of the thir-teenth centuries.

contended, the periodicity in this region had an inordinate effect on the cy-cles of other participants in the thirteenth-century world system.

China had her own cycle of development that began somewhat earlier—certainly by the eleventh- and twelfth-century Sung dynasty—and that did not finally retrench until the mid-fifteenth century. That cycle reached its apogee under the Yuan dynasty when the southern region (with its port out-lets to the Indian Ocean trade) was fully united with the northern zone (with its caravan links across Central Asia). When both of these lines to the world system were open, China flourished; when they closed, China de-clined, and, with her, the rest of the world system as it had been organized in the thirteenth century.

Given this variability, one must not reify "cycles." Rather, the theory we have been setting forth suggests that *when there was a period of congruence among the upward cycles of related regions,* these cycles moved synergistically. Upturns were the result, at least in part, of the linkages each region managed to forge with other parts of the world system, and feedbacks from that system, in turn, intensified local development.

The same was true in reverse. When separate regions experienced setbacks, either from unique or common underlying causes, the overall direction of the change vector was deflected. And just *because* the regions had become so interlinked, declines in one inevitably contributed to declines elsewhere, particularly in contiguous parts that formed "trading partnerships."

One of the most important systemic changes that occurred at mid-fourteenth century, of course, was the significant drop in population that occurred simultaneously and not independently in many parts of the world, as a result of the pandemic of the Bubonic Plague and/or other epidemics that ravaged much of the system. Although responses to these population declines varied from place to place (in some regions recovery was rapid, in others, recovery was slow or never occurred), two consequences were fairly universal. One was a reemphasis on agricultural production, which absorbed a higher proportion of the smaller population than it had even decades before. The other was a drop in the rate of urbanization. Both were symptoms of the fact that participants were no longer able to generate the surpluses characteristic of the thirteenth century. Thus, there was also a drop, albeit temporary, in the overall volume and value of trade, particularly long-distance trade.

The second systemic change was geopolitical. In the course of the thirteenth century, the geopolitical medium through which merchants and their goods circulated had become increasingly frictionless and continuous. The simultaneous operation of two different routes across Central Asia (a southern and a northern) and two different routes between the Middle East and Asia via the Indian Ocean (the Red Sea and the Persian Gulf) meant that any blockages developing at specific synapses of the circulatory system could be bypassed. This flexibility not only kept the monopoly protection rent that guarders of individual routes exacted from passing traders within "bearable" limits, but it guaranteed that goods would go through, in spite of localized disturbances.

By the middle of the fourteenth century, however, the admittedly fractious unity of the Central Asian empire assembled by Genghis Khan and then bequeathed to multiple successors was in disarray. This eventually closed the Central Asian route that had earlier provided an alternative to the sea route. Finally, when the Mongols, severely weakened by the Black Death (or some other disastrous epidemic), "lost" China in 1368, the world lost the key link that had connected the overland route, terminating at Peking, with the sea routes through the Indian Ocean and South China Sea, terminating at the ports of southeast China. The repercussions of this disjunction at the eastern end of the world system were felt throughout the trading world.

During the late fourteenth and fifteenth centuries, the link between Europe and Asia, via the Mediterranean and the Indian Ocean, was sustained by the Venetian–Egyptian marriage of convenience. Indeed, the sea route they controlled gained additional strength because competing pathways were essentially closed. However, the south and southeast Asian systems to which this narrowed line connected were already in decline.

Internal developments in south and southeast Asia reduced the number of powers active in that system. In south India, the western coastal ports continued to play an important role in trade, but the east coast, ruled by the mountain-based Vijayanagar, became even more passive in the sea trade. There was an overextension of the trading circuit of Middle Eastern and western Indian traders and shippers into the Bay of Bengal circuit that had formerly constituted the natural sphere of Coromandel activity.

The slack created by the declining activities of Coromandel traders was belatedly and only partially taken up by the principalities along the strait, most notably Malacca. These principalities never had a truly independent base of power, however. Their vitality was the result of the motivation for trade on the part of India, on the one side, and China, on the other. Only during periods in which direct contact between the two giants was actively blocked by embargos or was passively reduced by declines in the shipping fleets at either end, did the straits region play, almost by default, a more active role. The limited independent power of the principalities of the strait was clearly demonstrated by the fact that they declined when overall trade diminished. This occurred in two phases, at least with respect to China.

When the Ming first came to power in China, their interest in trade was temporarily inhibited by a preoccupation with more pressing concerns and possibly, by a "change in philosophy." In the opening decades of the fifteenth century (1403-1430), there was a revival of interest in external contacts, but it was both ambivalent and, as seen, aborted. The withdrawal of the Chinese fleet after 1435, coupled with the overextension into the two easternmost circuits of the Indian Ocean trade of the Arab and Gujarati Indian merchants, neither protected by a strong navy, left a vacuum of power in the Indian Ocean. Eventually, this vacuum was filled—first by the Portuguese, then by the Dutch, and finally by the British.

Of crucial importance is the fact that the "Fall of the East" preceded the "Rise of the West," and it was this devolution of the preexisting system that facilitated Europe's easy conquest. It would be wrong, therefore, to view the "Rise of the West" as either a simple "takeover" of a prior functioning system or an event whose outcome was attributable exclusively to the internal characteristics of European society. Rather, two paradoxical forces were at work.

First, pathways and routes developed by the thirteenth century were later "conquered" and adapted by a succession of European powers. Europe did not need to *invent* the system, since the basic groundwork was already in place by the thirteenth century when Europe was still only a peripheral and recent participant. In this sense, the rise of the west was facilitated by the preexisting world economy that it restructured.

It must be recognized, however, that the "takeover" of that system was certainly not according to the old rules. The old world system that was deeply penetrated by Portuguese intruders in the early sixteenth century offered little resistance. Why? In part, it could not, since it was already at a low (albeit possibly temporary) point of organization. Perhaps it had adapted so completely to the coexistence of multiple trading partners that it was unprepared for players interested in short-term plunder rather than long-term exchange. More than anything else, then, it was the new European approach to trade-cum-plunder that caused a basic transformation in the world system that had developed and persisted over some five centuries.

In the earlier system, although there were certainly rivalries and no small amount of interregional conflict, the overall pattern of trade involved a large number of players whose power was relatively equal. No single participant in the thirteenth- and early fourteenth-century world system dominated the whole, and most participants (with the possible exception of the Mongols) benefited from coexistence and mutual tolerance. Individual rulers did jealously seek to control the terms of trade and the "foreign traders" in their own ports and inland centers, but the ambition to dominate the entire system seemed beyond their needs and aspirations (and probably capacities). The change in the "rules of the game" introduced by the European newcomers in the sixteenth century, therefore, caught the older players off guard.

The new rules were being imposed not only on the old world but, with even greater vigor, on the new. In this connection it is important to note that the European shift to the Atlantic had begun even before the closing decade of the fifteenth century when the voyages of Columbus and Vasco da Gama signaled a decisive break with the past. Although these journeys were sponsored by Atlantic rim monarchs of the Iberian peninsula, the groundwork for them had been laid by Genoa, from which Columbus originated.

Recall that the two rival sea powers, Venice and Genoa, had very different geographic "natural" advantages. Venice, on Italy's east coast, had easiest access to the eastern Mediterranean. Furthermore, her transalpine connections to the North Sea ran through (today's) Austria and Germany. She was thus poorly situated to exploit the Atlantic. In contrast, Genoa, on the west coast of the Italian boot, had a freer hand in the western Mediterranean, particularly after her Muslim North African rivals had been defeated after the middle of the thirteenth century, when Christian Spain "reconquered" Andalusia, which decreased the hazards of passage via Gibraltar. This permitted her expansion into the Atlantic, a "middle sea" that in the sixteenth century began to usurp the Mediterranean's key role. Thus, although Venice ostensibly defeated Genoa in their centuries-long rivalry, it was Genoa's "solution" to the eastern trade question that eventually triumphed in the next world system.

Recall that Genoese galleys had begun to enter the Atlantic by the late thirteenth and early fourteenth centuries to bypass a no longer hospitable or profitable land passage through France; the growth of Genoese Atlantic shipping was in inverse relation to the decline of the Champagne fairs, no longer "free" and no longer easily reached by the Flemish cloth merchants. Thus, Genoa's move into the Atlantic was primarily motivated by changes that were occurring within the local European subsystem, rather than in the "world system," and was at first directed only toward Europe.

Nevertheless, it eventually led to the total transformation of the larger system. It is not that the European navigators, by sailing down the coast of Africa or even westward to the Americas, "discovered" new routes. In the medieval period Arab navigators already knew the route around Africa and there is at least some evidence that landfalls in the Americas had, from time to time, been made by earlier sailors from the Middle East. But Middle Eastern traders did not need this circuitous route since they controlled the shorter one.

It was not until Venice consolidated her relations with Egypt, the state that guarded that shorter route, that her rivals—at first only Genoa but later also the naval powers on the Atlantic rim—sought alternative paths to the east. Eventually they found them, and this, more than any institutional or motivational characteristics of European culture, changed world history.❖

RECOMMENDED READINGS

Thomas R. Shannon, *An Introduction to the World-System Perspective* (Boulder, CO: Westview Press, 1989), and Terence K. Hopkins, *World-Systems Analysis: Theory and Methodology* (Beverly Hills, CA: Sage, 1982), each offer an introduction to the methodology and approach that distinguish world systems analysis; *World System Structure: Continuity and Change,* ed. W. Ladd Hollist and James N. Rosenau (Beverly Hills, CA: Sage, 1981), discusses the internal logic of the system. *The Rise of Merchant Empires: Long-Distance Trade in the Early Modern World, 1350-1750,* ed. James D. Tracy (Cambridge, UK, and New York: Cambridge University Press, 1990), and Alan K. Smith, *Creating a World Economy: Merchant Capital, Colonialism, and World Trade, 1400-1825* (Boulder, CO: Westview Press, 1991), each offer a world systems perspective on European expansion.

DISCUSSION QUESTIONS

PART THREE: EXPANDING HORIZONS: CHALLENGES TO THE CLASSICAL HERITAGE, A.D. 500 to 1350

1. Sports are an important aspect of human life and can tell the perceptive observer a great deal about the societies pursuing them. Drawing on "The First Olympics" in Part II and "The Medieval Tournament" in this part, discuss the similarities and differences between these two events. Consider a modern football game from start to finish, with all of its accompanying activities; do you consider it valid to say that most sports today, especially team competitions, are basically social rituals? If not, what function do you think sports serve in our society, and why are we willing to devote so much time and money to them?

2. In both "The First Olympics" and "The Medieval Tournament," participants competed primarily for glory, but the entire tenor of the two kinds of competition was different. How did Olympic competition and medieval tournaments compare, and how would you account for their differences? What role did each play in its society?

3. Returning to the question of "aristocratizing" and "democratizing" technological innovations, how were the development of the great horse and the stirrup aristocratizing innovations, and how did they shape the world of "Bodo: The Life of a Peasant"? How did they lead to the cumbersome and complex rituals of the medieval tournament? Was the clock a democratizing or an aristocratizing innovation, and how did it influence European society?

4. "The Development of Gunpowder and Firearms in Medieval China" discusses technological developments that were basically democratizing. How was this so? Why was the feudal society of Europe particularly vulnerable to these sorts of weapons? Medieval China was much less affected by these innovations than Europe was. Was China less aristocratic than Europe and, if so, in what sense?

5. "The Natural History of Medieval Women" demonstrates how the position of women can be influenced by general economic conditions. What can we deduce about the economies of early Israel, Han China, and medieval Europe from the status of women in those societies? Herlihy suggests that the status of women declined in the later medieval period. How does this agree with the apparent freedom enjoyed by

Margery Kempe in "The Life and Times of Margery Kempe" (see Part IV), or is Margery a thoroughly unrepresentative example?

6. If you were to ask Bodo the peasant, Sānudāsa the merchant, and a Heian nobleman what they considered "the good life" and how one went about obtaining it, what might they answer? How would their views of duty, wealth, family, and religion compare?

7. In "Jewish-Muslim Relations: The Formative Years," we can see that the situation in the oasis of Medina in 622 was dangerous. Was conflict between the Jews and Muslims unavoidable? If you had been a Jewish leader during that period, what would you have done? Was the position of the Muslim minority so precarious that they could have been destroyed? Why was Muhammad able to use the Jewish communities to serve his own purposes?

8. By and large, technology during the medieval period seems to have been much more advanced in China than in western Europe. How do you account for this difference? Was it solely the result of Europe's isolation, military preoccupations, and relative poverty, or were there other possible reasons?

9. Sānudāsa the merchant strove for glory and fulfillment in much the same way as the competitors in the Olympics and medieval tournaments did, but the nature of his fulfillment was much different. In what ways is "The Travels of Sānudāsa the Merchant" an allegory, and what lessons is it intended to teach? Is it significant that the West normally casts fighting men in the role played here by a merchant?

10. In "The Impact of the Crusades on Moslem Lands," we can see that military defeat is not always a bad thing. What advantages do defeated states and societies enjoy as a result of being beaten? What difficulties do the victors face? Considering the indirect consequences of warfare, did the Crusades play a part in helping to create "The Thirteenth-Century World System"?

11. Part III of this book is subtitled "Challenges to the Classical Heritage." In what sense were the societies of western Europe, China, and India heirs to the classical empires of Rome, Maurya, and Han? How have these heritages been preserved in these culture centers?

PART IV

Worlds of Change:
The Crisis of the
Classical Cultures

❖ ❖ ❖

A.D. 1350 TO 1650

	1350	1400	1450
EUROPE	**1340–1453** Hundred Years' War **1340–1400** Geoffrey Chaucer **1348** Bubonic plague **ca. 1373** *The Life and Times of Margery Kempe* **1378–1417** Great Schism	**1410** Battle of Tannenberg **1416** Execution of John Hus	**1462–1505** Ivan III, first Russian tsar **1469-1527** Niccolo Machiavelli **1479** *A Plague Doctor* **1492** Columbus sails west
SOUTHWEST ASIA AND AFRICA	**1355–1591** Kingdom of Songhay **1370–1405** Timur **1375** Abraham Cresques produces a map of Africa	**1413–1421** Mohammed I **1415** Prince Henry of Portugal captures Ceuta	**ca. 1450–1528** Songhai Empire, West Africa **1453** Ottomans capture Constantinople **1453–1918** Ottoman Empire **1488** Bartholomew Diaz rounds Cape of Good Hope
SOUTH AND SOUTHEAST ASIA	**ca. 1350–1550** *India and Islam: A Study in Defeat* **1398** Timur invades India		**1483–1530** Babur, founder of Mughal Empire, India **1498** *Why Not the Arabs?* **1499** Vasco da Gama reaches India
EAST ASIA	**1368–1644** Ming dynasty, China	**ca. 1400** Tea ceremony, Japan **1402** Battle of Angora, Turkey **1405–1433** Ming maritime expeditions; *The Maritime Expeditions of Chêng Ho*	**1467–1477** Onin War, Japan **1472–1529** Wang Yangming, Neo-Confucianism **1478–1573** Epoch of the Warring Countries, Japan
THE AMERICAS AND THE PACIFIC	**ca. 300–1500** *America's Ball Game*		**1460** Rise of Inca Empire **1492** Columbus discovers New World **1493** First Spanish colony, Hispaniola **1493** Treaty of Tordesillas

1500	1550	1600 1660
1509–1564 John Calvin **1517** Martin Luther's 95 theses **1519** Magellan sets sail around world **1520** Mayan ball game introduced to Europe **1534** Luther translates Bible into German Henry VIII heads English church	**1545–1563** Council of Trent **1558–1603** Elizabeth I **1561–1626** Sir Francis Bacon **1550** *Impact of War on Civilians* **1588** Spanish Armada	**1600** British East India Company founded **1648** Peace of Westphalia **1660** *Population Structures*
1500 *Incentives and Patterns of African Trade* **1500** Benin, West Africa **1501–1722** Safavid Empire **1520–1566** Sultan Suleiman **1520** The Chronicle of Kilwa (written in Arabic) **1528** 10,000 Africans in new world	**1571** Battle of Lepanto, Gulf of Corinth **1571** Portuguese found Angola **1573–1603** Empire of Bornu at Height under Idiris III, Africa **1588–1629** Shah Abbasi **1591** Timbuktu becomes Muslim	**ca. 1600** First known King of Ashanti, Africa **1620–1640** Dutch settle West and South Africa.
1511 Portuguese capture Malacca, Malaysia, Southeast Asia **1526–1739** Mughal Empire	**1556–1605** Akbar, Mughal emperor	**ca. 1600** Hindu recreation of *Ramayana* epic **1632–1652** Taj Mahal **1640–1680** Overthrow of Shah Jahan
1528–1588 *Ch'i Chi-kuang and the Japanese Pirates* **1542** Introduction of European firearms to Japan	**1573–1600** Unification of Japan **1592, 1597** Japanese expeditions to Korea	**ca. 1600** *Japan's Early Modern Transformation* **1603–1867** Tokugawa shogunate, Japan **1644–1911** Qing dynasty, China
1510 First African slaves in New World **1519** Hernando Cortés conquers Aztecs **1520** Magellan crosses Pacific **1530** *Conquistador y Pestilencia* **1533** Pizarro conquers Incas	**1571** Spanish conquer Philippines **1580** Virginia Company founded, North America	**1600** Franciscans establish missions in Florida **1605** Kingdom of Palmares founded by runaway slaves, Brazil **1600–1620** Jamestown and Quebec founded

INTRODUCTION

By 1350, the stability and relative isolation that had characterized the civilizations of the Old World in the previous era had disappeared, and the balance of power between those civilizations changed dramatically. This process had begun with the appearance of new waves of invaders from Central Asia. The most prominent of them were the Mongols, who had risen from nomadic origins to become a power that had dominated virtually the entire Eurasian continent. These conquests proved ephemeral, however. Mongol rulers everywhere generally followed a path of acculturation, and the conquerors were quickly absorbed into the native cultures of the regions in which they resided.

The Mongol expansion nevertheless had some enduring consequences. One of the more significant was to bring the civilizations of the Old World, including western Europe, into closer contact. Although technological progress was stimulated everywhere, the progress was not uniform. Innovation and a willingness to adopt technological advances often depend on cultural and social factors. Whereas other civilizations resisted change to a greater or lesser degree, Europe appeared peculiarly open to innovation and progressed steadily during the premodern era.

Many reasons could be suggested for the European adaptability, but perhaps the most significant was the fact that the dominant institutions of European society were in a state of dissolution. The waves of deadly epidemic diseases that regularly washed over Europe, each time killing a significant part of the population, had a profound effect on European society and culture. The reading selections entitled "A Plague Doctor," "The Direct Impact of War on Civilians," and "Population Structures" provide three different views of the stresses to which traditional European institutions were subjected by these demographic and personal disasters.

Fifteenth-century European society was in a state of flux, and prescribed patterns of behavior could scarcely be enforced under the prevailing conditions. "The Life and Times of Margery Kempe" demonstrates that a high degree of individualism was tolerated, and the reading exemplifies, in its way, Europe's receptivity to new forms of expression. Restrictive institutions were crumbling everywhere; advances in military technology had doomed the mounted warrior of feudal society, and the unitary religion of Europe had split into a number of conflicting sects by the middle of the sixteenth century.

At a time when Europe was increasingly willing and able to participate in the Old World economic system, the other civilizations of the Old World rejected foreign commerce as a profitable venture and turned their attention almost solely to internal improvements. "The Chinese Reach Out: The Maritime Expeditions of Chêng Ho" and "Ch'i Chi-kuang and the Japanese Pirates" discuss two episodes in what some historians have called China's

Great Withdrawal. "Why Not the Arabs?" suggests some of the reasons why the Muslims failed to capitalize on their technology and experience to gain dominance of the world's waterways.

By the end of the fifteenth century, the Europeans had begun to take to the sea. With their superiority in metallurgy, shipbuilding, and navigation, the Europeans were able slowly to establish control over world trade. Except in the Americas, they were not opening new routes, but simply taking over old commercial lanes that the Muslims, Chinese, and others had abandoned. The Americas were quite different. Here the Europeans encountered societies that had been generally isolated from the Old World for thousands of years. "Conquistador y Pestilencia" recounts one result of the end of this long isolation, the devastating spread of Old World diseases against which the native population had built no immunity. This factor eliminated most of the resistance that the Europeans might have met in exploiting the natural resources of these lands. In the course of this exploitation, they discovered new materials and foodstuffs that greatly increased their wealth. As is suggested in "America's Ball Game," substances such as rubber were a great impetus to European industry and manufacturing.

During most of the period up to 1650, the advanced civilizations of Islam, India, and China managed to control the European presence and limit their contacts with the outsiders. The Westerners expanded at the expense of only those societies or states lacking the numbers or the military capacity to resist them. They grew richer and more powerful as a result of their discoveries and conquests, and the influx of new ideas and goods transformed European society. Other Old World civilizations, by contrast, withdrew even more deeply into seclusion. "Japan's Early Modern Transformation" traces the steps by which the Japanese closed themselves off from any but the most limited foreign contacts, and "India and Islam: A Study in Defeat" considers how Muslim dominance destroyed the confidence and receptiveness of Hindu society.

By 1650, however, Europe was well on the way to becoming the dominant military and cultural power in the world. To an increasing extent, the other civilizations of the Old World could no longer resist European influences. The next three centuries would see the unification of the world under the force of the European example.

England, A.D. 1414

THE LIFE AND TIMES OF MARGERY KEMPE

H. S. Bennett

The chance discovery of the only surviving manuscript copy of the auto-biography of Margery Kempe has provided us with a remarkable oppor-tunity to learn what a middle-class Englishwoman of the fourteenth century did, thought, and said. The historian might wish that Margery had been more representative of her kind, but she was not. Writers of au-tobiographies are rarely run of the mill, and Margery was no exception to that rule. She carried on dialogues with God, wore the wrong sort of clothes, wept loudly on the most inappropriate occasions, went off alone on pilgrimages all over Europe, and generally meddled in everybody's business.

Some of her contemporaries considered her unbalanced, and some readers of the following selection may agree with that view. Her ambiva-lent status, however, reveals an interesting aspect of medieval society. It was an era when zealous people, such as the flagellants, Franciscans, her-mits, and ascetics, went to great extremes in their search for unity with God. The lines between divine zeal, religious dissent, and emotional dis-turbance were sometimes so fine that it was difficult to determine where they lay. Margery had no such difficulty; Jesus and God the Father were her personal friends and had assured her that she was singularly blessed. All she had to do was to get other people to accept that simple fact. And, after all, what can you do when God tells you to give away all of your money, or not eat herring, or reprove sinners in high places?

This selection not only offers us a picture of Margery's pilgrimage to Jerusalem but gives us an introduction to a priceless and quite impossible person.

READING QUESTIONS

1. What events preceded Margery's visions of Jesus?

2. What did she want from the bishop of Lincoln?

3. What preparations were necessary for a pilgrimage to Jerusalem?

4. How did Margery's pilgrimage affect her?

 mong the many little books—scarcely more than pamphlets—printed by Wynkyn de Worde in his efforts to provide reading matter for the growing literate public of his day, was a small eight-page quarto pamphlet—'A short treatise of contemplation taught by Our Lord, Jesu Christ, taken out of the book of Margery Kempe of Lynn'. Wynkyn de Worde may have printed some five hundred copies of this work, but in the course of centuries all of these save one seem to have perished, and from a study of the only known copy in the University Library, Cambridge, it was long thought that the work was a condensed version of a book of devotions, similar to that of other religious writers of the time, such as Hilton's *Scale of Perfection,* or the *Revelations* of Dame Juliana of Norwich. In 1934, however, Miss Hope Emily Allen, well known for her work on Robert Rolle and other mystics, announced her identification of a manuscript in the library of Colonel Butler-Bowdon of Pleasington Old Hall, Lancashire, as the autobiography of Margery Kempe, from which Wynkyn de Worde had extracted a mere handful of sentences.

Here then we have what Professor R. W. Chambers called 'our first biography in English'—a work in which the life, thoughts and experiences of a religious enthusiast are set out in detail. A generation earlier Geoffrey Chaucer had set down the thoughts and experiences of a sensual woman of the bourgeoisie in his portrait of the Wife of Bath. In her autobiography Margery Kempe, with a similar bourgeois background, unfolds for us the anxieties and experiences of a religious woman whose life was dedicated to the service of God. No English writer, hitherto, had committed to writing so intimate, revealing and human an account of his life and thoughts.

It would, of course, be easy to make a figure of fun out of Margery, who so frankly reveals herself. Even so sympathetic a writer as Father Herbert Thurston speaks of her 'terrible hysteria', while Miss Hope Allen says: 'she was petty, neurotic, vain, illiterate, physically and nervously overstrained.' These things often betrayed her into outrageous and undignified behaviour, unworthy of herself or of her dedicated aims. The self-portrait of a minor mystic remains, however, the more credible for its merciless honesty and its fidelity to life.

Lynn in the fourteenth-century was a prosperous town with a flourishing trade with Scandinavia, Germany and the Low Countries. Its great church of St Margaret, the Guildhall and other buildings told of the wealth of

From H. S. Bennett, *Six Medieval Men and Women* (New York: Atheneum, 1972), pp. 124–140.

its citizens who had contributed so handsomely to the funds for their construction. Among the leading citizens was John Burnham, the father of Margery, a man who had been elected mayor no less than five times and was for long an alderman of the borough. At one time he represented Lynn in Parliament, and was associated with the influential Corpus Christi Gild of the town. It was into this good bourgeois family that Margery was born about 1373, and about her twentieth year she was married to another *bon bourgeois,* John Kempe, a freeman of the borough, a member also of the Corpus Christi Gild, and soon after his marriage one of the borough chamberlains. More than that we know little of him and of the part he played in the municipal and commercial life of the town, although members of his family (and probably himself) were engaged in trade with various seaboard towns of Germany from time to time.

We may imagine, however, that on marrying John Kempe, Margery could look forward with confidence to the normal life of one of the town aristocracy, blessed with money and family connexions as she was. So far as her private life went, however, it opened badly, for her first-born caused her much suffering and illness—so much so, that, fearing she would not survive, and wishing to clear her conscience of a matter that had long been haunting her, she sent for her confessor and began to unburden herself. Before she had got very far, or had reached the principal matter that was troubling her, her confessor began to reprove her so sharply that she feared to go on and was silenced. Overwhelmed by her confessor's reproaches and burdened by a sense of guilt, her mind gave way, and for some seven months she was the victim of fears and hallucinations. At this time, she tells us, she saw; as she thought, devils open their mouths flaming with burning tongues of fire as if they would have swallowed her, sometimes ramping at her, sometimes threatening her, sometimes pulling and tugging at her both night and day. In her madness she slandered her husband and her friends, tried to destroy herself and lacerated her body with her nails, so that for a while she had to be bound and constantly watched. The day came, she believed, when sanity returned for, when she lay alone, Christ appeared to her in the likeness of a young man, clad in a mantle of blue silk, and sitting upon the bedside said: 'Daughter, why has thou forsaken Me, and I forsook thee never?' After this she recovered, and though her attendants remonstrated with him, her husband, 'having tenderness and compassion for her, commanded that they should deliver to her the keys', and she began to eat and drink and her bodily strength returned.

Once she was recovered, she seems to have led a worldly life, and was notorious for the finery of her garments, cut in the latest fashion and made of brightly contrasting materials, so that men stared at her as she passed and her husband begged her to be more moderate. All in vain: she told him he should never have married above his station and that she would continue in her ways, hoping to outdo other wives in her array; she was for ever seeking the admiration and esteem of all beholders.

To increase her resources and to show that she was as good as another at practical affairs, she set up a common brewery and for three or four years was one of the greatest brewers in town. She was dogged with ill luck, however, and turned to milling. To this end she hired a man, and bought a pair of horses, and hoped with this horse-mill to make money, but here again she was unsuccessful: some said she was accursed and that it was God's vengeance on her, while others saw in it a call to her from worldly things to those of the spirit. Margery took the latter view, and henceforth her life was more and more given over to prayer and contemplation.

By this time some fifteen or sixteen years of married life had passed and many children had come, but henceforth Margery more and more longed for the celibate life. For a time, all her pleas to her husband were vain. He at least, had no such wish. The most he would say was that 'it were good to do so, but he might not yet. He would when God willed it.' In the meantime Margery increased her devotions. She would rise at two in the morning, go to church and stay there till noon or later. She fasted, wore a hair-cloth for mortification of the flesh, and ever prayed that a chaste life might soon be hers. At this time began that 'plentyous and continual weeping' that was to be with her for so many years, and which was to evoke such fierce and hostile criticism, for as she tells us: 'Many people thought that she could weep or leave off at will, and therefore called her a false hypocrite.'

Margery cared little then or later for such criticism. She went her own way, seeing visions, having rapturous communications with Christ: at times in great quiet of spirit, at others sunk in distress and despair. Temptations came, but were so easily repulsed that she fell into the sin of vainglory. Then to punish her, as it seemed, God tempted her with lecherous desires, to which in the end she was anxious to succumb, but was humiliated when she approached her would-be lover who now repudiated her, and said that he would never consent for all the gold in the world: 'he would rather be hewn as small as flesh for the pot.' Further tribulations of this kind assailed her, but after much prayer and meditation an end came to this period of trial in due course: she and her husband went from place to place for her soul's health, until on one of their journeys, as they came from York in very hot weather on Midsummer eve, the old question of marital chastity was raised between them and Margery declared that she would rather see her husband slain than yield again to him. Later, as they sat by a wayside cross on the way to Bridlington, they came to a final agreement that he should not come again to her bed, on condition that she should pay all his debts before she started on her projected pilgrimage to Jerusalem. They solemnized their agreement by saying three paternosters kneeling beneath a cross in a field, and then with great gladness of spirit ate of the cake carried in his bosom and drank the beer from the bottle in her hand. Her emancipation was complete: henceforth, her husband was but a secondary figure in her life. She was the spouse of Christ, and her every waking hour was only profitable if spent in his service.

As we have seen, the great pilgrimage to Jerusalem was already in her mind, but, before this could be arranged, she spent much time moving about the country, at times impressing people by her sincerity and devotion, but often she ran into trouble by her outspokenness and scorn of religious men. At Canterbury she was accused of being a Lollard and threatened with the stake; at other times it was said an evil spirit vexed her or that some bodily sickness occasioned her behaviour, for she was wont to fall down in convulsions, making wondrous faces and gestures, all the time sobbing bitterly and crying loudly. At this period of her life two desires were uppermost in her mind. First, she wished to take a formal vow of chastity before a bishop, and to receive the mantle and ring of widowhood as a sign of her new estate: and secondly, she desired to dress in white, as a sign of virtue and purity. To this end she went to Lincoln to ask Bishop Philip Repington to grant to her her wishes. After waiting three weeks for the bishop to return to his palace she was received by him, and gave him an account of her meditations and contemplations, which so impressed him that he advised her to have them written down. This she was unwilling to do, and twenty years were to pass before she felt the time was ripe for this. When she made her request to be professed with mantle and ring and given the white robe, the bishop took advice of his council, and endeavoured to put her off until she returned from Jerusalem when, he said, she would be 'better proved and known'. In so doing he displayed worldly prudence, for to have afforded official recognition to this eccentric woman might have given his enemies a handle against him. This decision did not suit Margery, and on the next day she

> went to church and prayed to God with all her spirit that she might have knowledge how she might be governed in this matter, and what answer she might give to the Bishop.
> Our Lord Jesus Christ answered to her mind in this manner:
> Daughter, say to the Bishop that he fears the shames of the world more than the perfect love of God. . . . Therefore, daughter, tell him though he will not do it now, it shall be done another time when God willeth.

The bishop apparently took no offence at this bold speech, but advised her to go to the archbishop of Canterbury 'and to pray him to grant leave to me, the bishop of Lincoln, to give her the mantle and the ring, since she was not of his diocese. This cause he feigned through counsel of his clerks, for they loved her not.' Margery refused his advice, but said she would go to the archbishop 'for other causes and matters which I have to show to his reverence'. Even this ungracious answer failed to rouse Repington, who gave her a present of two marks (26s. 8d.) and asked her to pray for him.

Margery and her husband made their way to Lambeth Palace, and while waiting in the great hall heard the archbishop's clerks, squires and yeomen swearing and cursing among themselves. With characteristic lack of tact she rebuked them, whereupon a richly dressed woman turned on her with a fury of imprecations and concluded: 'I would thou wert in Smithfield, and I would carry a faggot to burn thee with. It is a pity that thou art alive!'

Then she was sent for by the archbishop, who kept her talking to him in his garden 'till stars appeared in the firmament'. Archbishop Arundel was a great prince of the Church and a relentless foe of Lollardy, and the fact that he talked so long with her and found no 'default in her' is the strongest possible evidence of the strength of her personality and the essential orthodoxy of her views. So impressed by her was Arundel that he suffered her to rebuke him for the behaviour of his servants, for whom she said 'ye shall answer, unless ye correct them, or else put them out of your service'. Arundel replied meekly and gave her a fair answer, and at length after much talk she came away.

As the autumn of the same year (1413) drew on Margery made the final preparations for her pilgrimage to the Holy Land. Her debts paid, she bade farewell to her husband and friends, and after praying at Norwich and again at Yarmouth, some time in November she sailed to the Netherlands and landed at Zealand. During the next month she and her companions travelled across Germany to Constance, and from there to Bologna, and so to Venice which she reached in January 1414. Here began a tedious wait of some months before the time came for the pilgrim galleys to set out. In the meantime, however, Margery had encountered plenty of trouble. First, she was reproved because she would eat no flesh and cried so loudly and constantly as to make herself a nuisance. Besides they said that she would talk of nothing but the love of the Lord at all times and places. Her fellow-pilgrims roundly abused her, and told her that they would not put up with her as her husband did, while one of them went so far as to say: 'I pray God that the devil's death may overcome thee soon.' Some deserted her and induced her handmaiden to leave her, while a fellow-pilgrim who had charge of her money gave her only a fraction of it, and told her to fend for herself. Fortunately others were kinder and took her along with them, but at Constance her persecutors rounded on her again and cut her gown so short that it came but little below the knee, while at the same time they gave her a piece of white canvas cut in the shape of an apron so that she should be thought a fool and despised. They also made her sit at the end of the table below everyone else, where she dared not utter a word. An English friar took her part and set her on her way to Bologna with an old Devonshire man, William Weaver. There her former companions found her, and a reconciliation was effected, Margery promising not to speak of the Gospel in their presence, and to be merry when they sat at meat. On reaching Venice, however, they quarrelled again, and for weeks she was alone until the time came to sail, probably some time in April. Further trouble then arose, for her companions secretly hired gear and places for themselves in one ship and were reluctant to take her with them. They changed their minds, however, when they later discovered that her 'voices' had warned her not to sail in that ship and they incontinently left it, and much against her will all sailed with her in the ship of her choice—an unwilling tribute to the spiritual power she exerted.

Although Margery tells us nothing, we know much about these pilgrim convoys from other fifteenth-century writers who made the pilgrimage or who wrote manuals for travellers. One of the fullest accounts is given by Friar Felix Fabri, who made his second journey in 1484, some seventy years later than Margery, but in essentials the conditions had remained unchanged, and we may gather from his account a vivid picture of what is meant to sail in a pilgrim galley during the fifteenth century. As the spring advanced, a number of galleys began to make ready for the voyage, and the first thing to do was to bargain for a place on one of these. Although they were private ventures, the Venetian State exercised a strict control over their masters, and saw to it that reasonable living conditions were provided for the pilgrims while at sea, and that the masters were responsible for their safe-conduct in the Holy Land itself. 'Venetian galleys are as like one to another as swallows' nests', we are told, and the pilgrims found on going on board that their quarters were in a 'cabin' below deck, which stretched the whole length of the ship, and was 'like a great and spacious chamber'. The friar tells us that 'the berths of the pilgrims are so arranged that all along the ship, or rather the cabin, one berth joins the next one without any space left between them, and one pilgrim lies by the side of another along both sides of the ship, having their heads towards the side of the ship, and their feet stretching out towards one another. As the cabin is wide, there stand along the middle of it, chests and trunks in which the pilgrims keep their own private property.' Once the pilgrim had struck his bargain with the master, he was alloted his place, according to what he had paid, and throughout the voyage made himself comfortable there as best he could.

Before embarking, however, he had to provide himself with a variety of articles necessary for his journey. He was advised to buy 'a little caldron, a frying-pan, dishes, plates, saucers, cups of glass, a grater for bread and such necessaries'. A chest to hold his clothes and barrels for water and wine were essentials, while many took coops of hens and a variety of victuals, for though the captain contracted to feed them throughout their journey, 'some time ye shall have feeble bread and feeble wine and stinking water, so that many times ye will be right fain to eat of your own'. Furthermore, a mattress and bedding were essential, for the captain provided nothing of this kind.

Once the journey had begun, the pilgrims settled down to the tedium of the voyage, which lasted about a month, depending on the number of places called at *en route* for fresh provisions, water and trading; on the delays caused by storms and by the appearance of pirates and other enemy vessels from time to time. These things enlivened the journey which otherwise passed slowly enough in talking, reading, praying or writing. Some meditated, others took violent exercise, climbing the rigging or lifting heavy weights. At times all seemed at peace one with another: at times quarrels and disputes broke out, making the galley like hell, says Friar

Felix, with the sound and fury of men's cursing and blasphemies. And finally 'there is among all the occupations of the seafarers one which, albeit loathsome, is yet very common, daily and necessary—I mean the hunting and catching of lice and vermin. Unless a man spends several hours in this work when he is on a pilgrimage, he will have but unquiet slumbers.' Games of chance, gambling and wine-drinking helped the hours to pass for some, while they waited for the call of the trumpet, summoning them to meals. On hearing this, all rushed to secure a place at one of the tables, 'for he who comes late gets a bad seat'. The meal is quickly served—salad, meat and some form of cereal and cheese, washed down by copious draughts of wine and water. A few noble or distinguished pilgrims had their own mess, and paid the cooks extra to cook for them, and the friar remarks on the noise and ill temper that comes from the close, over-heated cooks' galley as men struggle at the crowded fire-places to contrive a little space for their own pots and pans.

At nightfall with everyone trying to get to bed in very cramped quarters, all is noise and confusion. Quarrels easily arise, as each pilgrim tries to keep or win back the little space allotted to him. Those who have drunk too much are a particular nuisance, while the snores, moans and coughing of others, and the movements of the sailors overhead, prevent sleep coming easily, particularly as the heat steadily mounts in the crowded space and the scamperings of rats and mice help to take away the pilgrims' rest. As if this were not enough, some come to bed late and keep others awake by their chatter and by their refusal to put out their candles. Missiles and entreaties fail to move them: they only shout the louder and begin a new quarrel.

By day life also has its difficulties: petty theft is rampant; moving about the ship requires care, for things fall from above on the unwary pilgrim, and to walk carelessly in certain places involves the risk of being pitched overboard. The sailors are no respecters of persons, and when at work will roughly push aside or knock down those who get in their way. Hats are quickly blown away, while it is only too easy to drop valuable things into the sea when standing at the side of the boat.

From time to time the galley would put into some port so that fresh water, bread and other supplies could be laid in, and also to allow the master and his crew to buy and to sell, for all of them were determined and experienced bargainers. The pilgrims would also land to replenish their own stores, to see the sights and to pray at shrines and churches until the trumpets warned them that the ship was about to sail and that they must return at once. So the days wore on until the Holy Land drew near, and from the look-out an eager watch was kept, while the more ardent pilgrims stood hour by hour straining to see the sacred land of their desire. As soon as it was dawn they rushed on deck, and at last the watchman gave the long-expected signal, and gradually more and more of the pilgrims could see the land as the galley drew nearer, until at last it came to its anchorage in the harbour of Jaffa.

Now began a tedious wait for the pilgrims, anxious as they were to get on their way to Jerusalem, for they could not land until a safe-conduct had been received from the various Moslem officials who were the officers of the Mameluke sultans of Egypt. The master had first to get word sent to the governors of Jerusalem and of the other towns they would pass through for permission to proceed, and not until they had struck their bargains with the master was a single pilgrim safe to land. When finally they did so, they were herded like animals before the officials who entered their names on the roll, after which they were hustled along by Saracens into a series of caves, known as St Peter's cellars. Here the Christian dogs were roughly treated by their guards, who forbade them to wander outside although the caves were stinking with filth which lapped about their feet, and which they had to clear as best they could to make any space whereon they could lie. Their sufferings were eased by the arrival of traders who brought rushes and branches of trees which they placed on the miry ground while others brought sweet-smelling herbs, unguents and perfumes to solace the pilgrims. Others again brought bread and eggs, water, fruit and salads, which they willingly bought, and afterwards settled down to rest, but not before a fierce looking Saracen had exacted a penny from each of them in the way of rent—an operation he repeated early the next morning before he would allow anyone to leave the cave. Throughout the day young Turkish men moved in and out, provoking the pilgrims by their insults and outrageous behaviour, and if they struck back haling them before the Turkish officials so that they might be fined.

No term could be fixed to these delays: they were at the mercy of the various overlords, and until these were satisfied they were cooped up like beasts in the caves. At last, however, the period of waiting was over. The convoy was formed, and mounted on asses, with an escort of Saracens, the captains and governors leading the way, the pilgrims set out for Jerusalem. Their journey was often an eventful one, for the countryside was full of Arabs watching for an opportunity to rob or pillage. They would fall upon any small group if unprotected, or would attach themselves to the caravan and steal scrips, clothes and the like if these fell to the ground or were left unguarded. As the pilgrims passed through the villages they were often met with curses or even with volleys of stones. In addition the cavalcade raised clouds of dust, and this and the great heat made nightfall and rest in one of the pilgrim houses particularly grateful. There they were able to buy food and drink from the villagers—bread, eggs, rice cooked in milk, fruit and wine—but had to be extremely careful not to provoke them in any way.

So they gradually made their way to Jerusalem: on viewing the city many of the pilgrims wept for joy, knelt and bowed their faces to the earth, and above all, says Friar Felix, 'the women pilgrims shrieked as though in labour, cried aloud and wept'. Within the city there was much to see, and all the many places associated with the sacred story were visited, culminating in the Church of the Holy Sepulchre, or the Temple as it was sometimes called. Here the pilgrims were shown the chamber in which was the supposed tomb of Christ, and in another part of the building was the hole that received the base of the Cross. Here also they spent the night in contemplation and prayer, Margery Kempe and her party staying within the Sepulchre from one evensong to the next.

On arrival in the Holy Land Margery's religious zeal and emotion knew no bounds. She could scarcely ride on her ass at times, so acutely did she feel, while Mount Calvary and other holy places provoked tremendous displays: she wept and sobbed plenteously; she fell down because she could not stand or kneel, and rolled and wrestled with her body, and cried as though her heart would burst asunder. This crying, indeed, became part of her for many years, for as she says:

> This manner of crying endured many years after this time for aught that any man might do, and therefore she suffered much despite and reproof. The crying was so loud and so wonderful that it astounded people unless they had heard it before, or unless they knew the cause of the crying. First she had her cryings at Jerusalem and also in Rome. And when she came home to England, they came once a month, then once a week, then daily, and once she had fourteen in a day! and so on as God would visit her. She never knew the time or the hour when they would come, and as soon as she found that she would cry, she would suppress it as much as possible so as not to annoy people. For some said it was a wicked spirit vexed her: some said it was a sickness: some said she had drunk too much wine: some wished she had been in the haven: some would she had been at sea in a bottomless boat: and thus each man had his own thoughts.

Obviously, Margery was not easy to live with, and the pilgrims again deserted her on their return to Venice, some of them saying that they would go with her no further for a hundred pounds. The Lord told her to go to Rome, whither she was led by a broken-backed, poverty-stricken man, Richard of Ireland, and finally she reached Rome about September 1414 and was there until the following spring. While there, she assumed the white habit she had so long desired to wear, and lived as best she could, since she gave away all her money at one point in obedience to the Lord's command. Richard, not unnaturally, was 'greatly moved and evil pleased because of this, and spake right sharply to her', but she pacified him, and went about serving the people, declaring the faith, begging from door to door, welcomed here and repulsed there as the event fell. She gives many examples of all this, and was sustained throughout by her constant communings and messages from the Lord, and finally at Easter 1415 set off for England. Despite fears of thieves assailing her and her party on the way, she reached Middelburg in Zealand by mid-May, and crossed over to England safely in a little boat in less than two days. She knelt and kissed the land on coming on shore, and happily passed on to offer the three-halfpence given to her then at the cathedral at Norwich.

So ended her first and greatest pilgrimage. She had been absent from England some eighteen months and had survived difficulties and dangers which would have overwhelmed one less convinced of her divinely controlled life.❖

RECOMMENDED READINGS

Margery Kempe's autobiography has been translated into modern English by B. A. Windeatt, *The Book of Margery Kempe* (New York: Penguin Books, 1986), and a fuller biography has been provided by Louise Collins, *Memoirs of a Medieval Woman: The Life and Times of Margery Kempe* (New York: Thomas Y. Crowell, 1964). Eileen Power has sketched the lives of other interesting medieval women in *Medieval Women,* ed. M. M. Postan (Cambridge: Cambridge University Press, 1975). The devotional writings of a contemporary of Margery are available in Julian of Norwich, *Revelations of Divine Love,* trans. Clifton Wolters (New York: Penguin Books, 1966). Those who are intrigued by the circumstances of Miss Allen's discovery of Margery's manuscript will enjoy Richard D. Altick's stories of adventures in literary scholarship, *The Scholar Adventurers* (New York: The Free Press, 1977).

Indian Ocean, A.D. 1433

THE CHINESE REACH OUT
THE MARITIME EXPEDITIONS OF CHÊNG HO

Daniel J. Boorstin

We have already noted that the European expansion beginning in 1500 and the ensuing European global domination were perhaps the most important fact in the history of the modern world. In the selection entitled "The Thirteenth-Century World System," Janet Abu-Lughod argues that the Europeans did not create a commercial network, but took over one that already existed and were able to do so because of their aggressive approach to trade.

If European predominance did not come about because of any technological or scientific superiority, it follows that one or another of the other great civilizations of the Old World—Islam, Hindu, or Chinese—might have anticipated the Europeans by launching their own explorations and dominating the world's sea-lanes themselves. In this and a later selection, Daniel Boorstin considers why the Chinese and the Muslims did not do so.

The Chinese certainly had the technology and ability to do so. Between 1405 and 1433, the Ming emperors sent out seven great naval expeditions under the court eunuch and admiral, Chêng Ho. These fleets were composed of immense ships and were guided by excellent maps and advanced navigational equipment. During this quarter century, Chinese ships visited almost the entire littoral of the Indian Ocean and were not far from the tip of Africa. Compared to these great expeditions, the Portuguese fleet of Vasco da Gama that reached the region a half century later was a paltry affair.

But da Gama's fleet was only the first of many, and European naval activity continued to grow. After 1433, by contrast, the Chinese ceased to send out naval expeditions and concentrated instead on internal improvements. By 1550, the Chinese oceangoing fleet was broken up and Chinese were forbidden to travel on the high seas. In the following selection, Boorstin examines the reasons for the Great Withdrawal and for Chinese failure to seize the opportunity for world leadership.

READING QUESTIONS

1. Why was it significant that Chêng Ho was a eunuch?

2. Why was there friction between state officials and court eunuchs?

3. What was the purpose of Chêng Ho's expeditions?

4. What was the nature of the Chinese tributary system?

5. Why did the Chinese government abandon its maritime ventures?

hen Prince Henry the Navigator was sending his ships inching down the west coast of Africa, on the other side of the planet Chinese navigators possessed a navy unparalleled in numbers, in skills, and in technology. Their grand fleet had already sailed beyond the China Sea and around the Indian Ocean, reaching down the east coast of Africa to the very tip of the Dark Continent. But while the exploits of Prince Henry's ships were a prologue to seafaring voyages that would discover a whole New World and circumnavigate the globe, the grander Chinese expeditions of the same era were a dead end. They prefaced the catastrophic withdrawal of the Chinese into their own borders, with consequences we still see today.

What made the Great Withdrawal of 1433 so dramatic was that the Chinese seafaring outreach had been so spectacular. The hero, whose name became a byword for Chinese seafaring power, the designer and commander of the most remarkable of these wide-ranging ventures, was Chêng Ho, the Admiral of the Triple Treasure, commonly known as the Three-Jewel Eunuch, perhaps from the three precious elements of Buddhism—the Buddha, the Dharma, and the Sangha—or from the gems he gave as gifts and received as tribute. The fact that Chêng Ho was a eunuch, as we shall see, helps explain how he managed to develop these grand adventures, and also why they were so abruptly concluded.

In the West, *castrati* are known to history not for their political influence but mainly for their vocal peculiarities. In addition to removing the power to procreate, the castrating operation retards the deepening of the voice, and leaves the eunuch a soprano. From Constantinople the practice spread of using eunuchs in choirs. In the eighteenth century Handel's operas featured *castrati,* who then began to dominate the opera scene, sometimes requiring composers to write in parts especially for them. Until the early nineteenth century *castrati* sang in the papal choir in Rome. The Italian practice of castrating boys to prepare them to become adult male sopranos did not end till the reign of Pope Leo XIII in the late nineteenth century.

From Daniel J. Boorstin, *The Discoverers* (New York: Vintage Books, 1985), pp. 186–193, 199–201.

Religious dogma led some pious men to emasculate themselves to avoid sexual sin or temptation. "There be eunuchs," preached the Gospel according to St. Matthew (19:12), "which have made themselves eunuchs for the kingdom of heaven's sake. He that is able to receive it, let him receive it." The Church Father Origen (A.D. 185?–254) followed this advice, and after him there grew up a whole sect who castrated themselves the better to enter the kingdom of heaven. Such a sect persisted into twentieth-century Russia.

Wherever eunuchs have been able to exercise political influence, it has been a symptom both of the secluded position of women and of despotic government. The surgical act that deprived the eunuch of his sexual powers qualified him to be "keeper of the couch" ("eunuch" is from Greek "bed-watcher"). Where the monarch maintained a harem of wives and concubines, only members of his immediate family were permitted to reside within the palace precincts. The eunuchs detailed to attend on the women of the harem, being no menace to the purity of the imperial line or to the chastity of the royal consorts, were an exception. They became a privileged class. Knowledge of the daily habits and personal tastes of the emperors gave eunuchs a peculiar opportunity to anticipate the monarch's whims. In the arbitrary governments of the East this meant an opportunity to seize power. The power of eunuchs was conspicuous under the Byzantine emperors, when the brilliant Justinian I, codifier and preserver of Roman law, made the eunuch Narses (478?–573?) one of his generals. This choice was justified when Narses led the Byzantine armies in Italy to drive out the Goths, Alamanni, and Franks (553). The Ottoman sultans also put their eunuchs in commanding positions. The institutionalized influence of eunuchs over their royal masters became so familiar in Egypt that the term "eunuch" came to be used for any officer of the court, whether castrated or not. At times people were tempted to call their government a "Eunarchy."

Chinese imperial institutions proved peculiarly favorable to the power of eunuchs. The rigid court etiquette, as early as Han times in the reign (126–144) of Han Shun Ti, confined the emperor to his palace and the palace garden, like that where the Heavenly Clockwork would be displayed. On the rare occasions when he left those confines the emperor's advance men cleared the road of the populace and he was protected from the public gaze. Even the ministers of state could not converse with him familiarly. They saw him only at formal audiences when they were expected to address him through other officials also "below the steps" who stood nearer to the emperor's high throne. The term of respectful address to the emperor in Chinese *(Chieh Hsia),* the equivalent for the Western term "Your Majesty," meant "from below the steps." By contrast, the favored imperial eunuchs living inside the palace had daily converse with the emperor. Ministers of state could only offer formal reports and written memorials, but the eunuchs could whisper in the emperor's ear.

If the emperor had grown up outside the palace and came to the throne only as an adult, the eunuchs were less likely to exert political power. But again and again in later Chinese history the heir, born in the palace, grew up under constant tutelage of the eunuchs. When such an emperor, still a child, succeeded to the throne, the imperial eunuchs would control the child-emperor's decisions or those of the empress-regent. These eunuchs, who first became influential under the late Han emperors, were usually drawn from the lowest levels of society. Having no future outside the palace, they had no reason not to merit their reputation for being mercenary and un-scrupulous. They collected bribes, distributed honors, and meted out the punishments of the torture chamber.

But gradually a new scholarly class, disciples and interpreters of Confu-cius, also recruited from the poorer classes, became organized into a civil service. The lines between the pro- and anti-eunuch forces were now clearly drawn. The scholar-bureaucrats feared, envied, and despised the eu-nuchs who excelled them in power, even without being able to recite a sin-gle passage from the Confucian classics. The military class, led by generals who had risen by their competence, had reasons of their own to feel con-tempt for these effeminate imperial confidants of the bedchamber who had never fought a battle. The scholars and the generals somehow never man-aged to combine against those advisers who lived where adversaries could not penetrate.

One of these strategically placed eunuchs was Chêng Ho. For reasons that are themselves a part of our story, we know far less about Chêng Ho than about Henry the Navigator, Vasco da Gama, Columbus, Vespucci, or Magellan, who were his European counterparts. We do know that he was born a Muslim, but we know little else, except that he probably was a person of low birth who came from the south-China province of Yunnan.

The setting for Chêng Ho's exploits on the sea had been prepared a cen-tury earlier, when the last Mongol emperor was driven from Peking by the upstart "Chinese Napoleon." Chu Yüan-chang, the clever son of a poor farm laborer, was born in the eastern province of Anhwei, where his whole fam-ily died in an epidemic when he was only seventeen. He entered a Buddhist monastery, but when he was twenty-five, he took off his saffron robes and went out to lead his province against the Mongol intruders. After thirteen years of struggle his forces finally occupied Peking in 1368. Still only forty, he proclaimed himself the first emperor of the new Ming dynasty. While keeping his own capital in Nanking, the Southern Capital, he sent officials from the north to administer the south and officials from the south to ad-minister the north, hoping in that way to draw the nation together. During his thirty-year rule he managed to consolidate the nation, which had long been split by Mongol domination of the north.

The Emperor Chu Yüan-chang never ceased to resent reference to his lowly origins or his early years as a Buddhist monk. When two unlucky Con-fucian scholars in a congratulatory message made the mistake of using the word "birth" *(sheng)* which might have been misconstrued to be a pun for the word "monk" *(seng)*, they were sentenced to death. No religious crusader, he surrounded himself with Buddhist monks at the same time that he promoted Confucian academies and Confucian rituals.

As he grew older he suspected plots everywhere. It became a capital crime even to petition against any of his policies, and when he thought he noticed a rebellious spirit in Nanking he executed fifteen thousand people at one swoop.

The person who filled the post of prime minister, though appointed by the emperor, was usually promoted upward from the bureaucracy. Since the prime ministers had come from outside the palace circle, often having risen from the common people, they reached their position by academic attainments and personal competence. The prime minister thus was a wholesome check on the whims of the emperor and on the influence of the palace clique. But Chu Yüan-chang consolidated his personal rule by putting an end to the post of prime minister. When he suspected his prime minister of treason, he summarily abolished the post, providing that "anyone who dares to petition for its reestablishment will be ordered to perish immediately together with the rest of his family." This inevitably increased the power of the others who had the Emperor's ear, who of course were the eunuchs.

At the same time that this first Ming emperor took steps to lessen the powers of the bureaucracy he inaugurated other policies which hardened into hatred the suspicions that the regular civil servants had long felt against the eunuchs. In a peculiarly contemptuous gesture, he defied the ancient Chinese tradition, reinforced by Confucian teachings, that a gentleman or scholar should never be humiliated. If a scholar failed in his duty he could be ordered to his death, and was expected to commit suicide, but he was not to be publicly degraded. But the parvenu Chu Yüan-chang seemed to enjoy humiliating his intellectual superiors. At his court he made a public ritual of the flogging of high officials who seemed independent-minded or insufficiently sycophantic. All the court were required to be present in their ceremonial robes to watch their colleague stripped and beaten to death by scores of blows with a wooden rod. The Emperor's defenders argued that this practice actually did reduce bribery among the bureaucracy. It was the eunuchs, with their intimate access to the Emperor, who controlled and assigned these ritual floggings.

After the thirty-year rule of Chu Yüan-chang, and the brief reign of his reformist son who championed the Confucian way, a palace revolt was engineered by Yung Lo (1359–1424), the Emperor's uncle, with the assistance of the court eunuchs. Just as Kublai Khan had tried to build a Chinese empire for the Mongols, so Yung Lo now set out to encompass the Mongol Empire for the Chinese. In 1409 he boldly moved his headquarters northward from Nanking, the Southern Capital, to Peking, the Northern Capital, on the very borders of Mongol power, defiantly close to the Great Wall. He reshaped Peking into a rectangle-dominated imperial capital with a "Violet-purple Forbidden City," the abode of the Emperor, at its very center, embellished by a splendid ensemble of palaces, terraces, artificial lakes and hills, gardens, and vistas of shrubs and flowers brought from the far corners of the empire.

The megalomaniac Yung Lo soon decided to send out naval expeditions with messages of his grandeur into all the surrounding seas. For the command he chose Chêng Ho. These expeditions (1405–33), the vastest until then seen on our planet, enlisted some thirty-seven thousand in their crews, in flotillas of as many as three hundred and seventeen ships. Vessels ranged in size from the largest, the Treasure Ship carrying nine masts, 444 feet long with a beam of 180 feet, down through the ranks of Horse Ship, Supply Ship, Billet Ship, to the smallest, the Combat Ship, which carried five masts and measured 180 feet by 68 feet. Ibn Battuta, a century earlier, and Nicolo de' Conti, who was a passenger on a Chinese ship about this time, were both astonished that these vessels were so much larger than any they had seen in the West.

Westerners also noted the remarkable construction that prevented water in one part of the hull from flooding the whole ship. Bulkheads, a series of upright partitions dividing the ship's hold into compartments to prevent spread of leakage or fire, though then novel to Europe were an old story in China. They were probably suggested by the septa, the transverse membranes of the bamboo. Already in ancient pre-Han China, this design gave the strength and resiliency that made possible the multistoried ships which dazzled visitors from abroad with their high overhanging stern gallery, from which was suspended a gargantuan rudder with a blade of 450 square feet. These were only a few of the remarkable features of Chêng Ho's navy. Of course he used the compass, and perhaps other directional instruments, along with elaborate navigational charts showing detailed compass bearings. Though the Chinese had long been using the grid for charting the land, Chêng Ho's maps yield no evidence that they used latitude and longitude at sea.

Chêng Ho took his navy—we must not call it an armada, for it was not designed for battle—to nearly every inhabited land bordering the China Sea and the Indian Ocean. For at least five hundred years, since the glorious renaissance in the T'ang dynasty, the Chinese had been trading overseas with the Islamic world. To their own maps they had added the Nile, the Sudan, Zanzibar, and even some south Mediterranean places. Perhaps this knowledge came indirectly from Arab traders, but recent finds of T'ang and Sung coins and porcelain all along the African coast from Somalia to Zanzibar suggest that the Chinese themselves were there. Chêng Ho's expeditions were so well equipped with Chinese speaking the languages of these places that they must have had a long experience of dealing overseas.

Seven expeditions reached farther and farther west. The first, which set out in 1405, visited Java and Sumatra, then Ceylon and Calicut. The following expeditions reached Siam, made Malacca a headquarters for visiting the East Indies, then went on to Bengal, to the Maldive Islands and as far west as the Persian sultanate of Ormuz at the entrance to the Persian Gulf. Pacific squadrons visited Ryukyu and Brunei, while others went farther westward from Ormuz to Aden at the mouth of the Red Sea, then southwestward down the African coast to Mogadishu in Somaliland, to Malindi north of Mombasa, and to the Zanzibar coast. The adventuring sixth expedition (1421–22), within only two years, visited thirty-six states stretching the full width of the Indian Ocean from Borneo to Zanzibar. It was an ill omen for the grand enterprise when Chêng Ho's patron, the emperor Yung Lo, died in 1424. His successor supported the anti-maritime party by stopping the voyage planned for that year.

Chêng Ho's voyages then became pawns of the imperial succession. After the anti-maritime emperor's short reign his successor, a maritime enthusiast, supported the seventh and most expansive of all the voyages. Carrying 27,550 officers and men, this two-year expedition ranging farther than any of its predecessors, on its return in 1433 had established diplomatic or tributary relations with twenty realms and sultanates from Java on the east through the Nicobar Islands all the way to Mecca on the northwest and far down the east coast of Africa. Now these distant peoples, who for a thousand years had known small Chinese junks in their waters, were overwhelmed by many-storied ships, vaster than any seen before or any that the Portuguese would bring their way. They must have been puzzled that so potent a navy should pretend to have no warlike mission.

The purpose of these Grand Treasure Fleets is difficult for the Western mind to grasp. Chêng Ho's interests and aims were as far apart as the poles from those of the European fleets of the Age of Discovery. The Portuguese voyaging down the west African coast and around the Cape to India hoped to increase their nation's wealth, to secure the staples and the luxuries of the East, and to convert the heathen to Christianity. For his trading goods, as we have seen, Vasco da Gama brought bolts of striped cloth, washbasins, strings of beads, and lumps of sugar—which made the Samuri of Calicut laugh in contempt. The "goods" the Portuguese extracted included slaves by the thousands, who from Angola alone before the mid-seventeenth century numbered one and a third million. With ships heavily armed for battle, they were uninhibited in using terror. We have seen how Vasco da Gama cut up the bodies of casually captured traders and fishermen, and sent a basketful of their hands, feet and heads to the Samuri of Calicut simply to persuade him into a quick surrender. Once in power, the Portuguese governed their India in the same spirit. When Viceroy Almeida was suspicious of a messenger who came under a safe-conduct to see him, he tore out the messenger's eyes. Viceroy Albuquerque subdued the peoples along the Arabian coast by cutting off the noses of their women and the hands of their men. Portuguese ships sailing into remote harbors for the first time would display the corpses of recent captives hanging from the yardarms to show that they meant business.

Chêng Ho's navy came from another world. The purpose of his vast, costly, and far-ranging expeditions was not to collect treasure or trade or convert or conquer or gather scientific information. Few naval expeditions in recent history have had any other purpose. Chinese chroniclers repeated the report that Chêng Ho was first sent out to track down Emperor Yung Lo's nephew, whose throne Yung Lo had usurped, who had fled from Nanking and was said to be wandering abroad. But other, larger motives developed as the expeditions proceeded.

The voyages became an institution in themselves, designed to display the splendor and power of the new Ming dynasty. And the voyages proved that ritualized and nonviolent techniques of persuasion could extract tribute from remote states. The Chinese would not establish their own permanent bases within the tributary states, but instead hoped to make "the whole world" into voluntary admirers of the one and only center of civilization.

With this in mind, the Chinese navy dared not loot the states that it visited. Chêng Ho would not seek slaves or gold or silver or spices. Nothing would suggest that the Chinese needed what other nations had. While peoples of Asia would be struck by the Portuguese power to seize, the Chinese would impress by their power to give. They would unwittingly dramatize the Christian axiom that it was nobler to give than to receive. Instead of shoddy trinkets and childish gewgaws, they offered treasures of the finest craftsmanship. European expeditions to Asia revealed how desperately Europeans wanted the peculiar products of the East, but the prodigal gestures of Chinese expeditions would show how content the Chinese were with what they already had. This "tribute" system, which then dominated Chinese relations with other Asian states, was bafflingly different from any to which the Western mind has become accustomed. A state bringing tribute to China was not submitting to a conqueror. Rather, it was acknowledging that China, by definition the *only* truly civilized state, was beyond the need for assistance. Tributes therefore were less economic than symbolic. A tributary state declared its willingness to enjoy the benevolence of Chinese culture, and in return China demonstrated "the generosity and abundance of the Central Kingdom." No wonder the Chinese found it hard to imagine a community of sovereign nations! Only China was truly sovereign, for only China was worthy of sovereignty. The corrosive consequences of this frame of mind persisted into the twentieth century.

During the days of Chêng Ho the Chinese practiced what they preached, with costly consequences. The lopsided logic of the tributary system required China to pay out more than China received. Every new tributary state worsened the imbalance of Chinese trade. The accidents of history that cast Chinese public relations in this curious frame help explain why Chinese communication with the outside world was stultified for centuries to come. Meanwhile, the tributary system became a blind for the burgeoning commercial demands of other nations. Foreign sovereigns were not reticent to receive "gifts" from the Chinese emperor which were really bribes to encourage them to give peacefully what might have been taken violently. The Chinese government became the cat's-paw for foreign powers. Over the centuries the weakening Chinese government continued to receive foreign traders in the flattering guise of "tributaries." But in the time of Chêng Ho the Chinese Emperor managed, at least for a while, to give substance to his assertion that the Central Kingdom needed nothing from anybody and had nothing to learn from anybody.

No less remarkable than Chêng Ho's far-flung naval enterprises themselves was the suddenness with which they came to an end. Had this Chinese Columbus been followed by a procession of Chinese Vespuccis, Balboas, Magellans, Cabots, Corteses, and Pizarros, then the history of the world might have been quite different. But Chêng Ho had no successor, and Chinese naval activity abroad came to a sudden halt. Energies formerly spent sending out expeditions were all at once spent enforcing withdrawal. The Europeans' race for colonies and their quest for *terra incognita* had no counterpart in modern Chinese history. And the exploring spirit remained alien to China.

Chinese reclusiveness was an old story. The Great Wall, which goes back to antiquity, the third century B.C., was given its present form in the Ming dynasty, in the age of Chêng Ho. There is nothing like it in scale or in chronological continuity anywhere else in the world. The spirit of the Great Wall was expressed in countless other ways. One was the Great Withdrawal, when the emperor forbade his subjects to go abroad. Chinese seen outside their country were there illegally, and indiscreet travelers were punished with beheading. Chêng Ho's grand seventh voyage was China's last. His return home in 1433 marked an end to his country's organized seafaring adventures. An imperial edict in that year, and others that followed (1449, 1452) imposed increasingly savage punishments on Chinese who ventured abroad.

Of course there were practical reasons for the Great Withdrawal. Adding and maintaining tributary states was costly. For, as we have seen, the burden of the Chinese tribute system lay mostly on the "receiver." Impressing so many countries at such a distance was a heavy expense with meager economic return. Was so costly an ego trip for the nation, for the Emperor, and for his eunuchs really necessary? If China really was the all-perfect Center, was not such expensive reassurance superfluous?

Opposition to Chêng Ho's exploits was only another skirmish in the age-old battle of the Confucian bureaucrats against the court eunuchs. The centralized bureaucracy, dominated by scholars in the Confucian tradition, had been one of the most precocious of Chinese achievements. The bureaucrats sensibly argued that the imperial treasure be spent on water-conservation projects to help farmers, on granary projects to forestall famine, or on canals to improve internal communication, and not on pompous and reckless maritime adventures. What had these brought in, besides a few precious gems, and useless curiosities like rhinoceroses and giraffes?

Some incidental advantages did come from opening communications with all the countries around the Indian Ocean and the China Sea. But the Chinese balance of trade remained adverse, and when a drastic currency depreciation brought paper money down to 0.1 percent of face value, overseas trade relations could be kept up only by exporting gold and silver. Meanwhile, the thousand-mile-long Grand Canal reaching from Tientsin in the north to Hangchow in the south, begun two thousand years earlier, was perfected into a full-capacity, all-season seaway. Canal shipping displaced the seafaring vessels formerly needed to carry food from one part of the country to another, and maritime transport of grain was abolished.

At the same time, threats from Mongols and Tartars on the northwest frontiers required heavy military expenditures. The 1,500-mile-long Great Wall had to be repaired, and it was rebuilt into its present shape. Within fifteen years after Chêng Ho's return from his last voyage, the same Chinese emperor who had suppressed the Grand Treasure Fleets would be captured by Mongol and Tartar armies. By 1474 the main fleet of 400 warships had declined to 140. Shipyards disintegrated, sailors deserted, and shipwrights, fearing to become accomplices in the crime of seafaring, were hard to find. The ban on foreign maritime ventures was extended to include coastal shipping. Within a few years "there was not an inch of planking on the sea." Within a century—the century of Henry the Navigator, when European conquistadores and circumnavigators were reaching across the oceans and around the world—the Chinese were perfecting laws and organizing officials to suppress all seafaring. By 1500 it had been made a capital offense even to build a seagoing junk with more than two masts. In 1525 coastal officials were ordered to destroy all such ships and to arrest mariners who continued to sail in them. In 1551 the crime of espionage was redefined to include all who went to sea in multiple-masted ships, even if they went only to trade. The party of anti-maritime bureaucrats had triumphed. China turned back on herself.

The Chinese had long since developed their own version of the *oikoumene,* the habitable world, which put them at the center. They were their own Jerusalem. Since the Ming emperors were the Sons of Heaven, they were by definition supreme rulers and superiors of all other people on earth. While other peoples would exclude foreigners because they were not of their tribe, the Chinese automatically incorporated the rest of the world into theirs, in the role of barbarian acolytes. How natural that all non-Chinese peoples should pay tribute! And how obvious that the Chinese had little to gain overseas! Commerce abroad was beneath the needs of the Sons of Heaven.

When Europeans were sailing out with enthusiasm and high hopes, landbound China was sealing her borders. Within her physical and intellectual Great Wall, she avoided encounter with the unexpected. The unit of Chinese geographic description had long been the *kuo,* or "country," an inhabited land under an established government. And only such a government could be a tributary to the Sons of Heaven. The Chinese therefore showed little interest in lands uninhabited or out of reach. Confucian orthodoxy since the second century had confirmed their inward emphasis.

Why should Confucian scholars concern themselves with the mere physical layout of the outer world? The sphericity of the earth interested them less as a phenomenon of geography than as a fact of astronomy. The Greek notion of five bands of *climata* extending around the globe and companion doctrines characterizing the plants and animals that grew in each zone were not congenial. Instead, they described the cultural features of all parts of the globe by their relationship to the one Central Kingdom, and felt no impulse to find seaways to exotic lands or to quest for *terra incognita*. Fully equipped with the technology, the intelligence, and the national resources to become discoverers, the Chinese doomed themselves to be the discovered.❖

RECOMMENDED READINGS

The history and achievements of the Ming dynasty are covered in a series of excellent scholarly studies: Charles O. Hucker, *The Ming Dynasty, Its Origins and Evolving Institutions* (Ann Arbor: Center for Chinese Studies, University of Michigan, 1978); Edward L. Dreyer, *Early Ming China: A Political History, 1355-1435* (Stanford, CA: Stanford University Press, 1982); and Albert Chan, *The Glory and Fall of the Ming Dynasty* (Norman: University of Oklahoma Press, 1982). A journal entitled *Ming Studies* has been published from Minneapolis since 1975, and articles on major figures of the Ming period have been collected in *Dictionary of Ming Biography, 1368-1644,* ed. Carrington Goodrich (New York: Columbia University Press, 1976).

Accounts of medieval Chinese travelers to the West and of China's relations with the peoples of central and southern Asia may be found in an old but useful work by E. Bretschneider, *Mediaeval Researches from Eastern Asiatic Sources* (London: K. Paul, Trench, Trubner, 1887). China's African connections are the subject of J. J. L. Duyvendak, *China's Discovery of Africa* (London: A. Probsthain, 1949), and a technical, but illuminating study of one aspect of that trade may be found in Caroline Sassoon, *Chinese Porcelain Marks from Coastal Sites in Kenya: Aspects of Trade in the Indian Ocean, XIV–XIX Centuries* (Oxford, UK: BAR, 1978).

The best available early account is that of Ma Huan, *Ying-yai Sheng-lan: "The Overall Survey of the Ocean's Shores [1433],"* trans. J. V. G. Mills (Cambridge, UK: Published for the Hakluyt Society by the University Press, 1970).

Italy, A.D. 1479

A PLAGUE DOCTOR

Carlo M. Cipolla

Historians generally state that western Europe was relatively isolated from the rest of the Old World and was protected from the plagues that periodically swept up and down its complex of trade routes. Western Europe was thus free from severe epidemics from A.D. 543 until the coming of the Black Death in 1347. This is not quite true; the Crusades brought western Europe into close contact with the East. One of the results of the Second Crusade was the introduction of a contagious variety of leprosy, and a deadly form of dysentery swept Europe in the wake of the Third Crusade. The cities and towns of western Europe developed means of combating these onslaughts in the form of charity hospitals, nursing orders for men and women, quarantine laws, emergency burial regulations, rudimentary public health offices, and the like. Europe was not completely unprepared for the Black Death and the regular recurrence of deadly epidemics thereafter.

In the following selection, Carlo Cipolla discusses how one such institution, the plague doctor, had evolved by the close of the medieval period and the eve of the Age of Discovery and Exploration. The story of Master Ventura's negotiations with the officials of the city of Pavia illustrates two aspects of European life that would be significant elements in the future.

The first is that Europe had become a great repository of disease microorganisms. Waves of disease had weeded out the weaker members of the society, but even the strong survivors were carriers of various illnesses, including measles, chicken pox, tuberculosis, diphtheria, malaria, and even more. Wherever the Europeans went, they carried their complex baggage of bacteria and viruses with them.

The second aspect is illustrated by Ventura's willingness to risk death to gain an economic advantage. Untimely death had become so common that life, even one's own life, was not regarded as particularly valuable. The Europeans had come to hold human life cheap; this explains a good deal about both the courage and brutality of the discoverers and conquerors.

READING QUESTIONS

1. What was a plague doctor?

2. In their negotiations with Ventura, what were the major concerns of representatives of the city of Pavia?

3. What were Ventura's major concerns?

4. What did Ventura have to gain from his dangerous deal with Pavia?

T he Medieval and Renaissance city was afflicted with a problem which was essentially ecological in nature, namely a violent disequilibrium between the density of the population and the prevailing levels of hygiene and public health. The dire result of this disequilibrium was the recurrence of epidemics, mostly of bubonic plague, which at closely spaced intervals wiped out a large portion of the population. Ever since the outbreak of the great pandemic of 1347–51 people recognized the infectious nature of plague, but because they were totally ignorant of the sequence rat → rat's flea → man they overrated the possibility of man to man infection. Thus it was not easy in time of epidemic to find doctors willing to treat plague patients. On the other hand, if the plague were so highly contagious, a doctor visiting a patient—it was argued—would not only easily contract the infection but would also carry it to other people or to patients suffering from other ailments. The solution to this double-edged problem was found with the institution of the community plague doctors. These were physicians or surgeons, especially hired by an infected town or village in time of an epidemic, who were responsible for the treatment of the plague patients only and had to refrain from intercourse with the rest of the population. Their job was not only particularly dangerous but also very unpleasant because the plague doctor was quarantined, so to speak, for the entire period of the epidemic and some time thereafter. Those who applied for such positions were normally either second rate doctors who had not been particularly successful in their practice or young doctors trying to establish themselves. Texts of agreements between town administrations and plague doctors are not difficult to find in the archives and some have been published. Although they inform us about the terms

From Carlo M. Cipolla, "A Plague Doctor," in Harry A. Miskimin, David Herlihy, and A. L. Udovitch, eds., *The Medieval City* (New Haven and London: Yale University Press, 1977), pp. 65–72.

eventually agreed upon by the parties involved, the cold and detached juridical prose of the notaries hardly reveals the bargaining which always preceded the final settlements. The bargaining was often hard. On May 10, 1630, the town council of Torino considered the conditions requested by one Dr. Maletto to serve as a plague doctor. After some discussion the council instructed its representatives "to deal promptly with Dr. Maletto. They should try to reduce his pretenses and extract the best possible deal for this community but they ought to be careful not to lose the opportunity of hiring Dr. Maletto because it would be difficult to find a substitute at the same salary."

In the Communal Archive at Pavia (Lombardy) there is the original draft of an agreement reached between the community and a plague doctor. The document is of special interest because it shows a series of corrections and additions to the original text that are suggestive of the bargaining that took place.

The document is dated May 6, 1479, and it contains the "conditions agreed upon between the magnificent Community of Pavia and the doctor of medicine Giovanni de Ventura in order to treat the patients suffering from the plague."

The first clause deals with the salary. The community promised to pay to the doctor a monthly salary of 30 florins, which, as we shall see, had to be net of living expenses.

The second clause originally provided that the community would pay the salary two months in advance. This amounted to an interest-free deposit equivalent to two months' salary in favor of the doctor. However, in the bargaining that followed, the clause was modified, and the town's representatives managed to cut the advance to one month's salary.

Obviously the doctor had some doubts about the solvency of the community, and he was not satisfied with the advance payment. He wanted more guarantees, and the third clause of the contract stipulates that the community had to give the doctor an adequate pledge for the payment of his salary. On this point there seems to have been no further discussion.

A fourth clause also raised no difficulties. It was common practice in the hiring of an immigrant community doctor, whether plague doctor or not, that the community would provide him with a convenient house free of charge or at a reduced rent. In this particular case, the community of Pavia promised to provide Dr. Ventura with "an adequate house in an adequate location," completely furnished, at the community's expense. The clause suggests that Dr. Ventura had not been living in Pavia.

Disagreement must have flared up again on the fifth clause. Originally it had been stipulated that the city administration would continue to pay the doctor his salary for two months after the termination of his employment. Later on, however, the town's representatives backed out, and in the subsequent bargaining, as in the matter of the advance, they managed to reduce the extra pay to one month's salary.

In both clause two and clause five, the final text is less favorable to Giovanni Ventura than the original draft. Were the administrators beginning to feel some doubts about the quality of the doctor's services? Or, having brought the doctor to the verge of acceptance, did they feel that toughness might extract from him an even better deal? We shall never know, but the modifications to the original text of clauses six and seven seem to favor the first hypothesis. The sixth clause originally specified the duties of the doctor, emphasizing the limits of his obligation. It stipulated that "the said master Giovanni shall not be bound nor held under obligation except only in attending the plague patients." Later on, however, the town's representatives felt that they needed a better guarantee of a satisfactory performance and pressed for an addition which specified the doctor's duties in more positive terms: "namely, the doctor must treat all patients and visit infected places as it shall be found to be necessary." With the seventh clause the town's administration committed itself to give a free grant of Pavian citizenship to the doctor in appreciation for his good services. But again, at the time of the final draft, it was felt necessary to qualify the original text by the conditioning clause "according to how he shall behave himself."

What kind of man was Master Giovanni Ventura? We have no information on him and all we can do is to speculate on the limited basis of the agreement he made with the town of Pavia during a time of a social tragedy. He was ready to risk his life for some 30 florins a month, and it is doubtful whether he assumed this risk for purely humanitarian reasons. He was obviously anxious to obtain the citizenship of Pavia. One is tempted to think of him as an uprooted adventurer. But I doubt that that was the case. More likely he was an obscure doctor from the countryside, and the fact that he was normally addressed as "master" clearly shows that he was of humble social standing. There were in the villages young men who, thanks to scholarships or to the economic sacrifices of their parents or to both, managed to obtain a university degree. But it was not easy for them to practice in the cities because the city doctors did not welcome competition, and they therefore resisted the immigration of more doctors. On the other hand, as the memoirs of Jerome Cardano testify, toward the end of the fifteenth century a physician did not fare well in the countryside where peasants often had recourse to barbers and quacks. The dream of a young country doctor was to be admitted to the city. Perhaps Dr. Ventura was such a one, and when the plague hit the city, he played his version of Russian roulette: if all went well, he would have obtained the citizenship of Pavia, thus establishing there both his residence and practice.

Did Dr. Ventura have a family? In all likelihood he had neither wife nor children; otherwise their presence would have been mentioned in the clause referring to the house that the community had to provide for him. Yet Dr. Ventura must have had relatives in mind when he made the stipulations in the agreement. The chances of survival of a plague doctor during an epidemic were not high, and in clause eight, with obvious reference to the advance payment granted by clause two, Dr. Ventura obtained the promise that "in the event—may God forbid it—that the said Master Giovanni should die in the exercise of these duties, that then and in that case his heirs should not be required to make restitution of any part of his salary that might remain unearned." Was he thinking of his parents?

The institution of the community doctor in the Italian cities dated back to at least the end of the twelfth century. The idea behind the institution was to make available free medical treatment and care for the poor. The community plague doctor was but a special kind of community doctor and clause nine is similar to the analogous clauses that one finds in all agreements relating to the hiring of community doctors: "the said Master Giovanni shall not be able to ask a fee from anyone, unless the plague victim himself or his relatives shall freely offer it."

A plague epidemic was not only a human tragedy for a city; it was also an economic disaster. All too often, enormously swollen expenditures on public health measures were accompanied by drastic diminution of revenues, and all this meant bankruptcy for the frail public finances. Reading the agreement, one has the impression that Master Giovanni was more worried about the solvency of the city than about his chances of survival. With clause two he had obtained an advance payment. With clause three he had obtained from the city a special pledge to guarantee his salary. With clause ten he obtained that "whenever and however it shall come about—God forbid that it should—that because of a plague of this kind the city may be brought so low that Master Giovanni cannot have his wage nor the things necessary to his existence, that then and in that case Master Giovanni may be released from his obligation without any penalty."

By the end of the fifteenth century the gulf between physicians and barber-surgeons was widening in Italy; the physicians were more and more regarded as upper class while the barber-surgeons were increasingly considered part of the lower orders. By the end of the sixteenth century a physician was no longer addressed as "master"; that title being normally reserved to the barber-surgeons. In 1479, things had not yet gone so far, although even then it would have been unusual for a high-ranking, distinguished physician to be addressed with the title of "master." Dr. Ventura was obviously neither distinguished nor high-ranking. However, he was a physician and not a barber-surgeon, because clause eleven stipulates that "the Community is under obligation to maintain a barber who should be at least adequate and capable." The reason for the clause is obvious: a main task in the treatment of plague patients was lancing their suppurating bubos and the operation was normally performed by a barber-surgeon and not by a physician.

A city infected with plague was quarantined by all other places; trade and communications were halted, victuals became scarce and difficult and expensive to obtain. Many of those who were spared by the plague could hardly escape starvation. Dr. Ventura protected himself against these unpleasant events with clause twelve, which stipulates that "the Community has and is under the obligation to provide said Master Giovanni with all and everything which is necessary for his life, paying and exbursing the money therefore." Master Bernardino di Francesco Rinaldi obtained a similar clause when he was hired as plague doctor by the city of Volterra in 1527.

With clause four Dr. Ventura had already secured for himself free housing facilities: clause eleven took care of all other living expenditures. Thus the 30 florins of the monthly salary could be left untouched and put aside. When one's life is at stake, it is hard to decide whether pecuniary compensation is adequate or not. As we shall see below, however, by the standards of the time, the financial terms extracted by Dr. Ventura were reasonably adequate. But he kept worrying about the solvency of the community. He had already obtained the promise of an advance payment (clause two). He wanted a special pledge to guarantee his salary (clause three). He had made certain that in case of insolvency he would be released of his obligation (clause ten). But these guarantees were seemingly not enough to set his mind at rest. In a final assault on the problem he extracted clause thirteen, which stipulates that "however the community would not observe the previously agreed conditions, either partially or totally, then and in that case it would be possible to said Master Giovanni to be totally free from any engagement, notwithstanding the previous clauses or others to be made." Clause thirteen practically repeats what was already established by clause ten. What the town's administrators thought of this obsession of Dr. Ventura and of his being more concerned with the possible insolvency of the Community than with the probability of his catching the plague we shall never know. We know, though, that after they had accepted clause thirteen and had recognized the doctor's right to leave the job under the aforesaid conditions, the administrators pressed to have this addition inserted: "that the doctor should notify the community at least ten days in advance so that the Community would be in the condition to provide (for a substitute)."

While Giovanni could not take his mind off the community's possible insolvency, the town's administrators kept worrying about the kind of service that the doctor would provide to the patients. The minds of the two parties were following different logics and as the doctor persistently returned to his own point, the administrators felt that they had to reiterate their own. They had already managed to add to clause six the condition that "the doctor must treat all patients and visit infected places as it shall be found to be necessary." They had also succeeded in emphasizing that the grant of citizenship would be dependent on "how shall he behave himself" (addition to clause seven). But they were still uneasy. They therefore requested the insertion of clause fourteen, which stipulates that "said Master Giovanni would have and should be obliged to do his best and visit the plague patients, twice, or three times or more times per day, as it will be found to be necessary."

The town administrators were understandably concerned with the capacity of the doctor to resist the assault of the infection and to deliver his

services. This concern was not motivated by pure humanitarianism. Clause
fifteen stipulates that "in the case—may God forbid it—that the said Master
Giovanni would fall ill, and could not perform his office, that then and in
such case he should receive a salary only for the time of effective service."

The last clause stipulated that "said Master Giovanni will not be allowed
to move around the city in order to treat patients unless accompanied by a
man especially designated by the Community." The explanation offered is
that Dr. Ventura when accompanied by the deputy would be "identified as
the doctor appointed to that office," but the real reason behind the clause
was to ensure that the doctor would not intermingle with other people. The
deputy's function was to monitor Giovanni's movements. In Prato, in December 1527, the community made an inquiry on the behavior of the local
plague doctor Stefano Mezzettino. It was noticed that, according to the
rules, "when the community plague doctors move around they always have
to be accompanied by a custodian especially appointed, but said Master Stefano went to treat a patient in Pinzidemoli and went there alone, without the
custodian, with great danger for all concerned." He was reprimanded and
fined. A plague doctor was regarded as a contact and all contacts had to live
in isolation.

From the remarks I have made on some of the clauses, it will be apparent
that the agreement made between Dr. Ventura and the city of Pavia was not
dissimilar from analogous agreements made in other cities. One has, indeed,
the distinct impression that by the last quarter of the fifteenth century a
standard formula had evolved. This formula was adopted, with minor variations, in places as different as Turin in Piedmont, Pavia in Lombardy, and
Volterra and Prato in Tuscany. The pecuniary reward, however, varied considerably from place to place, largely depending on the quality and prestige
of the doctor, the availability of substitutes, the severity of the epidemic,
and the urgency of the town's needs. Dr. Ventura, we have seen, was granted
30 florins per month, the free use of a house, and his living expenses.

The florins mentioned in the contract were units of account. Thirty
such florins corresponded to 11½ gold florins and therefore to approximately 40 grams of pure gold. What this meant in terms of purchasing
power is difficult to say because the price structure of those days was totally different from the price structure of today. Books of medicine were
then valued in Lombardy between 5 and 13 florins each, with many having
the value of 6.5 florins. Thus the 30 florins that Dr. Ventura received each
month hardly bought five books of medicine. But manuscripts cannot be
compared with the printed books of today, and few doctors owned more
than some dozen books. Compared to other salaries, the salary of Dr. Ventura was not at all bad. A skilled worker, if he managed to be employed 200
days a year—which was virtually impossible—hardly made 60 florins in a
year. The accountant of the community made 84 florins a year. The mayor
of the city made 540 florins. At the university there were two or three

famous professors who earned more than 1,000 florins per year, but 75 percent of the lecturers earned less than 200 florins per year.

A contemporary living in a developed country may think that 40 grams of gold per month do not represent an exceptionally attractive salary. But in fifteenth century Europe gold was a scarcer commodity. Life was often brutish and short, and death was a more familiar event. Our story proves that a monthly salary of 40 grams of gold plus living expenses was high enough to attract a doctor to a job which bordered on suicide.❖

RECOMMENDED READINGS

Two studies that discuss the general effect of disease on the course of history are William H. McNeill, *Plagues and Peoples* (Garden City, NY: Anchor Press, 1976), and Charles-Edward Winslow, *Man and Epidemics* (Princeton, NJ: Princeton University Press, 1952). Specific epidemic diseases are considered by K. David Patterson, *Pandemic Influenza, 1700–1900: A Study in Historical Epidemiology* (Totowa, NJ: Rowan & Littlefield, 1986), and Hans Zinsser, *Rats, Lice and History; Being a Study in Biography, Which, After Twelve Preliminary Chapters Indispensable for the Preparation of the Lay Reader, Deals with the Life History of Typhus Fever* (Boston; Printed and published for the Atlantic Monthly Press by Little, Brown, 1935).

Most historical studies of epidemic disease treat the bubonic plague. One of the more controversial of these is Graham Twigg, *The Black Death: A Biological Reappraisal* (London: Batsford, 1984), who questions the identification of the Black Death with bubonic plague. Although old, Johannes Nohl, *The Black Death: A Chronicle of the Plague, Compiled by Johannes Nohl from Contemporary Sources,* trans. C. H. Clarke (London: Allen & Unwin, 1926), provides some dramatic eyewitness accounts of the devastation caused by the disease.

Among the most evocative of the eyewitness accounts of plague are Daniel Defoe, *A Journal of the Plague Year* (many editions), who recounts the plague of 1665 in London, and Miquel Parets, *A Journal of the Plague Year: The Diary of the Barcelona Tanner Miquel Parets, 1651,* ed. and trans. James S. Amelang (New York: Oxford University Press, 1991). Albert Camus, *The Plague* (many editions), provides an engrossing fictional tale of a plague-ridden city. Finally, Ann F. Ramenofsky, *Vectors of Death: The Archaeology of European Contact* (Albuquerque: University of New Mexico Press, 1987) offers evidence of the devastation caused by European disease among the native population of the American Southwest.

Indian Ocean, A.D. 1498

WHY NOT THE ARABS?

Daniel J. Boorstin

Over the centuries, western Europe had become dependent in many ways on certain imports from the East. Among these were spices. Some spices were almost a necessity; pepper, for instance, was often used to disguise the flavor of tainted meats, an important function in a protein-poor society without adequate means of food preservation. But western Europeans went far beyond simple needs; recipes from the later medieval period often call for a bewildering variety of spices, such as cloves, mace, cinnamon, nutmeg, and ginger in a single dish. These spices passed through numerous middlemen, and were quite costly as a result.

Beginning in the early fifteenth century, the small kingdom of Portugal began to send out expeditions along the African coast, slowly feeling its way southward in the hopes of opening an all-water route to the spices of the East. In 1498, the Portuguese admiral Vasco da Gama was successful in rounding the Cape of Good Hope, sailing through the Madagascar Straits, and entering the Indian Ocean. He found the entire region teeming with Muslim ships and traders, and discovered Muslim trading settlements almost everywhere his fleet touched land.

We have seen in "The Travels of Sānudāsa the Merchant" that the Hindus had once dominated these waterways. With the defeats they suffered at the hands of the Muslims, the culmination of which is discussed in "India and Islam: A Study in Defeat," the Hindus withdrew into themselves, and dominance of the region fell to Muslim mariners. In the following selection, Daniel Boorstin discusses the question of why the Muslims had not seized the initiative in discovery and exploration for which they were so much better equipped than the Europeans.

READING QUESTIONS

1. What was the Muslims' general attitude toward seafaring?

2. Why did Muslim mariners not penetrate the Madagascar Straits?

3. Who was Ibn Majid, and why was he a famous figure?

4. Why did the Muslims not seek to open an all-water route to the West?

I f, as it turned out, Africa was a peninsula, if there really was an open sea passage from the Atlantic Ocean to the Indian Ocean, as we are accustomed to say, then obviously there also was a sea passage from the Indian Ocean to the Atlantic Ocean. The Arabs who lived around the western and northwestern borders of the Indian Ocean were at least as far advanced in the seafaring sciences—in astronomy, geography, mathematics, and the arts of navigation—as their European contemporaries. Why didn't the Arabs take the sea passage westward?

One answer could be the same as that given by a Boston lady of an old New England family who was asked why she never traveled. "Why should I?" she replied. "I'm already there!" When Vasco da Gama finally arrived on the Malabar coast, as we have seen, he was greeted by Arabs from Tunis. These were members of a considerable Arab community, merchants and shipowners, who already dominated foreign commerce at Calicut. Long before a continuous sea passage was found between West and East, Arabs of North Africa and the Middle East were firmly rooted in India.

Taboos of caste, it seems, prevented Hindus from freely joining in overseas commerce. Some were forbidden by their religion from passing over salt water. Meanwhile, the astonishing expansion of Islam in the generations after Muhammad carried the Muslim empire across the Indus River and into India before the mid-eighth century. Arab traders swarmed into the cities of the Malabar coast.

Muslims from anywhere were remarkably at home wherever they went in Allah's commonwealth. Ibn Battuta, the Marco Polo of the Arab world who had been born in Tangier, during his extensive travels served comfortably as a judge in Delhi and in the Maldive Islands and was sent by an Indian sultan as ambassador to China. The Calicut that Gama saw included a prospering Arab quarter. Arab-operated warehouses and shops were found all over the city, and the Arab community was judged by its own cadis. Hindu rulers remained tolerant of the religion of the merchants who kept their city's commerce flourishing. Many a Hindu family hoped their daughter would become the wife of a rich Arab merchant. It was hardly surprising that the Arabs of Calicut did not welcome the Portuguese intruders.

From Daniel J. Boorstin, *The Discoverers* (New York: Vintage Books, 1983), pp. 178–185.

Seafaring in the Indian Ocean had flourished long before the birth of the Prophet Muhammad. At first the trip from Egypt and the Red Sea to India was made by following along the coast. The sailing traffic was enormously increased when the monsoons were discovered and put to use. A characteristic feature of the Indian Ocean, the monsoon (from Arabic *mausim*, meaning season) is a wind system that reverses direction seasonally. From a planetary perspective, it is a product of the special relations of land, sea, and atmosphere—a result of the differences in heating or cooling of land masses in contrast to that of the oceans. In India and in Southeast Asia, the monsoon blows in one direction at one season and contrariwise at another, and so offers convenient motive power both for going eastward in the Indian Ocean and for returning. *The Periplus of the Erythraean [Indian] Sea* (c. A.D. 80) credited a Greek pilot named Hippalus, who steered ships a century before under the late Ptolemaic kings of Egypt, as "the pilot who by observing the location of the ports and the conditions of the sea, first discovered how to lay his course straight across the ocean." After Hippalus showed how to use the southwest monsoon that blows across the Indian Ocean from June to October, to carry ships from the Red Sea to the shores of India, that wind came to be called the Hippalus.

Under the Roman Empire of Augustus the thriving sea trade between the Red Sea and India reached a hundred and twenty ships a year. Pliny complained, during the reign of Nero, that the empire was being drained of its currency in exchange for the baubles of India. The large hoards of Roman coins found in India prove how widespread that trade must have been.

Arab merchants were a familiar sight in India long before the landward expansion of Islam, but after the Prophet Muhammad the crusading motive was added to the commercial. In the mid-fourteenth century Ibn Battuta noted that Arab merchants were being carried from the Malabar coast to China in Chinese ships. In Canton as early as the ninth century there had been a Muslim community with its own cadi, and we have early records of Muslims as far north as Korea.

From the European perspective we have formed the stereotype that the Arabs have never been enthusiastic or successful seafarers. And the story of the Arabs in the Mediterranean does lend some substance to this notion. Caliph Omar I (581–644), who organized Muslim power and carried on the great landward expansion of the Muslim Empire into Persia and into Egypt, was wary of the sea. His Governor of Syria asked permission to raid Cyprus. "The isles of the Levant," the Governor argued, "are close to the Syrian shores; you might almost hear the barking of the dogs and the cackling of the hens; give me leave to attack them." Omar sought the advice of his wisest general. "The sea is a boundless expanse," General 'Amribn-al-As warned, "whereon great ships look tiny specks; nought but the heavens above and the waters beneath; when calm, the sailor's heart is broken; when tempestuous, his senses reel. Trust it little, fear it much. Man at sea is an insect on a splinter, now engulfed, now scared to death." When Omar forbade the excursion, he expressed the traditional Arab distrust of the sea. In Arabic, you "rode a ship" (*rakaba markab*) as you rode a camel, and when Muslims reached the shore around the Arabian peninsula, they saw the sea as a desert to be crossed en route to raid or to trade. There the northern Arabs rarely felt at home. The seafaring adventures of the ancient Arabs in the Mediterranean were sallies of commerce or of piracy, then not sharply distinguished from each other. They did not build a seafaring empire.

But even in the Mediterranean the Arabs were forced to go to sea. After a Byzantine fleet retook Alexandria (A.D. 645), it was plain that the Muslim Empire could not do without a navy. Alexandria became their maritime center, a new headquarters for naval training and for building ships with timber brought from Syria. By 655 the Arab fleet at Dhat al-Sawari defeated a Byzantine force of five hundred vessels. According to Arab tradition, the Arabs would have preferred to fight these enemies, too, on land, but the Byzantines preferred the sea. The Arabs, however, maneuvered the encounter into a kind of land battle conducted on shipboard. While Byzantine and Arab vessels were locked together, the Arabs slaughtered their enemies with swords and arrows.

The Arab-Muslim Empire spread landward around the Mediterranean. The Iberian peninsula, where the land of Europe came down to meet the land of Africa, was the part of the west European mainland that came under the Muslim sway. Historians, stirred especially by Henri Pirenne, still debate whether the Mediterranean ever really became a Muslim lake. It was the land-based strength of the Arabs who controlled both ends of the Mediterranean, whether or not they dominated the traffic inside, that shaped the future of seafaring in and from Europe.

With the minor exceptions of the islands of Cyprus, Crete, and Sicily, it was not necessary for the Arabs to cross a sea to pass from one part of their empire to another. If the Arabs of the north, those who settled and expanded around the southern shores of the Mediterranean, had been more like the Romans, more adept and more at home on the sea, less fearful of wide expanses of water, the later history and even the religion of Europe might have been quite different. Alexandria might have become a Muslim Venice. But instead, that once great metropolis, which in its earlier heyday contained a population of 600,000, had only 100,000 in the late ninth century. The caliphs of the ninth and tenth centuries allowed the city to decay. The famous Pharos lighthouse, marking Alexandria's harbor, which had been one of the Seven Wonders of the ancient world, became a ruin. Then even its ruins were appropriately destroyed by an earthquake in the fourteenth century. Arabic thought and Arabic literature looked landward.

But in the Mediterranean, empires were repeatedly won and lost on the water. There the ship was the sword of empire builders. During the centuries when Allah's empire was retreating in the West, the Indian Ocean, an area of nature's turmoil, remained remarkably peaceful. That was where Arab maritime prowess developed freely. The brilliant embodiment of that prowess, Ibn Majid, son and grandson of eminent Arab navigators, who called himself "The Lion of the Sea in Fury," achieved fame as the man who knew most about navigation in the dread Red Sea and in the Indian Ocean. He became a Muslim patron saint of seamen, in whose memory orthodox mariners would recite the first chapter of the Koran, the Fatiha, before venturing out on dangerous waters. Author of thirty-eight works in prose and poetry, he covered every maritime topic of his day. Most useful to Arab navigators was his *Kitab al-Fawa'id,* or Nautical Directory (1490), a compendium of everything then known of nautical science, which included information to guide seamen through the Red Sea and the Indian Ocean. Even today, for some areas, his work is said to be unequaled.

A divine providence must have been watching over Vasco da Gama on his first voyage. By an astonishing coincidence, when on reaching Malindi he finally secured a competent and trustworthy Arab pilot to steer his fleet across the Indian Ocean, it was this very same Ibn Majid. The Portuguese captain did not know how lucky he was. Nor could Ibn Majid have realized, as they sailed into Calicut harbor, that they were enacting one of the majestic ironies in history. The great Arab master of navigation was unwittingly guiding the great European sea captain to a success that meant the defeat of Arab navigation in the Indian Ocean. Later Arab historians have tried to explain away Ibn Majid's role by saying he must have been drunk to confide to Vasco da Gama the information that would guide him safely to his Indian destination.

Once admitted, the Portuguese and their European successors were not to be expelled from that ocean. In the later nineteenth century the Suez Canal would make the passage to India easier than ever for European sailors. By the mid-twentieth century Arabs still sailing from Kuwait and Aden to East Africa and to India seem to have forgotten much that Ibn Majid knew, for they were once again clinging to the coast.

Long before Prince Henry the Navigator had even begun to reach down the west coast of Africa, the Arabs knew the east coast of Africa all the way down to Sofala, opposite the island of Madagascar, and less than a thousand miles north of the Cape. There, at the Mozambique Channel, they found *their* Cape Bojador. Dare not to go beyond! The Koran twice declared that God had separated "the two seas" by a barrier that man could not overcome. Scholars explained that these two enclosed bodies of water were the Mediterranean Sea and the Indian Ocean, including the Red Sea. But the Prophet had also said, "Seek knowledge, even in China." Somehow, during the later Middle Ages, the Arab scholars were less securely imprisoned by their Muslim faith than the European scholars were by their Christian dogmas. Arab scholars proved willing to criticize and even to alter some revered classical texts, including Ptolemy's *Geography.*

The distinctive broadener of Muslim vistas was, as we have seen, the pilgrimage—the duty of every Muslim, man or woman, wherever living, to visit Mecca once before dying. We must recall the narrow orbit at that time of the life of a Scottish or Norwegian or French peasant, who might never journey beyond the nearest fair. But while the pilgrim tradition focused Arab-Muslim travel, it did not encourage exploratory seafaring.

Yet Arab geography flourished. And while medieval European cosmographers reposed in dogmatic slumber, Arab geographers were at home in the works of Ptolemy, which the West kept buried for a thousand years. The Arabs were even beginning to revise Ptolemy, suggesting that the Indian Ocean was not Ptolemy's closed sea but that it actually flowed into the Atlantic. One of the most influential of these pioneer Arab geographers was the versatile Al-Biruni (973–1050?), one of the greatest Muslim scientists of the Middle Ages. He combined precise observation with omnivorous curiosity, and even before he was seventeen he had made an improved device for determining latitude. Though born in central Asia, Al-Biruni became entangled in the far-ranging political intrigues of the rival dynasties of Persia, Turkey, and Iraq. "After I had barely settled down for a few years," he wrote, "I was permitted by the Lord of Time to go back home, but I was compelled to participate in worldly affairs, which excited the envy of fools, but which made the wise pity me." He expressed some of the more advanced Arab speculations about the shape of Africa.

> The Southern Sea commences at China and flows along the shores of India towards the country of the Zendj (Zanzibar). . . . Navigators have not passed this limit, the reason being that the sea on the north-east penetrates into the land . . . while on the south-west, as if by way of compensation, the continent projects into the sea. . . . Beyond this point, the sea penetrates between the mountains and valleys which alternate with one another. The water is continually set in motion by the ebb and flow of the tide, the waves for ever surging to and fro, so that ships are broken in pieces. This is why the sea is not navigated. But this does not prevent the Southern Sea from communicating with the Ocean through a gap in the mountains along the south coast [of Africa]. One has certain proofs of this communication although no one has been able to confirm it by sight. It is because of this inter-communication that the habitable part of the world has been placed in the centre of a vast area environed on all sides by the sea.

Since this controversial version of the linking of the oceans was known to Ibn Majid, who apparently accepted it, he could not have been unduly surprised to meet Vasco da Gama's fleet at Malindi. Ibn Majid himself was pleased to be able to point out that Al-Biruni's notions and his own had now been proven by the Portuguese, "the experienced ones." Since these "Franks" (a name in the East for all Europeans) had entered the Indian Ocean through *al-madkhal* (the place of entry), the perilous channel between the island of Madagascar and the African coast of Mozambique, Ibn Majid christened that sea path "the passage of the Franks."

For the Arabs, the Mozambique Channel, like Cape Bojador, had accumulated legendary menaces with the passing centuries. *The Arabian Nights* had embroidered the real perils with terrifying tales of a gigantic bird, the ruc or gryphon. Marco Polo reported what his reliable sources told him of Madagascar:

> You must know that this Island lies so far south that ships cannot go further south or visit other Islands in that direction, except this one, and that other of which we have to tell you, called Zanghibar [Zanzibar]. This is because the sea-current runs so strong towards the south that the ships which should attempt it never would get back again. . . .
>
> 'Tis said that in those other Islands to the south, which the ships are unable to visit because this strong current prevents their return, is found the bird *Gryphon,* which appears there at certain seasons. The description given of it is however entirely different from what our stories and pictures make it. For persons who had been there and had seen it told Messer Marco Polo that it was for all the world like an eagle, but one indeed of enormous size; so big in fact that its wings covered an extent of 30 paces, and its quills were 12 paces long, and thick in proportion. And it is so strong that it will seize an elephant in its talons and carry him high into the air, and drop him so that he is smashed to pieces; having so killed him the bird gryphon swoops down on him and eats him at leisure. The people of those isles call the bird *Ruc,* and it has no other name. So I wot not if this be the real gryphon, or if there be another manner of bird as great. But this I can tell you for certain, that they are not half lion and half bird as our stories do relate; but enormous as they be they are fashioned just like an eagle.

The Great Khan, he added, had received the gift of a Ruc's feather "which was stated to measure 90 spans, whilst the quill part was two palms in circumference, a marvelous object!" Oddly enough, the name of the rook in chess, though its modern guise gives no clue, appears originally to have come from the name of this bird.

The technology of Arab shipbuilding in the Indian Ocean in that era before the Portuguese arrived was a curious combination of strengths and weaknesses. The lateen sail, which the Arabs brought to the Mediterranean, by its adeptness at sailing into the wind had made the Portuguese ventures possible. The Arabs also pioneered in developing the stern rudder, which made any ship more maneuverable. They were skilled at using the stars for navigation. "He it is," said the Koran, "who hath appointed for you the stars that ye guide yourselves thereby in the darkness of land and sea; we have made the signs distinct for a people who have knowledge."

For reasons still unclear, instead of using nails in their ships, Arabs stitched together planks with cords made from coconut husks. Ships held together in this fashion would not long survive the buffeting of winds or the scraping of rocks. Why did they build their ships in this way? There was a widespread legend that magnetic rocks, or lodestones, in the sea would pull out iron fastenings and so drag apart ships held together by nails. And the high cost and scarcity of nails must also have had something to do with it. Once a distinctive style was adopted, naturally conservative seamen made it into a firm tradition.

Certain special features of the Arabian peninsula, homeland of the Arabs and of Islam, remind us of the difficulties faced by their seamen. Arabia possesses almost none of the naval stores—neither wood nor resin nor iron nor textiles—required for shipbuilding. To a man of the sea, the geography of Arabia could hardly have been more uncongenial. There were no navigable rivers, few good harbors, nor any populous or hospitable hinterland. Coral reefs surrounding the coasts produced wrecks to encourage pirates, from whom there was no convenient refuge. There was no easy source of fresh water. And the menacing northerly winds came down without respite the year round.

All these features of Arab lands and Arab civilization help us understand why they were not inclined to take their sailing ships around Africa and up the west coast to Europe. The best explanation, perhaps, is the most obvious. Why organize a continuous venture into the unknown? The modern organized exploring enterprise initiated by Prince Henry the Navigator was without known precedent. Seamen, eminently practical men, had habitually embarked because they had a cargo or passengers for a particular destination. Or they arrived to pick up a particular cargo somewhere. The seaman, like the landman, generally does not go in quest of the unknown, nor to confirm some concept of the earth or the oceans, but, as E. G. R. Taylor explains, "goes to sea like a man to his office, along a set route for a set purpose, his livelihood." Just as, on land, people dreaded mountaintops and preferred familiar paths, so too there were familiar paths on the sea.

The Arabs in the Indian Ocean were "already there." Both in the East and in the West. Why would they have wanted to go by sea to Portugal or northern Europe? Muslims were already just across the Straits of Gibraltar from the Christian world. Their domain already included the rich tropical variety of plants and animals and minerals and incense-laden ways. What the Arab world had to gain from the Europeans had already been tested and tried in the Iberian peninsula. Their encounters with the crusaders in the Middle East seemed to promise only a vast reservoir of infidels in need of conversion. ❖

RECOMMENDED READINGS

The Cambridge History of Islam, 2 vols., eds. P. M. Holt, Ann K. S. Lambton, and Bernard Lewis, (Cambridge, UK: Cambridge University Press, 1970), is the standard general history of Islam and the Islamic empire; Andre Clot, *Harun al-Rashid and the World of the Thousand and One Nights,* trans. John Howe (London: Saqi, 1989), offers an excellent study of the empire during its tenth-century golden age. The expansion of Muslim maritime activity and its results are portrayed in K. N. Chaudhuri, *Asia Before Europe: Economy and Civilisation of the Indian Ocean from the Rise of Islam to 1750* (Cambridge: Cambridge University Press, 1990), and Andre Wink, *Al-Hind: The*

Making of the Indo-Islamic World (Leiden: E. J. Brill, 1990), addresses the growth of Muslim power and commerce in India.

Relatively little had been written about Muslim discovery and exploration, but something of the spirit of the era may be caught in the fabulous adventures of Sindbad the Sailor and some of the tales of *The Thousand and One Nights*. Another suggestion of the wide world of the Muslims may be found in the works of two eminent tenth-century geographers, Masudi and al-Muqaddasi, in Basil A. Collins, *Al-Muqaddasi: The Man and His Work: With Selected Passages Translated from the Arabic* (Ann Arbor: Department of Geography, University of Michigan, 1974), and *The Meadows of Gold: The Abbasids*, trans. and ed. Paul Lunde and Caroline Stone (London: Kegan Paul, 1989).

Much more attention has been devoted to European expansion. Pierre Chaunu discusses the time just prior to the great age of European discovery in *European Expansion in the Later Middle Ages*, trans. Kattarine Bertram (Amsterdam: North Holland, 1979); an overview of the age itself may be found in David J. Arnold, *The Age of Discovery, 1400-1600* (London: Methuen, 1983). The Portuguese were the initiators of the era of discovery, and there is a considerable body of literature about their accomplishments. C. Raymond Beazley, *Prince Henry the Navigator: The Hero of Portugal and of Modern Discovery, 1394-1460 A.D.* (London: Putman, 1923); Eric Axelson, *Congo to Cape: Early Portuguese Explorers*, ed. George Woodcock (New York: Barnes & Noble, 1973); and Christopher R. V. Bell, *Portugal and the Quest for the Indies* (London: Constable, 1974) are only a sampling of this literature. *The Lusiads* (many editions) is the epic poem celebrating Portugal's great adventure.

INCENTIVES AND PATTERNS OF AFRICAN TRADE

Philip D. Curtin

To a large degree, the realities of Africa in the eighteenth and nineteenth centuries have been swallowed up in the myths of the twentieth. The European explorers and settlers knew full well that the interior of Africa was the scene of bustling activity—wars, trade, and simply social exchanges— among well-established and, at least in certain regards, quite advanced peoples. They were also aware, and deplored the fact, that the continent was crisscrossed by Arab trade routes along which ivory, cloth, salt, spices, manufactured goods, and slaves had moved for centuries. They were moving into dangerous territories unexplored by Europeans, however, and popular imagination was kindled by the element of the unknown. This aspect of Africa became its dominant characteristic for Westerners, and the interior of Africa became "the Dark Continent," "Darkest Africa," or even Joseph Conrad's Heart of Darkness. *The fact that the region was "dark" only from the European point of view tended to be forgotten as time passed, and the general Western view of Africa was fixed by such sources as the novels* The Lost Continent, She, *and* Tarzan, *and numerous B-grade motion pictures that portrayed the interior of Africa as unexplored by anyone, and its native residents as primitive, superstitious, and ignorant.*

At the same time, Western "defenders" of the Africans attempted to picture them as an uncomplicated people, whose peaceful isolation and traditional patterns of life were being destroyed by the pernicious effects of European-instigated trade and commerce.

Neither view of the history of the sub-Saharan African interior is anything like the truth of the matter. The region had been in indirect commercial contact with the rest of the trading world for centuries and was the site of highly complex and shifting patterns of industry and commerce. There were environmental impediments to such trade, of course, but the Africans had succeeded in accommodating to the difficulties they faced. This selection on the internal trade of sub-Saharan Africa provides an excellent overview of an aspect of African history of which most Americans are still ignorant. In addition, it provides a fascinating insight into the social processes of industrial development, processes which must have been quite similar to those of other societies, including that of Westerners.

READING QUESTIONS

1. What were the impediments to trade and travel in sub-Saharan Africa?

2. In what sort of areas did trade arise, and why?

3. What was the status of industrial workers? What were the advantages and disadvantages of this status?

4. How was trade adapted to traditional patterns of life?

S ub-Saharan Africa remained isolated from the main currents of world trade far longer than most of the rest of the Afro-Eurasian landmass. Even though Asian sailors reached much of the eastern coast by about 200 B.C., North Africans regularly crossed the Sahara by about 800 A.D., and European sailors reached the western coasts in the fifteenth century, much of the interior remained comparatively isolated until the eighteenth and nineteenth centuries—cut off by the aridity of the Sahara and its own patterns of disease environment. Tsetse flies and the trypanosomes they carried made pack animals useless through much of the African tropics, thus impeding long-distance trade. Other diseases, especially falciparum malaria and yellow fever, were so fatal to humans from other disease environments that Africa remained the continent least known to outsiders until the second half of the nineteenth century.

Textbooks and other summary treatments of African economic history sometimes illustrate the "penetration" of Africa with maps showing arrows leading from the coasts into the interior—from Egypt up the Nile valley, from the east coast into the highland lake region, from the Maghrib across the Sahara to the western Sudan, from the Atlantic coast into the Congo basin. Such maps are accurate enough to show the flow of foreign goods. Arrows in the opposite direction could also show how African goods and people moved along trade routes to the outside world. But intercontinental trade was only part of the whole. In Africa, as elsewhere in the world, local exchange was more important than long-distance trade. As a general proposition, the longer the distance, the more trade had to be confined to products of comparatively high value and low bulk, though bulkier goods could be carried farther as the technology of transportation improved over time.

From Philip D. Curtin, *Cross-Cultural Trade in World History* (Cambridge: Cambridge University Press, 1984), pp. 15–20.

Overemphasis on external trade can also lead to an overemphasis on external initiative. One of the myths of African history is the old view that commerce in Africa was largely pioneered by outsiders who penetrated a stagnant continent. In fact, trade beyond the village level began on local, African initiative. Traders moved out along the trade routes, set up trade diasporas that crisscrossed the continent in patterns of increasing complexity. When the European "explorers" of the nineteenth century *did* travel from the coast into the interior, they did so with the help and guidance of established African merchants who were already in the business of long-distance trade.

INCENTIVES TO TRADE

The most obvious and ancient explanation of why some people take up commerce and others do not is the differing resource endowments. Where people lived in a homogeneous environment stretching over some distance, there was no obvious incentive to trade beyond the village level; nor was there much reason for specialization within the village where almost everyone was necessarily involved in food production. Where different environments lie side by side, specialization and trade become likely. One of the most dramatic and important dividing lines between diverse environments in any part of the world is the desert edge, the *sahel,* separating land where agriculture can be practiced from the arid steppe and desert where only pastoral nomadism is possible. Nomads are specialized producers from necessity, with meat and milk but little or no access to grain, or fiber to make cloth. A sedentary, farming household can produce for itself most of the goods it will consume. Nomads must move with their cattle, which makes it very hard for them to raise anything else. Although people can, in a pinch, live on animal products alone, most nomads prefer to trade with sedentary people for grain, cloth, and metals. The result through history has been a long struggle of competitive cooperation between sedentary societies and their nomadic neighbors. Relations across the desert fringe could be those of peaceful trade, or those of violence represented symbolically by the story of Cain and Abel, but goods normally pass across this ecological divide with greater intensity than they do in more homogeneous environments.

In Africa, the Sahara has a desert edge to the north and to the south. Across the southern sahel lies the great savanna belt. Still farther south is another ecological dividing line where the savanna meets the tropical forest. There, too, diverse environments made for exchange of products like the yams or palm oil of the forest for the shea-nut oil and peanuts that grew better in the savanna. In this case, however, the communities on both sides of the line were sedentary farmers; neither was as specialized as the nomadic pastoralists were; and early trade across the ecological frontier can be assumed to have been less than it was across the sahel.

Other ecological frontiers come from differences in altitude. In East Africa, linguistic evidence suggests that some of the earliest markets originated where Mount Kilimanjaro and Mount Kenya provide a rich and well-watered environment nearly surrounded by a comparatively arid and lightly populated plain. Similar differences abound in the Ethiopian highlands and along the mountain chain that reaches south toward the Cape of Good Hope.

SALT, IRON, AND FISH

Resources still more unevenly distributed across the landscape were also important inducements to early trade. Archaeological evidence shows that copper, iron, and certain kinds of shells entered trade at a very early date, though the record is necessarily silent as to who carried them and how. Much of the earliest trade is assumed to have been a relay trade, carried on by people who bought and resold, without going far from home. Goods could move a long way in a series of short stages. The known sources of a natural product like salt could also serve as an attraction for many different groups for miles around. In many, perhaps most, recorded instances, however, it was the owners or specialist producers of the rare commodity who made it their business to move out along the trade routes in order to sell to strangers, founding a trade diaspora in the process, which later evolved to handle a greater variety of products. Several interior peoples in tropical Africa, both east and west, founded trade diasporas based initially on salt deposits but then moved on to become specialists in long-distance trade in a much greater variety of products. The Dendi of southern Niger, for example, began with salt but then spread their trade network so widely that by the nineteenth century, the Dendi language had become the dominant trade language over much of the present Republics of Togo and Benin.

Sea salt was available along all the coasts of Africa, either by boiling seawater or allowing natural evaporation from specially constructed pools. Several coastal peoples in West Africa, who later became important traders, seem to have begun the commercial penetration of the hinterland in order to take advantage of their local salt monopoly. The Avikam and Alladian peoples of the southern Ivory Coast and the Ijo of the Niger delta are notable examples. Where salt was especially scarce, as it was in the savanna country of West Africa, it was sometimes the interior people who created and operated trade routes for access to coastal supplies. Two such routes from the Mande heartland—one westward to the mouth of the Gambia, the other south through what is now Liberia—have left their imprint on the distribution of African peoples. A ribbon of Malinke-speaking people, whose homeland was southern Mali, are still found to the west along the line of the Gambia River, where their ancestors first went in search of sea salt. And the Vai of southern Liberia are thought to be a similar linguistic remnant of an old Malinke trade route to the Liberian coast, a remnant that was later cut off from the main body of Malinke-speaking people.

In Africa, iron is far more widely distributed than salt, but specialized skills in iron production and smith's work lay behind several trade diasporas. Whether it did so or not depended on the way iron production fitted other social patterns. In West Africa generally, iron workers were often considered to be a group apart from the rest of society, one of a half-dozen or so special, occupational castes that could only marry among themselves. They were respected for their technical knowledge, but they were also feared; to work with iron called for dangerous interference with the gods—with those of the earth they dug for ore and those of the trees they killed to make charcoal. Like merchants in ancient Greece, such a dangerous occupation made smiths simultaneously feared and despised. In much of West Africa they were relegated to a subordinate position.

In Wasulu, however, a group of merchant-blacksmiths who came to be called Kooroko were able to turn this low social position to their own advantage. Wasulu was a region in present-day Mali near the frontiers with Guinea-Conakry and the Ivory Coast. It lay near the ecological boundary between the savanna and the forest. The rulers of the several small states that made up Wasulu regarded hunting, cattle keeping, and agriculture as the only occupations worthy of free people. They relegated minstrels, wood workers, leather workers, and blacksmiths to a separate and subordinate status. Merchants were not a separate caste, nor were they respected, but the ancestors of the Kooroko gained one advantage from their low status. They could circulate freely within Wasulu, as high-status people could not. A noble away from home was a threat to the local nobility and ran the risk of death or enslavement.

The Kooroko emerged in the nineteenth century as an important trading group within a limited sphere. At first, they circulated mainly within Wasulu, selling their own ironware, pottery, and leather products. They then moved into the transit trade, buying kola nuts on the southern frontiers of Wasulu in return for the salt they had bought in the north. Their larger success came only in the twentieth century, when they moved out from Wasulu and began to settle as diaspora merchants in the larger towns of the French Sudan (now Mali), and especially in Bamako. In the colonial setting, they were no longer a cross-cultural trade diaspora so much as a skilled commercial community that was able to take advantage of trucks and telegrams to succeed in the fiercely competitive kola-nut trade from the producing zone in the forest to a broader market throughout savanna country.

The Yao from the vicinity of Malawi in southeast Africa also founded an important trade on the basis of iron production. Before the sixteenth century, the Yao had been farmers with hunting as an important sideline. Then the Wachisi, a group of skilled iron workers, immigrated into Yao society and adopted Yao culture. They began to make iron tools and to sell them locally. Other Yao then began iron production combined with trading expeditions, taking over the occupational niche previously assigned to hunting. The sexual division of labor had made hunting possible by leaving much of the agricultural work to women. Other customs that allowed prolonged absence to hunting parties could be easily shifted to do the same for trading expeditions. Village chiefs who had once headed hunting parties now led trading parties. Old ways to secure protective medicine and ritual ablution, and to prevent adultery by the wives of the absent, were transferred to commercial travel. By the sixteenth century, the Yao had pioneered a trade route from their homeland west of Lake Malawi to the coast near Mozambique City and on to Kilwa, in Tanzania. As trade developed, iron decreased in importance, replaced by an exchange of ivory for sea salt and imported goods. Like the Kooroko, the Yao began to draw goods from the far interior into their operations, until they had become one segment of a much more complex commercial network between the Indian Ocean coast and the heart of southern Africa.

Fishermen on the seacoast or along rivers were drawn into trade for the same reason pastoral nomads were. They had a specialized product that could be exchanged for a better-balanced diet. They had boats they could use to take their own product to market or carry other goods for profit. On all the major rivers, cultures evolved early on that have been categorized as "aquatic." They differed a good deal from one another, just as pastoral nomadism had many variants, but the Bobangi of the middle Congo or Zaire can serve as an example of the type.

The Bobangi came in time to dominate a 500-kilometer stretch of the river southward from the equator to Stanley Pool, or Pool Malebo. In the early eighteenth century, however, they were only one among several culture groups with similar aquatic cultures living along this stretch of the river. They kept permanent villages on high ground. Then, when the water level dropped with the dry season, they moved out to temporary villages, more convenient to the low-water fishing possibilities. They were therefore able to fish all year round, producing large quantities of surplus fish for sale in return for the manioc, yams, and other vegetable products of their agricultural neighbors. In one sense, they were semi-nomads using their boats as cattle nomads used pack oxen to move their tents.

When river trade on the Congo began to increase in the late eighteenth century, the Bobangi began to expand their trade area up and down the river, making alliances with similar aquatic people as they did so. The result was not a normal trade diaspora, stretching into alien territory—or, if so, only in the short run. The Bobangi assimilated the other peoples along this stretch of the river so that they all became Bobangi, distinguished politically and culturally from their nonaquatic neighbors who lived back from the river along the full length of the Bobangi river dominion.

This success came from technological superiority, not military power. Bobangi freight boats, about 10 meters long and capable of carrying up to

1.5 metric tons, won an easy victory in competition with head porterage, the only alternative for carrying goods. Their trade could therefore include bulky commodities like African-made iron and copper, manioc and fish, camwood, barkcloth, several kinds of palm mats, tobacco, palm oil, and palm wine. Intercontinental exports like ivory and slaves and intercontinental imports like Indian or European cloth were only a small part of the total by either quantity or value.❖

RECOMMENDED READINGS

Although the historical literature on sub-Saharan Africa is growing rapidly, some of it is tendentious or ill informed. This is not strange, given the lack of information in many areas, the relative paucity of archaeological materials or written sources, African nationalists' desires for a glorious and ancient past, and a certain inability on the part of European scholars to judge the achievements of peoples of antiquity largely on the basis of their material remains. UNESCO has sponsored a multivolume history of Africa, and the *Cambridge History of Africa* maintains the high standards of the press's other historical projects.

The Cambridge History of Africa, ed. J. D. Fage and Roland Oliver (London and New York: Cambridge University Press, 1975–); Roland Anthony Oliver, *The African Middle Ages, 1400–1800* (Cambridge and New York: Cambridge University Press, 1981); and *Africa in the Nineteenth Century Until the 1880's,* ed. J. F. Ade Ajayi (Oxford, UK: Jordan Hill; Berkeley: Heinemann, University of California Press; and Paris: UNESCO, 1989), offer broad and yet detailed accounts of the development of Africa and its peoples over the last five hundred years. David Robinson, *Sources of the African Past: Case Studies of Five Nineteenth-Century African Societies* (New York: Africana, 1979), provides some relatively short, but perceptive studies that illustrate both the differences between early modern African peoples and their underlying similarities.

Central America, About A.D. 1525

AMERICA'S BALL GAME

Stephan F. De Borhegyi

The Spanish explorers and conquistadors who arrived in the Mesoameri-can region of Mexico and Central America during the fifteenth and six-teenth centuries were amazed to find sophisticated civilizations with rich cultural legacies. These native societies were diverse in size, complexity, language, and customs, but they shared certain characteristics. Notable among the similarities was a passion for a sport played in ball courts throughout Mesoamerica. Basically, the game involved two competing teams whose objective was to knock a solid rubber ball through a stone ring placed midway along the walls of the court. The players never used their hands, only their hips, shoulders, or forearms.

That ball game, as suggested in the following selection by Stephan F. De Borhegyi, appears to have left a lasting influence on European and American modern sport. It is likely that the Mesoamerican ball game was the ancestor of certain modern ball games played in Europe and America, in particular such kicking games as soccer and football. The author fur-ther speculates that the concept of team play, or two teams competing against each other, was introduced to European society through the influ-ence of the Mesoamerican ball game.

The characteristics of a sport generally reflect the social, economic, and political institutions of its time, and that is certainly the case with the Mesoamerican ball game. The participants were restricted solely to the upper classes. The use of sport by the ruling classes to emphasize their mil-itary skills or perpetuate the affinities of their class was common among premodern societies. That, however, does not appear to apply to the Mesoamerican ball game, which stressed team play and an aggressive but nonmilitaristic nature. Both the lower and the upper classes had a strong affection for the ball game. Star players were held in great esteem, and, as was the case with the Greek Olympics and the medieval tournament, the participants competed primarily for glory and/or personal reward. Both players and spectators wagered incredibly high stakes on the outcome of games—even on occasion wagering themselves. The ball game, as could be expected in a society in which religion played such a key role, was not a completely secular affair. Each ball court was a temple because, like the

Greek Olympics, various religious ceremonies were connected with the game.

De Borhegyi's article offers a brief look at one of the most fascinating sporting events of the premodern world. From the author's description, the influence of the Mesoamerican ball game on modern sport appears significant, and its similarities and dissimilarities with other premodern sports are apparent.

READING QUESTIONS

1. What distinguished the Mesoamerican ball from pre-Conquest European balls?

2. How was the Mesoamerican game played?

3. What role did gambling play?

4. Where does it appear that the game originated?

5. What may have been the relationship between the Mesoamerican game and modern basketball?

But for the sporting enthusiasm of our Indian predecessors in the New World, competitive rubber ball games—as we know them today—might never have come into existence. Not only were the enterprising people of Mesoamerica responsible for the discovery of rubber—and its usefulness in the form of an ingenious, bounding, rubber ball—they may also have done much to influence the form in which some of our modern games of ball are played.

When the Spanish conquerors arrived early in the sixteenth century, they first witnessed a New World ball game in the Antilles, on the island of Haiti. Later, they saw ball games played on the Mexican mainland. They especially marveled at the ball (*olin*), which was solid and heavy and yet bounced so vigorously. The Spanish chronicler Torquemada (in 1613) described this unusual object from hearsay: "These Indian peoples know (as among us was known) the ball game, although different from ours. The place where it is played is called *tlachco,* which is like tennis among us. They make the ball from the sap of a tree which grows in the hot country,

From Stephan F. De Borhegyi, "America's Ball Game," *Natural History,* January 1960, pp. 48–59.

from which trickle some white thick drops when it is punctured, and which very' soon jell, which when mixed and kneaded, turns out blacker than pitch. Of this *ulli* they make their balls which although heavy . . . were very fitted for the way in which they played. They bounced and jumped as lightly as air-filled balls, and were better because there was no necessity for blowing them up."

An earlier account, by the chronicler Duran (1585), combines direct observations with detailed reporting: "This ball is—as some people may have seen—as large as a small ball used in playing nine-pins. The material of which the ball is made is called *olin,* which I have heard to be called *'batel'* in our Spanish, which is a resin of a special tree which when boiled becomes like sinews. It is plentiful and used . . . both as medicines and as offering. It has one property which is that it jumps and rebounds upwards, and continues jumping from here to there so that those who run after it become tired before they catch it."

It is no surprise, then, that Columbus brought back an example of such a ball, along with other wonders from the New World. Las Casas, writing from New Spain in 1560, remarked, "I saw one, as big as a small jug, which the old Admiral brought to Seville." It can therefore be assumed that, not long after Columbus' second voyage, rubber—and the rubber ball—were brought back in some quantities to Spain and to the rest of Europe, along with various accounts of the New World ball games. The game itself seems to have been introduced to Europe in the year 1528 by Cortes, who staged several games for the court of Charles V. One of these performances was witnessed by the German traveler Christoph Weiditz, on a trip to Spain in 1529. Shortly afterward, he published a description of his trip, the excellent illustrations of which included a sketch of two Indian ball game players and, in the text, some brief rules.

In Torquemada's description of New World ball games, which he calls *"juego de pelota,"* he mentions their similarity with the essentially sportive European ball games—in particular, court tennis and the *pelota vasca,* or *jai-alai.* However, prior to the Spanish Conquest, all the ball games that were played in Europe made use of leather balls that were either filled with hair or contained an inflated bladder. Indeed, the Spanish word for ball is still *pelota*—deriving from the word *pelo,* meaning "hair." The most popular ball games in Spain, France, and Italy during the fifteenth century were *pallone* or *balon* (words that have the same root as the English word "balloon," since the game was played with an air-filled ball) and court tennis, which was a hand game (*jeu de paume*), played with a hair ball.

Both these games derived from Roman prototypes and had even earlier Mediterranean origins. These, and all of European ball games prior to the sixteenth century, seem to have originated in ancient, spring rites practiced in southern Europe, Egypt, and the Near East. The two-sided aspect of the game probably represented the philosophic dualism of nature. In this ritualistic pairing, we may have the origin of "teams"—mock combats and contests dramatizing the eternal conflict between day and night, or dying winter and approaching summer. However, the emphasis was apparently on each individual's skill: there seems to have been no serious attempt to organize the opposing players into cooperative teams. Thus, the New World idea of two teams engaged in competitive play was quite possibly an innovation to Europe.

The Middle American ball game, as described to us by the Spanish chroniclers, was a combination of our modern games of basketball, volley ball, soccer, and *jai-alai.* It was played in high-walled, paved courts (usually 100 to 125 feet long and 20 to 50 feet wide), called *tlachtli* or *tlachco,* the floor plans of which were in the shape of a "capital I." As described by the Spaniards, the game had as its key the knocking of a solid, five-pound rubber ball, five to eight inches in diameter, through stone "hoops" set vertically in the center of each of the two long walls. The main objective of the play does not seem to have been to gain ground—as was the case with most of the sixteenth-century European ball games—but to score. Since the inner diameter of the stone hoop varied from six to twelve inches, making a "goal" was no easy task. However, the game varied from place to place, and in many areas, hoops were not used at all. In these cases, scoring must have been calculated on some other basis.

The number of players varied. There were amateur and professional teams and nearly every pre-Columbian settlement of any size boasted at least one ball court. In some contests, quite large teams—nine to eleven players strong—were used. In others, only two or three expert players took part. To quote Torquemada again: "They played in teams, so many against so many, such as two against two, and three against three, and sometimes two against three, and in main courts or *tlachco*'s the lords and nobles and great players, in order to embellish their markets principally on feast days and on many other days, went to play in them."

How the ball was first put into play remains unknown. But, once begun, the players performed with such skill and dexterity that there were times when the heavy rubber ball did not touch the ground for as long as an hour, during which it flew from one end of the ball court to the other. A team "scored" whenever the opposing ball-handlers missed a shot at the vertical hoop, or when the team made the ball reach the opponents' "end zone." Playing the ball off the side walls was quite important, and many of the finer tricks of the game were apparently based on the players' skill in this maneuver.

The most important score, however, was accomplished by putting the ball through one of the stone hoops. When this occurred, all other scoring points were discounted and the game was thereby concluded in great excitement and applause. Torquemada testifies: "This way of putting the ball through the hole, which we have seen, which seemed a miracle to the spectators (although it was by chance), they used to say and swear that the person must be a thief or an adulterer or that he would soon die, since he had

had so much luck; and the recollections of this victory lasted for many days until another happened which made it forgotten."

The star player who accomplished this remarkable feat not only won the game for his team but was entitled, for his skill, to collect the jewels and even the clothing of those who were watching. Generally, a merry scramble ensued and there was a mass exodus of all present.

Star players were highly honored by chiefs and commoners alike, but the game was so strenuous that it is hard to imagine that the stars could have remained at the top of their form for long. The heavy ball was not allowed to come into contact with bare hands, feet, or calves, but was kept in play with a sort of hand-held stone "flatiron" or with elbows, knees, and hips. Protection for the players consisted of quilted cotton elbow and knee pads, and around their waists they wore heavy belts, and yokes, of leather or basketry. Sculptures and paintings often show ball players equipped with these stone "gloves" and wearing yokes, as well as curious objects known as "palmate stones." Both yokes carved from stone and the palmate stones, themselves, have been discovered by archeologists. It is not known, however, whether this bulky equipment was actually worn in play, or whether the stone versions were made solely for ceremonial purposes. Evidence tends to show that the stone yokes—some weighing as much as fifty pounds—might have been used in some areas, to give the ball a better bounce. The palmate stones, on the other hand, are quite fragile, and it is unlikely that they could have survived the rigors of actual play.

For all their protective costume, casualties happened often during the course of the game. Says the eyewitness Duran: "Some of them were carried dead out of the place and the reason was that as they ran, tired, and out of breath, after the ball from one end to the other, they would see the ball come in the air and in order to reach it first before others would rebound on the pit of their stomach or in the hollow, so that they fell to the ground out of breath, and some of them died instantly, because of their ambition to reach the ball before anybody else. . . . They were so quick to hit their knees or seats that they returned the ball with an extraordinary velocity. With these thrusts they suffered great damage on the knees or on the thighs, with the results that those who for smartness often used them, got their haunches so mangled that they had those places cut with a small knife and extracted blood which the blows of the ball had gathered."

In spite of the fact that players often were severely hurt and occasionally were killed, the rewards of being a star were so great that such dangers were evidently considered inconsequential. Yet, there was even greater risk involved for the team captains. While the winning captain was overwhelmed with honors and gifts, the unfortunate captain of the losing team was not infrequently sacrificed to the gods! This fact we know from the Spanish chronicles. It may also be reflected in the dramatic depictions in low relief on the ball courts, at El Tajin, in Veracruz and at Chichen Itza, in Yucatan, and in the illustrations contained in such documents as the *Codex Boriga.*

Although such treatment of the losing captain may seem harsh, it was closely in keeping with the penalties imposed by the spectators upon themselves when they lost at the gambling that invariably accompanied the game. Both players and spectators laid wagers on the outcome of the contest, the stake varying with the status and wealth of the individual. As the chronicler Sahagun (1529) reports: "What the low class people gambled was jewelry of small value and worth and as he who has little wealth on hand usually loses it, they were in necessity of gambling their houses, fields, maize stores, maguey plants and of selling their children in order to gamble and even of gambling themselves away and of becoming slaves, to be sacrificed if they did not redeem themselves in time, as has already been told. Their way of gambling was that when they had finished losing the valuables which they carried, such as cloaks, beads and feathers, they would gamble on their word, saying that they had certain valuables in their houses."

Rulers might even play for principalities or kingdoms, as when Axayacatl, the ruler of Tenochtitlán (today, Mexico City), wagered his entire yearly income against that of Xihuitlemoc, the ruler of the neighboring city of Xochimilco. Lesser nobles and chiefs played for jades and turquoises, jewelry of gold, feather robes, articles of clothing, cocoa, cornfields, houses, and for slaves and concubines. With so much at issue, it is little wonder that there were times when, not content with the element of skill, such high-stake participants invoked the aid of the supernatural. According to Duran: ". . . these gamblers by nightfall took the ball and placed it on a clean plate with the leather loincloth and the gloves, hanging it all on a pole and, crouching before these instruments of the game, they worshipped them and spoke to them with certain words of superstition and incantations with much devotion, praying to the ball that it . . . be favorable that day."

All this might give the impression that, by the time of the Spanish Conquest, the Middle American ball game was a completely secular activity. Duran even describes it as ". . . a game of much recreation to them and enjoyment especially for those who took it as a pastime and entertainment." Nevertheless, the religious overtones that reflect the sacred origins of the game were apparent to Torquemada, who recalled: "Each ball court was a temple because they placed two images in it, the one was the god of the game and the other of the ball, on the top of the two lower walls, at midnight, on a day of good omen, with certain ceremony and witchcraft and in the middle of the floor they made similar ceremonies, while singing songs: thereafter one of the priests with some of his ministers came to bless it with certain words (if the detestable superstition can be called blessing); he threw the ball four times in the ball court and with this they said that the court was consecrated, and they could play in it and not before then."

In the codices, we continually see the gods associated with the ball court. Those most frequently illustrated are Quetzalcoatl, Texcatlipoca, Xochiquetzal, Xochipilli, Huitzilopochtli, Coatlicue, Xolotl, and the Lords of the Day and the Night. These divinities were even believed to be ardent players in their heavenly courts, like the vigorous, athletic gods of the Greeks, and the ball game was a favorite means of settling their divine disputes.

From the various legends, we learn that Quetzalcoatl was an unusually skilled player and had many ball courts dedicated to him. Historically, Quetzalcoatl seems to have been the culture hero of the Toltecs and ruler of the city of Tula. His defeat by his rival and arch-foe, Texcatlipoca, and his subsequent flight to the south has been passed on to us through a legend, recorded by Sahagun, which has this momentous conflict taking part on the royal ball court of Tula.

Moreover, the twin brother of Quetzalcoatl, Xolotl, was known throughout pre-Columbian Mexico as the divine patron of the game. In this, one may detect an inherent relationship between this god of twins or siblings and the duality implicit in competition: a factor that, as we have noted, was also present in the origins of Old World ball games. One can suspect that, as in Europe, the underlying motivation of the Mesoamerican ball games was to provide an outlet for aggressions toward neighboring groups and a means, short of warfare, for settling disputes.

In Middle America, the game was so immensely popular that almost every ceremonial center had at least one ball court and some of the larger ones held as many as ten to fifteen. Various versions of the ball game were played in pre-Columbian times from as far south as El Salvador to as far north as central Arizona, and throughout the islands of the Antilles.

Just where the game originated is yet to be determined. The invention of the rubber ball and its use in a ball game very likely took place through experimentation in an area where rubber-bearing plants were grown. This would suggest the lowland rain forests of Central America as a point of origin. Verifying this hypothesis, we find the earliest ball court known thus far at the important jungle site of Copan, in Honduras. This court has been dated at between A.D. 200 to 300, in the Early Classic period. Since there is nothing primitive about this Copan ball court, we can probably assume that others—representing the experimental beginnings of the game and so far not yet found—may pre-date it by several hundred years. As a matter of fact, archaic figurines, representing ball players, were found at Tlatilco, Mexico—which suggest that some form of the game was known in the Valley of Mexico as early as 1500 B.C., although it may not have been played in a formal ball court.

The type of classic ball court at Copan consists of an open-ended court, with a central playing alley between parallel, sloping side walls. Three elaborately carved, square or circular stone slabs apparently represented floor markers. At the top of each side wall were three vertically tenoned, stone parrot heads. Since these parrots were carved with large, round eyes, it is possible that they represent a precursor of the stone hoops found in later, Mexican courts. The floor markers were also important in scoring. This type of court was characteristic of the lowland Maya region of Guatemala, Honduras, and Mexico and survived to the end of the Classic period, possibly as late as A.D. 1000.

THE BALL GAME PRIOR TO A.D. 1500

LEGEND

Southwest U.S. courts—A.D. 800-1100

Game survived Conquest (no courts)

Mexican-type courts—A.D. post-1000

Lowland Maya courts—A.D. pre-900

Highland Maya courts—A.D. pre-900

Middle American ball games were played on varieties of courts during pre-Conquest period.

In the highlands of Guatemala and southern Mexico we find another type of ball court during the Classic period (A.D. 300 to 1000) that resembles a wash basin in its shape. This court is, in general, like that of the lowland Maya, but differs in being completely enclosed by a wall, which also incorporates some extra space, at both ends of the playing floor, to form end units. Although we find no evidence of stone floor markers, we cannot eliminate the possibility that goals of some sort may have been painted on the paved floor. The carved stone heads used to decorate these highland courts were characterized by horizontal—rather than vertical—tenons, frequently in the form of serpent and human heads, rather than parrots.

By the close of the Classic period, most of the lowland Maya centers were mysteriously abandoned. In the highlands of Guatemala and southern Mexico, after A.D. 1000, a new type of ball court came into fashion. Prior to this time, all ball courts were built on the ground level. But in these later courts the playing alley was lowered to a depth of several feet below the surface. It is very possible that this type of "sunken" court was introduced from

Mexico, where the game, as we have seen, may have been known since 1500 B.C. Since these post-Classic courts were built below ground level, they all had elaborate drainage systems. Although they retain the sloping side walls and the enclosed "capital I" shape, they show no signs of tenoned stone heads or floor markers. Goals, of course, may have been painted or made of perishable material.

While such "sunken" ball courts were characteristic of the post-Classic period (A.D. 1000 until the Spanish Conquest in 1524) throughout Guatemala and southern Mexico, still another type came into vogue in central and western Mexico and in Yucatan. It is this type that is described in detail by the Spanish chroniclers. Although the playing alley was in the "capital I" shape, it was built at ground level and the side walls were vertical rather than sloping. In the center of each side wall was an elaborately carved, horizontally tenoned, stone hoop.

Little is known of the ball courts in the region north of Mexico City. However, in Arizona, two types of courts have been recognized, both of the "sunken" variety. The one excavated at the Snaketown site is large and oblong and possesses end units. Apparently it was in use between A.D. 800 and 900. Smaller, circular courts—built during a later period (A.D. 900 to 1150)—are characteristic of the Flagstaff area. In these, the end units were replaced by small openings in the surrounding wall. There is hardly any doubt that the prehistoric inhabitants of Arizona learned of the ball game from their Mexican neighbors.

Since the shape of the courts varied in different periods and in different regions, it is easy to conjecture that the rules of the game must also have varied. Unfortunately, the only eyewitness accounts of the pre-Columbian ball game are those preserved in the Spanish chronicles. A variation, however, is still played today along the northwestern coast of Mexico—in the states of Sinaloa and Nayarit. No formal courts are used and the game has little of its former splendor. Nevertheless, the genetic relationship is clear: there is a corridor-like playing field, the ball is made of solid rubber and there is the obligation to strike it with the hip or thigh. Religious feast days are favored for play, accompanied by lavish betting.

The reason that only this one poor example of a once great game has survived to the present day is apparent in the chronicles. The historian Gomara states—and is corroborated by Cervantes-Salazar and Torquemada—that: "Each court was like a temple, because they put two images of the god of the ball game on the lower walls." Montolinia adds, ". . . and for this reason they were destroyed." Later historians piously argue that the ball game was destroyed by the conquerors out of a desire to protect the Indians from the very real dangers of play: however, such an assumption of altruistic motivation is, at the very least, open to suspicion.

In spite of its virtual extinction, the competitive ball game of Middle America lives on through its influence on the modern ball games of Europe and America. Although there is no indication that the rules of the New World game were ever incorporated directly into any European sport, it is obvious that the element of a vigorously bouncing rubber ball considerably altered the rules of the ancient game of tennis, and had its effect on the formulation of rules for such kicking games as soccer and football. Team effort to keep the ball constantly flying from side to side survives in modern volley ball.

There is also some reason to suspect a connection with the distinctly American game of basketball—which owed its beginnings, in 1891, to Dr. James E. Naismith, a physical education instructor at the Young Men's Christian Association Training School at Springfield, Massachusetts. In the late 1800's, a great stir was caused in this country with the rediscovery of the ruins of the ancient Maya ceremonial center, Chichen Itza. In 1891, the English archeologist Maudsley published the first article on the ball court there, calling it a tennis court or gymnasium. Dr. Naismith, understandably interested in any new type of sport, may well have read about the ancient ball games of Mexico and incorporated the idea of putting the ball through a hoop—albeit horizontal rather than vertical—in his ingenious new game of basketball.

Today, three types of ball games—football, soccer, and basketball—are played throughout most of the Western world. Now thoroughly secularized, they often are accompanied by the same excitement—and gambling—that once characterized the Middle American ball game. ❖

RECOMMENDED READINGS

For readings dealing with the Aztecs, see Alfonso Caso, *The Aztecs: People of the Sun* (Norman: University of Oklahoma Press, 1959), and Jacques Soustelle, *Daily Life of the Aztecs* (New York: Macmillan, 1962). For the Mayan civilization, see Sylvanus G. Morley, *Ancient Maya* (Stanford, CA: Stanford University Press, 1983), and J. Eric Thompson, *The Rise and Fall of Maya Civilization* (Norman: University of Oklahoma Press, 1954). For the Incas, see John Alden Mason, *The Ancient Civilizations of Peru* (Baltimore: Penguin Books, 1961), and Paul Kosok, *Life, Land and Water in Ancient Peru* (New York: Long Island University Press, 1965).

CONQUISTADOR Y PESTILENCIA

Alfred W. Crosby, Jr.

We note in the introduction to "A Plague Doctor" that the recurrent epidemics that swept over Europe were a factor of natural selection that bred a disease-resistant, but disease-carrying European. In the following selection, Alfred Crosby discusses the effect of the introduction of European bacteria and viruses on the pre-Discovery inhabitants of the New World. Drawing on a wide variety of sources, he concludes that the aboriginals died in great numbers immediately after their contact with Europeans, and that this mortality was a primary factor in the ease with which the Europeans conquered the Aztec and Inca civilizations.

Crosby's emphasis on the effect of contact on the native populations should not obscure the fact that epidemics occur with almost every massive contact between societies, and we should note that the mortality is not always one sided. It has been estimated, for instance, that fully half of the early European immigrants to the New World succumbed within two years after their arrival. One of the major reasons for the importation of African slaves is that they appeared to live longer under working conditions than either natives or Europeans. Europe itself appeared to pay a price in disease for the new lands it controlled. There is ample evidence that returning sailors from Columbus's first expedition introduced syphilis and perhaps other venereal diseases into western Europe.

On balance, however, the discovery was a medical disaster for the native populations of the New World. Having been isolated for so long from contact with other societies, the inhabitants of the New World had not developed the immunities that their conquerors possessed. The Europeans had acquired their immunity by suffering a century and a half of recurrent plagues; the New World natives had to pay that price in a single generation.

READING QUESTIONS

1. What explanations are given for the Europeans' relatively easy conquest of the inhabitants of the New World?

2. What causes epidemics?

3. How did contact with Europeans affect native populations?

W hy were the Europeans able to conquer America so easily? In our formal histories and in our legends, we always emphasize the ferocity and stubbornness of the resistance of the Aztec, Sioux, Apache, Tupinamba, Araucanian, and so on, but the really amazing thing about their resistance was its ineffectiveness. The Orientals held out against the Europeans much more successfully; they, of course, had the advantage of vast numbers and a technology much more advanced than that of the Indians. The Africans, however, were not "thousands of years ahead" of the Indians, except in possessing iron weapons, and yet the great mass of black Africans did not succumb to European conquest until the nineteenth century.

There are many explanations for the Europeans' success in America: the advantage of steel over stone, of cannon and firearms over bows and arrows and slings; the terrorizing effect of horses on foot soldiers who have never seen such beasts before; the lack of unity among the Indians, even within their empires; the prophecies in Indian mythology about the arrival of white gods. All these factors combined to deal to the Indian a shock such as only H. G. Wells's *War of the Worlds* can suggest to us. Each factor was undoubtedly worth many hundreds of soldiers to Cortés and Pizarro and other great Indian-killers.

For all of that, one might have at least expected the highly organized, militaristic societies of Mexico and the Andean highlands to survive the initial contact with the European societies. Thousands of Indian warriors, even if confused and frightened and wielding only obsidian-studded war clubs, should have been able to repel the first few hundred Spaniards to arrive. And what is the explanation for the fact that Indians were really only a little more successful in defending themselves and their lands after they learned that the invaders were not gods, after they obtained their own horses and guns and developed tactics to deal with the Europeans?

After the Spanish conquest an Indian of Yucatan wrote of his people in the happier days before the advent of the European:

> There was then no sickness; they had no aching bones; they had then no high fever; they had then no smallpox; they had then no burning chest; they had then no abdominal pain; they had then no consumption; they had

From Alfred W. Crosby, Jr., *The Columbian Exchange: Biological and Cultural Consequences of 1492* (Westport, CT: Greenwood Press, 1972), pp. 35–42.

then no headache. At that time the course of humanity was orderly. The foreigners made it otherwise when they arrived here.[1]

It would be easy to attribute this statement to the nostalgia that the conquered always feel for the time before the conqueror appeared, but the statement is probably in part true. During the millennia before the European brought together the compass and the three-masted vessel to revolutionize world history, men moved slowly, seldom over long distances and rarely across the great oceans. Men lived in the same continents where their great-grandfathers had lived and seldom caused violent and rapid changes in the delicate balance between themselves and their environments. Diseases tended to be endemic rather than epidemic. It is true that man did not achieve perfect accommodation with his microscopic parasites. Mutation, ecological changes, and migration brought the Black Death to Europe, and few men lived to the proverbial age of three-score years and ten without knowing epidemic disease. Yet ecological stability did tend to create a crude kind of mutual toleration between human host and parasite. Most Europeans, for instance, survived measles and tuberculosis, and most West Africans survived yellow fever and malaria.

Migration of man and his maladies is the chief cause of epidemics. And when migration takes place, those creatures who have been longest in isolation suffer most, for their genetic material has been least tempered by the variety of world diseases. Among the major divisions of the species homo sapiens, with the possible exception of the Australian aborigine, the American Indian probably had the dangerous privilege of longest isolation from the rest of mankind. Medical historians guess that few of the first rank killers among the diseases are native to the Americas.[2]

These killers came to the New World with the explorers and the conquistadors. The fatal diseases of the Old World killed more effectively in the New, and the comparatively benign diseases of the Old World turned killer in the New. There is little exaggeration in the statement of a German missionary in 1699 that "the Indians die so easily that the bare look and smell of a Spaniard causes them to give up the ghost."[3]

The most spectacular period of mortality among the American Indians occurred during the first hundred years of contact with the Europeans and

---

[1] *The Book of Chilam Balam of Chumayel,* trans. Ralph L. Roy, 83.

[2] P. M. Ashburn, *The Ranks of Death. A Medical History of the Conquest of America,* passim; Henry H. Scott, *A History of Tropical Medicine,* 1:128, 283; Sherburne F. Cook, "The Incidence and Significance of Disease Among the Aztecs and Related Tribes," 321, 335; Jehan Vellard, "Causas Biológicas de la Desparición de los Indios Americanos," 77–93; Woodrow Borah, "America as Model: The Demographic Impact of European Expansion upon the Non-European World," 379–387.

[3] Quoted in E. Wagner Stern and Allen E. Stern, *The Effect of Smallpox on the Destiny of the Amerindian,* 17.

Africans. Almost all the contemporary historians of the early settlements, from Bartolomé de las Casas to William Bradford of Plymouth Plantation, were awed by the ravages of epidemic disease among the native populations of America. In Mexico and Peru, where there were more Europeans and Africans—and, therefore, more contact with the Old World—and a more careful chronicle of events kept than in most other areas of America, the record shows something like fourteen epidemics in the former and perhaps as many as seventeen in the latter between 1520 and 1600.[4]

The annals of the early Spanish empire are filled with complaints about the catastrophic decline in the number of native American subjects. When Antonio de Herrera wrote his multivolume history of that empire at the beginning of the seventeenth century, he noted as one of the main differences between the Old and New Worlds the extreme susceptibility of the natives of the latter to diseases, especially smallpox. Indian women, he wrote, were especially quick to succumb to it, but it rarely infected anyone of European birth. The Indians became so enraged by the invulnerability of the Spaniards to epidemic disease that they kneaded infected blood into their masters' bread and secreted corpses in their wells—to little effect.[5]

The victims of disease were probably greatest in number in the heavily populated highlands of New Spain (Mexico) and Peru, but, as a percentage of the resident population, were probably greatest in the hot, wet lowlands. By the 1580s disease, ably assisted by Spanish brutality, had killed off or driven away most of the peoples of the Antilles and the lowlands of New Spain, Peru, and the Caribbean littoral, "the habitation of which coasts is . . . so wasted and condemned, that of thirty parts of the people that inhabit it, there wants twenty-nine; and it is likely the rest of the Indians will in short time decay."[6]

It has often been suggested that the high mortality rates of these post-Columbian epidemics were due more to the brutal treatment of the Indians by the Europeans than to the Indians' lack of resistance to imported maladies.

---

[4] Charles Gibson, *The Aztecs Under Spanish Rule*, 448-451; Henry F. Dobyns, "An Outline of Andean Epidemic History to 1720," 494.

[5] Antonio de Herrera y Tordesillas, *Historia General*, 2:35; Charles Gibson, *Spain in America*, 141-142.

[6] Joseph de Acosta, *The Natural and Moral History of the Indies*, 1:160. For specific references on depopulation see Antonio Vazquez de Espinosa, *Compendium and Description of the West Indies*, paragraphs 98, 102, 115, 271, 279, 334, 339, 695, 699, 934, 945, 1025, 1075, 1079, 1081, 1102, 1147, 1189, 1217, 1332, 1342, 1384, 1480, 1643, 1652, 1685, 1852, 1864, 1894, 1945, 1992, and 2050. An interesting comparison can be made between Spanish America and the Spanish Philippines. The aborigines of each suffered exploitation, but there were fewer epidemics and much less depopulation in the Philippines. Contact between these islands and the mainland of Asia had existed for many generations, and the Filipinos had acquired mainland immunities. See John L. Phelan, *The Hispanization of the Philippines*, 105-107; Emma H. Blair and James A. Robertson, eds., *Philippine Islands*, 12:311; 13:71; 30:309; 32:93-94; 34:292.

But the early chroniclers reported that the first epidemics following the arrival of Old World peoples in a given area of the New World were the worst, or at least among the worst. European exploitation had not yet had time to destroy the Indians' health.

The record shows that several generations of Indian contact with Europeans and Africans seemed to lead not to the total destruction of the Indians, but only to a sharp diminution of numbers, which was then followed by renewed population growth among the aborigines.[7] The relationships between these phenomena are too complex to be explained by any one theory. However, their sequence is perfectly compatible with the theory that the Indians had little or no resistance to many diseases brought from the Old World, and so first died in great numbers upon first contact with immigrants from Europe and Africa; and when those Indians with the weakest resistance to those maladies had died, interbreeding among the hardy survivors and, to some unmeasured extent, with the immigrants, led to the beginning of population recovery.

The record of early post-Columbian medical history of America was never kept carefully and much of it has been erased since, but it does seem to show a greater number of epidemics, characterized by a higher mortality rate, than was typical even in insalubrious Europe of that time. The very first was a pandemic which began in 1519 in the Greater Antilles and swept through Mexico, Central America, and—probably—Peru. It caused "in all likelihood the most severe single loss of aboriginal population that ever occurred," to quote one expert who has examined its history carefully.[8] It is the best documented of all of the first epidemics. We have no more than snatches of information on the others. Hans Staden, captive to the Tupinamba of Brazil in the early 1550s, was—ironically—saved from death by what may have been an epidemic. He convinced the local chief that the malady carrying off many of the Indians had been sent by the Christian God to punish them for their intention to eat Staden. In 1552 a respiratory disease killed many natives around Pernambuco. In the same decade epidemic broke out among the famished Frenchmen at Río de Janeiro, spread to the mission Indians there and killed eight hundred of them. In 1558 pleurisy and bloody flux spread along the coast from Río to Espírito Santo. In 1558 and 1560 smallpox arrived in Río de la Plata and swept off thousands of Indians, without touching a single Spaniard. Smallpox came to Brazil in 1562 and 1563 and carried off tens of thousands of Indians, but left the Portuguese unscathed. In some villages no one was left

[7] Sherburne F. Cook and Woodrow Borah, *The Indian Population of Central Mexico, 1531-1610;* Sherburne F. Cook and Woodrow Borah, *The Aboriginal Population of Central Mexico on the Eve of the Spanish Conquest.*

[8] Dobyns, "Andean Epidemic History," 514.

who was healthy enough to tend the sick, "not even someone who could go to the fountain for a gourdfull of water."[9]

The English were as efficient disease carriers as the Latins. In 1585 Sir Francis Drake led a large expedition against Spain's overseas possessions. His men picked up some highly contagious fever—probably typhus—in the Cape Verde Islands and brought it along with them to the Caribbean and Florida. The malady spread to the Indians in the environs of St. Augustine and, "The wilde people . . . died verie fast and said amongest themselves, it was the Inglisshe God that made them die so faste."[10]

In 1587 the English founded a colony at Roanoke Island, a few hundred miles north of St. Augustine. The colonists' diagnoses of their immediate and fatal effect on many of the Indians was similar in medical philosophy to that expressed by the Florida Indians. Thomas Hariot wrote that there was no Indian village where hostility, open or hidden, had been shown,

> but that within a few dayes after our departure from everies such townes, that people began to die very fast, and many in short space; in some townes about twentie, in some fourtie, in some sixtie, & in one sixe score, which in trueth was very manie in respect to their numbers. . . . The disease also was so strange that they neither knew what it was, nor how to cure it; the like by report of the oldest men in the countrey never happened before, time out of mind.[11]

The natives of what is now the Atlantic coast of Canada had contact with Europeans—fishermen and fur traders—from very early in the sixteenth century, long before the English attempted colonization at Roanoke or any other place in America. Depopulation was already apparent among their tribes by the time of French settlement. The Jesuit *Relations* contain a report dated 1616 from which the following paragraph is extracted. The Indians, it states,

> are astonished and often complain that, since the French mingle with and carry on trade with them, they are dying fast and the population is thinning out. For they assert that, before this association and intercourse, all their countries were very populous and they tell how one by one the different coasts, according as they have begun to traffic with us, have been more reduced by disease.[12]

---

[9] *Hans Staden, The True History of His Captivity,* trans. Malcolm Letts, 85–89; Alexander Marchant, *From Barter to Slavery: The Economic Relations of the Portuguese and Indians in the Settlement of Brazil, 1500–1580,* 116–117; Claude Lévi-Strauss, *A World on the Wane,* 87; Juan López de Velasco, *Geografía y Descripción Universal de las Indias,* 552.

[10] David B. Quinn, ed., *The Roanoke Voyages,* 1:378.

[11] Ibid.

[12] Quoted in Alfred G. Bailey, *The Conflict of European and Eastern Algonkian Cultures, 1504–1700: A Study in Canadian Civilization,* 13.

These Indians looked south enviously to New England, where tribes were not diminishing. The turn of these Armouchiquois, as the Canadian Indians called them, came in the same year that the above report was written. In 1616 and 1617 a pestilence swept through New England, clearing the woods, in the words of Cotton Mather, "of those pernicious creatures, to make room for better growth." Whatever the sickness was, Europeans were immune to it. The handful of whites who passed the winter of 1616–1617 with the Indians of coastal Maine "lay in the cabins with those people that died, [but] not one of them ever felt their heads to ache, while they stayed there." The Massachusetts tribe was nearly completely exterminated, depopulating the area of Plymouth Bay at just about the same time that the Pilgrims were deciding to come to America. The same epidemic also swept the environs of Boston Bay. A European who lived in that area in 1622 wrote that the Indians had

> died on heapes, as they lay in their houses; and the living, that were able to shift for themselves, would runne away and let them dy, and let there Carkases ly above the ground without burial. . . . And the bones and skulls upon the severall places of their habitations made such a spectacle after my coming into those partes, that, as I travailed in the Forrest nere the Massachusetts, it seemed to me a new found Golgotha.

There is no need to continue this lugubrious catalog. The records of every European people who have had prolonged contact with the native peoples of America are full of references to the devastating impact of Old World diseases. ❖

RECOMMENDED READINGS

There are a number of detailed accounts of the European conquest of the New World. The following bibliography concentrates on those relating to the overthrow of the Aztec Empire.

Five official reports in the form of letters written by Cortes and detailing his conquest and subjugation of Mexico between the years 1519 and 1526 are available in *Conquest: Dispatches of Cortes from the New World,* ed. Harry Rosen (New York: Grosset & Dunlap, 1962), and *Letters from Mexico,* ed. A. R. Pagden (New York: Grossman, 1971). A classic presentation of the conquest is William Hickling Prescott's *History of the Conquest of Mexico* (many editions). An interesting examination of the spiritual side of the venture is available in Charles Samuel Braden's *Religious Aspects of the Conquest of Mexico* (New York: AMS Press, 1966).

Herbert Cerwin, *Bernal Diaz, Historian of the Conquest* (Norman: University of Oklahoma Press, 1963), is a helpful biographical study of Diaz. A contemporary account of Cortes's conquests is provided by his secretary, Francisco Lopez de Gomara, *Cortes: The Life of a Conqueror by His Secretary*, ed. and trans. Lesley Byrd Simpson (Berkeley: University of California Press, 1965). Some of the best biographies of Cortes are William Weber Johnson, *Cortes* (Boston: Little, Brown, 1975); Henry Morton Robinson, *Stout Cortes* (New York: The Century Co., 1931); and J. E. M. White, *Cortes and the Downfall of the Aztec Empire* (London: H. Hamilton, 1971).

Aztec accounts of the conquest are collected in *The Broken Spears: The Aztec Account of the Conquest of Mexico,* ed. Miguel Leon Portilla, English trans. Lyander Kemp (Boston: Beacon Press, 1962). Aztec social conditions at the time of the conquest are described in R. A. M. van Zantwjk, *The Aztec Arrangement* (Norman: University of Oklahoma Press, 1985). General studies of the Aztecs are Jacques Soustelle, *The Daily Life of the Aztecs,* trans. Patrick O'Brian (Stanford, CA: Stanford University Press, 1970), and Nigel Davis, *The Aztecs* (Norman: University of Oklahoma Press, 1980).

For the effects of disease on history, see also the recommended readings for Carlo Cipolla, "A Plague Doctor."

THE DIRECT IMPACT OF WAR ON CIVILIANS

J. R. Hale

The famous Four Horsemen of the Apocalypse recorded in the Book of Revelations are identified as Famine, Pestilence, War, and Death. War brings on famine and pestilence, and these two factors account for far more deaths than all of the war's battles combined. The battles of World War I were probably the bloodiest in history; it has been estimated that possibly as many as thirty million died of wounds and disease during the years 1914 to 1918. In 1919–20, over fifty million died of the influenza spread across the world by returning combatants.

The loss of life among the civilian population has probably always been greater than that among the military, but the toll of civilians increased markedly with the appearance of the massive and voracious armies and almost continuous campaigning of the modern era. In the following selection, J. R. Hale examines the effect of the emergence of modern warfare on the civilian populations of sixteenth-century Europe.

One of the salient features of modern warfare would appear to be the degree to which war became a logistical matter. The larger, better equipped, and better supplied army always had the advantage, so leaders would drain the resources of their own civilian population while at the same time attempting to destroy their enemies' sources of supply. Since the armies had to be fed at any cost, civilians paid the price by starving to death. At the same time, the close quarters, fatigue, and exposure of army life bred disease, and the movement of troops spread these sicknesses among a malnourished civilian population.

The fact that early modern warfare affected civilians to such an extent may well have been a factor in the growth of both nationalism and the concept of total war. The clear realization that the essential difference between civilians and soldiers was that the soldiers suffered comparatively less may well have led people to accept the idea of universal military service much more readily than might otherwise have been the case.

READING QUESTIONS

1. How did warfare in the sixteenth century differ from that of earlier periods?

2. What were the effects of warfare on public health?

3. How did warfare affect the civilian economy?

4. How did warfare lead to famine?

5. Did civilians fare better under the conditions of siege warfare?

L arger, ill-disciplined armies, extended campaigning seasons, prolonged sieges: the brush-strokes of war in the sixteenth century were broader than formerly, and probably leached out more widely into the fabric of civilian society. Compared with the spasmodic nature of the Hundred Years War, the Wars of Italy and the Netherlands were almost unremitting molestations of normal life. Guicciardini noted in the 1530s the changed impact of war on civilians who, especially after 1509, 'saw nothing but scenes of infinite slaughter, plunder and destruction of multitudes of towns and cities, attended with the licentiousness of soldiers no less destructive to friends and foes'. And as a Dutch popular ballad of the 1580s put it:

> Our fathers were in their time
> Also chastised by war's strong rod.
> But never endured its punishment for so long a time,
> Nor suffered so much ill as we unfortunates do.

There was a similar difference in intensity and scale between the French civil wars and those of the Roses. It was overall damage to life and property that forced Bodin to conclude that 'the only way to maintain the community is to make war [abroad] and to invent an enemy if there is not one to hand'.

Worse was to come with the even larger and still poorly controlled and supplied armies of the Thirty Years War of 1618–48, and their need to exploit non-combatants as the source of food, shelter and criminous or sexual diversion. But what there was was bad enough. Towards the end of the sixteenth century wolf packs, symbols of the breakdown of civilization, were reported as attacking the starving peasantry of the southern Netherlands and Brittany. Of course contemporaries exaggerated. It was in an unwonted mood of optimism that La Noue remarked that 'France is so populous and so

---

From J. R. Hale, *War and Society in Renaissance Europe* (New York: St. Martin's Press, 1985), pp. 179–184, 191–193.

fertile that what the war has damaged in one year is restored in two'. Little credence can be given to the pioneer statistician of war casualties, Nicholas Froumenteau, who in 1581 recorded the destruction by fire of 252 villages, the death of 765,200 civilians (out of a population which had by then reached about 16 million), 12,300 rapes; war does not hold out a clean slate to such ineluctables as fire, death and ravishment. But soberer figures give a gaunt picture of what happened in areas most directly and consistently hit by war. The population of Pavia fell from 16,000 in 1500 to less than 7000 in 1529 when there were 'chyldren kreyeng abowt the streates for bred, and yet dying for hungre'. That of the Dutch textile centre Hondschoote fell from 18,000 in the 1560s to 385 in 1584. 'The voice of the poor peasant cries out to God,' recorded the Estates of Flanders in 1604, and with reason. Not just a life-or-death reason; it was emigration, precautionary or forced, that accounted for by far the greatest part of local population losses. This could lead not only to survival but occasionally to a better livelihood elsewhere. But the impact of war registered on emotion as well as on life and limb. Any estimate of war's impact on civilians must allow for the effects of flight, humiliation, privation and fear. These are all the more to be borne in mind because populations generally picked up again on the return of peace as refugees returned and new immigrants arrived (Hondschoote was almost as prosperous by 1620 as it had been before the wars engulfed it), because statistically, deaths caused directly by war are scarcely discernible amidst the still rising tide of population figures as a whole, and because the great majority were not caused directly by sack or pillage or casual brutality but through a conspiracy between war and those more impersonal and far more effective killers, epidemic disease and famine.

In the seven years between 1567 and 1574 some 43,000 men left Castile to fight in the Netherlands; perhaps a quarter were to die there. The Castilian outbreak of bubonic plague in 1598–1602 caused 600,000 deaths over those four years. Plague bred fastest in overcrowded, insanitary cities. There is no clear evidence that it was fostered by the comparable concentrations of men in camp or siege-line, but diseases like influenza, dysentery and hepatitis certainly were, and they were passed, through marketing and billeting contacts and the wandering of deserters, into a civilian bloodstream often too weak to resist them. It has been estimated that the diseases spread in 1627–8 by a French army of 6000, as they marched and camped between La Rochelle and Montferrat, led to the deaths of over 1 million civilians.

Too weak because undernourished. It was by exacerbating existing food shortages that war won its most pathetic trophies. It won them partly by engrossing foodstuffs for military hordes whose presence upset the local balance of production and consumption even in a good year. These increases were not limited to a war zone, but could affect, for example, the local price of the residue of salt beef and grain that had been bought in bulk in Naples for shipment to the Netherlands; the feeding of a garrison in Flanders could thus break the budget of a peasant in Calabria. Hunger riots in the English counties of Hampshire, Gloucester and Suffolk followed their stripping of grain for the army in Ireland and meat for the Netherlands expeditionary force. And meanwhile wars had to be paid for by increased personal taxation and by heavier tolls and sales taxes on the transport and purchase of essential commodities: wine, grain, meat, cloth, firewood, salt. Tax collectors, customs men, clerks of the market: these were the officers of war's financial alter ego and, though unarmed (if sometimes supported by armed guards), they contributed to its casualty lists.

Prices rose, too, because of 'unofficial' shortages caused by the devastation of the countryside by armies fanning out from the march or marauding from camp, as well as by the loss of the age's only fertilizer, manure, after the driving off of livestock to provide armies with meat on the hoof. When epidemics eased, reduced numbers could set to in unspoiled fields and intact workshops: war left proportionately greater numbers to face capital damage that made recovery a more painful process. Meanwhile purchasing power was falling, especially in towns, as a result of the loss of artisan jobs that followed the interruption of trade: underemployment was another 'normal' problem intensified by war. Through its effect on prices and purchasing power, bullet war's connection with social war (bread riots, peasant insurrections) had never been closer. The sense of shock expressed by contemporaries when Englishmen came to blows with one another during the Wars of the Roses was out of proportion to the scale of actual military campaigns, which amounted to sixty-one weeks over a period of thirty years, but the battles gave publicity to long-familiar non-war-related miseries and resentments: hunger and joblessness, haves and have-nots. The peasant revolt which convulsed Inner Austria in 1515 was triggered by the extra taxation Maximilian I had been imposing to fund his anti-Venetian wars. But the peasants' list of complaints only mentioned the underlying grievances that were goaded into violent expression: the misappropriation of tax revenue by its collectors, excessive labour services, unreasonable fines imposed by local courts, falsified scales and measures in markets, debasement of the coinage so that the kreutzer no longer bought the same amount of food as it had in the past, limitations by landlords on the traditional rights of the peasantry to fish, hunt and collect wood. If there was so little challenge to a ruler's right to go to war, or considered protest against war as such, this was because war, for all its dramatic apparatus, was experienced as a last straw on the burden of familiar forms of deprivation.

Much of the suffering inflicted by the soldiery on non-combatants arose from the inability of civilian society to deal with large numbers of men on the move. Even mass pilgrimages, which provided the only comparable concentrations of transients needing to be fed and housed, were regarded fearfully, and led to outbreaks of violence at their destination, Compostela or Rome. Yet pilgrims were, in theory at least, meek and peaceable folk, representing one of the best instincts of the populations through which they moved; moreover, their routes, goals and timetables were—in contrast to the peregrinations of armies—regular and could be anticipated well in advance. The military routes which most resembled pilgrim ways, the Dauphiné corridor used by French armies en route to or returning from Italy in the first half of the sixteenth century, the 'Spanish Road' between Savoy and Luxembourg used by troops going to the Netherlands in the second half, both led to military-civilian friction, although we have seen that food stores were accumulated in advance at their stopping points and the legal and financial modes for settling claims to compensation for theft and damage had been carefully elaborated.

No system, however ingenious or responsible, could protect a breadline community from an artificial population surge. The legal situation was clear: anything soldiers took that had not been bought in advance by the army's commissary service, whether food or drink, straw or firewood, should have been paid for. In the ordinances of war issued by Henry VII in 1487 at the start of his campaign against Lambert Simnel, he forbade any soldier to 'presume to take any manner of victual, horse meat, or man's meat, without paying therefor the reasonable price thereof assigned by the clerk of the market or other king's officer therefor ordained, upon pain of death'. His billeting order was similarly designed to protect civilians: so that 'no manner of person or persons, whatsoever they be, take upon them to lodge themselves nor take no manner of lodging nor harborage but such as shall be assigned unto him or them by the King's harbinger, nor dislodge no man, nor change no lodging after that to be assigned, without advice and assent of the said harbinger, upon pain of imprisonment and to be punished at the will of our said sovereign lord'.

Similar ordinances were proclaimed for armies of all nationalities throughout the century, it being in no commander's interest, save when deliberately scorching the earth or when entirely deprived of cash or credit, to alienate the population who possessed the rations and roofs to keep his army fed, reasonably comfortable and, in poor weather, fit. Implementing them was another matter.

The 'reasonable price' of foodstuffs could be maintained in camp or town by victualling officers when distributing bulk supplies earmarked for troops; and if the latter could not pay, they might be given credit. But official purchases were seldom adequate, especially when foul weather or sickness delayed the march. So additional 'official' purchases on the spot created shortages which raised prices for civilian consumers (producers, if they could organize transport fast enough, could make good short-term profits), and private transactions might be made clamorous, often violent, by the discrepancy between official and 'free' prices which no clerk of the market could control, particularly when the 'purchasers' had already gambled and drunk themselves out of credit with their captains and shopped with threats and blows rather than money. Even when the army had moved on, scarcity prices continued to oppress the poor because of the aftermath of crop destruction and beast-stealing caused by its troops and camp-followers when on the road. The cutting of fruit trees and timber for fires and shelters along the line of march also added its mite of interest to the cost of living.

These generalizations seem applicable to the period as a whole, though each campaign had its own timbre of civilian-soldier relationships. Relations varied within single campaigns. The main force of Henry VIII's French invasion of 1544, directed against Boulogne, in great measure owed its success, and, in the main, its acceptance by locals, to efficient victualling, whereas the division sent against Montreuil, not only because of poor official victualling failed to achieve its object, but left the countryside stripped and destitute: when a woman, begging for bread, was offered money by a soldier, her reply was 'God in heaven, what should I do with money, or anything else but bread, and only a little of that, so that we can eat it now, because we do not dare to store it for fear of the wild men.'

The most drastic and direct civilian confrontation with the military was the siege. Outside the walls the effect on the peasant and village economy was literally devastating if the operation were a prolonged one; many lasted several months, some for years. The Spanish siege of Ostend, for instance, started on 15 July 1601 and ended with its capture on 25 September 1604. However effective was the organization of long-distance supply trains, the hordes in the siege-lines and perimeter base camps always needed more. They took animals and fowl first because the trains only brought salt meat; then came grain, finally straw from thatch and wood from any farm buildings not used for billets; for sieges, from that of Pavia in 1524–5 and Florence in 1529–30, to those of Metz in 1552–3 and of Haarlem in 1572–3, came to follow a logistic rather than a seasonal calendar, and cold nights were more dangerous to the troops than the besieged's raiding parties.

Inside the walls there was, by contrast, a necessary collaboration between the populace and their garrison. Armed to defend their families and property, citizen patrols could keep the proclivity of troops to break into shops as supplies ran short within bounds; indeed, there seem to have been almost as many cases of citizens profiteering at their fellows' expense. The lives of the professional soldiers depended on the support on the ramparts of all males capable of bearing arms, and also on the labour of women in repairing breaches and building secondary lines of defence behind sections of the wall that had been made vulnerable by bombardment. In Charles the Bold's unsuccessful siege of Beauvais in 1472 the women's contribution was such as to prompt Louis XI to exempt them from the sumptuary laws (a particularly relevant form of decoration). Women of all ranks toiled with spades and wheelbarrows during the Imperialist siege of Marseilles in 1524. During the eighteen-month siege of Siena in 1552–3 every girl and woman, noble and common, between twelve and fifty was registered, issued with baskets and shovels or picks and organized into district labour gangs, pledged on pain of death to drop their household tasks and hasten to the walls when the order was shouted through the streets. By thus helping to protect their lives, civilians were also putting them at risk. To a conquering siege-army there was little distinction between a soldier who fired a shot and the men and women who plied a spade against them.

It is difficult to estimate how many civilians in sieges were killed by enemy action, either in repelling assaults or through cannon and (from the last third of the sixteenth century) mortar fire. Clearer, because recorded in wails of protest and claims for compensation, was the destruction of suburbs for one and a half or two miles to ensure a clear field of sight and fire from the walls: monasteries, farms, mills, orchards, all had to go. But everyone suffered financially. Even if food convoys could occasionally break through the lines (brought over the snow by sled to Haarlem), shortages forced prices up; 'Give us bread or peace!' an armed throng chanted at the military governor of Rouen during the winter siege of 1591-2. In this case the garrison was still well fed enough to agree to charge and break it up, but only too often the military and civic authorities had anticipated such protests by reducing the number of 'useless mouths'.

In 1495, when Novara, occupied by Charles VIII's lieutenant Louis d'Orléans, was besieged by its dispossessed owner Lodovico Sforza, duke of Milan, a diarist recorded that 'the people began to eat bran bread because food was very scarce, and for this reason the duke of Orléans drove out all those of the populace who were poor and useless'. When Coligny's defence of St Quentin in 1557 was reaching crisis point he, again presumably with a divided conscience, expelled the 'useless mouths', children and the unfit. Nowhere is this logistic tactic so coolly and movingly described as in Monluc's account of what he had to do during the defence he conducted in Siena in 1553. He went to the chief civic council and announced, 'You must put the useless mouths out of town.' There was not protest. 'I thereupon created', he goes on, 'six commissaries to take a list of all the useless people. . . . The list of these useless people I do assure you amounted to 4400 or more, which of all the miseries and desolations that I have ever seen was the greatest my eyes ever yet beheld . . . and these poor wretches were to go through the enemy who beat them back again towards the city, the whole camp continuing night and day in arms to that only end: for that they drove them up to the very foot of the walls that they might the sooner consume the little bread we had left, and to see if the city out of compassion to those miserable creatures would revolt. But that prevailed nothing, though they lay eight days in this condition, when they had nothing to eat but herbs and grass, and above the one half of them perished. . . . There were a great many maids and handsome women, indeed, who found means to escape, the Spaniards by night stealing them into their quarters . . . and some strong and vigorous men also forced their way and escaped by night. But all those did not amount to the fourth part, and all the rest miserably perished.' 'These', he concluded, 'are the effects of war. We must of necessity sometimes be cruel to frustrate the designs of an enemy. God has need to be merciful to men of our trade who commit so many sins, and are the cause of many miseries and mischiefs.' The expulsion of the useless mouths did not save Siena.

Horrible as such expulsions were, and as were the sacks that too frequently celebrated the success of a final assault, the most consequential impact of siege warfare on citizens was oblique and insidious. Far more died from the effects of malnutrition and disease (intensification of endemic ones and others introduced by garrison reinforcements or a conquering army, almost always sick itself from the rigours of the siege) than from wounds. Some 13,000 died of starvation during Henry IV's siege of Paris in 1590. And the effects lingered, with siege deaths occurring long after a chronicler had closed his account. ❖

RECOMMENDED READINGS

John R. Hale, the author of this selection, has also produced a more restricted study, *The Art of War and Renaissance England* (Washington, DC: Folger Shakespeare Library, 1961), as has Michael E. Mallett, *The Military Organization of a Renaissance State: Venice, c. 1400 to 1617* (Cambridge: UK, and New York: Cambridge University Press, 1984). A more general consideration from a somewhat later period may be found in *Adapting to Conditions: War and Society in the Eighteenth Century*, ed. Maarten Ultee (University: University of Alabama Press, 1986).

This was an age of military theorists. One of the greatest was perhaps Niccolò Machiavelli, *The Art of War* (many editions), and Sir John Smythe (1534?–1607), *Certain Discourses Military*, ed. J. R. Hale (Ithaca, NY: Published for the Folger Shakespeare Library by Cornell University Press, 1964), was perhaps more representative.

Even while society suffered from the new, less restricted mode of warfare of modern times, European jurists began to establish laws to regulate war's destruction. The most eminent of these was Hugo Grotius, *The Law of War and Peace*. trans. Francis W. Kelsey et al. (Indianapolis: Bobbs-Merrill, 1962), but the evolution of the laws of war continued, and their evolution is represented by the sources published in *The Law of War, a Documentary History*, ed. Leon Friedman (New York: Random House, 1972). The reader who wishes to pursue these ideas might reread Shakespeare's *King Henry V*, in which the justifications for waging war and the proper manner of conducting hostilities are recurrent themes.

India, About A.D. 1550

INDIA AND ISLAM

A STUDY IN DEFEAT

Subhayu Dasgupta

Of all of the civilizations of the Old World, the Indian was in most ways the least receptive to innovation and change. Lacking a strong central government or an inflexible faith, the Indians nevertheless proved to be highly resistant to foreign influences, even of the most useful and beneficial sort. As late as the opening of the nineteenth century, for example, the Indians had yet to adopt printing, and their culture was overwhelmingly oral. Historians have suggested many reasons for India's inability or unwillingness to adopt and benefit from the numerous technological and organizational innovations that had become increasingly available since the twelfth century. Among the factors that have been advanced are a restrictive caste system, a preference for speculative rather than practical thought, and a fatalistic view of life.

In the following reading Dasgupta presents India's failure to meet the military challenge posed by Islam after the year 1000 as a key factor in stultifying its later development. Faced with defeats caused by poor organization, outmoded tactics, and obsolete technology, Hindu society did not respond by modernizing in order to compete effectively. There was, instead, an increased insistence on traditional patterns of behavior and less tolerance of the sort of individual originality and creativity necessary for social progress. This was the way Hindu culture defended itself against foreign influences. Although politically subjugated, the Indians refused to be culturally dominated. Dasgupta maintains that such an attitude has continued to the present day and still impedes India's development.

READING QUESTIONS

1. What were some of the cultural causes of Hindu defeats at the hands of the Muslims?

2. What were the weaknesses of Hindu military organization?

3. How did Muslim weapons compare to those of the Hindus?

4. How did the Hindu states react to their defeat?

T he opening year of the millennium, that is, A.D. 1001, the last century of which was just running out was conspicuous in the history of India as it witnessed the defeat of the Indian King Jaipal by Mahmud of Ghazni, an event that was the dark herald of the numerous defeats of Hindu arms to follow. As the millennium since the birth of Buddha (c. 596 B.C.) to the death of Harsha Vardhana (A.D. 646) saw the growth and the establishing of a mighty civilisation followed by a doldrum existence of nearly three and a half centuries, so the millennium that started with A.D. 1000 saw the steady erosion of Hindu political power. Till the rise of Shivaji in the seventeenth century the history of India since A.D. 1001 is the history of the steady ascendency of Islamic power and the military and political decline of the Hindus in their own home land. The series of defeats that the Hindus sustained and the fact that in spite of frequent defeats at the hands of an enemy fully committed to iconoclasm and proselytisation, Hindu society yet maintained its identity in proud defiance of the superior arms of the Muslims had a deep effect and led virtually to mutation in the Hindu psychology. The military defeats which created terrible anxiety situations and conditions of great insecurity brought about psychological reactions which had a far-reaching impact on Hindu culture, norms, values, attitudes to this life and the life hereafter. The already existing trends of casteism were accentuated and the cultural barriers built to preserve the social mores also prevented social growth. It gave new powers to social tradition and strengthened the forbidding aspect of the superego. The defeats were all the more poignant as they took place despite the larger number of the defenders and the smaller size of the invading army. It was almost always a defeat of strategy due to a psychological condition that prevented them from learning from defeats and innovating for victory. It displayed the triumph of the Muslim strategy of divide and rule and the failure of the Hindus to unite even though defeats meant severe punishment at the hands of the enemy. The defeats, though they always took place despite Hindu valour, were due to adherence to obsolete tactics, lack of swiftness in battle, lack of organisation, casteism, puritanism about washing, bathing and eating even when the engagement was around the corner. Many battles were lost because the Hindus used elephants, a war animal of doubtful value. The entire organisation of the Hindu army in the battle field depended upon the leader's being perched on the back of an elephant and remaining in sight of the fighting men. The absence of the leader from the usual seat even due to an emergency almost inevitably led to panic and rout. The organisation of the Hindu army veered entirely around the

From Subhayu Dasgupta, *Hindu Ethos and the Challenge of Change*, rev. ed. (New Delhi: Arnold-Heinemann, 1977), pp. 145–155.

leader. The loss of one man could lead to the defeat of the entire army. But it must be noted that once the invaders settled down in the country they adapted themselves to the climate and ethos and ceased to be the drive-hard soldiers that their predecessors were. The invaders who came from across the frontier in the West were almost invariably hardy men of stamina and strategy and they overthrew the local princes, gone soft with easy life or weakened by baronial rebellions and intrigues in the court.

The Muslim invasion of India, in fact, started with Mahmud of Ghazni. There had been an earlier settlement of Arabs in Sind, but the advance of this was checked and it was not in an expansionist mood. As Stanley Lane-Pool remarked, it was 'an episode in the history of India and of Islam, a triumph without results'.

While the call of Islam to proselytise the world carried the Arabs westward up to Spain, in the east the Turko-Afghans steadily made inroads into India whose ancient civilisation already nearly two thousand years old (not counting the Indus Valley civilisation) was unable to match the strategy, determination, military equipment and the social organisation of the youthful Islam. Battles between Hinduism and Islam were essentially battles between a defensive conservatism and orthodoxy on the one hand and aggressive strategy and youthful thrusts on the other.

The military strategy of the Muslim invaders was largely the tactics of the Persian empire as developed by Darius, and called 'Talquama'. The formation of the army was in the shape of a crescent. As the battle raged, the two horns of the crescent advanced and joined, encircling the enemy. The strategy which Shihabuddin Ghori adopted to defeat Prithviraj A.D. 1190 *circa* was the almost invariable pattern of all Muslim offensives. The method of waging the battle was to harass the enemy by intensive archery which was followed by a powerful cavalry charge—a method which was not only decisive in India against the Hindus but also against the Eastern Roman Emperor Romanus who was squarely defeated by these simple tactics of the Turkish Squadrons in A.D. 1071.

The maintainance of a powerful reserve force called the 'Iltimish' was another notable feature of Turkish strategy. The reserve force which consisted of picked soldiers was kept on leash, ready to come to assistance if any wing was weakening or to be released at last as the decisive final blow, if the battle was raging at par. Organisation of the Turkish army and of the Muslim army in general was thorough. Nothing was left to chance or arbitrary whims. Co-ordination of artillery, cavalry and infantry, as well as of the divisions led by different generals with the controlling centre was effected through parades, mock battles, organised hunts and routine drills. The army was kept fighting fit at all times. Timur's war machine which was a model for all the armies of the age was organised on 'rational basis'. Whatever may be Timur's personal shortcomings in the field of battle and in handling his army he was a rationalist. It is because of this basic rationalism that his choice of lieutenants was always right. Merit alone counted. No other consideration prevailed but the need of the army and victory. The armies of Babar and Akbar were also modeled on the

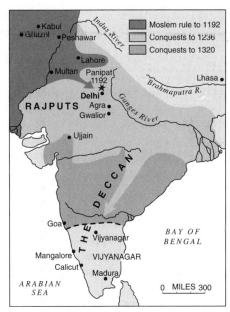

The Moslem conquest of India.

armies of Timur by and large and achieved remarkable results. Along with excellent co-ordination, outstanding leadership that had stood the tests of many
wars, was given iron discipline that brooked no deviation and exacted complete identification with the supreme commander and with the goal. Disobedi-
ence was out of the question being punishable by a most painful death.

The invading army again was always much swifter than the host army
even when the latter were Muslims. Muslims who settled down as conquerors in India steadily took to a life of comfort and became sedentary and
easy going like their Hindu counterparts. Thus, Ibrahim Lody would march
two to three miles and then stop and rest for two to three days, carrying
with him a vast and moving city, while Babar and his small but compact
forces dashed forward to meet him, an encounter in which the small but the
agile delivered a crushing blow to the large and the ponderous.

The size of the army too was very important. The Indian fondness for a
large army and disregard of co-ordination and compactness led to many defeats and much carnage. From the shadowy war between Alexander and Puru
(Porus) in 326 B.C. to the battle of Talikota in 1565 between Vijayanagara and
the Islamic confederacy, far too many battles were lost by the large army to the
small but better organised and compact one. Alexander faced Puru's 30,000
with his 15,000, the result of the attrition being on the estimates of Arrian as
follows: 'Nearly 20,000 of the Indian infantry were killed in this battle, and
about 3,000 of their cavalry. All their war-chariots were destroyed . . . out of
Alexander's original 6,000 infantry, some eighty were killed; in addition to

these he lost ten of the mounted archers . . . about 20 of the mounted Hetaeri and 200 of the other cavalry'. In Talikota the large and disorganised army of Vijayanagara was defeated and the Vijayanagara kingdom entirely destroyed by a much smaller army of the Islamic confederacy—the Hindu losses running into '16,000 slain and thrice that number wounded', the Muslim loss being negligible. The large size of the army was due chiefly to the recruiting of novices—anyone able to collect a knife or a bamboo pole being drafted into the army. Secondly, the gay and easy-going life of the Indian princes called for an increasing number of comforts and amenities while on the march. A large Mogul army, during the decline of the Mogul power, was thus a moving township with shops, nautch girls, money-lenders, news-reporters, besides of course the curious, the onlookers and the bystanders. Often non-combatants exceeded the combatants to a ratio of 10 to 1.

Thus in a large army, the fighting strength did not go up as the number would suggest—as the largeness was due to non-combatants coming in numbers reducing the manoeuvreability of the army and often interfering with the military operations. In the battle between Sher Shah and Humayun (1539) the latter's 40,000 men fled before the former's 10,000 even though a gun was not fired mainly because a large number of camp-followers made almost impossible the movement of Humayun's army. An officer in Humayun's army commanding a hundred troopers had a retinue of five hundred servants to look after him.

The immense advantage of delivering the first blow, often decisive for victory, characterised the tactics of the invading army from the days of Alexander to those of the British. As J. N. Sarkar puts it, describing Alexander's tactics against Puru: 'The Indian Army lay on the defensive, a huge inert mass waiting to observe their enemy's action. Alexander on the other hand seized the initiative, thus enjoying the advantage of attacking or drawing back at any point as suited his interest and varying his tactics with every change in the tide of the battle.' Again nearly 1500 years later around (A.D. 1193–99), says J. N. Sarkar describing the tactics of Shihabuddin Ghori against the Indian prince Prithviraj, 'He seized the tactical initiative and forced the Hindus to fight on the ground and in the manner of the Turk's own choosing instead of the defenders delivering an attack planned and prepared from before. In fact all day long Rajputs had to dance exactly as Shihabuddin played the tune.' Timur the great conqueror 'always followed the strategy of delivering the first blow' and carried the day. Referring to Sher Shah's battle with Humayun J. N. Sarkar comments, 'This battle proved that the army that cannot take the offensive is doomed and purely passive defence is futile.'

However, though the Indian army was by and large inert and on the defensive, Rana Pratap and Shivaji are notable exceptions. Rana Pratap at Haldighat with scarcely a quarter of the size of the Mogul army held the Moguls at bay for a good part of the day simply because of the all-out massive offensive with which he opened the engagement (1576). Though the battle was ultimately lost to superior numbers and superior strategy without the initial offensive it would have been lost much earlier.

In the area of military equipment the Muslims again displayed their superiority as they did in strategy and organisation. In all the four major equipments for war, (a) the horse, (b) the bow and arrow, (c) the artillery, and (d) the armour and shield, the Muslims were by far superior to the defenders of the country.

The Central Asian bow also called composite bow 'made of steel or two horns joined together with a metal clasp' was a terror to the enemy till it was replaced by musketry. The missiles delivered from the bow could pierce shields and breastplates. The bow which played havoc on the enemy in the hands of the Macedonians for generations, brought defeat to defenders in India. Even as late as 1565 in the battle of Talikota, these bows, in the hands of the Muslim confederacy fighting the army of Vijayanagara, played a vital role as they were much superior to the bamboo bows of the Hindus whose arrows neither in range nor in power of penetration were any match for these composite bows.

The Turkoman horse, a noble steed and one of the most spirited creatures on earth, gave the Muslim army coming from central Asia a speed and a stamina which the country ponies used in large numbers by Indian princes, Hindus and Muslims could not match. The 'Horse' and the 'Sawar' (rider) called 'Turusk Sawars' became a byword for 'superbly mounted dashing cavalry of any race.' Not only could these horses swim across streams but they were as hardy as those who rode them living on worm wood and covering, as Timur's horsemen did, 150 miles a day and night and 80 miles a day for a week.

The artillery, again, which came to India with Babur and decided many battles was not fully adapted by the Hindus and not used to its maximum advantage. The Hindu army depended largely on the sword and the traditional bow and arrow: artillery, even when maintained was neglected and not integrated into the military machine. The Muslims, on the other hand, made full use of the artillery and musketry. The development of the cannon from being a dead weight carried to the field on carts to a mobile and wheeled artillery was followed and adopted to great advantage in war.

The development of Turko-Afghan strategy and organisation in battle was inspired largely by the social, cultural and religious revolution through which they passed since their baptism into Islam. The clarion call of the prophet to proselytise the infidels was a command to do or die if persuasion failed. Therefore death in battle for the holy cause was to be amply rewarded in paradise. As Fisher puts it, 'Muslim faith in the all powerful Allah and His will also gave them a sense of fatalism that life or death was but His wish and all that he could do was to serve His cause'. The social equality of Islam also integrated the people of diverse races and languages into one homogeneous unity, a contrast with the caste-ridden Hindu society they sought to crush. Rigorous prohibition of drinking further gave the soldiers of Islam advantage over their enemies. Absence of drunkenness made alertness and vigilance omni-present qualities among the invaders.

We have the picture of a youthful and an aggressive people who were raiding the ancient civilisations from India to Spain. Hindus faced the challenge with a great deal of valour but not with stratagem and unity. Though Puru suffered a major disaster in the hands of Alexander, indeed the greatest general of antiquity and a veteran of many wars, yet the Hindu mind in the second century B.C. was still plastic and capable of learning from experience. Thus the chariot which in the past was a major organ of the Hindu army, a charioteer having about the status of a knight, was steadily discarded as it proved too bulky and unwieldy in the changing tactics of battle. Chariots are last mentioned in the Deccan campaign of Kharvela around 170 B.C. In the campaigns of Samudra Gupta or Harshavardhana chariots are not mentioned any more.

Many victories that the Indian army and military leadership secured against the Sakas (Scythians), Huns and Greeks were possible only because Indian strategy was geared to the needs of the hour. Yet, with the ossification of the Hindu culture, attitude and values, the flexibility and plasticity of mind was deteriorating. The Hindu tactics of the battle, for example, remained unchanged despite repeated encounters with the Muslims. They generally charged straight ahead if they were not on the defensive. They scarcely held back any reserve, or what the Turks called 'Iltimish' for emergency.

The Hindus made no effort to reorganise the army, to provide training to recruits, and to integrate different military functions on a plan to have a co-ordinated action of the entire army in the battlefield as the Muslims did. No effort was made to standardise the size and quality of the weaponry so that at the time of action none would be left with sub-standard arms. The Hindu army continued to remain in part regular troops and in part rabble who had neither training nor proper arms and were a positive hindrance to the successful conduct of war.

The Hindu response to artillery and muskets was cold. The Marhattas for example, who developed superb tactics of warfare and delivered many crushing blows on much better equipped enemies, depended largely on lances and swords. The Muslim invaders in conducting a war were bent upon victory and handled the rules as well as the equipment of war pragmatically. A battle like any other human endeavour was to be judged by the result. There was to be no question of conformity to rules or scriptures having precedence over the final objective—victory.

Describing the battle of Talikota, Jadunath Sarkar describes how pragmatic the Muslims were in handling artillery, 'As soon as the wild Hindu multitude came within point-blank range he discharged his guns, loaded with bags full of thick slug-like copper coins instead of shots and after this one salvo 5000 Hindus lay dead and writhing in a human mound before the Muslim centre—this "whiff of grape" finished the Hindus and their last venture was quenched in blood.' This use of artillery shows indeed how innovative the Muslim leadership was and how in their hands artillery came as easily as a tool being adjusted with ease according to the needs of the hour.

As Scheerer puts it in his article on 'Problem solving', in the Scientific American, 'Duncker discovered that fixation often interferes when the solution of a test problem requires the use of a familiar object in a novel way. Suppose someone needs a screw driver and one is not available. He could make do with any thin and sufficiently hard object—a coin for example. But to see this possibility he must shift from his normal idea of "Coin as money" to the new functional concept of "coin as screw driver", and this is a difficult kind of shift for many people to make . . . a person who thinks of it independently should be credited with a truly creative insight'.

The leadership of the Muslim confederacy thus passes the exacting tests of creativity of the modern psychologists. The essence of strategy is free-wheeling of ideas, continuous and uninhibited combination and recombination of parts to create new wholes. No one personifies the spirit of creative leadership and strategy better than Alexander the Great, whose relentless organisation and reorganisation of the army is an example for all times. 'To the very end of his life Alexander was making experimental changes and developments in army organisation, and all the changes in the direction of increased mobility and away from the technical supremacy of the phalanx of heavy infantry armed with pikes. His pitched battles he won (like Cromwell, as historians have already pointed out) by rapid flanking cavalry movement, keeping the heavy infantry in reserve; his sieges by breaching the enemy defences with siege artillery, followed by a rush of light infantry through the breach'.

Our analysis will however remain incomplete if we do not mention treason and the lack of unity among Indian princes as factors that contributed heavily to the Indian debacles. Both lack of unity and large scale treason point to a divided society where gain of one group is loss to the other. Private gain had precedence over the social, and probably the implicit social sanction of corruption that we see even today around us had deep roots in the Indian tradition. It is maintained that the main reason why the Indians in general and specifically the Hindus failed to rise up to the occasion was that they had become a closed society, men with closed minds. Certain repressive tendencies like pollution on touch or even pollution on approaching near, were present since the time of Samudra Gupta or even earlier. If these tendencies led to poor performance of Hindu arms, the military defeats one upon the other only accentuated further the narrowness, the defeatism, the gloomy view of life which created nationwide despondency and lack of confidence. The military performance of the Hindus thus highlights two major weaknesses—failure to innovate and inability to meet the challenge of organisation and co-ordination. Despite the fact that defeats took place because of the Hindu inability to discard fixed ideas and dogmatic belief-systems yet the Hindu reaction was not to reject the blinkers and to come out of the shell but to retreat deeper into the shell and make the existing belief-systems even more rigid and dogmatic. Basham who fully corroborates the diagnosis of the Hindu predicament with arms observes as follows:

'The Kingdom of medieval Hindu India, incapable either of empire building or of firm alliances and maintaining enormous unruly armies which were continuously at war, indeed produced their heroes but they were quite incapable of withstanding the Turks, whose military science was not burdened by pedantic or ancient tradition'.

In the relatively open societies of Europe, however, military challenges led a broadening of the cultural and technological base. As Mumford puts it, 'The effect of fire arms upon technics was threefold. To begin with, they necessitated the large scale use of iron both for the guns themselves as well as cannon balls'—requiring necessarily expansion of the ferrous industry. 'Second, the gun was the starting point of a new type of power machine, it was mechanically speaking, a one cylinder internal combustion engine . . . Because of the accuracy and effectiveness of the new projectiles, these machines had still another result: they were responsible for the development of heavy fortification, with elaborate outworks, moats . . . The business of defence became complicated in proportion as the tactics of offense became more deadly: road building, canal building, pontoon building, bridge building became necessary adjuncts of warfare'.

Again, says Mumford, 'The pressure of military demand not merely hastened factory organisation at the beginning: it has remained persistent throughout its entire development. As warfare increased in scope and large armies were brought into the field, their equipment became a much heavier task. And as their tactics became mechanised, the instruments needed to make their movements precise and well-timed were necessarily reduced to unformity too. Hence along with factory organisation there came standardisation on a larger scale than was to be found in any other departments of tactics except perhaps printing'.

In India however, none of these things happened. What provided stimulus to spectacular social change elsewhere, failed to provoke an ossified society into action. War and military defeats led the Hindus only to greater proscription of deviant ways, the enforcing of conformism to tradition and to the growth of a retreating personality. ❖

RECOMMENDED READINGS

For a general background, one may consult Romila Thapar, *A History of India,* Vol. I (New York: Penguin Books, n.d.), which provides a history of India from the Aryan invasions to the coming of the Mughals in 1526. The *Mahābhārata,* the great Indian epic, is in the process of translation by J. A. B. van Buitenen (Chicago: University of Chicago Press, 1973-). The *Bhagavad Gita,* a portion of the *Mahābhārata,* which many consider the epitome of classical Indian philosophy, religion, and culture, is available in an excellent translation by Juan Mascaro (New York: Penguin Books, n.d.). The culture of classical India is reconstructed in Jeannine Auboyer, *Daily Life in Ancient India: From Approximately 200 BC TO 700 AD,* trans. S. W. Taylor (New York: Macmillan, 1965).

China, A.D. 1588

CH'I CHI-KUANG AND THE JAPANESE PIRATES

Ray Huang

The Ming dynasty (1368–1644) was the only truly Chinese dynasty to rule China between the thirteenth century and the Revolution of 1911. The establishment of the Ming followed a century of Mongol dominance, and the dynasty endured for two and a half centuries before yielding to the conquering Manchus. The Ming gave China a renewed independence and pride and raised it to a previously unparalleled preeminence in East Asian affairs. The Ming period represented the culmination of China's age-old institutional and cultural traditions. The stability of the regime and the general prosperity of the people showed the vitality of the Chinese tradition and its capacity for growth and change.

Ray Huang's biographical sketch of the Chinese general Ch'i Chi-kuang (1528–1588) depicts an important period in the life of one of the greatest military leaders and reformers of the Ming period. Born of a hereditary military family, Ch'i early distinguished himself and achieved rapid advancement. By the mid-1500s he had been granted a command against the formidable Japanese and Chinese pirates active along China's eastern seacoast. Ch'i produced amazing results against the pirates, but his contribution went beyond their defeat. Through a series of reforms, he established an entirely new military organization. Prior to his innovations, the army had been totally unprepared to deal with external pressures on China's borders. Chi's efforts produced a well-trained and disciplined army that succeeded in eliminating the pirates and bringing calm to the northern frontier.

The following account of Ch'i's early years and his efforts against the pirates gives a perceptive glimpse into the internal workings of the Ming military system and, in addition, includes an examination of the incompatibility between the military and civilian elements of the Ming government. The author points out the differences in philosophy and practice between the two branches of service. The dissension created by the resulting bureaucratic infighting and corruption eventually extracted a heavy toll in both governmental and military efficiency.

READING QUESTIONS

1. Why were successful generals and their junior officers continually falling into disgrace?

2. What were the defects of the military system when Ch'i Chi-kuang began his command career?

3. How did the Japanese pirates operate?

4. How did Ch'i Chi-kuang develop and train his army?

5. Why didn't the Chinese develop more modern weapons and tactics?

6. How did Ch'i Chi-kuang adapt his organization and training to the special needs of his men?

h'i Chi-kuang's death on January 17, 1588, fell in the Year of the Pig, as by the lunar calendar it was the twentieth day of the twelfth month of the previous year. The event was not taken notice of by the court. If it was ever reported to the emperor, it was presumably by the Secret Police. The dispatch therefore never turned up in the palace archives.

Three months before his death, Ch'i's name was mentioned to the Wan-li emperor for the last time by an investigating censor who wanted the throne to consider the general's reappointment. That suggestion cost the censor three months' salary. The imperial rescript on his memorial reminded him that he was endorsing an officer who had recently been impeached. In reality almost three years had lapsed since Ch'i's censure and dismissal. If the emperor had been willing to forgive the general, one of the most capable for many centuries, he could have let the reinstatement take effect without referring to the past. Since in this case he did refer to the past, this meant that Ch'i Chi-kuang had not been forgiven. His close association with Chang Chü-cheng had made him unforgivable—at least throughout Wan-li's reign.

But even without a state burial or a posthumous restoration of honor many decades later, Ch'i Chi-kuang still fared better than other generals. His senior officer and close friend, Yü Ta-yu, was subject to all kinds of criticism

From Ray Huang, *1587: A Year of No Significance: The Ming Dynasty in Decline* (New Haven and London: Yale University Press, 1981), pp. 156–174.

Ming China.

and never allowed to hold a responsible position for long, even though he had repeatedly distinguished himself on the battlefield and his effort at reviving the dynasty's military power could be matched only by Ch'i's. Another general, Lu T'ang, was detained before being dismissed. T'ang K'o-ku'an was likewise arrested but was told to redeem himself in combat, which eventually led to his death in an ambush set by the Mongols on the steppes. Ch'i's own lieutenants, including Hu Shou-jen, Wang Yü-lung, Chu Yü, and Chin K'o, were either abruptly discharged from service or exiled to the frontier. Only Liu Hsien, also Ch'i's contemporary, managed to weather many rounds of impeachment and censure. He did so largely because he was directing a protracted campaign against the aborigines in Szechuan and his service was indispensable. After his death his son Liu T'ing inherited his position with reduced rank. He, too, survived many censuring actions and career crises as he gained prominence, only to perish in the ill-directed campaign against Nurhaci in 1619.

The unhappy experiences of these generals could not have been entirely coincidental. There were basic incompatibilities between military operations and the dynasty's style of bureaucratic rule. In essence, the army had to deal with a situation arising from an imbalance. Wars and battles resulted from the uneven growth of socioeconomic forces which had gone beyond the point where they could be politically reconciled. Or sometimes armed conflict was necessary because of a peculiar and extremely distressing situation requiring immediate relief that could not be secured by usual and peaceful means. These military solutions challenged the primary purpose of the bureaucracy of the empire, which had been geared to the principles of stability and balance. In the minds of the bureaucrats strength was not power, regional interests should be minimized rather than freely championed, and there was no distress that could not be relieved by the spirit of sharing.

Although in practice the moral objectives of the government were often compromised, its approach still presented a serious technical handicap to the armed forces. Military commanders, in order to be successful, had to habituate themselves to maintaining a selective vision and be willing to take extreme measures. When facing the enemy they must deliver concentrated and lethal blows; when on the defensive they had to concern themselves with vital points only, generally considering life expendable that could be traded for time and space; and when victorious, they could spare no effort to widen the path of success. None of these strategies could have met with the approval of civil officials preoccupied with the dogmas of restraint and moderation, and whose sense of history, virtually timeless as it was, made them most reluctant to accept the merit of any drastic action based on physical force, which to them led only to temporary and localized gains.

Even the maintenance of army installations in peacetime had to an extent conflicted with the style of civil administration peculiar to the dynasty. A separate system of army logistics which lay outside the control of the civil bureaucracy would have been out of order. Yet to set up a network of supply depots with strategic emphasis and geographical preference also ran counter to the homogeneous development that the Civil Service was determined to encourage. The presence of soldiery was never favorably regarded by a large agrarian population governed in the spirit of simplicity, as both recruitment and discharge tended to create social problems. In numerous cases a soldier entering the service was a farm laborer leaving the productive force. And his eventual return to his village usually added an undesirable element to the local community, as his newly acquired skills and living habits hardly enabled him to resume his former life with ease and comfort. Such problems were compounded in the case of army officers. Unlike other societies where a retired officer could reappear as a man of proven ability entitled to leadership roles in the local community, or become a civil administrator backed by prestige and expertise, the empire offered no such advantages to a commander discharged from the armed forces. Trained to deal with technical precision, he would soon find that elsewhere value was placed on serenity, literary accomplishment, the powers of moral persuasion, and skill in subtle maneuvers—all qualities diametrically opposed to his own talents.

These fundamental incompatibilities were too profound to be overlooked. Not only did civil officials react to army officers with feelings of rivalry and disdain, but also they could, in matters of high-level command, raise questions as to the latter's wisdom. There was room for controversy in every individual case: one outlaw should have been persuaded to lay down arms rather than fight; another, however, should have been quickly crushed with incessant blows rather than being allowed to rest and gain breathing space. Logistical problems could also add to the complexities. A commander could, of course, be punished when his soldiers mutinied and looted the general population. Yet a continual cause of uprising was pay arrearage, which could be completely out of the commanding officer's control.

The dynasty's Civil Service had gained maturity roughly within the hundred years from the mid-fifteenth century to the mid-sixteenth century. During the same period the prestige of army officers had sunk to the lowest level, extreme even by our own standards. The technical difficulty of raising sufficient funds to maintain the military units cannot be ignored as a cause of the decline. But on the other hand, the unitary structure of the government, with its emphasis on ideological cohesion, could never have reached such a final stage of development had it not constantly advanced at the expense of the armed forces. The differences between the two branches of service were too great to allow them to coexist as equals. Yet, before there was any contest for hegemony, the military bureaucracy had been destined to defeat. For a settled empire such as this, an accomplishment of the most valiant general had to be temporary and localized. And of course army officers were no match for civil officials in gaining influence through rhetoric.

In 1555, when Ch'i Chi-kuang was transferred to Chekiang, the coastal province that was being scourged by Japanese pirates, on the northern frontier the Mongol leader Altan Khan was penetrating Chinese defense lines at will and, when he left, taking the captured population and its movable goods along with him. The decline of the dynasty's military power was not a surprise, but the extent of it was. While despair and confusion reigned along the east coast, a band of pirates, reportedly fifty or seventy men, was bold enough to maraud inland on a route that encircled the southern capital, which—unbelievably—had a garrison boasting, at least on paper, 120,000 men.

A general conclusion could be drawn that the defense installations of the empire, along with their logistical framework, had largely vanished. Ch'i Chi-kuang's contribution was not only the defeat of the pirates. Before the pirates could effectively be dealt with, he had virtually to organize a new army. His book, *Chi-hsiao Hsin-shu,* reveals that Ch'i himself settled the recruiting procedure, decided the pay scale, devised general rules governing personnel assignment, standardized the organization of combat formations, selected weapons, outlined the duties of individual soldiers and their officers, designed his own banners and coordinating signals, invented his own tactics and schemes of maneuver, prescribed military etiquette, and issued his own orders of court martial, which, based on the principle of group responsibility, compelled both officers and men to guarantee one another's performance in combat on threat of the death penalty. He even handed out a recipe for making field rations! But other aspects of army logistics remained under the control of civil officials. The fact that Ch'i had to take responsibility for these details revealed that, until then, the empire had failed to institutionalize its military establishment. There were no military handbooks or field manuals, no schools that specialized in the martial arts, not even an effective ordnance department. If there had been any organizational tables, maintenance charts, and articles of war, they must have been inoperative for a long time.

These historical facts made Ch'i Chi-kuang's remarkable creation nothing less than a personal command, regardless of what he might have wished it to be. Significantly, thirty years later his command still appeared to be more personal than institutional—in fact, to many stability-minded civil officials a potential threat to the dynasty rather than a safeguard of it.

It was extremely paradoxical that in the middle of the sixteenth century the Japanese could violate China's security on the eastern seaboard. In many respects it seemed that the invasion should have been reversed. Not only was Japan much smaller and less populous than China, but also for decades its home islands had been in a state of anarchy. Law and order had completely broken down; the territorial lords were embroiled in warfare with one another, at times even betrayed and dislodged by their own lieutenants. China, on the other hand, was governed by a highly integrated civil bureaucracy; the emperor's orders extended to the remotest corners of his realm. Moreover, the centralized state was supposed to maintain the largest army in the world, backed up by close to two million hereditary military households, each of which was required by law to furnish a soldier for active service at all times.

But there was a huge gulf between theory and practice, and in the case of Ming China between reality and the projected ideal. The registration of hereditary military households had not been put on a sound basis even at the founding of the dynasty, although it was designed to shield the general population from the disturbance of conscription. At the very beginning, large numbers of households were pressed into service; desertion and absconding started as soon as the military colonies were organized. In later centuries the tax-exempt land assigned to these households was sold and mortgaged by the users at will. Increased mobility of the population had made the original concept unworkable. It was not unusual for a colony to be reduced to a skeleton, in some extreme cases a tiny fraction of its former self, such as 2 to 3 percent of its originally recorded strength. As the dwindling manpower could not be advantageously deployed, it was more likely for soldiers to be used by their commanders as construction workers and porters, and no less frequently as domestic servants.

Also responsible was the supply system. Army logistics was integrated with the civil administration, which operated on the principle of lateral transmission of supplies at the lowest possible level. The Ministry of Revenue was really a huge accounting office, which supervised the scheduled and automatic deliveries of revenue-collecting agencies directly to the corresponding disbursing agencies. The services and supplies were by no means assembled and routed at intermediate depots. They were channeled into numerous short and interlinking supply lines which covered the empire like a closely woven net. The number of intermediate agencies must have been greatly reduced as a result. But the lowest civil office, that of county magistrate, could be required to make deliveries at a score of disbursing agencies, each of which would in turn receive consignments from a score of suppliers. This system permanently deprived the higher echelon of the opportunity to develop a logistical capacity to keep pace with changing conditions, at the same time ensuring the likelihood of shortage in all units, as apparently some of the many delivering agencies for one reason or another would become delinquent, while others were neither able nor required to make up the deficiencies. After the system had been in operation for over two hundred years, the accounts also drifted away from reality.

This way of managing supplies, with its centralized direction but decentralized execution, had a more profound effect than was generally realized. The annual moving of grain to Peking was a good example. The foodstuff was collected from the land-tax quotas of a large number of counties and prefectures in the southern provinces. Nominally, a special transportation corps within the army was organized to haul the supplies on the Grand Canal; this comprised 120,000 officers and men operating close to 12,000 grain boats. Yet, no supporting services were ever set up within the transportation corps. Army captains and lieutenants commanding individual ships, who had received the quantities of grain from the tax-paying communities, were held directly responsible to the imperial government. More illustrative was the construction of grain boats, due to be rebuilt every ten years. A "dockyard" was established on the Huai River, which in its heyday had an annual capacity of over 700 craft. But inasmuch as the services and supplies that were to contribute to the ship construction program had never been fiscally organized, the divided resources could not be pulled together under a central administering body. The so-called dockyard had to be divided into eighty-two separate units—in effect eighty-two boat-yards. Its site on the riverbank was a long strip of land only thirty yards wide. But the adjacent constructional units with their individual housing facilities extended over two and a half miles.

Needless to say, such an organization had little sophistication, linked as it was to the technological level of the village. A case in point was the turning out of high-quality shirts of mail by palace artisans for the emperor's bodyguards; the armor used by field troops generally consisted of quilted cotton garments, some reinforced with iron strips, others stuffed with wastepaper. This was a situation that even Ch'i Chi-kuang could not correct. Toward the end of his career, the basic equipment at his command was still submitted by numerous communities as a part of their tax quotas. The crude manufacture and lack of standardization of gear must have accounted for the quality of the field army. It could not be significantly different from a large force of militia.

Furthermore, army officers, including high commanders, were not required to be profound thinking men. In them, gallantry in action was much more highly valued. Liu T'ing, who had yet to die in Liaotung, was famous for the long-handled sword he wielded, which weighed no less than 160 pounds. Tu Sung, another general who laid down his life in the same campaign, was even more brutish and unschooled. Never lacking dash when at the head of charging troops, in times of defeat and humiliation he would not hesitate to destroy his own weapons, armor, and saddle, threaten to commit suicide, or shave his head, declaring himself an ordained Buddhist abbot.

Almost all officers had inherited their positions from their forefathers. By a complicated procedure, men of junior grade received their commissions without diminution; but descendants of general officers inherited reduced ranks. The military service examination, intended to open army commissions to all qualified candidates, fell short of this goal, as commanders originating outside of hereditary circles were rare. The examination itself emphasized archery and horsemanship. The written portion, given by civil officials, never really dealt with military science. The so-called military school also offered a curriculum that gave preponderant attention to the Confucian canon. Its primary concern, furthermore, was "to teach the student to write 100 characters daily."

In order to compensate for the lack of generalship among the generals, the court of Peking empowered governors and governors-general to give orders to army commanders. Under them, censorial officials commissioned as military circuit intendants extended their power of surveillance to take full charge of operations. This setup merged well with the bureaucratic structure of the government, as both logistics and communication had to be integrated under civil leadership. Territorial control had to be stressed. After all, the army was organized with the principal aim of pacifying provincial districts, not meeting or launching full-scale invasions. This preconsideration held especially true in the southern provinces, the coastline hitherto having been regarded as an insulated barrier.

Civil officials, nevertheless, lacked intrinsic and professional interest in the affairs of the army. In those territories where the military colonies were in a state of decline they let them fall into further inactivity. It was the mid-century Japanese invasion that changed the picture: it dramatized the risk of an undefended coastline and showed that, in order to mend the situation, general officers had to be selected from groups of individuals who possessed qualities more sophisticated than those expected of the best sergeants and platoon leaders.

The marauders who rampaged on the eastern seaboard in the sixteenth century were not exactly pirates. Onshore they built inland bases and besieged walled cities. Their incessant raids lasted for at least two decades. Nor were they exclusively Japanese. Most of the time they cooperated with mixed bands of Chinese; on many occasions the latter predominated. Their leadership was even supplied by Chinese adventurers. But within the fighting element, the role played by the natives could not be more than auxiliary.

The invasion was based in Japan; and the Japanese furnished all the military skill and military equipment.

The problem of piracy was inseparable from international trade, which, even though proscribed by law, had been flourishing on the eastern coast for some time, engaging adventurers of different nationalities. The most impressive junks in the traffic measured 100 feet in length and 30 feet in width, with shells 7 inches thick, and were therefore unmatched by the government's warships. It was said that on a busy day during the trading season as many as 1,200 large and small ships hugged China's coastline, extending their trade routes on a huge arc that ran from the Japanese islands to the Gulf of Siam. Ports of call were designated on the desolate offshore islands not covered by official patrols. In the absence of a court system to enforce contractual obligations and settle cases of indebtedness, a score of sea captains, most of them Chinese but some of them undoubtedly of mixed parentage, acted as armed arbiters in an attempt to fill the legal vacuum. They eventually rose to be pirate leaders.

Before the officials moved in to confiscate their ships and seal off their harbors, some of the pirate leaders had already extended their influence inland by marrying into families of the gentry and inducing the latter to join in their adventures. But when they began to service their ships inland and, as de facto authorities on the seaboard, summoned villagers to their "courts" for questioning, the imperial government was forced to act. Such a maritime power, however embryonic, threatened the agrarian-based dynasty in theory as well as in practice.

Yet, when the showdown came, the weakness of the imperial government was thoroughly exposed: its formidableness appeared only on paper. Senior commanders had no inkling of the number of soldiers at their service, or the number of ships. Regional commanders demanded cash payments from the general population before they would consent to function. Soldiers characteristically started to flee at the first glimpse of the enemy. Combat units had not had a field maneuver for so long that they marched in close formation. "When one man was lost, ten thousand stampeded." The distressing situation soon became universal. The most heroic resistance to the invading pirates was put up by civilians hastily organized on city walls.

On the other hand, the Japanese, comprised of fighting men from Yamaguchi, Bungo, Ozumi, Satsuma, Hakata Bay, and Tsushima and Gotto islands, were noted for their lack of a unified command. Unable to develop a war aim, in the early stages of the campaign they followed their Chinese leaders in the vague hope that the devastation they wrought would force the court of Peking to open trade, perhaps granting army and naval commissions to those leaders. Once this hope was dashed by Governor-General Hu Tsung-hsein, who trapped the traitors at negotiations and delivered their heads to the capital, the subsequent waves of invasion from Japan gradually developed into a senseless affair, serving no purpose other than to satisfy the predatory urge of the warriors.

But China's weakness was Japan's strength. While lacking unity at the top, the Japanese demonstrated remarkable organizational ability on the battleground, indicating that, however warlike, there was a certain solidarity within their social order which, in contrast to China's, was rooted at the bottom. Chinese writers were unanimously impressed by the stern discipline the invaders were able to impose on their fighting men, in action and in camp. Uniformity of military skill marked the pirates more than the temporarily recruited mercenaries. Unlike rebelling Chinese peasants, they repeatedly defeated the government forces, which were overwhelmingly superior in number.

The invaders arrived on the Chinese coast in ships carrying about a hundred men each. Though small landing parties were reported, a major wave involved scores of such ships, and therefore several thousand men. At the high point of their marauding, the pirates were said to be able to set up an enclave of 20,000 men. Natives were either enticed or forced to join the ranks. But subsequently some of those captured were sold in Japan's slave market. The pirates maintained their mobility by seizing inland shipping. Their loot included not only valuables but also bulky cargo. At least one source indicates that they collected silk cocoons in quantity and assigned village women to work on them, thus showing themselves enterprising enough to enter the area of manufacture. When the ships could not be conveniently moored they were burned on the beaches. In all events, the invaders made the systematic pillage of the coastal provinces a long-term project, and with the profits they reaped, were ready to quarter in China for the winter. In the spring they would be relieved by new waves of invaders. There were also instances where the Japanese constructed their ships for the return voyage on Chinese shores.

The invincibility of the Japanese was based on the skillful handling of contact weapons and close teamwork within small units the size of platoons and squads. Infantry tactics, in fact, accounted for most of their field performance. The twin swords, in particular, were wielded with such dexterity that onlookers "could see only the flash of the weapon, not the man." Squad leaders gave commands with folding fans. Usually they directed the swordmen to lift their weapons upward, and as soon as the attention of the enemy was distracted, they would signal the lowering of the blades, the sharpness of which exceeded anything of Chinese make. Since each swordsman in action could cover as large an area as eighteen feet in diameter, this skill gave the invaders an advantage in close combat. Chinese observers also noted that the Japanese used bows eight feet long and arrowheads two inches wide, and that their javelins "were thrown before they could be seen." Firearms had never been considered vital by the pirates. Ch'i Chi-kuang himself mentioned that the Japanese had introduced the musket to China, but there is no evidence that they themselves used it effectively. Scattered evidence indicates that the heavier guns in their possession had been captured from the Chinese.

In the early phase of the campaign Chinese officials persistently overlooked the importance of teamwork. As the Japanese were recognized as being superior in soldiery, an effort was made by those officials to recruit Chinese individuals capable of acrobatic performance—including boxing instructors, Buddhist monks, salt smugglers, and aborigines from the southwest—as an answer to the challenge. Only after their troops were repeatedly ambushed and annihilated by the enemy did the organizers for the defense come to the conclusion that the problem was far more fundamental than they had thought.

Although the Japanese usually entered the field in bands of no more than thirty men each, such platoons were well coordinated, even when they were operating at a distance from each other. Signals were given by blowing seashells. The invaders were experienced at using native guides, sending out patrols, deploying in depth, creating deception, and driving refugees in front of them to harass and confuse the defenders. Ironically, the government forces were not versed in such basic tactics. At best, the stout-minded would dash toward the enemy unaided, only to fall victim to the better trained pirates, who would then proceed to encircle and mop up the remaining government troops. The numerous rivers, creeks, and lakes in the territory were the source of yet more woe for the routed units. Once the men started to flee, many of them eventually died in water—an infamous fate that Supreme Commander Hu Tsung-hsien himself once narrowly escaped.

Holding the advantage, the pirates usually assumed defensive positions if they had the choice. They preferred to wait for the Chinese to make mistakes. Ch'i Chi-kuang made the following observation:

> The numerous battles I have fought over the past several years give me the impression that the pirates always manage to sit on the heights waiting for us. Usually they hold on until evening, when our soldiers become tired. Then they dash out. Or else, when we start to withdraw, they will catch us out of step to launch their counterattack. It seems that they always manage to send forth their units when they are fresh and spirited. They adorn their helmets with colored strings and animal horns of metallic colors and ghostly shapes to frighten our soldiers. Many of them carry mirrors. Their spears and swords are polished to a shine and look dazzling under the sun. Our soldiers, therefore, are awed by them during the hours of delay before contact.

Thus, despite what official circles called the "campaign by government forces to suppress the pirates," in terms of military proficiency such a phrase was misleading. At least until Ch'i Chi-kuang perfected his tactical command, the engagement could better be described as a contest between Japanese professionals and Chinese amateurs.

When organizing his command, Ch'i Chi-kuang turned his back on the hereditary families and military colonies. His volunteers were recruited from the inland districts in Chekiang. This was possible because the government, facing a protracted campaign, had authorized a surtax on all existing revenues to finance it. Ch'i exhorted his soldiers:

> Any day you are in the service, even a rainy and windy day when you are sitting there with folded arms, no one can do away with the three cents of silver due you. But every bit of this silver comes from the tax money turned in by the general population, some from your own local districts. At home you are farmers yourselves. Who of you is not? You must now think of the toil and trouble of working in the field to raise the tax money, and be glad to have the present easy time of receiving silver payments. The taxpayers feed you for a whole year without asking you to work. All they expect is that you beat off the pirates in one engagement or two. If you do not even try to kill the pirates to give those people protection, what are they feeding you for? You might get by with a court martial, but even then, Heaven would let someone somewhere put you to death.

With this combination of moral suasion and the threats of popular religion Ch'i established combat discipline among his recruits. He declared that he would execute an officer if his entire unit ran away from the enemy, or his subordinate commanders if the stampede occurred and the officer perished in his effort to halt the retreat. If a squad leader should die without the support of his men, the death penalty would be applied to all the soldiers in the squad. Although such extreme measures could not be put into effect in more than a few selected cases, its intimidating effect achieved the purpose and Ch'i's command became most difficult to beat. To keep conditions this way he had frequently to invoke this article of war. He pointed out that even in the midst of disastrous defeat there had to be some deserving individuals whose merit must be recognized. Conversely, even after an overwhelming victory the few officers and men who had failed to perform their duties should never be allowed to go unpunished. In a memorial to the emperor, Ch'i recounted the battle of 1562, when his troops tried to recapture a stone bridge from the Japanese. The first attempt failed and all thirty-six men in the platoon died. The second platoon, following it up, also lost half of its men. At this time the survivors began to fall back. Ch'i, on the spot, personally cut down the retreating platoon leader in order to renew the attack. Eventually the enemy was overpowered and the battle ended with one of the most satisfying victories of Ch'i's career.

Ch'i's discipline was sometimes terrifying. He left many instructions to cut off the ears of his own soldiers for a number of offenses. An unconfirmed story held that he actually ordered the execution of his second son. But brutal or not, with his persistence and constant personal supervision he built up an army that was truly invincible. He could assemble a whole division of troops in the rain and they would stay in the drizzle for hours without shirking their duty.

Discipline, especially discipline in combat, nevertheless went hand in hand with pride and self-confidence, which cannot be sustained without skill and proficiency. Ch'i Chi-kuang had to work hard with his men on the training ground. Like the Japanese, he focused his attention on contact weapons. All these weapons, he further stressed, could be mastered through learning the technique of wielding a simple wooden pole—the basic of basics.

The techniques adopted by Ch'i had been handed down through oral tradition by individuals, some of them working as army instructors. Yü Ta-yu had made some effort to narrate the techniques; but it was Ch'i who put the instructions together in the form of a technical manual. The fundamental principle could be said to take a "dialectic approach" to the art. Every posture had its duality: the static and kinetic aspects, the guarded and unguarded portions of the body, the frontal and lateral alignment, the defensive and offensive potentials—in short, the yin and yang. One could also maneuver a contact weapon consonantly with the techniques used in dancing and boxing, since every motion involved three phases: the start, the pause or reversal, and the continuation until the recess. Whether for effectiveness or gracefulness, the mastery of the art depended upon proper rhythm—or perfect timing in transforming the yin to the yang. The general emphatically reminded his officers and men that in dueling with an enemy with a contact weapon, the cardinal rule was to maneuver the opponent into a false move before delivering the fatal blow. In more detailed analysis he gave fancy designations to different poses and gestures, such as "riding the tiger," "a hermit fishing," "the maiden's embroidery needle," "an iron buffalo plowing the land," and so on. Each case was a study of motion at the instant of equilibrium before reversal.

The more creative part of his tactics had to do with teamwork, embodied in the concept that each infantry squad must coordinate the use of long and short, offensive and defensive weapons. In dealing with the pirates, the most effective weapon of all was the lance, which had an overall length of twelve feet or even longer. Ideal for making deceptive movements, it nevertheless had to be manipulated at some distance from the enemy. Once the lancer missed his target and came within striking distance of the opposing swordsman he was virtually disarmed. In order to provide a protective screen for the four lancers in the squad, Ch'i assigned four soldiers to walk ahead of them, one carrying an elongated pentagon shield on the right and one carrying a small round shield on the left, to be followed by two carrying bamboo trees complete with upper branches. Behind the lancers were two rear-guard men with three-pronged, fork-shaped weapons, from which arrows propelled by firecrackers could also be fired. Including a corporal and a cook-porter, a squad consisted of twelve men.

The symmetry of the squad earned it the name of the "mandarin duck formation." Yet, though both shield-men carried swords, the one on the right with the longer shield was supposed to dig in to hold the advance position of the squad. The man on the left with the round shield must throw javelins, crawl on the ground until he reached the enemy, and lure him out into the open. That done, the bamboo-tree carriers would pin the opposing pirates down at a distance to permit the lancers to throw more easily. The last two soldiers guarded the flanks and rear, and when needed, supplied a second line of striking power. Their fork-shaped weapons, however, could not be maneuvered to create deception.

Obviously, the success of this operation depended upon the cooperation of the soldiers; there was little opportunity for individual heroism. Instructions were repeatedly given by Ch'i Chi-kuang that soldiers in each squad must be rewarded or punished collectively and that under no circumstances should the lancers be separated from their protective screen. But when the terrain and position of the enemy justified it, the squad might split itself into two identical sections and proceed abreast; or leaving the fork carriers behind, it could line up the eight soldiers in a continuous front line, with the lancers alternating with those carrying shields and bamboo trees.

The use of rattan shields, pitchforks, and bamboo trees as standard weapons suggests that Ch'i's command had never separated itself from its peasant outlook. Later the bamboo tree was replaced in some instances by an antler-shaped metal weapon; but its function was still to obstruct the opponent rather than to inflict wounds. Using two soldiers to perform the work of one, his tactics could never earn a high efficiency rating by any objective standard.

It would be inexplicable if Ch'i Chi-kuang had been unaware of the significance of firearms. He used them satisfactorily in engagements, lectured on their importance before his officers and men, and brought them to the attention of the emperor. Yet he never abandoned the formation and fighting methods of his infantry squad, which, compared with contemporary uses of weapons, seemed to be lagging a hundred years behind. This incongruity was a very complicated matter, however. . . .

Ch'i Chi-kuang's command started in 1559 with 3,000 men. Two years later its authorized strength doubled. In 1562 it was further expanded to 10,000 men. But Ch'i never had a supply officer, a quarter-master general, or a commissariat's office within the civil government with which he could deal. As the maintenance of his troops was contributed to by many counties and prefectures, no unified or permanent factory capable of producing advanced types of weapons was ever created. The normal procurement procedure called for the assigning of quotas to the local districts by provincial officials. As commanding general Ch'i produced samples; the local officials then copied these models using whatever resources they had at their disposal. The muskets thus manufactured had a tendency to explode, as Ch'i related. Soldiers therefore did not dare hold them with both hands to steady their aim. It often occurred that lead shot did not suit the gun barrels they were made for and fuses would not ignite. Given the loading time of the muskets, Ch'i Chi-kuang could not help but see their limitations. Even in the later years of his career, his authorized only two muskets for each infantry squad and maintained that each company of musketeers must be accompanied by a company of soldiers carrying contact weapons. Any ratio that favored firearms would be unrealistic and might endanger the army as a whole. . . .

The record of Ch'i's tactical command accredited it, from the time of its inception in 1559, with having attacked heavily defended positions, fought in confrontations, relieved sieges, and pursued the pirates to offshore islands without losing a battle. Ch'i Chi-kuang never attempted anything overly ambitious or even truly innovative; but when he was committed to anything he thought it over well. His handbook went into such practical details as that on the march he anticipated that some soldiers would use the need to urinate as an excuse to leave their units, and that under enemy attack some of the men's "faces would turn yellow and throats run dry," and they would "forget everything they had ever learned about combat." He predicted the percentage of firearms that would never fire, and the number of shots that would be fired but do no damage to the enemy. On the battlefield, he candidly pointed out, few could put more than 20 percent of their skill to work. "Whoever could put out 50 percent would have no rival." All this, however, was not intended to be pessimistic. The grim realities only called for more intensive drilling and deliberate planning before contact with the enemy.

Two or three days before a battle, Ch'i Chi-kuang demanded up-to-date intelligence reports every two hours. He maintained a reconnaissance company under his own control. Maps sketched in red and black ink were prepared for briefing his officers, whenever possible along with clay models to simulate the terrain. His units carried charts showing the hours of sunrise and sunset on specific days of the year. A string of 740 beads was used as a timepiece, to be counted in synchronization with an ordinary walking pace. In these ways Ch'i prepared himself for the engagement from every conceivable angle before jump-off, in which on many occasions he personally took part. As commanding general Ch'i knew his men and knew them well. Many years later he could still reel off the names of individuals who led the first waves of assault in his major and minor battles.

Even though Ch'i Chi-kuang became commander-in-chief in Fukien Province in 1563, his operations involved little strategic planning. His corps of volunteers remained essentially a tactical command. With firearms not playing any significant role in the fighting and cavalry charges also unfeasible in the rice-paddy-covered south, there was no chance to develop the kind of variety characteristic of combined arms in action. Field maneuvers were generally restricted. Ch'i's own favorite tactic was to storm the strongholds of the enemy line. The risk of attacking the more substantial portion of the opponent's entrenchment was greatly reduced by selecting unexpected avenues of approach and striking with high speed. Ch'i's men had the endurance to suffer the hardships of rough terrain in order to employ the element of surprise. Ambushes were laid by them whenever possible. Their simple equipment enabled them to move briskly.

Again and again, the commanding general was willing to sustain the initial loss of a battle. His experience had convinced him that once the hardest fighting was over, the lines held by the pirates would disintegrate. Many of their followers, especially Chinese natives, would lose the will to resist and would lay down their arms. Its continual success established the reputation of Ch'i's command of being able to annihilate in a matter of hours divisions of pirates that other government troops had been unable to subdue in months. In these operations Ch'i usually employed numerical superiority to achieve his swift and sweeping victories, with the obvious exception of the winter of 1563–64, when he was seriously outnumbered and the battle dragged on for fifty days.

Yet, when the siege of Hsien-yu was lifted in the spring of 1564, the campaign against the pirates changed its complexion. The Japanese, realizing that armed raids on the coast were no longer profitable, gradually withdrew from the adventure. Those that continued were made largely by Chinese bands who now drifted to Kwangtung, away from the region where Sino-Japanese trade had once flourished. Without a formal declaration, the empire had finally achieved its military objective. Now the amphibious bandits could be dealt with strictly as internal insurgents.

In the course of events, Ch'i Chi-kuang had established himself as the most successful Ming general. Although not the most straightforward, he must be recognized as the most adaptable general. As such, he saw warfare first as a contest of will power and second as an application of military science and technology. For an agrarian nation managed by a civil bureaucracy whose object was to resist international trade, the use of technology should never be allowed to upset the empire's constitution and therefore to defeat its purpose.❖

RECOMMENDED READINGS

Six other biographies of figures from the Ming dynasty are included in Ray Huang, *1587: A Year of No Significance: The Ming Dynasty in Decline* (New Haven and London: Yale University Press, 1981). Two important references for the Ming period are L. Carrington Goodrich and Chaoying Fang, eds., *Dictionary of Ming Biography, 1368–1644)* (New York: Columbia University Press, 1976), and Wolfgang Franke, *An Introduction to the Sources of Ming History* (London: Oxford University Press, 1968). An interesting article that illustrates the interaction between Ming military and civilian interests is "The Maritime Adventures of Grand Eunuch Ho," *Journal of South-East Asian History*, Vol. 2 (1964): 31. Charles O. Hucker, *Chinese Government in Ming Times* (New York: Columbia University Press, 1969), is an informative treatment of the nature of Chinese government in the Ming period. Frank A. Kierman, Jr., and John K. Fairbank have assembled an interesting collection of essays in *Chinese Ways in Warfare* (Cambridge: Harvard University Press, 1974).

JAPAN'S EARLY MODERN TRANSFORMATION

John Whitney Hall

Although the emperor of Japan remained a sacred symbol of Japanese sovereignty at the beginning of the sixteenth century, power was in fact exercised by numerous local warlords struggling among themselves for supremacy. This situation was ended by a series of extraordinary leaders: Oda Nobunaga (1534–1582), Toyotomi Hideyoshi (1536–1598), and Tokugawa Ieyasu (1543–1616). In a long series of conflicts and intrigues, these men succeeded in defeating and eliminating the great clans, major landlords, and militant Buddhists who opposed the concentration of power in their hands. Tokugawa Ieyasu determined to establish institutions that would perpetuate his family's rule. He established a new capital at Edo, the modern Tokyo, and required his vassals either to reside there or to leave their families there as hostage. He formed councils of state, regularized the position of the warrior class (samurai), encouraged the development of a merchant class and money economy, and more. Such institutions made the rule of the Tokugawa family (1600–1868) unusually stable and peaceful.

Although the Japanese were quite receptive to European influences during most of the sixteenth century, the Tokugawa rulers began to limit foreign contacts during the course of the seventeenth. By 1641, Christianity had been suppressed, foreign traders expelled or sequestered, and the Japanese were forbidden to leave their country. Without a foothold in the country, the European powers were unable to expand their influence and control as they did in India. In 1853, Commodore Matthew Perry anchored in Tokyo harbor with a fleet of four ships, asking for ports of entry into Japan. Japanese leaders debated the matter hotly, but finally decided that their best course was to modernize their country. Foreign influences were accepted, but on Japanese terms.

In the following selection, John Whitney Hall discusses the sixteenth-century unification of the islands, the basis of Japan's ability—unique among East Asian states—to control and direct the foreign influences that would eventually make of it one of the economic superpowers of the world.

READING QUESTIONS

1. In what ways did Japan and Europe appear similar in the sixteenth century?

2. In what ways did they in fact differ?

3. What was the nature of the Japanese unification of the sixteenth century?

4. What were some of the accomplishments of the Tokugawa regime?

I n 1543 some Portuguese traders in a Chinese junk came ashore on the island of Tanegashima south of Kagoshima, the headquarters city of the Satsuma domain of southernmost Kyushu. This first, and presumably accidental, encounter between Europeans and Japanese proved to be an epochal event, for from the Portuguese the Japanese learned about Western firearms. Within three decades the Japanese civil war that had been growing in intensity among the regional military lords, or *daimyō,* was being fought with the new technology. In 1549 another Chinese vessel, this time purposefully, set on Japanese soil at Kagoshima the Jesuit priest Francis Xavier, one of the founders of the Society of Jesus. This marked the start of a vigorous effort by Jesuit missionaries to bring Christianity to Japan. For another hundred years Japan lay open to both traders and missionaries from the West. And conversely Japan became known to the world beyond its doors.[1]

From a strictly Japanese perspective, the century or so from the middle of the sixteenth century is distinguished by what can be called the "daimyo phenomenon," that is, the rise of local military lords who first carved out their own domains and then began to war among themselves for national hegemony. Between 1568 and 1590 two powerful lords, Oda Nobunaga (1534–82) and Toyotomi Hideyoshi (1536–98), managed to unite all daimyo

---

[1] The use of the term "Christian century" has been applied to this era by Western scholars, but I have avoided using it in this introduction because of its possible overemphasis on the foreign factor. The best-known general work on this subject in English is C. H. Boxer's *The Christian Century in Japan, 1549–1650* (Berkeley and Los Angeles: University of California Press, 1951).

From John Whitney Hall, "Japan's Early Modern Transformation," in John Whitney Hall, ed., *The Cambridge History of Japan* (Cambridge and New York: Cambridge University Press, 1991), pp. 1–6.

under a single military command, binding them together into a national confederation. The most important political development of these years was without question the achievement of military consolidation that led in 1603 to the establishment of a new shogunate, based in Edo. The shogunate itself, the government of the Tokugawa hegemony, gave form to the "Great Peace" that was to last until well into the nineteenth century.

Japan's sixteenth-century unification, as it was both observed by Europeans and influenced by the introduction of Western arms, has naturally suggested to historians various points of comparison between European and Japanese historical institutions. In fact, European visitors of the time found many similarities between the Europe they knew and the Japan they visited.[2] Will Adams (1564–1620), for one, who landed in Japan in 1600, found life there quite amenable. Japan to him was a country of law and order governed as well or better than any he had seen in his travels. Since his time, historians, both Western and Japanese, have given thought to whether Japan and Western Europe were basically comparable in the mid-sixteenth century. Was there in fact a universal process of historical development in which two societies, though on the opposite sides of the globe, could be seen to react to similar stimuli in comparable ways? The first generation of modern Japanese and Western historians to confront this question readily made the intellectual jump and put Japan on the same line of historical evolution as parts of Europe. The pioneer historian of medieval Japanese history, Asakawa Kan'ichi, typified this positivistic approach. As a member of the Yale University faculty from 1905 to 1946, he spent much of his scholarly life in search of a definition of feudalism that could be applied to both Europe and Japan.[3]

Historians today are more cautious about suggesting that a tangible continuum might underlie two such distant but seemingly similar societies. Yet they continue to be intrigued by questions of possible comparability in the Japanese case.[4] We think of early modern Western Europe in political terms as an age of the "absolute monarchs," starting with the heads of the Italian city-states, the monarchies of Spain and Portugal, and finally England under the Tudors and France under the Bourbons. Underlying these

---

[2] A conveniently arranged anthology of excerpts from the writings of European visitors to Japan is available in Michael Cooper, comp. and ed., *They Came to Japan: An Anthology of European Reports on Japan, 1543–1640* (Berkeley and Los Angeles: University of California Press, 1965).

[3] Kan'ichi Asakawa's most pertinent articles on the subject of feudalism in Japan have been gathered in *Land and Society in Medieval Japan* (Tokyo: Japan Society for the Promotion of Science, 1965).

[4] See the discussion of feudalism in Japan in Joseph R. Strayer, "The Tokugawa Period and Japanese Feudalism," and John W. Hall, "Feudalism in Japan—A Reassessment," in John W. Hall and Marius B. Jansen, eds., *Studies in the Institutional History of Early Modern Japan* (Princeton, N.J.: Princeton University Press, 1968).

state organizations were certain common features of government and social structure. First there was a notable centralization and expansion of
power in the hands of the monarchy, and this tended to be gained at the expense of the landed aristocracy and the church. Characteristic of these
states was the growth of centralized fiscal, police, and military organizations and the increasing bureaucratization of administration. There were
certain attendant social changes, particularly what is commonly described
as the "breakdown" of feudal social class divisions, and the "rise" of the
commercial and service classes. Often this process was furthered by an alliance between the monarchy and commercial wealth against the landed
aristocracy and the clergy. And finally, common to all, was the growing acceptance of the practice of representation in government. The establishment of diets or parliaments was the truest test of postfeudal society.

Japan during the sixteenth and seventeenth centuries underwent several similar political and social changes. The country achieved a new degree
of political unity. The Tokugawa hegemony gave rise to a highly centralized
power structure, capable of exerting nationwide enforcement over military
and fiscal institutions. Yet centralization did not go as far as it had in Europe. Daimyo were permitted to retain their own armies and also a considerable amount of administrative autonomy.

However, in contrast with Europe, Edo military government did not nur-
ture an independent and politically powerful commercial class. There was
no parliamentary representation of the "Third Estate." Rather, the samurai
were frozen in place as the "ruling class" and reinforced at the expense of
the merchant class. Although internal events in Japan showed certain patterns that invited comparison with Western Europe, the methodology for
making such comparisons has not been convincingly developed. To be sure,
there have been numerous attempts at one-on-one comparison based on the
premise that the unification of Japan under the Tokugawa hegemony was
comparable to the appearance of the monarchal states of Europe. Specifically, Marxist theory has been used to equate changes in sixteenth-century
Japan with the presumed universal passage of society from feudalism to the
absolute state.[5]

The effort to explain Japanese history using concepts of change derived from a reading of European history has its advocates as well as its
critics.

As more is discovered about the political and social institutions of the late
sixteenth century in Japan, the more complex the problem of comparison

---

[5] For a discussion of the controversy over concepts of periodization, see John Whitney Hall,
Keiji Nagahara, and Kozo Yamamura, eds., *Japan Before Tokugawa: Political Consolidation
and Economic Growth, 1500-1650* (Princeton, N.J.: Princeton University Press, 1981),
pp. 11-14.

across cultural boundaries appears to be. It is important to note that the vocabulary of historical explanation that has evolved among historians working strictly in documents primarily to Japan is perfectly capable of identifying and analyzing the Japanese case on its own terms.

The traditional landmarks of Japanese historical periodization help identify the primary boundary-setting events of the period. We start with the Ōnin-Bummei War of 1467 to 1477 that marked the beginning of the final downward slide of the Muromachi shogunate. According to traditional historiography, the period from the Ōnin War to 1568—the year in which Oda Nobunaga occupied Kyoto and thereby initiated the period of military consolidation—is referred to as the Sengoku period, the Age of the Country at War. Between this date and 1582, when Nobunaga was killed by one of his own generals, traditional historiography has applied the label *Azuchi,* the name of Nobunaga's imposing castle on Lake Biwa. The period from Nobunaga's death to 1598, during which Hideyoshi completed the unification of the daimyo, is given the name *Momoyama,* from the location of Hideyoshi's castle built between Osaka and Kyoto. The victory of Tokugawa Ieyasu's forces against the Toyotomi faction at the battle of Sekigahara in 1600 marked the beginning of the Tokugawa hegemony. Tokugawa Ieyasu (1542–1616) received appointment as shogun in 1603, but his status was not fully consummated until 1615, when he occupied Osaka Castle and destroyed the remnants of the Toyotomi house and its supporters. The Tokugawa, or Edo, period was to last until 1868.

The years covered do not conform to any single traditional historical era but, rather, include both the Azuchi and Momoyama periods and the first two centuries of the Edo, or Tokugawa, period. This time span is justified on the grounds that it covers the birth and the ultimate maturation of the form of political organization referred to by modern Japanese historians as *bakuhan,* namely, the structure of government in which the shogunate *(bakufu)* ruled the country through a subordinate coalition of daimyo, whose domains were referred to as *han.* Although historians have commonly treated the Azuchi–Momoyama and the Edo periods as distinct entities, more recently they have come to recognize that the origin of the Tokugawa hegemony and the formation of Edo polity cannot be explained without reference to the fundamental institutional changes that occurred under Oda Nobunaga and Toyotomi Hideyoshi. Hence, we now commonly link the earlier age as a preamble to the longer Edo period.[6]

There is, of course, no intent to deny the separate identities of the Azuchi-Momoyama and Edo periods as meaningful units of historical

---

[6] For recent studies of this transition era, see George Elison and Bardwell L. Smith, eds., *Warlords, Artists, & Commoners: Japan in the Sixteenth Century* (Honolulu: University of Hawaii Press, 1981). Pages 245 to 279 of this volume comprise an extensive bibliography of works in Western languages.

periodization, especially from the point of view of the cultural historian. Similarly, Azuchi–Momoyama still stands for half a century of massive military consolidation and political and social transformation, as the leading regional warlords created the compact domains that were eventually hammered together into a national coalition in 1590 by Toyotomi Hideyoshi.

Most of the events of this era have been described with superlatives and absolutes. Unification was not simply a matter of conquest by one all-powerful daimyo. Rather, unification was companion to a more universal development, namely, the establishment of the warrior estate (the *bushi* or samurai) as the primary ruling authority in the country. Gathered into the castle towns that served as headquarters for the more than two hundred daimyo, the samurai enforced a rigorous administration over disarmed peasant and merchant classes. Despite the weight of military rule, the general national mood was one of openness to social change and to the outside world. Japanese adventurers engaged in commerce and piracy along the China mainland and into the waters of Indochina and the Philippines. Conversely, when Japan's shores were first visited by European traders and missionaries, they were warmly welcomed. We have noted already that Japan learned of firearms and Christianity from the West. The first had an immediate bearing on the nature of domestic warfare, hastening appreciably the process of military consolidation. The spread of Christianity was basically divisive in its impact, giving rise to deep suspicions and tensions among Japanese of all classes. This ultimately became a contributory factor that led the authorities to close Japan's doors to all Europeans except the Dutch, adopting the so-called *sakoku,* or seclusion, policy. But that was not until 1639 and was the work of the more conservative Tokugawa shogunate.

More characteristic of the ages of Nobunaga and Hideyoshi were the private figures of the first two unifiers themselves. Nobunaga appears as the ruthless destroyer, wholly determined to eliminate all obstacles to his national unification. On the other hand, Hideyoshi is remembered as the creator of institutions that became the building blocks for the subsequent Tokugawa hegemony. Yet for all of this, he remains the colorful military upstart, indulging in flamboyant social displays, erecting gilded monuments to the emperor *(tennō)* or to himself. His most grandiose exploit was the controversial invasion of Korea in 1592-8.

The Edo period that followed also projected its own historical image exemplified in the figure of Ieyasu, the only one of the unifiers who succeeded in establishing a hegemony that survived his own death. National unity was institutionalized to safeguard a lasting peace. The major decisions made by Ieyasu and his first two successors as shogun were taken in the name of consolidation and stability. This was evident in the efforts to shape the bakufu as a national instrument of political control. Christianity was interdicted, and foreign contacts were brought under strict regulation. The stamp of *sakoku* that colored the Edo bakufu's relations with the outside world was a reversal of the previous mood of openness. But it should not be thought that all the policies of the Edo shogunate were negative in their intent. Indeed, it was under the Tokugawa that Japan successfully made the transition from military to civil government, something that Hideyoshi had had little time to consider. Moreover, it was Tokugawa policy that permitted or even encouraged the growth of a new urban class, the *chōnin,* and the urban cultural environment that it nurtured. In the area of foreign affairs, the Tokugawa shogunate was to continue to keep its eyes on the outside world indirectly through the Chinese, the Koreans, and the Dutch, who were given restricted access to Japan.❖

RECOMMENDED READINGS

John Whitney Hall, *Government and Local Power in Japan: 500 to 1700* (Princeton, NJ: Princeton University Press, 1966), discusses the origins of feudalism in Japan and the nature of provincial government and provides a useful background to the rise of the Tokugawa. *Medieval Japan: Essays in Institutional History,* eds. John W. Hall and Jeffrey P. Mass (New Haven, CT: Yale University Press, 1974), provides a collection of essays focusing on the political and institutional history of the period 794 to 1600. An examination of both the development of military government until the mid-fifteenth century and the effect of the Onin War is provided in H. Paul Varley, *The Onin War* (New York: Columbia University Press, 1967).

The Tokugawa period itself is the subject of a number of useful studies. Kenneth P. Kirkwood, *Renaissance in Japan* (Rutland, VT: C. E. Tuttle, 1970), provides a cultural survey of the seventeenth century. *Studies in the Institutional History of Early Modern Japan,* eds. John W. Hall and Marius B. Jansen (Princeton, NJ: Princeton University Press, 1968), is a valuable series of essays on the Tokugawa period. The educational system of the era is discussed in Ronald P. Dore, *Education in Tokugawa Japan* (Berkeley: University of California Press, 1965). Tetsuo Najita, *Visions of Virtue in Tokugawa Japan* (Chicago: University of Chicago Press, 1987), examines the intellectual history of the period.

H. Paul Varley, *The Samurai* (London: Weidenfeld and Nicolson, 1970), briefly discusses the origins of the samurai and the evolution of the class through Tokugawa times. Tsunetomo Yamamoto, *Bushido, Way of the Samurai,* trans. Minoru Tanaka and ed. Justin F. Stone (Albuquerque, NM: Sun Publishing, 1975), and Tsunetomo Yamamoto, *Hagakure. The Book of the Samurai,* trans. William Scott Wilson (Tokyo: Kodansha International, 1979), are two excellent translations of one of the basic works on the samurai ethic and way of life. A fascinating personal interpretation of the *Hagakure* written by the renowned Japanese author Yukio Mishima three years before his own suicide is available in Yukio Mishima, *The Way of the Samurai* (New York: Basic Books, 1977). Another work, contemporary with the *Hagakure,* is Miyamoto Musashi's famous treatise, *Book of Five Rings,* trans. Victor Harris (Woodstock, NY: The Overland Press, 1982). Musashi was a wandering samurai *(ronin)* of notable martial skill who retired to a life of seclusion and meditation in 1643. He composed his *Book of Five Rings* a few weeks before his death in 1645. It is unique among books on the martial arts in that it deals with the strategy of warfare and the methods of single combat in accordance with exactly the same principles.

Western Europe, A.D. 1660

POPULATION STRUCTURES

Henry Kamen

We have already had occasion—in the selections entitled "A Plague Doctor" and "Conquistador y Pestilencia"—to mention the steady mortality in Europe due to disease. Alfred Crosby, in "Conquistador y Pestilencia," suggests it was the susceptibility of the native population of the New World to the diseases the Europeans brought with them that made their subjugation so relatively easy. In this selection, Henry Kamen demonstrates the heavy toll that these same diseases took on the European population in the period 1550 to 1650.

It is difficult for the modern reader to imagine the effects of a mortality by disease and hunger that condemned every second child born to death before the age of twenty. One of the results particularly affected women. Given the relatively high mortality among young women from various causes, the sizable portion of the population that was sterile for one reason or another, and the large number of women who chose a life of chastity within the Church, fertile married women had to bear eight to ten children simply to maintain the population. Since the age of marriage was seldom less than twenty and birth and weaning were a matter of some two years, most such women spent twenty years of their lives—if they lived so long—pregnant, bearing, and suckling. This left little time or energy for professional or intellectual achievement.

Another consequence was that fully half of sixteenth-century society consisted of children and teenagers. This fact led to a vicious circle; children were unable to produce enough to support themselves and so contributed to the widespread malnutrition that lowered the average life span and required families to produce large numbers of children to maintain the population.

Kamen concentrates on yet another aspect of the situation, the contrast between the death rate of the poor and hungry and that of the well-to-do and well fed. The differential in death rates among the American population suggests that some such factor continues to work even today.

READING QUESTIONS

1. What was the death rate in sixteenth-century Europe?

2. What portion of the population were children?

3. What were the major epidemic diseases, and what were their mortality rates?

4. How did the effect of epidemics on the wealthy compare to that on the poor, and what were the consequences of this difference?

hat was the place of man in the Europe of this century? Perhaps the most obvious feature is that the time allotted to the average man was short in comparison with modern life expectation. Fewer children than now lived to grow old, and more adults than now died young. The situation would differ according to environment and social class, but on the whole it was a society (and, since the research so far done has been limited in area, we must say a western European society) in which the balance was heavily tilted in favour of youth, simply because the possibility of a ripe old age had been foreshortened.

One way of looking at the brevity of life is to consider what the average life expectancy at birth might have been. Evidence is most readily available for privileged and easily measurable minorities such as the aristocracy. A survey of the ruling families of western Europe over the whole seventeenth century suggests that the average male expectation of life at birth was twenty-eight years, and the female expectation thirty-four years. In the English peerage over the century 1575-1674 the average male expectation at birth was thirty-two years, the average female 34.8 years (figures which can be compared with the period 1900-24, when the life expectation of a male peer was sixty, of a female seventy years). Similarly, a study of nineteen of Geneva's leading bourgeois families shows that in the half-century 1600-49 the male child at birth could expect to live to thirty, the female to thirty-five years. By modern standards these figures are staggering, yet it is worth remembering that it is the privileged, those most likely to be protected against hunger and disease, who are represented here. The lot of the poorer people, for whom records are more difficult to come by, was certainly and indescribably worse.

From Henry Kamen, *The Iron Century, Social Change in Europe 1550-1660* (London: Weidenfeld and Nicolson, 1971), pp. 12-18, 24-32.

A study covering three thousand seven hundred children of all classes born in Paris at the end of the seventeenth century, for instance, arrives at an overall life expectancy of twenty-three years, a figure which begins to come closer to the condition of the mass of the population.

The picture seems bad enough when compared with a life expectancy of over sixty years for a modern British male child, but it becomes immeasurably worse when we look at the recorded child mortality of the time. The figures show that life expectancy was lowered principally by the very high death rate during infancy and childhood. In sixteenth-century Castile the mortality was notably high: in the rural areas round the city of Valladolid, in the villages of Simancas, Cabezón and Cigales, it appears that between forty and fifty per cent of all children died before their seventh year; while in the neighbouring city of Palencia as many as sixty-eight per cent of those born between 1576 and 1600 died before the age of seven. Comparable figures can be obtained for France. Generalising from the data available for the parish of Crulai in Normandy and the area round the cities of Beauvais and of Amiens, we can say that nearly twenty-five per cent of all children born in the north of France in the seventeenth century died during their first year of life, and that a possible average of fifty per cent of all babies failed to reach the age of twenty. This can be illustrated in detail from the Auneuil district of Beauvais, where over the period 1656–1735 out of one thousand live births there were only seven hundred and twelve survivors of both sexes at the end of the first year. At the end of five years there were five hundred and sixty-seven survivors, five hundred and twenty-nine at the end of ten, and four hundred and eighty-nine at the end of twenty. This indicates a levelling out of the incidence of mortality, and a rise in the rate of life expectancy after the years of infancy. The example of the Capdebosc family in the Condomois (France) is instructive. Jean Dudrot de Capdebosc married Margaride de Mouille on 19 May 1560. They had ten children, of whom five died before their tenth year. Odet, the eldest son, married Marie de la Crompe in 1595: of their eight children five did not reach their tenth year. Jean, the eldest, married twice. Jeanne, his first wife, had two children, one of whom died at nine years, the other at five weeks. Marie, the second wife, had thirteen children in the twenty-one years 1623–45. Of them six died in infancy, one was killed in war, two became nuns. Of the thirty-three children born to this prolific family during the century, only six founded a family. The principal reason: infant mortality.

The knowledge that life would be short, and that only a relatively small proportion of the population would survive into old age, must have made the quality of life differ appreciably from that of modern Europe. Without a large complement of aged people, the Europe of 1600 was predominantly a youthful one, a pre-industrial society in which natural forces conspired to keep life cruelly short. Children and young people must have been everywhere more in evidence than the aged. In Germany in 1538 we find Sebastian Franck complaining that 'the whole of Germany is teeming with children'. That this was not mere imagination is suggested by the calculation of the English demographer Gregory King in 1695 that over forty-five per cent of the people of England and Wales were children. Elsewhere in Europe the picture was similar. In four parishes of Cologne in 1574, thirty-five per cent of the people were children below the age of fifteen; in six districts of Jena in 1640 the proportion was an average thirty-eight per cent; while Leiden in 1622 seems to have had somewhere near forty-seven per cent. The predominant age group in society was therefore a surprisingly young one. Gregory King's figures for England put the average age of the population at about twenty-seven years, a calculation that is supported by other evidence. England was not exceptional in this low average. In Geneva in the period 1561–1600 the average age of the population was as low as twenty-three, and only in the years 1601–1700 did it rise to 27.5 years. This unusual age structure in society may be made clearer by comparing some figures. In the table below, some data for modern England are set beside figures for the earlier period.

AGE GROUP	VENICE 1610–20	ENGLAND AND WALES 1695 (KING)	ELBOGEN CIRCLE (BOHEMIA) LATE 17TH CENTURY	ENGLAND AND WALES 1958
		IN PERCENTAGES OF THE POPULATION		
0 to 9	18.5	27.6	26	14.8
10 to 9	18.2	20.2	20	14.2
20 to 9	15.4	15.5	18	13.8
30 to 9	15.7	11.7	14	14.1
40 to 9	11.0	8.4	9	13.9
50 to 9	8.3	5.8	13	13.2
60 +	12.9	10.7	13	16.9

If the dominant age group was young, it may be presumed that marriages occurred even earlier than they do now. Such an assumption, which at one time used to be made on the basis of literary evidence, can no longer be held. The carefully considered evidence of demographic historians now shows that, contrary to the earlier impression, people in fact tended to marry at a reasonably mature age, and that this was equally true of both urban and rural areas. The reasons for this are not entirely clear. It may be that, as in some modern communities, the partners delayed until they could achieve economic independence from their relatives; or it may be that late marriage was a conscious way of restricting the size of one's family. A few years could make quite a lot of difference. As one historian has observed, 'an average age at first marriage for women of, say, twenty-four might well produce two more children than marriages contracted at an average age of, say, twenty-nine'. Whatever the reasons, the available figures speak for themselves. The admittedly limited data obtained from an analysis of the Genevan bourgeoisie shows that in the late sixteenth century (1550–99) the girls tended to marry on the average at about twenty-two years, the men at about twenty-seven; by the early seventeenth century (1600–49) this had risen to nearly twenty-five for the girls, twenty-nine for the men. In Old Castile in the sixteenth century the ages were somewhat lower: girls married at about twenty, men at about twenty-five. None of these figures is representative enough to allow us to generalise about common practice: the Genevan ages apply to a small, perhaps untypical, class; the Castilian ages to a solid rural community.

When we get to the seventeenth century, however, we find the pattern largely unchanged. In the diocese of Canterbury between 1619 and 1660, out of a total of over one thousand recorded first marriages the mean age of brides was 23.9, of grooms 26.8 years. In the country parish of Colyton in Devon in the late sixteenth and early seventeenth centuries the average age at first marriage of both men and women was about twenty-seven years. The marriage habits of the English nobility differed from these figures only in that noblewomen tended to marry younger. While the age of noblemen at first marriage varied from about twenty-five years in 1560 to nearly twenty-seven in 1660, noblewomen in 1560 married at just over twenty years and in 1660 at just under twenty-two. The data for Crulai, Beauvais and Amiens in France give the same sort of conclusion for the mid-seventeenth century. Here the girls tended to marry at between twenty-four and twenty-five years, the men at twenty-seven or over.

When we consider the life expectancy of the period, these marriage ages seem to be late rather than early, and it would appear that the average couple could look forward to a relatively short married life. At Basel in the 1660s, for example, the average length of a marriage was just over twenty years. As a consequence of this and of high mortality, the unity of the family often had to be maintained by a second or even a third marriage. The upper classes were more in a position to afford this than anyone else. In the Genevan group, in 1550–99, out of every hundred marriages among men, seventy-four were for the first time and twenty-six were re-marriages. The English nobility also had a high re-marriage rate. In the period 1575–1674 as many as 21.8 per cent of those nobles of either sex who had married once, married again. Looking at a wider social spectrum than these privileged classes, we still find a very similar pattern, as in Amsterdam in 1600, where there were twenty-one re-marriages for every hundred first marriages among the population.

The relative brevity of married life, and the very high infant mortality, meant that the balance of birth over death was very precariously maintained. It only needed a disaster—say a war or an epidemic—to tilt the balance heavily in favour of death. Even without such disasters, in normal conditions in the early seventeenth century something like two live births were necessary to produce every adult human. Enormous importance must therefore be attached to the fertility rate at this period. For present purposes it is simplest to look at the size of the average western European family. One contrast with the modern condition stands out immediately. In twentieth-century Europe the economically privileged classes and nations tend to have small families, and the poorer communities tend to have large ones. In six-teenth- and seventeenth-century Europe, on the other hand, precisely the opposite held good: poorer people tended to have fewer children, while those high up the social scale had more. In sixteenth-century Old Castile, a study of the village of Villabañez shows that families on the average seldom had more than four children. In seventeenth-century France and England the same sort of size was maintained in small towns and rural communities, the average number of children in France being just over four per family. A cen-sus of the city of Norwich in the late sixteenth century suggests a figure of 2.3 as the average number of children in a family from the poor sectors of the population (as against 4.2 children among the wealthy burgesses). From evidence like this about the size of families and households it can be seen that the Europe of this time was far from having the large families usually as-sociated with underprivileged pre-industrial communities.

It is not until we turn to the privileged sector of the population, the rich bourgeoisie and the nobility, that we find it possible for parents to afford nu-merous children. The English aristocracy seem to have been fairly restrained in this respect, since over the century 1575-1674 they averaged five chil-dren per family. This moderate pattern was upset only seldom by the heroic few, such as the first Earl Ferrers (1650-1717), who had thirty bastards and twenty-seven legitimate children to his credit. It is when we come to the flourishing bourgeoisie of Geneva that we meet fairly large families as the rule rather than the exception. Here in the late sixteenth century we find that of families where the wife had married before the age of twenty, no less than forty-two per cent had nine to eleven children, and eleven per cent had over fifteen. Over the whole period 1550-1649 the average number of chil-dren in a family depended on the wife's age at marriage, as follows:

AGE AT MARRIAGE:	under 20	20-24	25-29	30-39
CHILDREN:	9.67	7.37	4.85	2.29

The imbalance in size of families between different sectors of the pop-ulation causes little discussion in an age like ours where birth control is a common practice. The clear difference between the number of live births in rich and poor families in the sixteenth century, however, suggests that some form of birth control was also practised then. The poor could not af-ford many children, and resorted to means of control. One of the biggest so-cial problems that St Vincent de Paul had to deal with in France, for example, was the number of abandoned babies, *enfants trouvés,* who could be found anywhere, in town or country, deliberately exposed to die, or ne-glected because no food could be found. More difficult to trace than this sort of practice was the actual prevention of conception. This was probably not widespread, and the full weight of Church disapproval lay against it, but evidence suggests that on certain occasions—during a famine, for example—a severe fall in the birth rate could be attributed not only to unusual mortality but also to some voluntary limitation. Even in normal times, as a study of the parish of Colyton in the early seventeenth century has shown, there is no doubt that limitation of births was undertaken, though the actual means used remains obscure.

The best documented cases of birth control refer not to the rural population so much as to people in the cities, middle-class people, and above all the court. Prostitutes, of course, had to be adept at contraception, but there were others. A French writer, Henri Estienne, refers in a 1566 work to women who utilise 'preservatives that prevent them becoming pregnant'; and another Frenchman of the period, Pierre de Bourdeille, quotes the case of a servant-maid who, on being unbraided by her master for becoming pregnant, claimed that it would not have happened 'if I had been as well instructed as most of my friends'. By the seventeenth century, according to a confessor's manual published in Paris in 1671, priests were instructed to enquire in the confessional whether the faithful had 'employed means to prevent generation', and whether 'women during their pregnancy had taken a drink or some other concoction to prevent conception'. Other evidence can be quoted along the same lines, such as the well-known anxiety of Madame de Sévigné over her daughter becoming pregnant too often. Hints of information like this make it certain that contraception was practised by both men and women in the early modern period. The interesting development, however, doubly so since it seems to take place at the same time as a slowing down in population growth towards the middle of the seventeenth century, is the rise among the upper classes of a prejudice against too many offspring. In England this attitude led to the publication in 1695 of a book called *Populaidias, or a Discourse concerning the having many children in which the prejudices against having a numerous offspring are removed, and the objections answered.* The author condemns those who 'nowadays are much wiser or much worse than in earlier generations they were; who are afraid of what they so much wished for; who look upon the fruitfulness of wives to be less eligible than their barrenness; and had rather their families should be none, than large'. Limitation of births because of moral pressures (the fear of illegitimacy) and poverty had been common; limitation in those circles where poverty and starvation was unknown was a novel trend, a move towards the standards and values of the modern age.

POPULATION CHECKS

The one great reality of life was death, readily accepted because always unavoidable, omnipresent not only in the ordinary course of living but also in the whole environment of the time: in the teaching and imagery of religion; in art, poetry and drama; in popular entertainment and public celebrations. The hand of death seemed all the more inevitable since it could not be controlled. Of the three scourges bewailed by the Litany—*a peste, fame et bello, libera nos Domine*—the first two could be considered only as natural cataclysms, though already there were suggestions that public policy could remedy their worst effects. The scale of infant mortality and the short span of life suggests that most households were familiar with the consequences of death through unlooked-for causes. Mortality came with ruthless regularity, so much so that even periods of population expansion or of civil peace were not necessarily free from serious loss of life.

EPIDEMICS

The first, and perhaps most serious, cause of untimely death was the epidemic. Since these were seldom continental in extent, it may help us to list the principal occasions when they occurred and the main areas known to have been affected:

1563-4:	London, Barcelona, Hamburg, Bohemia
1575-8:	Northern Italy, London, Bremen, Belgium
1580 :	Paris, Marseille, England
1595-9:	Spain, England, Germany
1625 :	England, Germany, Palermo
1630 :	Northern Italy, Bavaria, Saxony, Danzig, Montpellier
1635-6:	Holland, England, Germany
1655-6:	Holland, Naples, Rome, Genoa
1664-5:	London, Amsterdam

It is impossible to impose any pattern on the appearance of epidemics, for they came with great frequency but at very irregular periods, and even in the list above the only ones to devastate a wide area systematically were those of 1630 in northern Italy and 1635-6 in Germany. Great urban centres were naturally the places where they flourished most, and the data for some cities suggests that epidemics were the rule of life here rather than the exception. To take only a few cities at random, Bremen had severe epidemics in 1565, 1566, 1568, 1575-7, 1581-6, 1597-8, 1610-12, 1626, 1633 and 1653-7; Danzig had them in 1564, 1601-2, 1620, 1624, 1630, 1639-40, 1653, 1657 and 1661; Seville in 1571, 1582, 1595-9, 1616 and 1648-9; Amiens in 1582-4, 1596-8, 1619, 1627 and 1631-8; while London had its biggest outbreaks in 1563-4, 1577-83, 1592-3, 1603, 1625, 1636-7 and

1665. These dates show little regularity. The cities come from varying areas, but even within national boundaries there was seldom a rigid pattern to the outbreaks.

Why was mortality of this sort so common a feature of life? It is certain that not all the outbreaks can be attributed to 'plague', even though contemporaries habitually used the word to describe any particularly virulent epidemic. We can also blame influenza, typhus, typhoid and smallpox. An English observer in 1558, for example, reported that 'in the beginning of this year died many of the wealthiest men all England through, of a strange fever'. Historians have since tended to identify 'fevers' such as this with one or other of the diseases mentioned, principally with influenza. By distinguishing in this way between the several types of complaint, it becomes easier to explain the reasons for the high death-rate.

Plague struck seldom, and then with unusual ferocity. The savagery of its attacks caused it to be feared and remembered, but clearly it was in numerical terms a less persistent enemy than the daily toll of common diseases. In outbreaks for which records are not available, it is often difficult to decide whether plague or some other disease was responsible. Generally it is safe to say that the epidemics with highest mortality were the plague ones, and that they tended to be confined to towns. London's three great plague years illustrate this. In 1603 the plague victims were seventy-seven per cent of all deaths, in 1625 they were sixty-five per cent, while in 1665 the total of deaths was eight times that in a normal year, and the number of plague deaths was seventy per cent of the total.

It is not always easy to estimate what proportion of the population was lost in this way, but something like one-eighth was a minimum. The three London plagues just mentioned were of this dimension. The outbreaks in Amsterdam in 1624, 1636, 1655 and 1664 are estimated to have removed respectively one-ninth, one-seventh, one-eighth and one-sixth of the population. For an analysis of the impact on a small community, we can take the town of Uelzen in Lower Saxony. Here the plague of 1566 carried off twenty-three per cent of the population of one thousand one hundred and eighty, and another outbreak in 1597 carried off thirty-three per cent of a population numbering one thousand five hundred and forty. The high death-rate for plague may be contrasted with a dysentery epidemic in the same town in 1599, which carried off only about fourteen per cent. In large cities, thanks to overcrowding and extremly unhygienic conditions, the rate could be very much higher. Santander in Spain was virtually wiped off the map in 1599, losing two thousand five hundred of its three thousand inhabitants. Italian examples are particularly striking. Venice from July 1575 to July 1576 lost forty-six thousand seven hundred and twenty-one of its population of about one hundred and seventy thousand, a proportion of twenty-seven per cent; Mantua in 1630 lost nearly seventy per cent of a population of some thirty thousand; and both Naples and Genoa lost nearly half their population in the plague of 1656.

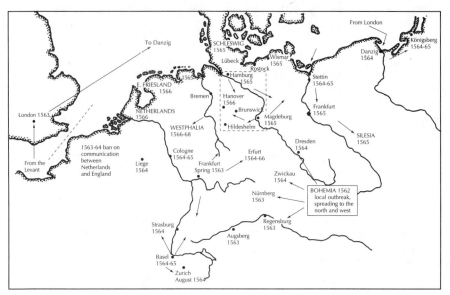

The spread of a plague epidemic.

What was peculiarly horrible about the plague was that there appeared to be no defence against it. In so far as it was understood to be transmitted through human agents, isolation was the surest insurance. During the 1563 plague in England, Queen Elizabeth ordered Windsor to be sealed off from London, and, we are informed by the annalist Stow, 'a gallows was set up in the market-place of Windsor to hang all such as should come there from London'. Isolation of humans, however, was no protection against the flea-infected rat, which was eventually recognised to be the principal carrier of the disease. The speed at which an epidemic could develop, thanks to this carrier, is shown by the following diagram, which illustrates the progress of the 1563–6 outbreak from its origins in the Middle East and its first European foothold in Bohemia.

The early eighteenth century saw the last appearance of the disease. London's 1665 outbreak was the last in England. There was a further epidemic in Spain in the late 1670s, and then severe outbreaks in the Baltic and in Provence in the early years of the next century. The epidemic at Messina in 1743 ended the reign of plague in Europe.

The social effects of plague have been imperfectly studied, but there can be no doubt that it discriminated among its victims. Thriving on filthy conditions, it struck first and foremost at the lowest classes in the towns. An analysis of the incidence of plague in Amiens has shown that the wealthier parts of the city were invariably spared during an outbreak, and it was the poorest quarters that were most hit. The same is true of London, where the Mortality Bills show the epidemics taking their origin in the poorest suburbs. When an epidemic struck Lyon in 1628 a contemporary comforted himself with the thought that 'only seven or eight persons of quality died, and five or six hundred of lower condition'. The pattern was a familiar one. We find a bourgeois of Toulouse observing in his journal in 1561: 'The contagion only ever hits the poor people . . . God by his grace will have it so. The rich protect themselves against it.' The low mortality among the rich and the upper classes may to some extent be explained by the fact that it was they, the guardians of the state, who were the first to take refuge in flight. When the plague hit Bilbao in the early autumn of 1598, says one report, 'only the totally impoverished remained' in the city. The bourgeoisie moved to other towns, the nobility to their country estates. Some of the rich who remained did so in the conviction that the plague was discriminatory and that they were largely immune. The banker Fabio Nelli, writing from Valladolid in July 1599, in a week when nearly a thousand people had died of the plague, observed that since only nine senior officials of the municipality had died, 'I don't intend to move from here . . . almost nobody of consideration has died.' Figures available for Venice just before and after the epidemic of 1630 give added proof that it was the common people who suffered principally, since their numbers as a proportion of the total population fell from 88.7 per cent to 85.4 per cent, while the proportion of nobles and bourgeois rose from 11.3 to 14.6 per cent. The result of this situation was aggravation of social tensions and class hatred. With the evidence plain before their eyes, the upper classes considered that the plague had been caused and spread by the poor. Their contempt for the unprivileged was matched on the other side by a bitter resentment that those who had never lacked material comforts should also be spared the vengeance of the scourge. In these circumstances, times of epidemic became potentially times of class violence.

Poverty and poor nutrition were the two principal features of the victims of any epidemic, and the same was true of plague. Examples from Spain in the crippling epidemic of 1599 illustrate this. Of the eighty victims of plague in Burgos on 22 April, 'from those who had food to eat only seven persons died'. In the town of Santo Tomé del Puerto, only five of the two hundred and five dead on 26 April were adequately fed. Of the three hundred who died in Aranda de Duero on 11 May, only two were well-off. In Sepúlveda on 26 April 'all those who have died in this town and its region were very poor and lacked all sustenance'. The connection between poverty and epidemics could hardly have failed to attract the attention of public authorities, who made some attempt to improve conditions of hygiene in towns and cities. It is doubtful, however, if any of the measures taken by municipalities were really effective. If the plague receded it was because of purely natural causes connected with the life-history of the rat. The fact that typhus, smallpox and other diseases went on from strength to strength shows how much remained to be fought for in the struggle for the preservation of life.

One important aspect of the social crisis precipitated by an epidemic is worth noting. In the absence of public authorities who deserted their posts as soon as an outbreak occurred, the citizens resorted to direct popular control. In Bilbao in 1598 and 1599 all major decisions were sanctioned by a general assembly of the citizens meeting in the church of St John. In several other towns the participation of citizens in government was enlarged so as to enable control measures to be taken more effectively. Emergency situations bred emergency measures, even concessions to democracy. Sometimes these concessions were inevitable: in Santander a popular riot occurred in January 1597 when the major deserted the town because of the plague, and thereafter a general assembly of the citizens was called for any important decisions.❖

RECOMMENDED READINGS

Henry Kamen, the author of this selection, provides an excellent overview in *European Society 1500-1700* (London: Hutchinson, 1984). Michael W. Flinn, *The European Demographic System, 1500-1820* (Baltimore, MD: Johns Hopkins University Press, 1981), discusses the general European population structure before the full impact of the Industrial Revolution was felt; Michael Anderson, *Population Change in North-Western Europe, 1750-1850* (Basingstoke, UK: Macmillan Education, 1988), covers much the same material with a somewhat more limited scope.

In *Plagues and Peoples* (Garden City, NY: Anchor Press, 1976), William H. McNeill, an eminent macrohistorian, offers a general consideration of the effect of disease on population and hence on history, and his *Population and Politics Since 1750* (Charlottesville: University Press of Virginia, 1990) deals directly with the issue of population as a factor in political history. The influence of diet on population is the subject of Massimo Livi Bacci, *Population and Nutrition: An Essay on European Demographic History,* trans. Tania Croft-Murray (New York: Cambridge University Press, 1990). The relationship between population and economic development is covered by *European Demography and Economic Growth,* ed. W. R. Lee (New York: St. Martin's Press, 1979), and H. J. Habakkuk, *Population Growth and Economic Development Since 1750* (Leicester: Leicester University Press, 1971).

DISCUSSION QUESTIONS

PART FOUR: WORLDS OF CHANGE: THE CRISIS OF THE CLASSICAL CULTURES, A.D. 1350 to 1650

1. "America's Ball Game" discusses the religious significance of Mesoamerican ball games. A similar connection between religion and sports can be found in "The First Olympics." Why do you think there seems to be such a close connection between one of the most solemn and, supposedly, one of the most frivolous of human activities? Consider the attitudes and behavior implied in the term *sportsmanship*. How are participants, at least as an ideal, supposed to approach a game? Against this background, what do you think of the phrase, "It's only a game"?

2. Travel has traditionally occupied an esteemed position among human activities, and has been highly regarded as a religious, recreational, or educational activity. The European upper classes of the early modern period felt their education was incomplete until they had taken the "Grand Tour." When we consider the events described in "The Travels of Sānudāsa the Merchant" or the details of the pilgrimage to Jerusalem portrayed in "The Life and Times of Margery Kempe," we see that travel in the past was often uncomfortable and dangerous. What was so appealing about travel to people of earlier times? What benefits did they hope to gain from wandering about in such a fashion? What part does travel play in modern life, and what purpose does it serve? Why should travel continue to be so important?

3. Human beings are regarded as naturally competitive, and so it should not be surprising to see competition as an important element in their sports. And yet, the competitive element in "The Medieval Tournament" sprang from martial origins, whereas the author of "America's Ball Game" suggests that here the competitive element had a religious origin. Is competition a natural element of sports? In any case, why is it such an important element in our pastimes today? What human need does this kind of activity satisfy? Is achievement of this sort a legitimate aspiration, or is it a misuse of human abilities? Betting on the outcome of sports events, either by the spectators or the participants, seems to be almost universal. Is it possible that gambling is an essential element of sports? In any case, what social or economic function does betting serve?

4. In "Conquistador y Pestilencia," Alfred Crosby suggests that the death toll among the natives of the Americas made the conquest of the New

World much easier for Europeans. But the death rate among the European conquerors was also very great. Why did the Europeans keep coming in the face of such a good chance of dying? Why was European society able to keep expanding under conditions that caused a virtual collapse of the native civilizations of the Americas?

5. Societies show widely different reactions to defeat. How did the Muslim reaction in "The Impact of the Crusades on Moslem Lands" differ from that of the Hindus in "India and Islam: A Study in Defeat"? What could account for such differences? To what extent may this factor have contributed to the collapse of Aztec and Inca resistance to the Spanish?

6. In "The Chinese Reach Out: The Maritime Expeditions of Chêng Ho," you have read of the rapid retreat of the Chinese from a policy of expansion and international relations to one of almost virtual seclusion, and have seen the same process occur in "Japan's Early Modern Transformation." What caused these reversals of policy and what benefits did China and Japan gain from their practice of seclusion and isolation? What were the short-term and the long-term implications of their actions? Are international contacts always a good thing? Under what conditions are they not?

7. Why did the Arabs fail to seize the opportunity to establish their supremacy at sea after the retreat of the Chinese? Would it be reasonable to say that the crucial European gains in sixteenth-century discovery and exploration were largely accidental? Why did the Europeans remain dynamic and expanding when the other civilizations of the Old World retreated within themselves?

8. By and large, the populations of the other Old World civilizations remained stable during the sixteenth and seventeenth centuries. European population, by contrast, increased steadily despite the severe losses of life through war, famine, and pestilence outlined in "The Direct Impact of War on Civilians." What was there about European "Population Structures" that permitted such increase?

9. By 1650, European technological, scientific, and military superiority to other societies of the world was clearly established. What had happened between 1350 and 1650 to bring this about? More particularly, what happened between 1500 and 1650 to place Europe in advance of the other world civilizations? What was it about the Europeans that allowed them to dominate the globe? What was it about European culture that posed such a threat to the traditional cultures of China, Japan, India, and Islam?